JESUS

A BIOGRAPHY

JESUS
A Biography

ARMAND PUIG i TÀRRECH

BAYLOR UNIVERSITY PRESS

Waco, Texas 76798-7363

Originally published as *Jesús: Una biografía*

Peu de la Creu, 4, 08001, Barcelona
www.grup62.cat

Cover Design by Natalya Balnova
Cover Image: "Cristo Salvator Mundi" (oil on panel) by Quentin Massys or Metsys (c. 1466–1530). Koninklijk Museum voor Schone Kunsten, Antwerp, Belgium / Giraudon / The Bridgeman Art Library

Library of Congress Cataloging-in-Publication Data

Puig i Tàrrech, Armand, 1953-
[Jesús. English]
Jesus : a biography / Armand Puig i Tàrrech.
p. cm.
Includes bibliographical references (p. 680) and index.
ISBN 978-1-60258-409-9 (pbk. : alk. paper)
1. Jesus Christ--Biography. I. Title.
BT301.3.P8413 2011
232.9›01--dc22
[B]

2011014139

Printed in the United States of America on acid-free paper with a minimum of 30% pcw recycled content.

In memory of Neus and Josep, Marian and Pere,
disciples of Jesus.

Contents

Foreword

"Sir, we wish to see Jesus" (John 12:21)—such was the godly desire expressed by some Greeks as they spoke with the Apostle Philip. This desire, which the Gospels wholly satisfy, is one that has existed throughout the entire history of the Church and continues up to the current day. However, in the past two and a half centuries the Gospels have been literally drained of their historical and theological content by aprioristic interpretations of a kind that are mythical, rationalist, fantastic, aesthetic, or skeptic. Fortunately, in recent decades, historical research has expanded its field of study and has been able to furnish more and better documentation that indicates that Christian sources are not a mythological creation of the first Christian community but have a solid and unequivocal historical basis rooted in the actual existence of Jesus of Nazareth. Indeed, it could be said that history is an indispensable key to the correct interpretation of the figure and message of Christ. The originality of Christianity is rooted precisely in the affirmation that human history has embraced the indescribable event of the presence of God as man, redeemer of mankind through his mysterious death and resurrection.

Someone has seen in the parable of the prodigal son a metaphor for the evolution of research into the historical Jesus in three stages. In the first, the youngest son personifies Leben Jesu Forschung—moving away from the traditional information that is considered unfounded and embarking on a quest for the "true" historical Jesus and failing because of its "rationalist" bias. In the second stage, the older son personifies dialectical theology, which prejudicially rejects any research into the historical Jesus. In the third stage, the father takes the youngest son and reconciles him with the older: historical research supports theology, but without rationalist or agnostic preconceptions.

Within the framework of this reconfirmed faith in the historical solidity of Christian sources, contemporary research has expanded with new perspectives such as, for example, the study of papyrus manuscripts, the evaluation of archaeological findings, and, most importantly, the comparative study of literature of the era. To this effect, scholars of literary criticism, particularly North American and English (Peter Georgi, David Laurence Barr and Judith L. Wentling, Gilbert G. Bilezikian), have long since overcome the twofold prejudice against the Gospels as either Kleinliteratur or legendary stories, and they have confirmed the abundant and reliable historical information of Christian sources in relation to the words, attitudes, and stories of Jesus of Nazareth. Within this area of historical precision and interpretative realism, mention should also be made of the "biographical" interpretation of the Gospels as proposed, among others, by Charles H. Talbert, Philip Shuler, Hubert Cancik, and, especially, Klaus Berger and Richard Burridge. The latter, having compared the Gospels to Greco-Roman biographies, considers that the Gospels belong to the literary genre *bios* (βίος): "The increasing tendency among New Testament scholars to refer to the gospels as 'biographical' is vindicated; indeed, the time has come to go on from the use of the adjective 'biographical,' for the gospels are *bioi* (βίος)."

Professor Armand Puig i Tàrrech's work, which sets out to portray the figure and message of Jesus, is presented within this new and broad area of research, without rationalist or ideological bias and confident in the historical reliability of Christian sources. As such, it presents a well-documented and detailed portrayal of a historical Jesus that best approximates reality. It is a reality that includes the words, the miracles, the preaching about the Kingdom of God, the passion of the cross, and the resurrection of Jesus, duly and irrefutably attested by entirely different sources. The author thus manifests his confidence in the possibility of sketching a biography of Jesus that is solid and consistent and of reaffirming an indispensable continuity between history and faith. This "reconstruction" is a beneficial antidote to the continual "deconstruction" of the historical Jesus that is not merely reminiscent of academic rationalist research but also an actual reproposal made on the internet of the belated and tendentious postulation of the "story of Christ."

The Jesus depicted by Puig i Tàrrech, like the analogous work of Joseph Ratzinger (Benedict XVI), not only adequately answers the thousands of questions on the life and work of Jesus of Nazareth but also presents us with a plausible portrayal of the founder of Christianity, who, while belonging to history, at the same time introduces into history his undeniable gift of true humanity, renewed by divine grace.

Cardinal Angelo Amato, SDB
January 3, 2011
Liturgical Memorial of the Name of Jesus

Preface

This book has been written with the broad aim of combining historical research, exegetical analysis, and spiritual reflection. The style is narrative in nature, meaning the reader does not have to wade through a mass of "wise" discussion; instead it looks closely at the passionate and complex figure of Jesus from the point of view of Judaism and of his impact on early Christianity. The book uses a global, summarized view and seeks to answer the main questions set by the life and death of Jesus of Nazareth. Ultimately, to use the phrase coined by B. Chilton, it is a "critical biography" of the founder of Christianity.

A book of this kind, which neither requires nor forbids its readers to have religious beliefs, cannot debate the great number of issues surrounding the figure of Jesus in depth. Often, we can assess only the results and conclusions as an integral part of the narrative discourse. Obviously, the fact that all aspects are not debated in detail, with all that that entails, does not mean that they have not been closely examined as part of current research into Jesus, and specifically in terms of the so-called Third Quest for the historical Jesus, which began some twenty years ago.

In this book, the fundamental approach to examining the figure of Jesus is historical criticism. The subject matter, however, is handled as a narrative, or series of deductions, which may at times seem "easy," or self-evident, or indeed which may seem to ignore certain problems. I am sure that experts in the field will be able to appreciate the reason for including or excluding certain elements and that they will be able to understand the delicate handling of the basic question of the historical accuracy of the words and deeds attributed to Jesus of Nazareth. Great care has been taken to overcome the obstacles of historicism, which blur the profile of Jesus, either because, in the name of rigor, they set restrictive parameters or, in the name of "truth," they lead to ill-founded reconstructions.

This book aims to give nonspecialist readers an insight into the key figure. To do so, they can leaf through it freely, choosing either to read it sequentially or, given its length, picking through the various subjects using the indices. The fact that there are a great many citations from the four canonical Gospels (Matthew, Mark, Luke, and John) invites readers to delve further into these fundamental literary documents. To an extent, the book acts even as an introduction to the reading of the four Gospels. In short, this is an "interactive" work, in that it provides an open dialogue and approach to examining the historical figure of Jesus.

* * *

H. I. Marrou once said that history is a spiritual adventure in which the character of the historian has to be completely immersed. The implication, in my case, as someone who believes in Jesus Christ, God and man, and as a priest in the Catholic Church, does not mean that the critical spirit or the procedures and methods of historical research can be overlooked. Quite the opposite, I feel that it is possible to undertake a study of the historical figure of Jesus Christ only by using these tools accurately and by being fully aware of the limitations of the research, whether attributable to missing data or insufficient sources.

I would like, here at the start, to set out my references, which belong to the three main cultural areas that have influenced me. From the Anglo-Saxon area, I have found the contributions by J. P. Meier (1991) and J. D. G. Dunn (2003) to be useful and stimulating. The German-speaking world has given us the work of G. Theissen and A. Merz (1996) and the studies by J. Schröter (2006) and J. Frey (2002). As far as the Latin world is concerned, I have found the following particularly valuable: C. Perrot (1993), J. Schlosser (1999), and G. Barbaglio (2002). The majority of these authors (Protestants and Catholics) are involved in the so-called Third Quest for the historical Jesus, which also acts as the framework for this book. In any case, the bibliography lists these and other works of reference. Furthermore, on some occasions a name is mentioned within the text itself so as to indicate that, for the point in question, that author's specific opinion has been taken into consideration in particular. However, the characteristics of the book (aimed at a wide-ranging audience and not just specialists) mean that the exegetic dialogue is not carried out through the usual system of footnotes.

A glass can be seen to be half full or half empty. I have to admit that my natural tendency is to see it half full. Applying a serious critical methodology to the study of the figure of Jesus does not necessarily mean highlighting the lack of evidence or knowledge. Highlighting certain areas can act as a guide toward truths and probabilities. Obviously, the sources constitute a vital aspect of this. With regard to these the Third Quest has led to a reassessment of the gospels, both canonical and otherwise, and of certain material handed down by the Church Fathers as historical sources on the life of Jesus. Some of the aforementioned authors or recent works are a sign of this, and to them should be added the book by Professor J. Becker, in which he focuses on Jesus' mother, Mary.

New data and research on the different trends in Judaism in the first century offer a more precise perspective on the world in which Jesus of Nazareth lived. However, the key factor in the progress, in my opinion, has been the "uninhibited" assessment of the canonical Gospels as the most important historical source on Jesus. The Gospel of Mark is not, indeed, a chronicle of the life of the rabbi of Nazareth, nor a daily log of his activities. But rather it offers an outline that often was not created after the event but in response to these events in his life. The same can be said of the Gospel according to John, which was overlooked to a great extent in the First and Second Quests: the historical material contained in the fourth Gospel constitutes a valuable contribution, in particular when it comes to the narrating of the Passion. Likewise, the source or collection of Jesus' sayings called Q, which has recently been the focus of a great amount of study, represents (despite the difficulties involved in its literary reconstruction) another solid rock that acts as a basis for the earliest traditions. In short, there is no element, no matter how insignificant it may seem, that can be dismissed out of hand when trying to establish the historical figure of Jesus.

I would like to thank various people who have enabled this book to see the light of day, particularly Professor Andrea Ricardi, founder of the Comunitat de Sant'Egidio. Likewise I am profoundly grateful to my parents, Armand (†) and Virginia, who always encouraged me, and to my teacher of biblical exegesis, Prof. Jacques Dupont (†), who gave me guidance in the study of the New Testament texts. My students at the Faculty of Theology of Catalunya (Barcelona) and at the Higher Institute for Religious Studies Sant Fructuòs (Tarragona) were the first recipients of many of the chapters of the book, before the latter assumed their current form. The English version has been the subject of a number of modifications to the Catalan original (2003), in respect to both chapters 1 and 2 and the bibliography. Professor Bruce Chilton (Bard College) and Dr. Carey C. Newman, director of Baylor University Press, have helped me enormously in bringing this version to fruition. I must also express my appreciation to David Cullen for his outstanding translation and to Sid Phipps for completing the task together with Dr. Jenny Read-Heimerdinger, who oversaw the production of the translation overall. Many thanks also go to Jenny Hunt of Baylor University Press, who prepared the manuscript for printing.

1
Introduction

What does it mean to write a history of Jesus of Nazareth? To what extent is it possible to recreate first-century Galilee with sufficient guarantees for the end results? Is it possible to write a book about someone who, while alive, was not a politician or victorious general, a renowned thinker or admired writer, nor a religious leader recognized by Israel, his own people? And despite all this, following his death, his memory has lived on, grown, and spread to the extent that the history of the world cannot be written without including him.

Many have tried to define the profile of the founder of Christianity. The first to do so was Mark, author of the first narrative about Jesus, followed by Matthew, Luke (or, possibly, Luke and then Matthew, as G. Segalla proposes), and John. Other later texts were also known as the gospels but were not accepted as canonical writings alongside these four. Details have been provided by further documents, such as two collections of Jesus' sayings known as Q and Thomas (or the Gospel of Thomas) and lesser texts including certain papyri. After the first century and the start of the second, literature on Jesus grew exponentially as each Christian writer (and those who wrote against Christianity, such as the philosopher Celsus) tried to portray Jesus' identity and the essence of his message. Western history, in its many artistic and literary expressions, shows a sustained interest in interpreting the figure of this Galilean prophet, capable of inspiring contradictory reactions and releasing the creativity of the human spirit.

The historical question, though, centers on a fundamental factor, both for those who believe and for those who do not, both for those who state that Jesus Christ is the son of God made man and for those who see him as just another prophet in the long line of key figures in the rise of the world's religions. Jesus of Nazareth can be subjected to the rigor of historical study, as he was a human being who lived a fragment of human history, from his birth to his death crucified at the gates of Jerusalem and buried near the hill of Golgotha.

History is not, as the positivism of the nineteenth century declared, a demonstration of what has been, a neutral and objective description of events just as they supposedly took place. Actually, the positivist illusion has contributed instead to creating a history that reflects the ideology of the moment. Historical science makes progress as a result of the hermeneutic cycle, which is established between what is objective and what is subjective, between the data and evidence left from the past and the ability to collect, sift, weigh, and blend this in a reasoned and reasonable explanation. We cannot look back at the past without a prior understanding and a particular and conditional point of view to guide the research—while remaining open to new perspectives. This explicit prior understanding requires an emotional closeness to the subject being studied; that is, without empathy and sympathy, historical analysis becomes cold and distant and thus less precise, despite an apparent veil of objectivity. The concerns of the present day, at the start of the twenty-first century, are not alien to the historical question of Jesus. This is also true of the concerns of those who attempt to answer this question.

In the case of Jesus, the historical sources are, contrary to popular belief, not few in number. The canonical Gospels and, to a lesser extent, certain subsequent apocryphal Christian texts, as well as some non-Christian sources, provide an extensive pool of data produced soon after the events narrated took place. Seventy years after Jesus' death, around the year 100, there were already four narratives dealing with his life and message. This is an unusual situation for someone from antiquity. Of course, this documentation is influenced by the faith of Jesus' first followers, the early Christian communities who believed in his death and resurrection, the Messiah of Israel and Lord on high. And this should be taken into account, if we are to respect the idiosyncrasies of the Gospels, which have formed the basis for the faith of the Christian Church throughout time. The Gospels cannot be substituted by any other historical source. Indeed, as G. Theissen states, "[T]he whole story of Jesus (the historical Jesus and the Christ believed to have risen) is the foundation of Christian faith" (2003, 513). This book focuses on the former, within the framework of a conviction: the need to ensure the continuity between history and faith. This book focuses on the Gospels within the framework of a conviction: that there is a need to ensure the continuity of history and faith. With this in mind then, it would seem unwise to employ either a fideist approach, which attempts to demonstrate the absolute historical authenticity of everything detailed by the Gospels, or a rationalist approach, which tries systematically to refute it.

The "supernatural" elements of the texts, rather than being dismissed out of hand, should be understood in terms of the narratives where they occur. Interpreting an ancient text does not mean that it has to be defended against every form of "attack"; rather it has to be understood as a whole, within the context of the methods and systems employed by the authors of the time. Thus, for example, the historian Plutarch, in the introduction to his *Life of Alexander* (1:1-3), reminds readers that his task is not to refer to all the celebrated events in the life of the protagonist, nor to explain each and every one of them in detail, but to provide a summary. This point of view was shared by the authors of the Gospels and the oral tradition surrounding Jesus that preceded them: to explain not everything but only what was most important and to express it in a summarized and concentrated form.

In short, a historical examination of Jesus cannot attempt to surgically scrutinize each and every verse of the Gospels, carefully separating out additions to Jesus' history added over time by the Christian community as a result of their faith. The attempts made in this area, such as that of the "Jesus Seminar" in the 1980s, have led to somewhat arbitrary solutions, despite their being presented as the result of a consensus in the exegetical world. The reconstruction of Jesus' profile has to be seen as an outline, opening up a range of interpretative possibilities, based on rigorous analysis of the texts.

The history of Jesus has to take into account the "subjectivity" of the Gospels, which, as with any historical source, act as a catalyst for the examination of the events narrated. Similarly, in the aforementioned example, the historical figure of Alexander the Great is created from the writings of Plutarch and others. Thus, all the historical sources have to be sifted using strict historical criticism. Indeed, this critical study of the sources shows that Jesus' life cannot be analyzed without taking into account the Gospels, the richest and most consistent documentary sources, and, alongside the early Christian community, the crucible for the tradition surrounding Jesus and the inspiration for the evangelical texts.

Therefore, Jesus cannot be separated from the Jewish tradition from which he comes nor from the lives of the first Christians, who forged the evangelical tradition. What comes after (Jesus) has to be understood in terms of what came before (the Jewish tradition); and, vice versa, what existed first (Jesus) has to be understood in terms of what came after (the Christian community). These three elements have to be distinguished but not contrasted. They have to be assessed separately, linked, and fit together, as you cannot explain one without the other. This book seeks to provide a historical profile of the character of Jesus of Nazareth. However, we have to bear in mind that his profile does not end with his death, but continues into the life of the early Christian community. Likewise, we have to take into account the Judaism of first-century Palestine, the background in which his figure is rooted.

As mentioned above, the historical question cannot be separated from the questions surrounding Jesus' overall identity, such as those set by Christian theology or those asked by the people who have faith in him. However, this question goes beyond the boundaries of Christianity or indeed the boundaries of religion. When addressing the question of Jesus, students from the different denominations of the Christian Church (Catholic, Evangelical, Anglican, or Orthodox) who employ fair judgment and a rigorous historical method can come together in the analysis of the biblical texts without their respective ecclesiastical dogmas representing an obstacle to working jointly toward a shared aim. Research into Jesus, as with many other areas of biblical exegesis, represents an example of practical and effective ecumenism, carried out with a sense of mutual respect and passion for the truth. Furthermore, Jewish scholars (G. Vermes, D. Flusser) have contributed to the research, as have researchers working in the field of nonreligious humanism, who examine the figure of Jesus with complete objectivity.

Indeed, the figure of Jesus has been the object of a great number of varied and often contradictory interpretations over the course of history. Each age has left its mark on the definition of the profile of Jesus, in a range of different languages: artistic, literary, and notional (philosophical and theological). Even social groups, especially in times of social or ideological turmoil, have been moved by the figure of Jesus and created their own profiles. Thus, in French literature, J. P. Jossua has shown the sharp contrasts between Pascal, for whom Jesus Christ is "the centre to which all tends" (*Pensées*), and Voltaire, who describes him as "an obscure Jew, from the dregs of the people" (*Dieu et les Hommes*). George Sand refers to Jesus as "a carpenter's son, poor, undistinguished, wandering the land, talking to miserable workers . . . who have neither money nor bread nor education" (*Le Compagnon du Tour de France*). His end is, according to de Vigny, terrible, as in the olive grove "the sky was black and God did not respond" (*Le Mont des Oliviers*). Victor Hugo, however, states that Jesus' redeeming death reaffirms that "God revealed himself (*se dévoile*) so that man could see Him," and that, on the cross, "as God bleeds, the human race, in dread, reflects" (*La Fin de Satan*).

In fact, between the French Revolution (1789) and the First World War (1914–1918), one depiction of Jesus quickly succeeded another, mirroring the social and political events of a turbulent century—varying between revolutionary and bourgeois interpretations. Jesus was the champion of the disinherited of the earth, the leader of those looking for emancipation from an oppressive God, or the sweet Master of Nazareth who offered his ethical wisdom to the societies of the Restoration after 1870, perfectly in tune with a pious and puritan bourgeoisie that wished to maintain the current social order. New ideas on Jesus as an apocalyptic prophet, proposed by A. Schweitzer (1906), represented the end of the purely ethical and sociological readings of Jesus that had characterized the nineteenth century and introduced the subject of the arrival of the Kingdom of God as the central point in interpreting Jesus' life. Schweitzer declared the failure of the so-called First Quest for the Historical Jesus started by Reimarus (1777) and based on the ideas of liberal theology. The bloody war of 1914–1918, of truly apocalyptic proportions, reinforced Schweitzer's proposal, which was accepted by R. Bultmann, the twentieth century's most influential exegete. Indeed, in a modified state, it has arisen again in current historical research into Jesus.

The ideas of the philosopher and linguist H. S. Reimarus, disseminated after his death by another philosopher, G. E. Lessing, anticipate what is still today the usual picture of Jesus among those who wish to "free" it from the dogma of the Christian churches and reduce it to its simple humanity. The Enlightenment separated what the Christian dogma brought together: the two sides of Christ. On the one hand, there is his divinity, which is supposedly an invention by the Christian Church based on the historical figure of Jesus, and on the other hand is his humanity, which needs to be analyzed independently of the "divinity" promulgated by the Church. The synthesis that the Council of Chalcedon (451) struggled to work out, and that forms the basis of Christian dogma, was thus called into question. Jesus is changed into a pious Jew who only wanted to reform his religion according to those universally valid moral principles found in the Sermon on the Mount: harmony, peace, love, goodness, happiness and piety. The prophet of Nazareth thus became an illustrious "deist," a preacher of eternal, spiritual truths, not a master of "higher mysteries or doctrines of the faith." However, Jesus would have failed completely: his violent death without popular support would mean only that his view of the imminent arrival of the heavenly Kingdom on earth was an illusion. It is at that point that his disciples would have turned Jesus' failure around and invented his miracles, his resurrection—having stolen his body from the tomb!—and his status as redeemer and Son of God. The actual historical facts would have been otherwise, according to those who claim to have an advanced understanding of the matter. G. E Lessing considers that the religion of Christ would be one thing and the religion of the Christians another. The most authentic religion of humanity, Jesus' humanity, that ever existed, would be something quite different from the religion based on faith in him, a falsification promulgated by the Church, according to J. G. Herder's critique. In short, with Reimarus a gulf is opened between the so-called "historical Jesus" and the so-called "Jesus of the faith" or "biblical Jesus," and this gulf has not been completely bridged yet.

Half a century after Reimarus, questions continue to abound about the role of divine intervention in the creation of the world, and D. F. Strauss analyzes the gospels, looking for an intermediate path between rationalism and faith-based theory. In his book in two volumes titled *The Life of Jesus Critically Examined* (1835–1836), the work on Jesus that had the most influence in the nineteenth century, Strauss distinguishes between the "myth" which needs interpretation (Jesus' birth, the miracles, his resurrection) and his "normal experience" that is readily understandable (the parables, the Sermon on the Mount, the message of the Kingdom, Jesus as Messiah and Son of Man). The early Church received a massive impetus from its founder, and its faith arose based on the "divine-human" condition of Jesus expressed by the Gospels, particularly regarding those "mythical" elements that embody eternal truths: the "myth" thus becomes the holder for a seminal idea, which is the idea of God as man. For Strauss, a follower of Kant and Hegel, Jesus' incarnation is the symbol of humanity comprising nature and spirit; the resurrection is the symbol of faith in the ongoing life of the person's will despite death. On the other hand, Strauss' critique questioned a number of reports in the Gospels, and it is understandable that its consequences had a devastating effect on many of his readers. This was the case for Ernest Renan, a Catholic seminarist, who left the Church and later wrote the most popular Life of Jesus of the nineteenth century. This was also the case for the young Nietzsche, the son of a Protestant pastor and theology student, who lost his faith after reading Strauss' book.

Renan's book (1863) is a typical biography of Jesus based on liberal theology. It owes its notable success—by the year 1864 it was already into its thirteenth edition!—to its novel-like character and its all-pervasive pathos. Curiously, a Frenchman and not a German wrote it. For Renan, Jesus is a charmer, admired and loved by all, especially women, who preaches a religion of the heart, aside from any doctrine, and consequently it reaps the enmity of the temple authorities and the Jewish religion. Jesus was an idealist, a preacher full of charisma, who wished to imbue the people with his apocalyptic visions and ended up crucified, having been sentenced by Pilate at the instigation of the orthodox Jews. His disciples, fascinated by his teachings, disseminated the faith in his resurrection. According to Renan, this is as much as can be said of Jesus. One can happily discount the other information in the Gospels, and some details, such as the miracles, can be said never to have existed.

The liberal theology propounded by H. J. Holtzmann and A. von Harnack and by B. Weiss and W. Bousset promotes a vision of Jesus dominated by the ethical teachings of the Master of Nazareth and, as G. Theissen points out, allows for a renovation of the Christian faith, leaving behind the dogma of the Church. For Harnack, for example, the Kingdom of God is a purely religious construct that pervades all of existence "since sin is forgiven and human misery is banished." However, the other elements of Jesus' life (miracles, resurrection) are relegated to second place, and his roots in Jewish soil are forgotten. Jesus' return to the Jewish fold takes place above all in the writings of J. Weiss (1892) and A. Schweitzer (1906). For these authors the Kingdom is a cosmic and apocalyptic reality, and not an individual or ethical one. Jesus announced the Kingdom as a reality that shakes the foundation of this world and takes it into a higher realm. Laws are surpassed and Jesus manifests himself as a radical figure who meets ordinary people and ends up unjustly crucified—a sign of a hope yet to be completed. But the world did not come to an end, despite the many signs that the arrival of the Kingdom was imminent. Schweitzer's ideas attest to the inadequacy of a quest—the First Quest (1777–1906)—which fashioned Jesus according to the ideas of the liberal theologians. Great caution therefore needed to be exercised. In the second edition of his book (1913), Schweitzer concludes that the enigma of Jesus is ongoing. Surely the challenge is, and will always be, to find a synthesis of the master and the prophet, of the mystic and the sage. In 1902 the Catalan poet Jacint Verdaguer died, a man who, from a profoundly spiritual starting point, attempted to bring together the social Jesus, a poor man among the poor, and the liberal Jesus, the master of wisdom. Verdaguer brings to the fore the two antagonistic worlds of the nineteenth century as they apply to Jesus, that of the worker and that of the bourgeois, which, despite the differences, were both committed to the most studied figure in human history.

Schweitzer's book was decisive for the first part of the past century (1906–1953). After this insightful contribution to the history of research into the life of Jesus, skepticism about the possibility of writing a "life" or "biography" of Jesus arose. The theology that developed thereafter, the so-called "dialectical theology," emphasizes the gulf between the world and God (the "wholly Other," as J. K. Barth puts it) and alerts us to the danger of converting an immediate earthly reality—the historical Jesus—into the exclusive object of faith to the detriment of the faith in the Jesus who died and was resurrected. Seen in this way, the study of the historical Jesus is a side issue and not substantive. Despite this, R. Bultmann, the most influential theologian of the twentieth century, wrote a short work on Jesus between the two World Wars (1929), which turned into a declaration of what he himself had considered to be impossible: the synthesis of the historical Jesus and the Christ of the Christian faith.

Bultmann's disciples reacted shortly after the end of the Second World War (1939–1945). In 1953 E. Käsemann started his "New Quest for the Historical Jesus" (*Neue Forschung*), which later came to be known as the "Second Quest for the Historical Jesus." Horizons were expanded. Käsemann's intention was certainly not to explain the historical Jesus. Rather, his question was of a theological nature: why did the early Church consider the man from Nazareth Lord and Savior? The answer is to be found in his wish to emphasize that the earthly, historical Jesus is the same as the Christ, the Lord of all things. Thus, faith needs history as its starting point. Belief in Jesus, as proposed by the Church, is possible only if faith is based on a valid history of Jesus and how he spoke of God—what is known as "implicit Christology" in the theological world. Thus, theology needs research into the historical figure of Jesus. The Second Quest overcomes the skepticism prevalent in the period 1906–1953, but it does not do much to further our knowledge of the historical Jesus, as is shown by the most popular work on Jesus between 1953 and 1985, written by G. Bornkamm (1956).

In the 1980s there was a slow paradigmatic shift with the beginning of what S. Neill and N. T. Wright called the "Third Quest for the Historical Jesus." With the growth of the domination of Anglo-Saxon culture, the political map of Europe and the world was turned on its head with the fall of the Soviet regimes (1989). Together with this upheaval, the new approach is characterized by an openness to the historical question, which relegates the theological issues to second place and, in some cases, causes them to become part of the former. The Third Quest was highly diversified in terms of both its methods and its results and led to a veritable explosion of works on the historical Jesus, some of which were widely acclaimed by the public and turned Jesus into a media personality. The common denominators of the Third Quest are the "Jewishness" of Jesus and his place in the Jewish and Galilean context of the first century, the use of noncanonical sources (the Gospel of Thomas, dismissed by the two previous quests), and a change to the main criterion of research—the criterion of discontinuity or dissimilarity gave way to the criterion of plausibility or sufficient reason.

However, the writers belonging to the Third Quest occupy a wide range of positions. Perhaps the diversity of approach to the Kingdom of God and its arrival/presence allows us to distinguish between a Third Quest that sees in Jesus only a master of wisdom with a certain cynical side (the "Jesus Seminar," Crossan) and another that sees in him the prophet of modern times (J. Schlosser). Currently, the first position that Jesus is a cynical master of wisdom is decidedly in the minority, and the great majority of European and North American authors adopt a so-called "eschatological" interpretation of Jesus. As a matter of fact, some European authors not adhering to Bultmann's views had already placed a great deal of confidence in the historical approach to Jesus that placed him in the Jewish framework of his time. I am referring to J. Jeremias and M. Hengel, for whom the kerygma (the proclamation of Jesus as Lord and Savior in the New Testament) could not be set against history, which is complementary. Jeremias calls it a "necessary condition." Thus, we must emphasize the continuity of Jesus and early Christianity and discard the notion that posterior "invention" or "mythologizing" helped to create the faith of the Apostolic Church. The book that you have in your hands naturally takes this view, and other exegetes, such as H. Schürmann and J. Dupont, support this opinion. N. T. Wright sets his work on the historical Jesus within the framework of rigorous historical research at the same time as attempting to answer the theological questions of the early days and of Christian theology as a whole. J. Frey also insists on maintaining the continuity of history and the kerygma, as do many other authors, who more or less explicitly discard the pre-Easter/post-Easter duality and emphasize the value of oral tradition in furthering the tradition of Jesus (J. D. G. Dunn) and point to the trust we can place in the four gospels as historically valid documents (R. Bauckham, C. S. Keener). Significantly, J. Schröter calls his book *Jesus of Nazareth: Jew of Galilee and Saviour of the World* (2006). The title of the recent work by P. Barnett is *Finding the Historical Christ* (2009).

Whatever the case, the fundamental question pertains to our understanding of Jesus in the context of the Palestinian Judaism of the first century: Jesus is "part of Judaism" (G. Theissen). Besides the studies on Galilee (S. Freyne) and on the time of Jesus as a whole (W. Stegemann), the archaeological and geographical approach has regained its importance (J. H. Charlesworth). This approach has allowed us to paint the "world of Jesus" and the context in which his work took place in a much more precise fashion and to define the terms of his "Jewishness" (C. A. Evans, S. E. Porter). The path opened up years ago by the Jewish scholar J. Klausner and subsequently followed by G. Vermes and D. Flusser has been fruitful and necessary. Among the early works of the "Third Quest," anticipated by B. F. Meyer's contribution, is the work of E. P. Sanders (1985), the central thesis of which is that Jesus belonged to a majority or "common" Judaism and sought the restoration of Israel. J. P. Meier, on the other hand, regards Jesus as a "marginal Jew" and places him on the periphery of the first-century Jewish movements and belief systems. G. Theissen, for his part, adopts an intermediate position and qualifies Jesus as a "marginal Jew" in his lifestyle, characterized by itinerant radicalism and charismatic prophecy, but as a "central Jew" in that he shares the basic Jewish beliefs common to all of Israel (G. Barbaglio). In fact, the debate about Jesus is also a debate about the Judaism of his time. Within this Judaism, Jesus shines with a light of his own as someone who was viewed as the Messiah of Israel (J. A. Fitzmyer, M. F. Bird) and who died as "King of the Jews" (P. Fredriksen) without being understood by his contemporaries (A.-J. Levine). However, it is worth pointing out that the interpretation of his life in a political sense is less than convincing (R. Horsley). But those approaches to his life as a mystic (M. Borg) or as an ascetic of a millennialistic kind (D. C. Allison) or as someone with a visionary penchant (B. Chilton) are worthy of attention.

In a word, a less rigid use of the literary sources, the archaeological discoveries in Galilee and throughout the Mediterranean, more detailed knowledge of the history of the Jewish people in the first century, and new exegetical methods and approaches have led to a renewed confidence being brought to the establishment of a well-founded historical profile of Jesus. This confidence is expressed in the following pages.

2
The Sources

After two thousand years, the oral tradition surrounding Jesus has been gobbled up by history. We are left with written sources, archaeological remains, literature, and geography to ascertain the personal and collective map of Jesus of Nazareth's life. Around 135 A.D., more than a century after Jesus' preaching, Papias, Bishop of Hierapolis in Phrygia, wrote a work on the Master's sayings that had reached him as part of the oral tradition, and Polycarp, Bishop of Smyrna in Asia Minor, martyred in 155 A.D., proudly stated that he had been a disciple of the disciples of Jesus. Nonetheless, at the same time, the Christian writer Justin of Rome did not have access to the oral tradition and needed the written texts for information on what Jesus had said and done. Later, at the end of the second century and during the third century, new Christian texts, known as the apocrypha because they did not belong to the canon of the New Testament, recovered some of the earliest traditions. At this time (ca. 180 A.D.), as shown by the Muratorian canon, the largest part of the New Testament, the touchstone for Jesus' life, already existed as a text recognized by the majority of the Christian churches.

2.1. Christian Sources

The sources on Jesus of Nazareth are almost exclusively literary in nature. However, an article published in *Biblical Archaeology Review*

(November–December 2002 issue) presented findings from an ossuary that contained the remains of James, Jesus' brother, and that, according to A. Lemaire, author and professor at the Sorbonne, dates back to the same time. The limestone ossuary (50 ¥ 27.5) with its simple design comes from the area around Jerusalem and corresponds to the type of ossuaries used in this area during the first century A.D. The practice of burying the dead first in a niche, tomb, or sarcophagus before, a year later, collecting the bones and keeping them in a stone urn or ossuary was common among Jews up to 70 A.D. The inscription engraved on one of the sides of the urn reads, "Jacob/James, son of Joseph, brother of Jesus." The language used for this inscription is Aramaic, widely spoken in Palestine, especially Galilee, and the language used by Jesus' family.

With regard to the three people mentioned on the ossuary, there are two possibilities regarding the relationship: Joseph, father of James and Jesus, or Joseph, father of James and brother of Jesus. In the first case, James and Jesus are brothers, while in the second case the brothers are Jesus and Joseph, James' father. In line with what has been suggested orally by J.A. Fitzmyer in the summer of 2003, the ossuary could have held a brother of Jesus or a nephew, both called James. Mark 6:3 (Matt 13:55) states that Jesus had four brothers, James, Joseph, Judas, and Simon, as well as sisters (see 4.3.4). However, the sources usually identify James as "Jesus' brother." Josephus talks of him as "the brother of Jesus, who was called Christ, whose name was James" (*A.J.* 20:200). In Galatians 1:19, Paul alludes to "James the Lord's brother." It seems that the first interpretation, that is, James and Jesus as sons of Joseph, is more likely than the second. In this case, the information from the ossuary fits perfectly with that provided by Josephus and the New Testament. The second name on the ossuary is that of Joseph. This name, which was very common at the time, corresponds to Jesus' legal father and one of his brothers. However, as the first possibility seems to be the more likely, the ossuary backs up the four gospels (in particular Luke 3:23 and John 1:45), namely that Jesus' father was called Joseph.

According to K. Fuchs, the parental relationship between the names of Joseph (father) and James and Jesus (brothers) is seen only three times in the Jewish historical sources between the years 20 and

70 A.D. The coinciding of these three names in the same inscription means that the ossuary can in all likelihood be identified as the urn holding James, head of the Christian community in Jerusalem and close relative to Jesus. According to Josephus, James was executed on the orders of the High Priest Annas in 62 A.D. As was the custom at the time, his remains were placed in the ossuary about a year later. Thus, the ossuary and inscription date back to 63 A.D. If the person buried in the ossuary was James, son of Joseph and brother of Jesus, or James, son of Joseph and nephew of Jesus, this archaeological find represents the oldest evidence on the history of Jesus.

The first problem arising from the ossuary is whether the inscription is genuine. This question has the experts diametrically opposed. For A. Lemaire and J. Fitzmyer, the inscription was the work of a single hand using the same type of writing, lowercase. In Aramaic this was used only between 10 and 70 A.D. Other researchers (E. Meyers, R. Altman, and P. Flesher) see the inscription as the work of two hands, and two different parts have to be distinguished: The first ("Jacob/James, son of Joseph") is deemed to have been carefully inscribed by an expert with experience in the typical lowercase style of inscriptions. The second ("brother of Jesus") is somewhat amateur, using a later, more commercial mix of lowercase lettering and an Aramaic that is not genuine. The first undoubtedly dates to the time around James' death (70 A.D.); the second part dates back only to a time before the second century (McCarter) or the third and fourth centuries (Altman). This theory proposes that the ossuary dates back to the first century but that it was subsequently retouched.

The second problem, which is decisive, arising from the ossuary is its authenticity. The Israel Antiquities Authority issued a statement on June 18, 2003, deeming the ossuary to be a forgery. Although the stone used is from the area, the inscription seems to have been added later by someone imitating the styles of writing from a number of ossuaries from the first century A.D. This is evident from the geochemical and microscopic analyses carried out on various patinas from the piece. A. Lemaire's conclusions are totally undermined by this evidence, as is the belief that this is the oldest historical evidence on the existence of Jesus and his family.

2.1.1. THE CANONICAL GOSPELS (MARK, MATTHEW, LUKE, AND JOHN) AND Q

2.1.1.1. The Manuscripts in Existence

The tradition surrounding Jesus that took shape in early Christianity was mostly based on written material that held the traditions started by Jesus himself. These traditions have been collected above all in the four canonical Gospels, written between 60 and 100 A.D. and published in the following order: Matthew, Mark, Luke, and John. The first papyrus with a gospel text is P52, which contains some fragments from John 18:31-33 and 37:38. This papyrus, dated to around 125 A.D., is held in the J. Rylands University Library (Gr. P. 457) in Manchester. The time difference between the date when the Gospel according to John was produced (95–100 A.D.) and the first existing evidence of this Gospel (125 A.D.) is extremely short when compared to the case of classical Greek authors, such as Homer, Aeschylus, and Aristotle. For example, the critical edition of Aristotle's Poetics (384–332 B.C.), published in the Budé collection, is based on three manuscripts, the earliest of which is the Arabic translation of the Greek philosopher's text produced by Abu Bishr Matta in the tenth century A.D., that is, some fourteen centuries(!) after Aristotle wrote it. However, the Arabic version is in fact a translation of a lost Syrian version, from the sixth century A.D., which was produced from the original Greek. Furthermore, the Arabic version is somewhat literal and so unintelligible that it often has to be compared to the two oldest Greek manuscripts of the Poetics in existence: Parisinus 1741 (10th to 11th centuries) and Riccardianus 46 (B) (14th c.).

Literary documents on Jesus were brought together very early at the end of the second century and made up the two large sections of the New Testament (the Gospels and the Acts of the Apostles on the one hand and Paul's epistles on the other). These sections were already in circulation as written collections and used in liturgical life in Christian communities. G. Stanton, in his book focusing on the truth of the Gospels, has highlighted a link among three fragments of papyri belonging to the same codex from the end of the second century. This contained copies of the four gospels. The papyri referred to are as follows: P64, kept in Magdalen College, Oxford (Gr. 18), containing certain fragments of chapter 26 of Matthew; P67, known as the Barcelona Papyrus 1, held in the Roca-Puig archive at the Library of the Abbey of Montserrat and containing fragments from chapters 3 and 5 of Matthew; and P4, held in the Bibliothèque Nationale in Paris (Suppl. Gr. 1120), containing a good part of chapters 1 to 6 of Luke. Stanton bases his conclusions on the results obtained by papyrus experts C. H. Roberts and T. C. Skeat. With reference to the collections of Paul's epistles, the oldest evidence is P46, a papyrus from around 200 A.D., which is held in Dublin (Chester Beatty Library, P. II) and in Michigan (Ann Arbor, Inv. 6238). The oldest document containing a copy of the Acts of the Apostles, alongside the four Gospels, is P45, a papyrus from the middle of the third century. Among the early papyri, P98 (Institut Français d'Archéologie Orientale, Cairo, Egypt, P.IFAO inv. 237b) contains Revelation 1:13-20 and seems to date back as far as the second century. Another important manuscript from the start of the third century is P75, belonging to the Bodmer collection (P. XIV and XV) and held in Cologny, Switzerland. It contains a good part of Luke and John. Thus, less than two hundred years from the death of Jesus, there were already works documenting his life, and they had even been brought together in collections.

As a result, it is difficult to accept the hypothesis of the Catalan Jesuit J. O'Callaghan, taken up by C. P. Thiede, that a small fragment of papyrus from the seventh cave of Qumran contains a few Greek letters (not words!) from Mark 6:52-53, which correspond to the word *Gennēsaret*, among others. This would mean that the Gospel of Mark existed before 50 A.D. Thiede has expanded the hypothesis to the Gospel of Matthew, stating that 7Q5 is a fragment of a codex and that P64 and P67 (papyri with fragments of this gospel) date back to a similar period before 70 A.D. This contradicts the opinion of the vast majority of exegetes in claiming that documentary evidence exists from the times of the apostles. However, the method used to count the letters is not sufficient when it comes to identifying 7Q5, as G. Stanton has shown. Furthermore, when it comes to dating the two Matthew papyri, the paleographic arguments (use of paragraphs, punctuation, style of writing, use of the *nomina sacra*) do not back up the idea of their coming from before the end of the second century A.D.

At the present time (2009) according to J. Chapa, the number of Greek manuscripts of the New Testament is close on 3,500: 127

papyri (all found in Egypt and dated between the 2nd and 8th centuries), 320 manuscripts in uncial or majuscule letters (dated between the 4th and 10th centuries), and 2,898 manuscripts in cursive or small letters (dated between the 9th and 18th centuries). Additionally, there are 2,438 lectionaries. The uncial manuscripts, written on parchment made from animal hides, represent the first attempt to "edit" a codex of the entire Bible as early as the fourth century, when Christianity was a tolerated religion promoted by the imperial powers and when the ecclesiastical network had had time to consolidate itself. Codex Sinaiticus, discovered in St. Catherine's Monastery and kept in the British Library in London, and Codex Vaticanus in Rome are examples, in particular the latter, of a very ancient kind of text that has become vital in current critical editions. Another important uncial manuscript from the fifth century, Codex Bezae, held in Cambridge, represents a type of text that existed in the second century. Ancient versions (particularly Syrian, Coptic, and Latin) were also in circulation from the second century onward, with biblical quotations inserted by the Apostolic Fathers in the first and second centuries and the Church Fathers from the second century onward. All this immense amount of material, much greater in volume that any other text in Greek or Latin from antiquity, has been the object of critical study and painstaking classification as part of the discipline known as biblical textual criticism. The basic list of manuscripts, produced by the Institute for New Testament Textual Research (Münster, Westphalia, Germany), can be found in the last pages of the *Novum Testamentum Graece* (Stuttgart: Deutsche Bibelgesellschaft, 1993).

Current critical textual studies applied to the New Testament have provided evidence that there were two or three types of text in circulation during the second century in regions of the Mediterranean, especially in the east. This diversification can be explained by the rapid rise of Christian communities inside and outside the Roman Empire and the large number of copies produced by an army of scribes dedicated to writing, with varying degrees of success, the papyri and parchments to be used by these communities. This diversification also came about due to the progressive centralization of ecclesiastical life in important cities, where there was a tendency to iron out the imperfections of the original text and correct the errors introduced by those copying them (Antioch or Alexandria). However, the Greek text deemed to be correct in the critical editions, and in the translations into modern languages, has to be studied in light of these variations. Investigations must be conducted carefully, as interpretations are always based on one text in particular.

Research into Jesus is based on a great amount of work to establish the literary documents that make up the most important source, the New Testament. The text of today's New Testament is the result of well-founded, critical, textual, and paleographical studies: the difference between this and the original copy of each book has to be small. Problems of any importance arise only in Codex Bezae, in particular in the book of the Acts of the Apostles, where the text of this manuscript is 10 percent longer than the corresponding text in Codex Vaticanus! This, however, is a unique situation in the New Testament. Apart from this, the most notable differences between the manuscripts affect only certain passages, and in the majority of cases these are resolved without causing too many concerns. There are some problems, nonetheless, that cannot be solved easily. A good example is the episode of the adulterous woman (John 7:53–8:11). Some manuscripts and early versions do not contain the section 7:53–8:11, and others place it after 7:36 or 7:44, some at the end of the Gospel of John. Some even place it after Luke (21:38), which may be the most apt location, as the style and vocabulary seem to correspond more closely to those in the Gospel according to Luke. This state of affairs shows that in the second century the episode of the adulterous woman was in circulation as a separate unit, aside from the text of the four gospels. It also shows that the scribes knew it was an authentic fragment from the tradition and introduced it to their copies of the gospels, obviously placing it in different locations. The reason for this situation may be the great force and radical nature of the scene, in which Jesus condemns the adulterer's sin ("do not sin again") but in which he does not condemn the person who has committed it ("Neither do I condemn you"). The scene ended up being placed after John 7:52.

2.1.1.2. In the Beginning, the Oral Tradition

At this point, the next question seems obvious. If we are to look at the historical figure of Jesus and we have stated that the gospels are the most important source of information, then we need guarantees that these documents truly reflect the life and message of Jesus of Nazareth. In other words, we need to track the process that leads from Jesus to the four gospels. Only in this way can we understand the relationship between Jesus and the early Christian community, the generation of the apostles, those who actually followed the Master from Nazareth.

All of Jesus' activities, from when he starts at around the age of thirty until they are cut short by his violent death, are underpinned by two threads: on the one hand, his chosen disciples and the people who come to listen to him and, on the other, the leaders who try to interrogate and at times contradict him. The closest is the circle of Twelve Disciples, who shared Jesus' life with him but left him on his own when he was arrested in the garden of Gethsemane. These Twelve Disciples were "eyewitnesses," that is, followers who accompanied the Master and who could recount what they had seen and heard. Jesus was a traveler, with no fixed address or abode. He spoke in people's homes and in the fields, by the lake or in the synagogues, on a boat or sitting at the table of his hosts; so his disciples collected what he said and did orally—they did not write it down.

We need to remember that the art of memorizing things in the ancient world was common practice, in education and in the transmission of culture in general. Quintilian tells us in his *Institutiones Oratoriae* (11:2:11) that Simonides of Ceos, an author from the sixth and fifth centuries B.C., had written an "Art of Memory." We know too that children by the age of seven had already memorized Homer. The disciples of the rabbis at the time of Jesus listened and memorized the words and interpretations of their masters and incorporated them into their own interpretations. The name given to the rabbis of the first and second centuries is a sign of this; they were called Tannaites, or "those who repeat the teachings" of the rabbis who went before them. Only at the end of this era, around 200 A.D., was a good part of this material written down, when the Mishnah was produced.

Oral culture was predominant in Galilee at the time of Jesus, when only a small number of people knew how to read (10 percent?) and information was usually communicated and kept orally, without being written down. This does not mean that such transmission of information was unreliable or nonexistent. Quite the contrary, the oral tradition represented the vibrant expression of the collective memory. This led to events being explained in different ways, not due to bad faith or carelessness but due to this oral transmission's inherently being, as J. D. G. Dunn states, "a blend of establishment and flexibility, of stability and diversity." The oral transmission of words or events not only means that they are not strictly governed from the outset, as in the case of a written (unique) official version, but also means that what is passed on must be important enough not to have been lost or to have become overly confused. Naturally, the person who recounts these events (telling) interprets them (retelling), but this is equally true in written language! The tradition that begins with Jesus is vibrant, as it is framed by respect for the person who started it while also possessing the freedom and variety characteristic of oral transmission. The tradition is based on Jesus of Nazareth but was started by the men and women who witnessed his activity. Jesus gave his words and deeds a noteworthy quality, but that was not his principal consideration. His disciples take on the role of eyewitnesses and thus become the recipients and transmitters of this tradition. The care taken by the disciples and the power of Jesus' mission are why, in many cases, the distance between the "transmitter" and the "origin" is very short. The portrayal and the message of Jesus do not hide behind a tradition that distorts them. It is rather the opposite: the tradition of Jesus acts as a path that leads to him.

Furthermore, there is a second factor at play in the step from Jesus (oral transmission) to the gospels (the written accounts): the life and growth of the early Christian community as a group that believes in Jesus, dead and resurrected, and that communicates its faith in him. This means that at a very early stage in Jerusalem, and almost certainly in Galilee, where Jesus' followers, all Jews, came together, the memory of the Master and his words and actions became an essential part of their meetings. However, this memory was centered neither on the precise examination of the small details nor on ultimately peripheral questions, such as the Master's physical appearance, his nature or character, and his moral or even religious virtues. The early Christians were most interested in communicating who Jesus was and who he had been: sent by God, able to defeat death, and able to bring new life and new hope. They were not interested in looking back nostalgically. Rather they wanted to spread the word here and now to those who wanted to listen, that God had spoken to mankind through this man, to the point where he had even been resurrected. Their prime objective was not to recreate Jesus' history but to broadcast the fact that he was the Lord of the living and the dead, and for that reason his memory was highly valued. For that reason, there are some very specific details that have been passed down by the tradition regarding Jesus, such as the cushion that supported his head while he slept during a storm (Mark 4:38) or the rooster that crowed when Peter denied knowing him (Matt 26:74; Mark 14:72; Luke 22:60; John 18:27). Furthermore, the authentic transmission of the words and deeds of Jesus and of the memory of him became a major purpose of the prologues, closing words, and epilogues of the gospels of Matthew, Luke, and John, written before 100 A.D., above all in the case of Luke. However, a future perspective is also present in Mark (14:7-9), written around 70 A.D.

The history of Jesus is present in a number of different episodes passed down by the tradition, but the literary form varies as to whether it is a parable or a miracle, whether it is a story from his childhood or a fragment of the Passion. What I mean to say is that, when it comes to giving shape to the oral tradition, the early community had to structure it in styles that began to repeat themselves. One of the most obvious cases is in the narration of the miracles, which often end with a thanksgiving to God from those present, introduced to highlight the divine gift to those people oppressed by illness. The potential of the oral tradition can also be seen in the level of variation or disagreement between separate accounts of the same event in different gospels. For example, the accounts of the birth and childhood of Jesus in the gospels of Luke and Matthew include a number of disagreements as to the actual event. This phenomenon is due in part to the fact that these events were told and retold many times before ultimately being written down. Finally, the tradition is the beating of the heart of the early community's faith in Jesus, Messiah and Lord. Jesus' words and acts were not passed on with a sense of skepticism or coldly; rather, they were passed on with the passion and enthusiasm of communities that recognized them as the testimony of the man they worshipped as the resurrected. These early Christian documents all reflect the impact of an event that, in the eyes of the first believers, had changed history for each and every person on earth: the resurrection of Jesus after his death on the cross. It is understandable that the vibrant and enthusiastic tones of Easter provide new dimensions for many of Jesus' acts and words. His history is inseparable from the life and faith of the first Christians.

The account of the Passion in the Gospel according to John (chaps. 18–19) is a clear example of the symbiosis between the history of Jesus and people's faith in him. At the end of the account, it says that the soldiers, following orders, sped up the death of the crucified by breaking their legs, but Jesus was already dead and one of the soldiers wanted to make sure by piercing his side with his spear. Blood and water sprang from Jesus' side. The author goes on to stress his faith and call on the faith of those who hear or read his gospel, saying, "He who saw it has borne witness—his testimony is true, and he knows that he tells the truth—that you also may believe" (John 19:35). We can find the historical truth about Jesus thanks to the oral and written traditions, which culminate in the Gospels. The history of Jesus is crucial in terms of the tradition that arises after his death, and thanks to this we can produce an outline of his profile with sufficient historical guarantees.

2.1.1.3. The Written Documents

Having tried to clarify how and why Jesus' acts and words have been passed down from the early Christian community, it is now time to look at the strata of the tradition and each of the documents one by one. We need to look at three periods in the first century. As P. R. Tragan has shown, immediately after Jesus' death, between the years 30 and 50 A.D., the oral tradition dominated. As the earliest Christian tradition began to take root, the communities were small and the areas to which Christianity spread were limited to the big cities—Jerusalem, Antioch, Damascus, and Rome—and the following regions: Judaea, Samaria, Galilee, Phoenicia, Syria, Cyprus, Asia Minor, and Egypt. Certain oral pieces used in the catechism and the liturgy of the Christian community, such as the Philippians hymn (Phil 2:6-11) or the formula on the death and resurrection of Jesus (1 Cor 15:3-5), may well come from this period. The period of the Gospels' literary prehistory begins around the year 50 A.D. with written collections of Jesus' words and sayings. The section on the miracles (Mark 6, Matt 8–9) and the chapter of parables (Mark 4, Matt 13) are probably examples from this period. The oldest nucleus of sayings collected in the so-called Gospel of Thomas is a gnostic manuscript from the second century. The early "narrative" of the Passion also comes from this period.

However, the most important contribution from the period 50–60 A.D. is the collection of sayings Q (named after the first letter of the German word *Quelle*, meaning "source"), which may have taken shape as a document at this time and subsequently been incorporated into the gospels of Matthew and Luke. This collection of Jesus' sayings (containing only one narrative, the healing of the centurion's son; Matt 8:5-13, Luke 7:1-10) was written in Greek and contained some 230 verses. Despite the great difficulties involved and the debatable results, the year 2000 saw a reproduction of Q by J. M. Robinson, P. Hoffmann, and J. S. Kloppenborg, which brought together a decade of work by an international team of biblical scholars. This reconstruction represents a conclusion to the research and a starting point for debate on the results obtained. Finally, between about 60 A.D. (some would say 70 A.D.) and the end of the first century came the arrival of the definitive written documents, that is, the four gospels. The first to be written was Mark and the last definitely John. It is more complicated to ascertain whether Matthew was completed before or after Luke.

2.1.1.4. The Source or Gospel of Q

We now need to take a closer look at the Q document, the oldest written source on Jesus. Although the existence of Q is based on solid information, it cannot be verified completely, or at least has not been to date. In any case, it is a valid and serious working hypothesis. Indeed, 85 percent of the Q traditions in the gospels of Matthew and Luke maintain the same order. Furthermore, in some cases the same Q tradition appears twice in the same passages in Matthew and Luke. All the evidence comes together to show that Q could have been a written document that was used separately for the gospels of Matthew and Luke. Q is interested in presenting the figure of

Jesus, Son of God, as a wise master who teaches a way of life and as a rejected prophet who announces the active, present, and future presence of God in human history.

However, Q does not explicitly or directly mention the events and activities of Jesus' life (especially the miracles, among which the healing of the centurion's son is an exception) or his end (death and resurrection). Thus, it is not a complete "biographical" account of Jesus in the style of Matthew, Mark, Luke, and John. For this reason it has to be differentiated from these four writings and is not deemed a gospel. Though some words ascribed to John the Baptist are found in Q, it is fundamentally a collection of Jesus' sayings reflecting people's faith in him as someone anointed by the Spirit and bringing good news to the poor and as the Son of God, resurrected from the dead. The audience for Q was people who shared this same faith.

There are many reasons why Q provides substance for the figure of Jesus. First, historical accuracy requires permanent written records, and oral and written cultures can coexist without any great difficulties. Second, the life and internal workings of the Christian community acted as an enthusiastic reflection of Jesus' life and created the oral tradition. For this reason Q does not need to focus on what is central to the faith of the early Christians (adherence to Jesus, who died and was resurrected) or the miracles that Jesus carried out. Rather it needed to focus on his teachings, which had to provide the basis of the lives of those who believed in him and who were marginalized for having this faith. As a result, Jesus' sayings in Q are very valuable, but not all of them can be said to have came from the mouth of Jesus exactly as they were written down. C. M. Tuckett has shown that the faith and life of the early Christian community echo through the Q document and that this echo is expressed in the way in which Q has recorded and passed on the collected sayings of Jesus. Despite all these conditioning factors, Q is still the earliest historical source on Jesus: Q was written as little as twenty years after the sayings it contains were first uttered. Q marks the start of the coexistence of written and oral materials, a situation that characterized the Christian tradition of the first decades.

2.1.1.5. The Canonical Gospels

The decade 60–70 A.D. saw an innovation that had important repercussions on the cultural history of the West: for the first time, a narrative of the life story of Jesus was put to paper, starting with his predecessor John the Baptist and ending with the announcement of his resurrection to a group of women. This narrative is called "the gospel," as can be seen in Mark 1:1: "The beginning of the gospel of Jesus Christ, the Son of God." Although the text does not mention the name of the author, chronologically speaking it is attributed to Mark, as part of the Christian tradition that dates back as far as the second century. This tradition also includes the names of the other three authors to whom the Gospels are attributed: two are direct disciples of Jesus (Matthew and John) and two belong to the second generation of Christians (Mark and Luke). It is worth noting that traditionally Mark and Luke are linked to Peter and Paul, respectively.

The impact that Mark's text represents for the first communities can be seen in the fact that the second (or third) Gospel written, Matthew, incorporates 90 percent of the episodes found in Mark. However, this does not mean that Matthew is simply a repetition of the first Gospel. Matthew is almost twice as long as Mark, including material coming from the Q document and material from other unique traditions (given the letter M by experts). The result is a compact, systematic text with Semitic undertones that focuses on Jesus' teachings, but without the vigor of Mark's narrative. It starts with Jesus' conception and ends with his appearance, after his resurrection, before the eleven disciples. The twelfth disciple, Judas, had betrayed him and met a tragic end.

A new development introduced by Luke begins the history of Jesus, as in Matthew, with his birth, but continues into the history of the early community. Luke wrote his work in two volumes (the Gospel and the Acts of the Apostles). The Gospel ends with Jesus' ascension into heaven; the second volume begins with the descent of the Holy Spirit coinciding with the Jewish festivities of Pentecost. This event represents the start of Paul's spreading the Word of the Gospel throughout the Mediterranean and as far as Rome. As with Matthew, Luke constructs his Gospel in accordance with his literary criteria (closely related to the Greek world) and based on the Gospel according to Mark, material from the Q document, and a significant amount of his own material (given the technical name L). This material is vital in retracing Jesus' historical profile.

The last Gospel to be written was John, which differs from the general pattern common to the other three. For this reason Matthew, Mark, and Luke are known as "synoptic" or "parallel Gospels," often echoing general themes or small details. The contents of John are all more stylized, concentrated, and full of important theological significance. His narrative presents a number of visits to Jerusalem by Jesus for the Jewish festivities, and a quarter of the text (chaps. 13–17) is devoted to one episode: Jesus' Last Supper with the disciples. Despite its unique and singular nature, its overriding desire to produce a dense and profound tone, the Gospel according to John provides historical details on Jesus that are of great importance, in particular those referring to the Passion and his death. John, as does Mark, starts his narrative with the figure of John the Baptist, Jesus' predecessor, and, like Matthew and Luke, ends it with Jesus' resurrection. The text has a fine opening: a majestic introduction, which is a hymn to Jesus Christ, the preexisting Word incarnate, only Son of the Father, who reveals the loving face of God (1:1-18).

Thus, between about 60 A.D. and the end of the first century A.D., a new literary form, known as a Gospel, appeared in four similar, but diverse, books, four extraordinary narratives, each with its own personality, presenting the figure, activities, acts, and words of Jesus of Nazareth, based on material passed down by the tradition. As G. Stanton points out, Justin of Rome (ca. 155 A.D.) calls them the "Memories of the Apostles," a term that echoes the "memories" (*memorabilia*) of Socrates, written by Xenophon. As far as the ancient world is concerned, the Gospels are a series of "memories," a widely accepted form of biography in Greco-Roman culture. In this case they focus on a Galilean Jew from the first century called Jesus of Nazareth. As with the Greco-Roman biographies, the Gospels aimed to provide insight into the identity of the leading character, that is, to tell of what he said and did by highlighting the small details of his actions and his words. Furthermore, given that knowing about Jesus' words and actions is essential and natural for those who wish to believe in him, the Gospels are narratives of his "life" and not simply summaries of an arcane wisdom or triumphant chronicles of some great man or fictional tales invented to entertain an audience. The Gospels are not literary fantasies or historical novels or even history in the strictest scientific sense of the word. They are biographies that focus on the complete identity of the leading character, Jesus. They are based on the sources available and talk about the words and deeds of the central character rather than digressing or making personal comments or attempting psychological descriptions. The aim of the four Gospels is never hidden or disguised. John ends his Gospel thus: "[T]hese [signs] are written that you may believe that Jesus is the Christ, the Son of God, and that believing you may have life in his name" (20:31). This is how Luke begins: ". . . having followed all things closely for some time past, to write an orderly account for you, most excellent Theophilus, that you may know the truth concerning the things of which you may have been informed" (1:3-4).

In conclusion, there are six fundamental Christian sources that have allowed us to form an outline of the historical profile of Jesus. They are as follows: Q (a collection of Jesus' words or sayings, which can be reconstructed from the Gospels of Matthew and Luke), Mark (Gospel), M (traditions belonging to Matthew, contained in his gospel), L (traditions belonging to Luke, contained in his Gospel), John (Gospel), and Thomas (a collection of Jesus' words or sayings, which calls itself a gospel). This last source is presented below, alongside the noncanonical sources. Finally, we need to ask ourselves about the criteria used to weigh and assess the materials contained in these sources (see 2.3).

2.1.2. The Noncanonical Gospels

Here we talk about noncanonical gospels rather than the Apocrypha, as this latter term is often linked to esoteric, or even heretical, literature. The noncanonical category covers a wide range of writings, some of which belong to circles that defended doctrines not accepted by the majority of Christianity. For this reason, these writings did not make up part of the canon of the New Testament. The apocryphal texts, whether or not they were included in the canon of the Christian churches, contain traditions dating back to antiquity and had an important effect on the liturgy and spirituality of the first centuries.

Indeed, they were highly regarded and esteemed. I am referring, for example, to the *Infancy Gospel of James* (ca. 200 A.D.) and the Pseudo-Matthew (6th c. to 8th c.), which is one of the sources for the "Golden Legend," a work by Jacobus de Voragine (13th c.). The common characteristic in all the noncanonical Gospels is that they are not narratives of Jesus' life, teachings, and acts. They refer to only certain fragments of his life or are limited to certain aspects of his preaching. It is impossible to read them as a separate entity from the canonical Gospels, to which they are indebted.

2.1.2.1. The Gospel of Thomas

The "Gospel according to Thomas," a term used at the end of the manuscript, or simply Thomas is one of the six most important sources for research into the history of Jesus. A complete copy in Coptic, found still intact in Nag Hammadi, Upper Egypt, in 1945, was dated to 350 A.D. Before this, at the start of the twentieth century, three Greek papyri had been found at Oxyrhynchus (nos. 1, 654, and 655), dated to the third century A.D. They contain fragments from Thomas, but the text differs substantially from the version in Coptic, a translation from the original Greek. Detailed study of the 114 sayings or words or logia attributed to Jesus in the Gospel of Thomas leads us to believe that the final Greek version was made in 150 A.D., although minor modifications were introduced around 200 A.D. Now, Thomas' final version is a mixture of materials: some are close to the canonical Gospels, especially the synoptic Gospels, and some differ widely from these and are closer to the gnostic doctrines. Thus, the best solution seems to be to distinguish between Thomas' final version, imbued with Gnosticism and far removed from the Apostolic Church, and his first version, which reflects Christianity with a Judeo-Christian stamp, close to the Gospel according to Matthew and the Gospel of the Hebrews. A. DeConick has proposed a similar distinction. The final version of Thomas with its 114 logia, as we have just said, appears to be from 150 A.D., while the first version with its 70 logia would be from around 100 A.D. In the time between, the text would have been augmented because of the progression from the more authentic tradition of Jesus to that of Christian Gnosticism. Thomas' first version—

a compilation of Jesus' sayings—appears to be a selection of his words that explains the radicalism of Christian life and presents Jesus as a model for the renunciation of family and goods. The disciple, he who "searches for the Kingdom," must accept the revelation of the Kingdom and has to live in accordance with this gift; furthermore, Jesus identifies himself with this Kingdom, and so finding him and finding the Kingdom are the same thing. The Pharisees are the opposite, those who have refused Jesus and who now fight his followers. We are in the middle of a struggle between Phariseeism and Christianity, typical of the end of the first century. As for the final version of Thomas, this represents a substantial change in beliefs and modus operandi. The community, which in 100 A.D. practiced a vigorous Christianity based on the message of the Kingdom and linked to the Judeo-Christian community of Jerusalem (and the memory of James, the brother of Jesus), which was in close contact with the other Christian communities (especially in Antioch), changed in its appearance. It changed into a notably gnostic community that understood "finding the Kingdom" as "finding the self" and promoted an elitist Christianity made up of spiritual, perfect beings, those who have overcome any duality and live in the plenitude of light and knowledge. The gnostics considered Thomas to be superior to Peter (the Apostolic Church) since the former had received a special revelation from Jesus—hence the name now given to his gospel, the Gospel of Thomas!

The Gospel of Thomas has been variously interpreted and evaluated. In spite of the clear differences between it and the canonical Gospels, some authors, such as H. Koester and J. D. Crossan, have proposed the idea of considering Thomas as the "fifth Gospel." Thomas, the oldest Gospel, would be a separate text from the other four canonical Gospels and thus the most authentic, as it would have existed by 50 A.D. Most authors, however, believe that Thomas contains only some of Jesus' words, passed down by the oral tradition, that were not contained in the Gospels of Mark, Matthew, Luke, and John. The majority of the sayings have either been taken from the tradition of Jesus, often just as they appear in the four canonical Gospels (revising or expanding them), or are typical gnostic sayings that have been attributed to Jesus. There is no doubt that in its current form Thomas is a gnostic Christian text, the contents of which have to be interpreted in terms of the gnostic myth and not in terms of the theology of the four canonical Gospels. This can be seen in the opening to the work (logion 1): "These are the words that Jesus the Living spoke. Thomas Didymus wrote them down. And he said: 'He who finds the interpretation of these words will not taste death.'" The contrast between this opening and that of the Gospel according to Mark (see 2.1.1.5) is marked.

In the sayings, systematically attributed to Jesus and as they are found in the final version of Thomas, is a typical example: "Jesus said, 'When you make the two one, you will become the sons of man, and when you say, "Mountain, move away," it will move away'" (logion 106). As G. Stanton stresses, Thomas is interested in the timeless and nonhistorical sayings of a divine and glorious Jesus and not in narrating a life spent on the roads of Galilee or his death on the cross. The final saying is a good example of the author's intentions with regard to his readers: that they come to understand the hidden meaning, that esoteric knowledge be revealed to them that can lead them to salvation, here and now and definitively. This can be seen here: "Simon Peter said: 'Mary (Magdalene) must go from our midst, as women are not worthy of life.' Jesus said to them: 'I will guide her and make her a man, so that she too can become a living spirit, as a man, just like you. Because every woman that becomes a man, will enter the Kingdom of Heaven'" (logion 114).

The most ardent defenders of the importance of Thomas in the quest for the authentic words that Jesus spoke have been the members of the Jesus Seminar, a seminar active in the United States since the 1980s. The belief that Thomas has to be dated to before Mark, around 50 A.D., has led to detailed analysis of this collection of Jesus' sayings and the separating out of those that supposedly are not contained in the four canonical Gospels. It is worthwhile reviewing the results obtained: among the 114 in Thomas, there are only five logia or sayings that are not contained in the four Gospels. They are as follows:

1. "Jesus said 'Be passersby'" (logion 42)
2. "Jesus said 'Let one who has become wealthy be king, and let one who has power renounce'" (logion 81)
3. "Jesus said 'Whoever is near me is near the fire, and whoever is far from me is close to the kingdom'" (logion 82)

4. "Jesus said 'The [Father's] kingdom is like a woman who was carrying a [jar] full of flour. While she was walking along [a] distant road, the handle of the jar broke and the flour spilled behind her [along] the road. She didn't know it; she hadn't noticed a problem. When she reached her house, she put the jar down and discovered that it was empty'" (logion 97)
5. "Jesus said 'The Father's kingdom is like a person who wanted to kill someone powerful. While still at home he drew his sword and thrust it into the wall to find out whether his hand would go in. Then he killed the powerful one'" (logion 98).

These are the only five literary units revealed by the critical research of the Jesus Seminar to have belonged to Jesus and to be found in this Gospel. The Seminar is incidentally highly in favor of demonstrating the independence and antiquity of Thomas. In my opinion, we should, however, exclude logion 81. We could, however, add a sixth text, a parable, which, according to J. Jeremias and O. Hofius, may belong to a tradition dating back to Jesus himself (analogous, in any case, to Matt 13:45-46 and Thomas 76):

6. "And Jesus said 'The person is like a wise fisherman who cast his net into the sea and drew it up from the sea full of little fish. Among them the wise fisherman discovered a fine large fish. He threw all the little fish back into the sea, and easily chose the large fish. Anyone here with two good ears had better listen!'" (logion 8).

In addition to logia 8, 42, 82, 97, and 98, we must attribute to the oldest tradition of Jesus two more logia (the second part of logion 19 and logion 102). Thus, in total Thomas compiled seven logia that are not in the material of the canonical Gospels: four sayings of a proverbial and graphical nature (19, 42, 82, and 102) and three parables (8, 97, and 98). Here is the text of logia 19.2 and 102: "Jesus said: 'If you become my disciples and pay attention to my words, these stones will serve you'" (logion 19.2); "Jesus said: 'Damn the Pharisees. They are like a dog sleeping in the cattle manger: the dog neither eats nor [lets] the cattle eat'" (login 102).

The fact that only some of the sayings from Thomas are directly useful for historical research does not mean that Thomas cannot offer some valuable information on the oldest forms of discursive texts (sayings and parables) in the canonical Gospels. However, the unique contribution offered by Thomas in the form of words actually spoken by a historical Jesus and not found in the canonical Gospels does not seem to go much beyond the seven texts mentioned above.

In other decidedly gnostic manuscripts, the results are even fewer and farther between, even though like Thomas they are called gospels. Thus, the Gospel of Philip, the Gospel of Mary, and the Gospel of Truth are renderings of the gnostic myth veiled in a more or less narrative style. They are theological treatises that offer no link to the tradition on Jesus. The results are no better from a series of gnostic manuscripts that refer to dialogues between the resurrected Jesus and his disciples. Again, these texts cannot strictly be considered gospels. These dialogues, in particular the Apocryphon of James (Nag Hammadi I/2) and the Dialogue of the Savior (Nag Hammadi III/5), written in the second century, form part of an attempt to reveal secret teachings. It cannot be discounted that they may contain some elements from the tradition relating to Jesus. This can be deduced from this brief parable: "For the kingdom of heaven is like an ear of grain after it had sprouted in a field. And when it ripened, it scattered its fruit and, in turn, filled the field with ears of grain for another year" (*Ap. Jas.* 12:22-27). The Gospel of the Egyptians, from the second century, mentioned by Clement of Alexandria and Encratite in nature, is another gnostic document where Jesus talks to a disciple, Salome.

2.1.2.2. The Gospel of Peter

A similar state of affairs to that of Thomas pertains to the so-called Gospel of Peter, an incomplete Greek manuscript that narrates certain parts of the Passion and resurrection of Jesus. The manuscript, dating back to the eighth to ninth centuries, was found at Akhmim, Upper Egypt, at the end of the nineteenth century. Here again, two papyri (no. 2949 and probably no. 4009) provide evidence that the Gospel of Peter already existed in the second century, although the textual differences compared to the manuscript are, as in the case of Thomas, quite obvious. We know that bishop Serapion of Antioch (ca. 190 A.D.) already knew about the Gospel of Peter and that he revoked permission to read it during liturgy on seeing that it was used by the Docetists (Christians who defended the idea that Jesus only appeared to be human). In the third century, the Christian theologian Origen also knew and quoted the Gospel of Peter.

It has been put forward that the Gospel of Peter may contain the oldest core of traditions surrounding the narration of the Passion and resurrection of Jesus (J. D. Crossan defends this hypothesis and calls this nucleus the gospel of the cross). However, the majority of authors believe that the Gospel of Peter, as it is found in the manuscript of Akhmim, may contain some very early elements but that, fundamentally, it is simply expanding on the text of the four canonical Gospels (Matthew, Mark, Luke, and John). R. E. Brown has been able to show this convincingly. The way in which the Gospel of Peter narrates Jesus' resurrection illustrates its secondary character: "[The soldiers who were standing guard by Jesus' tomb] again they see three men come forth from the tomb, and two of them supporting one, and a cross following them: and of the two the head reached unto the heaven, but the head of him that was led by them overpassed the heavens. And they heard a voice from the heavens, saying, Thou hast preached to them that sleep (i.e., those who have died). And a response was heard from the cross, Yea" (39–42). If to this we add the fact that the author shows an obvious ignorance of Jewish Law, it is clear that the value of the Gospel of Peter as a historical source is limited. However, it should be taken into account when examining the passion and resurrection of Jesus (see 6.2 and 6.3).

2.1.2.3. Papyrus Egerton 2

The third noncanonical manuscript is Papyrus Egerton 2. It is called by some the "Gospel of Egerton," was found in Egypt and dated to between 150 and 200 A.D., and was published in 1935. In 1987, it was proven that another small fragment of papyrus held in Cologne (no. 255) also belonged to Egerton 2. Papyrus Egerton 2 (four badly preserved folios, of which only two and a half are partially usable) contains some episodes from Jesus' life, all of which are linked to the canonical Gospels. Among these, the following stand out:

1. A discussion between Jesus and some scribes on Jesus' lawbreaking, which echoes phrases from the Gospel according to John, copied from chapters 5, 7, 9, 10, and 12;
2. The healing of the leper, which reminds us of the episode in the Gospel according to Mark (1:40-45) and the similar episodes in the Gospels of Matthew (8:1-4) and Luke (5:12-16), which include phrases from John (5:14); however, it also contains details that are implausible for a Jewish setting (the leper states that he ate with other lepers in an inn!);
3. The question about the payment of the tax "to the kings" (not to Caesar) is presented as a generic question and not as an alternative between God and the sovereign(s) of this world, as it is in the episode in Matthew (22:15-22) and the parallels in Mark (12:13-17) and Luke (20:20-26) and in the echoes in the Gospels of John (3:2, 10:25) and Luke (6:46);
4. Jesus' miracle at the river Jordan, which is not mentioned anywhere else, appears more akin to a magic trick than a miracle such as those seen in the four Gospels.

Can we state that all these materials have been passed down by the oral tradition from around 50 A.D. and are thus from a time very close to when Jesus was alive and preaching? Or, as E. Norelli states, do they represent a theological reconstruction of Jesus based on the Gospel according to John, which needs to be seen within the context of the Hellenized Christian setting of the second century A.D.? This would explain the similarities between Egerton 2 and the text of the canonical Gospels. Whichever alternative we choose, we have to recognize the fact that the words attributed to Jesus in Egerton 2 do not fit easily with the other sayings attributed to him. The principal value of the papyrus is probably seen in the fact that it can help us to understand the development of the tradition regarding Jesus.

2.1.2.4. "Papyrus" Oxyrhynchus 840

The fourth noncanonical source is Oxyrhynchus 840, a fragment of parchment found in the Egyptian town of the same name in 1905. The fragment can be dated to between the third and fifth centuries and probably belongs to a complete gospel copied out in small letters and is not an amulet. Its forty-five lines contain two episodes involving Jesus in Jerusalem:

1. The end of a discussion between Jesus and his disciples, telling them to avoid committing any kind of evil or injustice;
2. An argument between Jesus and Levi, a high priest close to the Pharisees, on the ritual cleansing required in the temple; this also appears in Mark (7) and Matthew (15 and 23), where Jesus ends up denouncing external cleanliness and internal unrighteousness and where he also talks about baptism as a form of purification of sins (John 4 and 7).

These texts confirm the different positions that Jesus and the Pharisees adopted toward ritual cleansing. This is highlighted by the way the Pharisee leader asks Jesus, "Who permitted you to wander in this place of purification [i.e., the temple] and to see these holy vessels, even though you have not bathed and the feet of your disciples have not been washed?"

2.1.2.5. Papyrus Oxyrhynchus 1224

The fifth noncanonical source is Oxyrhynchus 1224. This fragment of papyrus is all that remains of a complete document (of at least 176 pages), which may have been a gospel or collection of Jesus' sayings, resembling Q or Thomas. It contains four sayings attributed to Jesus. The first (the healthy do not need a doctor), with the introduction referring to those who eat with Jesus, is taken from Mark (2:15-17). The second and third resemble Matthew 5:44 and Luke 9:50. The fourth does not appear in any of the canonical Gospels: "[The one who] is faraway [today], tomorrow will be [near you]."

The Cairo Papyrus 10735, the Fayum Fragment, the Berlin Papyrus 11710, and the Coptic Papyrus of Strasbourg are of little significance for historical research on Jesus. Doubtlessly related to the last one of these is the so-called Unknown Berlin Gospel (Berlin Papyrus 22220) dating from the turn of the second and third centuries, containing ten legible pages, in which Jesus appears in conversation with the disciples in the upper room (John 13–17) and in the garden of Gethsemane (Matt 26:30-46), just at the beginning of the Passion. However, neither this gospel fragment nor any of the following fragments contain material that is directly relevant for the historical Jesus: the gnostic gospels of Mary and Judas, the gnostic texts of the Dialogue of the Savior or the First Apocalypse of James, or any other gnostic document taken from the Gospel of Thomas in its earliest form and already mentioned here. However, all these documents bear some kind of witness to the development of Christianity in the second and third centuries.

2.1.2.6. The Secret Gospel of Mark

The sixth noncanonical source is limited in its contribution, and its authenticity is also in great doubt. According to Morton Smith, the researcher who made it public in 1973, there was an unknown letter written by Clement of Alexandria around 200 A.D. that contained some twenty lines of text under the title the "Secret Gospel of Mark." Despite Smith's assurance that he had discovered the document at the Mar Saba Monastery in the Judaean Desert near Jerusalem, it is strange that no one has been able to see the original manuscript of this letter. For this reason, many believe that it is an early, or some would say late, falsification.

The letter in question says that, in addition to the canonical Gospel, Mark wrote a second epistle, a "secret gospel" that included a series of episodes not referred to in his Gospel. Thus, three episodes of this gospel have been conserved: the resurrection of the young man by Jesus in Bethany and the nocturnal visit of the young man to Jesus after six days (episodes introduced by the secret gospel after Mark 10:35) and a meeting that fails to take place between Jesus and some women in Jericho (mentioned after Mark 10:46). The first episode relates the resurrection of a young man from a well-to-do family, whose sister had asked Jesus to have pity on her. It would seem to be a "remake" of the resurrection of Lazarus, Martha and Mary's brother (John 11), with the introduction of other elements essentially originating in the canonical Gospel according to Mark. The same tone is maintained in the second episode, which, however, contains a surprising fact: Jesus, who was staying in the young man's house, is visited at night by this young man, who was "wearing a linen cloth over his naked body. And he remained with him that night, for Jesus taught him the mystery of the Kingdom of God." According to the letter from Clement made public by Morton Smith, the Carpocratian heretics wanted to interpret the passage sexually, but the reasons for the young man being dressed only in a linen cloth and his receiving Jesus' teachings at night can be explained by the Gospels of Mark (14:51) and John (3:2), where they talk of the disciple who removes his loincloth and runs naked from the Garden of Olives and the nighttime visit of Nicodemus, an important Pharisee, to see Jesus. Either the so-called Secret Gospel of Mark is a fabrication (and there are many reasons to think so), or it is a text based on the Gospels of John and Mark and, thus, not of use to us as a historical source on Jesus' life.

2.1.2.7. The Judeo-Christian Gospels

The seventh noncanonical source on the life of Jesus is the Judeo-Christian Gospels. The few fragments in existence are inserted into the works of the Church Fathers as quotations, and their textual accuracy cannot be strongly attested, given that the Fathers often cited somewhat imprecisely. According to numerous writers, there are three Judeo-Christian Gospels: those of the Nazarenes, of the Hebrews, and of the Ebionites. The Gospel of the Ebionites is attested to by Epiphanius of Salamis in the fourth century. In regard to the other two, Jerome recognizes only one, which he calls the Gospel according to the Hebrews, while Hegesippus distinguishes between the Gospel according to the Nazarenes in Aramaic and the Gospel according to the Hebrews. However, it is not totally clear that Hegesippus is actually referring to two different gospels. It is more likely that there was a single, large Judeo-Christian Gospel that existed in two different versions, both known to Hegesippus and Jerome: the original in Greek kept in Alexandria (Clement and Origen) originally addressed to the Judeo-Christian townspeople of Antioch in Syria, the other translated into Aramaic and kept in Caesarea and used by the Nazarenes of Beroea in Syria and by the other Judeo-Christians in Syria where the dominant tongue was not Greek but Syriac, a variant of Aramaic. The Judeo-Christian Gospel or the Gospel according to the Hebrews is dated to the beginning of the second century around 100 A.D. and was read by the Syrian Judeo-Christian communities jointly with the Gospel according to Matthew or maybe as a substitute for it. In any case, the proximity of the Gospel according to the Hebrews and the Gospel according to Matthew is best explained if we hold that, at the time, the Syrian Judeo-Christian communities considered both texts to be authorized narratives of the life of Jesus, the Messiah. The few fragments that have come down to us from the Gospel according to the Hebrews by way of the Church Fathers tend to confirm this proximity.

On the other hand, the Judeo-Christian Gospel according to the Hebrews contains certain material of a surprising nature about Jesus, which indicates that a part of the tradition about him may have ended up in the Syrian Judeo-Christian communities by way of Palestinian refugees around the time of the First Jewish War. The Judeo-Christian Gospel according to the Hebrews contains some remarkable episodes and sayings attributed to Jesus. One of the most famous of these, quoted by Clement of Alexandria and the Gospel of Thomas (logion 2), is as follows: "He who seeks must continue to seek until he finds, but when he finds he will be astonished. Astonished he will reign, and once he has started to reign, he will find rest" (Schneemelcher—*Hebräerevangelium* no. 4b). Also close to Thomas (logia 55 and 62), where it says that following Jesus is more important than one's own family, there is a saying, quoted by Eusebius of Caesarea, that seems to derive from Matthew (10:37-39) and John (17:6): "I have chosen the most worthy; and my worthy ones are the ones the Father has given me" (no. 23). Love of one's brother occupies a notable position in the Judeo-Christian Gospel. According to this gospel, "making one's brother sad is one of the gravest sins, and as a result, you will only be happy if you look upon your brother with love" (no. 5). These two sayings, quoted by Jerome, belong without doubt to the core of Jesus' message (e.g., Matt 18:10). Here too, a logion (logion 25) from Thomas is close to the Judeo-Christian Gospel: "Love your brother like your very own soul; keep him as the apple of your eye." The first version of the Gospel of Thomas and the Judeo-Christian Gospel belong to the same Judeo-Christian context.

The Judeo-Christian Gospel also contains some modifications that have not been dated with certainty. One modification is that of the man with the withered hand who is cured by Jesus (Matt 12:9-14): it states that he was a mason and that he pleaded to the healer, "I beseech thee, Jesus, to restore me to my health that I may not with ignominy have to beg for my bread" (quoted by St. Jerome, no. 10). A further example is, following the sentence in Matthew (18:22) where Jesus states that we have to forgive "seventy times seven" times, the Gospel of the Hebrews adds these words from the Master: "For in the prophets also after they were anointed with the Holy Spirit, the word of sin was found" (also quoted by St. Jerome, no. 15a).

On the other hand, when all of Jesus' family decides to be baptized by John the Baptist, Jesus says of himself that he is without sin: "What sin have I committed that I need to be baptized by him? Unless what I have just said is ignorance" (no. 2). The texture is similar to Matthew (3:14-15), where the Baptist recognizes Jesus' holiness, along with John (8:46): "Which of you convicts me of sin? If I tell the truth, why do you not believe me?" Logion 104 in the Gospel of Thomas takes a similar line: "What sin have I committed or how have I been undone." However, Jesus is baptized, and then the fullness of the Spirit, with which he is imbued (Luke 4:18-19, quoting Isa 61:1-2), becomes evident in a text of the Gospel according to the Hebrews, where the Holy Spirit appears as a feminine figure, as the mother of Jesus, since in Hebrew the word for spirit (*ruah*) is usually feminine. When the "Lord" Jesus, after being baptized, comes out of the water, there descends upon him "the whole fountain of the Holy Spirit" and says to him, "My son, I expected you among all the prophets that you should come and that I should rest upon you. For you are my rest, you are my first-born who shall reign in eternity" (*Hebräerevangelium* no. 2). Clearly the Holy Spirit resides in Jesus and he is the Son (also John 1:33-34). Again, in relation to the temptations (Matt 4:1 and 4:8), the Holy Spirit is called "mother" by Jesus himself: "My mother the Holy Spirit took me by one of my hairs up to the great mount Tabor" (*Hebräerevangelium* no. 3). This saying, attested by Origen and Jerome, can be interpreted gnostically (Christ engendered by the Holy Spirit within the pleroma). Matthew (1:18) and Luke (1:35) say that Jesus was conceived by the Holy Spirit ("she was found to be with child of the Holy Spirit"), and thus the Holy Spirit, by making Mary's motherhood possible, has a maternal influence on Jesus.

With regard to the Gospel of the Ebionites, a Judeo-Christian group in Jordan, Jesus' sayings, taken from Matthew, Mark, and Luke, are transformed to meet the group's sectarian theology, making it difficult to gain any useful material for research into Jesus' history.

In conclusion, the contribution made by the Gospel according to the Hebrews, the Judeo-Christian Gospel par excellence, cannot be underestimated, as it is an early witness to the tradition of Jesus and its development in a context as particular and difficult to understand as the Judeo-Christian one. However, it appears that words about himself that reflect particular theological doctrines and that do not belong to the oldest stages of the Jesus tradition are sometimes put into Jesus' mouth.

2.1.3. Other Christian Sources

2.1.3.1. Certain Gospel Manuscripts

Some fragments have not been included in the critical editions and translations of the canonical Gospels because they exist only in one or a small number of manuscripts. This is the case of the so-called Freer Logion, found in only one uncial manuscript, Codex Washingtonensis, which comes after Mark 16:14. It is a brief dialogue between Jesus and the disciples, in which they pity the fact that this world is under Satan's rule and full of injustice and disbelief, and they ask the Master to reveal his righteousness. Jesus responds thus: "The term of years for Satan's power has been fulfilled, but other terrible things draw near. And for those who have sinned I was handed over to death, that they may return to the truth and sin no more, that they may inherit the spiritual and imperishable glory of righteousness that is in heaven." The question is whether a fragment such as this reflects Jesus' words or whether it is instead a later theological interpretation.

Another question arises with regard to the sentence that Codex Bezae adds to Luke 6:4, where Jesus addresses a man working on a Saturday, the day of rest according to Jewish Law: "Man, if you know what you are doing, you are blessed; but if you do not know, you are cursed and a transgressor of the law."

Many manuscripts also include Jesus' chastising of James and John when these two disciples want to make fire come down from the heavens to consume the Samaritans who did not welcome him (Luke 9:55-56). These are his words: "You do not know what kind of spirit you are of, for the Son of man did not come to destroy men's lives but to save them." This sentence fits in with the context and Jesus' preaching. However, we cannot be sure that this is not an addition because there is no response in the original text in 9:55, which simply states, "But he turned and rebuked them." Two similar texts (Luke 19:10 and John 3:17) would have supported this addition.

2.1.3.2. The New Testament, Apart from the Gospels

Apart from the four gospels, the other books of the New Testament also contain some of Jesus' sayings. One of the most well known was inserted in Paul's address to the elders of the Ephesians gathered at Miletus: ". . . remembering the words of the Lord Jesus, how he said, 'It is more blessed to give than to receive'" (Acts 20:35).

The Apostle Paul does not include any direct quotations of Jesus' sayings in his epistles, but he does refer explicitly to Jesus' position on divorce (Mark 10:6-9, 11-12): "To the married I give charge, not I but the Lord, that the wife should not separate from her husband (but if she does, let her remain single or else be reconciled to her husband)—and that the husband should not divorce his wife" (1 Cor 7:10-11).

Regarding the gospel mission, Paul mentions the regulation enjoining Christian missionaries to live by this work (Matt 10:10 and Luke 10:7): "The Lord commanded that those who proclaim the gospel should get their living by the gospel" (1 Cor 9:14).

In the First Epistle to the Corinthians (11:23-25), Paul repeats the Eucharist given by Jesus at the Last Supper, also present with some variations in Luke (22:19-20), Matthew (26:26-29), and Mark (14:22-25). This is how Paul expresses it: "For I received from the Lord what I also delivered to you, that the Lord Jesus on the night when he was betrayed took bread, and when he had given thanks, he broke it, and said, 'This is my body which is for you. Do this in remembrance of me'" (see 6.1.3). In the First Epistle to the Thessalonians (4:15-17), the encounter with Jesus that is to take place at the end of history, with the rising of the dead and the addition of those who are alive to Jesus' triumphant and glorious entourage, is said to be "the word of the Lord."

A final example from the First Epistle to the Corinthians (15:3-8) does not contain any of Jesus' words, but it does provide a summary of his death and his appearances following his resurrection: "Christ died . . . [and] was buried, . . . he was raised on the third day . . . [and] he appeared to Cephas, then to the twelve. Then he appeared to more than 500 brethren at one time, most of whom are still alive, though some have fallen asleep. Then he appeared to James, then to all the apostles. Last of all, as to one untimely born, he appeared also to me" (see 6.3).

The rest of the texts (of which there are many), whether from Paul's epistles, the Epistle of James, or the First Epistle of Peter, offer allusions to Jesus' words in the gospels. However, these epistles, unlike the Acts of Apostles (20:35), the First Epistle to the Corinthians (7:10-11, 9:14, 11:23-25), and the First Epistle to the Thessalonians (4:15-17), do not explicitly mention that the words come from the Lord Jesus. For example, there is the reference to the commandment on love ("love your neighbor as yourself"), recorded both by Paul (Rom 13:9, Gal 5:14) and the Gospels (Matt 22:39 || Mark 12:31 || Luke 10:27) and also by the Epistle of James (2:8). The latter offers quite a few phrases that resemble those that the Gospels attribute to Jesus. Thus, the call to pray with confidence (". . . let him ask in faith with no doubting"; Jas 1:6) closely echoes Jesus' words in Mark (11:24): "[W]hatever you ask in prayer, believe that you have received it, and it will be yours." Likewise, the question asked by James (4:12) ("But who are you that you judge your neighbor?") brings to mind Jesus' statement: "Judge not, that you be not judged" (Matt 7:1 || Luke 6:37).

The echoes of Jesus' words can be seen in the First Epistle of Peter; for example, "but even if you do suffer for righteousness's sake, you will be blessed" (3:14) is an obvious parallel to the eighth Beatitude from the Gospel according to Matthew: "Blessed are those who are persecuted for righteousness's sake, for theirs is the kingdom of heaven" (5:10). The similarities between Matthew (5:16) (". . . that they may see your good works and give glory to your Father who is in heaven") and the First Epistle of Peter 2:12 (". . . [that] they may see your good deeds and glorify God on the day of visitation") are self-evident.

2.1.3.3. The Apostolic Fathers

The Christian writers at the end of the first century and the first half of the second century are known as the Apostolic Fathers. They retained and passed down some of Jesus' words and activities, which they themselves picked up from the oral tradition or from documents unknown to us. The surviving works are not great in number, but they do demonstrate that the case of Papias of Hierapolis in Phrygia, author of a large collection of the Lord's sayings, was not an isolated one. Evidence of this has reached us via Eusebius of Caesarea in his *Ecclesiastical History* (3:39:3-4). The last years of the first century and the first quarter of the second century were characterized by the coexistence of written traditions about Jesus, the majority, and oral traditions that lasted in the memory of those who had known the apostles. For example, one of the oldest Christian documents, although later than the Gospels, is the Didache, or Teaching of the Apostles. This is apparently a collection of instructions that Jesus gave. This writing contains interesting elements regarding the life of Jesus and his disciples. It is presented as a model for the Christian missionaries who were traveling through Syria at the end of the first century. Many of Jesus' words in the Didache resemble those in Matthew, which was probably produced in Antioch in Syria. However, even older material may be yet found. For example, Didache (1:5) says with respect to almsgiving, "Give to everyone who asks you, and ask it not back." This sentence, implicitly attributed to Jesus, is also attributed to him by Luke 6:30: "Give to everyone who begs from you; and of him who takes away your goods do not ask them again." In Matthew (5:42), the phrase is given a slightly different tone: "Give to him who begs from you, and do not refuse him who would borrow from you."

The First Epistle of Clement of Rome to the Corinthians has also survived from this same time (ca. 95 A.D.). This interesting document contains seven of Jesus' sayings, known as the Sermon on the Mount (Matthew) or on the Plain (Luke), but expressed in a very ancient style, possibly indicating a source other than Q and these two gospels. The text says, ". . . remembering the words of the Lord Jesus which He spake teaching forbearance and long-suffering: for thus He spake 'Have mercy, that ye may receive mercy: forgive, that it may be forgiven to you. As ye do, so shall it be done to you. As ye give, so shall it be given unto you. As ye judge, so shall ye be judged. As ye show kindness, so shall kindness be showed unto you. With what measure ye mete, it shall be measured withal to you'" (13:1-2).

Soon after (ca. 110 A.D.), the Epistle of Ignatius of Antioch to the Smyrnaeans (3:2) was influenced by traditions that were not connected to the four Gospels. This is seen in the narrative of the resurrected Jesus' meeting with his disciples, a scene that closely resembles Luke 24:36-43 and that Ignatius may have picked up from the oral tradition: "[A]nd when He [Jesus] came to Peter and his company, He said to them, 'Lay hold and handle me, and see that I am not a demon without body.' And straightway they touched Him, and they believed, being joined unto His flesh and His blood. . . . And after His resurrection, He [both] ate with them and drank with them as one in the flesh, though spiritually He was united with the Father."

2.1.3.4. The Church Fathers and Other Ancient Sources

Finally, some sayings attributed to Jesus are quoted in a range of ancient Christian sources, both literary and liturgical, or apocryphal manuscripts and ecclesiastical regulations, but their contribution to the historical discourse on Jesus is very limited, although they may well be authentic words of his. Here are six examples: (a) Justin Martyr, in his *Dialogue with the Jew Trypho* (35), quotes a phrase that undeniably echoes Matthew (chaps. 10 and 24): "There shall be schisms and heresies" (1 Cor 11:18-19); (b) Clement of Alexandria, in his *Stromata*, quotes the following phrase: "seek what is great, and the little things shall be added" (1:24:158) (Matt 6:33 and 7:7); (c) a number of Christian authors, including Origen, quote a short and somewhat enigmatic sentence attributed to Jesus, echoed in the First Epistle to the Thessalonians (5:21): "Be ye good money-changers" (*Pseudo-Clementine Homilies* 2:51:1); (d) Tertullian quotes a sentence that closely resembles the Acts of the Apostles (14:22): "no one untempted should attain the celestial kingdoms" (*On Baptism* 20:2); (e) in the Acts of Peter (10), there is a brief sentence that is similar to Mark (8:17): "They that are with me have not understood me"; (f) a Syriac homily provides us with another short sentence: "As you are found, so will you be led away to judgment" (*Liber Graduum* 3:3, 15:4) (Matt 5:25-26, 10:17, and 24:40-41).

2.2. Non-Christian Sources

2.2.1. Jewish Sources

2.2.1.1. Josephus

The Jewish historian Josephus, born in Jerusalem (37 A.D.) into a well-to-do family with sacerdotal ancestors, is, without doubt, the most important non-Christian source on the life and activities of Jesus of Nazareth and, in general, on Judaism in the first century. Josephus, associated as a young man with the Pharisees, was the leader of a Jewish revolt against the army of Vespasian in Galilee, but he was taken prisoner and went on to predict that the Roman general would become emperor. This prediction was interpreted as a good omen, and when it came to pass, the new imperial family, the Flavius, protected him and he, in their honor, took the Roman surname Flavius. He wrote his literary work in Greek in Rome. The highlights of this work include *Bellum judaicum* (or "The War of the Jews," originally written in Aramaic) and *Antiquitates Judaicae* (or "The Antiquities of the Jews"). Of the latter, which is the only one to provide information on Jesus, a dozen Greek manuscripts survive (the oldest from the 11th c.), as does an earlier Latin translation (5th to 6th c.). Josephus, who died around 100 A.D., made every effort to justify the causes of the First Jewish Revolt, blaming the Zealots and Sadducees and removing all responsibility from the Pharisees for any anti-Roman sentiment. This did not save him from the rebuke of his own countrymen, many of whom were Pharisees and accused him of being a collaborator and traitor. Those who most appreciated his work were the Christian authors, in the anti-Jewish attacks that continued throughout the Middle Ages.

We are interested in three of the texts from the Antiquities: one talks extensively about John the Baptist (*A.J.* 18:116-19), which we will examine later (see 4.5.2); the second refers to the violent death of James, Jesus' brother (*A.J.* 20:200); and the third, known as the *Testimonium Flavianum*, talks about Jesus directly (*A.J.* 18:63-64).

Josephus explains that in 62 A.D., four years before the First Jewish Revolt broke out, the High Priest Annas and the Sanhedrin of Jerusalem, or the Great Council of the Jewish people, condemned the leader of the city's Christian community, James, to death, alongside some well-known members of the group:

> [Annas] assembled the Sanhedrin of judges, and brought before them the brother of Jesus, who was called Christ [Greek, *khristou*], whose name was James, and some others; and when he had formed an accusation against them as breakers of the law, he delivered them to be stoned. (*A.J.* 20:200)

This brief text does not show any signs of subsequent Christian intervention (see 6.2.3.1). In effect, it is not talking about James in a Christian way as "the Lord's brother" (Gal 1:19), simply addressing him as "the brother of Jesus." As G. Theissen points out, Jesus is mentioned as an aside and merely so as to identify James, as Josephus assumes that he will be less well known to his readers. In fact, Jesus has already been mentioned (*A.J.* 18:63-64). Finally, when Josephus talks about "Jesus, who was called Christ," he does so to distinguish him from others with the same name, which was common among first-century Jews, and it may not have been intended as any form of special recognition. This text shows that Josephus had an impartial view of Jesus and, if anything, viewed him positively. The Jewish historian makes it clear that James' stoning was illegal. The Sanhedrin could not dictate death sentences, which were reserved for the Roman authorities alone, and many law-abiding Jews, and the Pharisees in particular, disapproved of executions.

The other text in which Josephus talks about Jesus presents us with more problems. Although all the manuscripts of the *Antiquitates Judaicae* include it in full (18:63-64) and it is also quoted by the Christian historian Eusebius of Caesarea (260–339 A.D.), it does not seem, as these sources make out, to be the work of Josephus. Experts since the Reformation have argued that the entire fragment is a subsequent Christian addition. Some of the phrases are distinctly Christian in nature, but the language and content of a good part of the fragment have little to do with what would be expected from a Christian author. Over recent years, the theory that the so-called *Testimonium Flavianum* is an authentic fragment of Josephus, with some additions of Christian origin, has gained ground. The resulting text, which the majority of today's experts accept as genuine, is as follows (the probable additions are underlined and the original Greek of the most important terms is in parentheses, as proposed by J. P. Meier):

> Now there was about this time [when Pilate was governor] Jesus, a wise man (*sofos anēr*), if it be lawful to call him a man; for he was a doer of wonderful works (*paradoxōn*), a teacher of such men as receive the truth (*talēthē*) with pleasure. He drew over to him both many of the Jews and many of the Gentiles. He was [the] Christ [Messiah] (*khristos*). And when Pilate, at the suggestion of the principal men amongst us, had condemned him to the cross [to die], those that loved him at the first did not forsake him; for he appeared to them alive again the third day; as the divine prophets had foretold these and ten thousand other wonderful things concerning him. And the tribe of the Christians, so named from him, are not extinct at this day. (*A.J.* 18:63-64)

What we have considered authentic in this text closely resembles the quotation from the *Testimonium Flavianum* in the Arabic translation of the universal history of Christianity written by Agapius, Bishop of Hierapolis, in the tenth century. Here is Agapius' text, rescued from obscurity by the Jewish historian S. Pines:

> [Flavius] Josephus says . . . "At this time there was a wise man who was called Jesus, and his conduct was good, and he was known to be virtuous. And many people from among the Jews and the other nations became his disciples. Pilate condemned him to be crucified and to die. And those who had become his disciples did not abandon their loyalty to him. They reported that he had appeared to them three days after his crucifixion, and that he was alive. Accordingly they believed that he was the Messiah, concerning whom the Prophets have recounted wonders."

Therefore, it seems that the hypothesis of the Christian additions has been proven: each of the three additions mentions Jesus' divine nature (the first), that he is the Messiah of Israel (the second), and that he was risen from the dead, as predicted by the prophets of Israel (the third). Obviously, only Christians can express themselves in this way. If we read the text without these additions, we can see the original words of the Jewish author Josephus, who does not seem to show himself contrary to the Christians. For him, Jesus was a "wise man," who performed miracles and taught true things to the people of his time, with an impressive influence both among his own people and among other peoples (the Gentiles). He was accused by the Jewish leaders and condemned by the Roman governor Pilate to die on the cross, but his followers did not abandon him; instead, they kept his memory alive.

2.2.1.2. Rabbinic Manuscripts

While Josephus talks impartially about Jesus, the rabbinic manuscripts speak of him as a result of the reaction and opposition to the Christian writings, in particular the canonical Gospels of the Christian Church, especially the Gospel according to John in the case of the Babylonian Talmud. As P. Schäfer points out, the Talmud enters the polemic against Christianity by presenting Jesus the other way around to the New Testament, although, in general, it does not reach the levels of malignancy found in the medieval work "Toledot Jesus." We need to add only that, in addition to the contempt and rejection of both Jesus and the disciples, rabbinical writings keep their silence: in the Babylonian Talmud explicit references to Jesus are censored or replaced by a vague "he" or by an offensive "son of the Panthera"—a Roman soldier with an invented name (the result of switching the order of the consonants of the Greek *parthenos*, virgin, which is applied to the mother of Jesus in the canonical Gospels). References to the figure of Jesus are rare (fifteen or so), scattered among six tractates of the Babylonian Talmud, two tractates of the Palestinian or Jerusalem Talmud, the tractate of Tosefta, and the Midrash Rabba to the book of Ecclesiastes. Despite this scarcity of references, the Babylon Talmud, written in Babylon under Sassanid domination—a dynasty fighting the eastern Christian empire, Byzantium—does refer to Jesus: his family (Jesus is a bastard, *mamzer*, the fruit of an adulterous relationship), his education (Jesus is a frivolous and libertine student), his status as interpreter of the Jewish Law (he has no authority), the healing of the sick attributed to him (without divine assistance), his fully justified execution for idolatry and blasphemy, the five disciples executed with him, and the eternal punishment that he and his followers have deserved. Clearly the rabbinical writings treat Jesus in a biased manner, and an anti-Christian polemic predominates. However, at certain points one could say that the Babylonian Talmud contains elements of the early Jewish tradition concerning Jesus, at the same time as it is strongly pervaded by the denial of Jesus as a messenger from God. We mention two baraitoth, that is, two early traditions forming part of the Tractate *Sanhedrin* of the Babylonian Talmud (written at the end of the 5th c.), which may have their origins in the second century. One of them refers to the execution of Jesus:

> On the eve of the Passover, Yeshu [i.e., Jesus], the Nazarene, was hanged. For 40 days before the execution took place, a herald went forth and cried, "He is going forth to be stoned because he has practised sorcery and enticed Israel to apostasy. Any one who can say anything in his favour, let him come forward and plead on his behalf." But since nothing was brought forward in his favour he was hanged on the eve of the Passover. Ulla retorted: "Do you suppose that he was one for whom a defence could be made? Was he not a Mesith [*enticer*], concerning whom scripture says, 'Neither shalt thou spare, neither shalt thou conceal him'? With Yeshu however it was different, for he [i.e., his case] was connected with the [Roman] government." (*Sanh.* 43a)

It is difficult to interpret every one of the details in this text. It talks of Jesus as someone who is executed (stoned and then hanged) on the eve of Passover, as someone who had magical powers (who performed miracles), and as someone who, ultimately, misled the Jewish people, who tricked them and enticed them and led them into idolatry, that is, to follow and to believe in a man (Jesus) who was a blasphemer, an enemy of God. The reasons why he was condemned are, in terms of rabbinic orthodoxy, made clear. Similar expressions to describe Jesus are seen in the second *baraita*, which also gives a clear idea of the disputes between Christians and Jews:

> One day, while Joshua was reciting the Shema [the daily Jewish prayer] Yeshu [i.e., Jesus] came to him. Joshua made a sign to him with his hand. Yeshu misunderstood, thinking he had been repulsed, so he went away, set up a brick and worshipped it. Joshua said to him "Repent!" Yeshu replied, "I learned this from you: 'Anyone who sins and causes the people to sin, is not allowed the possibility of repentance.'" The teacher said: "Yeshu practised sorcery and corrupted and misled Israel." (*Sanh.* 107b)

The portrayal of Jesus as a false prophet who had apostatized from the faith of Israel and led others to do the same and the mockery by the Jewish leaders are repeated, more virulently, in a text from the Tractate *Gittin* in the Babylonian Talmud (56b–57a). This text is also set within the context of anti-Christian attacks and does not provide any interesting contribution to the history of Jesus: Jesus is shown to be affiliated with two other great "blasphemers" (Titus and Balaam) and suffers terrible, infernal, and degrading punishment. The anti-Christian attacks against the Gospel doctrine of Jesus' virgin birth led to a tendentious and malevolent narrative on Jesus' origins, found in the Tractate *Shabbat* from the Babylonian Talmud (104b). Jesus is presented as the son of Miriam "the women's hairdresser" and Pandera, her lover. A similar version is recounted by Celsus, a philosopher from the second century who argued against Christianity: "[S]he [Jesus' mother] was turned out of doors by the carpenter to whom she had been betrothed, as having been guilty of adultery, and that she bore a child to a certain soldier named Panthera" (quoted by Origen in his book *Against Celsus* 1:32). These are biased accounts of Jesus' origins, designed simply to counter the reports of his virgin birth, as seen in the Gospels of Matthew and Luke.

2.2.2. Roman Sources

2.2.2.1. Tacitus

In 116–117 A.D., the Roman patrician Publius Cornelius Tacitus (56–ca. 120 A.D.) wrote the *Annals*, a work intended to be a history of Rome from the death of Augustus to the death of Nero. In the section dedicated to Nero, Tacitus describes the fire of Rome started by the emperor in 64 A.D., but for which the Christians of the city were unjustly held responsible. This accusation was intended to appease the people's indignation, and as a result, many Christians were executed. Tacitus does not condone Nero's opportunist cruelty, but he does call the Christians "criminals who deserved extreme and exemplary punishment." Christians are presented as people who hated mankind (*odium humani generis*), that is, that as Jews they did not meet the socially acceptable rules and customs. Furthermore, Tacitus says that they believed in a "mischievous superstition," in other words, that they professed a belief that negated the official worship of Rome's gods and thus represented a threat to the state. In short, the Christians were well known enough in Nero's Rome for him to be able to use them as a scapegoat. Tacitus explains why people call them *christiani* or *chrestiani*:

> Christus, from whom the name had its origin, suffered the extreme penalty [*supplicio adfectus erat*] during the reign of Tiberius at the hands of one of our procurators, Pontius Pilate, and a most mischievous superstition [*exitiabilis superstitio*], thus checked for the moment, again broke out not only in Judaea, the first source of the evil, but even in Rome, where all things hideous and shameful from every part of the world find their centre and become popular. (*Annals* 15:44)

2.2.2.2. Suetonius

Suetonius, another Roman historian (70–ca. 130 A.D.), also describes Christianity as a "new and impious superstition." He wrote the biography of twelve Caesars, or emperors, from Julius Caesar to Domitian. In this work, De vita Caesarum, written around 120 A.D., Gaius Suetonius Tranquillus mentions the expulsion of the Jews from Rome decreed by Claudius in 49 A.D. and also mentioned in Acts (18:2), where it says, "[In Corinth, Paul] found a Jew named Aquila, a native of Pontus, lately come from Italy with his wife Priscilla, because Claudius had commanded all the Jews to leave Rome." This is how Suetonius justifies this imperial measure:

> [Claudius] banished from Rome all the Jews, who were continually making disturbances at the instigation of one Chrestus [Christ] [*impulsore Chresto*]. (*Life of Claudius* 25)

This short note shows a lack of information or an error when Suetonius read his sources, as it assumes that this Christ ("Christus/Chrestus") was in Rome instigating these disturbances among the Jews of Rome when Claudius was emperor. In any case, Suetonius does let us know that this individual was the cause of the disorder among Rome's Jews. It is highly likely that this reference from the Roman historian is the result of bitter controversies arising within the Jewish community concerning the acceptance or denial of Jesus as the Messiah (Latin, *Christus*). The confrontations led to a decision by the emperor, who was not enamored of eastern religions, and he decreed that all the Jews be banished from the city or, according to another possible interpretation of the Latin, only those Jews who had taken part in the disturbances. Thus, the division among the Jews of Rome was produced as a result of the Christian mission, which had been particularly active among the Jews of the imperial capital, even though Jesus had been dead for only twenty years.

2.2.2.3. Pliny the Younger

Another Roman source on Jesus, called Christ in Roman texts, was produced at this time. Pliny the Younger (61–ca. 120 A.D.) had been sent by Emperor Trajan to Asia Minor, to the province of Bithynia-Pontus, to act as governor. He lived there from 111 to 113 A.D. and kept up prolific correspondence with the emperor from there. For Pliny, as for Tacitus and Suetonius, Christianity was a "superstition," which he described as "perverse and extravagant." The denunciations of Christians increased, and Pliny felt it was necessary to make Trajan aware of this and of his position of nonintervention ("I have never participated in trials of Christians"), although he had already started to condemn Christians for simply being such. Trajan merely advises his governor to intervene when a Christian had really broken the laws in force and adds that he should not pay attention to unfounded accusations: being a Christian was not a crime in itself.

During the course of their correspondence, Pliny mentions Jesus in passing; specifically, the word *Christus* appears threes times in letter 96 from book X of his *Letters to Trajan*. On the first occasion, Pliny stresses that the authentic Christians remain firm in not offering sacrifices to the gods and the emperor and thus refuse to renounce the name of Christ (*Christo male dicere*). On the second occasion, the governor compiles a series of declarations by former apostate Christians and two slave women, "servants" or possibly "deaconesses" (*ministrae*) of the community, submitted to torture. Here is a summary of the information gleaned by Pliny on the Christian practices in his provinces:

> They were accustomed to meet on a fixed day before dawn and sing responsively a hymn to Christ as to a god [*carmenque Christo quasi deo dicere*], and to bind themselves by oath, not to some crime, but not to commit fraud, theft, or adultery, not falsify their trust, nor to refuse to return a trust when called upon to do so. (*Letters* 10:96)

The references to Jesus, called *Christ* in the three Roman sources above, are undoubtedly made from a historical point of view. However, they do not offer more than brief reports, which can be summarized as follows: Christ (*Christus*), that is, Jesus, executed by Pontius Pilate, governor of Judaea, when Tiberius was emperor, founded the Christian group; this group, which had spread through the country of the Jews, where it began, and reached Asia Minor and Rome, worshipped Christ as a god.

2.2.3. Other Sources

2.2.3.1. Greek Sources

The remaining sources are few in number and offer less. Jesus appears only indirectly, as "the wise king of the Jews" or "the crucified one." The two non-Christian authors who mention him come from the same Hellenistic city in Syria, Samosata. They are Mara and Lucian.

The Stoic philosopher Mara bar Serapion, who was imprisoned in Rome, wrote a letter in Syriac to his son where he urges him to live in accordance with that which really matters, wisdom, by copying the models of the wise men. Alongside Socrates and the sculptor (or philosopher) Pythagoras, Mara apparently refers to Jesus (see W. Cureton, 43–48) as follows:

> What advantage did the Jews gain from executing their wise King? It was just after that their Kingdom was abolished. God justly avenged these three wise men [Socrates, Pythagoras, and Jesus]; . . . the Jews, ruined and driven from their land, live in complete dispersion. But

> Socrates did not die for good; he lived on in the teaching of Plato. Pythagoras did not die for good; he lived on in the statue of Hera. Nor did the wise King die for good; He lived on in the teaching which He had given.

This letter, which has to be dated after the destruction of Jerusalem (70 A.D.) and the disaster that hit the Jewish people who lived in Palestine, offers an important reference. The defeat of the Jews at the hand of the Roman general Titus and the subsequent deportation of the Jewish warriors that survived is seen as divine retribution, in the same way that other contemporary sources, both Christian (Matt 22:7, 23:35-36, 27:25) and Jewish (2 Bar 1–3 or the 4 Esd 2:1-14), viewed them. Mara knows the Christian tradition of Jesus' royalty, which is linked to the Passion; indeed, the plaque above Jesus' cross reads, "the king of the Jews" (see 6.2.5.3). However, this does not mean that Mara was necessarily a Christian since his description of the death of Jesus differs from his description of the death of Socrates and Pythagoras, whom he talks about as living on through their works. Mara stresses that Socrates' philosophy lives on thanks to Plato, who compiled it; and Pythagoras' art lasts thanks to his sculptures, such as that of the goddess Hera; Jesus has taught "new laws," in the Gospels, which contrast with the "old laws," in the Jewish Torah. These "laws," or wisdom, are considered to be the greatest contribution of the Jewish "King," the "Wise King."

A few years later (in the second half of the 2nd c. A.D.), also in Samosata, another author, Lucian, echoed the words of Mara bar Serapion. In his work, the *Passing of Peregrinus* (nos. 11 and 13), Lucian talks about the case of a man who was "crucified" in Palestine "because he introduced this new cult into the world." However, this man is presented as a "sophist," as someone who wanted to possess wisdom and who had inspired followers. According to Lucian, these followers, the Christians, still observed the "laws." Jesus, then, is presented as a philosopher who has propagated a particular doctrine and way of life, which have had an influence on Syria, the world that Lucian knows. The Christians, "worshipping this crucified sophist himself," live "under his laws," that is, the Gospels.

Both Mara and Lucian make it clear that Jesus suffered a violent death. Lucian talks about a crucifixion. A Greek, or possibly

Samaritan, author in the second half of the first century A.D. called Thallus, who wrote a universal history in three volumes, may also have referred to this. His work has reached us indirectly, via Julius Africanus, a Christian chronologist from the third century, who used Thallus' volumes in his historical work. Julius explains that, according to Thallus, there was a solar eclipse in 29 A.D. and that this eclipse should be linked to the darkness that covered the land while Jesus suffered on the cross (Luke 23:44-45). If we have correctly interpreted this somewhat confused text, it seems that Thallus wants to interpret this darkness as a natural event, while Julius Africanus refutes this and interprets this darkness as a wholly supernatural miracle. If our reading of the sources is correct, Thallus alludes to Jesus' crucifixion and tries to contradict the Christian belief that certain miraculous cosmic phenomena took place at the time of his death on the cross.

2.2.3.2. Islamic Sources

We also need to note the Islamic sources and, specifically, the Qur'an, a document from the seventh century. The Qur'an is a late historical source on Jesus and depends on Christian, canonical and apocryphal, and Jewish sources. Jesus is "Isa Ibn Mariam," that is, Jesus son of Mary, to whom Allah, or God, "gave clear miracles": God made him a holy prophet (sura 2:253). Jesus' power and holiness come from his being the son of a virgin mother and are seen in his extraordinary conception: "And she who guarded her chastity [Mary], so We [God] breathed into her of Our inspiration and made her and her son [Jesus] a sign for the nations" (sura 21:91). In a similar vein, in sura 19 of the Qur'an, which is titled "Marium" and is dedicated in its entirety to the mother of Jesus, there is a description of the announcement from the angel Gabriel. God's messenger tells Mary that God is to give her "a beautiful boy, young, strong, pure and perfect" (ayat 19).

The Qur'an recounts the disbelief and opposition that Jesus' miracles encountered and specifically denounces the Jewish accusation that he practiced magic. This, as we have seen (see 2.2.1.2), is found in the Talmud. The Qur'an says, ". . . [Y]ou [Jesus] came to them [the Jews] with clear arguments, but those who disbelieved among them said: This is nothing but clear enchantment" (sura 5:110; and, similarly, sura 61:6). The disputes between Christianity and Judaism in the Arabian peninsula, at the time of Muhammad, with regard to Jesus' origins (holy man or bastard) and the theological discussions among Christians themselves are echoed on various occasions in the Qur'an. The holy Islamic book stresses Jesus' holiness but does not recognize him as the Son of God, as "[i]t beseems not Allah that He should take to Himself a son" (sura 19:35).

However, according to the third sura, "Al-Imran," which offers a kind of summary of Jesus' life, Jesus has been sent by God and deserves the title "Al-Massih," that is, "Messiah" or "Christ." Here, Jesus is described as "a miracle," created, like Adam, by God himself. Jesus is "honourable and chaste," "he shall speak to the people when in the cradle and when of old age," and his power is such that he can "bring the dead to life with Allah's permission." The intrigues and tricks of the demons are useless against him, and God, who "vanquished" evil, says to him, "I am going to . . . cause you to ascend unto Me and purify you of those who disbelieve and make those who follow you above those who disbelieve to the day of resurrection." These words allude to Jesus' death and resurrection/ascension, as narrated in the Gospels.

According to the Qur'an, Jesus is a divine emissary whom God, Allah, has "taught . . . the Book and the wisdom and the Taurat [the Torah or Jewish Scriptures] and the Injeel [the Gospels or Christian Scriptures]" (sura 5:110). However, Jesus repeatedly foretold of the "Apostle who will come after me," the prophet Muhammad (sura 61:6). The historical references to Jesus in the Qur'an are blended with reinterpretations influenced by Islamic doctrine. The basis for these references includes the whole of the Bible, both the Old and New Testaments, and the Apocrypha.

2.3. The Value of the Sources on Jesus

This long journey through the historical sources on Jesus of Nazareth leads us to an undeniable conclusion: there is no doubt as to the historical existence of this individual. Denying the existence of Jesus would be irresponsible, even when based on painstaking and rigorous historical criticism; the figure of Jesus is not a construct, a product of the imagination of the early Christian community. Similarly, one cannot adopt an uncritical attitude toward the historical sources on Jesus that views these sources as completely unbiased. On the contrary, solid historical research neither discounts them nor accepts them blindly; rather, they have to be weighed and interpreted. This ensures that both sterile skepticism and naive apologetics can be avoided.

Questions about Jesus can be made based on the data that we have on him and on what surrounded him and his work. This is the key: to correctly situate Jesus in his time and to read the historical sources in terms of the corresponding context and circumstances. To be able to make progress with this undertaking, we need to fully understand the life of first-century and modern Jews and to take into account the Judaism that acted as the backdrop to Jesus' birth, life, and death and the early Christian community that continued his memory. In other words, Jesus has to be placed, plausibly, credibly, and convincingly, into the context of contemporary Judaism and Christianity.

All the material we have at our disposal must be considered in light of certain criteria and rules that enable us to analyze critically the Gospel texts and to discern what each of them contains with regard to the historicity of Jesus. The aim of putting forward these criteria is to refine our approach to the historical Jesus as far as possible and hence to measure how reliable the results obtained are. A criterion is a tool and has to be used not in a mechanical way but with tact and sensitivity, in the knowledge that it is not infallible but neither is it superfluous, since the direction of research into the historical Jesus largely depends on it. The so-called Second Quest for the historical Jesus had prioritized the criterion of discontinuity, combined with the criterion of coherence. It appears that these two criteria might result in what is true of and exclusive to Jesus, his "uniqueness." In fact, the criterion of discontinuity or dissimilarity postulated that, in order to reach the core of the life and message of Jesus, it was necessary to discard everything that depended on or was sympathetic to first-century Judaism and early Christianity. Once this sort of "purification" had been carried out, one had to construct, on the basis of "coherence," a global vision of Jesus that would gradually be completed as materials formerly under suspicion were recovered. These two criteria, complemented by other minor ones, brought to the table the three variants that compose the question on the historical Jesus: his contemporary Judaism, the Christian community that came into being after him, and his own person and message (acts and words according to the Gospels/Scriptures and other written sources). The two aforementioned criteria provide a way of relating Jesus to Judaism, on the one hand, and to the early Christian community, on the other.

The Third Quest for the historical Jesus revised and reformulated these two criteria. It is the same procedure, but the rules have been changed. In essence, the separation that grew up between the first stages in the research, in which the discontinuity was emphasized, and the later stages, in which a certain continuity was reestablished, isolated Jesus from his Jewish context and did not take into account the impact this had on the early Christian community. Continuity and discontinuity must both be taken into account simultaneously, thereby bringing out the concept of "authenticity." Historical material on Jesus cannot be reduced to a disjunctive statement of this type: Is this word attributed to Jesus authentic or not? Did the episode attributed to him really happen, or was it a fabrication? We need to introduce and manage the concept of the oral and written Jesus tradition that allows the Gospel material to be interpreted in a flexible and nuanced manner; this material is the fruit of the activities of the early Christian community and the result of authentic transmission of the message. We need to emphasize the weight and importance of Jesus' Jewishness, that is, his level of integration into the Judaism(s) of the first century, as a background that constantly emerges in the four canonical Gospels of the first century and as a background to his own personal characteristics.

The criterion of discontinuity or dissimilarity has been subsumed and transformed into the criterion of historical plausibility, as formulated by Theissen and Winter. Peculiar to the Third Quest, the criterion of plausibility has integrated the criteria of embarrassment and multiple attestation and partially the criterion of coherence. On the other hand, the criterion of coherence has been developed into the criterion of "charactericity" by J. Dunn. This writer maintains that those elements characteristic of the tradition of Jesus, even though they may be rather different from it, must be incorporated into it, and even though such elements may be central or peripheral to mainstream Judaism at the time of Jesus. In other words, a natural continuity is established between Jesus and the early Christian community, taking shape in the "Jesus tradition" that grew from the record of those who knew him firsthand. The continuity between Jesus and the early community is not an a posteriori "construction" but rather a theme common to any tradition: what is transmitted and recorded constantly reestablishes the relationship with the person behind this tradition. The Jesus tradition begins during his ministry and not after Easter.

The criterion of historical plausibility embodies a double plausibility: that of the context (the Jewish world in which Jesus lived) and that of his impact (the world of the early Christian community that came into being after him). In both cases, the similarities and the differences help us to understand the relationship between Jesus and his environment or the one that he helped to create. Thus, as far as the Jewish context is concerned, Jesus is clearly inseparable from Palestinian Judaism of the first century, and any tradition relating to him must take account of the Judaism of his time. An example: Jesus' baptism by John cannot be dissociated from the movement that the latter instigated in the decade beginning in 20 A.D. in the area of the Jordan. On the other hand, Jesus' integration into the Jewish context of the time does not negate his singularity; indeed, it reinforces it. The greater our knowledge of the Jewishness of Jesus, the greater our understanding of his particular character. An example: the laws relating to ritual washing on fasting days are scrupulously adhered to by the rabbis who are contemporaries of Jesus, but he does not share this position and does not desist from eating with public and notorious sinners, with whom no rabbi would share a table. Jesus' behavior is obviously very unsettling to the strictest of Jews.

Let us move on to the plausibility of the impact that Jesus had. The independent Christian sources that were not modified at a later date agree on elements that come from Jesus himself. However, we must be wary of drawing overly quick conclusions from the evidence of multiple sources. Sometimes a single source can constitute a very solid piece of evidence. For example, the parables of the Good Samaritan and the prodigal son are present only in Luke! The impact that Jesus had on the early community leads to both agreement among the many sources and disagreement among them.

We can see how historical plausibility works when applied to Jesus of Nazareth. We have shown how the Jesus tradition is spread among six literary sources, coming from the early Christian community: the Q collection of sayings, the Gospel of Mark, Matthew's own material, Luke's own material, the Gospel of John, and the collection of sayings included in Thomas. The expression the "Kingdom of God" appears in all six sources as well as in Paul's epistles. This repeated use indicates that it must be one of Jesus' authentic sayings (see 5.1). The converse is also the case, however. For example, the reference to Jesus as "a glutton and a drunkard" appears only in Q (Matt 11:19 and Luke 7:34). Such a surprising expression presents problems, and it seems unlikely that it would have been invented by the early Christians. In this case, we have to conclude that it comes from Jesus' time and from those who criticized him. Jesus clearly states that he is not ascetic like John the Baptist but rather that he keeps to normal eating habits.

We now need to look at the way Jesus fit into the Judaism of his time. Jesus' lifestyle was that of a pious Jew of this period. For example, Jesus went to the synagogue on Saturdays, the day of rest, where he heard the Scriptures and, on occasions, preached (Mark 6:2 and Luke 4:16). This was common practice among devout Jews. Jesus, however, was surprising in the unique way in which he acted. Even though it was Saturday and the Sabbath, he was happy to heal the sick, despite the opposition of the Pharisees (Mark 3:1-6 and Luke 14:1-6) (see 5.3.2.2). The case of the Sabbaths shows that a flexible interpretation of the historical sources relating to Jesus is required. This has to be combined with a close linking of Jesus to the Judaism of his time and the distance that grew between them.

The criterion of historical plausibility helps us to focus and clarify what we know about Jesus, contributing to a comprehensive perspective that is devoid of ambiguity and vagueness. The natural context for Jesus the person, a Jew in Galilee, is Judaism, or, more precisely, the Judaisms of the first century. In this context, his uniqueness becomes clear. Hence, we need to understand the social, geographical, historical, and religious context in which he lived. We need to understand his world at its innermost: the Judaism, or Judaisms, of the first century, which were active in the land in which he was born, lived, and died.

2.4. The Archaeological Data

Looking closely at the materials that provide information concerning Jesus, we can establish that the major part comes from written sources that are both direct and indirect and both internal and external to early Christianity. At the same time, we cannot ignore the information relating to the historical, social, political, economic, and religious context in which Jesus lived. Especially with respect to the next chapter, "Context," we must also mention the contribution made by archaeology to our understanding of Jesus' world. There are no actual material objects (artifacts, implements) that we can be absolutely sure belonged to Jesus, although there is a fair amount of certainty with regard to some objects, such as the Turin Shroud, where the imprint of a crucified body does point to the Passion of Jesus. On the other hand, there are places and locations referred to in the written materials but also known from geographical and topographical studies that support the concrete circumstances surrounding the life of Jesus and his disciples, of the people who followed him, and of his adversaries.

Stones and objects speak to us, and thus archaeological remains allow us to read and interpret the writings in ways that are more perceptive and at times quite surprising. James H. Charlesworth mentions the words of E. Robinson (1856): "Jesus' country is not a *terra incognita*." It is certainly a country that has preserved a large number of objects contemporaneous to Jesus' times, and these have been brought to light by the archaeological campaigns and discoveries of the past few decades. Despite the limitations and general opacity of certain hypotheses, it cannot be denied that archaeology has opened new paths, leading to a better understanding and sometimes interpretation of the general environment in which Jesus lived.

The book you have in your hands has attempted to make use of the data furnished by archaeology above all in the second of those areas we have just mentioned: the context and the environment of Jesus' life that shaped the times in which he lived. Of course, archaeological data cannot be separated from social history. What is more complex is the systematic use of sociology, anthropology, and even more so psychology. M. Sawicki's warning that research into Jesus has been too reverential toward sociology while remaining overly suspicious of the written word must be taken seriously. In other words, the necessary use of heuristic models clarifies and simplifies the task, but it suffers from the disadvantage of washing away the nuances and of applying an analytical framework that tends to iron out contrasts. Such models run the risk of reducing the natural scope of the writings and the meanings inherent in them. Research models do give rise to innovative and stimulating insights. However, the strictures imposed by the working hypotheses make the interpretation of the writings awkward and burdensome. This can lead to the acceptance or dismissal of interpretations that tend to be viewed as global. We need to be careful. S. Freyne has pointed out that beyond the heuristic models chosen—none of which are adequate—clearly the symbolic universe and the social world of Jesus have to be included in the interpretative quest.

In my view, the contribution made by archaeology has been most noteworthy in the field of contextual information, and it has served as confirmation of the facts contained in the written materials. Archaeological data bring concrete information, which may confirm or sometimes negate previous conclusions, to Jesus research. Naturally the text is the fixed point of reference for the artifact; the text always has the last word. Archaeology is not enough on its own, as it is but an additional and complementary source allowing us to gain a better understanding of the text. To the extent that the artifact helps us to understand history, it gives color to the text and contextualizes it within the life from which it comes, widening the interpretative horizons. Thus, archaeology is not just some sort of ethnographic covering, a mere top coat of paint—quite the contrary, an archaeological fact can become the key to interpreting a text.

Jerusalem and Galilee are the two fundamental archaeological areas for Jesus research. Let us stop a moment in the Holy City. We have to only pick up a recent work (*Jesus and Archaeology*) compiled by James H. Charlesworth to see for ourselves how the information available has increased over the past few years. Jesus' stay in Jerusalem (synoptic Gospels) or his several stays there (John) have been bathed in a new light, and the Jerusalem of Jesus' time is slowly opening up to us in front of our eyes. Specifically, the urban geography around 30 A.D. is portrayed with noteworthy clarity: the perimeter of the walls and the location of the city gates, the hill of Golgotha where the crucifixions took place outside the city walls, the nearby quarry that became a burial place (mound and tombs situated in what is now the church of the Holy Sepulchre or Anastasia), the enormous temple with all its facilities (underground stairways and the corridors going from the Gate of Hulda to the esplanade), the temple annexes (the massive stairway that rose from the city to the esplanade, the great baths for ritual purification or *miqvaot* to the south of the mount where the temple stood), the pools of Betzata or Bethesda (with the five porticoes to the north of the temple) and Siloe (to the south of the ancient city of David), and the praetorium of the Roman governor (on the site of what was Herod's palace, a fortified residence with a great stone courtyard to the west of the city). Houses, palaces, cut stone masonry, shops, (probably) theatre seats in stone, (probably) Theodotus' synagogue, within the city, and sepulchres with ossuaries, outside the city, inscriptions, paintings, and all manner of artifacts—all in all making a typical first-century city with great buildings, the trappings of the center of the Jewish religion—practiced by almost a tenth of the population of the Roman Empire, for whom the temple was the great symbol of its distinctive identity.

This picture of the Jerusalem of Jesus' time furnished by the science of archaeology has had various consequences. Undoubtedly, archaeology frequently portrays for us the social and symbolic context for the framework of Jesus' life. The framework is fundamentally and crucially linked to the written sources, above all the four Gospels of the first century—the so-called *canonical* Gospels—which give us direct access to the deeds and the words of Jesus of Nazareth. But it is archaeology that helps to verify what the writings tell us. Thus, the fact that archaeology has confirmed the historical accuracy of the Gospel according to John and has elevated it to the category of a historical source, on an equal footing with the three other, synoptic Gospels, is particularly relevant for the history of Jesus research. In a word, archaeology is laying claim to its rightful part in the research into Jesus; its contribution to this body of knowledge fully justifies it being considered a partner in this research.

3

The Context

The world inhabited by Jesus and his disciples was basically the region of Galilee as it was in the first century A.D. Its boundaries, according to S. Freyne, stretched from Lake Hula to the town of Nain, overlooking the valley of Jezreel, or Esdraelon (some sixty kilometers north to south), and from the river Jordan/Lake Galilee to Beit Shearim (on average, some forty kilometers east to west). Galilee was a mountainous country. The only areas without mountains were the fertile valleys surrounding the lake. This Jewish country was hemmed in between the Mediterranean plains to the west and the Plain of Esdraelon to the south, areas inhabited by non-Jews, and by the geological depression of the Jordan, to the east, where Lake Galilee is some two hundred meters below the level of the Mediterranean Sea. Beyond the Jordan to the east was another area dominated by non-Jewish races, as was the case to the north of the country, where Galilee was bordered by the great Phoenician cities (Tyre and Sidon, and Ptolemais) and by the land of Caesarea Philippi or Paneas, the Hellenistic metropolis at the source of the river Jordan.

The land of Galilee had belonged to Israel since the thirteenth to twelfth centuries B.C. when the Canaanites, the original inhabitants, were progressively substituted (not without some amount of cultural fusion) by a new displaced population, in part, from Egypt: the Hebrew people. As time went by, the Israelite tribes of Zebulun and Naphtali occupied and settled the land that would, subsequently, become known as Galilee. However, in 722 B.C., the Assyrians' destruction of one of the two Jewish kingdoms, the kingdom of the North or the kingdom of Israel, caused mass migration. The Assyrians deported the Israelites to Haran in northern Mesopotamia, and the people in these regions, who were not Jews but pagans, were moved by force to Galilee. This echoed Isaiah's ancient prophecy that foresaw "a great light," the light of the Messiah, David's descendant, which would light "the people who walked in darkness," a people who would be happy again following great hardship and grief. The ancient prophecy, reiterated in the Gospel of Matthew, says, "In the former time he brought into contempt the land of Zebulun and the land of Naphtali, but in the latter time he will make glorious the way of the sea, the land beyond Jordan, Galilee of the nations" (Isa 9:1).

The pagans, the non-Jews, would never leave this land again. Following this people from northern Mesopotamia, others were to arrive, this time speaking Greek, with the conquests of Alexander the Great (333 B.C.). Not even when Galilee was reconquered between the second and first centuries B.C. by the Hasmoneans, Jewish kings, and the land was dominated by Jews once more with their migration from Judaea to the north did the presence of the non-Jewish population disappear. This return of the Jews was the work of Aristobulus I, a Jewish king of the Hasmonean dynasty (104–103 B.C.), and his successor Alexander Jannaeus (103–76 B.C.). Nevertheless, soon after (63 B.C.), the Roman legions, led by Pompey, occupied the Hasmonean kingdom, and the whole of the territory including Galilee was annexed to the Roman Empire. The arrival of Pompey brought with it a wide-ranging political reorganization that affected the whole of David's ancient kingdom. The Roman general reduced the jurisdiction of the high priest in Jerusalem to the three areas where the Jews represented the majority of the population: Judaea, the mountainous region around Jerusalem, to the west of the Jordan; Peraea or Transjordan, the region to the east of the Jordan, on the other side of the river; and Galilee to the north. Jewish Law did not affect the citizens or their social lives in other neighboring regions, where the Jews were a minority, such as the free Hellenistic cities of the Decapolis or the Mediterranean coast, or indeed where they were nonexistent, such as Samaria.

The ancient land of the kingdom of David, the great king of Israel, was broken up into a mosaic of administrative units, each with different languages, cultures, races, and religions and all under the jurisdiction of the legate in Syria, the great Roman province of the east, the capital of which was the city of Antioch on the Orontes. Galilee was a small territory in this vast province, which in 37 B.C. became part of the new kingdom of an Edomite, Herod, whom the Romans recognized as a *rex socius et amicus populi romani*. The new rulers of the country showed their gratitude to Herod, who had defeated the Parthians, naming him sovereign of a territory that was nearly as large as the ancient kingdom of David. It was during Herod's reign as king of Judaea, Samaria and Edom, Peraea and Galilee, Trachonitis and Iturea, that Jesus was born, the "king of the Jews," member of the tribe of Judah and descendant of David, known at the time as Jesus of Nazareth, a small town in Galilee.

3.1. Galilee

3.1.1. The Towns and Cities

Galilee in the time of Jesus was primarily rural and inhabited in the most part by Jews, and it was here that Jesus lived almost all his life. The inhabitants who were not Jews were a minority and concentrated in just two cities: Sepphoris and Tiberias. These two cities were paid special attention by Herod Antipas, son of Herod the Great, who was tetrarch or sovereign of Galilee from the death of his father (4 B.C.) until 39 A.D.: forty-three years, almost Jesus' entire life. During the first part of his long reign, Antipas' capital was Sepphoris, in mountainous Galilee, which had been reconstructed and embellished following its destruction during the revolt against Rome in 4 B.C. and even given a new name: *Autocratoris*, "Imperial (city)," in honor of Augustus. Indeed, the history of Sepphoris has a before and after in terms of 4 B.C. From the time of Alexander Jannaeus (103–76 B.C.), a period when Galilee was repopulated with Jews, with the arrival of a great number of immigrants from Judaea, Sepphoris had been a strictly Jewish city. For this reason, it was the focus of the Galilean revolt that followed the death of Herod (4 B.C.) and became the stronghold for Judas, son of Hezekiah, one of the leaders of the uprising (see 3.3.3.1). The troops led by Varus, the governor of Syria, came down harshly on the Jews involved in the uprising; the city was set alight and its inhabitants sold as slaves. From then on, Sepphoris became a city with a mixed population, in which the Jews, still a majority, were to a great extent pro-Roman, and where the Sadducees were stronger than the Pharisees. Varus' bloody punishment may well have had its effect. Thus, Sepphoris, which according to Josephus was "the largest city of Galilee," was the only town in the land that opened its doors to Vespasian, asking to be protected by a Roman garrison and even offering to "assist him against their own countrymen" (*J.W.* 3:32–34).

The most interesting archaeological find in Sepphoris is a theatre with a capacity for 4,500 people. According to E. and C. Meyers, the construction of this theatre must date back to the first half of the second century A.D., but most archaeologists, including Z. Weiss (the current director of the dig), believe that the theatre was built at the start of the first century A.D., during Antipas' reign and as part of his building work, when Sepphoris was still the capital of Galilee. Josephus would seem to confirm this conclusion, as he calls the city "the security of all Galilee" (*A.J.* 18:27) and talks about the building work carried out by Herod's son. The commercial relations with the network of surrounding towns are attested to by the presence of ceramics found in rural areas.

As well as the theatre, enormous ritual Jewish baths (*mikvah*) have also been excavated in the city, which indicates that there was a sizeable Jewish population living here. However, and despite some opinions to the contrary, it would seem that Sepphoris was a Hellenized city, as can be seen in the urban geography, but not pagan, as no temples or statues to the Greco-Roman gods or pig bones have been found. The inhabitants must have been mostly Jewish and favorable to Roman power; this was made evident during the First Jewish Revolt against Rome. Thus, it is no mere coincidence that the Pharisees were few in number and the Sadducees, with a good number of sacerdotal families, widely installed.

Jesus seems to have had no links with Sepphoris. The city is never mentioned in the Gospels and cannot have been a place where Jesus preached. Whether he visited the city before beginning his public activities and whether he may even have worked there are questions we are unable to answer (see 4.4.1.2).

With respect to Tiberias, the other large city in Galilee, though located only sixteen kilometers from Capernaum (Jesus' second home after Nazareth), it was never visited by him either. Archaeology has not been of great help in the case of Tiberias. The newly constructed city on the banks of Lake Galilee was begun in 19 A.D. by Antipas to act as the new capital, instead of Sepphoris. Antipas called it Tiberias, in honor of the emperor Tiberius, who had succeeded Augustus in 14 A.D. We know from Josephus that the city was built on top of an old cemetery, which went against Jewish Law regulating ritual purity (*A.J.* 18:38). More so than in the case of Sepphoris, the construction of the city followed Hellenistic models. There were even figurative paintings of animals in Antipas' palace, which was expressly forbidden by Jewish Law. In Tiberias, the population was, as in Sepphoris, a mixture. But unlike in Sepphoris, when the revolt against Rome broke out in 66–70 A.D., the Jews who were in favor of the revolt won out and the minority non-Jews were massacred.

In building up Jesus' biographical profile, there are two towns of interest in Galilee: Nazareth, where he was brought up and lived until he started on his public activities, located in, and isolated by, the mountains of Lower Galilee; and Capernaum, his adopted hometown by Lake Galilee. They are two relatively unimportant towns that did not play any part in the political history of first-century Galilee. Nazareth was a small town (with three or four hundred inhabitants, most of whom were farmers or shepherds), clinging to the side of a mountain, with scattered homes that often took advantage of the caves formed in this rocky land, with an open veranda and roof terrace. Twenty-three Greco-Roman tombs have been found in Nazareth in a wide radius around the central point of the current Church of the Annunciation, which represented the focal point for the town and its limits. Recently, signs of vine cultivation have been found to the west of the town dating back to the first century A.D.: a wine press, stone walls, and three circular towers, also made out of stone (Mark 12:1).

Capernaum was bigger than Nazareth. The suggested numbers of inhabitants vary between one thousand (Loffreda and Bagatti) and fifteen thousand (Meyers). Reed believes there to have been seventeen hundred, scattered throughout an area of between six and ten hectares. It seems that the town must have had a population of around two thousand people. Capernaum had no town planning, public buildings, or defensive walls. The houses were poorly constructed, not using ashlars. However, this Jewish town of fishermen and farmers did have two buildings that made it stand out to an extent: a synagogue and a tax office (Mark 2:13-14). This office acted as a customs house, charging to let people pass. Some four kilometers to the east, the river Jordan acted as the border to Antipas' territory and the start of Philip's on the other side of the river, where travelers would soon reach Bethsaida.

The synagogue seems to have been paid for by a soldier from Antipas' army, a non-Jewish centurion living in the town (Luke 7:1-5). Reed describes this centurion as an official from the administrative section and a soldier of the tetrarch but refutes that he had one hundred soldiers under his orders residing in Capernaum. Basalt foundations to the synagogue from the time of Jesus have been found under the impressive archaeological remains of the synagogue built in the second to third centuries A.D. However, the most interesting archaeological find in Capernaum relating to Jesus is what is known as Peter's house, a poor fisherman's dwelling from the first century A.D., which has subsequently been embellished and adapted to make it into a Judeo-Christian domestic church. The walls have graffiti in honor of Jesus and Peter. In the Byzantine period, a splendid octagonal church was built over the house in order to perpetuate the memory of a local tradition, which no doubt dated back to the first century A.D. and which is linked to the narration in the Gospels (e.g., Mark 1:29-34, 2:1-12, 3:20).

Before continuing with the description of Galilee, I would like to spend a moment to focus on Bethsaida, a town in Gaulanitis that, in the times of Jesus, formed part of the tetrarchy of Philip, though the Jews who lived there were considered Galileans. Bethsaida was located on the lakeside and only two hundred meters from the river Jordan, which served as the natural border between the territories belonging to Philip and Antipas. Bethsaida, some four or five kilometers from Capernaum, was the hometown of three of Jesus' disciples: the brothers Simon (Peter), Andrew, and Philip (John 1:44, 12:21; "Bethsaida in Galilee"). Nowadays, Bethsaida is some two and a half kilometers from the lakeside, but in the times of Jesus it had direct access to the lake; Bethsaida, which in Aramaic means "the house of fishing," would have been right beside it.

In general, the houses in Bethsaida were of a higher quality than those in Capernaum, and its inhabitants were richer. There were even fish factories. The population was made up of Jews and non-Jews. This blend of races and the healthy economic situation led, according to J. H. Charlesworth, to its changing in 30 A.D. from what had been a village, a *kōmē* (Mark 8:23), to a Hellenistic city, a *polis* (see 3.4.1.1). Philip gave it the name of Julias, in honor of Julia Livia, Augustus' wife and mother of Emperor Tiberius. Josephus, who links the city to another Julia, Augustus' daughter (*A.J.* 18:28), knew it by both names, the Latin (*Juliada* or *Julias*) and the Aramaic (*Bethsaida*). R. Arav, the director of the excavations at Bethsaida, believes that they have discovered a Roman temple dedicated to Julia Livia.

3.1.2. The Languages

The language of the Jews of Galilee and a good number of Jews living in Judaea was Aramaic, the latter speaking it with an unmistakable accent. Aramaic was the mother tongue of Josephus, who was born in Jerusalem, and for this reason Titus sent him to speak to those defending the city to persuade them to surrender. Josephus used "their own language" (*J.W.* 5:361). Aramaic was also the language spoken in the courtyard of the house of the high priest, when Peter was swamped by the servants and guards who identified him as one of Jesus' followers. Those who were with him in Jerusalem, in the courtyard of the house of the high priest, said, "Certainly you are also one of them [a disciple of Jesus], for your [Galilean] accent betrays you" (Matt 26:73). Peter spoke with the accent and idiosyncrasies of the Galilean dialect, which were recognized by others who spoke Aramaic with a Judaean accent.

The Galileans had difficulty in pronouncing and distinguishing between guttural consonants, in both Aramaic and Hebrew, and this would explain, for example, why they pronounced the name of Jesus as Yeshu instead of Yeshua (see 4.1). Jesus' mother tongue was Galilean Aramaic, and this is the language he used to speak to his disciples and for preaching (see 4.4.1.1). As we have just seen, it was also the language used by Peter and Andrew, Jesus' disciples who came from Bethsaida. In any case, Aramaic and Hebrew are two different languages, and for this reason the Scriptures were read in Hebrew and the corresponding fragment was translated into Aramaic in the synagogue. Aramaic was also used for preaching.

The second language spoken in Galilee was Greek. The rural areas were exclusively inhabited by Jews, and only in the two capitals (Sepphoris, the old, and Tiberias, the new), with mixed populations of Jews and non-Jews, can we assume that Greek was spoken at least as much as Aramaic. The non-Jews in Galilee obviously spoke it, as did the tetrarch Herod Antipas and his court, officials, and civil servants, the most important people in the country, and all those who aspired to be such. It was also the language of the military, for both the Roman and Herodian troops, and of the low-level civil servants, such as the tax and customs collectors, who had to deal with people who spoke only Greek and who had to present their documentation to Herod's administration in this language. Greek was spoken, to very different degrees, by a number of Jews from Galilee and the surrounding areas, due to their belonging to the ruling classes, or simply for commercial reasons in order to use the language of the buyer, often a non-Jew.

The use of Greek was also on the rise in Jerusalem. The city was undergoing a certain level of Hellenization, and the upper classes and Jews coming to live there from throughout the Mediterranean Diaspora spoke the language with a certain level of fluency. Greek, the language of the dominant culture, the Roman administration, and commerce, was needed in a city that played home to pilgrims and merchants, curious visitors, and non-Jews who worshiped the God of Israel, people coming from around the empire and beyond. M. Hengel calculates that between 10 and 15 percent of the inhabitants of Jerusalem and the surrounding area spoke Greek. An important detail stands out: the inscriptions on the Jewish coins produced at the time of Herod's reign are only in Greek. Galilee, then, was a fairly diverse place.

The other Semitic language used, apart from Aramaic, was Hebrew, the language of the Jewish religion, the Bible, and prayer. All Jews living in the ancient land of Israel prayed from memory in Hebrew, and some of them knew by heart fragments from some sections of the Bible, including the Psalms or the most important prophecies. In Judaea, specifically Jerusalem, especially written Hebrew was still in use, as the ancestral language and that of the Jewish people. There may have been sectors where Hebrew was the actual spoken language. Sirach was written in Hebrew (180 B.C.); trilingualism exists in the book of Daniel, written shortly after, in Hebrew and Aramaic in equal parts, with some words in Greek. The Essenes at Qumran encouraged the recuperation of classical Hebrew, the language of the Scriptures, as a written and spoken language and resembled the rabbis or scribes, who used Hebrew in their teaching and dialogues with other rabbis.

Unlike Judaea, where Hebrew can be found in inscriptions on ossuaries and in written documents from the time of Jesus, it seems that the same cannot be said of Galilee. Hebrew was not used as a colloquial spoken language, as it was for the rabbis who would live there in the coming centuries. It seems that Aramaic was the only language used by the people at the start of the first century in Galilee.

To complete the picture of Galilee's languages, there remains only Latin, which was almost nonexistent in the territory. Latin was spoken by the entourage of the Roman governors living in Caesarea, the Roman capital of Judaea, and it was also the official language of the legion, but not for Antipas' troops, who spoke Greek. Other languages, such as Nabatean and Arabic, were heard occasionally in the country thanks to the caravans of merchants who crossed it on their way to Damascus or Phoenicia or in the large port of Caesarea Maritima, the commercial and military gateway to Rome (see 4.4.1.1).

3.1.3. THE ECONOMIC SITUATION

Galilee was essentially an agricultural area, with property belonging to a range of different owners. Most of the cultivation involved vineyards, olives, and cereals. Large estates belonged to people living outside the country, people who had invested in agricultural property and who had subsequently handed over its running to an administrator. The impressive fortified town of Ramat Hanadiv, located in the northern hills of the Carmel range beyond the borders of Galilee but still very close by, is a typical example of agriculture, stockbreeding, and housing at the end of the first century A.D. Side by side with these *latifundia* were small family holdings, which were handed down over the generations and worked on directly by the owners. Land was also leased, where tenants had to give part of their harvest to the owner. Each morning, a good number of day workers came together in the squares to wait for someone to give them work. The parables of the murderous tenants (Mark 12:1-12) and the workers in the vineyard (Matt 20:1-15), as told by Jesus, are examples of this situation.

The main economic problem for the smallholders, and the majority of the population in general, was taxation. Requests to reduce taxation were not infrequent, such as the uprising in Syria in 17 A.D. against the Emperor Tiberius, as told by Tacitus (*Annals* 2:42). Herod himself decreed a reduction in the taxes to be paid by his subjects in 20/19 B.C. From 6 A.D., taxes were collected in Judaea for the Roman governor, while in Galilee Antipas was solely responsible for taxation. It seems that he did not have to send any to Rome and the imperial exchequer. He was in sole charge of the taxes and, according to Josephus (*A.J.* 17:318), each year they provided him with an income of some two hundred talents, 4,500 kilos of silver, alongside what he received in extraordinary taxation and that taken from the harvests and commercial transactions. It does not seem, however, that the Jews in Galilee, unlike those in Judaea, had to pay to so-called *tributum soli*, or tax on agricultural property, which was one of the bases of the Roman fiscal system. Despite this, taxation amounted on average to 30 percent. For this reason, a bad harvest led to many having to face up to debts in order to pay the taxes. The application of two different fiscal systems from 6 A.D. onward, the Herodian in Galilee and the Roman in Judaea, led to serious conflicts and tensions, as seen, for example, in the episode involving the tribute or taxation for Caesar in Judaea, and specifically in Jerusalem (Mark 12:13-17) (see 3.3.3.2).

Galilee was an area rich in agriculture and fishing, and, unlike Jerusalem, there were no vastly rich Jews living here. Among the residents of Galilee, the richest was probably Herod Antipas, the tetrarch, popularly called "king." The other large agricultural landowners, first among whom was the emperor himself, lived abroad and had their properties managed by administrators. Obviously, fishing was the main business on the lake. The Greek cities around the lake and further afield, such as Tyre, were commercial centers that accounted for a good part of Galilean trade. Despite Josephus' emphatically highlighting the well-being of rural Galilee (*Life* 30), it cannot be said that the population was rolling in money. The agricultural smallholders and day workers often faced economic difficulties, usually related to taxes, with these problems possibly leading to the selling of land, emigration, or even banditry.

3.1.4. A LAND OF CONFLICTS?

In light of the above, the question of the social and political situation in Galilee in the times of Jesus arises: was it a land free of conflict (the position adopted by S. Freyne), or was there a continuous and growing social crisis (the opinion of G. Theissen)? The Roman historian Tacitus significantly summarizes the country's social and political situation with the terse phrase *sub Tiberio quies*, "[in the land of the Jews] all was quiet under Tiberius." Tiberius was emperor while John the Baptist and Jesus carried out their public activities (14–37 A.D.). The long reign of Herod Antipas (4 B.C.–39 A.D.) also seems to have been quiet. Galilee and Peraea were small worlds that Antipas could control closely and that he took care not to offend: Antipas' coins, unlike the Roman coins (or Philips'!), did not have an engraving of the figure of the emperor.

The government of his brother and neighbor, Philip, tetrarch of Iturea, Gaulanitis, and Trachonitis, lands to the north and east of Galilee, from 4 B.C. to 34 A.D., was also characterized by stability. Despite this, we have to assume that the reconstruction of Sepphoris, capital of Galilee until 20 A.D., and the building of Tiberias, the new capital, could not have been possible without heavy taxes imposed by Antipas and that this situation must have been the backdrop to Jesus' activities. The latent conflict between rural Galilee, the majority, and urban Galilee, in Herod Antipas' two capitals, must have grown constantly. The attitudes of John the Baptist and Jesus toward Herod, the former directly conflictive and the latter implicitly critical, give us an idea of the tensions existing between the sovereign and his subjects.

3.2. JERUSALEM

The focal point of Jewish life, for both Jews living in ancient Israel and those of the Diaspora, was Jerusalem. The holy city of Judaism was at the heart of the Jewish people and religion. For any Jew, whether from within or beyond the boundaries of the Roman Empire, traveling up to Jerusalem represented the fulfillment of the words of the psalm, "I was glad when they said to me 'Let us go to the house of the Lord!'" (122:1). Jerusalem is the fullest expression of Jewish history and identity, but it is also the city that encapsulates God's design and promise. This may be why Jesus says, "for it cannot be that a prophet should perish away from Jerusalem" (Luke 13:33). Indeed, although, as we will see (4.6), more than half of Jesus' public activities took place in Galilee, Jerusalem was always present in his life, especially toward the end: the city provided the background and the conclusion. In effect, it seems that Jesus visited Jerusalem on a number of occasions during the approximately three years of his public activities. The fact that Jesus decided to travel to Jerusalem at the end of his life for the Passover festivities was decisive.

Jerusalem had been the historical capital of Israel since King David conquered it from the Jebusites around 1000 B.C. (2 Sam 5:6-15), and his son Solomon built the temple (1 Kgs 6). However, in 931 B.C. the northern tribes separated from those of the south and Jerusalem became the capital simply of the kingdom of Judah, reigned over by one of David's descendants. It was destroyed in 587 B.C. by Nebuchadnezzar and rebuilt by Nehemiah between 445 and 433 B.C., though the temple had already been rebuilt (520–515 B.C.) by Zorobabel, with the consent of the Persian rulers. It acted as the capital of the province of Judaea under Persian, Ptolemaic, and Seleucid rule until the middle of the second century B.C., when it again became the capital of an independent Jewish state, now ruled by the Hasmonean dynasty. It lost its independence following the Roman invasion (63 B.C.) but remained the capital during the reign of Herod the Great (37–4 B.C.), the king imposed by the country's new powers. As Josephus states, "[With Pompey, the Roman general who occupied Jerusalem in 63 B.C.,] we lost our liberty, and became subject to the Romans" (*A.J.* 14:77). Following the arrival of the Roman governors in Judaea, in 6 A.D., the political capital for the province of Judaea became Caesarea Maritima.

3.2.1. Herod's Buildings: The Work on the Temple

Herod was an Edomite and thus from an eastern branch of Greco-Roman culture. He did not follow the Jewish Law closely despite legally being a Jew, having been circumcised in accordance with the Law, but, as king of the Jews, he had to behave as such. As a great number of his subjects were Jews, Herod could not ignore them when it came to planning his government. Herod started extensive building work, such as large fortresses (Herodium, Masada, and Machaerus) and new cities (Caesarea Maritima and Sebaste). Jerusalem, the capital of his kingdom, also benefited from his policy to promote public works. It seems that Herod developed three works in the Hellenistic style (a hippodrome, a theatre, and an amphitheatre) in and around the city. With regard to the defenses, some of the work carried out can be seen at the so-called Essene Gate, mentioned by Josephus, the Northern Gate in the second wall (now under the Damascus Gate), and the great palace, which was constructed in the northwest of the city, with three impressive towers, dedicated to Mariamne (his favorite wife, a Hasmonean princess), Phasael (his brother), and Hippicus (his friend). The foundations of one of these towers can still be seen today, as part of the Jaffa Gate. Herod's fortified royal palace could accommodate large military contingents and was subsequently made the praetorium, the official residence of the Roman governor when he visited Jerusalem, for example, for the Passover, the Jewish celebration par excellence. Herod's ancient palace held the main headquarters for the cohort or Roman military garrison stationed in Jerusalem, which was commanded by a tribune (John 18:2; Acts 21:31). The palace was a magnificent building that offered an excellent view from the towers over the temple area and the city as a whole—allowing for its direct control (see 6.2.4.1).

The most spectacular work was the extension and reconstruction of the small temple of Zorobabel, which Herod converted into an impressive monument. Thousands of workers were involved in the long reconstruction work on the temple, and the work certainly contributed to strengthening the economy of the inhabitants of Jerusalem and those of the surrounding area. The work on the temple began in 20–19 B.C. and was still going on in Jesus' time, as it says in John

2:20: "It has taken forty-six years to build this temple." In fact, the work on the temple was completed around the time of the penultimate Roman procurator Albinus (62–64 A.D.), only a few years before it was destroyed (70 A.D.). According to Josephus, the work permanently involved some eight thousand men (*A.J.* 20:9).

Today's Wailing Wall formed part of the outer section of the Herodian temple, the esplanade of which was covered by the building of the new retaining walls. Herod also rebuilt the sanctuary and built a large royal gateway at the south of the complex, which provided access to the south (the Hulda Gates) and to the west (in particular, the so-called Robinson's Arch, which supported an enormous staircase between the temple esplanade and the Lower City or Tyropoeon Valley). Herod also built ritual baths close to the temple area. We can cite two literary accounts of the Jerusalem temple. A Jewish proverb says, "He who has not seen the Temple of Herod has not seen a beautiful building" (Babylonian Talmud, *B. Bat.* 4a). In the Gospels, one of the disciples, referring to the temple, exclaims before Jesus, "Look, Teacher, what wonderful stones and what wonderful buildings!" (Mark 13:1). One of these stones, which is still in situ in the retaining wall, to the north of the Wailing Wall, seemingly weighs six hundred tons!

However, before starting on the reconstruction of the temple, Herod remodeled the ancient Baris citadel, which was in the northwest corner of the temple complex, and converted it into a large defensive building. This citadel opened onto the temple esplanade and was used as the quarters for the detachment of the Roman cohort in charge of closely controlling the holy Jewish area and Jerusalem as a whole. Herod named the fort the Antonia Tower, in honor of Mark Anthony, Caesar Augustus' rival and his first patron.

3.2.2. The Economic and Social Situation

Jerusalem was a city renowned throughout the Roman Empire. The Jews represented 10 percent (!) of the total population of the empire and made the city well known. While Galilee was a region rich in agriculture, agricultural activity in Jerusalem and in Judaea in general was more akin to a subsistence economy; however, stockbreeding was a prosperous activity, especially in the so-called Judaean Desert between the mountain range of the center and the Dead Sea. Water was abundant on the Jericho plain, where production focused on dates and citrus fruit. Nearby, the famous balsam was produced in the Engedi oasis to be exported around the empire.

Jerusalem's economy focused on the temple. Jerusalem was a city of commerce and services: accommodation for pilgrims, the slaughterhouses for the sale of animals used in sacrifices, money-changers (the only currency accepted in the temple were the shekels of Tyre), employment directly linked to the temple (the priests offering sacrifices, the Levites in charge of preparing them and maintaining the temple complex and who aided worship, and the members of the guard), and employment related indirectly (bakers, craftsmen, blacksmiths, potters, jewelers, spice sellers) all contributed to the temple as a great economic stimulus. In addition, each adult Jew, whether living in Israel or the Diaspora, was obliged to pay an annual tribute to the temple. This tribute consisted of one *didrachma* (or half a shekel), the equivalent of two days of work (Matt 17:24-27). Though we do not know the actual level of response to this obligation, it would seem to be quite high, with Jerusalem receiving large quantities of money for worship at the temple.

This economic system centered on the temple led to the formation of an upper class, limited to a small number of families, which shared out the positions of responsibility at the temple (the so-called high priests in the Gospels) and which, at least in part, paralleled the economic oligarchy in the city (the so-called nobles in the Gospels). At the top of the pyramid was the high priest, head of the temple and the Sanhedrin, or great Jewish council, who was named by the political governor in power. The most characteristic case was that of Annas, who was nominated by the legate of Syria, Quirinius, and who held the position from 6 to 15 A.D. Five of his sons (Eleazar, Jonathan, Theophilus, Matthias, and Annas) and, possibly, two of his grandsons (Elioneus and Matthias) were also made high priests for short periods between 16 and 66 A.D. So was Joseph Caiaphas, Annas' son-in-law, as John (18:13) points out. Caiaphas, nominated by Varius Gratus, was the high priest who lasted longest in the position: eighteen years (from 18 to 36 A.D.). His involvement in Jesus' trial and condemnation to death was crucial (see 6.2.3.1).

While the poor agrarian proletariat dominated in the rural areas of Judaea, Jerusalem was a prosperous city and even had a somewhat cosmopolitan air, at least within the Jewish world. In Herod's time, a number of families from the Jewish communities in Egypt and Babylonia had immigrated to Jerusalem, where they soon became part of the elites in Judaea. Even Greek-speaking Jews from the Diaspora came to the city, where they built their own synagogues. This is the case of the Theodotus synagogue (*Corpus Inscriptionum Judaicarum* II:1404) and the synagogue of the Freedmen (Acts 6:9). Jerusalem attracted many Jews thanks to its academies or "study houses," directed by renowned scribes, such as Hillel, and the important Jewish festivities saw the city turned into a microcosm of different cultures. This is clear from the list of countries and towns from which the Jews came to Jerusalem for the Pentecost festivities (Acts 2:9-11). However, alongside the great fortunes, the majority of the population had to support heavy taxation and a difficult economic situation. Among these were many priests who practiced in the temple for only one or two weeks a year and who had to survive the rest of the time with manual work normally outside Jerusalem. Their situation was very different from that of the sacerdotal aristocracy, members of the influential sacerdotal families who controlled the income and tithes received by the most important institution in Israel. Evidently, the Jewish revolt that started in 66 A.D. was caused by high levels of social unrest, which affected the temple and contributed to its ruin.

Around 30 A.D., when Jesus was present in Jerusalem with his disciples, the city can be described using Tacitus' phrase, applied earlier to Galilee, *sub Tiberio quies*. It was this peace and the desire of the temple's leaders to maintain the status quo that led to the tragic end to the life of the prophet from Nazareth. The contrast between town and country and, more specifically, the contrast between the anti-Roman leanings of Galilee and the pro-Roman sentiment of Jerusalem, which aimed to maintain collaboration with the Romans, helps explain the mistrust inspired by a Galilean prophet who arrived in the city accompanied by a group of followers. His last visit was particularly uncomfortable as he entered the city triumphantly, welcomed as the Messiah and envoy of God. It had been less than twenty-five years (6 A.D.) since another Galilean, Judas, had arrived in Jerusalem, inciting the people not to register in Quirinius' census and not to pay the taxes demanded by the Roman administration. Judas the Galilean confronted Roman power. Jesus of Nazareth, another Galilean, did not confront it but preferred to suffer capital punishment decreed by the Roman governor, Pontius Pilate, the prefect of Judaea.

3.3. THE JEWISH RELIGION

The religious unity of the whole of the Jewish people needs to be underlined, despite the inevitable differences due to geography; Jews lived in Palestine and in the Diaspora, whether Greco-Roman or Eastern, beyond the borders of the empire. Jerusalem acted as the focal point for a cohesive faith based on a series of shared foundations. E. P. Sanders defines them thus: adoration of one God manifest in the daily reciting of the prayer "Listen, Israel" (*Shema Yisrael*); worship in the main sanctuary in Jerusalem, especially for the important pilgrimage festivities; daily prayer in the family and weekly at the synagogue with the reading of the Law or Torah; observation of the ritual precepts of the Law (circumcision, rest on the Sabbath, rules on ritual cleanliness); and observation of moral regulations.

Recent archaeological discoveries have provided evidence of this cultural and religious unity among the Jews of Galilee and Judaea, dating back to the times of the Hasmoneans. For example, coins from this dynasty are found in both territories. According to J. H. Charlesworth, the archaeology highlights three signs that link Galilee and Judaea: identical systems for ritual cleansing (use of stone sinks for ablutions and baths [*mikvah*]), the same techniques for burials, and a lack of pig bones among the animal remains. The written sources frequently stress the sense of superiority felt by the Jews of Judaea over the Jews of Galilee. G. Vermes mentions a statement attributed to rabbi Johanan ben Zakkai (second half of the 1st c. A.D.), where he criticizes the Galileans for not keeping to the Law: "Galilee, Galilee, you hate the Torah [Law]!" (Jerusalem Talmud, *Šabb.* XVI:15d). This opinion is echoed by the Jewish leaders addressing Nicodemus in reference to Jesus: "Search [the Scriptures] and you will see that no prophet is to rise from Galilee" (John 7:52).

3.3.1. The Pillars of the Jewish Religion: The Law, the Temple, and the Land and Family

3.3.1.1. The Law

Jewish life and piety revolve around unconditional fulfillment of the Law held in the Torah and seen to be the expression of God's wishes for Israel, his people, as shown by the Holy Scripture, the Bible. Observation of the Law is the source of well-being and happiness. As it says in the psalm, "Blessed are they whose ways are blameless, who walk according to the Law of the Lord" (119:1). Or, in the words of Josephus, "[B]y living under that Law as under a father and a master, we might be guilty of no sin, neither voluntarily nor out of ignorance" (*Ag. Ap.* 2:174). For Jews, the Law is the holy principle for life, observing it is a source of happiness; the Law is immortal. All virtue is contained in the Law, as one's whole life should be guided by it in order to glorify one unique God through the fulfillment of the laws he has established. The stipulations of the Law cover all areas of existence, both social and personal, and thus the Law acts as a form of wall that defends Israel from evil and from being led astray by the customs of other peoples. For this reason, it has to be listened to at the synagogue and learned, so that it can be put into practice and taught. As Hillel said, "An ignorant person [of the Law] cannot be pious" (*Avot* 2:6).

The Law's commandments start with the recognition of God, as perfect creator, so great that he cannot be represented by material figures. The Law also includes absolute respect for elders, conjugal fidelity within monogamist marriage, prohibition of abortion, the need to bury the dead, help for the needy, prayer and fasting, welcoming non-Jews who are interested in the Law, sacrifices to the temple, ritual purification of food, sexuality, contact with dead bodies, impure people and things, and so on. This legislation derives from the five books of Moses, the Pentateuch (Genesis, Exodus, Leviticus, Numbers, and Deuteronomy).

This last point includes one of the fundamental differences between the Pharisees and Sadducees, the two groups or schools of thought and the leading tendencies in first-century Judaism, which we will talk about further in section 3.3.2. For the Sadducee scribes, fulfilling the Law meant keeping to it exactly as it was written in the

Pentateuch without exception. This was the only writing that was worthy of being called Law or Torah, and all the rules and regulations for life had to be taken from here. The Pharisees included alongside the written Law of the Pentateuch the books of the prophets, which also contained certain regulations, though these were not as important as those in the Pentateuch. The Pharisees maintained that a "tradition" had begun with Moses of interpreting the Law, a tradition handed down by subsequent scribes, both ancient (Ezra) and modern (e.g., Hillel). These scribes had reinterpreted and expanded this tradition so as to accommodate new and changing lifestyles and to make them more practical. Therefore, according to scribes with Pharisee leanings, both the written Law (the biblical Pentateuch) and the tradition of the elders, later known as the oral law, were valid.

Pharisees and Sadducees fought for control in the Sanhedrin, or great Jewish council, which came together in Jerusalem and was the highest legislative and judicial authority for the Jews around the world, and not just those who lived in the lands with a Jewish majority (Judaea, Galilee, and Peraea). Although the decisions of the Sanhedrin were recognized by the Roman authorities as compulsory only in Judaea, Jews, wherever they lived, were morally obliged to respect its decrees. Jerusalem's Sanhedrin comprised seventy-one members and was headed by the high priest, the public leader of the Jewish nation. The sacerdotal aristocracy, the "high priests," or members of their families ran the temple and dominated the Sanhedrin together with the "nobles," or members of the well-to-do families in the city, who were almost all Sadducees. Yet the Pharisee scribes were influential. They were much more popular than their Sadducee counterparts and were increasingly improving their position vis-à-vis the Sadducees.

There was a dispute for influence and dominance in Jerusalem in particular, where the leaders of these two groups lived. We do not know to what extent the numerous synagogues constituted the scenario for the struggles between these two groups to introduce their doctrines, but they represented an ideal setting given the large number of people willing to hear the preaching and interpretations of these synagogues' leaders and the scribes or rabbis who spoke there.

We do not have much information on the Galilean rabbis of the first century, as we know hardly anything about the scribes of Jesus' times who taught in the Galilean synagogues. We can deduce that the

Galileans had more problems in observing ritual purification, as their main activities included agriculture and stockbreeding. This naturally entailed ritual impurity on a regular basis (touching dead animals that had not been sacrificed, physical contact with animals forbidden by the Law, etc.). At least, as G. Vermes highlights, these were the accusations made from Judaea. Obviously, a simple people found it difficult to meticulously fulfill all the tenets of the Law because, no doubt, of their great number rather than bad faith. Nevertheless, Galilee remained a very Jewish land that tried to observe the commandments of Moses' Law.

The synagogue was at the heart of Jewish life in middle-sized Galilean towns, such as Capernaum, and, probably, small ones too, such as Nazareth. Though archaeology has yet to offer us a precise map of the synagogues in first-century Galilee, it is clear that going to the synagogue every Saturday morning was a common and established custom. The synagogues were the meeting point for the community, to read the Law, for teaching and prayer. An inscription found at the Theodotus synagogue in Jerusalem states, "Theodotus . . . built the synagogue for the reading of the Law and the teaching of the commandments" (*Corpus Inscriptionum Judaicarum* II:1404). The synagogue buildings in rural Galilee were small and simple, and in some cases larger private houses must have been used as the synagogue. With a rectangular floor plan, the synagogues had stone or brick benches attached to the walls and, on occasions, a small platform for the reader with a special seat for the person giving the homily (Luke 4:20). The adornments were the bare minimum: an ark to hold the scrolls wrapped in cloth, which included copies of the books of the Law (the Pentateuch) and the prophets (from Joshua to Malachi), and possibly an ambo (raised platform), to place the scrolls on when they were being read. Men and women prayed separately: the men at the front and the women behind. There may have been a ritual bath and sinks near the synagogue for washing before prayers.

The highest authority in the community and the synagogue was the council of elders or nobles (Luke 7:3, in reference to Capernaum). The leader or leaders of the synagogue were chosen from among these. They were in charge of supervising the worship and the liturgical service and managing the building in general. The synagogue's leaders decided who among those present should lead the prayers and who should be invited to preach to those present (Mark 5:22, which mentions Jairus, "one of the rulers of the synagogue"). However, the person who managed the prayer in the synagogue most directly and the school for children associated with the synagogue was the "attendant" (see 4.4.2). They also took charge of a number of tasks including the storing of the scroll or volume used in the reading (Luke 4:20) or blowing the horn on the Sabbath and for the main festivities (above all, New Year). The liturgical service began with the *Shema* prayers and the Eighteen Blessings (compulsory daily prayers for every Jew), which were recited by one and echoed by the rest. Then there was the reading of a fragment of the Law or Pentateuch and the reading of a fragment from the book of the prophets. After the readings came the translation of the Hebrew biblical texts into Aramaic, the language spoken by the people; there followed a homily, or commentary on the texts read, also translated into Aramaic. The service at the synagogue ended with a final blessing (if, a rarity in Galilee, a priest was present). The Galilean synagogue was the heart and soul of a people that lived surrounded by a non-Jewish culture and way of life, far from the temple in Jerusalem. The synagogue was the house of the Law, the place where the Law was read and discussed, the place where people were taught and grew in their understanding of God's will.

3.3.1.2. The Temple

The high level of respect shown by the Galilean Jews for the Law also applies to their relationship with the temple in Jerusalem. We have already mentioned that the temple was the most important institution in the city from an economic point of view. At the time of Jesus the city numbered between twenty-five thousand and fifty thousand inhabitants. However, the temple was much more than that: Judaism identified itself with the temple as the place where the Lord on high had chosen to reside. This was proclaimed in the psalms ("For the Lord has chosen Zion, he has desired it for his dwelling"; Ps 132:13) and echoed endlessly throughout Jewish literature ("the Lord did not choose the nation for the sake of the holy place, but the place for the sake of the nation"; 2 Macc 5:19). Therefore, there is an unquestionable and unconditional respect for a place that made the divine presence visible, a place that serves as a bridge between God and Israel. This is the function of the sacrifices and worship, offered to a unique God on a unique altar, in Jerusalem (*A.J.* 4:200–201). Above all, the supreme head of the temple, the high priest, transcended his temporal obligations and always represented the Jewish nation before Rome and the people of the covenant, Israel, before God himself.

The people honored the priests who sacrificed animals and made offerings of products of the land—oil, flour, and wine, as stipulated by the Law—and who blessed those before them. The daily perpetual sacrifice at dusk, offered for all of Israel, represented the constant link between the people and their God. A victim was also offered every day for the Roman emperor. Even non-Jews visited the splendid temple complex in Jerusalem, and many of them, sympathetic to Judaism, prayed and made donations. Certain inscriptions on stones in the Court of Gentiles marked the "wall of separation," the boundary in the complex that could not be passed by non-Jews, on punishment of death. Once in the part of the complex reserved for Jews (by race and religion), there were separate courtyards reserved for women and men. The altar of holocausts burned before the sanctuary, a building in two parts: the holy place contained the altar of perfumes, the candelabrum with seven branches, and the table for offerings of bread; the holy of holies was empty in the first century but in ancient times had been designed to contain the ark of the covenant. The holy of holies could be entered only by the high priest, wearing special clothes, on the Day of Atonement, or Yom Kippur. The splendor of the ceremonies and magnificence of the buildings clearly reflected the devotion that the Jews had for the temple. Even when people were critical of its functioning or the abuse of power by the leaders, they were never left indifferent by Israel's holiest place!

In Galilee, devotion to the temple was expressed in pilgrimages to Jerusalem for the most important festivities (Passover and Tabernacles, in particular; Luke 2:41-52). Furthermore, the Galilean Jews were happy to pay the annual tribute to the temple, though we do not know how many people actually paid it, given the difficult economic situation of the region's poorest people. The Pharisee rabbis urged payment of the tithes to the temple for worship; they even tithed the smallest of herbs, such as mint and rue or legumes (Luke 11:42). The Galileans' affection for the temple can be seen in the events described by Josephus. In 39 A.D., a mass protest by Galilean and Judaean Jews in Tiberias, the capital of Galilee at the time, arose when they found out that the emperor Caligula wanted to erect a statue to himself in the temple at Jerusalem (*A.J.* 18:269–74). The Jewish protests led to the abandonment of the project.

3.3.1.3. The Land and Family

The land and family constitute the third pillar of the Jewish religion. The family is the natural setting for the passing on of the religion of Abraham and Moses. The Law rests on the close relationships at the heart of the family, in its widest sense, and on the belief system that this transmits. The family is the first place that the Law is observed, and the most important Jewish celebrations are always based on the family. The celebration of Passover in spring to commemorate Israel's release and the exodus from Egypt often requires families to come together for a dinner, as the Law stipulates that there must be at least ten men present (excluding the women and children). The seven days of the Tabernacle's festivities, when huts are constructed using palms and reeds beside houses or on the roofs as reminders of Israel's journey through the desert, formed a happy family celebration taking place in the autumn following the harvest. The weekly feast, the Sabbath, commemorates the exodus from Egypt, made possible by the intervention of God and the seventh day of creation, when God "rested from all his work which he had done in creation" (Gen 2:3). The main element in the weekly feast (the Sabbath) is the family meal on Friday at dusk, which marks the start of the new day. The Sabbath rest begins at sunset on Friday and ends at sunset on Saturday.

The family was where children learned to live in accordance with the Law and to pray, to carry remembrance of God in their heart: "And these words which I command you this day shall be upon your heart; and you shall teach them diligently to your children, and shall talk of them when you sit in your house, and when you walk by the way, and when you lie down, and when you rise. . . . And you shall write them on the doorposts of your house" (Deut 6:6-9). Entering the community of Israel requires circumcision, a ceremony that consisted in the cutting of the infant male's foreskin some eight days after birth.

Circumcision was carried out at home and included giving the child a name. It confirmed the alliance of the people of Israel with God and was an unequivocal sign of belonging to the Jewish race. The dominant Greco-Roman culture mocked circumcision and considered it an embarrassing mutilation. For the Jews, however, it marked their identity, to the extent that they happily called themselves the people of the circumcision. From life's beginnings, parents are the first people responsible for the religious education of their children. Philo of Alexandria expressed it thus: "[F]or [the Jews] looking upon their laws as oracles directly given to them by God himself, and having been instructed in this doctrine from their very earliest infancy they bear in their souls the images of the commandments contained in these laws as sacred" (*Embassy* 210).

The land of Israel represents a precious gift that God promised and gave to Abraham, the father of the Jewish people, and his descendants. The first time that Moses had a divine revelation, the words he received from God were, "I have come down to deliver them [my people] out of the hand of the Egyptians, and to bring them up out of that land to a good and broad land, a land flowing with milk and honey" (Exod 3:8). The land belongs to God, and those who invade it, the Romans, defile the name of the God of Israel: the whole country is included in the holiness of the temple and the city of Jerusalem. This leads to the unbreakable link between the Jewish people and the land and the need to cleanse it of the gods and customs of other peoples, eventually leading to the radical extreme of war.

The Jews of Galilee in particular strongly objected to the occupation of the land that belonged to God and his people and which they now felt was being defiled and sullied by the non-Jewish population. Galilee was a Jewish enclave among lands inhabited by pagans, non-Jews: Samaria, Gaulinitis, and Decapolis. Protests broke out increasingly as the first century went on, often violently, until they led to the great conflict of the First Jewish Revolt, in which a good number of Galilean Jews took part. Disrespect for the Romans and the desire for freedom were two constants in the Galilean national character. The Galileans were the most nationalistic Jews. Jewish identity was strong in the land situated furthest from Jerusalem. When Jesus was born, only a century had passed since Jews mostly from Judaea represented the majority in Galilee once again.

3.3.2. The Religious Groups: Pharisees, Sadducees, Essenes

The Jewish authors Josephus and Philo of Alexandria and the Roman author Pliny the Elder provide ample information on the various trends or groups within first-century Judaism in the times of Jesus. Some experts insist even on talking of Judaisms in the plural in order to stress the diversity and pluralism that characterized them. This use of the plural is not entirely misleading. Following the Maccabean revolt in 167 B.C. against Antiochus IV Epiphanes, the Seleucid king, and until the destruction of the temple in Jerusalem in 70 A.D., Judaism could be seen in different lights depending on the various trends and sensibilities: the Pharisees, workers and intellectuals, leaders and guides for the popular classes; the Sadducees, the elite with links to the sacerdotal aristocracy and the well-to-do classes of Jerusalem; and the Essenes, a group formed from the sacerdotal aristocracy of Jerusalem who set themselves apart from the rest in the monastery at Qumran by the Dead Sea. Josephus, with considerable imaginativeness, wanted to equate these groups to three "philosophies" or Greek philosophical schools, relating the Essenes to the Pythagoreans, the Sadducees to the Epicureans, and the Pharisees to the Stoics. The last is, without doubt, the best comparison. This is evident from the literary and conceptual links between Paul, the great Christian missionary and a "Pharisee" converted to the new faith (Phil 3:5), and popular Stoic thought.

3.3.2.1. Historical Precedents (175–152 B.C.)

The fight against Hellenization

The common denominator among these three groups is the desire to renovate Judaism in the face of the challenge from first Greek and subsequently Roman cultures, religions, and ways of life. The starting point has to be Antiochus III the Great's victory over Ptolemy V in 200 B.C., when the Seleucids became the new rulers of the Jewish people. While Antiochus III awarded the Jews privileges and protected their religion, his son, Antiochus IV Epiphanes (175–164 B.C.), sparked a great crisis by initiating a methodical program for the Hellenization of Judaism: "[T]he king wrote to his whole kingdom that all should be one people, and that each should give up his customs" (1 Macc 1:41-42). The campaign initially achieved notable success. Hellenism had arrived in Israel in 332 B.C. with Alexander the Great; this success led to a traumatic division within the Jewish people. It seems that on the king's orders, some Jews in favor of adapting Judaism to Hellenism started to offer sacrifices in a Grecian style, thus equating the God of Israel with the Greek gods, and no longer rested on the Sabbath. There were already some who had not circumcised their sons and who ate pork and other animals forbidden by the Law of Moses.

In Antiochus IV's plans, Jerusalem was to become a completely Hellenistic city (urban planning, customs, beliefs). This required the support of the ruling class, the city's sacerdotal and lay aristocracy. The ruling sacerdotal families linked to the temple were divided between those who, to varying degrees, accepted Antiochus IV's projects and those who opposed them head-on. The High Priest Jason (175 B.C.), a descendant of Zadok, perhaps with the intention of breaking away from the king, sided with the moderate reformers. These reformers suggested that aspects of the dominant Greek culture be introduced, rather than a radical transformation of the Jewish religion; for example, they proposed Greek methods for educating the young. However, Antiochus wanted to go further and named Menelaus high priest in place of Jason (172 B.C.). Menelaus was a member of the sacerdotal aristocracy, but not a descendant of Zadok, and thus usurped the most important position in Judaism illegitimately. Menelaus' appointment brought to the fore those who bluntly promoted the syncretism of Moses' religion with the Greek beliefs and gods, as had happened with the autochthonous religions in the countries neighboring Israel. This idea was shared by Antiochus: to equate the God of Israel with the gods of the Greek pantheon, specifically Zeus, father of the gods.

The king increased the pressure on those who strictly followed the Jewish religion and started to persecute those who opposed him with threats of death or the burning of the scrolls containing the Jewish holy works. The Hellenization program culminated in December of 167 B.C. when Antiochus IV built a new altar on top of the altar of holocausts in the temple in Jerusalem and dedicated it to Olympian Zeus, the greatest of the Greek pantheon gods. This was meant to unite the religious beliefs of all of his subjects. However, the king had gone too far, and Mattathias Maccabee (whose surname means "hammers"), a priest from Jerusalem who had left to live outside the city with his five sons in the town of Modein, started a revolt in the name of loyalty to the Law and to the religion of his forefathers.

The rebels installed themselves in the caves and hideouts of the Judaean Desert and began a successful guerrilla campaign, which saw them gain control of some parts of the country. Antiochus IV died in 164 B.C., and Judas Maccabee finally gained control of part of Jerusalem, including the hill on which the temple had been built. He immediately set about having the holy Jewish building purified and restored. The altar of holocausts, reconstructed beautifully, was dedicated once again to the worship of the God of Israel. Shortly after, Antiochus V Eupator (164–162 B.C.), successor to Epiphanes, offered the Jews peace and "agreed to let them live by their laws as they did before," in accordance with the laws of their forefathers (1 Macc 6:59).

The revolt led by Mattathias and his sons against King Antiochus had immediate support from the Assideans or Hasidim, meaning "pious," or those "who offered [themselves] willingly for the Law" (1 Macc 2:42). These groups represented an extensive movement for the renewal of the Jewish religion and piety. As pro-Hellenistic pressure grew under Antiochus IV Epiphanes, the feeling of belonging to the religion of their ancestors and the desire to defend their customs also grew among the people. For many of them, refusing any kind of syncretism with the Greek religion had to be total, as the very existence of the Jewish religion was on the line.

As P. Grelot points out, the threat represented by Antiochus IV is forcefully stressed in the book of Daniel, written in an apocalyptic style and with Hasidic leanings. Faced with a seemingly calamitous present, the work contains a series of divine revelations regarding human history, the setting for God's triumph. Thus, with the hope of establishing God's kingdom, there is the belief that after death comes a reward for those who have loyally resisted. Another text, the Book of Dreams (included as part of an apocryphal manuscript, the First Book of Enoch, chaps. 83–90), deals with the magnificent end to human history, with the building of a new temple where all those who have respected the Law to the end come together. These ideas were popular among the people, and Jesus made use of them to express how God had begun to make himself present in the history of mankind;

in other words, that his Kingdom was already here: "The time is fulfilled, and the Kingdom of God is at hand" (Mark 1:15).

One of the driving forces behind the Hasidim movement was the scribes, laymen versed in the Holy Scriptures who dedicated their time to studying the Law and interpreting it. Bit by bit alongside the priests who also knew the Law and who guided the people on how to keep to it, other lay experts began to appear who helped spread observance of the Law as the hallmark of the religion of Israel. As well as keeping to the Law, the Assideans stressed that history was where God would manifest himself definitively and that this manifestation could not be far off. History had to be examined with the eyes of a prophet to see the tracks left by God's promise.

The Assideans, religious reformers, were not involved in political strategies, which meant they became increasingly distanced from the Maccabees and those who fought with them for the triumph of a specific political project. In particular, the Assidean groups disassociated themselves from the Maccabees when Alcimus, belonging to the legitimate sacerdotal dynasty of Zadok, was named high priest by Demetrius I Soter in 162 B.C.: many Assideans made peace with him, while the Maccabees opposed him. The Maccabees continued their military and political struggle against the increasingly weakened Seleucid kings. Judas, the mythical military leader of the Maccabees, died in 160 B.C. while fighting against Bacchides, the governor of West Euphrates, a Seleucid province belonging to Judaea. Command passed to his brother Jonathan, a skillful politician who knew how to make the most of the constant changes and intrigue in the Seleucid monarchy until 152 B.C., when the Seleucid monarch named him high priest. He thus achieved his aim of becoming the leader of the Jewish nation, with direct jurisdiction over the land of Judaea.

The rise of different groups

The above summary of the complex history of the Jewish people between 175 B.C., the year that Antiochus IV Epiphanes succeeded to the throne, and 152 B.C., the date when Jonathan Maccabee was made high priest, should be used to set the scene for the origin of the three most important Jewish groups of Jesus' age: the Pharisees, Sadducees, and Essenes. Jonathan's nomination as high priest shook the bases of power. We should not forget that the high priest represented the highest political and religious Jewish authority. It was a position that up to then had maintained a certain level of independence while in the hands of Zadok's descendants, as king Solomon had decreed over eight hundred years before. From a popular perspective, the nomination of Jonathan could be interpreted as a victory for the defenders of the Law against Hellenization, the enemy of Jewish principles, and as a possible step toward a future Jewish state. From the point of view of the ruling sacerdotal classes, this nomination represented the usurpation of the legitimate high priest (a descendant of Zadok), with the only aim being to consolidate the political power of the Maccabees, the new masters of the situation. Subsequent events support both interpretations: ten years later, with Simon Maccabee (142–134 B.C.), Jonathan's brother, came an independent Jewish state and the Hasmonean monarchy, which lasted until 63 B.C. and the Roman occupation of the country.

The balance of forces, then, was shaken up by Jonathan's coming to power. All of them were affected, but particularly so Jerusalem's sacerdotal aristocracy, which until then had had complete control over the temple, and lay aristocracy, which had dominated the city's economy. This ruling class, led until then by descendants of Zadok acting as high priests, reacted in three ways when faced with this situation of change.

First, the members of the Onias family, of the Zadok dynasty, who until 175 B.C. had acted as high priests and who had been removed from the position by Antiochus IV, now saw that their possibilities were coming to an end, and as a result they went into exile in a friendly country, Egypt. They founded a schismatic temple in Leontopolis. This temple, which was never more than the family's private chapel, as Tcherikover rightly points out, was closed by Vespasian between 72 and 74 B.C. The last high priest from this family active in Jerusalem was Onias III ("the laws were very well observed because of the piety of the High Priest Onias and his hatred of wickedness" and "a zealot for the laws" [2 Macc 3:1; 4:2], "the prince of the covenant" [Dan 11:22]), who was killed at Antioch on the Orontes. This charismatic character represented Israel's most genuine tradition of loyalty to the covenant and opposition to any compromise with Hellenism.

The second reaction had an anonymous leader, the Teacher of Righteousness, the rival to the Wicked Priest, according to the

Qumran scrolls, who would found the Essene group. When Jonathan (probably the Wicked Priest) was unjustly named high priest, the person who until then had carried out the functions or thought that he was the candidate to carry them out, the Teacher of Righteousness, suffered a form of domestic exile. Subsequently, this Teacher (or, more likely, one of his successors as leader of the Essenes) opted to retreat to the Dead Sea coast, to Qumran, where he brought together a cultural and sacerdotal monastic community, which was a spiritual replica of the temple in Jerusalem. This great anonymous leader, who continued the Zadok dynasty, shared the fundamental aim of Hasidism, strict observance of the Law, supported by rigorous study, taken to radical extremes. It should come as no surprise that many of the "pious" felt spiritually close to the Qumran community and a certain number joined the ranks of this marginal sectarian Judaism, which challenged the priests who controlled the temple in Jerusalem.

The third reaction was that of the sacerdotal aristocracy that remained in Jerusalem, willing to collaborate with the new power of the Maccabees/Hasmoneans, as they had earlier collaborated with the Seleucid monarchy. Now, however, the Hasidim movement had spiritually shaken the Jewish people, focusing it once again on the Law and its stipulations. The members of the most important sacerdotal families stressed their role in society and, as "sons" or descendants of Zadok/Tzadok (both forms are interchangeable in Hebrew), called themselves Zadokites or Sadducees. As with the "pious" movement, they proclaimed observance of the Law, though they did tolerate the Hellenized or autocratic leanings of some of the Hasmonean governors, such as John Hyrcanus and Alexander Jannaeus. Two factors contributed to the rise of the Sadducee group: the fact that the Pharisee group was already organized, as Josephus states (*A.J.* 13:5), and the need to form a lobby group to work with the new Hasmonean governors who also occupied the position of high priest. The pragmatism of the sacerdotal aristocracy ensured that the Sadducees kept control of the Sanhedrin and leadership of the temple, although they did not hold the position of high priest, reserved for the Hasmonean sovereign. Subsequently, in the time of Herod and the Romans, following the fall of the Hasmoneans, they were able to recover all their influence and, ultimately, the position of high priest.

The most direct successors to the Hasidim movement were the Pharisees. It is likely that in the new situation brought on by Jonathan's nomination as high priest, the first to organize themselves were those furthest from power. These, the Pharisees, were concerned with maintaining the principles that had allowed them to overcome the crisis brought on by Antiochus IV: devotion to the religion of their forefathers through the defense to the extreme of the fulfillment of the Law. Antiochus' persecution, accompanied by the martyrdom of certain individuals devoted to the Law, left a deep mark in the soul of the people. This spirit of being linked to the Law, which had inspired such enthusiasm in an important part of the Jewish people, had to be kept alive. The "pious" from the upper strata of society, including scribes (the intellectuals of the time), were concerned by Jonathan's projects, which camouflaged a purely political agenda. The Pharisees were convinced that what was needed to save Israel was, above all, the holiness of the life of the people, achieved by keeping to each and every one of the stipulations of the Law. The name *Pharisee* means "those distinguishing with precision" (*paroixim*), those of scrupulous exactitude and detail in observance of the Law. This interpretation of the name is preferable to another possible meaning, "the separated" (*peruixim*).

3.3.2.2. The Pharisees

Interpretation of the Law

It is likely that the Pharisees were the first of the groups to form. The fact that they were the first to take on the spirit and followers of the Hasidim, or "pious," movement shows that they were the first to react to the new situation. Possibly, before Jonathan gained power, the Pharisees, coming together in "brotherhoods" (*haburot*), already constituted a differentiated group. Right from the start, the mostly laymen Pharisees showed themselves to be loyal to the covenant, strictly keeping to the Law (and the Ten Commandments, in particular) and focusing their attention on specific questions: the rules of ritual purity relating to food and liquids and contact with dead bodies; the ritual rules on worship in the temple; the payment of tithes; resting on the

Sabbath and feast days; the rules on divorce; and carrying out pious works (prayer, fasting, almsgiving). This is how they were distinguished and wanted to distinguish themselves from those Jews who were unable to follow the Torah: the uncivilized, "who do not know the Law, [and] are accursed" (John 7:49), those who lived sinfully (tax collectors, prostitutes, etc.). For this reason, they felt it necessary to avoid any kind of contact with foreigners and Samaritans, in particular.

The Pharisees found support among the people, as their approach to the Law was full of humanity, given that their ultimate goal was to make it practical in any situation and circumstance in life. They combined extreme attention to detail (according to the Pharisee teachers, the Law was broken down into 613 commandments that had to be strictly met) and a flexible and innovative interpretation of these commandments, which aimed to adapt them and make them practicable. For example, every seventh year was sabbatical and required the fields to be left fallow or uncultivated, regardless of the crop (Exod 23:10-11). This led to serious problems for farmers who, every seven years, had to go without their harvests. For this reason, Hillel, the most renowned scribe of the time, produced a particular interpretation of this stipulation that allowed farmers to ignore this sabbatical year: the so-called *prozbol.*

This and other regulations resulting from the Pharisees' interpretations of the Law (*halakot*) formed the "tradition of the elders," to which the Pharisees ascribed an almost similar level of importance as they did to the Holy Scriptures or written Law. As Josephus says, "[T]he Pharisees have delivered to the people a great many observances by succession from their fathers, which are not written in the laws of Moses" (*A.J.* 13:297). Over time, the "tradition of the elders" became known as the oral law, which was highly developed at the time of Jesus and was written down around 200 A.D. and called the Mishnah. The Mishnah constituted the basis of the Talmud. The Pharisees' position on the importance of the "tradition of the elders" (Mark 7:5) was strongly opposed by the Sadducees, as it would be by Jesus himself. A second important factor in the differences between the Pharisees and the Sadducees can be seen in some of the specific doctrines found in the so-called Writings, the most recent biblical books: the doctrine on resurrection and immortality as a reward for those who opened themselves up to good (Dan 12:2) and the doctrine on angels as personal beings acting as messengers between God and mankind (Dan 10:20-21). Jesus and Christianity accepted these two doctrines, while the Sadducees opposed them strongly: according to them "souls die with the bodies" (*A.J.* 18:1).

Their influence over the people

At the end of the first century B.C., the Pharisees, thanks to their scribes, had become the spiritual leaders of the Jewish people, spreading from Jerusalem to the other urban centers within and beyond the borders of the country of the Jews. Their activities were not limited to promoting the spiritual renewal of Judaism in Palestine, as their influence also stretched to the important Jewish communities in the Syrian Diaspora (Damascus, Antioch). In the first century A.D., the Pharisees probably represented a form of Judaism that was not marginalized but rather struck a chord with the people, even though not all of their proposals relating to the observance of the Law enjoyed the same levels of acceptance.

The Pharisees were an innovative group, with a strong drive, despite the differences among the scribes representing the various schools of thought. This led to it constantly undergoing change and growth and can be seen in the tradition of having five pairs of scribes, the heads of their respective schools of interpretation of the Law (150 B.C.–30 A.D.). According to a text in the Mishnah (*Avot* 1:4-15), the most famous pair was made up of Hillel, with more open leanings, and Shammai, who was more rigid, direct disciples of whom lived when Jesus was alive. The Pharisees overcame the atavisms and acquired customs that were more strongly defended by the Sadducees and the interpretations of the Law propounded by the priests most closely connected to the temple. However, there is no evidence to show whether the leading form of Judaism, in global terms, was more akin to that seen around the temple, as E. P. Sanders proposes, or whether it was that put forward by the Pharisees. If we have to judge by the Gospels and Josephus, then it would seem that Jewish religious life benefited most from the scribes who belonged to or were close to the Pharisees, especially in Galilee, the Jewish land farthest from Jerusalem. In Judaea, the weight of acquired customs and the sacerdotal influence must have been greater, despite the growing force of the Pharisees. In any case, they were not many in number (some six thousand, according to Josephus in *A.J.* 18:42), but their influence was still felt among the people.

Respected and listened to even by the Sadducees, their natural adversaries, and those who supported Herod and his sons, the Pharisees were able to win people over. There were three reasons for this. First, they did not belong to the sacerdotal or lay aristocracy of Jerusalem, although there were Pharisees closely linked to the ruling classes (e.g., Nicodemus, a follower of Jesus, or Josephus himself). The second reason was that the Pharisees publicly and openly confessed devotion to the Law, characterized by a sincere and demanding observance of the religion: "[T]hey live meanly" (*A.J.* 18:12). The tirades against them in the early Christian tradition and specifically the Q document (Luke 11:39-52 and Matt 23:13-33) respond to Jesus' denunciation of a religiousness that is overly sure of itself and self-satisfied and that tends to exclude those who do not observe the Law. In other cases, the attacks in the Gospels are an expression of the disputes following the destruction of Jerusalem's temple between the early Christian community and the Pharisee-dominated Judaism of the time. The third reason for the Pharisees' success derives from one of the aforementioned factors: their closeness to the specific day-to-day problems affecting those who wanted to strictly keep to the Law. The Pharisee scribes resolved these problems creatively and openly, but they also built up a series of rules and regulations. This meant that observance of the Law became more complex and detailed and, thus, further removed from the people with the simplest lifestyles. However, compared to the Essenes, the Pharisees adopted wide-ranging and balanced positions, which were not elitist. We can see the contrast between the different positions in terms of the theology of free will. According to Josephus (*A.J.* 13:171–73), while the Essenes deemed that "nothing befalls men but what is according to [fate's] determination," the Sadducees stated that "we are ourselves the causes of what is good, and receive what is evil from our own folly," and the Pharisees believed that "some actions, but not all, are the work of fate [divine providence], and some of them are in our own power."

Their political position

The Pharisees actively intervened in Jewish life, often on the back of the Sadducee influence, dominating the circles of power. During the early days of John Hyrcanus (134–104 B.C.), son of Simon Maccabee, the Pharisees were in favor with the Hasmonean sovereign, but they subsequently lost out and were forced into opposition. This change occurred because John Hyrcanus started to act like a Hellenistic governor, far removed from the ideals held in the Pharisee camp. Simultaneously, Jerusalem's aristocratic lobby, linked to the Sadducees, became Hyrcanus' great ally. The situation worsened during the reign of Alexander Jannaeus' (103–76 B.C.), Hyrcanus' son, who ordered the crucifixion of eight hundred of his opponents, including many Pharisees (*A.J.* 13:176). Only in the days of Queen Salome Alexandra (76–67 B.C.) did the Pharisees regain their position. Thus, they used to take revenge by eliminating their former persecutors and reinstating the legal regulations that they had put forward and that John Hyrcanus had abolished. From then on, the Pharisees formed part of the Sanhedrin alongside the Sadducees and continued to have an active influence on the lives of the Jewish people.

As we have seen, the Pharisees were "activists" in the observance of the Law, but this conviction had a religious, a political, and both a public and private bias. For example, they refused to swear loyalty to Herod (*A.J.* 17:42); some Pharisees supported the popular revolt against the tribute for Caesar, led by Judas of Galilee in 6 A.D. (*A.J.* 18:4). The Pharisees shared the popular hope in a powerful messiah from the house of David, who would expel the Romans from the country using armed force, as stated in the Song of Solomon (chaps. 17 and 18), written in the first century B.C. and probably Pharisaic in origin.

Obviously, for a Jew convinced of the royalty of God and the supreme nature of the Law, it was embarrassing to have the people of the covenant subjugated to the rule of pagans and obliged to pay a tribute to Caesar. However, it was also true that if their observance of the Law was not overly affected by the governor in power, then they could tolerate a compromise and accept their domination. Phariseeism in the time of Herod and the Romans was somewhat ambiguous in regard to the popular hopes for liberation shared by all Jews and to its practical achievement. It may be this ambiguity that saved the Pharisees from being dragged along and enveloped in the defeat following the First Jewish Revolt, unlike the Sadducees and Essenes, who disappeared forever from history. The Pharisees chose the opportunist path and avoided the radicalism of the zealots. For this reason, after the disaster of 70 A.D., the Pharisees were key in the formation of Rabbinic Judaism. The scribes close to Phariseeism, the experts in the Torah, became sole leaders of the Jewish people and promoted survival and reconfiguration of a Judaism without the temple. They were protected by a wall that was not material but spiritual: the study and strict observance of the Law.

3.3.2.3. The Sadducees

The lack of materials on the Sadducees and the difficulty in interpreting those that do exist mean that we cannot sketch a very precise image of this important Jewish group at the time of Jesus. The main reason for this is that the Sadducees disappeared at around the time that the temple in Jerusalem was destroyed by the Roman legions (70 A.D.), without leaving any documents on their tradition. In this, they differ from the Pharisees and Essenes. The Sadducee traditions contained in Josephus, the New Testament, and Rabbinic literature (the Mishnah and Talmud) are few in number, and the information they provide is fragmented. Alongside all this are the biased images, produced in modern times, presenting the Sadducees as dark and sinister individuals, blending a fictitious religiousness, a lifestyle that was more Greek than Jewish, and a self-interested collaboration with the Romans.

The Sadducee identity

The reality, however, is somewhat different. The Sadducee group originated as a lobby for the well-to-do and ruling classes of Jerusalem, both the sacerdotal aristocracy and the city's lay oligarchy, united by family ties and common interests. As Josephus says, the Sadducees "are able to persuade none but the rich" (*A.J.* 13:10), though, obviously, not all the members of the upper classes belonged to this group. In any case, the Sadducees are always linked to the successive political powers (Hasmoneans, Herodians, Romans), ensuring control of the temple. From 6 A.D., when Judaea was made a Roman province, the position of high priest was almost exclusively their preserve. Furthermore, from the times of John Hyrcanus onward they dominated the Sanhedrin in Jerusalem, though, following the Pharisees' victory in the times of the Hasmonean Queen Salome Alexandra (76–67 B.C.), they had to accept the presence of Pharisees on the great Jewish council. As the first century A.D. went on, the Pharisees gained increasing power and prestige among the people, and this led to a balance of power within the Sanhedrin, a balance that was tipped in the favor of the Sadducees, thanks to their holding the position of high priest.

While the Pharisees represented the feelings of the popular classes, the powerful and small Sadducee elite was linked to the opulent and the well-to-do. However, the influence of the Sadducees among the people should not be underestimated, especially in Judaea because the temple acted as a meeting point and center for teaching, where people went not only to pray and to present their sacrifices and offerings but also to listen to the priests.

We have already said how the Sadducees were formed during the great crisis arising from Antiochus IV's program of Hellenization and from the reaction led by the Hasidim, or Assidean, movement. The Sadducees aimed to carry on the legacy of the Zadokites, that is, of the sacerdotal families who had provided the high priests. A good example of a Sadducee, *avant la lettre*, is that of Jesus, son of Sirach and grandson of Eleazar, a scribe living in Jerusalem, who was professionally employed in instructing the children of the city's well-to-do families and who summarized his teachings in the Book of Sirach or Ben Sira, which takes his name.

This individual, who lived around 200 B.C., is presented as a cosmopolitan man and someone who kept strictly to the Law of Israel, a devoutly religious man who worshipped in the temple and was steeped in the wisdom linked to the love of God the generous creator, externalized in prayer. Ben Sira praises those who dedicate their lives to the study of the Law and is quick to provide a eulogy to the great figures of Israel, from Adam and Enoch to Nehemiah and the High Priest Simon, a contemporary of his. The acts of these individuals are compared to those of the more famous Greek heroes. Responsibility for their own actions, just and sincere behavior, social relations (family, friends, public life, government), virtues (modesty, prudence, generosity, self-control), and vices (pride, lies, greed) all play an important part in his discourse. All those subjects relating to immortality and resurrection, reward and punishment after death, are missing. The figure emerging from the Book of Sirach is one of a Law-abiding

Jew caught between two worlds: the Jewish and the Greek. This person is simultaneously tied to the faith of his forefathers and close to the Greek way of life and culture that are so attractive to the new generations of the well-to-do in Jerusalem. Ben Sira's position is that of a moderate Hellenist writing in Hebrew and not Greek, of someone who moves in a rich and elitist society, the upper classes of Jerusalem who want to form part of the Hellenic world.

The Sadducees and Rome

Ben Sira's account shows with a good level of precision the religious and cultural substrata of the Sadducees. However, following the crisis brought on by Antiochus IV Epiphanes and the subsequent Hasidim reaction, it would be modified to reflect a greater focus on observance of the Law. The political perspective also needs to be added. The Sadducees from the time of Jesus have often be labeled simply as collaborators with the Romans, people who took advantage of their position of power to maintain their status and to gain as much as they possibly could. The reality is that the Sadducees acted with an obvious sense of responsibility as leaders of the temple and Sanhedrin, the two most important institutions for the Jewish people. Their love of their country and their religion cannot be doubted. They made their decisions for the good of the community, or what they understood to be so. This can be seen in the words of the High Priest Caiaphas before the Sanhedrin when he justified the need to eliminate Jesus as "it is expedient . . . that one man should die for the people, and that the whole nation should not perish"; if not "the Romans will come and destroy both our holy place [the temple] and our nation" (John 11:50, 11:48).

The temple was the visible center of Judaism and the Sadducees' raison d'être: without the temple, they would have disappeared, as was seen in 70 A.D. The Sadducees considered themselves the guardians of the Jewish nation, and their political pragmatism was based on this conviction. Religion and state formed, in their case more than in any other, an inseparable whole that could lead them to acts of self-interested prudence, or even flagrant injustice. It could also lead them to a radical and violent nationalism, as with the zealots, self-destructing in a theocratic ideal taken to extremes: God as the only Lord of Israel, the Romans as enemies of God. The temple and the Sadducees would be destroyed as one.

Interpretation of the Law

The Sadducee group disappeared in 70 A.D., enveloped in the catastrophe of the First Jewish Revolt, which had also led to the destruction of the Qumran Essenes, two years earlier. The Sadducees' political strategy aimed at a pact with the Romans and adapting to the circumstances, no matter how difficult, while their religious ideals were stubbornly based on the popular hopes for a radical change in the current reality of oppression and injustice. Apocalyptic ideas relating to decisive divine intervention in history, with divine justice offering eternal reward for one side and eternal punishment for the other, and the resurrection of the dead burned in the souls of many of them. However, while the Pharisees, and Jesus, accepted the resurrection of the dead and, to an extent, some of the ideas related to the apocalyptic discourse (the Messiah, the Kingdom of God), the Sadducees strongly opposed them: "Sadducees, those who say that there is no resurrection" (Luke 20:27). The reason for this is simple: in the five books of the Pentateuch, the only biblical books that the Sadducees considered to be Law, there is no mention of the resurrection of the dead. According to Acts (23:8), the Sadducees also denied the existence of angels and spirits, that is, demons. However, in the Pentateuch, angels appear as God's messengers (e.g., in Genesis 28:12, Jacob sees God's angels in his dreams as they ascend and descend between heaven and earth). What the Sadducees may be denying is that all human beings have their own guardian angel, those who "behold the face of my Father who is in heaven" (Matt 18:10). The Sadducees' refusal to acknowledge the existence of guardian angels (and not simply angels) could be explained by their desire to ensure against the lessening of the value of each individual's will and freedom.

From what we have just seen, we can deduce that the Sadducees considered the Pentateuch or the Torah (the Law, in its strictest sense) as the only Scriptures that could be considered regulatory in the fullest sense. The other biblical books, especially the books of the prophets, were valuable only in terms of piety and exhortation. For this reason, the Sadducees looked to only the Pentateuch for the bases of their arguments. Unlike the Pharisees, they never looked to the sentences or opinions of the scribes of the past, to the "tradition of the elders," as an authoritative argument to justify a given interpretation. Josephus expressed this idea saying that the Sadducees "dispute with

[the] teachers of philosophy" (*A.J.* 18:16). Jesus is said to have "taught them as one who had authority, and not as the scribes" (Mark 1:22). This does not mean that there were not interpretations of the Law shared by all the Sadducees. The point that needs to be stressed is that the opinions of the Sadducee scribes were not seen as Law, not even by these scribes themselves, and thus according to them there was no authoritative "tradition of the elders." In other words, the Sadducees believed that the opinions of their own scribes had a temporary and circumstantial value and that they could be modified: the only untouchable thing is the Law as is. There could be no additions made to the written Torah.

Obviously, the questions raised in daily life are varied, and not all of them can be answered directly by the Pentateuch. However, the Sadducees always provided an answer, as did the Pharisees. Unfortunately, the materials available were very few in number. The most explicit, the Mishnah's tractate Yadayim (4:6-8), refers to a number of questions that led to controversy between the Pharisees and the Sadducees: the rules of ritual purity (animal bones, glasses, water coming from a cemetery), owners' responsibility for their slaves, and the way in which a divorce document should be written. This text shows the Sadducees to be more flexible than the Pharisees! In another case relating to easing rules on the Sabbath rest, known as erub, the Pharisees were the more flexible (*'Erub.* 6:2). These and other cases, including the use of the death penalty for false testimony (*Mak.* 1:6), show how the emphasis placed by the Pharisees and Sadducees varied but that the exegetic procedures employed by both were similar. The difference came from the value, regulatory or not, given to the sentences laid down by the "elders," the famous scribes. For this reason, the Sadducees never produced a tradition of their own sentences and interpretations, unlike the Pharisees. This is one of the other reasons why, as J. P. Meier points out, they have become figures lost in the mists of time.

3.3.2.4. The Essenes

The Essenes and Qumran

Despite the prejudices shown by some experts, the Qumran community, located on the Dead Sea coast, was the Essenes' headquarters.

The Essenes were a Jewish group mentioned by Pliny the Elder, Philo of Alexandria, and naturally Josephus. As mentioned above (3.3.2.1), the origin of the Essenes has to be dated to around 150 B.C. (some believe ca. 140–130), when a faction of Jerusalem's sacerdotal aristocracy broke off relations with the Maccabees/Hasmoneans. This probably occurred at the time of Jonathan, known as the Wicked Priest in the documents found at Qumran, who had been illegitimately named high priest. He had usurped a descendant of Zadok's who occupied or had occupied this position or who had carried out the functions: the somewhat cryptically named Teacher of Righteousness. This unknown figure confronted Jonathan, broke the ties with his class, Jerusalem's sacerdotal aristocracy, and founded the Essenes.

Between 150 and 135 B.C. a small group of people installed themselves in an abandoned fortress at Khirbet Qumran, on the Dead Sea coast. It was only later, between 125 and 100 B.C., that a considerable number of people, the central nucleus of the Essenes, definitively installed themselves in the Qumran complex some thirty kilometers from Jerusalem. This complex consisted of a large house with a refectory, an office, a pottery workshop, large meeting rooms (also used as dormitories?), storerooms, three large cisterns (supplied with water from an aqueduct), a number of ritual baths, and a lookout tower. We do not know whether the monastery was built while the founder was still the leader or, more likely, whether the group was then led by one of his successors, who was still known as the Teacher of Righteousness and who continued to challenge the Hasmonean ruler in power and the high priest (John Hyrcanus?), the Wicked Priest of the Qumran texts.

The exact causes of the breakaway and self-marginalizing of the Essenes and their history can be clarified from the documentation produced by the Qumran community. This clearly shows that the Teacher of Righteousness wanted to "separate from the congregation of the men of falsehood" (Community Rule 5:1-2). Pliny the Elder confirms this with his own brand of exoticism: "[The Essenes are] a people that live apart from the world, and marvellous beyond all others . . . the palm-trees [of the western Dead Sea] are their only companions" (*Natural History* 5:15). The Qumran community acted and behaved like a "sect" and was structured around a sacerdotal and cultural model, where ritual purifications were central.

Study and observance of the Law were taken to radical extremes and performed in an exceptionally rigorous manner. Communal life was monastic in style and carried out in an atmosphere of profound spirituality, alongside a tense eschatology: those at Qumran considered themselves to be the authentic Israel, their mission being to prepare for the great struggle at the end of history, which would see a resounding victory for those loyal to God. The ancient writers were naturally very respectful when they talked about the Essenes. Josephus writes, "[H]ow much they [the Essenes] exceed all other men that addict themselves to virtue, and this in righteousness; and indeed to such a degree, that as it hath never appeared among any other men, neither Greeks nor barbarians" (*A.J.* 18:20). Now able to read firsthand an important part of the Qumran library, today's reader has to be impressed by the spiritual and literary richness of works such as the Thanksgiving Hymns (*Hodayot*), found in the first cave, or the liturgical prayers, a highlight among which are the Songs of the Sabbath Sacrifice, from the fourth cave, which reflect the angelic and celestial liturgy that these angels, the members of the Qumran community, took part in.

An isolated community

The Essene group, however, was not limited to the members of the Qumran community, who, as Pliny put it, "have no women among them . . . [and] money they have none." Beyond Qumran, in towns and cities in Palestine and, possibly, the Diaspora, there were other Essene communities who practiced the Jewish religion in accordance with their laws and principles, but who married ("they do not marry out of regard to pleasure, but for the sake of posterity," as Josephus stresses; *J.W.* 2:161) and had private property for agricultural work and commercial activities. They were obliged to contribute to the communal funds each month, providing the equivalent of two days of work. They had to accommodate any members of the group who might visit them. We know this from the so-called *Damascus Document*, which was found in El Cairo's synagogue in 1896. This document contains rules for the Essene communities living away from Qumran. The Essenes' austere behavior, strong sense of brotherhood, and extreme generosity to others were, once again, praised by Josephus: "[E]very one of them gives what he hath that wanteth it, and receives from him again in lieu of it what may be convenient for himself" (*J.W.* 2:127).

The Essenes saw themselves and the rest of Israel as the chosen among the chosen, for whom God had provided a Teacher of Righteousness "to guide them in the way of His heart" (*Damascus Document* 1:11). God had formed an eternal alliance with them and shown them the way of holiness and truth. It may be for this reason that Philo tries to explain the name Essenes (*essaioi*) with reference to the word holy (Greek, *hosioi*) (*Hypoth.* 11:1). The Essenes are those who drink from the abundant well that is the Law, excavated by priests and laymen (the "wise men of Israel"), those who have broken away from the temple in Jerusalem and retreated to the desert, where they have developed "the exact interpretation of the Law" (*Damascus Document* 4:8).

What were the regulations for life, the specific, just and pious, behavior of the men and women of the Essene communities? The Essenes believed in monogamous and faithful marriage, thought little of riches, and kept to the moral laws (e.g., helping the poor, widowed, orphans, and strangers). They strictly observed the ritual laws, for example, not having sexual relations during the period of menstruation and celebrating the festivities according to the Essene calendar and rules. They looked "to return to the Law of Moses, for in it everything can be learnt" (*Damascus Document* 16:2).

Forming part of the community required a profound spiritual renewal, based on peace and the constructive criticism of one's brother. Reading the *Damascus Document* provides an image of a hierarchical community, which was tightly knit and with a brotherly spirit that led to their sharing all their possessions: there are no poor people among the Essenes, though they are forbidden from marrying before the age of twenty (Rule of Congregation 1:9-11). In view of these qualities they have often been praised by contemporary experts, such as E. P. Sanders, who qualifies them as the Jews who were "most pious, most rigorous and devout in their observance of the Law, the most conscious of human weakness, those who most trusted in the grace of God, the most radical, the most exclusive." Josephus provides us with their number: some four thousand (*A.J.* 18:20).

One of the mixed Essene communities, with women and children, may have been located at the site of the current Ain Feshka, a few kilometers to the south of Qumran, where enclosures have been found for growing crops and keeping animals, as well as a cemetery with male and female remains. This small Essene settlement could have provided support for the monastery itself at Qumran, inhabited solely by men. According to the sect's own documents, discovered in eleven caves close to the monastery, only celibate men lived there. It has often been stated that the reason for this practice, unique in the Jewish groups, is because they viewed sexual relations as something that made people impure. Those at Qumran had taken the rule on sexual abstinence for priests while they were at work at the temple's altar to the extreme: now, the rule was to affect the whole of their lives. Not marrying (and chastity) was a clear means of constantly ensuring ritual purity.

There may have been another reason, too: those at Qumran were considered soldiers of Israel who had to fight against God's enemies in the great battle at the end of time, and accordingly they had to be "pure of spirit and flesh" in order to fight alongside the holy angels, who knew nothing of carnal relations (War Scroll 7:5-7). Spiritual preparation for this decisive conflict required living in celibacy and avoiding behavior that led to sexual desire (e.g., being naked unnecessarily; Community Rule 7:12). They cannot have abstained from sexual relations in self-defense against the supposed salaciousness of women, which is the reason given by Josephus: "they guard against the lascivious behavior of women" (*J.W.* 2:121). Philo of Alexandria employed similar terms (*Hypoth.* 11:14-17). Celibacy for these misogynous reasons does not fit with the statement in the Rule of Congregation that says that the whole of Israel "in the last days," the Essene community, includes "women and children," who have to be educated "in the precepts of the covenant" (1:1-5).

With regard to wealth, the situation for the Essenes living at Qumran was obviously much stricter than for those who lived scattered among the towns and cities of the country. At Qumran, they positively prohibited private property: people definitively admitted to the community had to give up their belongings to the community. This is confirmed by Josephus (*J.W.* 2:122) and the Community Rule found in the first cave: following two years at the monastery, novices are voted upon, and if they are successful, they enter the community's brotherhood: "he shall be registered in the order of his rank among the brothers, for Torah [Law], judgement and purity and his property shall be assimilated" (6:22). These are the four basic commitments that a new member of the Qumran monastery has to take on: observe the Law fully in accordance with the sect's rules and interpretations, be listened to in community decisions, comply with the stipulations relating to the strict ritual purity (those at Qumran followed the same regulations for cleanliness required for worship in the temple, whether they were priests or not), and renounce the possession of any goods, which were to be handed over to the community. The only private belongings were a hoe to bury their own excrement, some underwear, and a white tunic for mealtimes and community meetings.

The communal property was managed by the community's members of sacerdotal descent. These formed the rectorial council and had complete authority in decisions, implementation, and, where necessary, punishment of wrongdoing (punishment could ultimately lead to expulsion). This was the case for those who slandered the founder or leaders, those who blasphemed or who broke a serious precept of the Law. The Qumran organization's strict hierarchy could lead us to believe that the leaders' arbitrary whims dominated life in the commune. Nothing could be further from the truth. This can be seen in the guidelines that had to be followed by the Teacher, who presided over the community's council: a wise man who followed God's will. The Teacher had to support and encourage the brothers, discerning what was best for them, instructing and guiding them with love, as "this is the time for the preparation of the way into the wilderness," before the last days (Community Rule 9:19-20).

Observance of the Law

A fundamental element at Qumran was the maintenance of the regulations on ritual cleanliness and a very strict observance of the Law. For example, the Essenes interpreted the Law on rest on the Sabbath so rigorously that, if an animal fell in the cistern or pit that day, it could not be removed (*Damascus Document* 11:13-14). This is not the position adopted by the scribes close to the Pharisees, nor is it the position adopted by Jesus. In contrast to the those at Qumran, he states, "Which of you, having a son or an ox that has fallen into a well, will not immediately pull him out on a Sabbath day?" (Luke 14:5; Matt 12:11). A Qumran document, called the *halakhic* letter, found in the fourth cave and preserved as fragments in six different copies, is particularly enlightening with regard to the ritual and judicial regulations of the Essene scribes, which were clearly differentiated from those of the Pharisees and, from what little we know, the Sadducee interpretations. Questions relating to the temple, such as the sacrifices and offerings made by pagans, the red heifer (Num 19:1-10), the animal skins used to transport liquids in the temple, the type of animals that could be sacrificed, the tithes for fruit trees and cattle that had to be paid to the priests, and so on, and, above all, the calendar indicate that the reason for the self-imposed exile of the Teacher of Righteousness, the founder of the Essenes, came from a confrontation within Jerusalem's sacerdotal aristocracy concerning these questions.

As we have seen, Jonathan's appointment as high priest represented the victory of one faction, the future Zadokites or Sadducees, and the defeat of another, led by the Teacher of Righteousness, who also claimed to belong to the Zadok dynasty. In effect, we can see in the Community Rule that those who wanted to convert themselves from everything wicked had to separate themselves from "the men of falsehood" (or "the men of the pit"; 10:19) and form a community "under the authority of the sons of Zadok, the Priests who keep the Covenant" (5:1-2).

The most virulently contested point between the two sacerdotal groups was, without a shadow of a doubt, the question of the calendar to be used in the temple to show when the festivities were to be celebrated in Israel. In the first half of the second century B.C., the lunar calendar, based on the full moons (and used before the Babylonian exile), replaced the solar calendar (twelve months of 30 days, plus 4 days to take it to 364), which had, until then, been the official calendar in the temple. This change meant that the main festivities changed date and were celebrated, in the opinion of the Essenes, on the wrong day. As may be expected, at Qumran a dozen copies of the Book of Jubilees have been found based on a solar calendar and quite a number of astronomical texts. These texts are very fragmented and contain certain esoteric elements, including a mixture of alphabets in the same text. They are related to the movements of the celestial bodies and the setting of the Jewish festivities and the turns taken by the priests in the temple.

The Essenes' domestic exile comes, in great part, from the confrontation between two factions of Jerusalem's sacerdotal aristocracy over legal and cultural matters: the Sadducees, allied with Jonathan and his successors, and the Essenes, who considered themselves to be the authentic descendants of the covenant and defenders of the purity of worship, in contrast to a profane temple, which could be restored only by the Teacher of Righteousness. The Temple Scroll, found in the eleventh cave, which blends elements from the book of Deuteronomy with nonbiblical laws, is presented as a divine revelation, with God speaking in the first person: the Qumranic belief of their being chosen leads us to believe that they saw themselves as the guardians of the word of God. The fact that many other biblical books found in the library at Qumran have been rewritten and have had new material added indicates the apocalyptic leanings of those at Qumran: the community was led, ultimately, by "all that has been revealed [by God] concerning their appointed times" (Community Rule 1:9).

The authentic Israel

We now turn our attention to how the Essenes at Qumran defined themselves: "a community of truth and virtuous humility, of loving kindness and good intent," which came about following "the conversion of . . . life" which overcomes the "stubborn heart" (Community Rule 2:24, 3:1-3). Entering "the covenant of God" has to be pure and sincere. Anyone who should refuse the knowledge he is provided with and who cannot remain firm in his decision to change his life, "he shall not be justified . . . nor cleansed by purifying waters" (3:3-5). Heartfelt honor and sincerity in life are fundamental factors in belonging to the "sons of light" and being saved by "His mercy." Despite affliction and misfortune befalling them, God's salvation and kind justice will come, as stated by the Community Rule: "He will pardon all my sins. Through His righteousness He will cleanse me of the uncleanness of man" (11:14-15).

A perfect balance is thus established between what the individual has to do and what God makes possible in his or her heart. In effect, there are two spirits in conflict within the hearts of everyone, the spirit of truth and the spirit of falsehood, which originate from light and darkness, both created by God, but each opposed to the other. "The nature of all the children of men is ruled by these" two spirits (4:15). The end of time is characterized as the end of injustice and falsehood and the triumph of holiness and truth. The ferocious battle is ongoing and will be resolved only later: as determined by God "in the mysteries of His understanding, and in His glorious wisdom" (4:18). Hope flourishes in the end, when the Messiah, sent by God, arrives and a new world comes to pass: the just are rewarded, the ill cured, and the dead brought to life. God himself aids the weak and ultimately "brings good news to the poor." This is how it is described in an interesting fragment from the fourth cave (4Q521), which evokes some of the passages from the prophet Isaiah and a text in the Gospels in which Jesus sums up his mission: "the blind receive their sight and the lame walk, lepers are cleansed and the deaf hear, and the dead are raised up, and the poor have good news preached to them" (Matt 11:5 || Luke 7:22).

The Essenes considered themselves to be the authentic and only Israel, "the People of God" (War Rule 3:13), "the sons of light," "all the rest of the people," called together "that every Israelite may know his place in the community of God according to the everlasting [divine] plan" (Community Rule 2:22-23). The only possible option when faced with history is for all of Israel to abandon the ways of perdition, avoid those who have led them astray, and follow the guidance from the priests at Qumran. From among these will come the high priest who, on the day of the final combat, will lead the army made up of the other priests, the Levites and the men of the community, converted into soldiers to crush the army of God's enemies: "the king of the Kittim [i.e., the Romans] and all the forces of Belial," "the prince of the realm of wickedness" (War Rule 15:2-4, 17:5).

Other texts talk of the sacerdotal Messiah, or Aaron, and of Israel's Messiah, who sit together at the banquet for the community, though the sacerdotal Messiah always ranks higher (Congregation Rule 2:12-21). The Community Rule also mentions the eventual coming of "the Prophet and the Messiahs of Aaron and Israel" (9:11), but the *Damascus Document* seems to describe only one Messiah (12:23–13:1). Whatever the case, a clear division is established between the Essene community, chosen to fight the final battle, aided by God and his angels, and the enemy forces: the aim of the victory is "to bring darkness low and to lend might to light" (War Rule 13:15), that God be recognized as the Lord of lords throughout the world.

Alongside this complete antagonism toward past, present, and future enemies of Israel, there is a deep divide within Israel itself.

On the one hand, there are those who have freely agreed to "practise truth, righteousness and justice upon earth" and, for this reason, have joined the community and entered the covenant with God (Community Rule 1:5-6); and on the other, there is "the congregation of the men of falsehood" (5:1-2) who have to be avoided and who must not be contacted. This separation of the holy from the false, "the sons of darkness," is absolute: those from Qumran are aware of the fact that they have been called to "perfect holiness" (8:20) and, thus, have to ignore the "men of the pit" and maintain an internalized feeling of "everlasting hatred" toward them (9:21-22). The Teacher of Righteousness writes to his fellow believers, "We have separated from the mainstream of the people" (4Q *halakhic* letter, frr. 7 and 8).

The intense brotherly love within the community contrasts with the unspeakable hate for those who do not belong: the Essenes are a tight-knit group, who refuse or distrust those from outside. It is understandable then that the Essene elite should not show, as with the Sadducees and unlike the Pharisees, any interest in proselytism. This system of separation obviously also included those who, by nature and according to the Law, were impure and could not enter the temple. The paralytic, the blind, the lame, lepers, and those with a physical disability could not enter Qumran. Members of the community who were seen to be ritually impure, even temporarily, were also excluded: they were not allowed to enter the community assembly, as they had to purify themselves beforehand (Congregation Rule 2:3-4). Obviously, being impure meant they could not take part in the great battle at the end of history, alongside the holy angels, as stated in the War Rule (7:4-6).

A dramatic end

We do not know what happened exactly at the end of the year 68 A.D. when a detachment from the *Decima Fretensis* legion, which had just conquered Jericho, marched on Qumran. Though the men at Qumran did not manufacture weapons, and, for this reason, Josephus calls them "ministers of peace" (*J.W.* 2:135), it seems that Vespasian's army came up against armed resistance from the members of the community. There is evidence of this in the layer of ashes and arrowheads found by archaeologists and dated to this time. Those who faced the Romans did not constitute thousands of men perfectly trained and equipped, as described in the War Rule. The reality must have been somewhat less impressive and intimidating for the legionaries who sacked and destroyed Qumran. For the Qumranites, it may have been considered the final great battle against the Kittim, as mentioned above, the cryptic name given to the Romans in the War Rule, which stated that the Kittim would be crushed (18:3).

We do not know whether the Qumranites resisted, believing that this was the decisive battle between Michael and Belial, between the sons of light and the sons of darkness, the battle that was to end the "dominion of the Kittim" (War Rule 1:6) and lead to universal peace and the "dominion of Israel among all flesh" (17:7). In any case, the Essenes disappeared completely from human history, after having hidden their library in the neighboring caves in the Judaean Desert. Thanks to this providential planning, we have access to firsthand accounts of the thoughts and lives of a unique and remarkable Jewish group from the times of Jesus. There are still many difficulties involved in interpreting the Qumranite texts, which have now all been published. For example, the meaning of the famous and enigmatic Copper Scroll still has to be worked out. Found in the third cave, it seems to be an inventory of fabulous treasures hidden throughout the land.

3.3.3. The Popular and Resistance Movements

Herod's long reign (37–4 B.C.), with an iron fist and frequent bloodletting, did not allow for even the slightest opposition. Herod learned the lesson early in his reign when he had to fight, and even risk death, before defeating those who rose up against him. Only in this way was he able to start governing, de facto, the kingdom that Rome had entrusted to him. However, as soon as he had the situation under control, he cruelly crushed any attempt at dissent. Josephus does not provide information on opposition groups, and it is likely that during Herod's reign opposition to both him and the Roman emperor was not given the slightest chance to manifest itself (*A.J.* 15:366–69). However, on his death (4 B.C.) and until the Romans conquered Jerusalem (70 A.D.), each political change was accompanied by attempts at popular revolts, initially local and subsequently general, until, in 66 A.D., a full-scale rising against the Romans was organized. This does not mean, however, that the first century A.D. was characterized by continual uprisings. The main problems did not start until around 50 A.D., with the progressive consolidation of the armed resistance movement against Rome. Before this, there was a diversified protest and revolt against Roman power, though only on a few occasions did this lead to a popular uprising, with messianic, theocratic, or prophetic undertones.

3.3.3.1. Popular Messianic Movements

Following Herod's death (4 B.C.)

The death of the tyrant Herod and the subsequent power vacuum led to a series of spontaneous uprisings. There were those who proclaimed themselves to be "king," and one of these, a certain Simon, one of Herod's slaves, even managed to put on the royal diadem (*A.J.* 17:273–76). The popular fervor that this obscure figure stirred up is a sign of the resentment and anger inspired by a governor who only acted like a Jew, without ever feeling like one on the inside. Simon, and his followers, from Peraea ("a disordered body of men [who] fought rather in a bold than in a skilful manner," according to Josephus) sacked a few of the royal palaces that Herod had built, starting with the one in Jericho. Gratus, one of Herod's officers, confronted Simon with the dead king's army and, with the help of the Romans, defeated the movement and executed him.

Another pretender to the throne who took advantage of Herod's death was Athronges, an unknown shepherd from Emmaus in Judaea, who, according to Josephus (*A.J.* 17:278–81), brought together a band of men that was "very numerous." Apparently Athronges, having put the royal crown on, was able to keep power "a great while" and eliminated a great many of Herod's supporters and Romans, accused of arrogance and injustice. Varus, the Syrian legate, ended the revolt led by Athronges, who had presented himself as the new David, the mythical king of Israel, who had also been a shepherd and who, like Athronges, had some strong and courageous brothers.

A third pretender, also from the popular classes, was active in Galilee. His name was Judas, son of Hezekiah, and he was the leader of a group of bandits. He and his followers, "a multitude of men of a profligate character" in the words of Josephus (*A.J.* 17:271–72), assaulted the royal palace of Sepphoris, then the capital of Galilee, taking the arms from the arsenal and everything else they could get their hands on. Subsequently, Judas focused on banditry and extortion, despite having "an ambitious desire of the royal dignity." His followers included those whom the Herodian administration had left with nothing. Judas, who had strengthened his position in Sepphoris, was finally defeated by Varus' army. Sepphoris was destroyed, and those who lived there, all followers of Judas, were enslaved (*J.W.* 2:68).

Religious and social motives were present in all of these armed uprisings against Rome. Not even the revolt led by Judas, son of Hezekiah and leader of bandits, was without its religious references regarding Israel's traditional heritage (e.g., King David). Those who followed these spontaneous leaders were people in a desperate economic situation, day workers or smallholders, who had had to bear the greatest strain of Herod's taxation. Judas, Athronges, and Simon came from the country's rural areas and attacked the urban areas and centers of power. The momentary success of these "messiahs," who were able to mobilize a good number of farmers from Peraea, Judaea, and Galilee, can be explained only by the fact that they offered a specific figurehead for popular hopes in terms of an immediate release from their oppressors and the reestablishment of social justice. The old apocalyptic aspiration becomes a reality, though only for a short time.

During the First Jewish Revolt (66–70 A.D.)

The messianic figures reappeared strongly during the First Jewish Revolt (66–70 A.D.), in particular in Jerusalem. Among the leaders of the armed resistance against the Romans who adopted the stance of pretenders to the throne was Menahem, the leader of the guerrilla group that had occupied the fortress at Masada, and who traveled to Jerusalem where he became the leader of the uprising against Rome. Menahem, who walked through the city in royal robes, was assassinated by zealots from the group led by Eleazar, son of Simon, a priest (*J.W.* 2:445–49). The fact that radical zealotry had problems accepting a monarchical figure who, to a certain extent, occupied the place of God may have been a factor.

A second pretender to the throne in this period was probably Simon bar Giora, who came from southern Judaea or, possibly, Gerasa in the Decapolis. Simon led a powerful militia that aided the release of prisoners, a typical messianic activity, throughout Judaea before arriving and settling in Jerusalem. Simon bar Giora's group took up a strong position in Herod's royal palace, the last focus for Jewish resistance in the capital, which the legions of the Roman general Titus could occupy only for a few days following the destruction of the temple. Taken to Rome as a prisoner of war, Simon was paraded in chains by the Roman general's triumphant entourage; he was then executed as a pretender to the throne and for an act of high treason against Caesar.

3.3.3.2. Popular Theocratic Movements

Judas the Galilean (6 A.D.)

We cannot be completely sure that the messianic claimants arising after Herod's death (4 B.C.) had theocratic ideas, that is, that they fought to establish a political regime governed only by the Law of God, the only Lord of the earth (and not the blasphemous intruder, the Roman emperor!). However, religious motivations dominated the popular movement led by Judas the Galilean, which began in 6 A.D. coinciding with another important political change: the deposing of Archelaus, Herod's son, from his position as ethnarch of Judaea and the reconverting of Judaea into a Roman province.

Judas came from Gaulanitis, the land bordering Galilee, thus the surname "Galilean," but he carried out his activities in Judaea, stirring up the population against Rome and encouraging an uprising inspired by the issue of the *tributum soli*, which the Romans wanted to impose. The principle employed by Judas was clear: the land belonged to God and not to the emperor. Therefore, the latter had no right to tax possession of the land. The movement led by Judas was a combination of theocratic ideals and social protest against the suffocating tax burden on the population and against the new demands that the Romans were making.

The issue of taxation had already emerged as part of the popular complaints addressed to Archelaus when he was named *ethnarch* in 4 B.C. Josephus explains, "[S]ome made a clamour that he would ease them in their taxes; others, that he would take off the duties upon commodities; and some, that he would loose those that were in prison" (*J.W.* 2:4). Ten years later, matters worsened when, with Archelaus exiled, Judaea (with Edom) and Samaria were converted into the Roman province of Judaea and governed directly by a prefect or governor, a high-ranking imperial officer, who had direct judicial and fiscal jurisdiction. At this time, Quirinus, the Roman legate in Syria, ordered a census of the population in this new province in order to set the bases for the payment of taxes, which from this point on would go toward swelling the coffers of the Roman Empire. Taxation in the other two Jewish territories (Galilee and Peraea) was collected by Antipas, a Herodian governor and a Jew.

However, this fiscal measure went against Jewish religious principles, as interpreted by Judas the Galilean, a "scribe," and, according to Josephus (*A.J.* 2:117–18), a Pharisee named Zadok who joined him. For Judas, the Roman census went against the holy principles that the land belonged to God alone by attempting to value it and set the corresponding *tributum soli*. According to Judas, this valuation (*apotimēsis*) was a degrading slavery for Israel (*A.J.* 18:4) and went against God's laws and the usual Jewish census system, designed simply for the payment of the *tributum capitis*, the per capita tax. With regard to the question of the census, see 4.2.

We may consider Judas the Galilean's doctrine, which later went on to constitute the theoretical basis for the zealot and resistance groups, a radicalization of the political and religious theories of the Pharisees. As M. Hengel points out, some Pharisees close to the scribe Shammai sympathized with the revolutionary violence. Judas the Galilean was no zealot (this group was not organized as such until the First Jewish Revolt), but the ideas of this scribe would be put into practice and contribute to promoting direct military opposition to the Romans. In a more modern definition, we could say that Judas the Galilean took the nonviolent nationalism of the Pharisees and converted it into the decidedly more violent nationalism of the zealots, who fought against Rome. The problem is not limited to political theory; indeed, it is essentially religious, despite the obvious political consequences involved. It does not seem that Judas the Galilean was a political activist in the strictest sense, although, as it states in the Acts of the Apostles (5:37), he had a great many followers and his death may have been violent. Some authors consider

Judas the Galilean to have had a certain messianic leadership, but the messianic idea need not necessarily be tied to theocracy, or the radical affirmation of God as the only government.

We can understand why Josephus describes Judas the Galilean as the founder of the "fourth sect of Jewish philosophy" (*A.J.* 18:23), which he places alongside the doctrines or "philosophies" of the Pharisees, Sadducees, and Essenes. The aims of the doctrines of Judas the Galilean succeeded in the uprising against Rome (soon leading to a break in relations with the Emperor): the daily sacrifice offered to him in the temple in Jerusalem was stopped, and all payment of Roman taxes ended. In accordance with Judas' freedom theories for the Jewish nation, the coins minted in Jerusalem during the First Jewish Revolt (66–70 A.D.) were inscribed with the words "Freedom/Redemption of Zion."

The tribute to Caesar was paid in denarii, the Roman currency, and was inscribed with his figure. This went against the first commandment of the Law, which prohibits idolatry: "[Y]ou shall not make for yourself a graven image, or any likeness of anything that is . . . in the earth beneath" (Exod 20:4; Deut 5:8). The fundamental dogma of the Jewish religion, the unique nature of God, which each Israelite repeats daily in prayer ("Hear, O Israel: the Lord our God is one Lord"; Deut 6:4), was interpreted eschatologically. It was as if we were at the end of time and the authority of any of the rulers on earth, including the Roman emperor, was in no way valid. For Judas, no one here on earth could be called lord, because God, and not Caesar, was the Lord of Israel and the whole world. The Law had to be kept faithfully and unerringly. If the fight to ensure respect for God's reign led to the loss of one's own life, then so be it, given that there was surely a future life for those who committed themselves to serving God and no one else. Belief in resurrection, as defended by the Pharisees, also formed part of the theocratic hopes of those involved in the resistance.

The question of the tribute to Caesar

Judas' theocratic ideas increasingly made their mark, especially in Judaea. A sign of this is the political and religious question put to Jesus by some Pharisees and Herodians regarding the payment of the tribute to the Roman emperor (Mark 12:13-17 || Matt 22:15-22 || Luke 20:20-26). Jesus was in Jerusalem in the years 29–30 A.D. The

Pharisees were interested in the religious aspect of the issue: "Is it lawful to pay taxes to Caesar, or not?" (Mark 12:14). In other words they are asking Jesus his opinion on the interpretation of the Law as proposed by Judas the Galilean.

The Pharisees were accompanied by Herodians, supporters of the rulers from the Herodian dynasty: Herod Antipas, the then tetrarch of Galilee and Peraea, and Herod Philip, who governed Gaulinitis and other territories northeast of the Jordan. These Herodian rulers collected taxes from the people, which meant that their Jewish subjects did not have to pay tribute to Caesar directly. For the Herodians, then, Jesus' position on the tribute also had political implications: "Should we pay them or should we not?" (Mark 12:15). This second question was much more pragmatic, and the Herodians, like the Pharisees, wanted to find out if Jesus agreed with Judas' ideas. Essentially they wanted to find out whether he would come down against Rome, or provide a politically correct answer (an "it depends"), distinguishing between the Roman taxation system and the Herodian system. If he chose the second answer, Jesus, as a scribe and defender of the rights of God and not of Caesar, would notably undermine the radical ideas he was supposed to support in the eyes of the people.

Jesus' answer encapsulates the unquestionable religious principle contained in Judas the Galilean's doctrine, proclaiming, "Give to God what is God's." However, he does not link this principle to direct and violent opposition to the emperor, or to the defense of Israel's political freedom, as Judas does. Jesus does not sign up to a theocracy; nor does he take sides for or against Roman political power. The phrase "render to Caesar the things that are Caesar's" is ambiguous and an appropriate response to the malicious question set. The political options are left completely open. It is not clear whether the meaning of the sentence is that they should refuse to pay, phrased ironically ("take this coin and return it to Caesar; let him have it, it is his!"), or whether it is a more prudent acceptance ("pay the tax to those who are in power; we would not want them to come and make matters worse"). Indeed the phrase may even show a certain level of indifference ("let each individual do what they think is best with their money: in the greater scheme of things this is irrelevant"). According to Jesus, what is important is the recognition of the supremacy of God and the need to give him what is his: heartfelt unconditional devotion. For this reason, the weight of the answer rests on the final statement: "Give to God what is God's." G. Theissen rightly compares this answer to a similar statement made by Jesus: "You cannot serve God and mammon" (Matt 6:24 || Luke 16:13).

In 44 A.D., Agrippa I, who had managed to reunify the lands of his grandfather Herod into a single kingdom and who had been well accepted by the Jews, died and thus brought to an end the dream of a nonforeign sovereign. All three territories with a majority Jewish population (Judaea, Galilee, and Peraea) came under the direct control of a Roman procurator (see 3.4.2), and the issue of the tribute came under renewed scrutiny. These were years of famine in various regions of the empire, and also in Palestine. In this context, two sons of Judas the Galilean, James and Simon, took up their father's theocratic doctrines once more and led an uprising against Rome. We do not know the level of the popular reaction; the only thing we know for sure is that Tiberius Alexander, governor of Judaea between 46 and 48 A.D. and an Alexandrian Jew who had renounced his faith, had them crucified (*A.J.* 20:102).

3.3.3.3. Popular Prophetic Movements

John the Baptist and Jesus of Nazareth (20–30 A.D.)

The first known prophetic figure in the first century A.D. was John the Baptist, who was active in the Judaean Desert and the region of the Jordan, specifically Peraea and possibly Judaea during the decade 20–30 A.D. Peraea or Transjordan was then a region ruled by Herod Antipas (4 B.C.–39 A.D.); it was this ruler who had John killed following his preaching of conversion in view of the imminent arrival of the end. John was an eschatological prophet, who identified with this role, lived an austere lifestyle that contrasted with the luxury of Antipas, and preached openly to everyone, rich and poor, just and sinner, those who kept to the Law and those did not. His figure, which mirrored that of the great prophets of Israel, impressed for its authenticity and inspired people's sympathy—people who all came from Jewish territories. John, "a righteous and holy man," brought together a good number of followers and baptized them. They baptized their followers too and kept the memory alive, even after his violent death.

Everything seems to lead us to believe that, between the years 28 and 29 A.D., John was executed by Antipas, a death instigated by the latter's second wife, Herodias, granddaughter of Herod the Great and, thus, Antipas' own niece. The fact that John publicly criticized a matrimonial situation that went against Jewish Law and the religious sentiments of the people led to his death (see 4.5.2.3).

Jesus of Nazareth, whom John had baptized, also took part in the prophetic spirit that surrounded the latter. His preaching began with the announcement of the royal manifestation of God, the kingdom of God, here and now. This good news, for everyone, but particularly well received by the poor and marginalized, the ill and sinners, required conversion. Jesus acted within and beyond the borders of Galilee, and eventually traveled to Jerusalem. He did not lead an ascetic life in the desert but moved from one place to another, above all in the rural areas of Lower Galilee, followed by a group of disciples who shared his life. His work involved healings, exorcisms, and other extraordinary signs that were acclaimed by the people, who brought him their ills and listened to his preaching. Jesus avoided direct confrontation with Antipas and the Roman powers and aimed his prophetic words on justice toward Jerusalem, demanding spiritual purification. It was, then, the temple's sacerdotal aristocracy that considered him a threat and pressured the circle surrounding the Roman governor, Pontius Pilate (26–36 A.D.), to have him condemned to death. Jesus of Nazareth was to die crucified on the cross on the eve of Passover: most probably Friday, April 7, 30 A.D.

The period before the First Jewish Revolt (30–66 A.D.)

Around the year 36 A.D. came extraordinary news of a Samaritan prophet who had rallied people on Mount Gerizim claiming that the holy vessels that Moses had buried would be found there. It was an inoffensive gathering, but the Roman governor Pontius Pilate ordered them to be massacred. The Samaritan protests led to Pilate's being relieved of his position (*A.J.* 18:85–89).

There were other prophets who were all Jewish. Under the procurator Cuspius Fadus (44–46 A.D.), Theudas persuaded a great number of people (Acts 5:36 talks of four hundred men) to follow him through the desert to the river Jordan. He said he was a prophet and that, on his orders, the river would part in two and they could walk across without getting wet. Fadus attacked and killed some of Theudas' followers and Theudas himself, whose head was brought to Jerusalem and put on public show (*A.J.* 20:97–99). Theudas wanted to carry out a prophetic sign, repeating the momentous crossing of the Jordan that had taken place in the time of Joshua. This prodigious act was intended to signal a new conquest of the country, this time over the Romans, the current occupiers.

During the government of the procurator Antonius Felix (52–60 A.D.), a figure known as the Egyptian appeared uniting "four thousand men of the Assassins," according to Acts 21:38 (Josephus talks of thirty thousand; *J.W.* 2:258), and leading them out into the desert and from there to the Mount of Olives. The Egyptian, who "pretended to be a prophet," announced that, on his orders, the walls of Jerusalem would fall, as had those at Jericho momentously in the times of Joshua, and that they would then enter Jerusalem triumphantly, crushing the Roman garrison and installing a religious and political regime based exclusively on Jewish Law (*A.J.* 20:168–71). However, the Roman troops stationed in the city came out and slaughtered those involved in the uprising, while the instigator escaped.

Still with Felix in power, an anonymous prophet announced that there would be signs of liberation seen in the desert, in reference to the time of the exodus (*A.J.* 20:167–68; *J.W.* 2:259).

Another individual, an "impostor" according to Josephus, led people out into the desert when the procurator Porcius Festus was in power (60–62 A.D.), promising them redemption and liberation from all their problems, announcing a new exodus (*A.J.* 20:188). It all ended with another massacre by the Roman troops.

We should note that the circumstances in which all these prophets are acting in the decades spanning 40 A.D. to about 70 A.D. are fairly similar. Josephus summarizes the activities during the time of Felix: "[I]mpostors and deceivers persuaded the multitude to follow them into the wilderness, and pretended that they would exhibit manifest wonders and signs, that should be performed by the providence of God" (*A.J.* 20:168). This description is valid for the whole of the period during which Roman procurators were in control (44–66 A.D.). History repeated itself. Charismatic individuals announced that God's final liberating action was imminent and encouraged everyone to take part. The omen for this long-awaited liberation would be a marvelous sign, which could be explained only through divine intervention and which would evoke one of the great wonders produced by God during the exodus: the passage through the desert and the arrival in the promised land thanks to Moses and/or Joshua. This is the reason why the exodus was often mentioned in the promises offered by these prophets. The revolutionary element consisted in the conviction that the enemy, the Romans, be removed and that social justice be restored. Furthermore, this would be a momentous event, with the powerful intervention of God, as seen in the gestures he made in the past: the parting of the Jordan or the fall of the walls at Jericho.

The simple people, the popular classes, looked forward to the definitive event that would bring an end to the social inequalities and the injustice in their lives, stirred up by the ineptitude and corruption of the Roman authorities; divine liberation would bring with it the immediate end to all their ills. The prophetic fever, a sign of the desperation of many, did not end even in the last days of the siege of Jerusalem, when, while the temple burned, some still waited for a sign from the heavens of the liberation that they so craved.

In contrast to all these prophetic figures who mobilized the masses and the marginalized and downtrodden leading them off to disaster, the figure of a charismatic prophet appeared in 62 A.D., Jesus, son of Annas. Josephus explains that he was an uncultured peasant who went through the streets of Jerusalem announcing the destruction of the city and the temple. Savagely attacked, he neither defended himself nor complained, he simply repeated his warning of misfortune for the city. Brought before the procurator, he did not demand pity, nor did he cry. The procurator, having had him whipped, let him go thinking him mad. The prophet continued to prophesy the city's destruction until his death during the siege of Jerusalem (*J.W.* 6:300–309) (see 6.2.1.3).

G. Theissen rightly points out that, of all these prophets, only John the Baptist, Jesus of Nazareth, and Jesus son of Annas proclaim a message of justice that requires the conversion of all the people before the imminent or actual arrival of God. The other prophetic figures promise salvation for all miraculously, with the most momentous events from the history of Israel being repeated just as they had taken place down the ages. The outcome was, however, quite the contrary.

3.3.3.4. Resistance Groups: The Zealots

It is likely that armed resistance against the Romans began, as a common phenomenon, only after the death of Agrippa I (44 A.D.), the king who had represented, in the eyes of many Jews, the more or less immediate hopes for liberation from the yoke of Roman occupation. It should not be forgotten that Agrippa was the grandson of the popular Mariamne, the last princess of the Hasmonean dynasty, sovereigns of an independent state. Herod, an Edomite, had married her in order to join forces with the Jewish royal family. Relations between the king, an affable character, and his Jewish subjects were smooth and propitious.

Agrippa was seen as someone who scrupulously kept the Law and took part in the worship at the temple. On one occasion during the festival of Tabernacles in 41 A.D., he publicly read a fragment from the Holy Scriptures. He frequently resided in Jerusalem and started work on the third wall, designed to reinforce the northern flank, the weakest part of the city's defenses. The coins minted in Jerusalem did not have any human figure upon them, in line with Jewish Law and theocratic requirements. In contrast, those minted in Greco-Jewish cities such as Tiberias had an effigy of the emperor, and those from Caesarea Maritima were engraved with his own effigy. Despite his political guile these, Josephus often praises Agrippa's practice of the Jewish religion. He says, "[Agrippa] offered all the sacrifices that belonged to him, and omitted nothing which the Law required" (*A.J.* 19:231). The Pharisees, in particular, showed themselves to be strong supporters of this wholly Jewish king. Agrippa stood up to the Christian community in Jerusalem: he had James, son of Zebedee, killed and imprisoned Peter, the leader of the Twelve.

Agrippa had been educated in the imperial court and personally knew the emperor (first Gaius Caligula and then Claudius). The trust he enjoyed from the emperors led to his power over the same territories as his grandfather, Herod. However, Agrippa, like Herod, had a two-headed kingdom, part Jewish and part Greek, and he had to satisfy all his subjects. Reading between the lines in Josephus, we can see that Agrippa, like Herod, acted like a Greek sovereign when necessary, without this leading to any particular backlash. Josephus (*A.J.*

19:343–52) and the New Testament (Acts 12:19-23) explain how the sudden death of the king was preceded by a crowd acclaiming him in the theatre at Caesarea Maritima, where he spoke in public wearing silver robes with "the voice of a god, and not a man!" Agrippa's political ambitions seem clear. While still alive, Claudius forbade him from completing Jerusalem's third wall, and after his death, the emperor's councillors did not allow his son, the young Agrippa II (*A.J.* 19:362), to inherit his kingdom. The Jewish frustration was immense and rekindled a stronger fire that would spread throughout the country, destroying it with the disastrous First Jewish Revolt. In 44 A.D., Judaea, this time along with Galilee and Peraea, would fall under the direct control of a Roman procurator.

During the second period of Roman governors (44–66 A.D.)

The return of the governors, following the parenthesis of Agrippa I, brought immediate popular reactions, which involved much desperation (as in the case of the Egyptian). However, the revolts against Rome intensified with the procurator Felix in power, in the decade starting in 50 A.D., of whom Tacitus says, "Antonius Felix, indulging in every kind of barbarity and lust, exercised the power of a king in the spirit of a slave [*servili ingenio*]" (*History* 5:9). Ignoring the Jewish Law that prohibits mixed marriages, Felix married Drusilla, daughter of Agrippa I, and he continued to act arrogantly and vex the Jewish population. The anger against Rome became increasingly intense, especially among the popular classes. Until then, the violence against the occupiers had been sporadic, but it now began to move throughout the country with bands of "robbers," a derogatory term used by Josephus to define groups that were increasingly linked to the political protest. These "robbers" were presented as the enemies of the well-to-do as well as the Roman occupiers. Felix's repression was very harsh, with crucifixions and all kinds of punishments.

These bands of robbers acting throughout the land were soon joined by groups of *Sicarii* (assassins), especially in the urban areas. They used a small dagger (*sica*). According to Acts (21:38), a leader, such as the Egyptian, managed to unite some four thousand of these assassins. Though these assassins eliminated Romans or people considered their collaborators, the border between these acts and organized crime was a grey area. Josephus tells of the case of the High

Priest Jonathan, son of Annas, who was assassinated by a Sicarius on the orders of the procurator Felix himself (*A.J.* 20:163).

The bands of robbers and *Sicarii* were not completely new. During Jesus' trial (30 A.D.), we are introduced to Barabbas, a "robber" (John 18:40), a "notorious" individual (Matt 27:16) who, according to Mark (15:7) and Luke (23:19), had been imprisoned with a group of rebels for murder during the insurrection in Jerusalem (see 6.2.4.4). The situation, however, was now worsening due to the actions of the Roman governors, who were increasingly corrupt and incapable, and the intervention of the prophetic figures, who proclaimed spectacular divine liberation, with the ultimate aim of gaining freedom from the Roman occupiers and independence for the country. Behind all these figures and groups were messianic-type hopes that grew and faded in accordance with the circumstances but that formed a constant backdrop to the life of the Jewish people. The confrontations within Jerusalem itself involved even the sacerdotal aristocracy. This class, which was well connected with Felix, constantly took liberties and even took some of the tithes meant for priests in lower classes. When the revolt began in 66 A.D., there was also a social revolt within the ranks of the temple's priests, during which a great many of their leaders were killed.

During the First Jewish Revolt (66–70 A.D.)

The history of the First Jewish Revolt (66–70 A.D.) involves a series of brave and somewhat desperate acts against a far superior enemy, made up of three or four legions, auxiliary cohorts, cavalry, and extra troops from the kings allied to Rome (among which there was a Jew, Agrippa II, then ruler of part of Galilee and Peraea). The revolt also involved internal struggles among the Jews themselves, which ended only when the common foe arrived at the gates of Jerusalem, the last stronghold apart from Masada. Once the whole of Galilee was in Roman hands (and Josephus, the Jewish commander, taken prisoner), the focus turned to the siege of Jerusalem.

John of Giscala, fleeing from the disastrous campaign in Galilee, took refuge in the Jewish capital. John was not overly scrupulous and, with his armed band, soon took control of the city. The well-to-do classes of Jerusalem, with the Sanhedrin as their highest authority and who had shared responsibility for directing operations against the Romans, were overtaken by events. John of Giscala's men eliminated Annas and Jesus, son of Gamaliel, who had held the position of high priest, as well as other members of the lay and sacerdotal aristocracy. Now more than ever, the Jewish Revolt became a popular and unstructured war, directed by charismatic leaders who held the political destiny of Judaism in their hands. The arrival of another resistance leader, Simon bar Giora, saw Jerusalem become a battlefield between his and John of Giscala's rival factions. These factions, along with Eleazar's faction, divided the city into areas of influence. The situation was under the complete control of the Zealots, the generic name given by Josephus to the resistance groups, who came from all parts of the country and took part in the defense of Jerusalem against the Romans.

In fact, only John of Giscala, a Galilean, and Eleazar, son of Simon, a priest, could truly be called Zealots, while Simon bar Giora and Menahem were messianic-type leaders who presented themselves as pretenders to the throne (see 3.3.3.1). The Zealots were the most radical rebels. Their zeal for God's cause, the temple, and the Law was absolute and without concessions, as with Phinehas, grandson of Aaron, who killed an apostate Jew who had worshipped the Moabite gods (Num 25:1-15). The hope of imminent and decisive intervention from God against the Romans gave them extraordinary courage to overcome ills and insupportable suffering. The great trials and tribulations of the siege of Jerusalem were interpreted by the Zealots as a sign of the coming of the end. The ferocious fight against the Romans had an eschatological edge.

There were obvious similarities between the Zealots and the Essenes, and it is not beyond the realms of possibility to suppose that any Essenes surviving the destruction of Qumran may have traveled to Jerusalem. The Romans had destroyed their monastery on the Dead Sea, and this was a sign from their point of view that the end of the world was approaching. This profound conviction in the imminent arrival of the end and the victorious and crushing manifestation of God should be taken into account when interpreting the Zealots' burning of their own provisions during the siege: "[A]s they saw the city on fire, they appeared cheerful, and put on joyful countenances, in expectation, as they said, of death to end their miseries" (*J.W.* 6:364). Josephus even explains that when the Romans had occupied and destroyed the sanctuary, the Zealots, defeated and captured, unsuccessfully asked General

Titus to be allowed to retreat to the desert. Here, so they believed, they would await what was about to pass: the divine liberation that had to coincide with the end of history and that was signaled, in their view and in accordance with popular apocalyptic ideas (Mark 13), by the destruction of Jerusalem and the temple.

Resistance in the time of Jesus?

The above reflections on the resistance in the period after Jesus serve to distinguish between the situation in the years between 40 and 70 A.D. and that at the time when Jesus was alive. The armed resistance groups, who continually acted against the Roman powers, appeared only in the decade starting in 50 A.D. The Zealots, the most radical resistance group, were only active and organized once the revolt against Rome had begun (66 A.D.). It is an anachronism to talk of the Zealots before 50 A.D. In the time of Jesus, there was no systematic armed resistance against Rome or warlike action led by the Zealots.

The difficult and much-debated issues of the day comprised (see 3.3.3.2) the tribute to Caesar, social protest and banditry, many dashed hopes, and people and groups, including Barabbas, who were active in the grey area between banditry and anti-Roman resistance. Defense of the Law characterized all the Jewish religious groups of the period, with the Pharisees as their head. As in the case of the Pharisees, there were other "militants" for the Law, Zealots who combined religious radicalism and political nationalism; they were prepared to justify their beliefs without violence, at least in theory. One of these people may have been Simon the Zealot (not the Zealous), a member of the group of Twelve Disciples (Mark 3:18). Once he responded to Jesus' calling, things were probably not particularly easy for Simon, or for Nathanael Bartholomew, "an Israelite indeed" (John 1:47); this expression could indicate an empathy between these two disciples (see 4.5.3.3). In any case, the renunciation of violence, the love for their enemies, the friendliness toward strangers (especially the Samaritans), the reasonable observance of the Sabbath, and the fact that they sat with publicly renowned sinners, such as prostitutes and tax collectors (even one of these was the disciple Levi), all went to represent an important change in perspective for the zealous followers of the Mosaic Law called to be disciples of Jesus (see 4.5.3.3).

3.4. Jews and Non-Jews

3.4.1. The Jews' Relations with the Greeks (or Pagans)

The three Jewish territories in Palestine were surrounded by peoples, cultures, and lifestyles that were not Jewish. The rural areas were exclusively Jewish, but the cities, although theoretically Jewish, had both Jewish and "Greek" inhabitants. This was the case of the two capitals of Galilee: the old, Sepphoris, and the new, Tiberias (see 3.1.1). This was also the case of Julias-Livias (the biblical Betharan), the city in Peraea where Herod had a palace built, which was destroyed during the uprisings following his death and rebuilt by his son Antipas and named in honor of Julia-Livia, Augustus' wife and Tiberius' mother (*A.J.* 18:27).

3.4.1.1. The Greek Cities

A similar situation held in the cities neighboring the three territories, although they were administratively Hellenistic cities. Jamnia, a free city in the province of Judaea, which had become the private property of the Emperor Tiberius as a gift from Salome, daughter of Herod, had a mixed population, with the Jews in the majority. Jaffa, like Jamnia, on the Mediterranean coast and probably ruled over by the Roman governor of Judaea, also had a Jewish majority, as can be seen in the First Jewish Revolt, when the city became a focus of anti-Roman resistance and was destroyed twice.

Lake Galilee was divided into two parts: the western shore was Jewish, and the eastern shore was Greek. There were two Jewish cities on the lake: Tiberias, to the west, and Taricheae, to the south. Here the population was mixed and focused on fishing. The eastern shore was non-Jewish, with the Hellenistic cities of Gergesa, Hippos, and Gadara; the latter two formed part of the Decapolis, a confederation of cities established by Pompey when the country fell into the hands of the Romans (64–63 B.C.). To the northeast of the lake, near the mouth of the Jordan, there was the Jewish town of Bethsaida, converted into Julias, the new Hellenistic city that Philip had built (see 3.1.1). We do not know whether Philip built the Greek city beside

Bethsaida or whether, as Josephus seems to suggest, he converted a small fishing village into a new city. Nor are the size and status of the city clear, if indeed it even had a status, as its name does not appear at all during the First Jewish Revolt.

The two important cities on the eastern shore of the lake were the Decapolis cities of Hippos and Gadara. Jesus may have healed a possessed man in the area of Gadara. He lived a base life in the burial caves by a cliff over the lake (Matt 8:28 and Mark 5:1, though the latter talks of Gerasa, another city in the Decapolis, located fifty-five kilometers to the south of the lake). Gadara was a great Hellenistic city, located beside famous hot water springs and home to a small Jewish community. Josephus calls it a "Grecian city" (*A.J.* 17:320; *J.W.* 2:97). Strabo tells us about the illustrious people who were born there; among these the poet Meleager stands out, who wrote in an epigram, "[T]he Attic land that lies in Syrian Gadara is the country of my birth." In an inscription on a tomb, Gadara is praised as a "city of letters," home of writers and orators. The coins had a boat engraved on them, as the territory reached the shores of Lake Galilee; the city itself was some nine kilometers away. The coins of another Greek city, Hippos, had a horse engraved on them. Although both Gadara and Hippos were free cities, they had belonged to Herod's kingdom but on his death became part of the Roman province of Syria. The Jews considered them two enemy cities, and during the First Jewish Revolt against Rome their territories (not the cities) were devastated by Galileans. The revenge was the massacre of the Jewish minorities living in both Hippos and Gadara.

A different situation pertained in another of the Greco-Roman cities, Caesarea Philippi or Paneas. It had been founded by Philip, Herod's son, by the sources of the river Jordan, where, since the third century B.C., there had been a cave dedicated to the god Pan (which was the inspiration for its second name). Jesus traveled there with his disciples. Mark mentions that Jesus traveled to "the villages of Caesarea Philippi"; but, as with Gadara, it is very unlikely that he entered the city itself (8:27). Herod had built a splendid temple dedicated to Augustus by Pan's cave. The city was so pretty and agreeable, surrounded by water and greenery at the foot of Mount Hermon, that Vespasian and Titus went there to rest between campaigns during the First Jewish Revolt. There were practically no Jews in the newly constructed city of Caesarea Philippi.

3.4.1.2. A Difficult Relationship

The levels of Jewish presence varied in the cities in first-century Palestine. As D. Flusser points out, not even the immigrants from Greece and Macedonia would have felt out of place in this country. These immigrants included the army veterans from other areas, who had colonized the country under Hellenist rulers; or those in the autochthonous non-Jewish settlements which, with the arrival of the Greeks with their culture, language, and religion, had become more Hellenized. Though we have not analyzed the situation in each Palestinian city, the non-Jews adapted themselves to the lifestyles, religion, and civil organization of the Greco-Roman world, as was the case in other parts of the East. The areas with an exclusively Jewish population were fairly concentrated, that is, Herod's kingdom: Judaea, Galilee, and Peraea were strongholds of Judaism within a wider area where they were outnumbered by the non-Jewish.

The Jews, and above all the Galileans, did not take well to the large Greek presence in the country, which was very visible on the trade routes and less significant inland. The land was one of the pillars of the Jewish religion, and the fact that pagans, non-Jews, were installed there led to feelings of scorn and uncomfortable impotence. For this reason, when the revolt against the Romans spread throughout Galilee in 66 A.D., the non-Jewish minorities in cities such as Tiberias and Jaffa were massacred and bands of Galileans attacked the areas around the Greek cities of Hippos and Gadara. An exceptional case was that of Scythopolis (formerly Beth-shan) in the Jordan Valley. It was an independent city that belonged to the Decapolis confederation where the Jewish minority in the city sided with the rest of the city's inhabitants against the Jewish bands from Galilee. Their unwonted gesture did not serve for much, as the city's inhabitants, once saved from the attack, turned on the Jewish minority and slaughtered them.

The unbounded hate on both sides during the First Jewish Revolt showed the latent tension that existed between the Jews and non-Jews, which manifested itself in mutual ignorance and disrespect. The Greek cities suffered under Jewish political expansionism while the Hasmoneans were in power, being conquered and integrated into a Jewish kingdom that had Jerusalem as its capital. Pompey freed them, but in the times of Herod and his grandson Agrippa I, they were governed once again by Jews, although the Herodian family originally came from Edom. The Jews, especially in Galilee and Peraea, had to live in close physical proximity to non-Jews and the powerful economies of the cities, both Greek and mixed, which determined the economic activities of these two regions. Judaea, located in the mountainous area between the coastal plain and the river Jordan with the Negev to the south, was more "immune" to contact with the non-Jewish population. Lake Galilee was on the trade routes between the rich valleys of Esdraelon and the Jordan to the south and the regions of the north and the east: Syria, Golan, and the Decapolis. The movement of goods increased with the passing of Nabatean caravans and the relative proximity to the port of Caesarea Maritima, from which Roman exports left Palestine. The productive economy, more than simply subsistence, obliged the mainly rural Jewish population to come into contact with the economically stronger non-Jewish population.

The greatest cause for discomfort came from their religious beliefs. The strictly monotheist Jews had to support the presence of the Greek religion, with its temples and cults. For the Jews, this represented intolerable profanity in the holy land of Israel, an attack that they could not counter. The ancient Canaanite and Syrian gods had been incorporated into the Greek pantheon, and the Greek-speaking immigrants had integrated the local gods. The resulting syncretism, typical throughout the Hellenistic world, came into direct conflict with the Jewish religious sensibility and, in particular, with the Jewish rules on ritual cleanliness that prohibited physical contact with any idolatrous representation or object.

The mainly Law-abiding Galilean Jews did not set foot in pagan cities that were full of temples and memorials dedicated to Greek gods, nor did they travel much to the areas around these cities with their columns (*hermae*), burial mounds, and votive religious monuments at crossroads. A devout Jew would have had great difficulty coexisting with the Greek world and its abundant and expansive religiosity. They were two physically close but mentally distant worlds that related with each other through a mutual ignorance. However, this distance guaranteed the survival of the weaker, Jewish culture, which remained immune to the dangers of syncretism. The bridges for dialogue and harmony that the Judaism of the Diaspora tried to build up with the Hellenistic world, with Philo of Alexandria as the most charactistic case, highlights the notable difference between the Judaism of Palestine and that beyond the borders of ancient Israel.

Regarding relations between Jews and non-Jews in Palestine, we should note the lack of disputes between the Jewish scribes and non-Jewish thinkers on religious issues. The Talmud does include some answers offered by rabbis to pagans asking questions or putting forward problems involving the nature of the Jewish religion, but the initiative never comes from the Jewish side. It is understandable that Jesus restricted his activities to the Jewish population and that he did not maintain much contact with non-Jews. Jesus did not live in a pagan land, and when he traveled, he had contact with non-Jewish people only if a healing was involved. On his journey to Tyre, the great Phoenician metropolis, Jesus wanted to pass incognito but was approached by a non-Jewish woman (a "Syrophoenician," according to the Gospel of Mark) who begged him to heal her possessed daughter. Jesus' response, which is evasive or even indifferent, reflects the difference between the "children" (the Jews) and the "dogs" (the pagans) (Mark 7:24-30 || Matt 15:21-28). Jews and pagans, as D. Flusser stresses, each went their own way, despite living side by side. There were very few proselytes in Palestine, pagans who converted to Judaism and adopted some (or all!) of its customs and beliefs.

Jerusalem did, however, attract many Jews and proselytes from other countries, anxious to learn about Judaism and the doctrine of one God and the strict moral commitments of the Jewish religion. For the most important festivities in particular, the city filled with pilgrims who went up to the temple to pray, offer sacrifices, and present offerings. Only ethnic Jews, or Greeks who had become Jews through circumcision and acceptance of the Law, had access to the atria or courtyards of the temple surrounding the sanctuary. The other Gentiles, who sympathized with Judaism to different degrees and in different ways, had to remain in the outer courtyard (the so-called Court of the Gentiles) (see 3.3.1.2). This is the reason why the request from "some Greeks" who wish to see Jesus is given such importance in the Gospel of John (12:21).

3.4.2. The Jews' Relations with the Romans: The Herodians

In 6 A.D., the new Roman province of Judaea was created. It depended directly on the emperor and was governed by a prefect with strong military backing. Despite being independent, it was overseen by the legate of Syria on the Orontes in Antioch. The governor resided in Caesarea Maritima, the largest port on the Mediterranean coast to the south of Tyre. Caesarea had been rebuilt to act as the bridging point to Rome. Caesarea, in honor of Julius Caesar, was to be from then on and, in the words of Tacitus, Iudaeae caput ("the capital of Judaea") (*History* 2:78). Naturally this was from a Roman point of view given that Jerusalem was the capital for the Jews.

3.4.2.1. The Roman Governors

Judaea was the official name given to the Roman province that included Archelaus' lands (Judaea, Edom, and Samaria). The inscription *Praefectus Iuda[ea]e* was found in the theatre at Caesarea Maritima, where Pontius Pilate received the title of Roman governor (26–36 A.D.). It was he who decreed the death sentence for Jesus, the Galilean prophet. The prefects, known as procurators from the time of Emperor Claudius, held the highest judicial and military authority over the non-Roman citizens and managed the financial administration, that is, taxation. Both the Roman governor and, in their territories, the Herodian rulers (Antipas and Philip) had full powers over military, administrative, and judicial issues.

Philo of Alexandria, a Jewish writer from the first century A.D., is not very complimentary toward Pilate. Philo considered him to be inflexible, hard and corrupt, and cruel and vengeful (*Embassy* 302–3). As a governor, he knew how to be obsequious before the emperor, lasting ten years in the post, but he was unable to win over his subjects, especially the Jews, whose special religious sensibility he never came to terms with. His errors generally show a lack of tact, but no particular malice. For example, he made the Roman troops enter Jerusalem with their insignia of the figure of the emperor held high, which went against the strict monotheism of the Jews. He also attempted to use the temple's treasures to build an aqueduct to Jerusalem; this was intolerable since this treasure consisted of the people's donations and offerings (see 6.2.4.4). However, Pilate could be enterprising and calculating when he needed to be. For example, some Samaritans had met for religious reasons by Mount Gerizim and were killed for no reason, as if they were political rebels (*A.J.* 18:87). This led to a spirited protest by the Samaritans and Pilate's removal by Vitellius, legate of Syria.

3.4.2.2. The Army

Only on questions of great importance, when the security of the empire was at stake, was it necessary for the Roman legate in Syria to intervene as head of the army of the Euphrates, which watched over the difficult eastern border of the empire and kept a close eye on events in Judaea. We have already seen how between the death of Herod (4 B.C.) and the First Jewish Revolt (66–70 A.D.), legions had had to intervene on several occasions in this Jewish land in order to put down uprisings or to impose order. In the first century A.D., the army of the East comprised four legions of professional soldiers mostly recruited from among the Eastern subjects and no longer exclusively Italian soldiers. The only true Romans were the superior officers, such as the captains of the cohorts (John 18:12) or the cavalry's squadron commanders. The situation was much the same in the Roman province of Judaea (which included Samaria and Edom) and Philip's territory, where the Jewish subjects were a minority.

The Jewish race was exempt from the levies and could not be enrolled in the Roman army. This special status, unique throughout the empire, was granted by Julius Caesar to all Jews, in both Palestine and the Diaspora. It aimed to avoid forcing the Jews to break the Jewish Law, the regulations relating to food, ritual cleanliness, and rest on the Sabbath (which would have been impossible to keep to in the Roman army). Neither did the Jews have to pay homage to the eagles and standards, which were both military and religious symbols. This meant that there were no Jews in the military forces controlled by the Roman procurators.

The military presence in day-to-day life was considerable. Some four or five cohorts of auxiliary troops (*auxilia*) and a detachment of the cavalry (*ala*) were stationed in Caesarea Maritima, representing over three thousand men, a little over half a legion. There were also small garrisons in cities and forts throughout the country. Cohorts were always stationed in Ashkelon, in the ancient Philistia, which belonged to the imperial family, and Jerusalem. The cohort in Jerusalem had its quarters in Herod's old palace, to the west of the city. This was also the praetorium or residence for the Roman governor when he traveled to Jerusalem. A detachment of soldiers permanently controlled the temple area from the Antonia Tower, in the northwest corner of the city. Jesus' trial probably took place in Herod's old palace (see 6.2.4.1).

The military structure in the tetrarchies of Antipas and Philip was probably much the same. Both had regular and permanent military forces, spread throughout the land, above all in the cities and forts such as Tiberias and Machaerus. These forces often aided the Roman legions when they carried out special campaigns against the Parthians or the Arabs. They rarely fought against the neighboring rulers associated with Rome, although Antipas, in a border dispute in 36 A.D., did disastrously fight the Nabatean king Aretas, an ally of Rome. Antipas' and Philip's troops had to ensure the country's security, particularly protecting the lines of communication from attack. Small garrisons commanded by a centurion ensured the safety of towns such as Capernaum, which had a tax collection office that probably acted as a customs house between the territories of Antipas and Philip (Matt 8:5-13 and Luke 7:1-10).

We have seen that the military forces stationed in the three Jewish territories in Palestine were predominantly non-Jewish. However, they did not all came from abroad; they included inhabitants of Palestine who had enrolled in the Roman army as a modus vivendi. In the case of Judaea, many soldiers came from the cities of Caesarea and Sebaste, especially the latter, the capital of Samaria. These troops held anti-Jewish sentiments, as was seen in 44 A.D. with the stentorian explosion of satisfaction shown on the death of Agrippa I, a king who had been favorable to the Jews. This led to reproach from Emperor Claudius himself. We do not know the exact origin of the soldiers belonging to Antipas' small army, which was organized along Roman lines. His superior officers were known as "tribunes" (Mark 6:21) or captains of a cohort, while the centurions, for example at Capernaum, commanded small garrisons or detachments. Among the professional soldiers under the orders of a governor allied to Rome, as was Antipas, there may have been Jews, at a time when many had little or no means of income. Enlisting into a "local" army, such as Antipas', which did not keep to the same regulations as the Roman army or legionary cohorts, may have been an attractive proposition for more than one unemployed Jew in Galilee or Peraea (Luke 3:14).

Not all the soldiers were so favorable toward Judaism as the centurion at the garrison in Capernaum, who according to Luke (7:5) paid for the construction of the synagogue in this town. Normally, it was quite the contrary. Antipas' soldiers carried out both surveillance and policing missions, with the latter opening up possibilities for abuse and extortion: John the Baptist urged them to "rob no one by violence or by false accusation" (Luke 3:14). Forced labor involving men and animals for public works (*angaria*) was frequently used by the military (or civil servants in public administration). With a clear conscience, they made people provide services from time to time, for example, transporting materials or pulling the yoke for a mile (Matt 5:41). Simon, a Jew from Cyrenaica, a Roman province now a part of Libya, was returning from the fields on the eve of Passover when he came across a group of prisoners on their way to Golgotha to be executed. He was made to "carry [the] cross" of Jesus of Nazareth. The centurion who was in charge of the execution was worried, no doubt, that the accused would die before he arrived at the place of his punishment and for this reason enlisted Simon, a Jewish immigrant from Cyrene (Mark 15:21). This was common practice at the time (see 6.2.5.2).

3.4.3. The Jews' Relations with the Samaritans

3.4.3.1. The Origin of the Samaritans

Samaria is the land between Galilee and Judaea. The Greco-Roman capital of Samaria was Sebaste, a Greek name that corresponds to the Latin Augustus. Herod named it in honor of Caesar Augustus, to whom he dedicated a temple in this Hellenistic city, which had been splendidly rebuilt following its destruction by John Hyrcanus, the Hasmonean king. Herod then repopulated the city with former soldiers and people from the surrounding area, and, for this reason, its inhabitants were truly heterogeneous.

This was true of the whole of Samaria. The complex history of the Samaritan land explains its impressive blend of races and beliefs. As J. P. Meier stresses, we need to make a distinction between race and religion: ethnically speaking, the region of Samaria has a fairly homogeneous blend of people, in which the Greek colonists, or the Hellenized and those who practiced the Greco-Roman religions, dominated, especially in the cities (and above all the capital, Samaria). The Samaritans were the majority in rural areas and worshipped Israel's God and followed the Law of Moses with their own variations and to a greater or lesser extent. The focus for the Samaritan religion was Mount Gerizim, near Shechem. To a degree, the scene in Galilee is repeated, but in reverse: in Samaria, those who follow the monotheism of the Torah are not the majority but a minority tolerated in a Hellenized world.

In the first century A.D., the fundamental beliefs of the Samaritans did not differ greatly from those of the Jews. For example, both the Samaritans and the Sadducees believed that only the five books of the Pentateuch were Holy Scriptures, revealed by God for his people; even the text of the Samaritan Pentateuch was very similar to the Hebrew Pentateuch until the turn of the second century B.C., when the country was bloodily destroyed by the Jewish ruler John Hyrcanus. At this point, relations between Jews and Samaritans cooled rapidly, before eventually turning to hatred. And yet, the Samaritans continued to practice the religion of Moses and the fathers, worshipping one God, circumcising boys, and observing the Sabbath and the festivities, above all Passover. However, they did not seem to have been particularly strict in keeping to the regulations regarding ritual cleanliness, which distinguishes the different groups within the renewal of the Jewish faith between the second century B.C. and the first century A.D., following the crisis brought on by Antiochus IV Epiphanes. The Samaritans also shared the messianic hopes held by the Jewish people, though they had their own figures: later Samaritan texts do not mention the sacerdotal and royal messiahs, instead talking of a prophet who will come at the end of days called simply *taheb* ("he who has to return"), a kind of new Moses (Deut 18:15).

3.4.3.2. The Conflict between Jews and Samaritans

The division and conflict between the Jews and Samaritans was produced around 330 B.C., when the Samaritans built an altar (rather than a temple) on Mount Gerizim near Shechem. From this time on, there were major disputes between the two, as seen in the words addressed to Jesus by the Samaritan: "[O]ur fathers worshipped on this mountain [Gerizim], and you [the Jews] say that in Jerusalem is the place where men ought to worship" (John 4:20). The expression "our fathers" refers to Moses, who had indeed ordered the building of "an altar to the Lord" on Mount Gerizim so as to be able to make sacrifices and offerings (Deut 27:4-13). The decision of the Samaritans, however, clashed with the legitimacy that the Old Testament bestowed on Jerusalem and its temple alone as the place where God was to be worshipped (e.g., Ps 132).

The hostile feelings of the Jews toward the Samaritans are evident in the last numerical proverb of the Sirach: "With two nations my soul is vexed, and the third is no nation: Those who live on Mount Seir [the Edomites], and the Philistines, and the foolish people that dwell in Shechem [the Samaritans]" (50:25-26). The long history of disagreements between Jews and Samaritans can be seen in the few texts in the Gospels that mention the latter. In the Gospel according to John, the Jewish leaders, who refuse to accept that Jesus came from God, speak harshly of them, saying, "Are we not right in saying that you are a Samaritan and have a demon?" (8:48). This invective is due to the bitter arguments between Jews and Christians seen at the end of the first century A.D., which also involved the Samaritans, as the Christian mission had made some progress among the Samaritan population.

However, not only the Jewish authorities were hostile toward the Samaritans. Two of Jesus' disciples show that they share the feelings common to Jews at this time. Jesus was traveling to Jerusalem for the Passover, starting off on the journey that was to end in his death. Initially, he tried to stay in a Samaritan town, but the inhabitants did not want to put him up "because his face was set toward Jerusalem." This reason or excuse clearly shows the feelings of the Samaritans and their animosity toward Jews traveling to Jerusalem, their holy city. Faced with this snub from the Samaritans, James and John, two disciples Jesus calls "sons of thunder," live up to their nickname and demand the immediate and violent destruction of the people in the town: "bid fire come down from heaven and consume them" (Luke 9:51-56). Jesus roundly refuses and, apparently, changes his route so as not to pass through Samaria.

From a less contentious point of view, the Samaritans were simply considered "foreigners" by the Jews. Thus, Jesus commented when he saw that of the ten lepers healed (nine Jews and a Samaritan) only the Samaritan came back to glorify God and give thanks to the healer, "Was no one found to return and give praise to God except this foreigner?" (Luke 17:18). The Gospel according to John expresses the state of affairs thus: "Jews have no dealings with Samaritans" (4:9). Despite all this, in the parable of the Good Samaritan (Luke 10:30-37), Jesus shows his sympathetic attitude toward the Samaritan who risked his life to aid someone he did not know but who had been beaten and left to die by the side of the road.

4
The Person

4.1. His Name

All the historical sources agree on the name of Jesus when discussing the object of study in this book. The name derives from the Latin Jesus, which comes from the Greek *Iēsous*. The Hebrew or Aramaic version is *Yeshua*, and in the Galilean dialect of Aramaic, Jesus' mother tongue, the name was pronounced as *Yeshu*. From the third century onward, in Babylonian Aramaic and in Syrian, the stress moved to the first syllable, and the name was pronounced as *Yeishu*. The name *Yeishua* is an abbreviation of *Yehoshua*, used only up until the time of the Babylonian exile (6th c. B.C.): this was the name of the charismatic leader who succeeded Moses, Joshua.

It was a well-known biblical name, given to a number of figures in the Jewish Scriptures, and was common among the Jews living in Palestine in the first centuries B.C. and A.D. This is evident from the inscriptions on the ossuaries from the period and in the work of Josephus who uses it some twenty times in the Greek form (*Iēsous*). As G. Barbaglio stresses, it is a name given to both anti-Roman rebels (Jesus, son of Shaphat; *J.W.* 3:450) and prophets (Jesus, son of Ananus; *J.W.* 6:288–309), and we even know of a high priest at the temple in Jerusalem called Jesus: Jesus, son of Phabet (*A.J.* 15:322).

This abundant use means that we must add more information in order to determine the individual in question. Jesus is known by his hometown (Nazareth) or by a second name (Christ, *Khristos*, which means "anointed," the Greek translation of Messiah). This name soon replaced his first name, with Josephus referring to Jesus as he "who was called Christ" (2.2.1.1), as do the Roman authors Tacitus, Pliny, and Suetonius (2.2.2). The early Christian communities, arising in the environment of Judaism (the Pauline communities), used both his first and second names indiscriminately, and the mixed form first appeared here: "Jesus, the Christ" or simply "Jesus Christ."

The Gospels of Matthew and Luke state that Jesus' name was not given casually or by accident. As is often the case with important biblical figures, their name is closely linked to their mission and ultimately reflects divine intention. The explanation given by the Gospel according to Matthew relates the name Jesus (*Yeishua*) to the word for salvation (*yeishua*). "You shall call his name Jesus, for he will save his people from their sins," says the angel, sent by God to Joseph, husband of Mary, Jesus' mother (Matt 1:21). A similar etymology, understandable only in Hebrew, can be seen in the works of Philo of Alexandria, a Jew in a Hellenistic culture (10 B.C.–60 A.D.). He explains the etymology of Joshua, Moses' successor: "Joshua [Jesus] means 'the salvation of the Lord'" (*Names* 121). The Gospel of Luke follows a similar line, talking of the angel's visit to Mary and announcing that she is to conceive and have a son, adding, "[Y]ou shall call his name Jesus" (1:31). Later in the same Gospel, Mary's son is linked three times to the idea of salvation (1:69, 1:77, and 2:11). The last of these three, another announcement from the angel, relates to Jesus' birth, on this occasion to the shepherds: "[F]or to you is born this day . . . a Saviour [*sōtēr*]." The Gospel of Luke preempts Jesus' actual name giving on the day of his circumcision (2:21).

The name Jesus is chosen by his parents, though according to the Gospels they are guided by a divine messenger in their decision: Joseph (according to Matthew) and Mary (according to Luke). Would Joseph and Mary not have followed the customs of the time and given their child a name belonging to the great heroes of Israel, at a time when the Jewish identity was striving to gain ground against the powerful Roman occupiers? Was it not Joshua who had led the people of Israel triumphantly into the land promised by God and who expelled their enemies? The reasons offered by Matthew and Luke, who narrate episodes from Jesus' childhood, agree that the name given to the child came from a divine revelation and point toward a mission that transcends everything, including political freedom. A common name, such as Jesus in first-century Galilee, is made unique by the individuality of the person it is given to. Ultimately, Jesus' life lived up to the scope of the name he was given.

4.2. His Place and Date of Birth

The historical sources are unanimous on Jesus' town of origin: Nazareth. The documents in the New Testament, the Gospels, and the Acts of the Apostles (2:22, 3:6, 4:10, 6:14, etc.) state this explicitly. Nazareth is "his own country" (Mark 6:1 || Matt 13:54) and "their own city," that of Joseph and Mary (Luke 2:39), the place where his relatives lived. Nathanael, a Galilean like Jesus and a future disciple of his, asked ironically, "Can anything good come out of Nazareth?" (John 1:46). The crowds that accompanied Jesus on his triumphal entrance into Jerusalem, a few days before the Passion, said, "This is the prophet Jesus from Nazareth of Galilee" (Matt 21:11). At the other extreme, the religious authorities in Jerusalem replied thus to Nicodemus, a Jewish leader who had dared to visit Jesus: "Are you from Galilee too? Search and you will see that no prophet is to rise from Galilee" (John 7:52).

In the Talmud, Jesus (*Yeishu*) is invariably described as *ha-notsrí*, an adjective meaning "the Nazarene." This is the case in the Tractate *Sanhedrin* (43a, 107b) from the Babylonian Talmud (2.2.1.2). Despite their differences, the Greek adjectives *nazarēnos* and *nazōraios*, both present in the Greek text of the New Testament, follow similar lines, as does the Greek noun *Nazara*, which appears alongside Nazareth, the most common Greek name. In modern Hebrew, Christians are known as *ha-notsrim*, "the Nazarenes," in line with the Talmud and the New Testament, "the sect of the Nazarenes"; this is the expression used by the lawyer Tertullus speaking on behalf of the members of the Sanhedrin in his allegations against Paul before the procurator Felix (Acts 24:5).

Faced with this impressive number of parallel testimonies, many experts have defended this exclusive link between Jesus and the Galilean town of Nazareth. Jesus, a Galilean, was born and lived in this town in Lower Galilee until he was thirty years old. However, the Gospels of Matthew and Luke make a distinction between his place of birth and his hometown. They state that Jesus was born in Bethlehem in Judaea and that he was brought up and passed his childhood, adolescence, and youth in Nazareth. The Gospel according to Luke states that Nazareth is "where he [Jesus] had been brought up" (4:16), and it situates his birth in Bethlehem (2:4, 2:6-7; as does Matt 2:1).

We need to ask ourselves where Jesus was born: in Nazareth of Galilee or Bethlehem of Judaea. What is the historical validity of the Christian tradition that states that Jesus was born in Bethlehem, the town of David, the great king of Israel?

4.2.1. The Place: Bethlehem

The Gospels of Matthew and Luke relating to Jesus' childhood have many points in common, but also some differences. The two most important points where they differ are the sequence of events and Mary and Joseph's legal situation when Jesus was born.

In Matthew, the report of the birth and Jesus' first days are associated exclusively with Bethlehem, though the angel appearing to Joseph in his dreams does so at an unnamed place. From the start of the Gospel, Bethlehem is the only town mentioned, and it is in a "house" in Bethlehem of Judaea where the wise men from the East find Mary and her child Jesus (2:11). Does this house belong to Joseph, a descendant of David and member of his family, or are Joseph, Mary, and Jesus staying in the house of one of Joseph's relatives, who was a member of the Davidic dynasty? Matthew explains that Herod had killed "all the male children and all those under the age of two in Bethlehem, according to the time stated by the wise men" (2:16). From this we can infer that the wise men's visit took place some time after the birth of Jesus, but not immediately after. As soon as the wise men leave the scene, Herod's persecution begins. Matthew relates that Joseph, Mary, and the child have to leave hurriedly by night, finding exile in Egypt. They did not return to Bethlehem: Joseph "was afraid to go there," to Judaea (2:22), as it was then ruled over by Archelaus, the son of Herod, the persecutor who had just died. He took his family to Nazareth, a small town in Galilee, where they could start a new life.

Luke's view is distinctive. Mary lived in Nazareth and was visited in her own house by the angel Gabriel. We are not told explicitly where Joseph was from or where he lived, but, according to Luke, he had to go to Bethlehem of Judaea to register; he "went up from Galilee, from the city of Nazareth" (2:4) "to be enrolled, each [in] his own city" (2:3). When they returned to Nazareth from Judaea after Jesus' birth, Joseph and Mary went "to their own city, Nazareth" (2:39). It seems that Joseph had two hometowns: Bethlehem and Nazareth. Joseph had neither a house of his own in Bethlehem nor a relative to put him up as, according to Luke, Mary gave birth in the stable of an inn. Once Jesus was born, he was circumcised after eight days, in line with the Law of Moses, and this took place in Bethlehem. Forty days after the child's birth, they went to the temple in Jerusalem to carry out the ritual purification of the mother in line with the Law of Moses. From Jerusalem, they did not return to Bethlehem, but to their hometown of Nazareth (2:39). They returned to the town they had left to travel to Bethlehem.

The second difference between Matthew and Luke relates to the legal situation in which Joseph and Mary found themselves on Jesus' birth. Both Gospels agree that, when Jesus was conceived in Mary's womb, they were "betrothed," legally man and wife though not living together (Matt 1:18; Luke 1:34). The question rests on when exactly they began to live together as man and wife. According to Matthew, they were living together before Jesus was born. The angel of God invited Joseph to take Mary as his legally wedded wife (1:20), and Joseph obeyed immediately (1:24). Joseph and Mary become man and wife in the fullest sense, legally and socially, as they lived under the same roof. The situation put forward by the Gospel of Matthew corresponds to the Jewish customs of the time: the ketubah or marriage agreement was signed, but the newlyweds did not live together immediately, rather they prepared their new home; the wife lived with her parents for a year while the house was readied. After a year, the wedding party was celebrated, when the bride entered her new home.

According to Luke (1:27 and 2:5), when Joseph and Mary arrived in Bethlehem, where Jesus was born, they were still in the same situation as they had been in Nazareth. They were legally married, but the wedding ceremony had not taken place. Their situation would have been a talking point for people: Joseph was the legal father of the child (his marriage agreement was valid), but he was not yet living with his legitimate wife. In other words, there were social irregularities in Joseph and Mary's situation, as they had not followed the established nuptial customs. This may well have led to slanderous rumors as to the actual father of the newborn child. There were and would continue to be doubts: Joseph himself, faced with Mary's sudden pregnancy, wanted to divorce her (Matt 1:19); the people of Nazareth significantly talked of Jesus in terms of his mother and not his father: "the son of Mary" (Mark 6:3) (see 4.3).

There are, however, two points that Matthew and Luke share. The first relates to the place where Jesus was born. As we have already said, the narratives in Matthew and Luke both rest on the idea that Jesus was born in Bethlehem (Matt 2:1 and Luke 2:4, 2:15). So, why do two independent and diverse historical sources provide the same information? Where has it come from? According to some, the early Christian tradition placed Jesus' birth in Bethlehem, so as to justify and demonstrate (in response to Jewish objections) that Jesus really was Israel's long-awaited Messiah. The Messiah had to be a descendant of David's, and Bethlehem was David's town. The suggestion by Matthew (1:20, 2:6) and Luke (1:27, 1:32-33, 1:69, 2:4, 2:11) that Jesus was the Messiah and a descendant of David makes it more likely that Bethlehem was a theological, rather than a historical, suggestion. If this was intended to "prove" that Jesus was a descendant of David and it was created by the early Christian community, why are there not more similarities between Matthew and Luke's narratives, specifically in their handling of his place of birth: Bethlehem?

The second point shared by Matthew and Luke is their narrative of an untimely and arduous journey caused by the events surrounding Jesus' birth. Matthew (2:1-23) describes the journey as a sudden nighttime flight from Bethlehem and a treacherous journey to Egypt brought on by Herod's persecution, with the subsequent exile of all the family (parents and child) and lasting until the death of their persecutor. According to Luke, the journey took place because of the universal census ordered by the Roman Emperor Augustus. This necessitated a dangerous journey for a heavily pregnant woman from Nazareth, her place of residence, to Bethlehem, and led to her giving birth in difficult circumstances, far from home and without any kind of support. In Matthew's narrative, Jesus was a fugitive and an exile; while in Luke, he was homeless and a stranger, but Bethlehem was always at the center of events. In short, according to Luke, Jesus arrived in Bethlehem and was born, a child not welcomed by his relatives. According to Matthew, Mary's son, at the mercy of Herod, had to abandon Bethlehem at night and flee to Egypt. What historical evidence is there for Jesus' journey to Egypt and his stay there? It has often been remarked that the intention in Matthew's narrative of the flight to Egypt is to establish parallels between the fate of an exiled Jesus in Egypt and the fate of Israel, his people, enslaved during many years in this same country. Thus, Jesus' time in Egypt had little historical foundation. The Gospel of Luke does not mention it at all; he probably had "theological" reasons for remaining silent on this matter. Curiously Luke also avoids mentioning that the adult Jesus traveled beyond the borders of Israel: the journey to Phoenicia (Mark 7:24), his subsequent journey to the Decapolis (Mark 7:31), another prior visit to the Decapolis (Mark 5:20), and the journey to Caesarea Philippi (Mark 8:27). According to Luke, Jesus' journey began in Galilee and ended in Jerusalem. It was only the early Christian community that passed beyond the borders of Israel and preached the Gospel there: Samaria (Acts 8:5), Syria (9:22), Phoenicia (11:19), and so on. Therefore, if Matthew is interested in stressing Jesus' destiny as an exile, Luke has reason to keep Jesus within the borders of Israel. It remains open to debate from a historical point of view whether Jesus and his parents really fled to Egypt to escape Herod's death threats, culminating in the massacre of the children of Bethlehem.

The other two canonical Gospels, Mark and John, provide little information. There is no reference to Bethlehem in Mark. The narrative presents Jesus for the first time as coming from Nazareth of Galilee (Mark 1:9). It is an idea shared by all four Gospels and that, as we have said, should be accepted as proven: Nazareth is Jesus' hometown. Mark's silence regarding Bethlehem as Jesus' place of birth does not lead to any concrete conclusion. In the Gospel of John, the only reference we have is 7:42. J. P. Meier rightly stresses the ambiguity of this verse: "Has not the Scripture said that the Christ is descended from David, and comes from Bethlehem, the village where David was?" The question taken literally states that Jesus cannot be the Messiah because he was born in Bethlehem. However, taken ironically, the speaker seems to state what he is denying. One needs to assume only that the readers actually knew that Jesus was born in Bethlehem, while the speaker did not. As a result, the denial becomes an affirmation, proving that Jesus is in fact the Messiah. This is not the only example of this kind of irony in the Gospel of John. The soldiers demonstrate through their denial and mockery of Jesus, "Hail, King of the Jews!" (John 19:3), what the reader already knows and recognizes, that Jesus is king. The plaque over the cross has a similar effect ("Jesus of Nazareth, the King of the Jews"; 19:19). Therefore, in John 7:42, the speaker may prove what he wishes to deny, and this is exactly the message that the Gospel wishes to transmit. John 7:42 may refer, de facto, to Bethlehem, David's town, as the place where Jesus was born.

No decisive arguments can be made against Matthew's and Luke's assertion that Jesus was born in Bethlehem of Judaea. Mary finally arrived here, pregnant, with her legal husband Joseph, following a difficult journey of some two hundred kilometers. It was probably a complicated journey, given Mary's pregnancy, but we do not know how pregnant she was when she traveled to Bethlehem with Joseph. The duration of her stay in Bethlehem, which is unknown, saw Mary give birth to the child she was carrying before returning to Nazareth. They may have had to take refuge in Egypt when faced with the murderous threats from Herod. This forms the historical nucleus of the events surrounding the birth of Jesus.

4.2.2. The Reason: A Herodian Census at the Time of Augustus

Next we need to ask why Jesus was not born in Nazareth and what led Joseph and Mary to Bethlehem. The Gospel of Luke justifies the journey to Bethlehem with a "census" (*apografè*) decreed by the Emperor Augustus (2:1), which affected the whole of the empire and was linked to Quirinius, governor of Syria (see Luke 2:2). Joseph and Mary traveled to Bethlehem to register, in compliance with this decree. However, Augustus was emperor of Rome from 29 B.C. to 14 A.D., while Quirinius became governor of Syria only in 6 A.D., just when Archelaus, Herod's son, was deposed and Judaea became a Roman province (*A.J.* 17:35, 18:1-2, 18:26). Through Quirinius Augustus decreed a provincial census (not a general one for the whole of the empire) to raise imperial taxes in the new province of Judaea.

This excluded Galilee and Perea governed by Antipas and Trachonitis governed by Philip, both sons of Herod. The census caused a revolt led by Judas the Galilean and was put down by Quirinius himself (Acts 5:37; *A.J.* 18:10) (see 3.3.3.2). This cannot have been the census that led to Joseph and Mary's journey to Bethlehem, as Herod was king when Jesus was born (Matt 2:1; Luke 1:5) and died in 4 B.C., ten years before Quirinius' census.

Furthermore, during the final years of Herod's reign, Syria was governed not by Quirinius but by C. Sentius Saturninus (10/9–7/6 B.C.) and P. Quinctilius Varus (7/6–4 B.C.). We can conclude that the census mentioned in Luke 2:2 is the last of the censuses decreed by Herod in 7/6 B.C. for the whole of his kingdom designed to meet his government's fiscal needs and completely independent from Rome. However, it satisfied the wishes of Emperor Augustus. We know that Augustus often promoted censuses around the empire, both in provinces controlled by the empire, the case in Judaea in 6 A.D., and in those territories governed by Rome's allies. Augustus had just carried out a census of Roman citizens throughout the empire in 8 B.C. Herod was quick to agree with Augustus' view on censuses at a time when it was in his interests to improve relations with the emperor, following a series of political difficulties he had had with him.

There are two possible explanations for the general census for the whole of the empire described in Luke 2:1 and decreed by Augustus. Either Luke has amalgamated and magnified a number of provincial censuses into just one general census, which Augustus would never have actually decreed, or it refers to the general census of Roman citizens (not all the inhabitants of the empire), which took place in 8 B.C., decreed by the emperor. In any case, the Gospel wishes to stress the historical importance of Jesus' birth by relating it to Augustus' and Quirinius' census.

Furthermore fourteen years had passed since Herod's last census of his subjects. This last census was carried out in 20/19 B.C., and the registers needed to be updated. The census decreed by Herod in 7/6 B.C., which included the swearing of loyalty to Augustus and himself, is mentioned in Josephus (*A.J.* 15:368, 17:42). Luke 2:2 also alludes to Herod's census with this text: "[T]his census [Herod's, in 7/6 B.C.] came before what took place when Quirinius was governor of Syria [6 A.D.]." As Tertullian says (*Marc.* 4:19:10), the governor of

Syria was Saturninus when Herod, king of Judaea, decreed his final census.

Herod, an independent king though allied to Rome, probably carried out censuses according to traditional Jewish customs, and not in the style of the Roman provincial censuses. The traditional census system in Israel, maintained since 200 B.C. (and probably earlier, throughout the postexile period), required both men and women to register. The criteria for the census and taxation, unlike provincial Roman censuses, were based on the individual (*tributum capitis*) and not their property (*tributum soli*). The census carried out by Quirinius and ordered by Augustus was a typical Roman provincial census that, for the first time and with strong opposition from the Jews, produced a property register based on a sworn declaration (*akroasis*) (*A.J.* 18:3). According to Josephus, this procedure transgressed "that happiness and those laws which they [the inhabitants of Judaea] had anciently enjoyed" (*J.W.* 2:86). The traditional Jewish census, which Herod with his political pragmatism was wise enough not to change, was designed simply to register all those individuals between the ages of twelve to fourteen and sixty-five so that they could pay an annual and equal per capita tax. The Law of Moses stated that the census be egalitarian ("the rich shall not give more, and the poor shall not give less"; Exod 30:12-15).

Taxation of agrarian property was typically Roman, as according to the Jewish way of seeing things the land could belong only to God and, thus, could not be given a value or registered in a cadastre with fiscal ends. God gave the land to his people, and no other authority could rule over it or dominate it. God was its only owner (see 3.3.3.2). Taxation was high in Herod's times, given that the monarch required a high level of income to pay for the great public works in his kingdom and to pay for the gifts given to the Greek cities further afield. Herod decreed all kinds of taxes on harvests and trade, but the king did not go as far as to apply a *tributum soli*, which would have deeply upset Jewish sensibilities.

Thus, the journey by Joseph and Mary, residents of Nazareth, to Bethlehem makes more sense from the point of view of Herod's census in 7/6 B.C. The reason for the journey was to be registered in the *tributum capitis* for each inhabitant, adult man or woman, in Herod's kingdom. Everyone had to register, "each to his own city" (Luke 2:3).

Herod's decree left a degree of freedom in the interpretation of this point. Joseph could have registered in Nazareth, his place of residence, but he chose Bethlehem, his hometown. This choice is understandable for a pious Jew from the dynasty of David, the great king of Israel. Joseph's family came from Bethlehem, where their origins were known and respected; they had emigrated only a few generations earlier to Galilee. Joseph decided, in accordance with the regulations set by the Law of Moses and the possibilities offered by Herod, to register in the town of his tribe (Judah) and his dynasty (Davidic) and thus comply with Herod's decree for a census.

This decision was probably affected by their socially anomalous and irregular situation, faced with criticism and slander from the people of Nazareth: Joseph was betrothed to a girl from the same town, Mary, who was pregnant before they had celebrated the wedding and before they were living together. He did not, however, divorce Mary and instead kept to the marriage agreement. The strong social pressure and the malicious doubts over the actual father of the child were other reasons for Joseph to take his wife to Bethlehem. The reaction of Joseph's relatives in Bethlehem cannot have been positive, as Mary had to give birth in precarious conditions in a stable on the outskirts of the town.

The records stating that Jesus was born in Bethlehem were soon established in the Christian community in Judaea. This is the only explanation for the Emperor Hadrian's interest in eliminating all vestiges of it and paganizing the town. Immediately after the Second Jewish Revolt (132–135 A.D.), Hadrian ordered the removal of any remnants of Christian heritage in the place in Jerusalem where Jesus died and had been crucified. He ordered the construction of a Greco-Roman place of worship in an equally holy place for Judeo-Christians: the cave in Bethlehem, which acted as a memorial to Jesus' birth. The cave, as explained by Jerome (*Ad Paulinum* 58), was used for the worship of Tammuz-Adonis, Venus' lover, dead and mourned by the worshippers. There may even have been a small holy grove planted nearby that disappeared in the fourth century, when Constantine built the Basilica of the Nativity over the site of the cave.

Mary's stay with the newborn child in the stable where she had given birth cannot have lasted long as, according to the narrative in the Gospel of Matthew, when the wise men from the East visited

Bethlehem, they found Mary and the child in a "house" (2:11). The tradition links a house to the period following Jesus' birth. It is unlikely that this house belonged to Joseph, whose ancestors, despite coming from Bethlehem, had emigrated to Galilee. It seems more likely that the house belonged to one of his relatives, from the Davidic dynasty like Joseph himself. After a few days of life (Luke) or a few months (Matthew), Jesus left this house and, after some time in Egypt to escape Herod's persecution (Matt 2:1-23), went to live in Nazareth, the town that would become "his own city," "his own country." This house belonged to Joseph, his father, where he grew up under his care and that of his mother Mary.

4.2.3. The Date: 7/6 B.C.

Jesus was born when Emperor Augustus (29 B.C.–14 A.D.) and Herod, king of the Jews, were in power (37–4 B.C.) (Matt 2:1; Luke 1:5, 2:1). Since Herod died between the months of March and April in the year 750, counting from the foundation of Rome (*A.J.* 17:167), it could not have been later than 4 B.C. This curious chronological anomaly (Jesus was born before the beginning of the Christian era!) is due to an error made by Dionysius Exiguus in the sixth century. This monk's attempts to set the date for the start of the Christian era led to his selecting the year 754 from the foundation of Rome and not 750, the year of Herod's death, or earlier. In other words, he was four years or more too late. Furthermore, our reflections in the previous section on the census show that Jesus must have been born by 7/6 B.C. Herod's decision to kill all the male children in Bethlehem and the surrounding area "who were two years old or under" (Matt 2:16) indicates that Jesus' birth must have taken place no more than three years before the death of Herod. He died when Jesus and his family were in Egypt, according to Matthew 2:19. The time frame has to be some three years before Herod's death, between the years 7/6 and 4 B.C.

Can we be any more precise? It all depends on the chronological value attributed to the information in the Gospel according to Matthew and the phenomenon of the guiding star detected by the wise men (2:2, 2:9-10), which they identify as a sign that the king of the Jews "has been born." A star indicating the birth of a great figure is common in antiquity. For example, Cicero (*On Divination* 1:23:47) explains how on the night of Alexander the Great's birth the great temple of Artemis in Ephesus was burnt down and how the wise men of Persia saw this event as a sign of the birth of someone who would put the whole of Asia at risk. The births of Augustus and Mithridates were also accompanied by celestial signs. The idea of this star unquestionably has Hellenistic and Oriental precedents. The star mentioned in Matthew 2 could have been the result of four distinct astronomical events observed at the time. It could have been a very bright star or a nova, which appeared between March and April 5 B.C. according to Chinese and Korean astronomers, due to the alignment of Jupiter and Saturn in the constellation of Pisces. This occurred three times during 7 B.C. (May–June, September–October, and December). It could have been the alignment of Jupiter, Saturn, and Mars (February 6 B.C.), the alignment of Jupiter and the moon with an eclipse of the royal planet in the constellation of Pisces (the "Jewish" constellation; February 20, 5 B.C.), or, in all probability, a combination of all of these. M. Kidger has identified the star mentioned as "DO Aquilae."

The idea of the star involves an entirely Jewish literary tradition. The astronomical considerations have to take into account Balaam's prophecies. He was a non-Jewish wise man who prophesied the coming of a great king from among the Jewish people: "a star shall come forth out of Jacob, and a scepter shall rise out of Israel" (Num 24:17). We know that this passage was interpreted as foreseeing a messiah in the Targum, or the Aramaic translation of the Bible, common in first-century A.D. synagogues. The Targum "translated" this verse as follows: "a king shall rise from Jacob, and a Messiah shall be anointed from Israel" (Targum Onkelos). The motif of the star unites two points of view: the Greco-Roman and the Jewish.

According to the Syrian calculation, which Luke seems to use in his Gospel (3:1) in order to set the date of the start of Jesus' public activities, his birth took place between October 1, 7 B.C., and September 30, 6 B.C. (see 4.5.1). Further exactitude in terms of the month and day becomes increasingly hypothetical. All attempts to work out the exact date have come up against the lack of evidence. Despite all the efforts to solve this question, with both astronomical calculations and ancient calendars, the research usually ends more or less in conjecture. The main talking point for the Christians of the first centuries was when to celebrate Easter, a date that depended on the moons and was not a fixed date. The Christmas festivities, since their beginnings in the fourth century at the time of Constantine, were celebrated on a set date: December 25.

The Roman festivities for the Unconquered Sun (*sol invictus*), very popular throughout the empire during the third century, were already associated with the winter solstice, the time of the year when the day began to get longer and there was more sunlight. The unconquered sun was depicted in a number of figures, including Mithras, the god who carried a knife and a torch to illuminate the darkness. He was born from a stone and helped shepherds. However, the unconquered sun was also depicted in the figure of the emperor, comparing him to the sun and representing his qualities as ruler of the universe, truly a divine manifestation. The Christian festivities were also associated with the sun and the light that grew with Jesus Christ, "when the day shall dawn upon us from on high" (Luke 1:78), making him the only one worthy of worship as "God of God, Light of Light," as the Nicene Creed puts it (385 A.D.).

Due to the lack of information in the historical sources, we do not know the day on which Jesus was born, and December 25 has little value from the point of view of Jesus' history (the probability is one in 365!). The date is, however, very valuable in the history of Christianity. It marks the beginning of the commemoration of Jesus' birth, coinciding with the winter solstice and the Unconquered Sun festivities, and represents the decline in the Greco-Roman religion and the emergence of the Christian religion throughout the empire.

4.3. His Parents and Family

4.3.1. His Parents, Joseph and Mary

Jesus is presented in the documentary sources as "the son of Joseph" (Luke 3:23, 4:22; John 6:42), "Jesus of Nazareth, the son of Joseph" (John 1:45), "the carpenter's son" (Matt 13:55), "the son of Mary" (Mark 6:3). Obviously Jesus' mother is called Mary. This is also made clear in the Acts of the Apostles 1:14. The name Mary, as Jesus' mother, is absent from the Gospel according to John, for reasons inherent in the text, but present in Matthew (1:18, 2:11, 13:55), Mark (6:3), and Luke (1:41-42, 2:5-7, 2:34). This does not mean that there are not other references to Jesus' "mother," even in John, where she is not named. They are as follows: in the visit that she and his brothers make while Jesus is in Capernaum (Mark 3:31-35 || Matt 12:46-50 || Luke 8:19-21), in the Cana wedding scene (John 2:1-12), and the scene at the foot of the cross (John 19:25-27; see also 6:42). Joseph and Mary are a legitimately married couple, with a number of texts calling Joseph Mary's "husband" (Matt 1:16, 1:19) or stating that Mary and Joseph are "betrothed," which means they have a marriage agreement that binds them (Matt 1:18-19; Luke 1:27, 2:5).

There is, however, a problem with Jesus' birth stemming from this. Joseph and Mary are legally man and wife, but, before celebrating the wedding or living together, Mary becomes pregnant with the child, who is to be her firstborn son. This anomaly is noted in several ways. First, in Nazareth, his hometown, Jesus is called "the son of Mary" (Mark 6:3) as well as "the son of Joseph," the usual name given in the biblical and Jewish world, where the genealogical line is generally paternal. Luke 3:23 refers to Joseph precisely as "[Jesus], being the son (as was supposed) of Joseph." Matthew is even more explicit: "[Joseph] knew her not until she [Mary] had borne a son" (1:25). Jesus is a child conceived and, probably, born before his parents had conjugal relations and before they lived together, although they were legally married. He arrived into this world in singular circumstances, and his being called the son of Mary by other people in Nazareth seems to indicate this. Nevertheless, the use of the normal name "son of Joseph" also shows that the unusual situation did not become a stigma that affected Jesus throughout his life.

Completing the list of texts related to the subject, there is John 8:41, where Jewish leaders discuss Jesus, saying, "We are not born of fornication; we have one father, even God." As J. P. Meier states, the second part of this verse is an attempt at self-justification by Jesus' adversaries, whom he accuses of being the devil's children (John 8:44). The first part can be interpreted as reflecting the rumors going around about Jesus, highlighting the mystery that surrounded his conception and birth. The bitter controversy between Jews and Christians at the end of the first century, when the Gospel according to John was written in its current form, is echoed in chapters 7 and 8, in which the question of Jesus' origin is debated: his age (8:57-58), where he came from (7:27, 7:52), his brothers (7:3-4, 7:10), and the Messiah's belonging to David's dynasty and his birth in Bethlehem (7:42). In this context, full of references to Jesus' specific history, John 8:41 alludes to the unique nature of his origins. Part of first-century Judaism supported Jesus' illegitimate origins, which was the intention behind the use of the word *fornication*. For this reason, this portion of John is often translated as, "We are not bastards [implying: unlike you]." As seen in Matthew and Luke, this malicious interpretation of Jesus' origins assumes knowledge (and a burlesque twisting!) of the Christian tradition regarding the virgin birth, which was spread in some Jewish and non-Jewish circles from the second century onward (see 2.2.1.2).

The Gospels present Joseph and Mary as Jesus' parents during his childhood and adolescence in Nazareth. The last scene in which all three appear together is during the pilgrimage to Jerusalem: "[H]is parents went to Jerusalem every year at the feast of the Passover. And when he [Jesus] was 12 years old, they went up according to the custom" (Luke 2:41-42). Much later, when, over thirty years old, Jesus left Nazareth and started to preach throughout Galilee, there is no mention of Joseph. Only his mother Mary is talked about. The most likely cause for this silence is that, by this time, he had died. This is the only explanation for the fact that the texts make no mention of his father. It is likely then that Joseph died in Nazareth at an undetermined age of between fifty and seventy.

The tradition supporting the idea that Joseph died first can be seen indirectly in the *Infancy Gospel of James*, an apocryphal manuscript from around 200 A.D. that tells of the life of the Virgin Mary and the birth of her son, Jesus. Here, Joseph appears as an old man, widowed and with adult children, who agreed to take Mary, a twelve-year-old girl yet to give birth to Jesus, into his care as his wife (9:3, 19:1). By the fourth century, this tradition had been integrated fully into another apocryphal text, the History of Joseph the Carpenter, and by a number of Greek and Syrian writers, including Clement of Alexandria (3rd c.). It seems clear that, when Jesus began his activities away from Nazareth, Joseph had already died. Epiphanius dates his death to when Jesus was still an adolescent, just over twelve years old (*Panarion* 3:78). The reason is very simple: as we have just pointed out, Jesus traveled to Jerusalem at this time to celebrate the Passover, as part of a group of Galilean pilgrims, among whom are his mother and father together with other friends and family. However, if we base our decision on John 6:42, Joseph cannot have died when Jesus was very young. At the scene of the bread and the fishes by Lake Galilee, the people listening to Jesus make the following comment: "Is this not Jesus, the son of Joseph, whose father and mother we know?" The phrase does not necessarily imply that Joseph is still alive but that everyone in Galilee knows who Jesus is and who his parents are (or were).

Mary outlived her son for a short time. While Jesus was traveling through Galilee, his mother went on living in Nazareth with the rest of the family and kept in close contact with her stepchildren, Jesus' brothers and sisters. The Gospels present her at their side in a visit they made to see Jesus when he was in Capernaum (Mark 3:31-35 || Matt 12:46-50 || Luke 8:19-21). She also appeared with them at a wedding in a town close to Nazareth called Cana: "Jesus also was invited to the marriage, with his disciples" (John 2:2). When Jesus visited Nazareth when preaching, Mary appeared as an inhabitant of the town, whom everyone knew as Jesus' mother (Mark 6:3).

Mary lived in Nazareth until Jesus' death, when she traveled to Jerusalem, where she probably stayed. The Gospel of John describes her as a witness to her son's crucifixion and death. In the Acts of the Apostles, Luke shows her together with the disciples in a room in a house in the city, known as the "cenacle" (*cenaculum*) in the Christian tradition, after Jesus' resurrection and before the Pentecost (Acts 1:14, 2:1). According to Luke, Mary, the apostles, other disciples, some women, and Jesus' brothers waited there for the arrival of the Holy Spirit. All these Galileans ("about a hundred and twenty," according to Acts 1:15) had followed Jesus to Jerusalem on his final journey and did not move from here.

In accordance with most of the apocryphal books that explain her death (dormition) and her assumption into heaven, Mary must have died in Jerusalem two years after Jesus' death. Assuming that she gave birth at the age of sixteen, a common enough occurrence at the time, she was around fifty-five when she died. Mary was buried near the River Cedron, a place that is still venerated today as Mary's tomb. Another tradition, referred to by Irenaeus of Lyon, states that Mary died in Ephesus, where she had been staying with John, one of the Twelve. Both traditions agree that Mary experienced a celestial glorification after her death, which resembled the resurrection of Jesus, her son.

4.3.2. Jesus, An Unusual Child

Jesus' birth is set apart by a series of unusual and abnormal circumstances. This birth contained a "secret," a nucleus that rigorous historical criticism, devoid of a priori judgments, is unable to penetrate or resolve. There were three reactions to this "secret." The first and entirely positive reaction was Joseph's, who appears in all the texts as Jesus' father, having accepted the role of legal father to Mary's child. The second response, which was more disrespectful, came from Jesus' close relatives and the townspeople of Nazareth, who were uncomfortable with him and unbelieving (Mark 6:4; John 7:5). The third, positive, reaction was the Christian tradition, which has been passed down in two documentary sources: the two, unconnected, infancy narratives from Matthew and Luke, written before 90 A.D. This tradition clearly sets forth Mary's virgin conception, without the apologetic character of later texts, such as the *Infancy Gospel of James*. However, if Mary was alive and living in Jerusalem with Jesus' disciples and brothers when the early community started on its journey (Acts 1:14), nothing would have stopped this tradition from regenerating itself with its own words.

The angelic visits, received by Joseph (Matt 1:18-25) and Mary (Luke 1:26-38), underline the fact that Jesus' origins are the fruit of a powerful, decisive, and unique action by the Spirit of God, which creates life where there was none. This is how the two celestial messengers express themselves: "what is conceived in her [Mary] is of [Greek, *ek*] the Holy Spirit" (Matt 1:20) and "the Holy Spirit will come upon you [Mary] . . . therefore the child to be born will be called holy, the Son of God" (Luke 1:35). In other words, Mary's conception without human intervention, through the work of divine power, focuses on the identity of the child to be born: the Son of God. As G. Barbaglio states, the virgin conception makes faith in Jesus as the Son of God himself visible to the first Christians and thus manifests that "with

God nothing will be impossible" (Luke 1:37). A second singular and unique intervention by the Holy Spirit took place when Jesus was resurrected after his death. This intervention brought life not only where there was none but also where there had been only decay: "[Jesus], designated Son of God in power according to [Greek, *ek*] the Spirit of holiness by his resurrection from the dead" (Rom 1:4).

There is enough in this comparison to counter the idea that Mary's virgin conception is simply a Christian adaptation of a myth found in other religions. In the Gospels, the Holy Spirit (divine in origin) does not act as the masculine partner, sexually fecundating a woman from this world. This was, however, the case of Romulus, the founder of Rome, regarded as the son of Rhea Silvia and the god Mars, or Emperor Augustus, regarded as the son of Atia and the god Apollo. The narratives of the founders of the great religions, such as Krishna or Buddha, are of little help: in the case of Mary, the prodigious element is reduced to the divine word, brought by the angel who announced either what has passed (Matthew) or what would come to pass (Luke).

The narrative of Mary's virgin conception has arisen from the earliest strata of the Christian tradition in response to an irreducible and essential role played by the figure of Mary of Nazareth and, consequently, of Jesus, her son. The almost complete anonymity surrounding the figures (Mary, and Joseph as well) involved in the conception and birth of Jesus is another factor that supports what is put forward by the Gospels of Matthew and Luke. The narratives in these two Gospels are different, but the tradition behind them is ancient and unique. Matthew, always quick to see in the figure of Jesus the fulfillment of the prophecies of the Old Testament, alludes to Isaiah 7:14 (according to the Septuagint or ancient Greek version) and an oracle that he applies to Mary: "'Behold, a virgin shall conceive and bear a son, and his name shall be called Emmanuel' (which means, God with us)" (Matt 1:23). The Greek word parthenos can mean "virgin" or, simply, "nubile girl, of marrying age." It is difficult to be sure how to interpret the translation of the Septuagint. Matthew clearly applies the idea of virginity to Mary, who remains a virgin despite conceiving her son, Jesus, who is also called Emmanuel.

4.3.3. JESUS, DESCENDANT OF DAVID

The texts repeat time and again that Joseph, Jesus' legal father, is a descendant of David. J. P. Meier rightly stresses that, in the Jewish world (and the Greco-Roman and today's Western worlds), the legal father is the actual father, whether or not he is the biological father. Therefore, saying that Joseph is Jesus' father means that he is his legal father, not necessarily his biological father. Through Joseph, Jesus is a descendant of David, as seen in the Gospels of Matthew (1:6, 1:16, 1:20) and Luke (1:27, 2:4, 3:23, 3:31).

Calling Jesus, directly or indirectly, "son of David" is seen throughout the New Testament. Examples can be found in the Gospels of Matthew (9:27, 12:23, 15:22, 20:30-31, 21:9, 21:15), Mark (10:47-48, 11:10), and Luke (1:32, 1:69, 18:30, 18:39). However, two very early formulae, from early Christian confessions of faith, also state that Jesus is "descended from David according to the flesh" (Rom 1:3) and is "descended from David" (2 Tim 2:8). The author of the book of Revelation also includes this tradition in 3:7 (Jesus is he "who has the key of David") and 22:16 ("I am the root and the offspring of David"). Again in the New Testament, Jesus is linked to the tribe to which David and his descendants belonged: "our Lord was descended from Judah" (Heb 7:14); "the Lion of the tribe of Judah, the Root of David, has conquered" (Rev 5:5). Widening the field even further, there is evidence of Jesus being an Israelite, descended from the patriarchs (and, the patriarchs of the people include David, as seen in Acts 2:29): "to them belong the patriarchs, and of their race, according to the flesh, is the Christ" (Rom 9:5). Jesus' Davidic lineage is affirmed, among other sources, in the Didache, a Christian manuscript from the start of the second century.

Attempts are made to justify Jesus' lineage in the two genealogies in the canonical Gospels (Matt 1:1-17 and Luke 3:23-38). There are two singular, differing texts, each containing a genealogical list, one from Abraham to Jesus (Matthew) and the other from Jesus to Adam (Luke). As J. Jeremias points out, in the Bible a genealogy is no mere curiosity but rather an instrument that ensures the legitimate and clear belonging to the people of Israel and, thus, to a part in the future and definitive salvation. A genealogy is the result of meticulous research into a person's history and lineage, which were thus linked to the history of a people. The research follows different lines, though both come to the same conclusion: Jesus, son of Joseph, is a descendant of Zerubbabel, son of Shealtiel, and David, son of Jesse. They offer more or less one thousand years of the history of Israel, covered by twenty names (Luke) or fourteen names (Matthew) for every five hundred years. Between Jesus, Zerubbabel (during exile), and David (the start of the monarchy), there are almost no coinciding names. It seems that two different lines of ancestry were selected. Matthew follows the royal line, which includes Solomon, David's son, while Luke follows a nonroyal line, which begins with Nathan, another of David's sons (2 Sam 5:14). After Zerubbabel, Matthew produces a list from Abiud, while Luke starts with Rhesa, without either following any of the biblical models. It comes as a surprise that they cannot agree on even the name of Jesus' grandfather, who is called Heli, according to Luke, and Jacob, according to Matthew. However, the names of his great-grandfather (Mathtat and Matthan) are almost the same. Furthermore, Matthew's and Luke's lists are very similar in the period before David.

These genealogies are complex. The genealogical tradition, on which Matthew's is based, adopts a more "official" position and follows (not always precisely) the list of the kings of Judah in the two biblical books of Kings. Luke seems to be more authentic than Matthew. There are two possibilities. The first one is as follows: either they represent two separate attempts based on two different traditions, or Luke's older list has been significantly modified until it becomes the one produced by Matthew. This one is very symmetrical and attempts to force the names to fit into the various historical periods. The second position may be preferable, as there are some singular aspects, such as the identification of Shealtiel as Zerubbabel's father instead of Pedaiah (both names appear in 1 Chr 3:17-19); in both Luke and Matthew, Jechoniah is the father of Shealtiel.

The genealogies clearly show that the early community had made attempts to place Jesus in the Davidic line by reconstructing his ascendancy and thus justifying his belonging to David's line and the people of Abraham. Luke has widened the horizons by taking Jesus' genealogy back to Adam, placing him within the context of the whole of human history.

Beyond the New Testament, there is also a tradition that assigns Jesus to a family of David's dynasty. Hegesippus, a writer born in Palestine and writing around 180 A.D., quoted by Eusebius of Caesarea in his *Ecclesiastical History*, states that he knows the members of Jesus' family. With regard to Simeon, successor to James, "the brother of the Lord" and head of the Christian community in Jerusalem, Hegesippus explains that he was denounced as a descendant of David with possible messianic, and thus anti-Roman, pretensions. For this he was condemned to crucifixion under Trajan (98–117 A.D.). Two grandsons of Judas, another of Jesus' brothers (Mark 6:3), had more luck when they were called to appear before the Emperor Domitian (81–96 A.D.) for belonging to the family of David and thus under suspicion of being related to a messiah and enemies of Rome. In fact, they were two peasants who cultivated the small property on which they lived, and thanks to which they could pay their taxes. Domitian saw that they were inoffensive and let them go (*Eccl. Hist.* 3:20:1-6). According to Julius Africanus, in a letter to Aristides, Jesus' family boasted of their Davidic origins (*Eccl. Hist.* 1:7:13). Obviously, some rabbis also boasted, such as Hiyya the Elder (200 A.D.) (Babylonian Talmud, *Ket.* 62b).

4.3.4. Jesus' Brothers and Sisters

The ancient Christian and Jewish sources speak about Jesus' siblings, about "his brothers" and "his sisters," or refer to someone as "the brother of Jesus," "the brother of the Lord," and so on. Therefore, we would contradict the sources if we denied that Jesus had four "brothers" and at least two "sisters." Significantly, Jesus' four brothers have classical names, typical of patriarchal Israel and common following the Jewish reform movements of the second century B.C. James, the eldest, takes the name of the patriarch Jacob, and the other three are given the names of his three sons: Joseph (or Joses), Judah (Judas), and Simeon (or Simon) (Matt 13:55 and Mark 6:3). The names of his sisters are not mentioned in the canonical Gospels. How do we assess this evidence from a historical point of view? What can be ascertained from this undeniable and completely natural state of affairs in

Jewish society at this time? The question becomes more important because Jesus left his home, family, and town at the age of thirty. This breakaway did not take place without any tension, as can be seen in some of the evangelical texts. On one occasion, his relatives (probably not just his brothers) traveled from Nazareth to Capernaum: "[T]hey went out to seize him, for people were saying, 'He is beside himself'" (Mark 3:21).

Jesus' brothers form a well-identified group, set aside from the disciples, those whom Jesus freely called to share his life and mission with him. Both groups appeared separately at the wedding in Cana, which ends thus: "After this he [Jesus] went down to Capernaum, with his mother and his brothers and his disciples" (John 2:12). According to the Acts of the Apostles, the 120 people in the upper room in Jerusalem, after Jesus' death and resurrection, split into similar groups: the apostles (male disciples), some women (female disciples), and "Mary the mother of Jesus . . . with his brothers" (Acts 1:12-14). Later on, "his brothers" became "the brothers/brethren of the Lord." This is the wording that imposed itself in the early Christian community and is the way the Apostle Paul used it (1 Cor 9:5). "The brothers of the Lord" settled in Jerusalem and took on the tasks of leading the city's Christian community. We do not know whether they were also in charge of other parts of Judaea or Galilee, their home region.

The most important of all of Jesus' brothers was James, known in the Christian tradition under the glorious title of "the Lord's brother" (Gal 1:19). James is Jesus' brother par excellence, the first in the lists of brothers in Matthew and Mark and, as a result, the eldest. Despite the synonymy, this James must not be confused with one of Jesus' disciples, member of the group of Twelve. The disciple James, known as James the Minor or the Younger, was the son of Alphaeus and Mary, brother of Joseph, according to the account of the selection of the Twelve (Matt 10:3; Mark 3:18; and Luke 6:15) and elsewhere (Mark 15:40, 16:1; Matt 10:3; and Luke 24:10). Nor should this James be confused with another, one of the most important members of the group of Twelve: James, son of Zebedee and brother of John, traditionally known as the Great, who was executed by Agrippa I in Jerusalem in 43 or 44 A.D.

4.3.4.1. James, the Eldest Brother

James, the Lord's brother, appears in the book of the Acts of the Apostles (12:17, 21:18) as the leader of the community in Jerusalem. He is the leader of the Christians who are Jewish in origin, who speak Aramaic/Hebrew, and who scrupulously keep to the Law of Moses, believing that no Jew can transgress it (Gal 2:12). However, it seems that James did not make those non-Jews by birth who converted to the Christian faith observe this law (Gal 2:9), as others wished (Acts 15:1, 15:5). According to the Acts of the Apostles (15:13-21), this explains the decisive role that he played in the so-called Jerusalem assembly, the first large-scale meeting of the early Church. Paul himself called James a "pillar" of the early Church, alongside Peter/*Cephas* and John (Gal 2:9). Indeed, James, together with Peter and Paul, was one of only three people to whom the resurrected Jesus appeared individually, according to the First Epistle to the Corinthians 15:5.

From the time Peter left Jerusalem in 43 or 44 A.D., James became the only leader of the city's community until he was stoned to death in 62 A.D. at the instigation of the Sadducee High Priest Ananus. James' execution went against the wishes of the Pharisees, many of whose followers had converted to the incipient Christianity. The stoning of James, "the brother of Jesus, who was called Christ," is referred to indignantly by Josephus, a Pharisee who lamented that a Law-abiding and pious Jew had been executed (*A.J.* 20:200). The Judeo-Christian tradition also conserves this image of James. Hegesippus, around 180 A.D., describes him thus, "James the Just" (*Eccl. Hist.* 4:22:4), as well as referring to him with the name, common throughout early Christianity, of "James, the Lord's brother" (4:23:1).

Hegesippus also offers a brief report on Judas, Jesus' third brother in the order given by Mark (6:3) and fourth according to Matthew (13:55). Hegesippus merely says that "according to the flesh [*kata sarka*], he was called his [Jesus'] brother" and that he was a descendant of David (*Eccl. Hist.* 3:20:1). As we have mentioned before, two of Judas' grandsons were called to declare before the Emperor Domitian, though he set them free, seeing that they were inoffensive.

Hegesippus also refers to Simeon, son of Clopas or Cleopas, who succeeded James at the head of the community in Jerusalem, as a relative of Jesus. Cleopas was a brother of Joseph, Jesus' legal father.

Therefore, Simeon was a cousin to Jesus and probably James. If this is correct, then Jesus' other three brothers (Joseph, Judas, and Simon) must have been dead by the time James' successor was chosen (62 A.D.). In the succession, it had become necessary to look to a secondary level of relation, that of Jesus' cousins.

4.3.4.2. The Meaning of the Expression "Jesus' Brothers and Sisters"

There are four ways of interpreting this expression:

1. They are Jesus' brothers and sisters in the biological and legal sense. Joseph and Mary were the biological and legal parents of a large family with at least seven children: five men and two women (or possibly more). Jesus was the firstborn and thus the eldest child.
2. Jesus' siblings are, in fact, cousins. The terms "brothers" and "sisters" are used figuratively: Jesus' siblings were first cousins, children of other fathers (or one father) and other mothers (or one mother), and not Joseph and Mary. Joseph was only Jesus' legal, not biological, father, while Mary was his biological and legal mother as Joseph's wife. Jesus was an only child, without brothers or sisters, either biological or legal.
3. Jesus' brothers and sisters are half brothers and sisters, only from a legal point of view. Joseph was the legal father of all of them, but he was the biological father of only those children from his first marriage: all of them except Jesus. Mary was Joseph's second wife and the biological and legal mother of only Jesus. Thus, Jesus was the only child of Joseph and Mary and also the youngest in the family if we take into account his half brothers and sisters.
4. Jesus' brothers and sisters are half brothers and sisters, sharing a blood link. Mary was the biological and legal mother to all of them, but Joseph was only the legal, not biological, father of Jesus. At his birth, Jesus was the only child of Mary, Joseph's legal wife. After Jesus' birth, Joseph and Mary had at least six children: four boys and two girls (or possibly more). Jesus was their first and eldest child.

These four possibilities do not all have the same merits, as can be seen when they are compared to our historical sources.

The first possibility asserts that Jesus and his brothers and sisters are blood relatives. This position cannot be sustained if we respect the two most important unconnected sources on the subject: Matthew and Luke. Both Gospels assert, in words and intention, that Jesus was not born from a sexual union between Mary and Joseph. This is also the position adopted by the early Christian tradition, which predated Matthew and Luke. Neither does any other text in the New Testament contradict this.

Consequently, the full-blood relationship between Jesus and his siblings can be upheld only from the point of view of an a priori argument that forces the evidence we have. Matthew (1:25), the text that handles the subject most directly, assures us that when Mary gave birth to Jesus, she and Joseph had not had any sexual relations. Only some Judeo-Christian and gnostic groups from the second and third centuries assert that Jesus was conceived with human semen, specifically Joseph's (Epiphanius, *Panarion* 30:2-3). This position has resurfaced since the eighteenth century, with the Enlightenment and rationalism.

The second possibility puts forward the opposing argument, stating that Jesus' siblings were close relatives, specifically cousins. As Jerome, the author who first proposed this position at the end of the fourth century, says, Joseph was "a guardian (*custos*) rather than a husband" (*Against Helvidius* 4; the *Infancy Gospel of James* 9:1 already expressed this idea in the same terms). Jerome's argument is based on the Hebrew language and stresses that Lot is Abraham's nephew despite being called his "brother" (*'aḥ*) in the Hebrew Bible. Genesis (29:12) says that Jacob was Laban's "brother," when in fact he was his nephew, and this is how Laban treats him (Gen 29:15). Another text (unique in the entire Bible) talks of "brothers," when from the context it is clear that they are "cousins": Eleazar, Kish's brother, has his daughters marry the latter's sons, "their kinsmen [literally: brothers]" (1 Chr 23:21-22).

The reason for this linguistic confusion seems to stem from Hebrew's limited nature, which often leads to circumlocutions, such as "the daughter of the brother" to indicate niece (Gen 24:48) or "the wife of the brother" to indicate sister-in-law (Gen 38:8). In reality

Jesus' brothers and sisters were cousins, and Jesus an only child. The fact that he was called "first-born" (Luke 2:7, 2:23) does not affect this conclusion since, as Jerome stresses, the term is a legal designation for the first son, regardless of whether the mother has had more children or not. Jerome rightly highlights this in Exodus 12:29, Exodus 34:19-20, and Numbers 18:15-17.

This simple and well-founded argument focuses on linguistic usage in the Old Testament. In the New Testament, however, the context for the term brothers/sisters never clearly shows that it could refer to cousins. In Greek, there is a separate word for cousins (*anepsios*), used in Colossians 4:10 (though used only once in the whole of the New Testament!). However, Jerome's proposal cannot be dismissed since there is no specific word in Hebrew or Aramaic, Jesus' mother tongue, to specify the closeness of relations between first cousins. If they had wanted to indicate that Jesus' siblings were in fact cousins, we might have expected even minimal evidence of this in the New Testament, or at least somewhere in the early Christian tradition. As J. P. Meier stresses, Hegesippus clearly distinguishes between James, "the Lord's brother," and Simeon, "the Lord's cousin" (*Eccl. Hist.* 4:22:4, a text where the adjective second refers to the word "bishop" and not "cousin"). If we take into account Hegesippus writing in the second century, it is difficult to maintain that the Lord's brothers could also have been considered his cousins.

The cousin hypothesis seems, as far as we can tell, to have been produced by Jerome in a dispute with Helvidius, although we cannot discount that he had used an earlier account of Jesus' family, after having rejected what until then had been the traditional position, presented here as the third possibility: that Jesus' siblings were half brothers and sisters, legal siblings on the side of their shared father, Joseph. Jerome uses strong words (*apochryphorum deliramenta*) to attack this viewpoint, but he does not offer any arguments to undermine it. The great authority that Jerome enjoyed throughout the Middle Ages meant that his proposal, based ultimately on aspects of philology, imposed itself throughout the West (Bede, Thomas Aquinas). Even the reformers, Luther, Calvin, Zwingli, considered it the most appropriate explanation.

The third possibility is also the oldest, as it was the common interpretation throughout the East from the second century onward, as seen in the apocryphal manuscripts of the time: Origen, Clement of Alexandria, Eusebius, and Epiphanius. Three apocryphal books from the second half or possibly the end of the second century A.D. and originating in the area of Syria mention, completely naturally, as if it were something well known and generally accepted, that Jesus had siblings from Joseph's first marriage. In James' *Infancy Gospel*, a manuscript of this title is presented as the work of James, Jesus' brother. When the priest hands custody of Mary over to Joseph, he replies as an excuse, "I have sons" (9:2). Later on, when the time came for Joseph to travel to Bethlehem to register, his children and Mary are mentioned. Joseph said, "I will record my sons" (17:1). The donkey that Mary rode on the journey was led by Joseph's "son" (17:2). On arriving in Bethlehem, it says that Joseph "found a cave there and brought her into it, and set his sons by her" (18:1). A second text, the *Infancy Gospel of Thomas*, describes how James was bitten by a viper and the infant Jesus cured the fatal bite. James is presented as Joseph's (eldest) son, sent by his father to look for firewood (16:1). Only reports, not the fragment itself, remain of a third text, the so-called Gospel of Peter, provided by Origen in his Commentary on Matthew (10:17), according to which "the brethren of Jesus were sons of Joseph by a former wife, whom he married before Mary."

The belief that Jesus had siblings, children from Joseph's first marriage, is shared by other later apocryphal texts. For example, the *History of Joseph the Carpenter* (17:2) echoes the *Infancy Gospel of James* (8:3), when it says Joseph was a widower when he married Mary. The scene is completed with Joseph portrayed as an old man, with adult children from his first marriage. This traditional image of Joseph is reflected in the Christian iconography, literature, and folklore of Christmas in the East and West. A good example of this is the second verse of the Catalan Christmas Carol "Les dotze van tocant" (It's Twelve O'clock), which says, "Mother and child are freezing cold and the old man [i.e., Joseph] is shivering."

This opinion, which is a constant in the Eastern tradition and primarily Syrian and Greek, corresponds to the New Testament and the works of Josephus. This Jewish historian called James the brother of Jesus, echoing the Gospels and the earliest and most natural way of describing their relationship. However, the word "brother" (*adelfos*) can mean several things: someone who is the biological son of the same father and mother; half brother, the biological son of the same father or the same mother; an adopted sibling; or someone legally recognized as a son, but not a blood relation. Josephus tells us that Antipas and Philip were Herod's biological sons but that they had different mothers: Antipas' mother was the Samaritan Malthace, while Mariamne, daughter of the High Priest Simon, was Philip's mother. Anyway, Philip is described as Antipas' "brother" (Matt 14:3; Mark 6:17; Luke 3:1, 3:19). In the Greco-Roman world, cases of legal parenthood were common. Tiberius succeeded Augustus as emperor because, in the year 757 from the foundation of Rome, Augustus had adopted him as his son. In fact, Tiberius was the biological son of Tiberius Claudius Nero and Livia, who later became Augustus' second wife and took the name Julia. The inscriptions on the coins show this: *Tiberius divi Augusti filius*. Moses, son of Amran and Jochebed and brother of Aaron, was adopted by the daughter of the pharaoh, who gave him the name of Moses (Exod 2:10).

These cases of legal adoption were similar though not identical to Jesus' situation. On his birth, Joseph and Mary were already man and wife according to the law, and thus Jesus automatically became Joseph's son. Luke refers to Joseph and Mary as Jesus' "parents" in a quite matter-of-fact way, having made it clear that Joseph was not his biological father (Luke 2:27, 2:41, 2:43, 2:48). As R. Bauckham states, if Joseph was Jesus' father without being a blood relation, then Jesus' brothers and sisters did not necessarily share the same bloodline. However, all of them should be considered and were siblings, as they all shared the same father, Joseph. Legally, there is no difference between Jesus and his siblings. In addition to tradition, dating back to the second century, and the commonplace nature of legal adoption in the ancient and modern worlds, the relationship between Mary and Jesus' siblings, when Jesus left the family home, should be mentioned. Up to this point, Mary's only child had been his mother's main support. However, when he began his public activities in the area around the lake, far from Nazareth, Mary came under the protection of the family, very probably Joseph's sons and daughters, whom she raised from a very early age and accompanied as they grew up. Given this situation, it is significant that on the few occasions when Mary appears in the Gospels while Jesus is preaching away from Nazareth, she is always accompanied by family members and, in particular, those whom the texts call Jesus' "brothers." For example, only his "brothers" accompanied Mary on her visit to see Jesus in Capernaum (Mark 3:31-35 || Matt 12:46-50 || Luke 8:19-21). Later, when Jesus returned on a visit to Nazareth, the only family mentioned were, in this order, Mary, his four brothers, and his sisters (Mark 6:3 || Matt 13:55-56). At the wedding at Cana, a town close to Nazareth, Jesus' mother and brothers are mentioned, as are the disciples, who traveled with him from Capernaum (John 2:12). Finally, those who traveled to Jerusalem at the end of Jesus' life and who were still there before the early Christian community became active were "Mary the mother of Jesus, and . . . his brothers," together with some women and the male disciples (Acts 1:14). Some of these women, Mary's sister, her sister-in-law, and Mary Magdalene, and a male disciple were present near the cross together with Jesus' mother (John 19:25). The expression "[Jesus'] mother and his brothers" seems to be a traditional formula, as it is repeated in a range of different sources including Mark 3:31, John 2:12, and Acts 1:14. Mary's companions were probably not nephews and nieces. It all becomes more understandable if we consider them her adopted or legal sons and daughters, orphaned by their biological mother and father (Joseph) and who took Mary under their care.

Neither the language, the custom of legal adoption, nor the close links between Jesus' mother and brothers in the Gospels go against the position upheld by Epiphanius in the fourth century in his work *Panarion*; indeed, they only strengthen it. This position, reflected in the early Syrian tradition (2nd c.) and the Greek-language churches, seems to best interpret the evidence in the New Testament regarding "his brothers." Therefore, Jesus had four brothers, whose names we know, and two sisters, whose names we do not know (according to Epiphanius, Mary and Salome). They were all Joseph's children, with his first wife, whose name is also unknown.

The last of the four possibilities has gained some credence recently after the discovery of certain problems with the second possibility in this list, Jerome's hypothesis, and after being distanced from the traditional position, the third of the proposals. This proposal was first put forward by the great theologian Tertullian, a North African Christian writer of the second century, and not Irenaeus of Lyon, as some have suggested. In the fourth century, Helvidius, contemporary and adversary of Jerome, produced a systematic proposal: Jesus' siblings were Joseph and Mary's biological children born after Jesus, who was the eldest.

Tertullian looks at the question five times in his work, twice directly and three times indirectly, in his fierce defense of Jesus' humanity in the face of the Docetist positions upheld by Marcion and his followers. Among the arguments in Tertullian's powerful dialectics are references to Jesus' siblings. The clearest and most direct text is *Against Marcion* 4:19:6-12, which debates the interpretation of Luke 8:19-21 and, specifically, the question, "Who is my mother, and who are my brothers?" (a question also found in Matt 12:48). According to Tertullian, in this passage of the Gospel, Jesus "transferred the names of blood-relationship" (transtulit sanguinis nomina) from his mother and brothers to those who heard his words and "whom He judged to be more closely related to Him by reason of their faith" (*Marc.* 4:19:11). This blood relationship could not have come from Joseph, as "if He is not of a human father, it follows that He must be (the son) of a human mother . . . [He] a human father is not ascribed" (*ex matre filius est hominis quia ex patre non est . . . non ex patre homine*) (*Marc.* 4:10:7). In another text (*On the Veiling of Virgins* 6:6), Tertullian distinguishes between Mary's virginity before giving birth and her establishment of conjugal relations with Joseph afterward (*virum passam*).

Tertullian seems to accept that there were conjugal relations between Mary and Joseph after Jesus' birth. This period must also have witnessed the birth of Jesus' siblings, though this is never explicitly confirmed. Tertullian is a precursor to and indirectly points toward the Helvidian view: Jesus' siblings were, like him, Mary's children, born following the union between Mary and Joseph. The value of Tertullian's view can be only relative since it forms part of theological controversy and debate. His position arises from the need to defend monogamy, or to respond to those who denied that Jesus was indeed a man, such as Marcion and Apelles, two gnostic writers.

Helvidius mostly bases his ideas on Matthew 1:18-26 and verse 25 in particular. In his opinion this makes a distinction between the time when Jesus was born and the time following his birth, during which Joseph maintained conjugal relations with Mary. Matthew 1:25 describes only the time before Jesus' birth as a time when there were no conjugal relations between Joseph and Mary. Indeed, there is an eloquent silence in the Gospels on the events following Jesus' arrival in this world. Not even in Matthew 12:46 or 13:55, texts that fail to support or deny Jesus' blood relation with his siblings, is this silence broken. Obviously the question of the origin of Jesus' siblings would not be uncovered if we had to rely on the New Testament, and specifically the Gospel of Matthew, alone. It is vital to look at the early Christian tradition in order to affirm the perpetual virginity of Mary.

The third possibility is in agreement with the tradition's leading proposal from the second century onward, when the origin of Jesus' siblings was first explicitly looked at, and it does not have to forcefully adapt the information from the New Testament. On the contrary, this information adequately supports and explains this view. This is often called the Epiphanian view. It is based on tradition that only adds to its plausibility and makes it seem the most likely one: Jesus' four brothers and, at least, two sisters were the children of Joseph's first marriage. The fourth possibility, the Helvidian view, defended by Tertullian, according to which Mary had at least seven children (Jesus, and then four boys and two girls), is the result of "wise" reasoning and arises, in Tertullian, in response to those who deny Jesus' humanity and incarnation. However, in Helvidius' hands, it is the result of an individual and very questionable interpretation of Matthew 1:25. Jerome's proposal, the second we looked at, appears to be just the opposite and a response to Helvidius. However, Jerome does not return to the more traditional point of view that Jesus' siblings were the children of Joseph's first marriage. Rather, he bases his exegetical argument mainly on linguistic factors and maybe on an earlier report, and thus provides an explanation that we cannot dismiss: Jesus' siblings were his cousins. In my opinion, Jerome's explanation rests on a problematic identification of James and Joseph, Jesus' "brothers" (Mark 6:3), as James the Younger and Joses, sons of a certain Mary (Mark 15:40) (see 4.5.3.3). Some believe this Mary is the wife of Alphaeus/Clopas/Cleopas (Mark 3:18; John 19:25) and the mother of Jesus' four first cousins (James, Joses, Simon, and Judas). Others believe that this Mary was married to someone whose name we do not know and was the mother of only James and Joses; while Clopas/Cleopas was the father of Simon and Judas and married to an unknown woman. Those who have developed Jerome's view cannot agree. The view of the minority, already common during the second century among the Judeo-Christian and gnostic groups and which proposed that Joseph was Jesus' biological father, contradicts the narrative in Matthew 1–2 and Luke 1–2 and must be dismissed.

This sheds some light on the unusual expression "son of Mary" (Mark 6:3), attributed to the townspeople of Nazareth and the expression "son of Joseph"/"carpenter's son" (Matt 13:55; Luke 4:22; John 1:45, 6:42). The most likely reason for this dual use and, in particular, the expression "son of Mary" is the unusual fact that Jesus is Mary's only child, while other men and women are also "Joseph's children": Joseph has several children, whereas Mary only has one. Thus, if anything distinguished Jesus of Nazareth it was that he was the "[only] son of Mary." As well as being known as the "son of Joseph," his legal father, he was also known as the "son of Mary," which is what really set him apart. This description in Mark 6:3 is strengthened by the probability that Joseph was dead by the time that Jesus came back to visit Nazareth, as he was more than thirty years old then. This does not mean that Jesus was not known as Mary's son during Joseph's lifetime: Joseph's death did not lead to a change in what people called him. The expression "son of Mary" reflects the informal customs in Nazareth in relation to Jesus as her only child. It cannot be considered a creation of the early Christian community, aimed at providing a foundation for Mary's virgin birth. The other possible considerations here (Jesus' birth in irregular social circumstances as the only child of a widow or the child of Joseph's second wife) complement but do not replace the primordial focus of interest in Mark 6:3. A singular relationship exists between Mary and Jesus, which begins with his birth and continues because this is her only pregnancy.

Although we cannot say for sure that the expression "his brothers" does not actually mean "his cousins," we have good reason to believe that Jesus had real legal, though not biological, brothers and sisters.

4.4. The Nazareth Years

According to Matthew (2:22-23), Jesus arrived in Nazareth soon after the death of King Herod, who had attempted to kill him. Herod's son, Archelaus, had just been named by Augustus as ethnarch of Judaea, Samaria, and Edom. This was in at least 4 B.C. or possibly a year or so later. Matthew's description of Jesus' return to Israel from Egypt leads us to think that he must have arrived in Nazareth around the years 4/3 B.C., when he was still a small child of three or four. Luke (2:39-40) assumes that Jesus returned to Nazareth a few weeks after his birth. Whichever solution we adopt (it is not clear whether Luke's narrative is preferable to Matthew's), Jesus was still very young when he started his life in Nazareth. In all likelihood, he did not leave again until he reached the age of thirty, as Luke points out (3:23). The Galilean town of Nazareth was the setting for the infancy, adolescence, youth, and entry to adulthood as the son of Joseph and Mary.

4.4.1. The Home: Language and Work

If we had to narrate the life of a child in the twenty-first century, we would start by talking about his or her education. However, in first-century Nazareth, a small rural town in Lower Galilee, there was no regulated school education, and education and training initially took place in the home, handed down by the family, and subsequently at the synagogue. The family, especially pious families like Jesus', introduced the infants to the faith of Israel, teaching them how to pray and how to worship and follow God's Law. Both mother and father had active roles to play in these tasks, which were backed up by contributions from the rest of the family, close and distant relatives, and the townspeople in general. The religiousness of the Jews of Galilee was both profound and simple, and the children lived it and made it their own from an early age.

Jesus' parents, Joseph and Mary, accompanied him until he reached adulthood, as set by the Law, until he was twelve years of age. This can be deduced from their pilgrimage to the temple along with some other Galileans, as narrated by Luke (2:41-52). As we saw in the previous section (4.3), Jesus shared his childhood with his four brothers and two (or more) sisters. They were children of Joseph's first marriage and older than him. Apparently they lived with Jesus under the same roof. It is most likely that Jesus' brothers and sisters married and started families of their own in Nazareth. Once Jesus had started his life as a traveling preacher and returned to visit the town, most of his brothers and sisters still lived there, except Joseph, who had died. In Mark 6:3, the people of Nazareth comment, "[A]nd are not his [brothers and] sisters here with us?" Jesus in all likelihood grew up in a large family, with siblings who were quite a bit older than he was (James, the eldest) and others who must have been only a few years older.

We do not know the age difference between James, the eldest brother, and Jesus, the youngest; but, from the year of James' death (62 A.D.), in Josephus (*A.J.* 20:200), we can assume that it could not have been more than thirteen or fourteen years. By this estimate, James was born in 20 B.C. or 19 B.C. and died at the age of eighty-one or eighty-two. When Jesus reached twelve years of age and traveled to Jerusalem with his parents and some other people, including "kinsfolk and acquaintances" (Luke 2:44), his brother James was twenty-five or twenty-six and probably married. Generally speaking, since men married around the age of twenty and women sixteen, it is not beyond the realm of possibility that some other of Jesus' siblings may also have been married or old enough to consider it. Considering the age of James (Joseph's eldest son) and assuming Joseph married for first time around the age of twenty, we can deduce that he was around thirty-five when he became betrothed to Mary. At this time, he was probably a widower with six children from his first marriage (four boys and at least two girls), the eldest of whom was not more than twelve. Mary naturally acted as the mother to all of these children and her own son Jesus.

4.4.1.1. Three Languages

The language of the Jews in Galilee and Nazareth was a Galilean dialect of Aramaic (see 3.1.2). Aramaic, which had made major inroads in Israel from the sixth century B.C. during the Persian rule, became the language of the Jews throughout Palestine and the autochthonous language of the Roman province of Syria, alongside Greek. Aramaic was Jesus' mother tongue, a Jew from Galilee. But it was not the only language he spoke and understood. As with many Jews from this period, Jesus would have known three languages; in descending order, they were Aramaic, Hebrew, and Greek. He would have been trilingual.

Why three languages? M. Hengel summarizes the role of each of these languages in the life of Jews in first-century Palestine thus: "Whilst Aramaic was the common language spoken by the people and Hebrew the holy language of religious worship and debate amongst the scribes, Greek would have become, above all else, the linguistic tool for industry, commerce and administration." There was only one other language present in this Jewish country, Latin, which was spoken by the Roman officials, beginning with the governor and his family. It was also used for official monumental inscriptions. The people, however, did not know Latin, as it was the language of the Romans, the political and military power that ruled over the land of Israel. A knowledge of Greek was enough to be able to communicate with the Roman administration.

Aramaic was the everyday language of the Jews in the time of Jesus. It was the language Jesus used to compose the Lord's Prayer, the disciples' own prayer. As J. A. Fitzmyer has shown, the second part of this prayer contains the following request: "Forgive us our trespasses." The word "trespass" can be understood only in terms of the Aramaic, where the same word (*hoba'*) means "debt" and "fault," "offence" against another. In the New Testament, above all in the Gospel of Mark, the Aramaic words clearly show that this was the language used by Jesus. The word *abba* ("father"), which Jesus uses to address God (Mark 14:36), is echoed by the early Christians (Rom 8:15; Gal 4:6); the order given to Jairus' daughter who had died ("'*Talitha cumi*'; meaning 'Little girl, I say to you, arise'"; Mark 5:41); the word Jesus used to cure a deaf and dumb man ("'*Ephphatha*,' that is 'Be opened'"; Mark 7:34); and Psalm 22:2, where Jesus asked in Aramaic during his crucifixion ("'*Eloi, Eloi, lama sabachthani?*' which means, 'My God, my God, why hast thou forsaken me?'"; Mark 15:34); all these are fragmentary remains of the language that Jesus spoke and preached in, and which the Gospels have conserved and translated into Greek. People's nicknames (*Cephas*, *Boanerges*), the inscriptions on the ossuaries, and the place names in the area around Jerusalem (*Gabatha*, *Golgotha*, *Haceldama*) are often Aramaic. Aramaic was the mother tongue of the Jews living in Galilee in the first century and of Jesus.

The Jews living in ancient Israel used Hebrew as the language for individual and joint prayer, and especially those living in Judaea considered it their mother tongue. Though some prayers were in Aramaic, the language used in the synagogue or the community's place of worship was predominantly Hebrew. This is unlike the Jews who spread throughout the Roman Empire, the Diaspora, who listened to the Scriptures and prayed in Greek, their mother tongue. Using Hebrew in prayer was not a problem for the Jews in ancient Israel or even Babylonia, the Diaspora beyond the Roman Empire, given that Hebrew and Aramaic were Semitic languages and had many notable similarities. In Greek one word described them both (John 20:16; it states that Mary Magdalene addresses Jesus "in Hebrew," when the word *rabboni* is Aramaic!).

Jesus prayed in Hebrew and, as a rabbi, would have known the language of the Scriptures well enough to put forward his own interpretation of some of the biblical passages. This can be seen from his response to the Pharisees who questioned him because his disciples had plucked heads of grain on the Sabbath: "Have you never read what David did, when he was in need and was hungry, he and those who were with him: how he entered the house of God, when Abiathar was high priest" (Mark 2:25-26). Jesus was referring to the events in the First Book of Samuel 21:2-7. In Mark 12:36, Jesus refers to the text of Psalm 110:1, where, placing himself on an equal footing with the Scriptures, he pointed out a problem with the interpretation of the text. The fact that Jesus preached in Galilean synagogues (e.g., Luke 4:16-20) is hard to understand unless he knew the Scriptures and the language they were written in. Jesus probably knew how to read Hebrew and could use it to speak to other rabbis on interpretations of the Scriptures, but the language in which he preached and taught his disciples to pray would have been Aramaic, the language of Mary, his mother.

Knowledge of Greek for commercial transactions in the lake area, where the eastern shore was Greek speaking, was a prerequisite. We do not know the level of trade between the Jewish and non-Jewish areas, but in certain cases, such as Bethsaida, they were physically very close to one another. Greek was the lingua franca for the whole of Lake Galilee, but not that used in the strictly Jewish part. Nazareth, Jesus' hometown, was only six kilometers to the southeast of Sepphoris, a city with a majority of Jews, but also with Hellenistic elements and clearly pro-Roman leanings. Was there much commercial contact between one and the other? If so, we can assume that the people of Nazareth, or at least the most enterprising, went to Sepphoris to sell their agricultural produce and spoke some Greek with the city's non-Jewish inhabitants (and even with some Jews). However, Jesus was not a farmer but a craftsman. Did this increase or decrease the likelihood of his coming into contact with the people of Sepphoris?

We may wonder, as does S. Freyne, what a rural Galilean Jew felt inside about the language of those who had occupied Israel, introducing beliefs and ways of life that were the diametric opposite of Jewish Law and customs. We cannot rule out that Jesus may have had elementary knowledge of spoken Greek, which he used colloquially but not for public speaking. Greek was the language used by Pontius Pilate in the trial that led to Jesus' condemnation. It was also the language of the soldiers who tortured and then crucified him. Even the Gospel according to John (12:20-22) says that "some Greeks" wanted to meet Jesus on his final visit to Jerusalem (see 6.2.4 and 6.2.5).

The statements and evidence put forward so far seem to confirm that Jesus was trilingual, to varying degrees: he spoke his mother tongue, Aramaic, most often; he could read and write Hebrew, but he may not have been completely fluent in it; and he spoke a bit of Greek, though it seems he did not know how to read and write it.

4.4.1.2. Carpenter and Blacksmith

Jesus grew up and lived in a rural environment in a town in Lower Galilee where the families generally cultivated the land. Agriculture and to a lesser extent raising livestock were the main sources of employment for the people of Nazareth. Most of Jesus' relatives were farmers, and he himself formed part of an agrarian society. As already mentioned (see 4.3.3), two of Jesus' brother Judas' grandsons, who were farmers, had to declare before Domitian (*Eccl. Hist.* 3:20:1-6). Jesus did not work on the land. He was a trained craftsman, earning his living by a single trade in the small town of four hundred or five hundred inhabitants. His trade was the same as that of Joseph, his father, and they were probably the only family plying this trade in the town. Mark 6:3 and Matthew 13:55 call Jesus, respectively, "the carpenter [*ho tektōn*]" and "the carpenter's son [*ho tou tektonos huios*]."

However, what trade is described by the word normally translated as carpenter? This translation does not cover the wide range of possibilities offered by the word *tektōn*. This term can include work not only with wood but also with stone and even metal. Thus, some people suggest that it be translated as "builder" or "stonemason," but in the Nazareth of this period many people were able to build houses and walls: dry stone walling was a practice common enough among farmers not so long ago! In his Dialogue with Trypho (88), Justin states that Jesus made plows and yokes, equipment that combines metal and wood and vital tools for farmers who have to yoke the livestock to plow the land and carry their loads. Jesus himself said on one occasion, "For my yoke is easy, and my burden is light" (Matt 11:30). We know that oil and wine presses, common in Galilee (see 3.1), were structures that combined wood, stone, and metal. The trade of the *tektōn* required, in the words of Homer, "hands . . . skilled to fashion all manner of curious work" (*Iliad* 5:60-61).

Jesus was a craftsman who worked with wood and metal, someone who knew how to handle both materials and who earned his living in a workshop, inherited from his father and equipped with all the tools and instruments required. Curiously, in Mark 6:3 and Matthew 13:55, in the medieval Catalan and Arabic versions of the Gospels (Marmoutier and Peiresc manuscripts), Jesus is described as "the blacksmith's son." Jesus' craft required intelligence, skill, and a degree of physical robustness, as well as materials and facilities, including a house with a relatively large space for working with metals (forge and anvil) or wood (bench and tools), perhaps with a yard in front. A workshop of these characteristics would have been designed for the tasks related to agriculture (to produce carts and the tools needed to work the land or to shoe animals) and the home (pots, kneading troughs to make bread, trunks to hold clothes and valuables, doors and windows, hinges and railings, posts and measures for solids and liquids, locks and latches).

This raises the question of how many people worked in the carpenter-blacksmith's workshop in Nazareth and whether the workshop closed when Jesus left the town and moved to the area by the lake. First, it is likely that Jesus inherited his father's business and that Joseph had trained him in it. If Joseph's ancestors were already carpenter-blacksmiths, they could have left Bethlehem to set up in Nazareth, a town near Sepphoris, the capital of Galilee. At the start of the first century B.C., Sepphoris was already the most important town in Galilee and, around 57–55 B.C., it became the capital of one of the five districts into which Gabinius, governor of Syria, divided the Jewish territories (*J.W.* 1:170). This political promotion brought economic and demographic consequences, and Nazareth must have benefited. Therefore, there is good reason to believe that Joseph's father or grandfather, carpenter-blacksmiths by trade, moved from Bethlehem to Nazareth and set up a workshop there.

Joseph apparently had four sons from his first marriage, and the volume of business in the workshop must have affected whether all four or only some of them worked there. Another condition affecting this must have been the skills of each of the four brothers, their ability to learn the trade. We also need to take into account that they may have married well and gone to work the land belonging to their father-in-law. It is not likely that the workshop would have been sufficient to maintain the families of all four brothers, once they had married. Normally, the eldest son, James, would have inherited the family business and his father's home. We cannot be sure, however, whether he remained in the house of his father, with his second mother, Mary, and his half brother on his father's side, Jesus.

The Gospel narratives lead us to believe that Jesus worked in the family workshop in Nazareth until he was around thirty and that he lived with Joseph and Mary, his mother, until Joseph's death. The facts that James married some time before Joseph's death and that there were still at least eight people living in the home (Joseph and Mary, four sons, including Jesus, and two daughters) lead us to think that James did not live in his father's home. James and another of Jesus' brothers may have worked alongside Joseph and Jesus, provided there was enough business to make this worthwhile. If Jesus was not the only person working in the workshop when he decided to move to Capernaum, this would mean that one or more of Joseph's other sons could have continued the family business.

These reflections on the amount of business in the workshop in Nazareth have to be considered alongside the issue of commercial trade between the town and Sepphoris, the capital of Galilee between 57–55 B.C. and 19 A.D., when Antipas began construction of Tiberias, the new capital on the lakeside. Nazareth was a town located an hour's journey from Sepphoris and was influenced by it. Some have tried to connect the economic activities in the workshop in Nazareth, owned by Joseph, to the reconstruction work in Sepphoris, carried out under Antipas, ruler of Galilee from 4 B.C. We cannot dismiss that

Joseph and his sons, including Jesus, received orders from Sepphoris and maintained trade relations with the city: a journey of an hour was not excessive.

Nevertheless, it may not have been wholly commercial reasons that affected whether or not those at the workshop accepted orders from Sepphoris. Jesus' family, belonging to the dynasty of David, was devoutly Jewish. Sepphoris, despite the Jewish majority even comprising Sadducees, those who most strictly kept to the faith, encouraged Hellenistic ways of life that probably distanced its inhabitants mentally from the beliefs upheld in the rural areas, with their strong links to the ancestral Jewish customs and their inveterate respect for the Law. The mental distance between Sepphoris and Nazareth was much greater than the physical distance. Jesus' preaching always moved through the rural areas, and the only city included as part of his itinerant preaching was Jerusalem. Though the market in Sepphoris was adequate for the purchase of raw materials and supplies for the workshop, it seems unlikely that there was any regular commercial contact between the workers in Joseph's workshop in Nazareth and the people of Sepphoris. The area where Jesus plied his trade as a craftsman with wood and metal was probably Nazareth and the neighboring villages.

The social standing of Jesus and his family is linked to this trade. In a rural town where most of the families worked the land, the craftsman's trade set him apart: not everyone had the skills to work with wood and metal. A craftsman or tradesman in a town such as Nazareth, of fewer than five hundred people, was looked up to by the smallholders, who represented the majority of families in the town and had to work as hard as they could to reap their harvest. Social standing and respect had nothing to do with the wealth of a craftsman. The social status of Jesus' family was comparable to that of any of the smallholders in Nazareth. They were higher up the scale than the day workers, who waited each morning in the square for someone to hire them, the farm workers employed by others to work the leaseholds, the farmhands on large properties, traveling salesmen, and so on. For Jesus and any other craftsman, the simple knowledge of a trade provided a certain level of respect in the small world of Nazareth, as many had to struggle to survive as farmers.

The Gospel according to Luke (1:28) places Mary, Jesus' mother, indirectly in her home in Nazareth when she received the visit of the angel Gabriel, who "came in unto her." On marrying Joseph she left her parent's home to live with her husband and raise a large family: four boys and at least two girls, as well as Jesus, her son. The *Infancy Gospel of James* indicates that Mary's family were well-to-do people, who were friends with the high priest and other temple leaders, but that they lived in Jerusalem and not Nazareth. Mary's father, Joachim, was a rich livestock owner, with lambs and calves, and even shepherds under his orders, while his wife, Anna, had at least a midwife at her service (*Infancy Gospel of James* 1–6).

It is not easy to determine the social standing of Mary's family and the dowry she might have brought with her when she formed a new family with Joseph. It seems that Joseph needed a second wife to raise the small children from his first marriage, and so Mary could not have belonged to a particularly well-to-do Nazarene family. If Mary's father was a shepherd, as the nucleus of the tradition related in the *Infancy Gospel* would seem to suppose, then this did not represent any special social standing, either too high or too low, in a farming town such as Nazareth. Jesus talked sympathetically about farmers and shepherds, about farming work, including grain (sowing and reaping), vineyards (planting, cultivating, and harvesting the grape), and fruit trees, such as figs, and about plants, including mustard, vital in making a good seasoning. The image evoked by the story of the shepherd who leaves ninety-nine of his flock unattended "on the mountains" (Matt 18:12; Luke 15:4 talks of "the wilderness") to go in search of the lost sheep until he finds it and takes it on his shoulders seems very lifelike and intimate. Is this scene part of the inheritance from Jesus' maternal grandfather, a shepherd from Nazareth, whom the Christian tradition in the second century called Joachim?

4.4.2. His Education

4.4.2.1. During His Childhood

Jesus was brought up in a small town inhabited by Jewish families who actively kept to the religion of Moses, where their social life centered on the synagogue. The family and the synagogue were the two environments in which Jesus was educated. It is hard to imagine what kind of education Jesus received in a family descended from David, characterized by its strict devotion to the Law, and in a synagogue such as Nazareth's, which supported the people's simple and solid religiousness. There are many things we do not know about the Jewish education system in the time of Jesus (even if there was one), which may have been established by and linked to the synagogues. An organized system along these lines seems unlikely, but there is sufficient evidence to show the role of the synagogue in the education of children up to the age of thirteen, the time when they were deemed adults and boys were obliged to keep to the Law in its entirety.

Initiation into the Law took place within the family (see 3.3.1.3). We have already mentioned Philo of Alexandria's thoughts: "[The Jews] looking upon their laws as oracles directly given to them by God himself, and having been instructed in this doctrine from their very earliest infancy they bear in their souls the images of the commandments" (*Embassy* 210). Josephus echoes these words, saying, "[W]e think it to be the most necessary business of our whole life to observe the laws that have been given us, and to keep those rules of piety that have been delivered down to us" (*Ag. Ap.* 1:60). A great many children, before reaching adulthood, abided by many of the Law's commandments, especially in the most religious families. Parents taught their children to recite the simplest prayers from memory (e.g., the so-called Eighteen Blessings and, subsequently, the *Shema*), to keep the Sabbath, to observe the laws of ritual cleanliness, especially regarding the forbidden foods, to fast on the Day of Atonement, and to worship at the synagogue on Saturdays; and they told them the great biblical stories and about the lives of the heroes and leading figures of Israel.

The education children received in the home was religious since religion covered and shaped all ambits of Jewish life: the family was and still is the setting for the Passover meal, the most important liturgical ritual in Judaism, led by the head of the family. So Jesus' childhood was characterized throughout by the practice of the Law. His parents were his role models, and his siblings, on reaching adulthood, became role models for their youngest brother. The essential role of the child's father in teaching the Law is evident in numerous rabbinical texts. We have Sifre on Deuteronomy (46 [11:19]), a midrash from the third century A.D., which reads, "As soon as a child starts to speak, their father has to speak to them in the holy language [Hebrew] and instruct them in the Torah, because, if they do not, they would be better off buried."

In Judaism, the Torah is the focus and content of education and the reason for any learning. Accordingly, Shimon ben Sheta, a rabbi alive during the first quarter of the first century B.C., is said to have produced a set of guidelines whereby all children had to attend the *bet ha-sefer* (literally, "the house of the book," "the house of the Bible," the name given to primary schools for children up to the age of 12 in the 2nd c. A.D.). If Jesus read and learned the Law by heart, which is more than likely, then he did so in the synagogue at Nazareth. The person responsible for this training was probably the synagogue's "attendant," the person in charge of leading the synagogue's liturgical service and someone with a good understanding of the Law and the prophets, the two most important parts of the Hebrew Bible. As Luke explains, during Jesus' visit to the synagogue in Nazareth, when the Master had already started to preach in places faraway, this attendant appeared, handed Jesus the scroll of the prophet Isaiah, and then took it back (Luke 4:17.20) (see 3.3.1.1).

According to the Mishnah (*Šabb.* 1:3), each Saturday this attendant taught the children the Law by making them memorize it and also taught them to read from the texts of the laws themselves. We do not know whether this attendant taught the children only on the Sabbath or whether their activities took place regularly throughout the week, paid for by the community, as can be deduced from the decree issued, years after Jesus' birth, by Yehoshua ben Gamla or Jesus, son of Gamaliel, high priest between 63 and 65 A.D. (Babylonian Talmud, *B. Bat.* 21a).

Jesus, between the ages of six and twelve, learned a range of fragments from the Scriptures by heart (first, prayers, psalms, and proverbs) and was also able to read them. Other children of the time had the same level of skill, if their parents were interested in encouraging this learning and wanted their children to know and observe the Law of God. In Jesus' case, this education probably included learning to write, but this was an art that required time and resources, and the number of people who knew how to write was less than the number who knew how to read. Jewish towns and villages had a scribe, paid to write documents for those who could not. Jesus also knew how to work wood and metal, which is another sign that he knew how to write for his work. The episode of the adulterous woman does not prove anything, where the sentence "Jesus bent down and wrote with his finger on the ground" (John 8:6) is elliptic, since it does not specify what Jesus wrote: words, signs alluding to the hidden sins of those accusing the woman, meaningless lines to show his disgust for the calls for her death?

Jesus' familiarity with the words and practice of the Torah, the Jewish Scriptures, began early in his life and at the hands of his parents, Joseph and Mary, and continued at the synagogue in his hometown, where he was taught to memorize passages from the Scriptures. They probably taught him and other children from Nazareth to write (though not all of them), perhaps including some of his brothers. In one of the tractates from the Mishnah, written around 100 A.D., it says, "At five [the age is reached for the study of the] Scripture, at ten for [the study of] the Mishnah, at 13 for [the fulfillment of] the commandments . . ." (*Avot* 5:21). Jesus' familiarity with the Scriptures continued and increased throughout his time in Nazareth, the hometown he left only much later, when he was older than thirty (Luke 3:23).

4.4.2.2. During His Youth and Adulthood

After the age of twelve, Jesus immersed himself into his education at the synagogue in Nazareth, where he was not led or taught, as far as we know, by any renowned teacher. Individual study of the Scriptures was common, as can be seen in the Tractate Avot in the Mishnah (3:6): the *Shechinah* (the presence of God) rests among those who sit dedicated to the study of the Torah, whether they be ten, five, three, or just one. When he started preaching, Jesus knew the Scriptures well and was up to date with the most important issues that concerned the scribes and rabbis of the time. The only rabbi's name mentioned in the Talmud as one of Jesus' teachers is Yehoshua ben Perahyah, who lived in the second half of the second century (Babylonian Talmud, *Sanh.* 107b and *Sotah* 47a). It is, however, an anachronous reference. E. Renan believed that Hillel was Jesus' teacher. This is an even more flagrant anachronism. However, recent comparison of the figures of Jesus and

Hillel has highlighted important parallels showing that much of what Jesus taught was being discussed by the rabbis of the day.

Does this mean that Jesus had the chance to hear rabbis who came to preach at the synagogue in Nazareth, or did he travel to Sepphoris, where Sadducee rabbis dominated or another of the neighboring towns, such as Arbela? Arbela was the hometown to the only Galilean rabbi before Jesus that we know about: Nittai (or Mattai), from around 125 B.C., who is mentioned in a list of famous rabbis in the Mishnah (*Avot* 1:6-7). The immense majority of rabbis were from Jerusalem or active in the city, which was home to the schools of the great teachers. Only occasionally did some of their disciples travel to Galilee (the periphery of Palestinian Judaism): Jerusalem was undoubtedly the center for religious people and groups (Pharisees and Sadducees). John the Baptist himself, as we shall see, carried out his activities not far from Jerusalem in the valley of the Jordan. Many of those who went to find him came from the holy city.

The figure of John the Baptist has received the attention of many experts, including B. Chilton, who believes that Jesus left home at twelve and, after a short period as a wanderer in Jerusalem, joined John the Baptist's circle as a disciple to the rabbi. Alongside the Baptist's other disciples there, he learned the interpretation of the Law advocated by John and, going against his master's ideas, shaped his own beliefs. According to Chilton, Jesus would not have become what he did (a "passionate religious genius") if he had simply taken on the "conventional piety" of a town such as Nazareth. A conclusion of this kind would aid matters, as it sets the name and location of Jesus' teacher and "explains" his training and knowledge. But it is not the only possible one (see 4.5.2.2, below).

We must keep to the map set out by the four Gospels, where Jesus was raised and grew up in Nazareth, where he lived and worked into his adulthood. Therefore, he was not a disciple to any rabbi: if his plan for life had been to become a rabbi, he would have had to go to Jerusalem, instead of staying in his small hometown. If we look closely at John 7:15, they knew well enough in Jerusalem that Jesus had taught himself: "How is it that this man has learning, when he has never studied?" This sentence may allude to the knowledge of the Scriptures that Jesus showed in his discussions with the Jews. The surprise comes, however, because Jesus had not had a teacher. A similar surprise, again mixed with a degree of disrespect, is evidenced in the reaction of the people of Nazareth, when Jesus was presented and prepared to teach at the synagogue: "Where did this man get all this? What is the wisdom given to him? . . . Is not this the carpenter?" (Mark 6:2-3; and likewise Matt 13:54-55). In Luke 4:22, the question is not negative, but it is similar: "Is not this Joseph's son?" The surprised tone is the result of Jesus wanting to teach the people of his own town. The people of Nazareth knew full well that Jesus had not studied anywhere and, despite this, saw that he expressed himself with an extraordinary and inexplicable "wisdom": for years he had been just a carpenter in Nazareth, but someone who had never had a teacher now spoke like a rabbi!

The people of Nazareth also found out that Joseph and Mary's son, since leaving the town and moving to Capernaum, performed miracles: he healed the sick and exorcised demons. The bewilderment was repeated (Mark 6:2): Where did he learn all this? Who taught him? And they asked, "Where did this man get this wisdom and these mighty works?" (Matt 13:54). Luke has the townspeople of Nazareth saying words that reflect their feelings toward Jesus: "[W]hat we have heard you did at Capernaum, do here also in your country" (4:23). This bewilderment came from the fact that Jesus had always lived at home, and now that he had started preaching, he showed them that he had two hitherto unknown skill sets: those of the rabbi and those of the healer. Neither of these skill sets can be attributed to formal training, school education, or the instruction of a teacher who could have initiated Jesus in arcane secrets.

The Galilean rabbi Chanina ben Dosa may have lived at the same time as Jesus. He healed people and exorcised demons, but there is no mention of his initiating anyone in magical arts or rituals. Chanina, Jesus, and the Greek miracle worker Apollonius of Tyana were charismatic healers who based their activities on the authority inspired by their character and the force of their words, received as a gift from God and accompanied by as little a ritual element as possible (e.g., the laying on of hands). Magic was completely different; here the key element was the learning of the secrets and rituals from experienced teachers, who introduced their disciples to the world of conjuring and esoteric spells. The charismatic healer helped only those who asked for help, restoring their life and dignity. Those who practiced magic used procedures, which could be very harmful, as they put themselves at the mercy of the dark forces. Furthermore, there was no need for any form of personal relationship between the magician and the person affected by the magician's arts, unlike the healer, who acted out of trust and welcome.

The accusation aimed at Jesus was that his healing powers arose from a pact with Satan. The scribes who traveled from Jerusalem to rule on his exorcisms confirm this: "He is possessed by Beelzebul, and by the prince of demons he casts out the demons" (Mark 3:22 || Matt 12:24 || Luke 11:15). This accusation is also echoed in the Gospel according to John: "You have a demon" (7:20). It continued in the rabbinical tradition, which accused Jesus of practicing sorcery (see 2.2.1). One rabbinical text (Babylonian Talmud, *Šabb.* 104b) even states that Jesus learned magic in Egypt, where he gained magical formulae by tattooing them on his skin.

The miracles performed by Jesus made people uncomfortable and were interpreted by some, those who did not accept him, as signs of a pact with Satan and not as power granted by God to do good. However, none of the miracles performed by Jesus require the invocation of dark forces, nor deceptive or esoteric formulae: Jesus' miracles took place as part of his preaching, announcing a God among men (see 5.2.1).

The people surrounding Jesus identified him, above all else, as a rabbi. This description as evidenced by his public activities helps us understand what sort of image he projected. He was an unusual rabbi, as he was not a member of a school of any of the famous rabbis, as were the majority at the time. The Pharisee group especially saw themselves as disciples of Hillel or Shammai and supported the interpretations proposed by them. The people rightly perceived that "he taught them as one who had authority, and not as the scribes," who based their words on the authority of their renowned predecessors to justify their interpretation of the Scriptures (Mark 1:22). Rabbis always considered themselves disciples of other rabbis. Jesus did not share this common characteristic. As we shall see later (4.5.2), the only rabbi mentioned and praised by Jesus is John the Baptist, whom he considered the greatest of the prophets and from whom he took a great many of his teachings. But he never said that John was his teacher: Jesus did not talk of the Baptist as if he were an unquestionable authority or as if he were his point of reference.

4.4.2.3. Knowing the Scriptures

Jesus was often called rabbi or *rabboni*, lord and teacher, by people, friends, and enemies, and he seemed happy with this name. The term *rabbi*, however, did not have the formal and technical character that it subsequently acquired in post-70 A.D. Judaism. The fact that he was called a rabbi indicates that his behavior reflected elements that justified this title, above all an adequate knowledge of the Scriptures, which allowed him to dialogue and discuss interpretations of the Law and Torah with other rabbis.

Without this knowledge, gained during his time in Nazareth by listening to the Torah and by reading and studying it, he would not have been able to participate in the debates: working on the Sabbath; David's eating of the bread meant as an offering, when he had no alternative (Mark 2:25-26 || Matt 12:3-4 || Luke 6:3-4); divorce and his reference to what God desired from the start of creation (Mark 10:6-9 || Matt 19:5-6); resurrection and the principle that God is of the living and not the dead (Mark 12:26-27 || Matt 22:31-32 || Luke 20:37-38); the Messiah and the interpretation of Psalm 110 (Mark 12:35-37 || Matt 22:41-45 || Luke 20:41-44). As C. A. Evans points out, Jesus created his own formula ("Have you never read in the Scriptures?"), which makes sense only if he himself had read the biblical texts and knew what he was trying to remind his audience of. This statement occurs some fifteen times in the Gospels (Mark 12:10; Matt 21:42). There are others that refer to what "is written" or what it says "in the Scriptures" (Luke 20:17). Even though Luke 4:16-20 does not explicitly state that Jesus "read" the fragment from Isaiah 61 cited, this is the most likely and natural explanation for this report of his visit to the synagogue in Nazareth.

One last observation completes the picture relating to Jesus' impressive knowledge of the Scriptures: the references to the books of the Old or First Testament attributed to him in the synoptic Gospels. Many are due to the influence of the early Christian tradition. These references include the five books of the Pentateuch, many of the books of the prophets (especially Isaiah) and some writings, above all the book of Psalms. The foundation for these references is Jesus' great familiarity with the Scriptures, because he had read and meditated on them in prayer and reflection. This familiarity also applied to his personal interpretations of the biblical texts, which remained within the framework set by contemporary rabbis but went beyond them in their originality (see 5.3.1.2).

Jesus had learned by listening to, reading, and probably copying from the Torah, the Jewish Scriptures, as it was being read in the synagogue (in Hebrew) and interpreted in the translations or targums and preaching afterward in Aramaic. This gradual accumulation over time took place in Nazareth and took up the greatest part of his life in quantitative terms. Only once he was older than thirty did the decisive change take place, when his silence gave way to the Word.

4.4.3. His Lifestyle: Celibate

4.4.3.1. Some Precedents

In the Mishnah's Tractate *Avot* (5:21), a man is considered ready for the nuptial bed at the age of eighteen. According to the rabbis, the age that men could marry was around twenty. The Qumran community's Congregation Rule stated that a man belonging to the Essene group and who did not want to remain celibate had to marry at the age of twenty (1:10). It decreed that matrimony should lead to procreation, as this is the divine wish expressed in the book of Genesis: "Be fruitful and multiply, and fill the earth and subdue it" (1:28). According to a sentence from Rabbi Eliezer ben Hyrcan, who lived during the first and second centuries A.D., not having descendants equates to homicide (Babylonian Talmud, *Yebam.* 63b). This teaching was kept unchanged by all rabbis.

There are however a number of exceptions. For example, Shimon ben Azzai, a rabbi from around the same time, stated, "[M]y soul is in love with the Torah; the world can be carried on by others" (Babylonian Talmud, *Yebam.* 63b). Celibacy was common practice among the Essenes themselves, at least among those who lived in the monastic community at Qumran (see 3.3.3.4). The same was true of the Therapeutae in Egypt, who shared many of the Essenes' ideas and practiced sexual abstinence. The Greco-Roman world counted those who were voluntarily celibate. The philosopher Epictetus stated that one needed to avoid distractions in order to be able to dedicate oneself completely to the service of God, as this was the only way in which one could be reborn so as to "maintain the character of an honourable and good man" (*Discourses* 3:22:69). Epictetus married only at the end of his life, in order to ensure that an abandoned child he had taken in was looked after. Philostratus wrote in his biography of Apollonius of Tyana that he had never wanted a wife and had always "mastered and gained control of the maddening passion" (1:13).

The references to some of the individuals in the Old Testament who remained celibate are more significant. The most famous case is that of the prophet Jeremiah, who was ordered by God not to marry or have any children (16:2). Faced with this and other demands related to his mission, the prophet lamented his situation: "Why did I come forth from the womb to see toil and sorrow, and spend my days in shame?" (20:18). The shame of being alone without the support of wife and children and of being taunted by everyone would have acted as a prophetic sign for the people of Israel. The people, who easily forgot God and the covenant, had to suffer the terrible death of mothers and their children, victims of their enemies and left even without a tomb. Jeremiah chose, despite himself, to remain celibate, though he did not hide his complaints at his situation from God, a situation that saw him living out the message he preached.

According to the Jewish tradition, Moses was celibate after he was chosen to act as the messenger between God and the people of Israel. As soon as Moses started speaking to God on a frequent basis, passing on his will to the people and delivering his Law, he stopped having sexual relations. This is the interpretation put forward by Philo of Alexandria (*Moses 2* 14.16) and the rabbis (Babylonian Talmud, *Šabb.* 87a). Moses had begun on the path of prophecy, and his life had undergone a radical change. From then on, as he had given himself over to God and his Word, sexual relations with his wife and looking after his children had to be relegated. His prophetic vocation took up his whole life and being, as the divine call required an exclusive relationship with the Lord.

4.4.3.2. Jesus' Choice

Jesus, involved from the start in a personal and very close relationship with God, the Father, took the same view. His prophetic vocation, which came to fruition only at a late stage in his life, gave weight to his decision to maintain voluntary celibacy. G. Vermes believes that Jesus married in Nazareth at the usual age (ca. 20) and, when he started his public activities, left the town and his wife and children. Unlike John the Baptist, who lived an ascetic life in the Judaean Desert and Jordan Valley, eating locusts and wild honey and abstaining from alcohol as a sign of his devotion to God, Jesus had made the same decisions as any other pious Jew, including those regarding his lifestyle.

Once he had started his activities, Jesus welcomed a visit from his closest relative in Capernaum, and when he went to Nazareth and preached in the synagogue, only his mother and brothers are mentioned (Mark 3:31-35, 6:1-6). If Jesus had had a wife and children, their presence would have been mentioned on these two occasions, in which his family is brought to the fore. And if this was the result of hypothetical censure by the subsequent Christian tradition, this still does not explain why this censorship would not have applied equally to the numerous women, both single and married, who are named and presented as members of the closest circles to Jesus. Thus, Jesus' celibacy is not unique: as J. P. Meier points out, it follows the pattern set by the prophet Jeremiah (and possibly the prophets Elijah and Elisha), John the Baptist, and the Essenes at Qumran. Moses abstained from sexual relations once he had received the prophetic call. Likewise, there were some Greco-Roman philosophers (Epictetus and Apollonius of Tyana) and rabbis (Shimon ben Azzai) who had made the same decision.

The next question is, what does this celibacy, that he has freely chosen, mean to Jesus? In the context of Nazareth, his decision would have been truly unique and unusual and would not have been approved of by the townspeople. It would have been seen as strange and disconcerting. Indeed, Mary's son was a figure surrounded by singularities. First, his birth had been preceded and accompanied by a series of unusual events that led to an uncomfortable situation, beyond the socially accepted norms. Second, less remarkable but still perplexing, was that Mary and Joseph had not had any children after Jesus: Mary's son was and continued to be the youngest of the boys and girls who apparently formed the carpenter's family. The third singularity took shape over the years: Jesus, a good and pious boy, healthy and hardworking, intelligent and able, member of a family respected by the people for being descendants of David, had not married, and no one could explain this surprising turn of events.

The reason for his celibacy is given by Jesus himself in a somewhat enigmatic statement seen in Matthew (19:12): "For there are eunuchs who have been so from birth, and there are eunuchs who have been made eunuchs by men, and there are eunuchs who have made themselves eunuchs for the sake of the kingdom of heaven." Jesus has decided not to get married "for the sake of the kingdom of heaven"; he has made himself a eunuch to focus his life on God and his Kingdom exclusively and completely. He has renounced sexuality and the ability to have children because, like Moses, as portrayed by Philo and the rabbis, he has placed his dialogue with God, his Father, and his mission to proclaim His Kingdom above all else. In the words of Paul, "The unmarried man is anxious about the affairs of the Lord, how to please the Lord" (1 Cor 7:32). Luke attributes to Jesus a similar expression when Mary and Joseph find him in the temple after having lost him: "Did you not know that I must be in my Father's house?" (Luke 2:49; another possible translation is, "Did you not know that I must be doing my Father's work?").

At heart is the reason given by rabbi Shimon ben Azzai, quoted above, justifying his decision not to procreate in terms of keeping to the first commandment given by God to man: "[M]y soul is in love with the Torah" (Babylonian Talmud, *Yebam.* 63b). Love of the Law is placed above all else. In the case of Jesus of Nazareth, another rabbi, God, and his Kingdom are what bring his life together. During his time in Nazareth, this defining and characteristic aspect of his life does not come to the fore, it remains for the time unexpressed, as, in the words of the Gospel according to John, the time for his manifestation has not yet come. Jesus' choices start to become apparent very subtly. One of the most important is his voluntary celibacy, which goes against the grain of the small world of Nazareth's established customs and religious beliefs: having a wife and children is a divine commandment, compulsory for any good Jew. Jesus' celibacy, his renouncing the chance to form a family of his own, precedes and aids another decision that would be decisive: to leave Nazareth, the home he lived in with Mary, his mother, and the smithy-carpenter workshop where he worked and earned his living, in order to start up his public activities, traveling around, far from home.

4.5. The Years of Public Activity

4.5.1. The Beginning (27/28 A.D.) and the End (30 A.D.)

4.5.1.1. The Start: 27/28 A.D.

The historical sources either do not agree or remain silent on the question of the duration of Jesus' public activities, from his leaving Nazareth in search of the Baptist to his final journey to Jerusalem, where he died. The two extremes between which he moves are, however, clear: Galilee and Jerusalem. The main point of difference resides in the duration of Jesus' itinerant preaching in the company of his disciples. The Gospels of Matthew, Mark, and Luke, the so-called synoptic Gospels, mention only one journey by Jesus to Jerusalem for the Passover, during which Jesus was crucified. Indirectly they point to Jesus' public activities lasting one year at most. The Gospel according to John states that Jesus was in the holy city to celebrate the Passover three times (2:13, 6:4, 11:55). This means that Jesus' public activities lasted for between two and three years. His activities alternated mostly between Galilee and Jerusalem, where he traveled for the most important Jewish festivals, such as Tabernacles (7:2) and the Dedication of the Temple (10:22). John 5:1 mentions an unnamed "feast" for which Jesus traveled to Jerusalem.

The only definitive data available show that John the Baptist's activities began in the region of the Jordan: "In the fifteenth year of the reign of Tiberius Caesar" (Luke 3:1). In this text (3:1-2), the author of the Gospel dates events with reference to the empire's highest authority and other lesser dependent political authorities in the style of contemporary historians: Pontius Pilate, Roman governor of the province of Judaea (26–36 A.D.); Herod Antipas, tetrarch of Galilee (4 B.C.–39 A.D.); Philip, tetrarch of Ituraea and Trachonitis (4 B.C.–34 A.D.); Lysanias, tetrarch of Abilene (14 A.D.?–37 A.D.). The highest Jewish religious authorities are also mentioned: Annas and Caiaphas, his son-in-law, held the position of high priest between 6 and 15 A.D. and 18 and 36 A.D., respectively. Bringing all these data together leads to the conclusion that the period in question was from 26 to 34 A.D.

Which year in the Christian calendar corresponds to Tiberius' fifteenth year in power? The answer seems simple. Tiberius became emperor on August 19, 14 A.D., the date on which Augustus died. According to the ancient chronographers his fifteenth year in office ran from August 19, 28 A.D. to August 18, 29 A.D. However, if Luke used the Syro-Macedonian calendar, then Tiberius' fifteenth year in power went from October 1, 27 A.D. to September 30, 28 A.D., dates that do not differ greatly from those of the ancient chronographers. It is less likely that he used the Julian calendar, according to which the fifteenth year was 28 A.D. or 29 A.D., from January 1 to December 31. Thus, there are two possibilities, 28/29 or 27/28 A.D. If considered together, they coincide in the year 28 A.D.

As J. P. Meier and G. Theissen point out, the year 28 A.D. seems to be the most likely, fitting in with the reference made to the first time Jesus celebrated the Passover in Jerusalem according to the Gospel of John (2:13). On this occasion, the Jews state, "It has taken forty-six years to build this temple" (2:20). We know from Josephus that the work on the temple was started by Herod in the year 20/19 B.C. (*A.J.* 15:380), though preparations for this work may have started earlier, 23/22 B.C. (*J.W.* 1:401). The priests took charge of the construction and remodeling of the holiest part of the complex, the temple itself, while Herod took charge of the rest. Josephus states that the temple was completed "in a year and six months" (*A.J.* 15:421), in other words, the summer of 18 B.C. Essentially this means that between the winter of 20/19 B.C. and Passover of 28 A.D., some forty-six years and a few months had passed.

Therefore, Luke 3:1 and John 2:20, together with the Syrian calendar and Josephus, point toward the period from October 27 A.D. to the spring of 28 A.D. as the time when John the Baptist preached in the Judaean Desert and baptized Jesus in the river Jordan. According to John 2:13, Jesus was in Jerusalem for his first Passover after leaving Nazareth to carry out his public activities. This Passover took place on Tuesday, March 30 (or possibly Wednesday, April 28) 28 A.D. This calculation is almost identical to the one used by the Jews and lends weight to Luke's having used the Syrian calendar, the most common throughout the Orient apart from Egypt. The Hebrew year began in the month of Tishri, which fell between September and October. As C. Perrot points out, the year 27/28 A.D. was a sabbatical year according to the Hebrew calendar, or even a Jubilee year, a year to leave the land fallow and pay homage to God (Lev 25:1-22). If this hypothesis is correct, this extraordinarily important year certainly affected the events in the synagogue in Nazareth, as narrated by the Gospel of Luke (4:16-30), where it says that Jesus fulfills Isaiah's prophecy "to proclaim the acceptable year of the Lord" (Luke 4:19).

The above conclusion on the year 27/28 A.D. as the time when Jesus started his activities fits with two somewhat nonspecific reports related to the chronology of his life. Luke 3:23 mentions, "Jesus, when he began his ministry, was about 30." If he was born in 7/6 B.C., this means that he started his ministry in the year 27/28 A.D. and was between thirty-three and thirty-five. This conclusion fits with the rhetorical, and ironic or argumentative, question set by the Jewish leaders addressing Jesus when he stated that Abraham had seen the day of his manifestation: "You are not yet fifty years old, and have you seen Abraham?" (John 8:57). According to his adversaries, Jesus, who had not reached fifty, claimed to have known the patriarch Abraham, who had lived in these lands many centuries before. Indeed, fifty is a round number that can only be approximate, though it does show that Jesus must have been younger than fifty during the period when he was carrying out his public activities.

4.5.1.2. The Date of Jesus' Death: April 7, 30 A.D.

It is clear that Jesus died on a Friday: "the day of Preparation, that is, the day before the Sabbath" (Mark 15:42). This is corroborated by all of the canonical Gospels, which also coincide on the day on which the Last Supper with the disciples took place: the day before, Thursday. This supper took place at dusk within the walls of Jerusalem, as stated by Mark (14:17), Matthew (26:20), Luke (22:14-15), and John (13:1-2). According to the Gospels, the day after his death and burial was a Saturday, when everyone rested as required by the Law. Only on Sunday morning, the first day of the week in the Jewish calendar, "when the Sabbath was past," did the women go to the tomb and find it empty. The discovery of the empty tomb is mentioned in all four canonical Gospels: Mark (16:1-2), Matthew (28:1), Luke (24:1), and John (20:1). It is also mentioned in the Gospel of Peter (50–57).

However, according to the Gospel of John, the Friday when Jesus died was the eve of the Passover and coincided with the fourteenth day of the Jewish month of Nisan, the day of Preparation. In this year, Passover, a feast that had no set date but coincided with the first full moon of spring, was on a Saturday. For this reason, it says in John 18:28 that the Jewish leaders "did not enter the [Pilate's] praetorium, so that they might not be defiled, but might eat the Passover [that Friday at dusk]." According to Jewish Law, entering the house of a pagan, such as Pilate, led to ritual impurity, which would have meant that the Jewish leaders could not have taken part in Judaism's most important religious festival, Passover. John 19:31 is even more explicit: "[That Friday] was the day of Preparation . . . for that Sabbath [the following day] was a high day." The Tractate Sanhedrin 43a in the Babylonian Talmud confirms this information: "On the eve of the Passover Yeshu [i.e., Jesus] was hanged" (see 2.2.1). The Gospel of Peter 5, an apocryphal writing from the second century A.D., says, "And he [Pilate] delivered him [Jesus] to the people on the day before the unleavened bread, their feast." Thus, Jesus died on a Friday that was also the eve of the Jewish festival of Passover, the fourteenth day of Nisan.

These details allow us to ascertain the exact day, month, and year of Jesus' death. In the period from 26 to 34 A.D., the eve of Passover or the fourteenth day of the month of Nisan fell on a Friday only in the years 30 A.D. (April 7) and 33 A.D. (April 3), using precise astronomical calculations to establish the first day of the month and the leap years. We have to choose one of these two dates. The first seems the more likely, since Jesus' public activities began in 27/28 A.D. and lasted three years. The Gospel according to John mentions three Passover feasts: at the start (2:13), in the middle (6:4), and at the end (11:55, 13:1) of this activity, in the years 28, 29, and 30 A.D. (see 4.6, below). Consequently, it is likely that Jesus died on Friday, April 7, the eve of Passover, in the year 30 A.D.

Nevertheless, some exegetes prefer to keep to the chronology of events set out in the synoptic Gospels. According to these, the Friday on which Jesus died was also Passover, the fifteenth day of Nisan. Jesus' Last Supper coincided, thus, with the Passover meal. Mark, Matthew, and Luke make it clear that Jesus wanted to eat the Passover meal with his disciples and that this was the last meal he shared with them, only a few hours before his arrest, trial, and execution.

Accordingly, Jesus died, despite some anachronisms, on April 27, 31 A.D. The years 27 A.D. and 34 A.D. also saw Passover fall on a Friday, but these two dates are difficult to justify if we consider 27/28 A.D. as the beginning of Jesus' public activities.

According to both the Gospel of John and the synoptic Gospels, all the events relating to the end of Jesus' life took place between dusk on Thursday and dusk on Friday, a twenty-four-hour period: the Last Supper and his arrest, trial, condemnation, execution, death, and burial. The difference of opinion concerns whether this Friday was the fourteenth of Nisan, the day before Passover, as the Gospel according to John states, or the fifteenth of Nisan, Passover, as the synoptic Gospels assume. Likewise, with regard to the Thursday the difference of opinion concerns whether Jesus' Last Supper coincided with the Passover meal for that year (as can be deduced from the synoptic Gospels) or the Last Supper with his disciples took place the day before the feast to celebrate the Jewish Passover (according to John's chronology).

The problems faced in trying to combine all the details found in the Gospel according to John and the synoptic Gospels seem to lead to the need to make a heads or tails decision. However, certain elements in the synoptic Gospels seem to be contradictory or disconcerting at least.

First, the Jewish leaders understood the love of the people for Jesus and were afraid of the large crowds of pilgrims in Jerusalem for the Passover celebrations and of their reaction to Jesus' execution on the day of the Passover feast (the fifteenth of Nisan), and during the following week (until the twenty-first of Nisan), which was equally popular and religiously important. According to Mark 14:1-2, the leaders decided to act astutely and have the affair sorted out before (!) Passover: "Not during the feast [between the fifteenth and twenty-first of Nisan], lest there be a tumult of the people" (also Matt 26:5 and Luke 22:2, 22:6). G. Theissen believes that this fear also affected Pilate, who did not want to risk crucifying three Jews, one of whom was accused of no less than being "King of the Jews"!, on the days that represented the highest expression of Israel's national and religious sentiment.

Second, it seems highly unlikely that the highest Jewish religious authorities, led by the high priest, spent the night of Passover involved in the arrest, interrogation, sentencing, and delivering to Pilate of a

Galilean prophet with messianic pretensions. It is also clear that the Roman governor would not have wanted to call a tribunal to judge and condemn Jesus and to execute the sentence on Passover, the day on which the Roman forces on duty in the Antonia Tower and the praetorium (Herod's former palace) had to increase their surveillance of the pilgrims who had come to Jerusalem: one hundred thousand people in a city that usually held twenty-five thousand.

Third, the release of a prisoner for the Passover festivities, mentioned in the synoptic Gospels (Mark 15:6-15; Matt 27:15-26; Luke 23:13-25) and in John (18:38-40), makes sense only for the fourteenth of Nisan, the day before the Passover, as only then could this person take part in the feast's main event, the Passover meal. Nor does it make much sense that for a Jew, such as Simon of Cyrene, to be returning from "the country" (Mark 15:21), and probably from work, on the morning of Passover. The involvement of the man from Cyrene, made to carry a load on a day of complete rest such as the day of the Passover, does not sit easily with the Jewish Law and the respect that the Romans should have paid them.

Finally, as we shall see later (6.1.3.1), it is not clear whether Jesus kept strictly to the Jewish rituals for Passover at the Last Supper with his disciples: as C. Perrot rightly points out, not even the lamb is mentioned as part of this meal! Another very different possibility is that Jesus' Last Supper with the Twelve was permeated by the symbolism of the Jewish Passover, part of the early Christian tradition in the synoptic Gospels. This symbolism was historicized, making both Jesus' Last Supper and the Jewish Passover meal coincide chronologically. However, the tradition in the Gospel according to John has maintained the meal's authentic historical characteristics: it was a special and extraordinary farewell meal, which Jesus had wanted and wished for.

In conclusion, the weight of evidence in play leads us to believe that the chronology proposed by the Gospel of John is more consistent and coherent than that of the synoptic Gospels. It is highly likely that Jesus' death can be pinpointed to Friday, April 7, 30 A.D., according to the Christian calendar, the fourteenth day of Nisan, eve of Passover in the year 3790 from the creation of the world, according to the Jewish calendar.

4.5.2. The Guidance of John the Baptist

The period between his reclusive and silent time in Nazareth and his sustained and intense years of public activity in Galilee and the neighboring areas, Perea, Judaea, and Jerusalem, was marked by his baptism at the hands of John. The Baptist, a renowned prophet, had begun baptizing in the Jordan Valley toward the end of the year 27 A.D. He had inhabited the desert for some time before this, if Luke (1:80) is anything to go by: "And the child [John] grew and became strong in spirit, and he was in the wilderness till the day of his manifestation to Israel," until the fifteenth year of the reign of Tiberius, which started in October 27 A.D. According to Luke (3), "[T]he word of God came to John the son of Zechariah in the wilderness."

It seems that John grew up in the wilderness, perhaps once his parents, Zechariah and Elizabeth, had died and he had become an orphan. Did this mean that the Essenes took him in and educated him, as they did with other orphans at the monastery at Qumran? Or was John, probably the son of a priestly dynasty (his father Zechariah was a priest), raised by members of his family until he decided to go off to lead an ascetic lifestyle in the wilderness? Did he meet a hermit in the desert to guide him spiritually, as Josephus was to be guided by Bannus (see 4.5.2.1)? At the start of the year 28 A.D., when Jesus arrived at the spot where John baptized people, John was already a famous prophet attracting crowds thanks to his holy lifestyle and the strength of his message: "a righteous and holy man" are the words used, according to Mark (6:20), by Antipas, the sovereign who had him executed!

The area that John kept to was Perea (Transjordan), belonging, like Galilee, to the tetrarchy of Antipas. The Baptist focused his activities in the southern end of the valley of the Jordan, a river that breaks the monotony of the arid Judaean Desert with its flow of water and the thick vegetation on its banks. Bethany, a town on the left or eastern side of the river, was where the Baptist carried out his activities (John 1:28). According to the Gospel of John (3:23), on occasions the Baptist traveled to baptize people further north along the Jordan Valley, to Aenon, near Salim, towns to the west of the river, some ten kilometers to the south of Scythopolis, a city of the Decapolis.

4.5.2.1. John, His Activity and His Person

The deserts surrounding the Jordan Valley were full of people who, like John, carried out ritual immersions, which were linked to an ascetic lifestyle. One of these, Bannus, lived in the wilderness austerely as a hermit; he ate, as did John, what the land produced from time to time and wore clothes made from plants; he bathed in accordance with the rituals using cold water both during the day and at night. Bannus attracted disciples; even Josephus, despite being a Pharisee, admitted to having been a follower during the three years he spent in the Jordan Valley (*Life* 11). However, according to Josephus (*A.J.* 18:116) and the New Testament, John was described as "the Baptist," the only one who was deemed worthy of this name among the many baptists apparently at work in the area in the first century. From the latter would arise the Mandaeans, a Judeo-Baptist sect from Mesopotamia.

People from a range of races and origins, those who kept scrupulously to the Law and those who did not, honest workers and extortionists, rich and poor, people from Judaea and Jerusalem and people from Galilee, all came in great numbers to be baptized by John. Renowned and notorious sinners, including "the tax collectors and the harlots," were among the first (Matt 21:32; Luke 7:29). John welcomed all without exception to his baptisms, as they were all "children of Abraham," those who saw themselves as holy and those who were sinners. However, no one could use this title without a complete renewal of their lives: trying to justify their behavior by saying that they "have Abraham as [their] father" (Matt 3:9 || Luke 3:8) was useless and did not free them from facing up to repentance and, ultimately, falling before God's inexorable justice.

John turned against any attempt at self-justification and strongly attacked those who felt sure of themselves because they belonged to the chosen people, Israel: "You brood of vipers!" (Matt 3:7 || Luke 3:7). The key was not the honor or the excuse of belonging to the people of Abraham but instead converting oneself truly to God. John emphasized his point with irony, saying that "God is able from these stones to raise up children to Abraham." This forceful image has a universalistic tone and is probably supposed to lead us to think that John would have welcomed even non-Jews who had a heartfelt desire to convert before the imminent coming of divine justice.

John's baptisms

The baptisms carried out by John were given only once in a person's life, once the supplicant had shown penitence for the sins he or she had committed and a willingness to bear fruit: "Bear fruit that befits repentance" (Matt 3:8 || Luke 3:8). According to Josephus, the fruit that John asked for is a life characterized for its "piety," veneration and fear of God and his "justice," in other words, the correct behavior unto others (*A.J.* 18:117; and similarly, *A.J.* 15:375).

John gave his baptismal ritual great depth and reach. According to Mark (1:4) and Luke (3:3), "John the baptizer appeared in the wilderness, preaching a baptism of repentance for the forgiveness of sins." The focus of John's baptisms was the imminent and severe judgment of God; those who publicly showed repentance for their sins and were willing to change their habits and behavior were welcomed and baptized with the promise of forgiveness: confession of their own failings was the condition for being allowed to undertake the ritual of complete immersion in the water (Mark 1:5 || Matt 3:6). Divine forgiveness was not given at the time of the baptism but rather on the final day of judgment with the filling of the Holy Spirit: this salvation was not the faraway future.

John's baptisms were a sign of repentance and a pledge from God for forgiveness in the near future, when history reached its end. Josephus states that John's baptisms were "not in order to the putting away of some sins [here and now]." Forgiveness was God's gift awarded at the end of time to those who had, through baptism in the present, received "purification of the body," provided that "the soul was thoroughly purified beforehand by righteousness" (*A.J.* 18:117). The baptism by water administered by John was a provisional sign that preceded the Spiritual baptism, the final, definitive, and eschatological baptism; it was not immediate in effect, as is the case of the Christian sacrament of baptism.

The end, which was imminent, is seen in the strong images borrowed from two common activities in rural life: felling of unproductive trees and threshing of the grain. Both images come from material contained in the Q collection of sayings. The first describes the moment before the felling of the tree, when "even now the axe is laid to the root of the trees," and tells of the destiny of this tree that failed to produce as it should have: "[E]very tree therefore that does not bear fruit is cut down and thrown into the fire" (Matt 3:10 || Luke 3:9). The second image, which like the first has apocalyptic overtones, illustrates a twofold possibility: the wheat is kept and chaff burned. An immediate response is required, as divine judgment is imminent: "His [God's? His envoy's?] winnowing fork is in his hand, and he will clear his threshing floor and gather his wheat into the granary, but the chaff he will burn with unquenchable fire" (Matt 3:12 || Luke 3:17). John's preaching places special emphasis on the coming judgment and the threat of punishment. The end of human history is to be dominated by God's inexorable justice, representing salvation for some and punishment for others. The Q source talks about a final baptism "with the Holy Spirit and with fire" (Matt 3:11 || Luke 3:16). John states ironically that some will remain immersed ("baptized") in the gift of the Spirit and be forgiven of their sins, while others will be buried in a terrible fire to live forever in hell: this is their immersion, their baptism!

John's baptisms are closely linked to the man. John was considered God's envoy sent to preach Israel's rebirth in light of God's imminent arrival, the day on which everyone would be judged. In order to fully renew one's life, a sincere and heartfelt commitment was required to act righteously and judiciously, truthfully and charitably. Luke describes the questions asked of John by people in general, and tax collectors and soldiers in particular (Luke 3:10-14). John is a messenger who has to prepare the way to God in the desert, as God's arrival represents the conclusion of human history as it says in Isaiah (40:3): "A voice cries: 'In the wilderness prepare the way of the Lord, make straight in the desert a highway for our God.'" John probably used these words to legitimize his prophetic mission in the Judaean Desert. An extremely strict religious group who lived in the desert made use of these words: the Essenes at Qumran also interpreted them in terms of the final coming of God (Community Rule 8:13-16) (see 3.3.3.4).

The announcing of someone greater

John's ideas were specific and simple and far removed from speculations on the coming of the end, visions and secrets, and celestial journeys: the usual contents of apocalyptic literature. Despite the apocalyptic overtones in his expressions, John's main concern centered on the need to repent before the imminent end. The Baptist linked an ethical commitment in the present, a life change, with judgment in the future. The baptisms represented conversion and prepared people to receive God's salvation. Through the baptisms John became an intermediary between God's will and people's decision in the world in which they lived; a world that in his opinion was entering its final stages. He was a prophet of the last days, sent by God to urge everyone to convert before the imminent forgiveness of sins.

However, the future that John spoke of involved the coming of a plenipotentiary, someone different and mysterious. John called him "he who is mightier than I" (Mark 1:7; Matt 3:11; Luke 3:16) or "he who is coming after me" (Matt 3:11; Mark 1:7; John 1:27). In comparison to him, the Baptist stresses his inferiority and, with a striking image (as all of his are!), states that he is not worthy to be his slave or to do what slaves do: untie his master's sandals. This is such a humiliating act that, according to the Babylonian Talmud, it is the only thing that disciples do not have to do for their master (Ketubot 96a). With this image, in the Gospels of Mark, Luke, and John (Matt 3:11 talks of carrying his sandals), the Baptist is alluding to a messianic figure, and one much more important than the rabbi or teacher: John talks of God's last emissary, the one who has to fulfill the hopes of the people.

When John was in prison, he sent some of disciples to Jesus to ask him if he was this individual, if he was "he who is to come" (Matt 11:3 || Luke 7:20). The question is revealing: John had doubts about Jesus; he had yet to recognize him as the Messiah. Jesus' response contained a certain questioning of the Baptist, given his doubts and reservations: "blessed is he who takes no offence at me" (Matt 11:6 || Luke 7:23). It was an invitation to accept him, to believe in him and his words, and to recognize him as God's plenipotentiary envoy. As J. P. Meier points out, John was sure that God would send someone with the mission of judging men at the end of days, someone to separate the wheat from the chaff, the saved from the condemned, but he did not know who this person would be. He used circumlocutions and vague periphrases; he avoided precise references. In any case, the Baptist considered himself insignificant in comparison to the one sent by God.

Jesus never left John's life completely, but John was never wholly convinced that his former follower represented the hope for Israel. The Christian tradition places words in John's mouth to express what he may have held in his heart but which he never dared speak out clearly:

"Behold, the Lamb of God . . . the Son of God" (John 1:29, 1:34, 1:36). The Christian tradition clearly refers to the name and great dignity of this figure: Jesus of Nazareth, the Messiah, the Lord. John was presented as the individual preparing "the Lord's way," the way for Jesus, as his "precursor," and it was he, not God, who fulfilled the prophecy in Isaiah 40 (Matt 3:3; Mark 1:2-3; Luke 3:4-6). The Gospel of Matthew goes even further and, when Jesus went to John to be baptized, placed the following words in the mouth of the Baptist: "I need to be baptized by you, and do you come to me?" (3:14).

John, ascetic and prophet

John's preaching was backed up by his ascetic way of life, which he practiced with others who were considered his disciples and who called him rabbi (John 3:26). John's clothes were somewhat different: he limited himself to a short kind of tunic (not a robe or cape) made of camel skin and a piece of skin (not a leather belt) around his waist, as is reported in Matthew 3:4 and Mark 1:6. John wanted to be known for wearing simple clothes, not the sumptuous or "soft raiment" worn by those who lived in "kings' houses" (Matt 11:8 || Luke 7:25). John's clothes were unique: a short tunic with a belt, but without a cloak, the vital outer garment needed to keep out the heat and the cold. The Baptist's tunic was not made from cotton, twill, or wool but from camel skin, a tough material offering little insulation, which left his arms unprotected as it had no sleeves.

The prophets of Israel wore clothing that resembled John's, and the typical material used was animal skins. For example, Elijah wore this clothing before rising to heaven and left his cloak on earth for Elisha, his disciple and successor (2 Kgs 1:8, 1:13). Unlike Elijah and as a sign of austerity, John the Baptist did not wear a cloak, and his tunic was made of camel skin. However, both used a piece of animal skin for a belt. John's clothing was an attempt to present himself as a prophet like Elijah but emphasizing the ascetic elements (not wearing a cloak).

John's asceticism was evident above all in the food he ate. Jesus said of John, "[H]e has come eating no bread and drinking no wine" (Luke 7:33 || Matt 11:18). John and his disciples avoided these two basic foodstuffs (bread and wine) and, like the Pharisees, kept to frequent and strict fasts (Mark 2:18 || Matt 9:14 || Luke 5:33, 18:12). John's diet was limited to what he could find in the desert: "locusts and wild honey" (Matt 3:4; Mark 1:6). As J. Gnilka points out, the Bedouins, the inhabitants of the desert, boiled locusts in water and salt and then roasted them on the fire. The honey was collected from the hives the bees built in the rocks and crannies. With regard to the wine, not drinking alcohol was something that set apart those people devoted to God, through the vow of a Nazirite (Num 6:3). As Luke (1:15) states, John may have been a Nazirite in its strictest sense. It is another sign that John's lifestyle was characterized by its extreme austerity.

A great many people were attracted to John to hear him preach and be baptized and then went home. However, some spontaneously formed a group of disciples around him and lived in accordance with the practices and teachings of their master. John was a hermit surrounded by a group of disciples, which varied in number, rather than the head of a monastery with a set community that followed a rule, as in the case at Qumran. John's disciples listened to the main teachings of their master relating to the urgent need to convert and the imminent Judgment Day, upon which the main ritual part of his activities was founded: the baptism or immersion in water by John himself or one of these disciples.

John's baptisms and ritual baths

John's baptisms were radically different from the purification rituals carried out by contemporaneous Jewish groups and individuals in accordance with the Law of Moses. The Essenes, Pharisees, and Sadducees, the three Jewish movements promoting religious renewal, ascribed great importance to the continuing ritual purification of both people and things, in line with the precise and strict regulations set down (see 3.3.2, above). The Pharisees, in particular, were concerned with educating people on how to keep to the rules on ritual cleanliness. The Sadducees' great care when it came to ritual purification can be seen in the small swimming pools found in the houses of the rich in Jerusalem that belonged to members of the sacerdotal aristocracy.

The community at Qumran probably shared similar feelings to those preached by the Baptist. For example, the Community Rule emphasized repentance and purification in the present in preparation for the imminent and definitive cleansing on the last day, carried out by the Spirit itself. However, ritual purification did not serve for anything if it was not accompanied, here and now, by repenting of one's wickedness (5:13-14): those who do not keep to these divine precepts shall remain impure, no matter how much they bathe. At the end of days (Mal 3:1), God is to purify men of all their wicked deeds with his spirit of holiness (Community Rule 4:21).

John the Baptist differs notably from those at Qumran in his message and his way of life. The entirely valid points of comparison do not mean that he can be considered as linked to the Essenes. At Qumran, the ritual purifications were carried out with extreme rigor; cleanliness was ensured by a program of obligatory, daily ritual baths, as can be seen in the archaeological finds from the Dead Sea monastery. Deep baths have been found at Qumran that allowed people to immerse themselves completely. The main point in John's teachings, however, was that the bathing took place only once: a single immersion to guarantee access to definitive salvation, as long as it was accompanied by sincere repentance.

Though John may not have explicitly gone against the system of repeated purifications, as required by the Law of Moses and practiced without exception, though with some variation, by the leaders of the Jewish religion (Pharisees, Sadducees, and Essenes), his baptisms do turn the tables on this system, for example the discussion "between John's disciples and a Jew over purifying" (John 3:25). John's baptisms were unusual at the time because they were not an immersion carried out alone (like the ritual purifications) but an immersion carried out by someone else and only once in one's life. This led to suspicions on the part of Israel's religious elites, including the Pharisees (Luke 7:30), fierce defenders of the laws on ritual purity, or the temple's Sadducee leaders (Matt 21:23, 21:32), jealous to hold sway at the Jewish people's most important institution. The temple was where the high priest carried out the ritual to atone the sins of all the people each year for Yom Kippur, the Day of Atonement.

Thus, John's single baptism was to some degree an attack on the importance of the complicated system of ritual purifications, carried out repeatedly, and the ritual of Yom Kippur repeated once a year. The people approved of this baptism, which guaranteed purification once and for all and which prepared them for the Final Judgment. Though the Baptist was a Law-abiding Jewish prophet, a teacher who interpreted the Law strictly (proposing, for example, strict fasting), his message did not focus on questions of ritual purity or keeping to each and every precept of the Law, which was the message of the Pharisees, Sadducees, and Essenes. As with Israel's great prophets, the nucleus of John's preaching was an urgent call for personal repentance before God, in the face of an imminent and Final Judgment. This repentance was to be carried out through baptism: immersion in the water in anticipation of the forgiveness of sins and being accorded the Spirit that God awards those whom he saves. This is what lent his words such force and made his message so attractive.

The people saw John as a prophet (Matt 14:5; Mark 11:32 || Matt 21:26 || Luke 20:6) and recognized his virtues (Mark 6:14). His group of disciples accompanied him on his mission, living in the wilderness with him or in the neighboring towns. Their devotion to the Baptist was unconditional: they went to see him in prison after his arrest (Matt 11:2, 11:4 || Luke 7:18-20) and took his body to the tomb after his execution (Mark 6:29 || Matt 14:12). Long after the death of John, some still said they had received his baptism, including Apollos, a Jew from Alexandria converted to Christianity (Acts 18:24-25) and some Christians whom Paul found in Ephesus (Acts 19:3).

4.5.2.2. John and Jesus

Jesus baptized by John

According to Luke (3:1-6), at the start of 28 A.D., some three months after John had started to make his message heard at the southern end of the Jordan, with his baptisms for repentance and the forgiveness of sins, people began to gather round him. John lived in the wilderness (Mark 1:4) and was renowned throughout the Jewish lands. People came from neighboring Judaea and Jerusalem in particular. They traveled down the Jordan Valley, crossed the river, and went to look for him in the land of Perea (Transjordan). Obviously there were also people from Perea itself. Bethany in Perea (John 1:28) was the point of reference, at the confluence of the Jordan where the wadis or gullies ran down from the highlands of the ancient Moab, and where the people came together to listen to his preaching and to be baptized by him. During this winter period, the rainy season, John immersed all those who wanted to be baptized, men and women, in the water from the river, gullies, or pools. The men wore only a piece of underwear and the women a tunic: this is also how Josephus describes the clothing worn by the Essenes for their ritual purifications (*J.W.* 2:161).

The Galileans, despite being further away, also came to John to be baptized. Some of them even became disciples of his. We know some of them by name: Andrew, from Bethsaida, a fishing village within the administrative boundaries of Philip's tetrarch, bordering Galilee; his brother Simon (Peter); Philip, also from Bethsaida; Nathanael, another Galilean, from Cana (John 21:2). Among the Galileans seeking baptism by John was a man who was coming up to thirty-five years of age: Jesus, from Nazareth, a small farming village near Cana surrounded by the mountains of Lower Galilee and far from the lake area of Andrew, Simon, and Philip. Jesus may not have come alone. The Gospel of the Hebrews (or Nazarenes), an apocryphal text from the start of the second century A.D., says that Jesus' mother and brethren also wished to travel to see John so that they could be baptized (Jerome, *Against the Pelagians* 3:2).

Alone or accompanied by his close relatives, he was certainly among other Galileans attracted by the Baptist's fame, and the carpenter's son from Nazareth was baptized by John in the river Jordan. This is an undeniable fact: "In those days Jesus came from Nazareth of Galilee and was baptized by John in the Jordan" (Mark 1:9 || Matt 3:13; and indirectly, Luke 3:21; John 1:32-33). Despite the dialogue between John and Jesus before the baptism in the Gospel according to Matthew and part of the Christian tradition (3:14-15), Jesus was baptized by John, without John knowing his identity. The Gospel of Mark maintains a conspicuous silence, and the Gospel of John states that the Baptist said of Jesus, "I myself did not know him" (John 1:33). The Gospel of Luke does not say anything about this, though it does refer to the fact that Jesus and John's mothers, Elisabeth and Mary, were related (1:36). Jesus may, therefore, have known that he was related to John, but he may not have wanted to identify himself before his baptism. Everything seems to lead us to think that Jesus' baptism was just one of the many baptisms that John undertook.

Why did Jesus want to be baptized?

The essential question pertains to how Jesus saw this baptism, which he freely and anonymously undertook. There were, fundamentally, three reasons that led people to ask John for baptism and requirements that this baptism brought with it: to confess their sins, heartfelt repentance and the desire to renew their lives, and the desire to seek God's forgiveness. This divine forgiveness would come on Judgment Day and the baptism was in preparation for this. Did Jesus undertake it with the same conscience and feelings? Did he go to be baptized because he wanted to change his life and gain divine forgiveness? Did he want to confess his sins?

We can see that at no time in his life did Jesus show any sign of guilt for his actions. He did not feel upset for having offended God or other men and, thus, he did not repent for any personal sin. It does not seem that Jesus wanted to be baptized because he needed forgiveness. Some, like J. P. Meier, believe that Jesus' baptism helped him form closer ties with his people, that he wanted to be recognized publicly as a member of a sinning Israel and to show the need for God's mercy; ultimately, he wanted to encourage a renewed community. Jesus' desire was to give an example of humility and solidarity, accepting the need to be just another of Israel's sinners, even though he may not have been or felt like one.

Above all else, Jesus wished to make clear his devotion to the two foundations on which the baptisms carried out by John, the most recent of the prophets sent by God, were based: the general call to conversion and the welcoming of God's final forgiveness. The "baptism of repentance for the forgiveness of sins" is how John's baptisms are described! These were also the two fundamental pillars of Jesus' message, two strong points in his preaching and activities: "Repent and believe in the gospel [the news that God heals and forgives]" (Mark 1:15). According to this, Jesus was baptized because he identified with John's message and saw this baptism as the starting point for his own mission. As we shall see (5.1.1), this mission can be summarized as a call: God has arrived in the world, his Kingdom is here, his forgiveness is spreading around the earth.

Jesus traveled to the Jordan because he was convinced that a new time had come: being baptized, Jesus became part of a movement for conversion led by John, who represented a sign of God's new will on earth. By this baptism, rather than showing his solidarity with the sin of humanity hoping for imminent forgiveness, Jesus was publicly acknowledging the arrival of this forgiveness and the immediate fulfillment of Israel's hope. Jesus experienced his baptism not as a personal expression of repentance for his sins but as the start of the times prophesied by John, as the beginning of the definitive forgiveness offered to all, for which he was to act as a plenipotentiary emissary. John spoke of God's imminent forgiveness; Jesus proclaimed that this forgiveness was, thankfully, here.

His baptism also meant that Jesus underwent an intense inner experience, as it represented the start of a new reality: God's presence on earth. This cosmic revelation in the Jordan (the divine voice speaks and the Spirit descends as a dove), as narrated by the Gospels, reflects two constants in Jesus' life: his closeness to God, the Father (see 5.4.2), and his position as the Messiah, anointed with the fullness of the Spirit (see 5.4.1). The Gospel narratives explain that, after Jesus' baptism, the heavens opened and the Holy Spirit descended toward him and a heavenly voice called him the Son of God (Mark 1:10-11 || Matt 3:16-17 || Luke 3:21-22; and with some differences, John 1:32-34). This extraordinary scene, deep in Jesus' internal experience, highlights his identity: God makes himself present in human history and life through the individual being baptized, a man like other men, yet different from them, the only Son of God, the Father. The baptism and revelation in the Jordan was the starting point for Jesus' mission.

Jesus allowed himself to receive John's baptism because he identified with the two main principles upon which it is based: repentance and forgiveness. However, he had a new conviction, which was quite different from John's: God is no longer what will soon come; instead, he has already arrived in the world and has started to spread his power. Jesus' activities testified to this conviction, especially manifesting itself in his miracles and healings. They were a sign that the Kingdom of God had arrived. This demonstrates that the force of evil has been defeated, that Satan has lost his power. The old world, controlled by evil, will fall, as a new world of good and salvation is on the way. The question is no longer waiting for the end of the world but welcoming the arrival of the new world.

Jesus tempted

Jesus was baptized in the wilderness where he underwent a long and complex spiritual trial, in which he was unceasingly exposed by Satan to temptations, which he overcame. Mark (1:12-13) and the Q source (Matt 4:1-11 || Luke 4:1-13) make the desert the scene for two episodes involving Jesus' inner turmoil, his spiritual biography: the heavenly and cosmic revelation following his baptism and the temptations, the cosmic fight between Jesus and Satan that involved forty days of fasting and from which he arose victorious, as we are told by the angels who serve him. Obviously Jesus was "tempted" on more occasions throughout his life: by the flattery he received from people who wanted to make him king (John 6:15), by his disciples who wanted to save him from his death on the cross (Mark 8:33), by the Jewish leaders who offered him the chance to save himself and escape death (Mark 15:31-32), by those who wanted him to allow the use of violence in revenge for disrespect (Luke 9:54-55), and by those who wanted to use force against their persecutors (Luke 22:38). However, the greatest temptation Jesus underwent was during the Passion, when faced with his imminent death; he alluded to "falling into the temptation," of trying to escape rather than accepting his death on the cross. There are two great temptations in Jesus' life: that of Gethsemane and that of the wilderness. In the temptation in the garden of Gethsemane, at the end of his life, his free will was put to the test when facing his upcoming violent death (Luke 22:3, 22:39-46). The temptation in the Judaean Desert, at the start of his public activities, shows Jesus' internal struggle as he began his prophetic mission to announce the Kingdom, a mission he accepted freely and which he carried out with words and prodigious deeds.

All the great prophets of Israel expressed difficulties when faced with their mission. In the narratives of their prophetic vocations, Isaiah was considered "a man of unclean lips," a sinner (6:5), and Jeremiah, like Moses, excused himself saying he was too young and did not know how to speak (1:6). Jesus, however, did not have these personal excuses or problems when starting the mission that he took on and accepted. It does not seem that Jesus received any sort of calling at the Jordan. Both the baptism and the temptations show that Jesus already knew where he was going by the time he reached the Jordan, or perhaps more accurately where God and the Holy Spirit were taking him. His struggle, his "temptation," should be considered a trial that aimed to dishearten him and make him abandon the mission he had accepted by turning things on their head and mystifying him. In the Q source narrative, Satan offered Jesus the chance to have power over the whole world, to take the place of God, to become, ultimately, Satan's subject ("If you, then, worship me, it shall all be yours"; Luke 4:7).

The early Christian community developed the spiritual struggle between Jesus and the prince of evil in the three temptations in the wilderness, convinced that Jesus had triumphed. Later, while he expelled demons and healed the sick, using an apocalyptic style, Jesus stated, "I saw Satan fall like lightning from heaven" (Luke 10:18). The Kingdom of God, which, with Jesus, is beginning to be built on earth, brings with it the annihilation of Evil, removing all its power. The temptation in the wilderness ended with Satan's retreat (Matt 4:11; Luke 4:13). Jesus triumphed and ensured that God could take his rightful place.

Jesus, John's follower and collaborator

The preceding considerations relate to the relationship between Jesus after his baptism and John. By listening to John's teachings and undergoing his baptism, Jesus had accepted his guidance, even though John did not know who Jesus was when he baptized him. Jesus did not return home to Nazareth but stayed with the Baptist for some time in Bethany of Perea, the area east of the Jordan governed by Antipas. If we take January 28 A.D. as the most plausible time for Jesus' baptism and the date of Jesus' journey to Jerusalem with his disciples for Passover that year, according to John (2:13-20), as valid, then a small group of followers grew up around Jesus between two and four months. As we have seen, Passover was on Tuesday, March 30 (or possibly Wednesday, April 28) that year.

Before he attracted his first group of disciples, Jesus formed part of the Baptist's circle. Immediately after his baptism, he probably shared the austere lifestyle of the whole group, a life of fasting, prayer, and aiding John in his baptismal mission in the region around the Jordan. The great number of people coming to be baptized made these tasks of support and welcome necessary. Jesus listened to John's preaching and teachings in a setting dominated by intense spiritual experiences, which included his temptations and the progressive affirmation of his own position as a teacher. This short period ended when Jesus, accompanied by four or five former disciples of John, now his disciples, left the Jordan area temporarily to travel to Jerusalem for the Passover celebrations (John 2:13).

These disciples were Galileans like Jesus, whom he had met as disciples, followers, or sympathizers of the Baptist. There were three from Bethsaida (Andrew, Simon-Peter, and Philip) and one from Cana (Nathanael), a man of strong convictions ("an Israelite indeed, in whom is no guile!"; John 1:47). The final disciple remained nameless (John 1:35, 1:40), but should probably be identified as John, son of Zebedee and brother of James. Both Andrew and Nathanael called Jesus rabbi (John 1:38, 1:49). This is also what John's disciples called him (John 3:26). Jesus was clearly recognized as an authority on par with the Baptist by some of his former followers. Jesus' group of disciples was beginning to take shape, and this meant that Jesus was not simply another of the Baptist's followers but someone who was emerging with a personality and teachings that were to set him apart.

We cannot be sure if Jesus, before traveling to Jerusalem, made a quick visit to Galilee with his mother and disciples to attend a wedding in Cana, Nathanael's hometown, after which he went on to Capernaum (John 2:1-12). The events in Cana make more sense in Jesus' life if they came after John the Baptist's imprisonment, when he traveled to Galilee to begin his activities.

The second phase of Jesus' relationship with the Baptist began after his return from celebrating Passover in Jerusalem with the small group of disciples, having had notable success in the city according to John 2:23–3:21. Even Nicodemus, one of the Pharisee leaders, a "teacher of Israel" (John 3:10), had shown interest in the teachings of this "rabbi" from Galilee (John 3:2). But instead of returning to Perea on the other side of the Jordan, "Jesus and his disciples went to Judaea" (John 3:22). Jesus stayed in an unnamed part of Judaea for some time "and baptized" (John 3:22, 3:26, 4:1). Like Jesus, John also baptized beyond the boundaries of Perea, in Aenon, in the territory of Scythopolis, a city of the Decapolis near Samaria in the southern part of the Jordan Valley. John and Jesus, and their respective disciples, had divided up the areas of influence; John looked to attract even the Samaritans, while Jesus had the area of Judaea. Whatever the case, both rabbis baptized far from each other, outside Perea, a land under the jurisdiction of Antipas, which was significant. The political situation had changed after Passover and prudence was required.

John's and Jesus' baptizing continued into the month of June 28 A.D., the time when John's first arrest probably took place, as decreed by Antipas (*A.J.* 18:118–19). Jesus immediately traveled to Galilee, according to Mark 1:14: "[A]fter John was arrested, Jesus came into Galilee." John (4:3) states, "[H]e [Jesus] left Judaea and departed again to Galilee." The threat of Antipas seems to echo through Matthew 4:12: "[W]hen he heard that John had been arrested, he withdrew into Galilee" (also Matt 14:13). Antipas had just imprisoned John the Baptist and Jesus may not have wanted to risk traveling in Perea. For this reason, he did not take the usual route used by Jews on journeys between Judaea and Galilee. Jesus and his disciples crossed Samaria, which Jews normally tried to avoid since it was considered a foreign and impure land. It was June, and Jesus invited his disciples to look at the fields, saying, "[T]he fields are already white for harvest" (John 4:35). The conversation between Jesus and a Samaritan woman by the well in the town of Sychar, not far from Shechem, the historical capital of Samaria, demonstrated the enthusiastic reception he received from the Samaritans, who recognized him as the Messiah (John 4:1-42). Jesus arrived shortly after in Galilee (John 4:43), and summer was about to begin.

John's memory would accompany Jesus throughout his public activities. The Q collection offers a good selection of material on John, making clear Jesus' opinion of John the Baptist, whom he lauded as one of the greatest people ever to have lived (Matt 11:2-19 || Luke 7:18-35). In one of the arguments between Jesus and the temple leaders and scribes in Jerusalem, John's baptisms, which came "from heaven," served as proof of the origin of his authority (Mark 11:27-33 || Matt 21:23-27 || Luke 20:1-8). Jesus' attitude toward John was so positive that during Jesus' life there was no evidence of any rivalry between the two rabbis, as a contentious reading of John 3:26 might imply. However, once John had been imprisoned, a distance grew between them, as the paths of both were to go off in different directions definitively.

This distancing came about due to an important event: Jesus stopped baptizing people as soon as he left Judaea and began preaching in Galilee. None of the Gospels show Jesus baptizing anyone following John's imprisonment. This imprisonment brought with it a radical change in Jesus' area of activity (moving from Judaea to Galilee) and in his activities (neither he nor his disciples baptized people any longer; John 4:2). If the baptisms had not ended, Jesus would undoubtedly have mentioned them in his response to John's disciples with regard to his messianic activities (Matt 11:2-6 || Luke 7:18-23). His silence has to be taken to be a clear sign that Jesus remained "loyal" to the baptismal practices of John, his guide, only for as long as the latter was able to perform them before his imprisonment.

Why did Jesus stop baptizing people when John was imprisoned? B. Chilton suggests that it was for political reasons: Jesus distanced himself from John, suspect in the eyes of Antipas, and reduced the risk of tension with the sovereign. Also according to Chilton, Jesus' journey to Galilee put distance between him and Antipas since, as we shall see later, the conflict between Antipas and John was centered on events that affected Perea and not Galilee. But these were not the definitive reasons. The baptisms carried out by John were a provisional sign that preceded the baptism by the Spirit and aimed at the imminent, not present, forgiveness of sins. Jesus proposed that God was manifesting all his compassionate and healing power here and now and that the time had come for the fulfillment of the prophecies: the sick were to be healed, the dead were to be resurrected, and the poor were to receive the good news. John's baptisms fell into the background as the healing of the sick, the freeing of the possessed of evil spirits, the welcoming the poor, and the sharing of the table with sinners became the focal points of Jesus' activities.

During the period between Passover and the summer of 28 A.D., when Jesus was active away from John but still under his influence, it is likely that he reduced the number of baptisms and let his disciples carry them out: "although Jesus himself did not baptize, but only his disciples" (John 4:2). Jesus, for his part, concentrated his activities on preaching and healings, the "prodigious signs" that produced such enthusiasm in the people of both Jerusalem (John 2:23) and Judaea (John 3:26, 4:1). Nicodemus saw the unmistakable sign of the divine presence: "[N]o one can do these signs that you do, unless God is with him" (John 3:2).

Jesus did not break away from John's baptismal practices; he simply handed them over to his disciples toward the end of the time they spent in Judaea, and once he had started preaching in Galilee, he suspended the practice. However, he maintained the full force of the message upon which John's baptisms were based: the call to conversion and the offer of forgiveness. When the disciples were sent on their mission throughout Galilee, they were told to preach to people to have them repent, to expel their demons and heal the sick (Mark 6:12-13). Jesus does not reject the practice of baptism. Proof of this is that the early Church restored the use of baptisms or immersions in water administered in the name of Jesus (Acts 2:38) or in the name of the Father, the Son, and the Holy Spirit (Matt 28:18-20). The case of fasting may well also help us to understand how the time in which Jesus was preaching was exceptional and unique in the minds of the first Christians. Jesus, when asked why his disciples did not fast like John's disciples, responded that the guests at a wedding did not fast while they were with the bridegroom: "[T]he days will come, when the bridegroom is taken away from them, and then they will fast that day" (Mark 2:20 || Matt 9:15 || Luke 5:35). The period of Jesus' activities was not the time for baptisms. All forces had to be reserved for what was most important: preaching and healing the sick and possessed. Later, when the bridegroom was no longer physically there, they could baptize again.

The distance between Jesus and John

Jesus did not end relations with John, but they did progressively grow apart. His teaching and preaching continued in their own style, linked to the Baptist's, but in many ways different. Jesus picked up many ideas that underlay John's preaching, but transformed them in an original way. He valued John's baptisms, but did not make them a part of his own mission. He shared John's ascetic way of life for a short while, but did not live this lifestyle while he preached and healed.

Josephus explains that both of them were individuals who taught people how to live ethically: John was "a good man, and commanded the Jews to exercise virtue" (*A.J.* 18:117), while Jesus was "a wise man . . . a teacher" (*A.J.* 18:63) (see the complete text in 2.2.1). However, he adds with regard to Jesus that "he was a doer of wonderful works," healings and exorcisms. Here lies the greatest contrast between the John's and Jesus' activities, and it has to be linked to another difference: the baptisms were John's defining activity; Josephus calls him the "Baptist" (*A.J.* 18:116–17), whereas they did not characterize Jesus' life and mission who, again according to Josephus, was known as Christ, the Messiah (*A.J.* 20:200).

In other words, what emerges following Jesus' baptism by John is his ability to overcome the power of evil, that which makes people ill with bodily ailments or destroys their inner structure and psyche (possession by evil spirits). A different way of talking about God and his actions in the world also emerged, involving the most common aspects of everyday life, used in narratives and images that touch and guide listeners toward a new world: the parables are a common means of expression used by the rabbi Jesus. As G. Theissen points out, John's strong images involving the tree to be cut down or the separating of the wheat from the chaff, referring to divine justice, have now changed. According to Jesus' teachings, the fig tree that does not bear fruit still has a chance before being chopped down (cf. Luke 13:6-9 and 3:9). Time is required for the seed sown to grow and for the grain to be harvested (Mark 4:26-29). The call to convert was shared by both John and Jesus, as are references to judgment, but the end of the world is no longer imminent, instead this end has been postponed: God's patience is great, and he is not concerned with destroying and judging this world.

Jesus does not place emphasis on God's judgment but on the salvation he offers everyone, and his special focus on the sinners. There is plenty of room left for compassion and forgiveness, and these are not conditioned by an imminent judgment or the threat of punishment: the definitive judgment exists, but there is plenty of time for salvation. The fundamental change is that John prophesies "the wrath [of God] to come," whereas Jesus starts by proclaiming that God's reign has begun ("the Kingdom of God is at hand," "the time is fulfilled"). The end of the world can wait. Forgiveness and salvation are not in the future but here and now, and they are already spreading around the earth. A good sign of this is the miracles that renew people and the words, pronounced with authority, that are capable of changing the people who hear them. John's importance derives from the fact that he represents the culmination of the prophets and that after him comes the Kingdom of God, which is made real thanks to the miraculous deeds and words of Jesus, which act as signs of power and mercy (Matt 11:12 || Luke 16:16).

Jesus modified John's fundamental concerns significantly. The emphasis changed; unsurprisingly, the people's response was enthusiastic. Jesus spoke and acted with authority. John's strong and prophetic words, calling for repentance, were converted into powerful words bringing happiness to the poor, health to the sick, and hope to everyone. The force of Jesus' words and actions led to a very special case, the healing of the deepest parts of the human spirit; and people spontaneously reacted with admiration: "With authority he commands even the unclean spirits, and they obey him" (Mark 1:27 || Luke 4:36). This is how the people of Capernaum in Galilee felt, but these words could equally have been used by the people of Judaea or Perea, before Jesus arrived at the lake.

Jesus' authority also derives from his interpretation of the Law, without having to be linked to any one group in particular (Pharisees, Sadducees, or Essenes) or any of the schools of the famous rabbis. John represented an important point of reference for Jesus, but Jesus made it clear that he was "he who is to come," the Messiah. He did not say so directly and avoided being acclaimed as such, but in the aforementioned scene with the envoys sent by John (Matt 11:2-6 || Luke 7:18-23) the message that he wanted to send his former guide was that he was to fulfill the prophesy of Isaiah 61, referring to the anointed one or Messiah, God's emissary: "Go and tell John what you have seen and heard" (Luke 7:22).

Jesus was concerned not only for the people's physical and mental (possession by evil spirits) health but also for their spiritual health. As part of his activities, Jesus reached out to those who were considered sinners and who were victims of social and religious ostracism, such as the sick or possessed. Sharing the meal table and unconditional friendship with public and notorious sinners was the way Jesus made his point. These sinners were ostracized by the most religious who wanted nothing to do with them. From his first days of public activity in Galilee, or maybe even before when he was in Perea and Judaea, Jesus was willing to sit down with tax collectors, people stigmatized for their means of employment, in which it was easy to act unjustly and commit fraud. Together with his disciples, Jesus was willing to share a table with all of them, to the protests and disbelief of the Pharisees who could not understand his behavior (Mark 2:16 || Matt 9:11 || Luke 5:30).

Jesus, unlike John, did not wait for the sinners to come to him, wanting to repent and asking to be baptized. Jesus offered God's forgiveness with no strings attached and the possibility of a plentiful conversion. For example, toward the end of his public activities Jesus stayed at the house of Zacchaeus, the rich chief tax collector in Jericho. Zacchaeus welcomed him with open arms and saw Jesus' visit as the chance to change his life and become a sedentary disciple (see 4.5.3.2). The chief tax collector was forgiven because, as Jesus said, "he also is a son of Abraham" (Luke 19:9). Another marginalized individual was also a daughter of Abraham, the hunched woman, who had as much right as Zacchaeus to regain her freedom, not from riches but from Satan, who had had her "bound for eighteen years" (Luke 13:16). As the Baptist had already said, "God is able from these stones to raise up children to Abraham" (Matt 3:9 || Luke 3:8). Renewed and liberated children may arise from among these people who were like stones, made hard by sin or illness. An image previously employed by the Baptist reappeared in a new form in the hands of Jesus, his former follower.

Jesus' willingness to go to sinners and offer them God's forgiveness explains why his activities no longer centered on baptisms, as John's did. Jesus decided against the ascetic lifestyle and mixed with the men and women of his time, making the sharing of the meal table an important part of his mission. He distanced himself from John because he saw God's forgiveness not as something in the future but as something that had to be proclaimed and offered to everyone immediately in their daily life, wherever they were. The rabbi, John the Baptist, traveled through the desert valley of the Jordan and settled in places with plentiful water for the baptisms (John 3:23). Jesus was also a traveling rabbi, who "has nowhere to lay his head," but he traveled through the populated areas of Galilee and the neighboring lands of Perea, Judaea, and Jerusalem, looking for people and being looked for by people to whom he proclaimed the arrival of the Kingdom of God.

The proclamation of the Kingdom, this good news, this gospel, dominated his activities, and John's ritual baptisms were superseded by the word, by a call to repent, by miracles that freed the body and spirit, and by a way of life that involved close contact with everyone, the good and the sinful, the upright and untrustworthy. Those who wanted to criticize him accused him of being "a glutton and a drunkard, a friend of tax collectors and sinners" (Matt 11:19 || Luke 7:34). The ritual baptisms and the ascetic lifestyle of John were overly restrictive for Jesus, who focused his life on communicating extraordinary news. The power of God, his compassion and forgiveness, illuminated this world, specifically through the life and works of the Master of Nazareth. The disciples of Jesus, the former follower of the Baptist, were soon more than four or five Galileans and former disciples of John who had decided to join up with the Galilean rabbi. Rather, they developed into a group of people, some called by him (the Twelve) and some constant or temporary followers who wanted to share in a prayer. These followers asked Jesus, "Lord, teach us to pray, as John taught his disciples" (Luke 11:1), and Jesus taught them the Lord's Prayer (Luke 11:2-4).

4.5.2.3. John, Martyred Prophet

John the Baptist's arrest probably took place in mid-28 A.D. The man responsible was Herod Antipas, tetrarch of Perea, the land where John had lived and carried out his activities. According to Luke (3:1-6), the region to the east of the river Jordan had been the setting for his preaching and baptisms since he started his activities (October of 27 A.D.) and remained so until around Passover of the following year. However, when Jesus returned to his former guide, after Passover of 28 A.D., which he had spent in Jerusalem, John was no longer baptizing in Bethany of Perea (John 1:28) but had moved to the west bank of the Jordan, to the town of Aenon, some 10 kilometers to the south of Scythopolis, part of the Decapolis. John the Baptist's problems with Antipas had just begun.

The conflict between the Baptist, who had until that point lived in Perea, and the sovereign Antipas is recounted by Josephus (*A.J.* 18:109–19) and by the Gospels (Mark 6:17-29; Matt 14:1-12). The conflict was above all due to politics: according to Josephus, Antipas was alarmed as he thought that the Baptist could lead a great number of people and "raise a rebellion (stasis)." Antipas, seeing that John had become a leader of the people, decided to have him eliminated "to prevent any mischief he might cause." The sovereign feared that the situation could get out of control and had John imprisoned.

However, what did John say that made Antipas fear a people's rebellion? John had not organized any form of political group, much less an armed one, designed to overthrow Antipas. Proof of this is that the tetrarch simply had him imprisoned, not judged. His followers were not affected in any way; indeed, they were free to visit their master in prison. Josephus does not give details about this point, but the Gospels are more specific and state that the conflict was fruit of the Baptist's publicly decrying Herod's behavior, as he had separated from his wife and now lived with "his brother Philip's wife," Herodias (Mark 6:17). This contravened the precept in God's Law: "You shall not uncover the nakedness of your brother's wife; she is your brother's nakedness" (Lev 18:16). For this reason the Baptist openly criticized the behavior of his ruler, Antipas, whom he reproached, saying, "It is not lawful for you to have your brother's wife" (Mark 6:18).

Josephus describes the background of this incident. Antipas had been married for some time to the daughter of the Nabatean king Aretas, whose kingdom bordered Perea. Probably around 20–25 A.D., Antipas fell in love with Herodias, wife of a Herod (but not Herod Philip, as both Mark and Matthew assume!), son of Herod the Great and his half brother. Antipas lived with someone who was both his sister-in-law and niece, since Herodias was the daughter of Aristobulus, another of Antipas' half brothers. When Herodias left her husband to be with Antipas, she had already had a daughter, Salome, who would marry the tetrarch Philip, yet another of Antipas' half brothers. When John was imprisoned and executed on Antipas' orders, both mother and daughter were married to two half brothers who were tetrarchs: Herodias to Antipas (to whom she was also his niece) and Salome to Philip (to whom she was also his great-niece). Given the complexity of the relations and matrimonial unions within the family of King Herod (who had ten wives!), it is understandable that the tradition in Mark and Matthew confused things: Herodias "became" Philip's wife when, in fact, Philip's wife was her daughter, Salome. Luke does not seem to make the same mistake (3:19).

In the words of Josephus, Herodias "divorced her husband while he was alive," and this was seen by the Jewish historian as "confounding the laws of our country," going against the Jewish Law (*A.J.* 18:136). It is a unique case in the extensive family of King Herod, which Josephus recounted with great displeasure. Josephus and the Gospel of Mark (chap. 6) thus coincide, though the Gospel focuses on the deeds of Antipas and Josephus centers on those of Herodias.

The harsh criticism by the Jewish historian of the union of Antipas and Herodias leads us to believe that this illegitimate marriage, denounced by a man of prophetic word and deed such as John, must have been one of the causes (but not the only one!) for Antipas' imprisonment of John. The Baptist was seen as the instigator of a possible uprising against him. A man such as John, who felt akin to the prophets of Israel, would have felt unable to hold his tongue when faced with arbitrary acts and abuse of the people by those in power: his call for justice must have resounded throughout the region of the Jordan. John was both admired and feared by Antipas, who had conflicting feelings when it came to John: he respected and even "gladly" listened to him, though "he was much perplexed" by him (Mark 6:20). Antipas recognized John's holiness, but he knew that he could represent problems for him and had him imprisoned.

Herodias, the person responsible for Antipas' matrimonial situation, was single-minded in her determination to take revenge on John. Herodias had left her first husband and plotted the whole affair. When faced with the Baptist's criticism, she convinced Antipas to have him imprisoned. Herodias was an energetic and highly ambitious woman, and she could not stand the Baptist's attacks, which touched a raw nerve in her and placed Antipas at a disadvantage before his subjects. Herodias' suspicions were not misplaced. According to Josephus, Jewish religious sensibilities did not appreciate the governor's open transgression of the Law and his moral conduct being the source of scandal. The Baptist's words not only were at heart an attack on an inadmissible flouting of Jewish Law, which Antipas and Herodias were obliged to respect, but also represented the *vox populi*, indignant at the arrogant nonobservance of these requirements. Indeed, these accusations had clear political implications, since Antipas would have been stripped of all authority before his subjects, the great majority of whom were Jews. In the words of B. Chilton, an illegitimate union signified an illegitimate government.

The Baptist's criticism raised a furor because it also affected the political balance between Antipas and Aretas, badly damaged by Antipas' betrayal of Aretas' daughter. Josephus explains how Antipas' first wife, having been betrayed by her husband, managed to escape from him and get to Machaerus, a fort located near the border between Perea and Nabatea. From there she was accompanied to her father's house (*A.J.* 18:111–12). Aretas' daughter left Antipas in a difficult position, as he was never able to gain a divorce and legitimately marry Herodias. The Baptist was preaching shortly after these events took place, when popular displeasure with Antipas was at its height and Aretas' hostility toward him evident.

These events did not leave the people indifferent, and this can be seen some years later, in 36 A.D., when Aretas and Antipas confronted each other over a border dispute and Aretas destroyed Antipas' troops (*A.J.* 18:113–14). For Aretas, this represented revenge for the insult his daughter had suffered. "Some of the Jews thought that the destruction of Herod's [Antipas'] army came from God, and that very justly, as a punishment of what he did against John, that was called the Baptist" (*A.J.* 18:116). This occurred seven or eight years after Antipas had had the prophet from the Judaean wilderness executed, at the request of Herodias, for having dared to publicly criticize their conduct.

Josephus recounts the execution: "Accordingly he [John] was sent a prisoner, out of Herod's suspicious temper, to Macherus, the castle . . . and was there put to death" (*A.J.* 18:119). Political reasons were behind John's imprisonment, but his execution was probably due to Herodias' personal motivations. Political and personal reasons underlie the Baptist's criticism of Antipas' behavior. John's voice was silenced as soon as he was imprisoned, despite continued contact with his disciples. They were able to visit him in prison and buried his body after his execution. John's execution took place some months after his imprisonment and can be attributed to pressure from Herodias, a personal enemy of the prophet.

According to Mark's (6:17-29) description of the Baptist's execution, it was Herodias who was in command: she decided, de facto, on John's death, and Antipas had to yield before her; he was forced to give in, having sworn solemnly before his guests at his fiftieth birthday celebration. His guests were "courtiers and officers and the leading men of Galilee" (Mark 6:21), the administration, army, and aristocracy of Antipas' tetrarchy, comprising the lands of Galilee and Perea. Mark mentions only Galilee and its capital Tiberias (also Luke 3:1 and *A.J.* 18:136) as the scene of the birthday celebration. However, according to Josephus, the setting is Machaerus, the great fort on the shores of the Dead Sea, in the dungeons of which John was held. All the guests from around the tetrarchy and possibly from abroad had come here to the far south of Perea.

The birthday celebrations for Antipas and the execution of the Baptist have been tampered with by the popular tradition from John the Baptist's disciples, and to which only Mark (6:17-29) and Matthew (14:3-13) make reference. Josephus does not mention it and says only that Antipas ordered John's execution. The scene centered on a girl, possibly Herodias' daughter, who entered the room full of all of Antipas' male guests and danced in front of them. Everyone was charmed by the dance. Antipas, a mere tetrarch, made a grandiloquent gesture in the style of a great king. In front of his guests, he swore he would give the girl whatever she demanded. The girl went off to find her mother, the hostess of the celebrations, Herodias, alongside other women. Herodias told her without a second thought that she should ask for "the head of John the baptizer" (Mark 6:24). Shortly after, the Baptist's head was presented on a platter to Herodias, his deadly enemy, who managed to silence the prophet from the Jordan forever.

The legend of the martyrdom, passed down orally, was added to and modified over the years. The most notable aspect was the identification of the "girl" (*korasion*) (Mark 6:22) who danced before Antipas as Salome, Herodias' daughter. At this point she was already the young wife of Philip, Antipas' brother and tetrarch of Trachonitis. It was well within the realm of possibility that a married woman would dance at a party in front of her brother-in-law/uncle/stepfather and his guests. It is also quite possible that one of the guests was Salome, his sister-in-law and daughter of Herodias, his wife: there were certainly enough justification in terms of their family ties! But we can also argue that this famous dance was not performed by Salome but by a young dancer, a "girl," as it states in Mark 6, whom Salome had brought with her to the party in order to dance in honor of Antipas and his guests. Popular tradition may well have unified these two figures (Salome and the dancer), which led to only one of them appearing in Mark's narrative.

The additions do not end here. The phrase "I will give you, even half of my kingdom" (Mark 6:23), addressed by Antipas to Herodias' daughter, is another addition and a sign of the popular hyperbolic tone. As G. Theissen points out, a similar phrase appears in another popular narrative, the book of Esther, where it is put into the mouth of Xerxes, the Persian king (5:3, 7:2). The observation that Herod Antipas was "sorry" (Mark 6:26) when he became aware that he had to fulfill his oath and execute the Baptist may be another popular addition designed to stress Herodias' evil. This ambitious and vengeful princess was, in fact, responsible for the death of "this righteous and holy man," as it says in Mark's narrative (6:20), whose only fault had been to criticize a serious transgression of the Law.

Matthew and Mark characterize Herodias as a perverse figure, while Antipas is absolved of responsibility, an admirer of the holy man, but forced to yield to his evil wife. Of course, Antipas was ultimately responsible for the Baptist's death. The historical sources are unanimous; it was Antipas who ordered John's decapitation (Mark 6:16; *A.J.* 18:119) and subsequently tried to kill Jesus (Luke 13:31; Matt 14:13).

The popular feelings regarding the violent death of the Baptist are described in the Gospels of Mark and Matthew and in the writings of Josephus. Mark (6:17-29) and Matthew (14:3-13) attack the figure of Herodias, presenting her as the figure who pulled the strings, rather than the inept Antipas who ended up having to execute John, almost against his own wishes. This narrative, which probably comes from the Baptist's disciples, is based on actual events (Herodias openly declared herself an enemy of the Baptist's!), though it has been revised and added to with certain sections that resemble the literary genre of the "courtly anecdote." Popular sentiment is also described by Josephus. The execution of the Baptist inspired sorrow and anger in the people, and these feelings remained for quite some time. The military defeat suffered by Antipas at the hands of Aretas in 36 A.D. was seen by many as divine punishment for his killing the Baptist (*A.J.* 18:116). Josephus also interprets Antipas' forced abdication and exile three years later (39 A.D.) as God's punishment for Herodias and Antipas: "And thus did God punish Herodias for her envy at her brother [whom the emperor had just given Antipas' tetrarchy], and Herod also for giving ear to the vain discourses of a woman" (*A.J.* 18:255). This was a reminder to the people of the Baptist, the martyred prophet, who had died at the hands of the unjust, the evil, and the powerful.

4.5.3. HIS FOLLOWERS

In the Gospels, the terms "follower" and "to follow" describe various ways of relating to Jesus. Those who are relatively distant or very close to him are said to follow him, listening to him and witnessing the prodigious deeds he performs. Despite the wide variety, they are all known as followers. The majority of experts writing currently distinguish among three groups or circles of people linked to Jesus in a variety of ways.

First, Jesus was surrounded by an outer, more numerous circle comprising the "multitudes" (*okhloi*), a term used by the Gospels to describe the general public who are attracted to him. Members of this circle are occasionally mentioned.

Second, there was an intermediate circle, the "disciples" (*mathētai*), men and women who felt closely linked to Jesus and accepted the difficulties and ostracism that loyalty to him entailed. There were two types of disciple: those who stayed in one place and those who traveled around. Those who stayed in one place continued to live with their families and offered support and accommodation for the traveling disciples. On occasions, they might go to be with Jesus and his traveling companions. The other type of disciples traveled round with Jesus under his guidance, while he proclaimed the Kingdom of God with his words and healings. The traveling disciples had left their homes, families, and jobs to share in Jesus' lifestyle. Among these traveling disciples, were people who had chosen to be Jesus' disciples and welcomed into this group by him and those whom he had called to be with him.

Third, there was the group of Twelve men whom Jesus had called directly to permanently take part in the whole life of the rabbi of Nazareth and who formed their own separate group within the disciples. Jesus occasionally sent them to announce the Kingdom and to heal the sick. This special group of disciples became known as "the Twelve" (*hoi dōdeka*), as it was made up of twelve people, and we know the name of each.

4.5.3.1. The Wider Circle: The People

The people surrounding Jesus were all very different, but the activities carried out by Jesus had a common backdrop: the crowds that followed him. The people who heard Jesus speak were never left indifferent; they were enthusiastic and reflective, taken up and brought back down. The healing of the bodily and spiritually ill, in particular, attracted lots of people: words and deeds were alternated, complementing each other in Jesus' activities (John 6:2). The firsthand witnesses of his words and actions praised and admired him. Jesus created an attractive force that took shape in those who listened to him, which he did not take advantage of for his own gain. Rather, he tried to ensure that the people held God above everything else in their lives. When a woman praised him by blessing his mother ("Blessed is the womb that bore you, and the breasts that you sucked!"), Jesus replied, "Blessed rather are those who hear the word of God and keep it!" (Luke 11:27-28).

While the Gospels overstate the people's positive reactions, especially regarding the miracles, people did go to great lengths to get to Jesus. At Capernaum, many people crowded before the doorway of the house where the Master and his disciples were staying (Mark 3:20); by the lake, Jesus had to get on a boat to escape the crush of people and be able speak without interruptions (Mark 3:9). People also pressed at the door of the house of Jairus, whose daughter had died. From among the crowd, a woman managed to get near to Jesus from behind and touch his cloak. Jesus realized this, and his disciples asked, "You see the crowd pressing around you, and yet you say, 'Who touched me?'" (Mark 5:31). People traveling around searching for Jesus were commonplace. One particular incident is the feeding of the five thousand: they knew where they had to go and, quickly, "they ran there on foot from all the towns, and got there ahead of them [Jesus and his disciples]" (Mark 6:33; likewise, John 6:5). People liked being near Jesus, and according to the Gospel of Mark, the rabbi from Nazareth pitied them all, "because they were like sheep without a shepherd" (6:34).

Jesus' ability to attract multitudes is not limited to his activities in Galilee, the setting for the aforementioned texts, but can also be seen on his visits to Jerusalem. People gladly listened to Jesus, hanging on to his every word. This led the religious leaders to admit their discomfort and to say that the only people who believed in Jesus were "this crowd, who do not know the Law, [and] are accursed" (John 7:49). Toward the end of Jesus' activities in Jerusalem and the surrounding area, people continued to come to him, captivated by his miracles and preaching. The climax to this feeling of mutual sympathy came with Jesus' triumphal entrance to Jerusalem, a few days before his death. A great number of people, with palms in their hands, hailed and acclaimed him as Israel's Messiah.

Jesus' success with the people is described by the Jewish historian Josephus, who wrote toward the end of the first century A.D., "[Jesus] drew over to him both many of the Jews and many of the Gentiles" (*A.J.* 18:63). The Jewish leaders must have been concerned by the positive attitude and enthusiasm of the people for Jesus. Therefore, crowds that accompanied him on his final entrance into Jerusalem may have been the last straw. Jesus' prestige among the people remained intact up until the last moment, and this undeniable fact determined the strategy of the Jerusalem authorities, who aimed to have him killed "[n]ot during the feast, lest there be a tumult of the people" (Mark 14:2) (see 6.2.1.1).

Jesus, like the Baptist and other popular prophetic figures who came after him (Theudas and the Egyptian), mobilized the people, inspired them, and filled them with hope. Josephus tells us how people listening to the Baptist "were very greatly moved by hearing his words" (*A.J.* 18:118). Theudas and the Egyptian convinced a great many people to follow them out into the Judaean Desert with the promise of a definitive prophetic sign that would bring an end to Roman domination (see 3.3.3.3). Jesus combined the strength of his words, in the style of the Baptist, with the messianic and prophetic force of his amazing healings. His was a language that the crowds in Galilee, Perea, and Judaea could understand. The two triumphant and climactic events in Jesus' life, the feeding of the five thousand in Galilee and his spectacular entrance into Jerusalem, were accompanied by similar reactions from the people: Jesus was acclaimed as the Messiah, David's descendant, the king of Israel, and the prophet they had been waiting for. This was the reaction of the thousands of people whom he fed (John 6:15); and this was way he was hailed by the crowds when he entered the holy city: "Blessed is he who comes in the name of the Lord!" (Mark 11:9 || Matt 21:9 || Luke 19:38 ||

John 12:13). However, Jesus did not allow them to make him king: in Galilee "Jesus withdrew again to the mountain by himself" (John 6:15), and after his triumphant entrance into Jerusalem, he left the city and went to Bethany (Mark 11:11; John 12:36).

We do not know to what extent Jesus' refusal to be considered a king led to disenchantment among his sympathizers. John (6:66) even goes so far as to say that "after this many of his disciples drew back and no longer went about with him." The only thing that seems certain is that there was a definite before and after in terms of Jesus' activities and the boom in his popularity surrounding the feeding of the five thousand (see 4.6.2, below). As we shall see, from this point on, Jesus changed his plans and, initially, avoided spending too much time in Galilee, up until then the land where he had centered his activities. Rather than the people defecting, we need to take into account the political reasons (the dangers represented by Antipas) that led him to leave Galilee or, at least, to get away temporarily. Jesus did return to Galilee from time to time and came into contact with the people, but as time went by he spent less and less time there, of his own volition (Mark 9:30).

The people's feelings for Jesus were fickle and inconsistent. The extraordinary deeds and healings that he carried out attracted people, but they did not lead to important changes in their lifestyles or attitudes (see 5.1.1.5). The most symbolic case concerned the towns near the lake where Jesus often preached: Capernaum, Chorazin, and Bethsaida. The townspeople had been privileged witnesses to Jesus' activities but had reacted indifferently (Matt 11:20-24 || Luke 10:12-15). With the zeal of the ancient prophets, he compared the small Galilean towns of Chorazin and Bethsaida to the two large, rich, and proud Phoenician cities of Tyre and Sidon. Capernaum, the luckiest of all and the center for Jesus' activities, was compared to Sodom, the city that had come to symbolize sin and depravation and was destroyed by fire and brimstone raining down from heaven, according to biblical tradition (Isa 23 and Gen 19:1-29). The conclusion was that Judgment Day would be more comfortable in these three foreign cities than in the three Galilean towns (Matt 11:20-24 || Luke 10:12-15).

The image of the boys playing in the square exemplified the attitude of "this generation": people who paid no attention to what was being said to them, who did not want to dance or laugh, who dismissed the ascetic lifestyle of the Baptist as that of someone possessed but also dismissed Jesus' lifestyle, considering him a glutton and a drunkard because he ate and drank in the company of sinners. People were reluctant to change their ways and cruelly criticized the prophets who preached repentance, whether in the wilderness (John the Baptist) or, like Jesus, in their own town squares (Matt 11:16-19 || Luke 7:35). They justified their lack of belief because they expected and demanded a sign from the heavens: a cosmic, definitive, and spectacular omen to indicate that Jesus really had been sent by God. Only thus could they believe in him and know that his words were worth paying heed to. Only then they would change. Nonetheless, Jesus refused to give them any such proof (Mark 8:11-12; also John 6:30; Matt 16:4).

This was the reasoning used by the people to justify their insensitivity to the words and invitation offered by Jesus. The problem was not something on the outside but within, in their hearts. They had the sign right in front of their eyes: if the Galileans only had known how to see it, they would have understood that Jesus' calling them to repent was echoing and adding to the calling that the prophet Jonah had addressed to the great city of Nineveh; and then they would have been able to overcome their indifference and self-sufficiency. The sign that they were looking for up in the heavens was down on earth in the words that Jesus spoke and the miracles he performed before them. They merely had to remember the example of the Queen of Sheba who went on a long journey just to hear the wisdom of Solomon (Matt 12:38-42 || Luke 11:29-32).

The people of Galilee were moved by the words and miracles of the rabbi of Nazareth, but they reacted lazily and unreceptively when it came to changing heart and their lifestyles. Despite their enthusiastic devotion at times, indifference and inertia characterized the people's attitude toward Jesus and his message. Jesus used the people in the parable of the sowing of the seeds; they are like the rocky ground "who, when they hear the word [the gospel], immediately receive it with joy; and they have no root in themselves, but endure for a while" (Mark 4:16-17). Jesus grew tired of "this generation" of nonbelievers, who were impervious to good and unable to change heart. He asked them somewhat ironically, "How long am I to be with you? How long am I to bear with you?" (Mark 9:19 || Matt 17:17 || Luke 9:41).

The point at which the fickle and arbitrary nature of the people's commitment to Jesus became most clear was during his trial before Pilate, the Roman governor. There, the people's sympathy for Jesus turned into hatred and the admiring praise turned into cries for him to be put to death. As we shall see (6.2.4.4 and 6.2.4.5), the Jewish authorities were particularly active in convincing people to demand Jesus' death (Mark 15:11 and Matt 27:20). The Jewish religious leaders had even made sure that there were people at their orders (the guards) or within their circle of influence who could tip the balance against him (John 19:6). Quite a number of the people had nothing to do with Jesus' trial. Many, including Jesus' disciples, went along with the tide of opinion, overcome with fear on seeing the decisiveness of the most conspicuous Jewish leaders in their desire to kill the Master. The people's silence is, however, easier to accept than the shameful way the disciples abandoned Jesus when he was arrested in the garden of Gethsemane.

4.5.3.2. The Intermediate Circle: The Disciples

Jesus was an unusual rabbi and teacher, as he did not keep to the school system: his teaching was itinerant, not always limited to his disciples but open to all those who wanted to listen. His invitations to people to listen were a common theme in his message: "He who has ears to hear, let him hear" (Mark 4:9 || Matt 13:9 || Luke 8:8). In one, highly significant, scene described only in the Gospel of Luke (10:38-42), Jesus visited the house of Martha and Mary, sisters of Lazarus. Martha complained to Jesus that Mary did nothing but listen to him instead of helping her to prepare what was to be given to their Master and friend. Jesus reminded Martha that listening is the only thing she needed to do. Listening to Jesus' words was more important than her anxiety, which seemed completely justified, as Mary had indeed chosen "the good portion." The identity of a disciple is shaped in terms of the words of the Master, which have to be listened to and experienced.

Jesus normally preached in public places, in buildings (such as the synagogue) or in the open air (a hill, road, or lakeside), but he also preached in private places (including homes). Jesus was not the head of any school or center for study, as his desire was not to teach a few students intellectually in the art of interpreting the Law; competent and renowned rabbis would come in the future. Jesus did not limit himself to a doctrinal message. He was a prophet, like the Baptist, but unlike him, he was also a healer, someone to whom many people came asking him to cure their body and spirit. Nevertheless, he did not manage a therapeutic center in one fixed place, like Aesclepius' sanctuaries in the Greek world, where the ill would go to be cured. He was a wandering preacher and lived with people, ate with them, and was within their reach, which meant they could find him easily.

As M. Hengel stresses, Jesus' disciples were able to establish a unique personal relationship with the Master, not only because many of them shared his nomadic lifestyle but also because their devotion was based on a permanent and stable relationship. The disciples were the "receptacle" for what Jesus said and did, and they represented the start of a tradition that would breathe life into the early Church and make the texts possible that we know today as the Gospels. They were the living memory of the teacher, as had been the disciples of the great rabbis of the time, Hillel and Shammai, or as had been the disciples of Epicurius, the Greek philosopher (341–271 B.C.). According to Diogenes Laertius, they were trained to memorize the writings of their teacher (10:12).

Jesus' disciples, itinerant or sedentary, had to make a wholehearted commitment to the Master and his activities. This tight bond was based on their voluntary decision and came in response to a calling they had received. It signified that they accepted their link to him. This link made them part of his spirit, and they entered a personal relationship with Jesus. The demands were great for both the itinerant and sedentary disciples: in the words of Matthew (5:13-14), disciples are called to be "the salt of the earth" and "light of the world," someone to bring happiness and warmth to the world. This calling is not in any way vainglorious, however: at the end of the day, the servants of the word acknowledged that they did not deserve any reward, as, they said, "we have only done what was our duty" (Luke 17:10).

What did being one of Jesus' disciples mean? The first evidence is found in Mark (8:34) and, slightly differently, in the Q source (Matt 10:38 || Luke 14:27). Mark's version states, "If any man would come after me, let him deny himself and take up his cross and follow me" (the same as Matt 16:24 and almost the same as Luke 9:23). Those who wanted to follow Jesus, who wanted to go with him and join him, had to say no to love for love's sake, had to relegate their own interests and ego. They had to deny themselves. Those who wanted to be disciples had to carry their own cross, the cross of the disciples; they had to place Jesus and the gospel above all else in this world. As life, the family, and one's own interests seem to be untouchable, Jesus described self-denial as the ostracism and shame of someone condemned to death. The image Jesus chose was no coincidence, given the way he himself was to die. However, the image of carrying one's own cross was not intended to be the way in which the disciples were to die but the way in which they had to live: by denying themselves. The idea of suffering is not the focus here, despite the reference to the cross. It should be linked to the text of the soprano's first aria in J. S. Bach's St. John Passion, which says, "I follow thee also with joyful step." This is the life of a disciple.

The paradoxical tone suggested by the above (those who wish to live as a disciple have to renounce living their lives in terms of their own ego) echoes another short and cutting statement from Jesus: "For whoever would save his life will lose it, and whoever loses his life [for my sake and the gospel's] will save it" (Mark 8:35). A similar statement also appears in the Q source (Matt 10:39 || Luke 17:33), and even in the Gospel of John (12:25). The square brackets around the phrase "for my sake and the gospel's" indicate that it was probably added by Mark with the intention of making the somewhat hermetic aphorism clearer. The addition helps people understand what was meant by "loses his life." It is the opposite of throwing it away or wasting it, ruining it for no reason or reward. The Gospel of Mark stresses that losing one's life means giving it up to Jesus and the gospel; thus, those who give it up preserve it and save it. The Gospel of John accentuates this paradox as much as possible: "He who loves his life loses it" (12:25). Those who truly want to love themselves and value their lives will lose their lives: love means not loving one's own ego but ignoring it. Whoever looks at life in terms of giving and losing will keep it forever. As John writes, taking up the idea found in Mark and Q, "[H]e who hates his life in this world will keep it for eternal life" (12:25).

When a life centered on love for oneself comes apart because of Jesus, the most immediate consequences affect the family. Disciples' strong commitment to Jesus leads to difficulties within their own home, whether they decide to leave or stay there. As S. Guijarro has shown, the family in rural Mediterranean societies plays a vital role as a cohesion and support structure. The institution of the family is held in high regard in Mediterranean countries even today. This is the background in first-century Galilee to the surprising statement found in the Q source: "If any one comes to me and does not hate his own father and mother and wife and children and brothers and sisters, yes, and even his own life, he cannot be my disciple" (Luke 14:26 || Matt 10:37). The strength of this phrase would have led to Matthew's assiduously replacing the verb hate with love more. The force expressed in this sentence in Luke shows that Jesus absolutely insisted on the principle of his disciples' commitment to Christianity ahead of their closest relatives. Blood ties are relegated when it comes to the commitment involved in following Jesus. The proclaiming of the Kingdom of God, the gospel, cannot wait.

In this conflict and division within the family itself, one question changes everything for those that have to answer it: "Do you think that I have come to give peace on earth?" (Luke 12:51). Out of context, this question does not make any sense as it is diametrically opposed to the happiness of those who bring peace. However, we need to consider what Jesus expected of his followers: this question warns people that their own families may impede their becoming a disciple. Jesus does not hide the difficulties that disciples will have with their families, to the point where division takes place between close relatives, people living under the same roof: fathers and sons, mothers and daughters, mothers-in-law and daughters-in-law. His words, reported in the Q source (Matt 10:35 || Luke 12:52-53), can be applied both to the sedentary disciples who accommodate the nomadic disciples in their homes and to those disciples who have left the family home.

The disciples' attitude toward their families was again mentioned by Jesus, in possibly even more surprising and exaggerated terms than the two above occasions, again in the Q source (Matt 9:21-22 || Luke 9:59-60). On the first occasion disciples' denial of their love for their closest relatives (parents, wife, children, brothers and sisters) was the priority in life; on the second occasion, he warned them of the consequences—serious conflicts within the families themselves (between fathers and sons, mothers and daughters, mothers-in-law and daughters-in-law). But now he questioned whether the role of disciple should be deemed more important than the burial of one's own father.

Ensuring one's father had a worthy burial and keeping the corresponding seven days of mourning were two of the most sacrosanct filial duties in Mediterranean societies and regulated by the fourth commandment of the Law ("honor your father and mother") (*A.J.* 17:200). A prospective disciple asked Jesus to be allowed to go home first (far from where they were?) to bury his father, lament for him as the customs decreed, and finally to return to join the disciples; he received this cutting response from Jesus: "Leave the dead to bury their own dead." He need not worry. His father will not go without the burial and mourning that he deserves, but there is only one thing to be done now: "go and proclaim the kingdom of God" (Luke 9:60). Time cannot be wasted on anything else.

With these exaggerated phrases and expressions, full of dialectic force, Jesus aimed to put the role of the family in a disciple's life into perspective and stressed that devotion to him and his project was central. For Jesus, the fulfillment of family duties is probably the greatest obstacle for those who want to become a disciple, for those who want to place the cause, the Kingdom of God, above all else. In the ancient world, the family kept people's life together (emotionally, socially, economically, and even the religious aspects of their life), providing them with identity, protection, and status. In first-century Galilee, Jesus' words on self-denial required breaking away completely from the interests of one's family, seen as paramount. Those who joined Jesus took on another identity: they were disciples. This identity, in a complex world, was a blend of purity of heart and a sense of reality: "be wise as serpents and innocent as doves" (Matt 10:16).

The itinerant disciples

Jesus was accompanied by a group of people who shared his nomadic lifestyle. The unity of Jesus' life and that of his disciples was complete: "He who receives you receives me" (Matt 10:40). Jesus had left his home, his family, and the town he grew up in, Nazareth, and the disciples knew that they had to do something similar. One of them said to him, "I will follow you wherever you go" (Matt 8:19 || Luke 9:57). Jesus' response reminded him that his followers would have no fixed home. The disciples had to stay wherever they could, wherever they were put up and fed, but unlike the birds that have their nests and foxes that have their holes, the disciples, like their Master, had nowhere to call their home: "[T]he Son of man has nowhere to lay his head" (Matt 8:20 || Luke 9:58 || Thomas 86).

Certain houses were used as refuges or lived in temporarily, for example, the house in Capernaum where Peter's mother-in-law, who was healed by Jesus, lived, the house that Mark calls "the house of Simon (Peter) and Andrew." There was the house that Jesus lived in provisionally when he was in the land of Tyre (Mark 7:20). Jesus spent time with his disciples in other houses in unnamed places and regions (Mark 7:17, 9:28). But the group had no fixed abode. The scene of the disciples eating the heads of grain they had gathered as they passed through the fields on the Sabbath was a clear example of this (Mark 2:23). The image represented the nomadic lifestyle of Jesus and his disciples, evidenced by the instructions to the disciples regarding their mission in the towns of Galilee: when they arrived in a town, they were to find a house where the family was willing to put them up, where they were to stay until they left the town.

Leaving home and physically following Jesus also meant leaving their families and jobs. There was another role model to follow here. The carpenter from Nazareth lived as a wandering prophet. Those who accompanied had to leave everything and follow him. Peter made this clear when he spoke for all the disciples on one occasion (Mark 10:28-29). Jesus answered his question by stating all that the disciples had left behind: their homes ("house"), families ("brothers or sisters or mother or father or children"), and jobs ("fields"). His response culminated in the abundant present, in which they were to receive one hundred times more than what they had, and a future of "eternal life" (Mark 10:30).

The reference to the "fields" leads us to think that most of the disciples came from farming families, but four of the group of Twelve (Simon and Andrew, James and John) were fishermen; these left behind the "nets," or "their father Zebedee in the boat with the hired servants" (Mark 1:18, 1:20), in the case of the last two. Work and family go together. Separation from the family requires a firm decision. As soon as this decision had been taken, there was no looking back, in the same way that, as soon as you have your hand on the plow the harvest has begun, your eyes can look only forward. Jesus used this agricultural image to respond to a man who wanted to become a disciple but first wanted to say goodbye to his family: devotion to Jesus and his mission was a decision that did not allow for any form of hesitation or second thoughts (Luke 9:61-62).

Jesus' call was direct and personal and required an immediate response. There was no time for dithering. A disciple of Jesus was overtaken by his loyalty to the Master. There was an exclusivity that could seem exaggerated or even disrespectful with regard to people's liberties. This is, however, an unjustified reaction. Not all those called to follow Jesus and become a wandering disciple took up the opportunity.

The Twelve did respond positively, although one of them, Judas, would betray him in the end. Other people also responded favorably, but we have less information on these, for example, a publican sitting in the tax collection office in Capernaum, Levi, son of Alphaeus. Jesus invited him to follow him, and Levi left his job (Mark 2:13-14). Two other Galileans were a similar case: Joseph Barsabbas, "the Just," and Matthias, who, as Luke explains in the Acts of the Apostles (1:21), had accompanied Jesus since "the baptism of John," from the start of his public activities to Jerusalem. Matthias was chosen to replace Judas in the group of the Twelve. Cleopas, probably Jesus' paternal uncle, a Galilean from Nazareth and married to Mary, was also linked to the group of disciples and was also in Jerusalem with his wife around the time of Jesus' death (Luke 24:18; John 19:25). The Q source reports the case of an unnamed disciple invited by Jesus to follow him, but we do not know whether he took up Jesus' offer or went to bury his father, as he initially wanted (Matt 8:22 || Luke 9:59).

The case of a rich man is a resounding failure. Jesus called him to be his disciple, but dispirited due to the amount of things he had amassed, he went away sad and dejected (Mark 10:17-21). Others were volunteers, and it was up to Jesus to set the conditions for their acceptance or to remind them of what they were committing themselves to. Some of the people Jesus healed may have ended up joining the group of traveling disciples. This may have been the case with the blind man Bartimaeus (Mark 10:52). Similarly, there were the women cured of their bodily and spiritual ills: Mary Magdalene, Joanna, the wife of one of Antipas' high-ranking officials, and Susanna (Luke 8:1-3). We shall look at this point again later on.

Jesus saw his disciples as people willing to put their own lives on hold in order to form part of his project. Jesus' closest model was the prophet Elijah. This great prophet of Israel went to find Elisha, a peasant who was plowing with some oxen, and "cast his mantle upon him" as a sign that he had chosen him as his disciple. Elisha had no second thoughts and immediately ran after Elijah, whom he asked only to say goodbye to his mother and father. The yoke he was plowing with was used as firewood to cook the meat of the oxen, and everyone was invited to a great feast. Elisha left his family and job: "[H]e arose and went after Elijah, and ministered to him" (1 Kgs 19:21). As with Jesus and his disciples, Elijah and his disciple Elisha had no fixed abode and, full of prophetic spirit, healed the sick miraculously. Jesus, however, did not aim to confront the rulers of his time, unlike Elijah. He stood up to the kings Ahab and Ahaziah, and Elisha took an active part in political affairs, crowning kings such as Jehu and Hazael.

The main aim of Jesus' activities was to proclaim the Kingdom of God to everyone, to all those who wanted to listen. This was also the disciples' task when they were sent out as missionaries. The Gospel according to Luke refers to the mission of seventy-two of these disciples. In addition to the Twelve, Jesus may have sent others to proclaim the Kingdom of God (Luke 10:1, 10:17). Clearly the mission to spread the Gospel could take up one's whole life and would have required sustenance: "for the laborer deserves his wages" (Luke 10:7; Matt 10:10; 1 Cor 9:14; 1 Tim 5:17-18; First Epistle of Clement 13:1-2). This was common practice among the early Christian communities. The proclamation of the Kingdom of God could not wait. Action was required quickly and urgently; nothing could be hidden and no time lost: "[W]hat you hear whispered, proclaim upon the housetops" (Matt 10:27). Elijah may have allowed Elisha to say goodbye to his parents before changing his life and following him, but Jesus was more radical: "No one who puts his hand to the plow and looks back is fit for the Kingdom of God" (Luke 9:62).

The sedentary disciples

In addition to Jesus' nomadic disciples, some did not leave their families, homes, and jobs but felt deeply committed to the Master and his project anyway. These people provided open houses and traveled to hear Jesus speak. Their fundamental contribution was the hospitality they offered Jesus and his disciples. This contribution was not insignificant, as Jesus and his itinerant disciples were not a group of aimless globetrotters but a group of missionaries who traveled from place to place with a specific message to communicate and healings to carry out.

Jesus' life model is not, as J. D. Crossan proposes, that of the cynical philosophers of the Greek world. Jesus and his disciples did not ask for charity; they relied on the support of others in the houses of friends, who offered their hospitality and their belongings. Jesus did not believe in social upheaval, or organizations that ridiculed the rich or showed disrespect for marriage. He did not advocate things that caused misery, nor did he respect only the laws of nature or admire people who lived arrogantly as beings apart. As G. Barbaglio rightly points out, Jesus was by no means like the self-sufficient, self-satisfied individuals who show off their superiority: "What do I want? Am I not without sorrow? Am I not without fear? Am I not free?" These words from Epictetus (*Discourses* 3:22:48) show the distance between the cynics' ideal (imperturbability) and the path that Jesus showed his disciples (self-denial, the gaining of one's life by losing it). The undoubted similarities with regard to some specific points, including riches or inner freedom, should not blind us to the fundamental differences: a life of self-sufficiency, such as that put forward by the cynics, has little in common with a life in which God is the focus and in which the essential inner feeling is trust in Him, expressed in terms of concern for others.

Jesus traveled around with a group of disciples who had given up everything to be with him and received support from a second group of people who continued to live at home but who offered their possessions to the Master. The phrase in Luke 14:33, which stresses giving up one's belongings for Jesus and those who are with him, applies to the followers who travel around with him and those who do not: "[W]hoever of you does not renounce all that he has cannot be my disciple." By doing so, they will gain new riches: "Let one who has become wealthy reign, and let one who has power renounce" (Thomas 81).

This twofold model of belonging also appears among the Essenes (see 3.3.2.4). The main group in the Essene community lived at Qumran by the Dead Sea, where they applied a strict monastic regime, were celibate, and shared their belongings. All who entered the community deposited what they had into a common fund. There were also

Essenes spread throughout the towns and cities, who were married and had property but who also showed impressive generosity toward the other members of the group, whether they lived at Qumran or not, offering them accommodation and support. The similarities to the model proposed by the Gospels are notable. However, Jesus did not ask for the belongings of his disciples who had left their homes and families to form part of communal reserves. The rich man called to be a disciple was asked to distribute the money from the sale of his belongings among the poor. The group's communal funds were fed by spontaneous offers that they received and not from the possessions that the disciples had deposited.

The people supporting Jesus were from two areas: Galilee and Jerusalem. The names we are given for the people from Galilee are, above all, of women: Mary Magdalene, Joanna, wife of Chuza, and Susanna (Luke 8:1-3), or Mary of Alphaeus, mother of James, one of the Twelve, and Joses (Mark 3:18, 15:40), and Salome, probably the mother of James and John, sons of Zebedee, two disciples from the group of Twelve (Matt 20:20, 27:56). We cannot be sure whether Simon the Pharisee, who may have lived in Magdala, should be included among the sedentary disciples. As for Jesus' accommodation, we know of the house in Capernaum that belonged to Peter and Andrew's family (Mark 1:29-31, 2:1, 9:33; Matt 17:25). Jesus may also have stayed with his disciples in Bethsaida, the town from which Peter, Andrew, and Philip came (Mark 6:45, 8:22; Luke 9:10).

We have a great deal of evidence for those who offered Jesus support in Jerusalem and the surrounding area. The majority came from the east of the city, toward the Jordan Valley. It was Zacchaeus, head of the tax collectors and comfortably off, who put Jesus up in Jericho, the most important city in the western part of the valley, according to Luke (19:1-10). Zacchaeus' case is particularly interesting, as Jesus took the initiative in staying in the house of someone he did not know personally. Zacchaeus had climbed to the top of a sycamore out of curiosity. Nothing makes us think that he wanted to invite Jesus to come and stay with him. It was Jesus who authoritatively made the suggestion, and Zacchaeus accepted immediately. This is spectacular, since this head of the tax collectors had publicly declared his faults and his repentance, which led him to return all the money he had made fraudulently (with an impressive addition: multiplying the amount by four!) and giving away half of his possessions to the poor. Jesus had asked another rich man to sell all his belongings and to give them to the poor and to join his traveling disciples, but he had turned down the offer. Zacchaeus, however, understood what Jesus was asking him to do; he understood his gospel and acted accordingly (see 5.2.2.1). Zacchaeus is probably the model sedentary disciple.

The second place that needs to be taken into consideration is Bethany. In this town in Judaea, some three kilometers to the east of Jerusalem (John 11:18), lived a family of a brother and two sisters, Lazarus, Martha, and Mary. This family was closely linked to Jesus. The house was the setting for some evangelical scenes in which Jesus sat down to eat with them. According to Luke 10:38-42, Martha was the hostess as she was probably the elder sister, who was busy and preoccupied with looking after Jesus and, though not explicitly stated, probably his disciples too. Mary was not concerned with the housework and concentrated on listening to the Master. Martha complained that her sister "has left [her] to serve alone" and asked Jesus to "tell her then to help me." Lazarus did not appear on this occasion, but he played a key part in the events according to the Gospel of John. This family from Bethany had a close friendship with Jesus: "Jesus loved Martha and her sister and Lazarus" (11:5). The family was a widely respected and could be considered upper class. They had important contacts in Jerusalem as we see in Lazarus' resurrection and the effects this had on the decision by the temple's leaders whether Jesus should be killed (11:53).

The Gospel of John also describes Lazarus' house in Bethany as the setting for the anointing of Jesus' feet by Mary, Lazarus' sister, who, in front of the shocked disciples, used "a pound of costly ointment of pure nard" worth "three hundred denarii" (12:3, 12:5). This anointing in preparation for Jesus' burial took place during a meal served to Jesus and his disciples by Martha. According to the Gospels of Mark and Matthew, this meal took place in the house of Simon the Leper (Mark 14:3-9; Matt 26:6-13), and "a woman" (unnamed) anointed Jesus' head (not his feet, in contrast to John 12:3). This version of events does not link the scene to the family of Lazarus, Martha, and Mary, though it still took place in Bethany.

The name of Simon crops up again in the episode reported in Luke (7:36-50), in which an unnamed woman, a "sinner," anointed

Jesus' feet with perfume despite the indignation of Simon, "a Pharisee," and the other guests. The scene ended with Jesus assuring the woman that she would be forgiven. The woman has been identified by the evangelical tradition as Mary Magdalene (Luke 8:2). There is no link here with Lazarus' family or Bethany, as the feast was given by Simon the Pharisee, not the leper(!), and took place in Galilee. These are apparently two separate occasions and different situations. The women who anointed Jesus are different: Mary Magdalene in Galilee and Mary, Lazarus' sister, in Bethany. The hosts are also different, despite the names: Simon the Pharisee (from Galilee) and Simon the Leper (from Bethany in Judaea). The latter was one of Jesus' sedentary disciples, offering food and shelter to the Master and his disciples.

Before Jesus' final, public, and jubilant entrance into Jerusalem, he was in Ephraim, a town some twenty kilometers to the north of Jerusalem, according to John (11:54). Jesus spent time there with his disciples because he was facing the open enmity of the temple authorities and Sanhedrin. Ephraim is not on the main routes into Jerusalem from the east (Jericho) or from the west (Joppa and the Mediterranean coast). The report in John (11:54) is very short, and we cannot tell exactly how long Jesus' group stayed in Ephraim or whether he was able to count on the support and hospitality of anyone there. However, he may have stayed there. At the start of his public activities, Jesus had baptized on the western banks of the Jordan probably to the north of Jericho, in the land of Judaea (John 3:22) close to Ephraim. According to the synoptic Gospels (Mark 10:46-52; Matt 20:29-34; Luke 18:35–19:27), the area around Jericho was where Jesus was active before he arrived in Jerusalem: Jesus cured Bartimaeus, a blind beggar, and stayed in the house of Zacchaeus, one of Jesus' sedentary disciples. It would not be surprising if Jesus had had other sedentary disciples in the town of Ephraim.

The fourth town could possibly be Bethphage on the western face of the Mount of Olives. Matthew (21:1-2) places the scene of the colt that Jesus was to ride for his public and triumphant entrance into Jerusalem. In Mark (11:1-6) and Luke (19:29-31) the setting is more ambiguous, as the town in question could have been Bethphage or Bethany. We can suppose that Jesus knew the place, people, and circumstances: the "colt tied at the door out in the open street," an animal "on which no one has ever sat" (Mark 11:2, 11:4). When the people heard that "the Lord [Jesus] has need of it," they let the disciples go in search of the colt and did not try to hinder them in any way. It all leads us to believe that the animal's owner was happy to let Jesus ride it to Jerusalem. This owner may not have been a disciple, but he must at least have been a sympathizer.

Something similar happened at Jesus' Last Supper with his disciples in Jerusalem. Two disciples had to find in the city "a man carrying a jar of water," who would take them to a house. The owner of this house already knew that Jesus, "the Master," had to dine with the disciples in his house, in "a large upper room furnished and ready" (Mark 14:13-15 || Luke 22:10-12; also Matt 26:18). It was obviously a spacious house with room for at least thirteen people. Everything seemed to be ready. The unnamed owner of the house had close links with Jesus; like Zacchaeus in Jericho and Lazarus, Martha, and Mary or Simon the Leper in Bethany, he agreed to accommodate the Master at a difficult time shortly before his arrest. We can assume that he was one of Jesus' sedentary disciples: his generous hospitality and commitment proved this. The hospitality offered was an unequivocal sign of his devotion. The same can be said of the owner of the garden on the Mount of Olives where Jesus often met his disciples (John 18:2) and where he was arrested the day before his death (Mark 14:32 || Matt 25:36 || Luke 22:40). We can see that the line between disciple and sympathizer is often blurred.

We need to take one last element into account, namely Jerusalem's leading classes who showed interest in or sympathy for Jesus but who did not dare show this publicly, probably due to the hostility of the city's religious authorities toward him. These people are known as secret disciples. According to the Gospel of John, the common denominator between Joseph of Arimathea and Nicodemus was that they had both been in contact with Jesus secretly. Nicodemus was "a teacher of Israel" (3:10), a rabbi belonging to the Pharisee group (3:1) who dared go out in search of Jesus only in the dark of night. Joseph was born in Arimathea, a town to the northwest of Judaea, but lived in Jerusalem, where he was the owner of a tomb that had yet to be used (and in which Jesus was to be buried). He was also on the Sanhedrin, or Great Jewish Council, where he was "a respected member" (Mark 15:43). Joseph was said to have been even "looking for the kingdom of God," which may indicate that he had close links to the Pharisees (Mark 15:43 || Luke 23:51). The Gospel of John states that Joseph was one of Jesus' disciples (19:38; also Matt 27:57), but only "secretly": his position as a leader would have allowed him only a secret devotion to his cause.

Joseph and Nicodemus appeared on the scene only after Jesus' death, and not during the brief interrogation before Caiaphas or while he was being judged by Pilate. Obviously, as Luke states (23:51), Joseph had not supported the Sanhedrin's decision to encourage Pilate to condemn Jesus to death; but he was not able to stop this initiative that had been agreed by the great majority of the supreme Jewish council (see 6.2.3.1). After Jesus' death, Joseph revealed himself to be a sympathizer and was concerned enough to offer him his tomb. He asked Pilate for permission to remove Jesus' body from the cross, and the Roman governor granted him his wishes. According to the Gospel of John, Nicodemus was also present on Golgotha, with one hundred pounds of aromatic spices to anoint Jesus' body with, and helped Joseph bury him (19:39-42) (see 6.2.6).

The women disciples

It is not easy to ascertain the status of Jesus' female disciples during his itinerant preaching. The first problem is the word (female disciple) in Greek, *mathētria*, which appears only in Acts 9:36, applied to Tabitha-Dorcas, a conspicuous member of the Christian community in Joppa, whom Peter resurrects. However, the masculine word (*mathētēs*) is clearly an all-inclusive term, not necessarily according to the philology but according to the numbers of men and women surrounding Jesus, those who were close or linked to him. This is the case with Mary, the sister of Lazarus and Martha, who is said to have "sat at the Lord's feet and listened to his teaching" (Luke 10:39). Mary's physical position and captive expression seem to indicate that she was one of Jesus' sedentary disciples since the scene took place in her house. The early Christian tradition and in this case Luke indicate that becoming one of Jesus' disciples was open to both men and women.

This belief is based on the eclectic nature of Jesus' audiences, which were made up of people of both sexes, adults and children, the healthy and the sick, the good and the sinful. In the feeding of the five thousand Matthew states that those fed included several thousand men "besides women and children" (14:21, 15:38). John tells us that Jesus fed the crowds with five barley loaves and two fish brought by a "lad" (*paidarion*) (6:9). Luke (11:27) reported significantly, "as he said this, a woman in the crowd raised her voice." Thus, anyone was welcome to listen to Jesus; whoever they were, they were a potential disciple.

Jesus' openness to anyone was evident in his treatment of notorious sinners. Jesus addressed them with great sympathy, which can at times even seem to amount to praise, since they were among the first to answer his calling and repent. The all-inclusive phrase "tax collectors [men] and prostitutes [women]" shows the effects that Jesus' words had on the most stigmatized in society, whether socially or religiously (Matt 21:31-32). A symbolic case is that of the public sinner, probably a prostitute, who came up to him to ask him for forgiveness and her captivating behavior that shocked the well thinking: she washed Jesus' feet with her tears, which she then dried with her hair, before kissing them and anointing them with perfume (Luke 7:36-50).

The crowds bring Jesus their sick so that he can heal them; among them there are both men and women of all ages and those suffering from all kinds of different illnesses. The Gospel narratives report many women being healed: one who suffered hemorrhages for twelve years and had spent everything she had on doctors; the daughter of a foreigner, a Syrophoenician, who suffered serious spiritual problems, possessed as she was by a demon; a woman who had been bent over since the age of eighteen and could not straighten herself (Mark 5:25-34; Mark 7:24-30; and Luke 13:10-17; respectively). We know the names of some of the women who were "healed of evil spirits and infirmities," the ills of body and spirit: Mary, who came from Magdala, a town on the banks of Lake Galilee, not far from Capernaum, from whom Jesus expelled "seven demons" (Luke 8:2; Mark 16:9); Joanna, who was married to Chuza, an administrator (*epitropos*) for Herod Antipas and high-ranking official in Galilee (Luke 8:3, 24:10); and Susanna, for whom we have no references (Luke 8:3).

According to Luke (8:1-3), these three women healed by Jesus and "many others" accompanied him and provided him with what he needed during his travels through Galilee. Luke (23:49) insists that there were "women who had followed him from Galilee" not far from the cross on which he had been crucified, though no names are given. Mark (15:40-41) expresses the situation in similar terms to Luke 8:1-3. According to Mark, three women took part in Jesus' activities in Galilee, and he offers us their names: Mary Magdalene, Mary, wife of Alphaeus and mother of James the Younger (one of the Twelve) and Joseph, and Salome. Matthew seems to identify Salome as "the mother of the sons of Zebedee," James and John, two important members of the group of Twelve (Matt 27:56; see also 20:20).

The only name common to the Gospels of Mark, Matthew, and Luke is that of Mary of Magdala or Magdalene, who always comes first and who, traditionally (and not unreasonably, as we have seen), has been identified as the anonymous prostitute mentioned in Luke (7:36-50). Mary was forgiven and was freed from the serious spiritual illness see suffered (the "seven demons" of Luke 8:2!). The other two names (Joanna and Susanna, from Luke, and Mary, mother of James and Joseph, and Salome, from Mark) are not common to all the Gospels, though Mary, mother of James and Joseph, is also mentioned alongside Mary Magdalene in Luke (24:10).

Undeniably, then, Jesus' activities in Galilee were characterized by the active presence of certain women who collaborated with him on a continual basis. They deserve to be called disciples. Their devotion to Jesus was evident because most of them traveled with him and the other disciples to Jerusalem. Unlike the male disciples, they remained at his side at the crucial times of his crucifixion, death, and burial. In the Passion, among the five names mentioned in Mark (15:40-41), Matthew (27:56), and Luke (8:1-3; 23:49), only Susanna is not mentioned. The women did not abandon their Master.

We know the names of at least four women who followed Jesus closely while he preached in Galilee and went with him to Jerusalem, accompanying him during the last moments of his life. One was single (Mary Magdalene, probably a former prostitute) and two were married (Mary, wife of Alphaeus, mother of James and Joseph, and Joanna, wife of Chuza, one of Antipas' high-ranking officials); there are doubts as to Salome's marital status, though according to the Gospel of Matthew she would seem to be the mother of the sons of Zebedee. The loyalty of these women to the Master led to their ensuring he had a dignified burial and they returned to the tomb to anoint his body with aromatic oils (Mark 16:1; Luke 24:10) on the third day after his death. They were the first to discover that Jesus' tomb was empty.

We do not know what two other women did during Jesus' mission in Galilee: Mary, the wife of Cleopas and thus Jesus' paternal aunt, and an unnamed maternal aunt ("his mother's sister"), mentioned together with Mary, Jesus' mother, and Mary Magdalene in John (19:25) (cf. also Acts 1:14). Possibly only the last of these women actively took part in Jesus' preaching in Galilee on a continual basis. The other three women (his mother and two aunts) joined Jesus' group only at the end of his life, when he was already near Jerusalem.

We need to ask ourselves about the way in which the female disciples helped Jesus while he was at work in Galilee. First, did these women accompany Jesus at all times, as did the male disciples (the Twelve and a few others), sharing the hardships of an itinerant lifestyle? Did Jesus' group walk from town to town in Galilee, staying wherever they were offered accommodation, regardless of the fact that they were men and women, single and married, and possibly even children? There is no proof to back this up. When Peter, in name of all the disciples, reminded Jesus that they had left "everything" behind, he specified those things that they had left behind (parents, siblings, and children), but he did not mention partners (husbands or wives) (Mark 10:29 || Matt 19:29). Only Luke mentions "wife and children" (14:26, 18:29), probably because he felt that wives were missing from the list that had been handed down by the tradition. Possibly Jesus did not include husbands or wives among those things that had to be left behind by his followers.

Does this mean that Jesus' married disciples followed him with their partners, while their children were in the provisional care of the grandparents or uncles and aunts? If Jesus referred to leaving children behind but did not mention wives (or husbands), it was because he did not allow any form of divorce. Jesus did not demand married disciples to abandon their partners; on the contrary, he demanded them to respect their marital status and not divorce. However, they could live away from their home and family temporarily for the cause of the Kingdom of God. Mark (10:29) tells us that Jesus did not make those disciples who shared his life with him end their marriages: the wives of married disciples who were traveling around stayed at home and looked after the children.

And what about the married women who accompanied Jesus, such as Mary, mother of James and Joseph, or Joanna? Were they given permission by their husbands (Alphaeus and Chuza, respectively)? The first case is easy to resolve, as James, known as the Younger, Mary's firstborn son, was one of the Twelve called by Jesus. Salome's case was equally simple, as she was probably the mother of two members of the group of Twelve (James and John) and wife of Zebedee. Joanna's case is somewhat more surprising, since she was married to one of the tetrarch Antipas' high-ranking officials. It all leads us to believe that the behavior of these women was tolerated socially, that there was nothing radically opposed to traditional customs or that could lead to malicious gossip with regard to the group of disciples. This would have been the case if these women, married or single, like Mary Magdalene, had joined them and shared the life of Jesus and his male disciples. Jesus believed in freedom, but not to the extent of provoking scandals and risking what to him was fundamental: the proclamation of the Kingdom of God in words and deeds. Jesus allowed women into his circle of disciples, but he did not ask them to share his life with him, as was the case with the Twelve and certain other male disciples. However, Jesus allowed a disreputable woman, a prostitute, to kiss his feet and to become one of his disciples, aware of the shock this inspired in his Pharisee host (Luke 7:39).

As with some of the male disciples, the women who accompanied Jesus in Galilee did not seem to have been called directly to follow him, nor were they sent by him as missionaries. These two things are among the aspects that set the Twelve apart (Mark 3:13-19, 6:7), though some other disciples were called on occasions, with differing results.

What Jesus asked for from the women who followed him as disciples was that they carried out a "service" (*diakonia*). This was constant and active support, which involved ensuring that there was food and accommodation for the group, and sorting out other organizational questions related to Jesus' itinerant preaching. The aid provided by the women mentioned in Mark (15:40-41) and Luke (8:1-3) may also have included financial support, especially in the case of Joanna, the wife of one of Antipas' administrators and someone with a high social standing. These women, however, did not "sponsor" the group. One disciple, Judas, looked after the group's money-box (John 12:6, 13:29). Jesus and the itinerant disciples received significant support from the sedentary disciples, who guaranteed them hospitality and contributed from their own pockets.

The four women mentioned by the Gospels in relation to Jesus' activities in Galilee (Mary of Magdala, Mary mother of James and Joseph, Joanna wife of Chuza, and Salome, probably, mother of James and Joseph) were halfway between the male and female sedentary disciples, who stayed at home and the all-male itinerant disciples, the nucleus of whom was the group of Twelve. These women looked after the logistics of the group of disciples and traveled around with Jesus, though not by his side. They accompanied him through Galilee, ensuring the basic living conditions for the Master and his disciples and, naturally, taking advantage of the opportunity to hear him and witness all he did. They traveled with Jesus, but not physically. They followed him, as he had given them specific tasks that allowed them to be close to the Master, though they could not always be by his side. In any case, their unconditional devotion to Jesus remained until the end.

Jesus' family

The people and the disciples form a circle of sympathy and friendship around Jesus. The fact that Jesus left Nazareth and began a life beyond the home and family is surprising and significant. Jesus did not have wife or children. Just after being baptized by the Baptist in the river Jordan, he attracted a number of men to him who had been until then disciples of John. Jesus quickly built up the foundations of a new family. All four Gospels relate when Jesus returned to Galilee, he was accompanied by a number of disciples. Jesus lived his life surrounded by his disciples. He wanted to start up a community of followers, as the Teacher of Righteousness had done with the Essene community, with the twofold aim of having people who were radically committed (the "monks" of Qumran) and having people to offer support while they continued to live at home. Similarly, Jesus allowed for a number of different types of followers and disciple in his circle: not everyone was called to the same thing.

They all formed part of the *familia Dei*, the "family of God," united by an active, practical, and inclusive fraternity. As we can see in Matthew (23:8), "you are all brethren." In the spirit of this fraternity, to be one of the pillars of the early Church, mutual assistance and service took on specific forms. One of Jesus' sayings graphically expresses the relation between members of this wide-reaching "family," made up of Jesus' followers, and all those, the poor, whom he considers closest to

God: "[W]hoever gives to one of these little ones even a cup of cold water . . . truly, I say to you, he shall not lose his reward" (Matt 10:42). Blood ties are no longer important, being replaced by a different link that everyone makes their own: a link to Jesus ultimately means listening to and safeguarding the word of God. Jesus reprimanded the woman who praised his mother for having had a son like him (Luke 11:27-28).

Jesus allowed himself to be "consumed" by the people who wanted to hear him preach and who were anxious to bring him their sick, asking for them to be healed. However, his family in Nazareth could not tolerate the good name of the descendants of David being brought into disrepute by one of its members, and they came up with an initial hypothesis regarding their relative, the former carpenter: "He is beside himself! He has gone mad!" (Mark 3:20-21). The first attempt to deal with him was made by the most important family members, Jesus' uncles and cousins, who traveled from Nazareth to Capernaum expressly. The second attempt was made by his closest relatives, his mother, brothers, and sisters, who went to the house in Capernaum where he taught. This second attempt was not successful either.

Jesus, faced with the pressure from his family in Nazareth, responded adroitly, calling to him those who listened to him and avoiding going out to find those who wanted to try and make him change his mind or who wanted to take him away by force if necessary. This was how Jesus avoided direct confrontation with his family, which would have vindicated those who had come from Nazareth. Without insulting them, but with conviction, he dissuaded them from choosing for him. Being his mother, brother, or sister entitled them to certain rights, but Jesus stressed, "who are my mother and brothers?" He himself responded, addressing those listening to him, saying, "whoever does the will of God is my brother, and sister, and mother" (Mark 3:35 || Matt 12:50 || Luke 8:21). Thus, all those who do as God wishes and listen to his Word, whether they share Jesus' blood or not, have to be considered a member of his family. Those who devote themselves to following God's will are relatives of Jesus! Naturally, his relatives in Nazareth, who were religious people, could not complain. They were not excluded by Jesus' response, but their rights over him, as blood relatives, were obviously relegated to the background; and they had to return without him.

These events did not lead to a break in the relations between Jesus and his family, but there was a distancing. This distancing can be seen clearly in Jesus' return visit. Some time later, Jesus, accompanied by his disciples, returned to the town where he had grown up and started teaching in the synagogue on the Sabbath. The people of Nazareth were confused by his words, full of wisdom, and by his miracles coming from someone who had never moved from the town. This bewilderment, however, did not turn into admiration but rejection. Their disrespect affected even his relatives, those who had attempted to dissuade him from the path he had chosen (Mark 3:20-21). The parochial antagonism was clear: what good could possibly come from the son of Mary and the brother of Jacob, Joseph, Judah, and Simeon, whom we all know? (Mark 6:1-6 || Matt 13:53-58). This was the same argument that Nathanael had used before he was called to become a disciple: "[C]an anything good come out of Nazareth?" (John 1:46). The author of the Gospel of Mark comments that Jesus had been surprised by this rejection. In fact, we do not know of any other visit by Jesus to his hometown, nor are there any reports about the relations between Jesus and his blood relatives following this somewhat unsuccessful visit to Nazareth. The lack of understanding was such that the Gospel according to Mark says, "[H]e could do no mighty work there, except that he laid his hands upon a few sick people and healed them" (Mark 6:5).

Jesus' family reappeared in his last journey to Jerusalem. His relatives and disciples, initially the Twelve but subsequently others, both men and women, come together in the city where he was to die crucified. Jesus' mother and most of his siblings were in Jerusalem for Passover 30 A.D. and ended up staying there (Acts 1:14). Mary was to die there (see 4.3.1). His eldest brother, James, even became the leader of the city's Christian community and a highly respected member of early Christianity until his martyrdom in 62 A.D. (see 4.3.4.1).

At the end of Jesus' life, his relations with his family seem to have been rebuilt and intensified. John (19:25) describes Mary, Jesus' mother, and two of his aunts, one on his father's side (Mary, wife of Cleopas) and one on his mother's side, who remains unnamed, by the cross witnessing the agony of their son and nephew. However, if the Cleopas in Luke (24:18) (one of the two disciples who traveled to Emmaus, disillusioned by the tragic end of the man who was to have freed Israel) was perhaps, according to Hegesippus, a brother of Joseph, Jesus' father, then Jesus' family must have changed their opinion of him and some of its members must have placed their messianic hopes in him at the end. Paul tells us that the resurrected Jesus appeared to James, his elder brother, after Peter, but before the rest of the apostles (1 Cor 15:7).

Jesus' break with his closest family may not have been definitive. The events in the synagogue in Nazareth show a definite distancing, but this must have been overcome gradually as they got closer to Passover 30 A.D. The opinion expressed by Cleopas, Jesus' uncle, in Luke (24:21; "we had hoped that he was the one to redeem Israel") may have reflected the sentiment shared by all the members of his family in Nazareth. Luke (19:11) makes it clear that there was a similar feeling among Jesus' disciples, as they saw that Passover was coming and as they were getting closer to Jerusalem ("they supposed that the kingdom of God was to appear immediately") (also Acts 1:6). At this time, James and John, Zebedee's sons, possibly with the intervention of their mother, Salome (Matt 20:20), were already asking Jesus for the first two places in the Kingdom (Mark 10:37 || Matt 20:21). The expectation raised by Jesus was growing as the Passover festivities approached, and this expectation may have led to his closest family traveling to Jerusalem. They all trusted in the prophet Jesus' great triumph; his triumphant entrance, heralded by palms and songs of praise, seemed to presage it. No one could have suspected that, only a few days later, he would be condemned to death and crucified as a criminal.

4.5.3.3. The Intimate Circle: The Twelve

One of the surest things we know about the history of Jesus is that he was accompanied by twelve men who shared his life with him and were always by his side from the start of his public activities. Some of John the Baptist's disciples were probably attracted to this man from Nazareth who had asked to be baptized by John and who, soon after John the Baptist's imprisonment, consolidated his position as a rabbi. He resembled the Baptist himself in certain ways; they both baptized people in different parts of the Jordan region (see 4.5.2.2). At the time, the disciples who baptized alongside Jesus in Judaea were few in number, as the group of Twelve took shape only once Jesus began his activities in Galilee after the Baptist's arrest.

The formation of the group of Twelve took place at the start of Jesus' activities in Galilee, possibly in mid-28 A.D. Mark (3:13) places the scene on a mountain, somewhere Jesus often went to find sanctuary and pray. There, with a certain degree of formality, Jesus created a specific group with a specific name and number: Twelve. According to Mark (3:13), these Twelve were not volunteers but men chosen by Jesus himself personally. They were given a twofold mission: to live alongside him and to go and preach, instilled with the power to heal both spiritual and bodily ills.

The Twelve were called to follow the Master physically wherever he went and to go wherever he told them to. The Twelve accompanied Jesus throughout the little more than two-year duration of his public activities, but when the Master fell into the hands of those who wanted to kill him, his closest disciples abandoned him shamefully. His arrest became a highly dramatic event, as he was betrayed by a member of this group, Judas Iscariot. During Jesus' Passion and death, the group of Twelve fell apart and reemerged only with the rumors announcing his resurrection.

However, the tight and direct relationship that Jesus maintained with his most intimate circle of disciples was not broken but remained intact. Paul reported this on Jesus' appearances following his resurrection: Peter, the leader and spokesman of the Twelve, he who denied knowing him during the Passion, was the first to receive a visit from the Master, followed by the whole group, "the Twelve" (1 Cor 15:5). Although they were only eleven at the time with the defection and suicide of Judas Iscariot, significantly the Christian tradition continued to call them "the Twelve," as seen in the Gospels of Mark and John. Luke stresses the importance of the Twelve as a group on the election of a twelfth member, Matthias, who took the place of Judas (Acts 1:15-26).

The evangelical sources provide the names of the Twelve in four lists (Mark 3:16-19; Matt 10:2-4; Luke 6:14-16; Acts 1:13); the Gospel according to John contains nine names, distributed here and there (all of them except Matthew, James son of Alphaeus, and Simon the Zealot, though James and John do appear as the "sons of Zebedee"). This comes as a surprise however since the Twelve, did not remain together as a group for a great length of time during early Christianity. Everything leads us to think that the members of the group went their own ways from Jerusalem shortly after Jesus' death, inspired by the desire to spread the gospel. Only the three most important disciples (Peter, James, and John) remained in Jerusalem and the neighboring territories, until in 43 or 44 A.D. James was beheaded on the orders of Agrippa I and Peter had to flee Jerusalem, undoubtedly traveling to Antioch. Peter, the first of the Twelve, traveled on from Antioch to Rome, possibly passing through Corinth and, according to all the evidence we have, died crucified in the imperial capital in the reign of Nero (between the years 64 and 68 A.D.).

Shortly before in 62 A.D., James, Jesus' elder brother, was stoned to death in Jerusalem at the instigation of the High Priest Ananus. James did not belong to the Twelve, but Paul described him as a "pillar" of Christianity, alongside Peter and John (Gal 2:9). Jesus' brother was undoubtedly the leader of the community in Jerusalem, at least as of 43 or 44 A.D., when Peter fled the city (see 4.3.4.1).

Another figure from the early Church who did not belong to the Twelve was Paul, a former Pharisee and the great missionary of the early decades of Christianity. Paul was a Jew from the Diaspora, was born in Tarsus in Cilicia, and had been a tenacious persecutor of Christians until he converted, and, like Peter, he was executed in Rome when Nero was in power.

Apart from Peter, James, and John, the other members of the Twelve do not appear again in the New Testament until after Jesus' death. The conclusion is obvious: the Twelve were a group of specific disciples from the time when Jesus was carrying out his public activities.

The names and identities of the Twelve can be derived from the four aforementioned lists. The Twelve names are grouped together in three blocks of four, headed, respectively and consistently, by Simon Peter, Philip, and James son of Alphaeus. In each of the lists, the last name given is that of Judas Iscariot, who betrayed Jesus. The order of the other names is not consistent.

Simon Peter, James, John, and Andrew

The first block of names is made up of two pairs of brothers: Simon (Peter) and Andrew, James and John. Everything points to Simon and James being the elder brothers, as Andrew and John respectively receive the qualification "his brother." They were four fishermen and Galilean Jews, the first two from Bethsaida (a town administratively beyond the boundaries of Galilee) and the other two from an unknown town not far from Capernaum. According to Luke (5:10), they were partners, but this is not corroborated by any other source. They were certainly fishermen from the same area, from the northeast of Lake Galilee, and it is highly likely that they already knew each other when Jesus called them. The boats they owned provided work for a number of men; Mark (1:20) says of James and John that "they left their father Zebedee in the boat with the hired servants," as soon as Jesus called them to follow him.

Luke (5:1-11) describes Simon as the owner of a boat on which several people worked. Boats such as this constituted small family businesses that, on occasions, provided work for other fishermen. The first-century boat discovered at the Kibbutz Ginosar, on the northwest coast of the lake, had a capacity for twelve to fourteen people. It was fragile with a low-cut hull and gives us an idea of how these small businesses must have worked, with five to seven fishermen to each boat (John 21:2-13). An abundant catch could easily destabilize one of these fragile boats, which were fairly vulnerable to storms: "they came and filled both the boats, so that they began to sink" (Luke 5:7).

Simon (Peter), son of Jonah (Matt 16:17) or John (John 21:25) and brother of Andrew, from Bethsaida, may have been married to a woman from Capernaum; but in the Gospels appears only his mother-in-law, whom Jesus cures of a fever in Capernaum itself, in "the house of Simon and Andrew" (Mark 1:29-31). Does this mean that the family had moved from Bethsaida to Capernaum? It is not clear whether Simon was a disciple of the Baptist like his brother, though it does seem likely that Jesus knew Simon (Peter) thanks to Andrew (John 1:40-42). Although Simon was his given name, Jesus gave him a nickname, *Cephas* (Aramaic, *Kepa'*), which translates into Greek as *Petros*, Peter. *Cephas* means stone or rock. Of these three names (Simon, *Cephas*, and Peter), he soon became known as Peter. The leader of the Twelve was, thus, known within the early Christian community by his nickname translated into Greek. As J. P. Meier points out, Jesus used to call him by his name, Simon, and this must have been how the other members of the Twelve usually addressed him.

Peter's role was crucial in an incident that took place in Caesarea Philippi (Mark 8:27; Matt 16:13) or Capernaum (John 6:59), although the latter is less likely. In the midst of his public activities and at a time when he was well known by many, Jesus asked his itinerant disciples their opinion of him. On behalf of all of them, Peter solemnly stated that he was the Christ (Mark 8:29; Luke 9:20) or (John 6:69) "the Holy One of God," the Son of God (Matt 16:16). Peter's complete devotion to Jesus was clear, as was his view on the identity of the one sent by God. This certainty was confirmed by Jesus when he urged him to "strengthen" his brothers (Luke 22:32). For Jesus, the nickname *Cephas*/Peter shows that Simon had to be a firm rock on which the faith of the other disciples could rest (see the same idea in Matt 16:17-19, referring to the construction of the Church: "[Y]ou are Peter, and on this rock I will build my church").

Although the nickname Peter means rock, it does not save the person from having to endure periods of weakness. Peter was to receive a harsh reprimand from Jesus when he contradicted him; Jesus also put him to the test concerning the suffering that the Master presaged for himself and the disciples. Peter could not accept that the cross would form part of the Master's future or that this could be the expression of God's wishes. Jesus rebuked him, calling him "Satan," and urged him to follow him as a disciple, without any kind of arrogance (Mark 8:32-33). On another occasion, a reference to Satan, "he who tempts," marked a trial that the Twelve had to undergo. The Passion, when they abandoned Jesus, vindicated a very expressive agricultural metaphor: "Simon, Simon, behold, Satan demanded to have you, that he might sift you like wheat" (Luke 22:31). The trial proved particularly difficult for Peter. Jesus said that Peter would repudiate him; in the midst of the Passion he publicly stated that he did not know the rabbi from Nazareth.

The saga of relations between Jesus and Peter, the Master and the leader of the Twelve, culminated in a reencounter after Jesus' resurrection. This reencounter is described in the words that Luke (22:32) attributed to Jesus at the Last Supper and that we have already mentioned. Jesus said to Peter, "I have prayed for you that your faith may not fail; and when you have turned again, strengthen your brethren." A similar idea can be seen in John (21:15-19), referring to Peter's role in the Church: "Feed my lambs."

Jesus also gave James and John, the two brothers known as "the sons of Zebedee," a nickname. He called them *Boanerges*, as Mark (3:17) explains, "sons of thunder." This qualification was used to describe someone with a strong and impetuous character, someone bold or even fiery. The sense here, though, refers above all to the behavior of the two brothers as disciples toward Jesus' way of doing things. The two brothers' reaction toward the Samaritan village, which did not want to put Jesus' group up for the night, seems a good example of why Jesus gave them this name somewhat ironically. They asked, "Lord, do you want us to bid fire come down from heaven and consume them?" (Luke 9:54). Jesus refused emphatically and publicly reprimanded the two brothers (see 3.4.3.2).

In a similar episode, John, speaking in the first person plural (on behalf of his brother James as well perhaps?), zealously attacked someone who was carrying out exorcisms in Jesus' name, despite not belonging to his group of itinerant followers. John, convinced that he had acted correctly, proudly stated that they "forbade him, because he was not following us." Jesus puts him right and replies, "Do not forbid him" (Mark 9:38-39; Luke 9:49-50).

In a third encounter, the two brothers proclaimed themselves as the two most important people in the Kingdom that Jesus was soon to establish: James wanted to sit at the right hand and John at the left hand of Jesus, the King. They asked for power and provoked indignation in "the ten," who were angered by the brothers' aspirations, which they openly and freely admitted. Jesus had to calm the impetuousness of the brothers and reminded them that the only thing they could aspire to as disciples was trial and suffering (Mark 10:35-45 || Matt 20:20-28). The two brothers showed that their zeal was sincere and that they were not simply moved by ambition by admitting their willingness to undergo whatever it took.

These three episodes outline the character of two extremely zealous disciples, with deeply held convictions for Jesus' cause, but with a fervor which, without their realizing, also brought into question their way of spreading the gospel. Jesus was obliged to refuse violence and revenge. He also refused to exclude anyone just so as to maintain a closed and reduced group. He denied that he was in a position to offer people power and control; in fact, what they were accepting was their cross to bear. The nickname "sons of thunder" shows that Jesus knew the sons of Zebedee very well, men who had given themselves over sincerely to the cause of the Master. But they needed to realize that what they had chosen was the opposite of what they thought; rather they needed to prepare themselves adequately for the task entrusted to them.

John, the younger of the two brothers, is clearly defined, if he is taken to be the unnamed disciple who appears in the Gospel according to John; he called them both "the disciple whom Jesus loved" or "the other disciple" (John 20:2). Furthermore, according to chapter 21 of this Gospel, the person in question is presented as the author of the whole document: "This is the disciple who is bearing witness to these things, and who has written these things" (21:24). Thus, we have to conclude that the unnamed "disciple" in the Gospel according to John is the same person throughout. The relationship he maintained with Jesus was centered on the closing stages of his life: the Last Supper (13:23), the interrogation by Annas (18:15-16), the crucifixion (19:26-27), the discovery of the empty tomb where Jesus had been buried (20:1-10), and the appearance of the resurrected Jesus in Jerusalem and by Lake Galilee (20:19-29, 21:1-23).

This "disciple" is described as being very close to the Master and showed signs of courage and decisiveness. He sat beside Jesus at the Last Supper and asked him directly for the identity of his betrayer. When Jesus was arrested, he did not flee like the others but accompanied him to the house of Annas, the former high priest, whom he knew. He then brought Peter in. He also ran with Peter to the tomb when Mary Magdalene alerted them to the disappearance of Jesus' body. The "disciple" was also nearby when Jesus was crucified on Golgotha. The affection that Jesus professed for him was so great that, just before he died, he entrusted the care of his own mother to him.

This information does not contradict the reports in the synoptic Gospels; namely that Jesus paid special attention to three disciples (Peter, James, and John). Neither does it contradict the public activities of Peter and John in the early days of the community in Jerusalem. The traditional identification of the unnamed "disciple" in the Gospel according to John (chaps. 13–21) as John, son of Zebedee and brother of James, is probably correct. This identification, comprehensively assessed, remains perfectly plausible historically.

Simon (Peter), James, and John are the only three members of the group of Twelve to receive nicknames from Jesus: *Cephas* (rock) and

Boanerges (sons of thunder), respectively (Mark 3:16-17). Jesus singled them out among the group with elements taken from nature (rock and thunder). The Master wanted them by his side at certain times of particular intensity. When he transfigured at the top of a mountain, he was accompanied only by Peter, James, and John, and it was Peter who spoke to Jesus on behalf of all three of them (Mark 9:2, 9:5 || Matt 17:1, 17:4 || Luke 9:28, 9:33). These three disciples accompanied him during a particularly dramatic scene when he resurrected Jairus' twelve-year-old daughter. This scene also shows Jesus' choice clearly: "And he allowed no one to follow him except Peter and James and John the brother of James" (Mark 5:37; Luke 8:51). Shortly before his arrest in the garden of Gethsemane, Jesus wanted to compose himself in prayer, and he took these three disciples with him. He ordered the other disciples to wait, but these three were singled out to come with him to pray. Unfortunately, Peter, James, and John tired and fell asleep. Jesus addressed Peter as their leader, saying, "Simon, are you asleep? . . . The spirit indeed is willing, but the flesh is weak" (Mark 14:33, 14:37-38 || Matt 26:37, 26:41).

Luke narrates the events in Gethsemane from the perspective of Jesus' inner experience and obviously summarizes the other events; for this reason, he does not mention these three disciples in particular (Luke 23:39-46). However, he does mention them in the miraculous fishing trip (5:10). In Jerusalem's early Christian community, Peter, James, and John were central; as we shall see, they took up from where Jesus left off. Peter and John, in particular, took on vital public roles during the early days of the incipient church (Acts 3–8). This can be the only reason why Agrippa I attacked the community's leadership by having James decapitated and putting Peter in prison with the intention of executing him (Acts 12:1-3). The "leadership" of the community is described as "three" even after the death of James, son of Zebedee. In Galatians 2:9, Paul talks of his visit to Jerusalem, where he met the early church's leaders (the "pillars"), Peter, John, and another James: the Lord's brother and head of the mother community in Jerusalem. It may have been for this reason that Paul places James at the head, above Peter (*Cephas*) and John.

In conclusion, there were three disciples in the group of Twelve whom Jesus singled out to be at his side at certain important times during his activities (the resurrection of Jairus' daughter, the transfiguration at the top of the mountain, the prayers in Gethsemane): Peter and the two sons of Zebedee, James and John. The preeminence of these three disciples is seen in the synoptic Gospels, and it presumably continued during the first years of the community in Jerusalem. It should be noted that the names of James and John do not appear in the Gospel according to John.

However, the first disciple to be called was, in fact, Andrew. The eastern tradition, rightly, calls him "the first to be called" (*ho protoklētos*). The synoptic Gospels and the Gospel according to John agree that Andrew was attributed a special place in the calling of the Twelve. He was the first disciple, together with another unnamed disciple, who accepted Jesus as the Teacher (John 1:38) and was called by Jesus alongside Peter (Mark 1:16 || Matt 4:18). The circumstances vary, but the nucleus of events remains the same: Andrew, the younger brother of Simon (Peter), son of Jonah (or John), from Bethsaida, met Jesus very early on, probably before his brother Simon did. According to John (1:41-42) it was Andrew who had been a disciple of John the Baptist's until that time and who presented Peter to Jesus when Jesus called him to follow.

Despite being Peter's brother, Andrew was not associated with him during the years when both accompanied Jesus as disciples. As we have just seen, the sons of Zebedee and Peter were the ones to take a special place by Jesus' side. The two pairs of brothers (Peter and Andrew, James and John) did appear, however, in Jesus' summons by Lake Galilee (Mark 1:16-20 || Matt 4:18-22) and in the lists of the Twelve. Andrew played second fiddle immediately after Peter (Luke 6:14; Matt 10:2) or was relegated to fourth place, behind James and John (Mark 3:16) or John and James (Acts 1:13). He also occupied fourth place (Mark 13:3) at the beginning of Jesus' speech on the destruction of Jerusalem and the end of the world. Obviously, the group of three are prominent enough on their own not to require Andrew.

Instead, Andrew, paired with Philip, plays an important role in the Gospel according to John, a much greater role than the one he plays in the synoptic Gospels. The connection between these two disciples seems to stem from their common origin in the same town: Bethsaida, "the city of Andrew and Peter" (John 1:44), known as "Bethsaida in Galilee" (12:21) in Jewish custom. Andrew, described as "Simon Peter's brother" (John 1:40; 6:8), and Philip appear three times together at the start, middle, and end of Jesus' activities, where Andrew is shown as slightly more preeminent than Philip.

According to John (1:35-51), the four disciples are called in this order: Andrew, Simon-Peter (*Cephas*), Philip, and Nathanael, or Andrew, Philip, Simon-Peter (*Cephas*), and Nathanael. It all depends on whether Philip is identified as the second of the "two disciples" (the other being Andrew) who "followed Jesus" (John 1:37). The second option is more likely. Indeed, Andrew and Philip acted as the middlemen in the relations with the other two disciples. Andrew found his brother Simon, and the following day Philip found Nathanael (John 1:40-51). In the feeding of the five thousand, both Philip and Andrew showed signs of impotence when faced with the task of feeding this great crowd of people, though it was Andrew who brought Jesus the boy with the bread and fishes to use to feed them all (John 6:5-9). The third incident took place in Jerusalem, following Jesus' triumphal entrance into the city. According to the Gospel of John, this was the last time Jesus showed himself in public before the Passion. Some "Greeks" and non-Jews who had come to celebrate the Passover told Philip they wished to see Jesus. Philip did not tell Jesus directly but passed the message on to Andrew and "Andrew went with Philip and they told Jesus" (John 12:22). In the Gospel according to John, Andrew and Philip appeared together in the shadow of Peter, despite all three being linked by the fact that they came from the same town of Bethsaida.

Philip, Judas Thomas, Nathanael Bartholomew, and Matthew

Philip was the member of the Twelve who headed the second group of four in the lists; this group comprised Philip himself, Bartholomew, Matthew, and Thomas (Mark 3:18; Matt 10:3; Luke 6:14-15; Acts 1:13). He should not be confused with a member of the group of seven, however, who were charged with the care of the Greek-speaking widows and orphans in the Jewish community in Jerusalem, and who would subsequently spread the gospel through the lands of Samaria and the plains of the Mediterranean coast (Acts 6:1-6, 8, 21:8). Philip, from Bethsaida, was a Galilean with a Greek name who may have had an average level of knowledge of the Greek language. Indeed, Andrew and Philip are the only two of the Twelve with Greek names. This may explain why it was these two who dealt with the

Greek pilgrims who wanted to see Jesus (John 12:20-22). Philip, like Andrew, had previously been a disciple of John the Baptist's, before deciding to follow another rabbi, Jesus of Nazareth, and it was he who called on Nathanael to do the same. Philip and Andrew also took part together in the feeding of the five thousand (John 6:6-9).

At the Last Supper (only according to the Gospel of John), Philip asked Jesus a question, as did three other members of the Twelve (Peter, Thomas, and Judas [not Iscariot]) once Judas the traitor had left the house. Philip was the third to ask (John 14:8). It is worth stressing that both the question asked by Philip and those asked by Thomas (14:5) and Judas (14:22) fit perfectly with the theological line of thought employed in the Gospel according to John, and it is difficult to derive any historical insight from them.

Thomas was another member of the Twelve who, like Andrew and Philip, received special attention in the Gospel of John alone. The synoptic Gospels mention only his name. This disciple was called Thomas, which like *Cephas*, comes from Aramaic (*te'oma'*) and means "twin" (Greek, *didymos*). This is what we are rightly told in John (11:16, 20:24, 21:2). Thus, Thomas may be a nickname that became the disciple's first name, and a great part of the tradition may not indeed know his actual name. However, the start of the gnostic Gospel of Thomas states, "These are the secret sayings that the living Jesus spoke and Didymus Judas Thomas recorded." This introduction gives Judas as the disciple's original name, while Didymus and Thomas (the Twin) act as nicknames or, indeed, redundant names. The four canonical Gospels use only the second name when talking about this disciple. However, the Gospel of Thomas, the Acts of Thomas, and a textual variation of John 14:22 found in certain Syriac manuscripts of the third century A.D. suggest that his first name was Judas.

The most likely explanation why this figure received the names Thomas or Didymus, the Twin, among the Twelve is that it was to avoid confusion with the other two Judases in the group: Judas, the traitor, with the second name Iscariot, son of Simon, and Judas, with the second name Thaddeus, son of James. While the last two Judases kept their first and second names (Iscariot and Thaddeus, respectively), the other Judas is known in the canonical Gospels only by his nickname (Thomas), while the apocryphal gospels also mention his first name: Judas. Whom was Thomas a twin of to merit this nickname? Was his twin someone also known to the group of Twelve? We do not know. The suggestion that he was Jesus' twin brother, made in the Acts of Thomas (an apocryphal manuscript from the 3rd century A.D.), lacks any kind of foundation. The use of the nickname reflects, as with the other two Judases, a practical solution within the group of Twelve rather than an express desire of Jesus. As we have pointed out, the Master gave only two nicknames: *Cephas* for Peter and *Boanerges* for James and John.

Thomas appears on three occasions in the Gospel according to John. The common denominator on each occasion shows him as both ironic and incisive, stubborn and disbelieving, who ends up being a model believer! We do not know to what extent the author of the Gospel modified the portrait of the person, but he is clearly given a well-founded and unique personality.

Thomas' first intervention is a clearly ironic observation. Jesus, who had found out about Lazarus' illness, told the disciples that he wished to return to Judaea despite the dangers for himself and his disciples. They tried to dissuade him, but faced with Jesus' insistence, Thomas replied, "Let us also go, that we may die with him" (John 11:16).

In a tone similar to the one at the Last Supper, Thomas complained about the path proposed to lead the disciples to Jesus: "Lord, we do not know where you are going; how can we know the way?" (John 14:5). The problem put forward by the disciple leads to one of Jesus' most important statements in the Gospel of John: "I am the way, and the truth, and the life" (John 14:6).

The argument between Jesus and Thomas ended with the two scenes of the resurrected Jesus' appearance before the disciples. Thomas' understandable refusal to believe that Jesus had been resurrected was vehement. First, Thomas could not accept the news that his fellow disciples had given him ("We have seen the Lord"), and he stubbornly demanded personal and complete proof of the fact: Thomas demanded to see the mark left by the nails in Jesus' hands, to touch it with his finger and place his hand over the wound in his chest left by the spear. But when Jesus appeared before the disciples for the second time and he invited Thomas to do what he had asked, he could only reply, "My Lord and my God!" (John 20:28). In the Gospel according to John, Thomas represents the move from doubt to faith, from ironic distance to sincere proximity.

Bartholomew (Greek, *Bartholomaios*; Latin, *Bartholomeus*) is a patronymic that was also used as a first name. In Aramaic *bar* means "son of" and *Tholomew* is a Grecian name derived from the Aramaic (*Tolmai* or *Talmai*). Exchanges and fusions between the Jewish and Greek worlds were constant in Israel, dating back to the arrival of Hellenistic culture in the country in the fourth century B.C. A similar fusion can be seen in the name of the blind man in Jericho who was healed by Jesus: Bartimaeus (*Bartimaios*). The Gospel translates this as the "son of Timaeus" (Mark 10:46). It was originally a patronymic that combined the Aramaic (*bar*) and the Hellenized name (*Timaios*) from the Aramaic (*Timmai*).

Bartholomew's identity has been suggested as Nathanael, one of Jesus' disciples from Cana in Galilee (John 21:2), whom Philip brought to Jesus (John 1:44-51). Significantly, when Jesus got to Galilee, one of the first things he did was to go Cana, Nathanael's hometown, as he, his disciples, and his mother had been invited to a wedding (John 2:1-2). Nathanael, then, met the Master thanks to another Galilean, Philip, who led him to Jesus, in the same way that Andrew had done for Peter. Indeed, in three of the four lists of the Twelve, Bartholomew is the name that comes directly after Philip.

The figure of Nathanael receives special attention from the Gospel according to John, where he is presented as an upright Jew, upstanding and Law-abiding, one of the pious who are waiting for the fulfillment of the prophecies and the arrival of the Kingdom of Israel, the Messiah who is to free his people, the prophet for the end of time. This is how Jesus described Nathanael: "Behold, an Israelite indeed, in whom is no guile!" (John 1:47). Nathanael could not hide his rural Galilean origins when he countered Philip's enthusiasm saying, "Can anything good come out of Nazareth?" (1:46). For someone from Cana, a town in Lower Galilee to the north of Sepphoris and relatively close to Nazareth, he could not believe that the Messiah came from such an insignificant town! Nonetheless, Nathanael, as with Thomas, passed from skepticism and a certain degree of disrespect to complete devotion to Jesus. These two figures, Nathanael at the start of the Gospel (1:49) and Thomas at the end (20:28), represent two personal journeys toward recognizing Jesus for what he was.

Thus from a historical point of view, there is every reason to believe that Bartholomew and Nathanael were one and the same member of the group of Twelve. It is still debatable, however, which of these two names should be considered that of the disciple. Bartholomew is a patronymic that was used as a first name, but not necessarily. Nathanael, in turn, is a Hebrew first name that has an important meaning ("gift from God") and that appears in Judith 8:1. Furthermore, a name like Nathanael fits with the image of the figure described in John 1:44-51. It seems best to conclude that the disciple's name was probably Nathanael, but, as the son of Tholomew, he was also known as "Bartholomew." As time went by, the second name became more common than the first, being rescued from obscurity only by the tradition based on John. A similar situation exists with the disciples James and John, to whom was applied the patronymic ("sons of Zebedee"), since their father was called Zebedee. In the case of Bartholomew, however, the patronymic (Bartholomew, "son of Tholomew") replaced the name (Nathanael) almost completely.

The last name from the second group of the Twelve is Matthew. This name, Jewish in origin, means "gift (from God)." While the Gospels of Mark (3:18) and Luke (6:15) simply name him, the Gospel according to Matthew identifies him with Levi, son of Alphaeus, a tax collector whom Jesus called upon to leave his work and become his disciple (Matt 9:9). In the list of the Twelve in Matthew (10:3), he is named "Matthew the tax collector." However, Mark and Luke consider these two to be different people: on the one hand, Matthew, one of the Twelve; on the other hand, Levi, son of Alphaeus, the tax collector (Mark 2:14 || Luke 5:27). Could he have changed his name as a result of a radical change in his life, once he had decided to join Jesus' mission? Did the Gospel according to Matthew know about a change of name affecting one of the Twelve, the only one who had been employed in a publicly reviled and sinful position, before joining Jesus? Even if the answer to these questions were in the affirmative, it would still be difficult to explain why two of the Gospels, Mark and Luke, do not identify Matthew as Levi.

James of Alphaeus, Simon the Zealot, Judas Thaddeus, and Judas Iscariot

The third and final series of four names from the group of Twelve always starts with James, a disciple and son of Mary and Alphaeus, a brother of Joseph. This figure is known in the lists of the Twelve as "the son of Alphaeus" (Mark 3:18; Matt 10:3; Luke 6:15), but the names of his mother and brother appear in the narratives of the Passion. Mark (15:40) talks about "Mary the mother of James the younger and Joses," or "Mary the mother of James and Joseph" (Matt 27:56), or simply "Mary the mother of James" (Mark 16:1; Luke 24:10) or even "the other Mary" (Matt 28:1); all these examples refer to the same person: the mother of one of the Twelve and wife of Alphaeus.

The identification of James, son of Alphaeus and James, son of Mary is proven because both are known as "the Younger," which appears only in Mark (15:40). This name (Greek, *mikros*) makes complete sense within the group of Twelve as an easy way to distinguish James, son of Alphaeus, from James, son of Zebedee, one of the three earliest disciples, alongside Peter and John, Zebedee's other son. Regardless, then, of any possible implication as to his small physical stature, Mark (15:40) has simply picked up on a name used within the Twelve that was not included in the group's "official" lists. The name "the Younger" received by James, son of Alphaeus, is one of the many details that the author of the Gospel of Mark has introduced into the narratives from his own experience.

The second member of the Twelve to appear in the final section of Luke's lists is Simon the Zealot (*zēlōtēs*) (Luke 6:15 and Acts 1:13). However, in Mark (3:18) and Matthew (10:4), he is placed third in this section, immediately before Judas Iscariot, and called Simon the Cananaean (*kananaios*). The two epithets added to his name, Cananaean and Zealot, are in fact one and the same thing: Cananaean comes from the transcription of the Aramaic *qan'ana'*, meaning zealous. This adjective, translated into Greek, is *zēlōtēs*. Luke preferred the translation of the Aramaic word in Greek, making it easier for his readers to understand.

Within the group of Twelve, where they spoke Aramaic, they obviously distinguished between Simon *qan'ana'* (Cananaean, zealous) and Simon *kepa'* (*Cephas* or Peter, rock). The designation the Cananaean or the Zealot works in the same way as another name, the Younger, which distinguished between James, son of Alphaeus, and James, son of Zebedee. These two familiar epithets were used within the circle of Twelve to distinguish between two sets of disciples who shared the same names: Simon and James. Again, it does not seem that the names the Cananaean/Zealot and the Younger were chosen by Jesus.

People have often wanted to interpret the appellations the Cananaean and Zealot used for Simon as a sign of his belonging to the group of Zealots, the armed resistance to Rome. There are those who believe that Simon was a disciple who had put down his arms in order to join the group following Jesus. We have seen, however, that this is anachronistic, since there was no serious armed resistance movement against Rome at the end of the decade beginning 20 A.D. (see 3.3.3.4). However, Galilee was full of zealous, Law-abiding people, active militants ensuring that the people kept to the regulations. On occasions, they shared theocratic ideals with Judas of Galilee, who directly and violently confronted the Roman occupation. However, zeal for the Law did not manifest itself in active violence but rather in a religious radicalism that tended to mark the boundaries between the pure and impure, national and foreign, the just and the sinful. From this point of view, Jesus' wide-ranging interpretation of the Law must have led to some surprise in people like Simon, or even Nathanael Bartholomew, solid Law-abiding Israelites, but who in the end were open to the Master's message to them. Before converting to Christianity, Paul had been, as he himself affirmed, "extremely zealous (*zēlōtēs*) . . . for the traditions of my fathers" (Gal 1:14), persecuting the Church due to his "zeal" for the Jewish faith (Phil 3:6).

The most common name in the group of Twelve is Judas. There are three disciples called Judas: Judas Thomas, Judas Thaddeus, and Judas Iscariot; one of Jesus' brothers was also called Judas (see 4.3.4). This is unsurprising since Judas (*Ioudas*) is the Greek version of the Hebrew name Judah (*Yehudà*), the name of Jacob's fourth son, a member of the dynasty in which King David was born and also, thus, the Messiah who would liberate Israel. Judas or Judah is also the name of the most famous of the Maccabees, the legendary Jewish leader who defeated Antioch IV Epiphanes, the foreign king who wanted to destroy the ancestral laws of Israel.

It was a very common name in the first century A.D. The most famous Judas from the era was another defender of the Law and Jewish freedom against foreign invaders: Judas of Galilee, the theocratic ideologue and resistance leader who was active against Roman power when the authorities sought to impose a census and taxes against the laws of God with regard to his people and the land (see 3.3.3.2).

We have talked about Judas Thomas above. The second Judas in the Twelve was Judas, son of James, who is mentioned in only two of the four lists (Luke 6:16 and Acts 1:13); in the other two lists (Mark 3:18 and Matt 10:3) his name is replaced by Thaddeus. This duality (Judas–Thaddeus) is unique in the lists of the Twelve, and we are within our rights to wonder whether they were in fact one and the same person. The most likely hypothesis is that they are the same person whose name was Judas and who was also called Thaddeus. This can be seen indirectly in the way he is described in the Gospel according to John: "Judas (not Iscariot)" (14:22). According to John's tradition, there are two Judases (Judas Thomas does not count, as he is almost always described by his two names): Iscariot and the other Judas. However, given the great number of second names, nicknames, patronymics, and epithets seen among the Twelve, Judas, son of James, may well have had the second name Thaddeus, especially as it was someone who could easily have been confused with two other disciples: Judas Iscariot and Judas Thomas.

The name Thaddeus (Greek, *Thaddaios*) originally comes from the Greek name *Theodotus*, which means "given by God," and became *Taddai* in Aramaic. This Aramaic form, however, was translated back into Greek as *Thaddeus*. The use of both Judas and Thaddeus to describe one single disciple is not an exceptional case among the Twelve. The spokesman and leader of the Twelve was also called both Simon (his name) and *Cephas*-Peter (his nickname). The disciple's first name (Judas) has been conserved by Luke, Acts, and John, whereas Mark and Matthew have kept only his second name (Thaddeus).

The last name on the lists of the Twelve is Judas, son of Simon Iscariot (John 6:71, 13:2, 13:26), also known as Judas Iscariot. Judas' defining characteristic is that he was the traitor, the man who saw to it that Jesus ended up in the hands of the temple authorities and the Sanhedrin, who wanted him killed. This surprising and upsetting fact meant that the name Judas soon became closely associated to this betrayal. He appears in all of the lists of the Twelve (Mark 3:19; Matt 10:4; Luke 6:16). There are no doubts as to his belonging to the group of Twelve: Judas "one of the Twelve, was to betray him" (John 6:71; see also Mark 14:10; Luke 22:3).

The word "Iscariot" may be a mix of the word *ix* ("man" in Hebrew) and *Cariot* or *Kerioth* (the name of a place), "man (coming from)

Kerioth." It is then some kind of family surname, and this explains why Judas' father, Simon, and Judas himself used it. English also has many surnames indicating a family's geographical origins: London, Lancaster, England, and so on. Locating Kerioth itself has proved difficult. Proposals include Kerioth-Hezron, in southern Judaea, in the Negev (see Josh 15:25), and Kartah, in the Esdraelon valley, near Galilee (Josh 21:34), or even the city of Jerusalem, as according to later targums, Iscariot may have meant "man of the city." None of these proposals has been proven to be definitive. In any case, as Jesus' other disciples were Galileans, Judas need not be an exception. The word Iscariot may well have been created as a patronymic in the town in Galilee where his father lived, or another of his ancestors (a man from Kerioth, the town in Judaea?). Nevertheless, we cannot rule out that the disciple and traitor may have come from Judaea.

Within the group of Twelve, Judas was in charge of the shared money-box (John 12:6, 13:29); his betrayal also involved an amount of money that the temple leaders promised to pay him (Mark 14:11; Luke 22:5). Matthew stresses Judas' greed, stating that the reward for his betrayal was thirty pieces of silver (26:15). Suspicions about money reappeared in relation to Judas when Mary anointed Jesus in Bethany. According to John (12:4-6), Judas showed his meanness by protesting emphatically at the misuse of the perfume being poured over Jesus: "Why was this ointment not sold for 300 denarii and given to the poor?" Mark (14:4-5) does not say who made this comment, and Matthew (26:8) seems to indicate that it is a thought shared by all of the disciples. Judas is presented as avaricious in Matthew (26:15) and as a thief in John (12:6).

In other sources, the real reason for his betrayal is not the money but his possession by demons. Luke starts his narrative of the Passion with these words: "Then Satan entered into Judas called Iscariot" (22:3). The disciple went on to offer his services to the high priests, the temple's leaders. John describes how Judas decided to betray Jesus because he was driven to do so by the devil (13:2). The devil's influence was seen in the piece of bread that Judas accepted from Jesus at the Last Supper. The Gospel of John says, "Then after the morsel, Satan entered into him" (13:27). In short, Judas "is a devil" (John 6:70). Judas' betrayal is incomprehensible for the Gospel writers, which only adds weight to its being a solid historical fact (see 6.2.2.5).

The sense and purpose of the Twelve

The Twelve Disciples, who were called and chosen by Jesus personally, were constant witnesses to his words and deeds, but they had a more wide-ranging purpose: the Twelve were to become a living extension of Jesus and his activities, in the present and in the future. Thus, we need to take into account what they represented rather than what they actually did. As we shall see, the Twelve do not appear to have left Jesus' side, apart from a short period when he sent them in pairs to act as missionaries in Galilee. Jesus wanted to choose twelve men above all others when he started his activities; twelve men who would form a set and stable group of disciples. As we have seen, there were other men and women who shared in his life and project in different ways and places, but the public image of the rabbi from Nazareth was indelibly linked to "the Twelve." These Twelve, at least their most conspicuous members (Peter, their spokesman, James, and John), also took part in the most important moments in Jesus' life. For example, the Twelve were probably the only people who ate with Jesus at the Last Supper on the day before his death.

Why did Jesus want to surround himself with a group of twelve men? First, a group of twelve, as E. P. Sanders stresses, harkens back to the twelve tribes of the restored Israel. The dream of bringing together all of God's scattered people to the promised land of Israel dominated a great part of Jewish hopes in the second and first centuries B.C. These hopes focused on the end of time, which was seen to be the moment when the people of Israel were to be fully reconstituted and restored, having overcome the test of this scattering.

A great many texts come from all schools of Jewish thought. From the start of the second century B.C., the Sirach contains this prayer: "Gather all the tribes of Jacob, and give them their inheritance, as at the beginning" (36:11). The subject was already common, following the destruction of the kingdom of Judah and its inhabitants' deportation to Babylonia. The prophet Ezekiel likened Israel to sheep scattered about the place and God was the shepherd, who promised to bring them back together: "I will bring them into their own land; and I will feed them on the mountains of Israel" (34:13). This view includes all the countries that the chosen people had been deported to and not just Babylonia. According to the prophet Isaiah,

God "will assemble the outcasts of Israel, and gather the dispersed of Judah from the four corners of the earth" (11:12).

From the second century B.C. onward, the idea of the restoration of Israel was strengthened by the growing religious nationalism against the attempts to Hellenize the region. The Second Book of Maccabees says, "For we have hope in God that he will soon have mercy upon us and will gather us from everywhere under heaven into this holy place" (2:18). In the first centuries B.C. and A.D., the figure to restore the twelve tribes was often the Messiah, the descendant of David. According to the Song of Solomon, this figure would "gather together a holy people, whom he shall lead in righteousness; and he shall judge the tribes of the people that has been sanctified by the Lord his God" (17:26).

This last text closely resembles a promise referring to the end of time that Jesus made to the Twelve. It is in the Q source (Matt 19:28 || Luke 22:30): "You who have followed me will also sit on 12 thrones, judging the 12 tribes of Israel." The role of the Twelve does not end in the present but continues on into the future, to the end of time, when all of Israel will be brought back together. The Twelve, swathed in Messianic authority, will take charge of governing Israel. As G. Theissen points out, Jesus has converted individual Messianism into group Messianism: the closeness of the Twelve leads to their taking part in the governing of the Israel at the end of time, when the Kingdom of the Messiah has begun. Unsurprisingly the two most impetuous and reckless disciples, the sons of thunder, James and John, asked if they could take the two places of honor, on either side of the main throne, where the King Messiah was to be seated: "Grant us to sit, one at your right hand and one at your left" (Mark 10:37 || Matt 20:21). In reply, Jesus avoided making any judgment: "to sit at my right hand or at my left is not mine to grant, but it is for those for whom it has been prepared" (Mark 10:40 || Matt 20:23). Only God knows who will hold these privileged positions in the future Kingdom.

It is certain that Jesus included the Twelve in his plans for the governing of Israel, once the Kingdom had been established. However, as J. D. G. Dunn points out and according to the aforementioned quotation (Matt 19:28 || Luke 22:30), the Twelve were to act only once Israel had been restored. Furthermore, Jesus' main aim was not to restore the people of Israel, when he proclaimed the coming of the

Kingdom of God. Contrary to the usual aspirations of the time, Jesus' hope was not directly focused on restoring Israel's religion, land, and people, the bases of the Jewish identity. It is difficult to find any references in the Gospels to the idea of a return from exile or of a new exodus for Israel. His aim was not set on reconstructing his people's national identity, which was suffering under the political domination of a foreign power. Instead, his proposal was fundamentally based on the reign of a God who was Father to the good and the bad, to the just and unjust. Indeed, there is nothing in the Gospels that mentions the restoration of Israel, as there is in the Jewish literature of the time. Even in the quotation from the Q source about the Twelve carrying out judgment of the twelve tribes of Israel, there is no actual mention of this restoration. It is an altogether different matter to interpret the exile-restoration duality in the sense of transference, that is to say, as it applies to Jesus, who would have identified with Israel's sufferings (N. T. Wright).

In order to understand how Jesus saw the end of time, it is not enough to simply point out the role of the Twelve as judges and governors of Israel. We also need to bear in mind another text from the Q source, which says, "[M]any will come from east and west and sit at table with Abraham, Isaac and Jacob" (Matt 8:11 || Luke 13:28-29). Jesus did not see the end of history simply in terms of Israel, but in universal terms, in terms of mankind as a whole. For this reason, Judgment Day will be favorable for Nineveh, the great capital of Assyria, which heard Jonah, Israel's prophet, preach and repented (Matt 12:41 || Luke 11:32). For Jesus, judgment is not Israel's triumph over the pagans, their enemies, but the moment when all people, Jews and non-Jews, place themselves before divine justice.

Jesus preferred to keep within the physical borders of Israel, though this was not always true. He considered the Jewish people to be the main audience for his activities. His choice of Twelve Disciples was a sign recognized by everyone, as the name "Twelve" was at the heart of Israel's collective imagination. Jesus did not relate this to ethnic or national borders because he wanted to spread his message across the whole of Israel. He did not propose to restore Israel from a political and religious point of view but to bring God's healing presence to all the men and women of Israel, without exception, starting with the poor, the sick, and the sinners, continuing with the Law-abiding and, subsequently, the foreigners, who were also to receive God's mercy. S. Freyne has pointed out that the norms of ritual purity (regarding bathing, the burial of the dead, and the preparation of food) were not practiced in the villages that Jesus commonly visited (e.g., Capernaum). This would indicate that his concept of restoration was primarily of an ethical nature.

Jesus' choice of twelve men, his formation of a group called the Twelve, was in actual fact a sign of the universality of his message and his intentions. It was not a sign of his concern for restoring Israel, in the way people understood this idea at the time. Jesus wanted to spread his message to all the sons and daughters of Abraham, especially to the sick, the sinners, and also foreigners, namely, to all those who needed to recover bodily and spiritually. Building an eschatological Israel, an Israel for the end of time, meant restoring people who needed saving immediately in body and spirit. For this reason, all who belonged to Israel (including those who believed themselves to be just!) had to repent. God is present in the world through what Jesus does and says, and people need to respond unselfishly. Heartfelt repentance was another of the names that Jesus gave to the restoration of Israel.

The Twelve were sent out to heal the sick of body and spirit and to preach repentance with splendid news: the Kingdom of God had already arrived! This meant that the restoration of Israel had already begun. This restoration would continue and culminate in the day when all of Israel and all those from further afield, from east and west, would come together again. "For I know their works and their thoughts, and I am coming to gather all nations and tongues, and they shall come and see my glory" (Isa 66:18). In this context, see also John 11:51-52 and 12:20-23. Note that the "restoration" is to be understood as the gathering of all peoples, the people of Israel and those of all nations.

Then, the Twelve would be rewarded for their work with a place of honor in the Kingdom: Jesus would maintain and continue his friendship with the Twelve and he would make them a part of his messianic mission. The Twelve represented Jesus' desire to spread his message to all of Israel and to promote the definitive and immediate restoration through the preaching of repentance and healing. Jesus' activities were universal (for everyone in Israel without exception) within the particular (almost entirely limited to Israel). In this he loyally continued John the Baptist's program. Fundamentally, the existence of the Twelve illustrated and accentuated this program shared by both rabbis of the Jordan and Nazareth, John and Jesus.

When Jesus sent the Twelve to visit all the towns of Galilee, they were acting as an extension of Jesus himself. They did the same things the Master did and acted in the way he told them to. This mission was limited in terms of space: the Twelve visited only some of the towns in Galilee, probably in an area they had already been to with Jesus. It was also limited in terms of time: nothing pointed to this mission of the Twelve lasting very long. Leaving aside the reasons Jesus sent the Twelve to travel through Galilee (see 4.6.2), these events are backed up by unquestionable historical evidence. Mark (6:7), Matthew (10:5), and Luke (9:1) specify that only the Twelve were sent in pairs by Jesus. Q does not mention who was sent. If Jesus sent the disciples on a mission probably only once, then those sent must have been a stable and consolidated group who constantly accompanied him: his inner circle. Jesus handed them a task of great responsibility.

If the Twelve traveled through a relatively small area mostly already known to them, and if their mission did not last more than a few weeks, then the harsh conditions that Jesus applied to carrying out this task become more understandable. The mission of the Twelve is reported in two versions: the Gospel according to Mark (6:7-13; see Luke 9:1-6) and the Q collection of sayings (Matt 9:37-38, 10:5-15; Luke 10:2-12; Luke 9:1-6). In both versions, the Twelve are confronted by many difficulties. Jesus tells them, "I send you out as lambs in the midst of wolves." They were not to expect any help in their work; on the contrary, they were only to come across problems and attempts to see them fail. They had to learn how to defeat evil, not with more evil but with righteousness. The golden rule of the mission was to have complete trust in God and his wisdom.

The Twelve sent by Jesus personally experienced the complete support that God guaranteed them in the hospitality they were freely offered. When they entered a town, they had to call at a house and, if they were welcomed, stay there, "eating and drinking what they provide," whether the host had much or not. This house, whether rich or poor, acted as the headquarters, from which their activities in the town would be based. The reason was, "for the laborer deserves his wages."

Understandably the rules set for the Twelve on their travels were reduced to a minimum. The Twelve did not have to walk long distances, instead visiting the towns and villages of Galilee's populated areas (especially, the region by the lake) and staying at the homes of willing hosts. They did not need to take anything with them: God ultimately gave them all they needed! They did not need a bag for food, money to buy it, or a purse to keep coins in. They did not need a change of clothing, sandals, or a staff to defend themselves from any bandits: the Twelve were not professional travelers, as were the cynics who showed off (!) about their poverty. The only thing the Twelve had to worry about was carrying out the mission that Jesus had entrusted them with. This meant that they could not waste time greeting people here and there, as this would delay them in their mission.

The instructions that Jesus gave the Twelve differed significantly from those that the Essenes adopted when they traveled and visited sedentary members of their group (*J.W.* 2:125–27). Their lifestyle also differed somewhat from that of the traveling cynics, who went from one place to the next with a bag, stick, and cloak with double lining. They also differed from the rules used by subsequent Christian missionaries, who had to make long journeys and were allowed to use sandals and a staff, as can be seen in Mark (6:8-9).

Once they arrived and had found somewhere to stay, they were to act in the way that Jesus ordered them to: healing the sick of body and spirit (expelling demons) and preaching repentance (Mark) and the coming of the Kingdom of God (the Q collection). This twofold task echoed Jesus' activities, as the Twelve acted as an extension of the Master himself, multiplying and spreading his activities. Those sent were given the same responsibility and dignity awarded to him who had sent them: "He who receives you receives me, and he who receives me receives him who sent me," God himself (Matt 10:40 || Luke 10:16; similarly, Mark 9:37 and John 13:20). If the Twelve encountered problems and were not welcomed in the towns they visited, they had to change the message of their preaching and show the people by means of a prophetic gesture that they needed to realize the imminence of the Day of Judgment: they removed the dust from their feet signifying that they had broken off any relations with the people of this town and could not be held responsible for the consequences. In an emphatic statement Jesus compared the attitude of this town to that of the people of Sodom, the depraved city where they wanted to harm even two of God's angels, and said, "Truly, I say to you, it shall be more tolerable on the day of judgment for the land of Sodom and Gomorrah than for that town." The mission of the Twelve was to continue Jesus' own mission, and Jesus gave them the same level of importance. Jesus' aim (to proclaim that God was present in the world and that the transformation had begun) also involved the Twelve, who were sent out to spread news of his words and deeds.

Jesus' aim was at the heart of the early community, following his death and resurrection: to spread the gospel to the whole of mankind (Mark 16:15). Luke used the term "apostle" when talking about the Twelve, which means emissary. The apostles became the basis of the Church. Others, such as Paul and Barnabas (Acts 14:14), were known as apostles to show that they were people who dedicated their lives to spreading the gospel of Jesus. Luke stressed the universal scope of the message preached by Jesus and reported on two missions: that of the Twelve apostles (Luke 6:13), and that of the seventy-two disciples (Luke 10:1, 10:17), a figure that represents all the people in the world according to the list given in chapter 10 of the book of Genesis.

4.5.4. The Competitors and Adversaries

As described above (see 3.3.2), the three most important religious groups at the time of Jesus were the Pharisees, Sadducees, and Essenes. We have also spoken about anti-Roman resistance and the Zealots in particular (see 3.3.3.4). We have outlined the distinctive traits of the Herodians, the defenders of Herod's dynasty and his sons, allies of the Romans, who controlled this Jewish country (see 3.4.2). We have briefly looked at the men who dedicated their lives to interpreting the Jewish Law, the so-called "scribes" or teachers of the Law, who were highly regarded by the people (see 3.3.1). We need now to return to the specific point of view of the relations between Jesus and the groups and collectives, who at different times and in different ways crossed his path during his activities. We need to pick up again on the terminology used by J. P. Meier, who calls them his "competitors and adversaries," given that the relations they maintained with Jesus varied from a marked affinity (some Pharisees) to ferocious opposition (the high priests and leaders of the temple in Jerusalem, for the most part Sadducees).

Let us begin with two considerations. Jesus did not accept any kind of description that could connect him to any given group or specific ideology, including, for example, the messianic ideology, as it was understood at the time. Nevertheless, he was happy for people to call him *rabbi* (a Hebrew word) or *rabboni* (an Aramaic word), which meant teacher. This was because, in the eyes of the people, Jesus was a teacher; someone who called them, taught them, and gave them rules how to behave, although he spoke differently from other contemporary teachers. However, presenting himself as a teacher did not mean that he identified himself with any particular group. Some scribes formed part of or sympathized with the Pharisees; others adopted positions that reflected those of the Sadducees, and others were not linked to either. Jesus belonged to this last group.

Second, we need to carefully distinguish between two types of information: the information on the historical figure of Jesus and the presentation of the relations between Jesus and his adversaries, as described by the Gospels. The image of Jesus' adversaries has undergone modifications by the Christian community, which wanted to distance itself from the Judaism of the time, with which it did not always enjoy the best of relations. Initially, those who believed in Jesus Christ were Jews who continued to rigorously practice the religion of Moses, while also recognizing Jesus as Israel's Messiah. The conflict grew because two divergent trends began, and the Jews who were devoted to Jesus' cause first became the object of suspicions, and then open attack within the synagogues. Around 50 A.D., the Q collection recounts that Christians who were Jewish in origin were being interrogated by the synagogue's leaders: "do not be anxious how you are to speak or what you are to say" (Matt 10:19 || Luke 12:11). Slowly but surely Christianity attracted those who were not of Jewish origin who, although Christian, were not committed to keeping to the Law of Moses.

The writings in the New Testament generally reflect situations of tension and conflict, or even open hostility, between the Jews who would not acknowledge Jesus' legitimacy and the Jews who had become Christians, followers of the resurrected Messiah of Israel. These differences are often reflected back on to Jesus' life, which leads only to the magnification of the contrasts between Jesus and other contemporary religious groups. For example, the report in John (9:22), "the Jews had already agreed that if any one should confess him to be Christ, he was to be put out of the synagogue," make sense only from the last decade of the first century A.D. onward. The Christian writings increasingly ignored the differences among the various Jewish groups, presenting them all equally as Jesus' adversaries. A good example of this comes in the Gospel according to Matthew, where the Pharisees and Sadducees are described as forming a common dialectic front against Jesus, which is highly unlikely from a historical point of view (Matt 16:1).

The Christian and Jewish texts accentuate the antagonism and increase the distance between Jesus and contemporary Jewish groups, presenting them all as far from supportive of him. Careful study of the evidence, however, shows that Jesus inspired both notable sympathies and deep antipathy among those who did not follow him. We cannot tar with the same brush all the religious and political groups and collectives when Jesus was active.

An attentive reader will notice that we shall not now talk about the Zealots or Essenes. The reason for this is simple: the historical sources on Jesus do not contain any direct reference to one or other of these groups. We have already seen that the second name of Simon, one of Jesus' disciples, is "the Zealot," but in the sense of zeal for the Law, not in the sense of belonging to any particular group. We have stressed that the Zealots, as a group or groups of armed militants fighting the Romans, did not exist when Jesus was alive. In 30 A.D., the distinction between anti-Roman resistance and bandits was still a very grey area, though the theocratic doctrines of Judas of Galilee, the ideologue for the Zealot movement, had made an impression on Jewish society. A good sign of this is the issue of payment of taxes to Caesar, which is mentioned in one of the questions put to Jesus by the Pharisees and Herodians (see 3.3.3.2). Later we shall see the significance of the figure of Barabbas, the bandit whom the people spared instead of Jesus of Nazareth (see 6.2.4.4).

Neither are the Essenes and their monastery at Qumran mentioned in the texts available. Jesus baptized people in the Jordan Valley to the north of Jericho in Judaea, and he even traveled to this city, not far from Qumran, but we have no evidence that he had any direct contact with the Essenes. When we looked at the Essenes earlier, the differences between their doctrines and Jesus' positions became clear, as did the differences with other contemporary Judaisms (see 3.3.2.4). J. P. Meier sums them up in five points: (a) strict interpretation of the Law, especially that relating to ritual purity and rest on the Sabbath, the meals restricted to members of the Essene community only, who respected the Law in the way that the priests would, although they were all laymen; (b) the use of the solar and not the lunar calendar, which was used by the majority Judaism and Jesus; (c) hatred of their enemies as an expression of the unbridgeable gulf between the members of the community and those who were not members, unlike a number of Jewish groups and Jesus' group, for whom membership of other groups was not anathema (the Sadducees were, however, strictly elitist); (d) the strict hierarchy of the Essenes based on the sacerdotal dynasty of the leaders, unlike Jesus' group or the Pharisees, who were strictly laymen; and (e) the study of astrology and dreams found in certain texts at Qumran, unlike Jesus' group (and certain rabbis including Hanina ben Dosa), who carried out healings, which do not exist in Essene texts. In conclusion, there is a significant distance between the sectarian Judaism of the Essenes and the other Judaisms of the first century A.D., and this distance is even greater when the Essenes are compared to Jesus of Nazareth.

4.5.4.1. The Scribes

Jesus and John the Baptist were considered and treated as rabbis, as teachers (John 1:38; 3:26). Jesus was called both rabbi and teacher by the people, his disciples or other religious leaders. On two occasions, the sources have maintained this name in the Aramaic, the language in which Jesus preached: Bartimaeus, the blind man Jesus healed in Jericho, and Mary Magdalene, his loyal disciple, addressed him as *rabboni* (Mark 10:51; John 20:16). However, the Hebrew word *rabbi*, used by the disciples, was also a common way to address him. Judas, when he betrayed him (Mark 14:45 || Matt 26:49), or Peter during Jesus' transfiguration on the mountaintop (Mark 9:5), used it quite naturally.

Jesus was a rabbi, a Jewish teacher from the first century A.D. The fact that he was accompanied by a relatively large number of disciples only added to his rabbinical image. Another detail also contributed to this image: Jesus wore a cloak, with fringes or knotted strings hanging off each of the four corners. Pious Jews would have recognized this as Jesus' desire to abide by the Law at all times (Mark 6:56 || Matt 14:36; Matt 9:20 || Luke 8:44). These fringes were not exclusive to rabbis, but this detail does fit completely with someone who has claimed for himself a position of religious leadership in Israel (see Mark 12:38).

The scribes did not form a group apart within Judaism. As we have said, Jesus was one of the nonaligned rabbis; he was not one of the scribes associated to either the Pharisees or Sadducees (nor to the Essenes, a closed group). We do not know if there were many "independent" rabbis, but we should stress that the renowned rabbis Hillel or Shammai were apparently not linked to the Pharisee group. The scribe who asked Jesus about the most important commandment in the Law was not attached to any religious group (Mark 12:28). Mark 2:16 highlights the situation perfectly when it refers to "the scribes of the Pharisees." The rabbis who spoke to and argued with Jesus were not always linked to the Pharisees. When Jesus found fault with the conduct of the Pharisees (Luke 11:39-44, a text belonging to the Q collection), he also criticized the behavior of the scribes (Luke 11:46-52).

Chapter 23 of Matthew, which associates the scribes with the Pharisees no fewer than seven times ("But woe to you, scribes and Pharisees, hypocrites!"), has to be attributed to the author of the Gospel and not to Jesus. Jesus did not refrain from publicly criticizing the spiritual vanity of the scribes, who liked to be treated with honor and be acknowledged as experts in the Law of Moses, the Law that all Jews had to keep (Mark 12:38-39).

The debate between Jesus and the rabbis focused ultimately on a fundamental question: the authority of his teaching (see Egerton 2). On what or on whom did Jesus base his doctrine and teachings, or the healings that accompanied them? In the words of the people themselves, who were astonished by his expelling an evil spirit: "What is this? A new teaching!" (Mark 1:27 || Luke 4:36). Jesus spoke with authority and did not need to base his ideas on those of earlier or contemporary rabbis. He did not justify his views by calling on those of other rabbis. He spoke on his own authority, freely referring to the Scriptures. He knew them, but his fundamental aim was not to interpret them. He was an expert in the Law, but he was not concerned about interpreting it.

Jesus was an unusual and unique rabbi who provoked contrasting reactions from other rabbis. In Mark 12:28-34 one of the rabbis actually agreed with Jesus on the central point of the Law: loving God and one another. Jesus told him, "You are not far from the kingdom of God." Nevertheless, Jesus' relations with the scribes were not always smooth. At times, Jesus overstepped the mark of what was deemed tolerable according to the common parameters of the Jewish religion. When he was in Capernaum, they brought him a paralytic man to be healed, and Jesus said to him, "My son, your sins are forgiven" (Mark 2:5). The scribes present considered these words a serious transgression, "blasphemy," as God is the only one who can forgive sins. For them, Jesus was a blasphemer who dared to do what only God can do, and this was incomprehensible and scandalous for people who always kept strictly to Moses' Law (see 6.2.1.1).

The opposition to Jesus from these qualified interpreters of the Law can be seen in the clearly hostile "sentence" handed down by the rabbis sent from Jerusalem to Capernaum, where Jesus had acted. The wise men of Israel concluded that if Jesus could successfully heal people's inner ills and expel evil spirits, it was because he had schemed with the lord of these spirits, with the devil himself (Mark 3:22). The next step after this accusation, also taken by the scribes in Jerusalem, was to have the rabbi from Nazareth eliminated (Mark 11:18).

The three synoptic Gospels show how throughout Jesus' trial and execution the scribes sided with the temple leaders, the high priests, and the nobility, Jerusalem's lay aristocracy, all of whom were linked to the Sadducee party. Many rabbis who had been in contact with Jesus may have acted on the orders of the religious authorities in Jerusalem, who had asked them, as "experts" in the Law, to take up positions on this awkward and unsettling figure. These scribes may have even belonged to the Sadducee group, who mainly came from Jerusalem's leading classes.

The Pharisees, the other important Jewish group of the time, may also have wanted to find out about Jesus' doctrines firsthand, and thus sent some of their rabbis to Galilee (Mark 7:1). Apparently the issue here was the obligation to ritually wash one's hands before eating, but there was another element in the background: Jesus was ignoring the tradition of the elders and acting on his own account. Once again there are echoes of the issue that most concerned the rabbis, the scholars of the Jewish people: "By what authority are you doing these things, or who gave you this authority to do them?" (Mark 11:28 || Matt 21:23 || Luke 20:2). This issue concerns the very heart of Jesus the person, and it is the fundamental sticking point between the rabbi of Nazareth and the other rabbis, between Christianity and Judaism.

The scribes did not all adopt the same position, but generally speaking, they opposed and accused Jesus. They were more akin to adversaries than to competitors.

4.5.4.2. The Pharisees

Of all the Jewish groups around when Jesus was alive, it has been rightly pointed out that the Pharisees were the ones closest to him. Jesus did not belong to the Pharisee group, but they did agree on some of the more specific doctrines: belief in the resurrection of the dead on Judgment Day, at the end of history; the influence of angels and demons on people's lives; the figure of the Messiah, who, at the end of time, would fulfill Jewish hopes; and the importance of the heart as the source of feelings, both good and bad. However, Jesus' preaching was framed by a new perspective: God has entered the history of mankind, and the establishment of his kingdom has turned everything on its head. This can be seen in the healings, visible signs of God's power, and in the defeat of evil and the devil, in all his forms.

The active presence of God in the history of man puts certain things into perspective, while making other things absolute. Accordingly Jesus, unlike the Pharisees, did not emphasize certain regulations and customs, and this was seen as scandalous, since they placed strict fulfillment of the Law above all else. In the Pharisees' view of the Law (and the Sadducees' and Essenes' view, for that matter), ritual purity was crucial. The Pharisees made every effort to make the laws known to everyone, introducing a great many reinterpretations in order to lessen the harshness of some of them, ensuring that they could all be put into practice. The Pharisees were authentic apostles of the fulfillment of the Law of Moses, whereas for Jesus obeying the

Law was subordinate to the bases or foundations of this Law: "justice and mercy and faith" (Matt 23:23 || Luke 11:42).

For the Pharisees, then, Jesus was a rabbi who promoted a "lax" interpretation of Moses' commandments. For Jesus, the Pharisees were concerned only with external purity and had forgotten about the purity of heart, thought, and intention (Mark 7:15). This would explain the relative value that the laws of ritual purity, the many fasts, the scrupulous payment of the tithes, and the strict observance of the festive and sabbatical rest had for Jesus (see 5.3.2.2). According to Jesus, the foremost priority should be given to other factors: saving sinners, the impure from a ritual point of view (Mark 2:18); proclaiming the Kingdom of God through words and deeds (Mark 2:19); justice, love, and faith (Matt 23:23); and that the life of a person was more important than observing the Sabbath (Mark 2:27, 3:4) (see 5.3.2.3).

The debate between Jesus and the Pharisees did not involve all of the Law's precepts (a total of 613, according to the Pharisee scribes), only those points that received a particular emphasis in the arguments that sprang up between the rabbis of different schools in the first century A.D. The differences were not great in number: Jesus and the Pharisees agreed on many issues! The problem lay in the priorities. An obvious example was that of divorce, which was relatively acceptable to the two important schools of thought led by Hillel and Shammai. Asked for his opinion, Jesus said that God's "first" concern was for man and woman to form a stable union and not to be separated (Mark 10:1-12). The typical scholarly debate (how and when can divorce be justified) was relegated to the background as Jesus took up a position that went beyond the boundaries of the initial question: the problem is not divorce, but matrimony, as a divine plan. Once again the rabbi Jesus left the Pharisee scribes "without a leg to stand on" (see 5.3.2.1).

The relations between Jesus and the Pharisees were, thus, much better than one would assume from a skim reading of the Gospels or a simply thematic reading. This is especially true of the Gospels of Matthew and John, which were written in the midst of the arguments going on at the end of the first century A.D. between a Judaism dominated by the Pharisees and a Christianity that still had strong Jewish roots. These arguments have had profound effects on both Matthew (23) and John (7–8). We should stress that Jesus had friends among the Pharisees, such as the Pharisee Simon (Luke 7), who invited him for meals, and the Pharisee scribes who visited him incognito, such as Nicodemus (John 3). Luke even described how some Pharisees saved Jesus when he was under threat from Antipas' criminal intentions, warning him to get away (13:31).

Jesus' criticism of the Pharisees was that they lived with an attitude of religious self-satisfaction and snobbishness. The clearest example comes in the parable of the Pharisee and the tax collector. Here, the Pharisee produced a very accurate description of himself: "I am not like other men, extortioners, unjust, adulterers. . . . I fast twice a week, I give tithes of all that I get" (Luke 18:11-12). The Pharisees lived irreproachable lifestyles and were eager to ensure that people kept to the Law, but they felt only disrespect for the marginalized, those who were so ignorant that they were unable to abide by the commandments (John 7:49). Naturally, they had to avoid sinners in order not to become impure and contaminated by their sin. The Pharisee Simon was shocked when Jesus let himself be touched by a sinner (Luke 7:39). Jesus, however, refused to segregate anyone. He criticized the Pharisees for not recognizing their own sin, the sin of the "virtuous": maintaining an excellent external appearance but allowing their heart to be filled with "extortion and rapacity" (Matt 23:25 || Luke 11:39). The Gospel of John (9:41) forcefully condemns this attitude of spiritual hypocrisy in pithy terms, saying, "If you were blind, you would have no guilt; but now that you see, 'We see,' your guilt remains."

Jesus had relations with Pharisees throughout the period when he was publicly active. Most of the six thousand Pharisees, a figure provided by Josephus, lived in or around Jerusalem, but there were also some Pharisee outposts in Galilee (Mark 8:11). But many of the discussions that Jesus had with the Pharisees must have taken place in Judaea and the area around Jerusalem in the months toward the end of his life. The Pharisees were an urban group with a major presence on the Sanhedrin, together with the Sadducees. Yet they did not appear during the trial and execution of Jesus (Matt 27:62 and John 18:3 are the only exceptions, and in both cases their involvement was peripheral). Thus, what Mark (3:6) says does not seem historically plausible. At the height of Jesus' activities in Galilee, the Pharisees could not have been scheming to have him killed, when they were not even actively calling for his head in Jerusalem (see 6.2.1.1).

This is an important detail because it shows, indirectly and once again, that the Pharisees were undoubtedly competitors but not adversaries.

4.5.4.3. The Herodians

Mark (3:6) also mentions the intentions of the Herodians, those siding with Herod Antipas, with regard to Jesus. Essentially, it states that they were planning to do away with him. The Herodians' desire to eliminate Jesus is confirmed in Luke (13:31). Here it says that "some Pharisees came, and said to him, 'Get away from here, for Herod [Antipas] wants to kill you.'" Antipas had already had John the Baptist killed, and now it could well be Jesus' turn: the tetrarch considered him to be a Johannes redivivus; he saw him as John the Baptist brought back to life (Mark 6:16 || Matt 14:2).

As a result, Mark (3:6) is partial confirmation of information that can be verified historically. The Pharisees are said to have been watching Jesus to see whether or not he respected the Sabbath, which can be confirmed by the historical sources. According to them, the healings that the rabbi of Nazareth performed were against the Law. However, there is no evidence that the Pharisees brought criminal charges against Jesus for this reason. Those who did show themselves to be against Jesus were the scribes in Galilee who accused him of blasphemy because he pardoned sins, thus usurping a function that only God can perform (see Mark 2:7 || Matt 9:3). Herod Antipas wanted to eliminate him too, but for political reasons relating to John the Baptist, under whose auspices Jesus began his activities. According to Antipas, the work carried out by John, who died for opposing him, was being continued by Jesus and represented a potential threat to his government. Thus, the scribes (not the Pharisees) and the Herodians agreed in believing that Jesus was dangerous: Mark 3:6 reflects this state of affairs to an extent. Matthew (12:14) says only that the Pharisees wanted Jesus out of the way. This view is the least likely of all, as can be seen in the way the Passion is reported by Matthew himself.

The Herodians appeared a second time in the Gospels in relation to the tax to be paid to Caesar (Mark 12:13 || Matt 22:16). Here the Herodians talked to Jesus directly. According to Mark 3:1-6, the only people present while Jesus healed the man's paralyzed hand on the Sabbath were Pharisees. The taxation issue involved two sets of people: "some of the Pharisees and some of the Herodians." The presence of the latter, people close to the Herodian dynasty and Antipas the tetrarch of Galilee and Perea, in particular, is confirmed by the political overtones of the question put to Jesus. The Pharisees were in charge of keeping an eye on the religious side of the issue, ascertaining whether or not Jesus interpreted the Law according to Judas the Galilean and refused to pay tribute to Rome; if this were the case, then the Herodians, defenders of the Roman cause in Palestine, would have good reason to accuse him. If he did not interpret the Law thus, then he would lose face with the majority of the Jewish people. (This issue is looked at in detail in section 3.3.3.2.)

The tax issue probably took place in Jerusalem, and the Herodians acted as witnesses to Jesus' words. They were sent to find out whether he was for or against Rome and represented the longa manus (long arm) of the established power. The Gospel explains that it was a difficult situation for Jesus; a form of trap had been prepared for him. The Herodians did not innocently ask him a question but in fact acted as spies, looking for evidence of high treason against the emperor, which could lead to the death penalty. The Herodians acted as agents for the Jewish authorities in Jerusalem, who wanted to catch Jesus and bring him before the courts of the Roman authorities. Their attempt failed spectacularly but demonstrated the combined religious and political strategy used to condemn Jesus to death.

In their few appearances, the Herodians are presented as Jesus' adversaries. They sided with Antipas, their leader, who concealed a desire to have him killed, and thus forced him to flee Galilee.

4.5.4.4. The Sadducees

Though there was probably a Sadducee presence in Sepphoris, the historical capital of Galilee, the vast majority of the Sadducees lived in Jerusalem. Indeed, Jesus debated in Jerusalem with the Sadducees directly in the last days of his life (Mark 12:18-27 || Matt 22:23-33 || Luke 20:27-38). As seen earlier, the references in Matthew (16:1, 16:6, 16:11) to combined action by the Pharisees and Sadducees are improbable and exist only in this Gospel, as can be deduced from a comparison with Mark 8:11-21, which mentions only the Pharisees: the Sadducees and Pharisees were, in fact, the two main opposing sides in Judaism from the second century B.C. to the first century A.D.

The events in question involved an argument started by the Sadducees, who were trying to trick Jesus. It focused on a theoretical problem aimed at ridiculing the beliefs held by Jesus (and by the Pharisees and Essenes!) with regard to the resurrection of the dead, a common point of discussion between Pharisees and Sadducees (see 3.3.2.3). The Sadducees, with an attitude somewhere between skepticism and scorn, put forward the case of seven brothers who successively marry the same woman, in accordance with the so-called levirate law. According to the Law of Moses, the dead man's brother had to marry the widow in order to ensure he had descendants (Deut 25:5). However, the Sadducees added mischievously that none of the brothers had children with this woman; thus, on everyone's resurrection, whom should she have sexual relations with? Which of the seven was actually her husband?

Jesus' response was twofold. First, he stated that relations between men and women (sexuality and procreation) would be completely different in the next life. There was no point looking at the question as if it were simply a continuation of the way we live our lives on earth. In an immortal eternal life, men and women would be "like angels in heaven," concerned only with praising and contemplating God, the source of happiness. Envisaging sexuality in the other world, as with other human activities (eating, drinking, dressing), became meaningless. The Sadducees' objection was nonsensical, and Jesus paid little attention to it. He merely needed to remind them of what is needed by those who have left the earth behind to live in heaven. Furthermore, his reference to the angels was ironic since the Sadducees also denied their existence (Acts 23:8). The dialectics of the rabbi from Nazareth proved to be highly effective.

Nonetheless, the main issue here was whether, at the end of time, the dead are resurrected. Jesus added to his response and turned on the offensive, criticizing the mistake made by the Sadducees in not believing in resurrection: they were people who "know neither the scriptures nor the power of God." Furthermore, Jesus accused those who saw themselves as deeply religious of lacking faith in the incomparable power of God, which is able to bring life to where there was only death. Once again this echoed Jesus' belief in the power of God, which feeds the birds in the sky and clothes the grass of the field, and, as John the Baptist proclaimed, can even raise up children to Abraham from stones.

Thus, for Jesus, this power manifests itself in all its majesty in the resurrection of the dead. The dead are returned to life because God's strength brings them life. Yet the Sadducees, self-acclaimed experts in the Scriptures, were unable to see this or interpret it correctly. Exodus 3:6 states, "I am the God of your father, the God of Abraham, the God of Isaac, and the God of Jacob" and shows who God is and how he acts. The Sadducees valued this text as it belongs to the Pentateuch, the only part of the Scriptures that they considered to be canonical. The reasoning is fairly simple. At the top of Horeb, God appeared before Moses inside a burning bush that was not consumed, and he identified himself as the God of the patriarchs who would save his people from the slavery of the Egyptians. However, can a God of the dead save? Can a God who is defined by his relationship with those who are no longer alive free people with his strong hand and powerful arm? What kind power would a "God of the dead" have? So, if only a God of the living makes sense and he presents himself as the God of Abraham, Isaac, and Jacob, the patriarchs and the whole of mankind are to be resurrected when the time comes. Once again, Jesus used a concise sentence to conclude: "He [the God of the fathers] is not the God of the dead, but of the living" (Mark 12:27).

In his response, Jesus talked of the "God of the living" and was referring to all of mankind. This can be seen in a text from the Q collection (Matt 8:11-12 || Luke 13:28-29) that describes the banquet in the Kingdom of God. The reference to the God of the living implies that the resurrection and Final Judgment are at hand. The result of these events at the end of history is, however, paradoxical: those who do not belong to the people of Israel, people "from east and west," shall sit at the table beside Abraham, Isaac, and Jacob, the fathers of Israel no less, while many of those from Israel shall be excluded. Another text from Q (Matt 11:21-23 || Luke 10:13-15) reflects the same idea of a Final Judgment day that will be very painful for those towns in Galilee that did not want to listen to Jesus. This concept, obviously, rests upon the idea of the resurrection of the dead.

Resurrection is implicit in all of the Gospel texts that mention the Final judgment or the ill-fated destiny of some people. For example, in the parable of the rich man and the poor man, Lazarus (Luke 16:19-31), a dialogue takes place between Abraham, who welcomes Lazarus among the blessed, and the rich man, who suffers pain and torment. The resurrection of the dead is, for Jesus and the Christian tradition, the resurrection of all of mankind, called to be "like angels in heaven." The dialectic debate between Jesus and the Sadducees was noteworthy in the force of the words uttered by the rabbi from Nazareth.

Jesus' relations with the Sadducees went from dialectic discussions to open hostility at the end of his life. Everything leads us to believe that the Sadducee faction on the Sanhedrin, represented by the temple leaders (the so-called "high priests," with Caiaphas as their head), and the city's lay aristocracy (the "nobles" in the Gospel texts) were directly responsible for Jesus' sentencing and death. While the Pharisees virtually disappeared from the scene during the Passion and Jesus' death, the two aforementioned groups and the "scribes" who sided with the Sadducees were actively involved throughout. These three groups agreed on the fundamental question that led to Jesus being accused of blasphemy: "By what authority are you doing these things?" (Mark 11:28).

As we shall see in 6.2, the Sadducee high priests led the machinations to have Jesus killed (Mark 14:1; John 12:10) and ensured that he ended up in the hands of Pilate, the Roman governor (Mark 15:1; John 18:35) and pressured him to sentence him to death (Mark 15:10; John 19:15). The Sadducees were Jesus of Nazareth's fiercest adversaries.

4.6. JESUS' LIFE'S JOURNEY

Anonymity characterized the first thirty or so years of Jesus' life. Apart from his birth in Bethlehem, his life in Nazareth did not involve any extraordinary events, outside of a normal life at the time. Jesus' conception and birth were not entirely normal, nor were they easy to accept for those who witnessed them firsthand, but the childhood, adolescence, and early adulthood of Mary's child were just like those of anyone else in his position.

The "normality" of his years in Nazareth did not offer any signs of the public activity that the carpenter's son was to undertake beyond his hometown and the surrounding area, nor his fame, which would spread through Galilee, arriving even as far as the other Jewish lands (Judaea, Perea) and the capital itself, Jerusalem. The initial reaction of those who had lived with Jesus in Nazareth, once he had begun his activities in Galilee upon his return, was surprise and disbelief: "Where did this man get all this?" (Mark 6:2), or as Matthew (13:54) puts it, "Where did this man get this wisdom and these mighty works?"

Jesus' only decision that surprised the people of Nazareth probably was that he did not want to get married (see 4.4.3). When Jesus left Nazareth, he was already over thirty, and the Jewish custom backed by the Law was that a man take a wife and produce descendants around the age of twenty. In Jesus' case, the need to get married was even greater since his mother was a widow and his brothers and sisters, who were older than he was, had probably left the family home. However, Mary, Jesus' mother, did have other relatives living in Nazareth: the children from Joseph's first marriage and her own brothers and/or sisters, or those of her dead husband. Jesus, however, surprisingly, did not form his own family. This decision undoubtedly led to and prepared him for the itinerant lifestyle that he took up with the group of Twelve. His reasoning can be seen in something he said and that seems to be somewhat autobiographical: "there are eunuchs [those who decide not to get married] who have made themselves eunuchs for the sake of the kingdom of heaven" (Matt 19:12). The prophet who proclaimed the Kingdom of God on earth had to focus his life exclusively on this Kingdom before he could start to proclaim it.

4.6.1. First Phase: The Jordan Region (Perea and Judaea; Late 27–Mid-28 A.D.)

Now in full adulthood, between the ages of thirty-three and thirty-five, Jesus left Nazareth and headed for the Jordan region to be baptized by John, the prophet who urgently called for people's repentance before the imminent arrival of God. John baptized in Bethany, a town to the east of the river Jordan, in the land of Perea, which like Galilee came under the jurisdiction of Antipas. The effects of John's preaching in the population of Galilee were notable; even Galileans from towns as diverse as Bethsaida and Cana had become disciples of his. The Baptist raised his voice in the desert and carried out baptisms as a sign of inner purification for the forgiveness of sins, which God would grant when he came and manifested himself. God's judgment would take shape in a mysterious figure whom even the Baptist himself did not know but whom he considered infinitely superior. This plenipotentiary emissary, "he who is to come," would be God's messenger for the last days. Jesus arrived at the Jordan, possibly accompanied by other Galileans, and asked John to baptize him. The Baptist did not know this man from Nazareth, though subsequently, when imprisoned, he sent his disciples to ask him if he was "he who is to come," or whether they had to wait for someone else (Matt 11:3 || Luke 7:20).

Once Jesus had been baptized by John, they established a relationship in which John guided him. Jesus became a follower and collaborator of his in his baptismal mission, which included welcoming those who came to be baptized. Soon, though, some of the Baptist's disciples recognized Jesus as their master and became disciples of the rabbi from Nazareth (John 1:38). The small group of four or five people were also from Galilee. They decided to join him and went with him to Jerusalem to celebrate the great Jewish festival of the Passover (John 2:13), which in that year of 28 A.D. fell on either March 30 or April 28.

This first journey to Jerusalem by Jesus and his disciples was a sign of how the paths of John and Jesus and their respective followers were to go their separate ways. Jesus was no longer one of John's coworkers. He was now an independent rabbi who had taken his first steps alongside the Baptist but who from now on would go his own way. His first step without John's guidance was to travel to Jerusalem, the center for the Jewish religion and people. There Jesus stirred up sympathy and concern among the city's authorities. He told them that he could destroy the temple and build another one in its place in three days (Mark 14:58; John 2:19). Was this a prophecy or irony? Whatever the case, it was used as one of the accusations against him when a good number of the Jewish leaders discussed the convenience of having him killed.

Because of the effect that his visit to Jerusalem had had—when even a rabbi, Nicodemus, had gone out to find him under the cover of night, because he was interested in the teachings of this Galilean "rabbi" (John 3:2)—Jesus did not go back to John's side. John was no longer baptizing in Bethany in Perea, having moved to Aenon, near Salim, very close to Perea and Samaria but under the jurisdiction of the free city of Scythopolis. The Baptist had moved to a strategic point among Perea, Samaria, and Galilee beyond the grasp of Antipas. Antipas' pressure on the Baptist, who had dared stand up to him and had criticized his irregular matrimonial situation, had almost certainly led to his move to the northern part of the Jordan Valley. Jesus, the Baptist's former follower, did not want to risk his mission either and decided to baptize not in Perea but in the land of Judaea, in the river's southern area (John 4:22). Jesus and John's separation was complete.

Jesus baptized in an unnamed part of Judaea in the Jordan Valley with a good degree of success, but his disciples increasingly administered the baptisms for repentance and the forgiveness of sins. Jesus dedicated his time to his tasks of preaching and healing the sick. The proclamation of the imminent arrival of God, one of the bases of John's preaching, became the proclamation of his presence, and thus liberation and salvation. The compassionate force of God could be seen in Jesus' healings, an unmistakable sign of the arrival of a new world of righteousness and forgiveness. He continued to preach repentance, but this repentance was for immediate forgiveness, not a future forgiveness from God. It was a forgiveness to be granted here and now. The time had come to fulfill the promises and prophecies. This fundamental change of perspective and the accompanying healings explain people's reaction to Jesus' activities. The Kingdom of God was already having an effect. The time of laws and prophets had been superseded by Jesus' preaching, heralding the arrival of the definitive Kingdom.

The concurrent baptisms carried out by John and Jesus' disciples ended abruptly when the former was imprisoned in the fort at Machaerus in Perea, to the southeast of the Dead Sea, on the orders of the sovereign Antipas. Jesus' reaction did not take long: he immediately left Judaea and headed to Galilee, no doubt passing through Samaria. This may have taken place in June 28 A.D., if we base our calculations on what the Gospel according to John has Jesus say when he is crossing through Samaria. Jesus asked his disciples to look at the fields and said, "[S]ee how the fields are already white for harvest" (John 4:35). This is the only possible clue for dating the events referred to in John 4:1-3.

Significantly, Jesus did not travel to Galilee following the normal route through Perea, avoiding the land of Samaria, which was considered impure by the Jews. The reason was Antipas' hostility; he did not hesitate to detain the Baptist, although the latter had taken precautions in getting away from Perea. The threat posed by Antipas can be seen in Matthew 4:12: "[W]hen he heard that John had been arrested, he withdrew into Galilee" (likewise Mark 1:14). Jesus opted to retreat to his homeland, which was safer for him, although it was also under Antipas' jurisdiction. There, far from Perea, he could continue with his activities. John the Baptist's imprisonment led to a change in Jesus' location (from Judaea to Galilee) and a change in the style of his activities: the rabbi from Nazareth was no longer sedentary, baptizing those who came to find him, but became itinerant. He had no fixed abode and began to travel from town to town proclaiming God's presence, with all his power and with all his mercy. "The Kingdom of God is at hand" (Mark 1:15 || Matt 4:17) was the phrase that marked his activities in Galilee.

4.6.2. Second Phase: Galilee (Based in Capernaum; Mid-28–Passover 29 A.D.)

Jesus' arrival in Galilee led to another decision. Jesus had left Nazareth at least six months before and had not gone back. Now, he made his new hometown Capernaum, on the northwest shore of Lake Galilee. Andrew, one of his first disciples and a former follower of the Baptist, had a house there together with his elder brother, Simon-Peter. This house became a focal point for Jesus' journeys. Jesus carried out his preaching and miracle working in the area surrounding Capernaum: the plain of Gennesaret to the west, the towns to the north of Capernaum, such as Chorazin, and Bethsaida to the east. Although some of his followers came from Tiberias, the new capital being built by Antipas, Jesus never set foot there. The area for his activities was exclusively rural and not urban.

Jesus only occasionally seemed to travel beyond this area, the northwestern quadrant of the lake. The Gospels mention three places in the mountainous area of Galilee, the part he came from: Cana, Nain, and Nazareth itself. John (2:1-12) refers to a journey Jesus made to Cana, where he, his disciples, and his mother had been invited to a wedding. Cana was on a mountainside overlooking the plain down to Sepphoris, some twelve kilometers to the north of Nazareth. With regard to Nain, a town some ten kilometers to the southeast of Nazareth, Luke (7:11-17) tells us about Jesus' time there with his disciples, when he resurrected a widow's only child. All three synoptic Gospels mention a visit by Jesus and the disciples to Nazareth, "his hometown," the place where he lived until he was over thirty (Mark 6:1-6 || Matt 13:53-58; Luke 4:16-30). This visit was dominated by a distancing from and friction with those who, until recently, had been his neighbors; indeed, many of them were probably his relatives. Jesus was shown disrespect by his own family and people he had known all his life to the extent that "he could do no mighty work there, except that he laid his hands upon a few sick people and healed them" (Mark 6:5).

There is evidence of a journey by Jesus and his disciples beyond Galilee to the eastern shore of the lake, to the non-Jewish territory of the Decapolis (Mark 4:35–5:20). Jesus healed a seriously ill man possessed by a legion of evil spirits who lived alone in the caves of a cemetery, far from the city. The evil spirits, some two thousand of them, ended up entering a herd of swine, which threw themselves into the lake and were drowned. The city where these spectacular events took place was probably Gadara, located some two hours from the lake (Matt 8:28). However, it may also have been Gergesa, nowadays Kursi, a town not far from the city of Hippos (in some manuscripts of Mark 5:1). Gerasa, fifty-five kilometers from the lake, seems, however, to be an unlikely setting (see Mark 5:1 and Luke 8:26).

Initially, Jesus' activities in Galilee inspired an enthusiastic response from the people of the northwestern part of the lake. Jesus was listened to by many people, some even coming from other areas. The healing of physical and spiritual (possessions) ills in particular attracted crowds of people who hailed Jesus as a prophet, as a man of God. The settings for his activities could be anywhere: the synagogues, where the people came together to pray and listen to the Scriptures; the house in Capernaum where he stayed on the lakeside (with a boat that acted as a "pulpit" to preach from); a mountain; the wayside; the plain; or the squares of the towns they visited. News of what was happening in Capernaum and the surrounding area traveled, reaching as far as Nazareth, where Jesus' relatives were alerted to his activities. They were intent on taking Jesus back home, with the excuse that he had lost his mind. Certain scribes were not very favorable either, reacting strongly to the healings that Jesus carried out. According to them, Jesus had been given these powers by Satan, the leader of the forces of evil. Nonetheless, the rabbi from Nazareth continued on his mission.

An essential element in Jesus' activities soon became apparent. Jesus had begun to preach in Judaea accompanied by a number of disciples, some of whom had been followers of the Baptist. However, in Galilee a group of Twelve men became formally defined, chosen by Jesus to share in his life. The number twelve relates to the twelve tribes of Israel, all the people of Israel, without exception, who were to receive the gifts of righteousness, peace, and hope that Jesus spread in return for repentance. Jesus actively related to his disciples, and, when the time came, he charged the Twelve with the task of going out in pairs to certain Galilean towns in order to repeat what he himself was doing: proclaiming with words and deeds (healing the physically and spiritually ill) that God and his Kingdom were here on earth and calling the people to repent in response to this final and definitive visit from God.

The people's devotion to Jesus increased, thanks to the force of his words and the divine power involved in bringing health to the sick. A popular movement formed around Jesus, which saw him as the one who was to bring happiness to everyone, especially to those who were suffering. However, those who were looked down upon because of the jobs they carried out, jobs that went against the Law, were not excluded either. These sinners were invited to sit down at the table with Jesus, despite the scandal that this led to in those who scrupulously kept to the Law, people who did not understand the behavior of the rabbi from Nazareth, who did not understand this attitude or other aspects of it, for example, his interpretation of the Sabbath rest.

Popular feeling probably reached its zenith at the time of the feeding of the five thousand (counting only the men!), which took place in the area near the lake around the time of Passover in 29 A.D. These events were highly symbolic since they had a resonance with the miracles performed by God in the desert when the people of Israel escaped slavery in Egypt. These events are remembered during the celebration of Passover and the wanderings of the people in the wilderness, when God nourished his famished people with bread (manna) and meat (quail) (Exod 16). Here, Jesus fed the hungry crowd with five loaves of bread and two fish. There was so much left over that the bread filled twelve baskets. The people responded quickly, proclaiming Jesus as the Messiah, the new king of Israel (John 6:15).

However, Jesus had no wish to head a messianic movement. The people did not understand the symbolism of the multiplication of the loaves: the miracle was designed for the table at the banquet in the Kingdom of God, as a symbol of the restoration of God's people, of everyone without exception and beyond any concerns relating to ritual purity. This prophetic symbol of God's friendship and Jesus' compassion became, in the eyes of the people, a messianic sign, interpreted as popular, political Messianism. Jesus did not see his mission as political and/or military leadership, and he did not accept the people's calls: calls to make him the unquestioned leader of the Israel's national and religious recovery. Faced with this misdirected popular enthusiasm, Jesus withdrew, getting away from the crowds (John 6:15). This enthusiasm may have quickly turned into disenchantment for this reason. The devotion of his followers turned into rejection or even disrespect. Jesus was left alone with the Twelve and a few other disciples (John 6:66-70). Meanwhile, Antipas, ruler of Galilee, became concerned by Jesus' ability to attract all these people and started to see the former follower of the Baptist, the prophet he had had executed in the fort of Machaerus, as a threat. Herod Antipas was convinced that Jesus was the Baptist resurrected and, thus, someone who had the power to perform miracles and to attract a great number of followers. The warning Jesus received from some Pharisee friends was well founded: "Get away from here, for Herod wants to kill you" (Luke 13:31).

Circumstances had quickly changed. Jesus faced a twofold challenge: getting away from the crowds who confused him with the Messiah and liberator of Israel and escaping the threat from the ruler of Galilee, Herod Antipas. The tetrarch saw Jesus as a pretender to the throne, an enemy, and he wanted to root out the threat of his mission, just as he had done with John the Baptist. However, Jesus did not wish to end up like John and prudently decided to change the focus of his activities. From then on, Capernaum was no longer the base for his itinerant preaching, and he began a life of constant change, where he was to be more exposed. He was to live a less stable life under the long shadow of Antipas within and beyond the borders of Galilee. This period began just after the Passover in 29 A.D.

4.6.3. Third Phase: Traveling through Galilee and Neighboring Lands (Passover 29–Tabernacles 29 A.D.)

Jesus celebrated the Passover of 29 A.D. on April 18 in Galilee. The feeding of the five thousand with the bread and fish took place before or after the festivities (John 6:4). Galilee, however, was no longer a safe or practical place for Jesus and his disciples. According to Matthew 14:13, Jesus withdrew to an unknown and unpopulated place as soon as he found out about John's execution. However, John 6:15 states that he fled to an isolated place, "to the mountain," because he wanted to avoid the popular cries that acclaimed him as Israel's liberator, God's messenger. We can get a better idea of what was going on if we combine these two reports: the pressures from the people (popular acclaim) and Antipas (a fate similar to John's) represented threats to Jesus' activities, as he saw them.

The path that Jesus chose was the only path available, if he really wanted to safeguard his mission from the twofold threat of political ideology and the violence of the man in power. In the subsequent months (April–September 29 A.D.) until the Tabernacles festivities, Jesus continued to carry out his activities, and he traveled more than ever. His group of followers was reduced practically to the Twelve, whose loyalty remained strong even during these "trials" (Luke 22:28).

We do not know the exact scope or intensity of the danger represented by Antipas, whom Jesus ironically called a "fox" (Luke 13:32). The rabbi from Nazareth was under close surveillance and he wanted to avoid, at all costs, falling into the hands of his sovereign and the sovereign of most of his disciples. For this reason, he said to them, "Take heed, beware of the . . . leaven of Herod" (Mark 8:15). Jesus continued his activities, healing the physically and mentally sick, but Capernaum no longer acted as the center for his travels around the lake. He traveled to different areas, both within and beyond the borders of Galilee, and even became somewhat clandestine. Greater tranquillity reigned in Jesus' group, and opportunities arose for the disciples to receive lessons from the Master. The previous phase that was one of fixed and intensive action in Capernaum and the surrounding area had been left behind. The Gospel according to Mark eloquently describes the great number of people involved in this new phase, so many indeed that "they could not even eat" (3:20, 6:31). This was a different period, when there were many more opportunities for exchanges between Jesus and the Twelve and also other disciples.

Jesus' travels in this period took him to the three lands neighboring Galilee: from west to east, Phoenicia, Philip's tetrarchy, and the Decapolis. They were three pagan, non-Jewish, lands, none of which fell under the jurisdiction of Antipas. Jesus and his disciples visited them occasionally and almost incognito. We do not know if he visited them in the order shown in chapters 7 and 8 of the Gospel according to Mark. As was his custom, the rabbi from Nazareth visited only the rural areas, not entering the cities. As a Law-abiding Jew, Jesus may not have wanted to incur the ritual impurity involved in visiting urban areas where the Jewish Law was not respected and, thus, where everyone who entered was considered impure. His decision not to enter the cities was possibly motivated by his desire not to risk falling into the hands of Antipas' men. The precedent of the Baptist influenced Jesus' obvious prudence.

The trip to the city of Tyre and to Phoenicia started in the north of Galilee, where they border one another. Apparently Jesus had sympathizers in the area, people who knew him from Lake Galilee. He stayed in the home of one of these (a Jew?) in an attempt to keep himself away from Antipas. However, his fame as a healer went before him, and as soon as he arrived in the region, as Mark 7:24 reports, "he could not be hid." There are reports of just one miracle performed by Jesus: the exorcism of a demon that tormented a non-Jewish, Syrophoenician girl, which he carried out from a distance without entering the patient's house. It was the girl's mother who went to find the Master and asked him to free her daughter from her serious illness. Jesus accepted, but not without some reservations, given that it involved healing a non-Jew. In the end, the woman's insistence won him over (Mark 7:24-30 || Matt 15:21-28). Everything leads us to believe that he spent a relatively short time in Phoenicia for, since people in the area recognized him, he did not want to stay for very long.

We have a somewhat surprising report of his visit to the Decapolis, a confederation of free cities controlled by Antipas, in Mark 7:31. Apparently Jesus went north from the land of Tyre to Sidon and crossed the territory of the Decapolis. However, traveling from the land of Sidon to the Decapolis, meant he had to pass through the tetrarchy of Philip, which comprised Iturea, Gaulanitis, and Trachonitis. Only later, in Mark 8:27, does it say that Jesus passed through this tetrarchy. Nonetheless, Jesus certainly went to the Decapolis, a Gentile land on the southeastern shore of the lake that he had already visited when he was in Galilee, having freed a man possessed by two thousand demons. He now healed a deaf man with a speech impediment using a ritual that was unusual for him and an order that ended in *Ephphatha* ("open"). This order was given in Aramaic, the local language, which may mean that the deaf man was a Jew. This episode, in the Gospel according to Mark (7:31-37), is the only mention of his short stay in the Decapolis. It seems that Jesus continued his travels incognito through the non-Jewish lands neighboring Galilee.

His trip to the tetrarchy of Philip, specifically to the capital Caesarea, is explained in a similar light. The main point of the journey is a very important scene reported directly in the three synoptic Gospels (Mark 8:27-30 || Matt 16:13-20 || Luke 9:18-21) and, somewhat differently, in John 6:68-69. Jesus questioned the disciples as to his identity: "Who do you men say that I am?" Simon-Peter, the spokesman for the Twelve, answered that Jesus was the Christ. This scene took place while the group traveled from town to town in the region around Caesarea. Jesus' activities during this journey are not mentioned, no preaching or healings. Everything took place within the group itself: Simon-Peter's faithful confession, on behalf of all of them, that Jesus was the Messiah, and possibly Jesus' first acknowledgment of his life's tragic destiny. Almost certainly, Jesus traveled incognito, never announcing himself to the people in the area. He must have stayed in this territory, under the jurisdiction of Philip, Antipas' brother, for only a short time.

In addition to these three journeys outside Galilee, Jesus visited a number of Galilean towns. The basic source of information is once again the Gospel according to Mark (chaps. 7–9). The Galilean towns mentioned in these chapters are Dalmanutha (8:10), Bethsaida (8:22;

also 6:45), and Capernaum (9:33). We do not know where Dalmanutha was, but Matthew 15:39, which echoes Mark 8:10, talks of Magadan: both of these names may relate to the town of Magdala, in the south of the plain of Gennesaret and Mary Magdalene's hometown. We can be sure only that Dalmanutha/Magadan was a town on the shores of Lake Galilee, like Bethsaida and Capernaum. Neither do we know the location of the "high mountain" where Jesus was transfigured before his disciples (Mark 9:2), though the tradition does point toward Tabor, the highest peak in Lower Galilee (588 meters). The incongruous nature of all these events reinforces the impression that Jesus and his itinerant disciples constantly moved from one place to the next and constantly received support from the sedentary disciples. This can be seen in the mention of a "house" in an unnamed place (9:28) or the "house" in Capernaum (9:33), which had been the base for his second phase of activities.

The third phase of Jesus' travels was characterized by constant movement throughout Galilee and the neighboring lands to the north and east. The distances involved were great but the time involved was quite short in proportion (some three months). Jesus did not lose contact with the people; two healings took place outside Galilee (Phoenicia and the Decapolis) and two in Galilee, in the area by the lake, where he had preached previously: the blind man in Bethsaida (Mark 8:22-26) and the boy possessed by an evil spirit, near the mountain where he had been transfigured (Mark 9:14-29).

This phase is dominated by the constant journeys, often incognito, and the scenes where Jesus was alone with his disciples and teaching them. The Pharisees appeared from time to time on Jesus' journeys or near the disciples. Nonetheless, he wanted to avoid them and those linked to Herod Antipas in order to safeguard his mission from obstacles and threats. His warning to the disciples was a strong indication of this: "Take heed, beware of the leaven of the Pharisees and the leaven of Herod" (Mark 8:15). Jesus took greater precautions, as his words were accepted less and less by the Pharisees and as Antipas' hostility increased. Jesus' activities were reduced, as were his opportunities in Galilee; so he decided to leave the land where he and his project had been most enthusiastically received.

4.6.4. Fourth Phase: Perea, Judaea, and Jerusalem (Tabernacles 29–Before Passover 30 A.D.)

Jesus left Galilee and the neighboring lands, which had been the setting for his journeys for two or three months, and headed south to the land of Perea, which he already knew from the time when he had been baptized by John and when he had been his follower. The Feast of Tabernacles was approaching, and he returned to Jerusalem. The last time he had been in the city was for Passover in 28 A.D. or, going by the information in John (5:1), for an unnamed "feast of the Jews" when Jesus healed a man at Bethzatha pool on the Sabbath. This healing may have taken place at some other time, possibly during the Tabernacles festivities in 29 A.D., when another healing also took place on the Sabbath: that of the man who had been blind since birth. This healing was linked to Siloam pool, also in Jerusalem (John 9).

Jesus decided to go to Jerusalem for the Tabernacles festivities, taking the necessary precautions and somewhat hesitantly, "not publicly but in private" (John 7:10). The difficulties and a certain amount of stealth continued. The Tabernacles festivities, like Passover, lasted for seven days. Jesus went up to the temple to teach at only "about the middle of the feast" (John 7:14). He did so again "on the last day of the feast, the great day" (John 7:37). This was a short public appearance in Jerusalem, which led to a deep divide among the people and hostility from the authorities, who openly argued with Jesus and even tried to have him arrested.

The tensions between Jesus and the Jewish leaders were preceded by a certain level of expectation. It was as if the people of Jerusalem knew that Jesus had started to act in areas nearby. There were those who asked, "Where is he?" (John 7:11). Jesus now moved in the parts of Perea and Judaea probably closest to Jerusalem, divided by the river Jordan. As we have said earlier, Jesus knew the area of Bethany in Perea from the time when the Baptist was active there. He also knew the Judaean territory on the other side of the Jordan Valley, as he had been there between Passover and the summer of 28 A.D. There is confirmation of the fact that Jesus was in this area in Mark (10:1): "[H]e left there [Capernaum] and went to the region of Judaea and beyond the Jordan [i.e., Perea]" (likewise, Matt 19:1). The error in this report, which seems to confuse Judaea and Perea, may have arisen because Jesus traveled equally in both of these areas, the former under the jurisdiction of Pontius Pilate, the Roman governor, and the latter belonging to Antipas. According to John 10:40, "He went away again across the Jordan to the place where John at first baptized, and there he remained."

This report, however, corresponds to the period after Jesus' second visit to Jerusalem, coinciding with another important Jewish festival, the Dedication of the Temple, which also lasted a week. This was probably in December 29 A.D., as John 10:23 points out: "it was winter." Once again, the temple was the setting for a dialectic confrontation between Jesus and the Jews. Opposition to the Galilean rabbi was increasing to such an extent that there was an attempt to even have him arrested. Jesus, however, "escaped from their hands" (John 10:39). It seems that they were not yet completely convinced that he had to be arrested!

Relations between Jesus and the Jewish leaders, Pharisees and Sadducees, scribes, high priests, and nobles, often ended in argument. Jesus was increasingly seen by the temple leaders as a dangerous and troublesome figure, capable of upsetting the political and religious balance that they were trying to maintain. The idea that Jesus was a nuisance and a danger to all of them began to spread. The Sanhedrin met in order to decide what to do with Jesus; they decided that he had to be killed when the opportunity arose. They had to act quickly then.

Other leaders, despite not sharing Jesus' points of view, did not go so far. This lack of unanimity is evident in the arguments that took place in the temple after Jesus had arrived in Jerusalem according to the synoptic Gospels (Mark 11:27–12:44 || Matt 21:23–22:46 [23:33] || Luke 20:1–21:4). Some of these arguments may have taken place during the two festivals celebrated at this time (Tabernacles and the Dedication), before Jesus' triumphant entrance into the city. With regard to what Jesus said privately to his disciples about the destruction of the temple and the end of the world (Mark 13 || Matt 24–25 || Luke 21), there are two possibilities: this scene may have taken place before the triumphal entrance into Jerusalem or after it. The synoptic Gospels and John agree in making the temple the setting for the fiercest discussions between Jesus and those who questioned or completely dismissed his teachings and words. In John 18:20 and Mark 14:49,

Jesus says of himself, "Day after day I was with you in the temple teaching."

The period of Jesus' travels through Judaea and Perea, before traveling to the city for the last time, seemed relatively normal. The people welcomed Jesus, surrounding him and listening to him. The disciples remained loyal to the Master, following him wherever he went. Jesus' competitors were rarely seen, discussions with them taking place only in Jerusalem. The events reported in Mark 10 do not mention healings; instead, there were only instructions for those who surrounded him, some of whom had traveled to Perea from Jerusalem (John 10:41). He continued to teach the disciples separately and in private. The belief in the imminent arrival of the Kingdom was probably growing among the disciples, as some of them dared to ask for a place of honor at Jesus' side. Jesus, however, stressed that the disciples' only aim should be to serve.

Jesus' stay in Judaea and Perea may well depend on a somewhat enigmatic statement that he had made some time before, when he had to increase his movements in order to escape from Antipas and his criminal intentions: "for it cannot be that a prophet should perish away from Jerusalem" (Luke 13:33). The last six months of Jesus' life were a form of "preparation" for his end. Jerusalem was the focus of Jesus' interests and intentions. His activities increasingly focused on the city, which he visited repeatedly. The image of the hen gathering up her chicks indicates his explicit desire to change the city's heart and the hearts of those who lived there: "O Jerusalem, Jerusalem. . . . How often would I have gathered your children together!" (Matt 23:37 || Luke 13:34).

Jesus had a mission aimed at Jerusalem, which was to end in failure: the city was to kill the one sent to them by God. Jesus included himself in a long list of messengers who had been spurned by Jerusalem, declaring, "Jerusalem, killing the prophets and stoning those who are sent to you" (Matt 23:37 || Luke 13:34). In the last months of his life, Jesus' activities were probably shared equally between the regions near Jerusalem (Perea and Judaea) and occasional stays (but more often than shown in the Gospels) in the city of Jerusalem, where his preaching won him some supporters. He also won supporters thanks to healings. According to the Gospel of John, he attracted a great many thanks to an amazing event: the resurrection of Lazarus, one of his friends (John 11:1-44).

In any case, Jesus and his disciples lived in Perea throughout this period (Mark 10:10 mentions a "house" where they stayed). When he found out about the serious condition of Lazarus, his friend, Jesus said, "Let us go into Judaea again" (John 11:7). Thus, he and his disciples set off for Bethany, where Lazarus lived and some three kilometers from Jerusalem. However, the fact that Jesus brought Lazarus back to life increased the Jewish leaders' concern that Jesus would lead a revolutionary movement against the Romans (!). There were constant misconceptions as to Jesus' leadership, among both his supporters and his adversaries. Jesus had no other option than to withdraw and avoid showing himself in public. After healing Lazarus, Jesus decided to leave Bethany and head "to the country near the wilderness, to a town called Ephraim; and there he stayed with the disciples" (John 11:54). Ephraim bordered the Judaean Desert, some twenty kilometers to the north of Jerusalem.

The last place that needs to be mentioned is Jericho, an important Judaean city in the Jordan Valley some twenty-five kilometers to the northeast of Jerusalem. The synoptic Gospels agree that two events took place here: the healing of a blind beggar called Bartimaeus (Mark 10:46-52 || Luke 18:35-43; Matt 20:29-34 talks of two blind men) and the hospitality that Jesus received at the house of Zacchaeus, the city's chief tax collector (Luke 19:1-10). Jesus had, however, begun his last journey to Jerusalem. Passover 30 A.D. was approaching, and the route he took from Jericho to Jerusalem was full of pilgrims from Galilee and Perea who were going to celebrate the festival and Judaean peasants who were going to Jerusalem "before the Passover, to purify themselves" (John 11:55). These rituals ensured the legal cleanliness required to celebrate the Passover and lasted seven days. Jesus and his disciples were among those who traveled to the city.

4.6.5. Fifth Phase: The Last Days in Jerusalem (Passover 30 A.D.)

Jesus arrived for the last time in Jerusalem along the Jericho road, which passed through Bethany, the hometown of Lazarus and his sisters, Martha and Mary, and then Bethphage on the flank of the mountain right in front of the city. Previously (4.5.3.2), we saw that Simon the Leper offered Jesus and his disciples a meal in his house in

Bethany, during which Mary, Lazarus' and Martha's sister, anointed Jesus with a great quantity of perfume. Jesus interpreted this anointing as preparation for his burial; according to Jewish custom, bodies were anointed with oil before being buried. Simon and the three siblings in Bethany were sedentary disciples and friends of the Master. These events took place, according to John 12:1, "six days before the Passover." The synoptic Gospels, however, say they took place "two days before" the feast (Mark 14:1, 14:3 || Matt 26:2, 26:6). In terms of the Passion, John's chronology appears to be the most appropriate. Thus, it was Sunday, April 2 or, the day before, April 1, 30 A.D. The meal in Simon's house took place on the evening of the Sabbath, in fact Sunday since the new day actually began at sunset.

Jesus and his disciples stayed at Bethany, three kilometers from Jerusalem, in the days before his death on the cross. According to the synoptic Gospels, Jesus went to the temple in Jerusalem each day to preach to the people, but when it got dark he returned to Bethany. The Jewish authorities, with Caiaphas the high priest as their head, had already decided to have Jesus killed (John 11:53), and there were "orders" out for his arrest (John 11:57), which were temporarily ineffective thanks to the popular enthusiasm that his triumphal entrance into Jerusalem had inspired (John 12:19). Mark also refers to the devotion of the people, people who listened intently to Jesus at the temple and who may have risen up had they known that the authorities wanted him killed (Mark 14:2). Despite the differences between the Gospel of John and the synoptic Gospels, the accuracy of the narratives is clear. The pressure on Jesus from the temple authorities increased, and he must have thought that he was safer not staying the night in Jerusalem, especially when he had loyal friends in Bethany. Nonetheless, the people showed themselves to be receptive to Jesus until the end (see Mark 12:37; John 12:18).

The people's closeness to Jesus culminated in his triumphant entrance into Jerusalem, which took place "the next day" (John 12:12). Initially, this seems to mean Monday, April 3, but it may also be Sunday, April 2, if we assume that the meal at Simon's house took place on Saturday evening. The information provided by Mark (chaps. 11 and 14) indicates that Jesus entered Jerusalem on Sunday, five days before Friday, the day when he died and, according to the synoptic Gospels,

Passover. Thus, it seems more likely that Jesus entered Jerusalem on Sunday, April 2.

Jesus entered the city to acclamations from his disciples and a group of pilgrims (with some locals), but the popular reception was fairly limited: if the Roman garrison stationed in the Antonia Tower had interpreted the reception as hostile, the cohort would have been sent out of the city to suppress those trying to get in. It is clear that his entrance was festive, "hosanna" being the most popular cry. It was an event that attracted a great many people, but it was peaceful in all respects and thus tolerated by the Romans. Those who did not take kindly to it were the Jewish authorities who saw sympathy for Jesus increasing among the people and, above all, how Jesus was opposed to the way the temple worked commercially, with his public protest against the money-changers and the pigeon sellers. Jesus, overcome with holy zeal, turned the tables and stalls over as a prophetic sign of how the temple had to be purified (Mark 11:15-16 || Matt 21:12 || Luke 19:45; also John 2:13-16, where the scene is intensified as he drives the sheep and oxen out using a whip, the only way of handling these large animals).

The days after Jesus' arrival in Jerusalem, Monday, Tuesday, and Wednesday (April 3, 4, and 5), were a time of waiting before the final events. They were decisive days for Jesus' future, as the plot was organized that would lead to his death: the betrayal, arrest, and trial before Pilate. The reaction of the temple authorities to Jesus' public denunciation of the commercialism was not long in coming. The authority with which Jesus acted surpassed their expectations and led to deep concern. Jesus was prudent, however (John 12:36), returning each day to the city to carry out the purification ceremonies in preparation for the Passover and speaking publicly in the temple, but each evening he left Jerusalem to spend the night in Bethany.

The place where he and the disciples stayed may have been the house of Simon the Leper or the house belonging to the three siblings (Lazarus, Martha, and Mary) or the house of some other sympathizers. Tensions with the religious authorities grew. Finally, the temple leaders and Judas, one of the Twelve, came to an agreement whereby the latter was to deliver Jesus to them when the occasion arose. The high priests were convinced that Jesus was a false prophet, who was opposed to the temple and who posed a threat to the status quo with Rome, the fragile political balance with the occupiers. They saw in him a potential political leader who would lead Israel toward certain disaster.

Events were now snowballing toward Thursday, April 6. Unlike his other activities up to that point, Jesus ordered two of his disciples to enter Jerusalem to prepare a supper that he wanted to have with the Twelve in the city that night. There was an air of precaution and stealth about the preparations for this supper. The disciples were to identify the house where the meal was to take place by a signal: a man with a jar of water was to take them to someone who would show them the room where the preparations were to be made. This room, readied with curtains and cushions and probably located in the Upper City, was to be the setting for Jesus' last meal with the Twelve. As evening fell, Jesus entered Jerusalem with his disciples.

The meal began at dusk, according to the Jewish custom, Friday, April 7th. All of a sudden in the middle of the meal and quite unexpectedly, Jesus removed his cloak and started washing the feet of his disciples. He then announced, to general astonishment, that one of the Twelve was to betray him and another would publicly deny knowing him. Jesus also blessed the bread and the wine, and shared them among the Twelve, saying that the bread was his body and the wine his blood.

Once the meal was over, Jesus left Jerusalem and headed down to the Kidron Valley, to the east of the city. He crossed to the other side and entered the garden of Gethsemane, at the foot of the Mount of Olives. This garden was well known to the group of Twelve, and obviously to Judas, the traitor, as well. Judas guided the detachment of temple guards there, placing Jesus in the hands of his enemies. Following some attempt at resistance from the disciples, whom Jesus himself told to desist, they fled. Jesus was arrested and taken before Annas and Caiaphas, the Jewish leaders. In the meantime, Peter, the spokesman for the Twelve who had followed Jesus from a distance, found himself identified as a disciple, but he repeatedly denied the fact.

Early on the morning of Friday, April 7, the day before Passover, the Roman governor Pontius Pilate received the temple leaders who brought Jesus with them as a prisoner, demanding that he be condemned to death. They accused him of being "the King of the Jews" and, thus, guilty of high treason against the emperor. Pilate, as often occurred, had recently arrived in Jerusalem to keep a close eye on public order during the weeklong Passover celebrations, staying in Herod's palace, which acted as his praetorium, the governor's official residence. Pilate interrogated Jesus but did not find sufficient reason to put him to death. He was then sent to Antipas, also in Jerusalem for the Passover; he did not find sufficient reason to put him to death either. The Jewish leaders, who had brought together a large crowd to put pressure on the governor, insisted that Jesus be condemned to death, and when Pilate had this crowd choose between Barabbas, a bandit, and Jesus, they unanimously chose to free the former. Finally, Pilate condemned Jesus to death on the cross, in accordance with Roman law.

Four soldiers took Jesus, who had been object of cruel insults, away to Golgotha beyond the city walls, the hill where the executions were carried out. Before this Jesus was whipped. Jesus had to carry the crossbar of his crucifix and was accompanied by two others condemned to death. He was so weak that the soldiers made a passerby carry his cross. When they reached Golgotha, a rocky hill near the walls of Jerusalem, Jesus was crucified amid insults from those who had wanted his death and the compassion of several women disciples of his, who looked on from afar. The agony ended at around three in the afternoon. This is the approximate time of his death. One of the soldiers ensured he was dead by passing a spear through his side. Subsequently, by permission of the governor, Joseph of Arimathea, an influential man and a sympathizer of Jesus', took his body down from the cross and buried him in a new tomb near Golgotha, the place where he had been executed. Nicodemus brought a blend of myrrh and aloes and helped him. It was the evening of Friday, April 7, 30 A.D.

4.7. Jesus, The Person

Jesus did not leave any written records; instead, his words have been handed down by the memory of the disciples. Great authors are renowned for their literary and artistic work or because an illustrious disciple of theirs has kept their work alive: it was Plato who made Socrates famous; Philostratus told us about the life of the miracle worker Apollonius of Tyana. Jesus' case is similar but different. It is similar because everything we know about him has come from the testimony of those who saw and heard him firsthand. It is different because, two thousand years on, the oral tradition has disappeared and our only direct records are the written testimonies, above all the four Gospels, which act as a bridge between him and us. These testimonies are the path that ensures safe access to Jesus, the fountains that those who want to know him have to drink from.

The Christian tradition has tried to break through the layers of dust that have accumulated throughout history and has stressed certain elements that highlight ancient and venerable paths. This tradition has led to such fascinating creations as the two letters between Jesus and Abgar, king of Edessa, which were written in the year 340 of the Seleucid era (28–29 A.D.), according to Eusebius of Caesarea (*Eccl. Hist.* 1:13:5-10), and which spread far and wide, even into medieval Catalan literature. There was the shroud with the reproduction "not made by human hands" (*akheiropoiētos*) of Jesus' face, the famous *mandylion*, which made it into the hands of Abgar and was taken to Constantinople in 944 A.D.; and the tradition of Jesus' agonized face imprinted on a handkerchief belonging to woman called Veronica, who had commiserated with the man about to be crucified; and the impression of the body of a man who had been tortured and crucified on the Turin Shroud, a piece of linen measuring some four meters, deemed to have been the shroud used by Joseph of Arimathea to cover Jesus' body once he had taken him down from the cross in the evening on Good Friday.

The treasures of the tradition and the imagination of artists and writers have been able to produce only approximate likenesses of the person of Jesus. These likenesses were marked by their time, and cultural and social influences. We have to return instead to the written sources, both Christian and non-Christian. These are the only sources that offer abundant insights that bring us closer to the person of Jesus. The problem is that these sources are only marginally interested in his physical and mental, or indeed spiritual, makeup. The reports about Jesus are often simply suggestions, or implications mixed in with other material describing his activities (his words and deeds). We have to interpret by paying more heed to our sensibility than to anything else.

For example, it is impossible to outline Jesus' psyche without employing a great amount of fantasy. No doubt, a historical novel on Jesus would have to make a great number of concessions in terms of the details, but that is not what we are concerned with here. We can avoid those areas that are too risky.

Nevertheless, we would not want to limit our wide-ranging profile of this figure by not looking more closely, carefully, and prudently at some of his characteristic traits, as seen in some of the historical texts. Prudence is required since the word enigma, already in use by D. F. Strauss in the middle of the nineteenth century, is often the best word when discussing Jesus. Obviously nothing allows us to look inside Jesus' soul. We know only what he wanted us to know. However, Gethsemane offers us an exceptional insight. Jesus was on the threshold of the final events in his life, and he opened up his soul to his three closest disciples: "My soul is very sorrowful, even to death" (Mark 14:34 || Matt 26:38). In the Gospel according to John, this feeling is expressed with these words: "Now is my soul troubled. And what shall I say? 'Father, save me from this hour?'" (12:27).

Apart from Gethsemane, the tradition closest to Jesus tried to plumb his feelings on a number of occasions. Mark stresses the feeling of discomfort and sadness that filled Jesus when he saw the hard-hearted reaction of those who did not want to understand or accept him: "[H]e looked round at them with anger, grieved at the hardness of heart" (3:5). A similar hardness of heart, and Jesus' profound sadness when faced with his tragic destiny in Jerusalem, led to the Master's bursting into tears on seeing the city (Luke 19:41). The Gospel of John describes Jesus' inner turmoil on two extreme and contrasting occasions. The Gospel's author points out the fairly obvious contrast between two friendships: the loyal friendship with Lazarus and his sisters and his betrayal by Judas, one of the Twelve. Jesus was also moved when he saw people crying at the death of his friend Lazarus (John 11:33, 11:35). However, during the Last Supper, distress dominated Jesus when he said, "Truly, truly, I say to you, one of you will betray me" (John 13:21).

Most of the time Jesus' feelings are projected outward. One of the most symbolic images of the Gospel is Jesus' compassion for the crowds who had come to listen to him and who needed to eat. In the Gospels of Mark (6:30-44; 8:1-9) and Matthew (14:13-21; 15:32-39), this compassion became the catalyst for a profoundly prophetic sign: the multiplying of the loaves in order to feed five thousand men. Luke (9:10-17) talks about welcoming and healing the sick as a preparatory step, and in John (6:1-15) the scene begins with the Master's concerns ("How are we to buy bread, so that these people may eat?"). This echoes Jesus' words to the Twelve in Mark (8:2 || Matt 15:32): "I have compassion on the crowd, because they have been with me now three days, and have nothing to eat." The people's needs move Jesus to act decisively. In essence, the healings implicitly or explicitly show an invincible and active closeness with those who are suffering. Jesus healed them through compassion, which thus became a form of resistance to the evil that had overcome them.

The healings are an example of the determination with which Jesus handled the decisions and options in his life. This is how the Gospel according to Luke interprets the transcendental decision that Jesus made when he traveled to Jerusalem for the last time, with a somewhat Semitic phrase: "[H]e set his face [resolved] to go to Jerusalem" (9:51). Ultimately, Jesus made his own decisions of his own free will, without regard for the circumstances. Jesus knew the consequences of his actions, but he did not base his decisions on conjecture. He was prudent and reckless, tender and demanding, patient and zealous. He was not single-minded, nor was he concerned with "political correctness." His inner freedom confused friends and enemies alike. Nothing took precedence over what he saw as his mission, or rather what he saw as God's will.

Many proverbs show a certain "union of opposites" in the lifestyle and savoir faire of the rabbi of Nazareth: "be wise as serpents and innocent as doves" (Matt 10:16). The Kingdom of God requires both astuteness and wisdom without presumptuousness, and innocence without naivety. Jesus needed a fair amount of prudence when faced with the threat from Antipas, a potential obstacle on his path as a prophet on the way to Jerusalem; but he did not think twice about taking risks. He was not concerned about being misunderstood; he refused to talk when they interrogated him and put him on trial.

Jesus acted as a friend to the weak, but there was an unquestionable strength in his undertaking. He defended the poor and downtrodden, safeguarded the right of children to be his friend, welcomed sinners unconditionally, but he was also demanding when it came to those who wanted to follow him. He did not hide the opposing forces in his message, such as those regarding God and money as the definitive raison d'être. His behavior involved a mixture of patient serenity and an intensity in the defense of God's cause, which was also his own. Jesus did not hesitate to upset the order of the commercial system that held sway in the temple; he turned over the tables of the money-changers and stallholders in order to show, using a gesture worthy of the prophets, the disorder in a temple that placed prayer and commercialism at the same level. Likewise, he was patient with his own disciples, who aspired to act as ministers in a kingdom designed for this world, at least until the last moment.

These contrasts make Jesus a particularly fascinating person. Nevertheless, the whole has a harmony that reflects the great sense of reality that he possessed. The dream of the Kingdom of God that Jesus brings to life for people is to be lived out in the lives of each. His imagination does not involve the otherworldly or the cosmic drama common in the visions of the apocalypse of the time. Jesus talks in terms of specifics with precise and explicit images, from day-to-day life; they are self-evident and the result of careful observation.

When he creates and uses parables (fictitious but lifelike stories), he borrows fragments of the reality around him to construct them; it is easy to feel at home with them. When he talks about the weather or the way seeds grow or the beauty of wild flowers, those who listen to him feel more akin to him. He is very clearly of this world when he talks wittily about the cunning of the steward who tricks people in order to receive favors once he has been fired or the insolence of a judge who does not want to hear the complaints from a poor widow. When he compares the Pharisee and the tax collector, the two extremes of religiosity (the most and the least), or when he compares the behavior of a priest and a Levite, servants of the legitimate temple in Jerusalem, and a Samaritan, a renegade who pays homage to God in the schismatic temple at Gerizim, he is simply telling things as they are.

Jesus has his feet firmly on the ground, and he does not want those who follow him to change that. The criticism he receives is, in fact, that people see him as too "grounded." His sharp response comes quickly: "For John came neither eating [bread] nor drinking [wine], and they say, 'He has a demon'; the Son of man came eating and drinking, and they say, 'Behold a glutton and a drunkard, a friend of tax collectors and sinners!'" (Matt 11:18-19 || Luke 7:33-34).

Jesus was a very dynamic man, a man who valued life in all its dimensions, someone who got close to people and things emotionally, with a sense of humanity, sympathy, and even humor. Among the words spoken by Jesus, there are many signs of these fundamental human qualities. Obviously, a sense of sympathy and humor does not mean that one does not take life seriously or that one makes fun of others. On the contrary, humor acknowledges the way things are and realizes that they will always be this way. Jesus introduces a dash of humor into what he says in order to stress the reality, and seriousness!, of his message about the Kingdom of God.

For example, the Gospels tell us that Jesus' disciples were concerned to know which of them was the most important, the finest disciple, the role model. Jesus insisted that the measure of personal holiness is service, not one's personal merits or qualities. Thus, the disciple who wishes to be considered first, has to come last. In order to get his point across and without warning, he takes one of the "last," a child, a small needy human being, someone who is growing, not an independent, free-standing adult. Jesus wanted to avoid telling them which one of them was the most virtuous or the best equipped, and he told them to look at the child. No one talks about greatness, virtues, or abilities when it comes to a child. Everyone sees a weak and vulnerable being who needs to be looked after and who has to be looked after as if he or she were Jesus himself (see Mark 9:33-37 || Matt 18:1-5 || Luke 9:46-48).

Another example: concerns about what to eat or wear are not exclusive to any one time or culture. Satisfying one's basic needs is something that no one, including Jesus, places in doubt. Nonetheless, can we thus assume that one's goals in life should be food, drink, and clothing; in other words, gastronomy and fashion? It is often said that those who do not work should not have the right to eat. Jesus, however, replied that there are those who live and eat without producing: the birds in the sky. The lilies in the field do not spend anything and yet wear a splendid and magnificent outfit, but they last only until they are thrown on the fire. Thus, what justifies living unhappily? Why bother eating and dressing? Is it not God himself who looks after the birds and the lilies? There is only one key: to believe in him.

Those who believe can live without these kinds of anxiety (see Matt 6:25-34 || Luke 12:22-31).

Jesus is a rabbi who has the purity of spirit necessary to have a proper grasp of reality while maintaining the right distance from it. Jesus does not avoid or try to escape the reality that surrounds him. His words often show that he has observed people and things; his observations are full of color, of exaggerated imagery, of paradoxes and insightful humor. Jesus does not distance himself from reality or look at it with histrionics, a sense of superiority or arrogance. He talks about situations in life using metaphors and similes from everyday life. Humor and realism are used together. Jesus is a perspicacious and wise man who uses his imagination to place a camel and the eye of a needle side by side, the largest animal in Palestine and the smallest hole that a housewife has to battle with. Difficult as it is to believe that an animal the size of a camel could fit through a hole so small, it is even more difficult to imagine that a rich man can enter into the Kingdom of God. A person's heart cannot be divided between these two desires (Mark 10:25 || Matt 19:24 || Luke 18:25).

Obviously, Jesus' heart was neither divided nor torn. As A. Men says, Jesus suffers the sufferings of others, he feels extraordinarily close to other people, but he does not suffer ups and downs. He does, however, undergo two complicated spiritual trials: the first, in the wilderness, at the start of his activities, and the second, in Gethsemane, at the end of his life. These two struggles crystallized his dilemma; did he keep to or dismiss what he wanted to do, or did he do what God wanted him to do: to carry out his mission and die on the cross (see 4.5.2.2). These trials, however, did not lead to dissatisfaction or distress, remorse or the victory of instinct. His actions were governed by a serenity that was rooted in his spiritual strength, not in the lack or cooling of his feelings and desires. These sentiments and desires continued to exist, but they were relegated to the background by a twofold concern that was the driving force in his life: his link to God and his care for the men and women who surrounded him. The twofold commandment of love, for God and for others, was the foundation stone of Jesus' message and his existence. Jesus communicated what he lived.

Jesus was not a mystic who experienced great highs of exaltation and terrible lows of abandonment and loss, days of brilliant light and nights of impenetrable darkness. There was a constant and perfect spiritual strength that emanated from God and spread and sustained compassion toward others. There was no form of dichotomy or tension here. He brought together prayer and healing. God, for Jesus, was not only the creator and Israel's liberator. Those around him were not just his people, the human companions needed for life and harmony. The God that Jesus talks about is familiar to him: his Father, a universal name that can be used by anyone, no matter where they come from. The people who address him will receive an intimate and direct response, no matter who they are or how they live, a response that liberates them from the stigma and hurt, both old and new, in their heart.

In short, as we shall see, what sustains Jesus the person is his absolute trust in God, whom he loves as the Father and as the Father of all mankind.

5

His Message

5.1. God, The Father, and His Kingdom

The focus of Jesus' message was the Kingdom of God. The expression "Kingdom of God" means that God is king and manifests his royalty in his kingdom. This unquestionable affirmation has to be complemented by another that takes us in the definitive direction: God is the Father. We can all call the one unique God by this name. In these two names (king and father, father and king), which Jesus took from the religion of Israel, we can see the image of God that he wanted to communicate. We do need, though, to bear one thing in mind: for Jesus, "Father" was indeed the name he gave God, and he may have used both as synonyms. However, Jesus did not describe God as king often (the only occurrence is in Matt 5:35). Jesus proclaimed the arrival of the Kingdom of God, but he called God Father.

5.1.1. God Is Manifest

5.1.1.1. The Kingdom Is at Hand

Jesus' message was radically new in that it offered a different view to that of John the Baptist and the prophetic and apocalyptic movements in Judaism: what they were waiting for in the near or distant future had already started to take place. Their hopes had come true. God had entered human history. A new opportunity never seen before had arisen: the chance to enjoy the virtues and happiness here and now, which had been reserved for later in theory. The future had melted into the present; history had changed shape and perspective. The Baptist had been on the threshold of the great news, preaching that God's arrival was imminent. Jesus stepped over this threshold and proclaimed that God was here and that everything in human history had started to change. It was a small start, the dawning of a new day; the Kingdom was here though not completely. The world had not come to an end; it was simply going to continue but in a different way.

The change had begun in the region of Judaea, where Jesus had performed baptisms with his disciples for a few months, away from the Baptist. It was here that changes were made to the Baptist's concerns and his way of saying and doing things. The forgiveness and salvation that John prophesied were now being seen in the present, in the words and deeds of the prophet Jesus: the sick were healed, hope returned, and joy grew (see 4.5.2.2). When Jesus arrived in Galilee, after John's imprisonment, everything was ready for an amazing announcement: "The time is fulfilled, and the kingdom of God is at hand [Greek, *ēggiken*]" (Mark 1:15; Matt 10:7 || Luke 10:9, 10:11). This Greek word, used by Mark and Q, showed not only that the Kingdom was on its way but also that it was already here; God's mighty action had begun in the world through Jesus' activities. Another expression, also from the Q collection, confirms that God was present among men: "the kingdom of God has come upon you [*efthasen*]" (Matt 12:28 || Luke 11:20). This presence is definitive and final: God is not going to go back on his decision. Nonetheless, his Kingdom has only just begun, and it is not complete; Jesus talked about the Kingdom as something that was both "at hand" and which "is here." In both cases, the unexpected new development took center stage: a new time in the history of man had begun, marked by the active presence of an active and loving God, victorious over evil.

Jesus talked about the "kingdom" or "reign" or "royalty" of God (Aramaic, *malkuta'*) in accordance with the Jewish beliefs of the time, which stressed his victory in the past, present, and future. There are no limits in time or space to God's power, which reaches around the world to all people and all their gods. We find in Psalm 145:13, "Thy kingdom is an everlasting kingdom, and thy dominion endures throughout all generations." Similarly, highlighting the universal royalty of God, Psalm 99:1 says, "The Lord reigns; let the peoples tremble! He sits enthroned upon the cherubim; let the earth quake!" According to a good part of Jewish thinking, the kingdom of God will appear only once Israel's enemies have been defeated. The everlasting kingdom of Israel would then be established, returning from exile and renewed in the covenant, the temple, and the Law, where the rights of the poor would be respected. The final return of God to the land of Israel included the Messiah ("the Lord of hosts will reign on Mount Zion and in Jerusalem"; Isa 24:23). "The Lord will become king over all the earth" (Zech 14:9). Or, as the Third of the Sibylline Oracles prophesies, there shall be a terrible war preceded by cosmic turbulence, and in the end "a kingdom over all mankind shall he [God] raise up for ages" (3:954–55).

In the Jewish apocalyptic texts, God's victory over Satan, Israel's worst enemy, was at the forefront. In the book of the Watchers, part of the First Book of Enoch, Azazyel (Satan) has his hands and feet tied by Raphael, the angel of God, and is buried in the desert until he is thrown into the fire (10:4-6) on Judgment Day. In the Testament of Dan, part of the Testaments of the Twelve Patriarchs, the defeat of Beliar (Satan) is overwhelming: "He [God? the Messiah?] shall make war against Beliar, and he shall give the vengeance of victory to our coasts. And the captivity shall he take from Beliar. . . . And no longer shall Jerusalem endure desolation, nor Israel be led captive; for the Lord shall be in the midst of her, dwelling among men, even the Holy One of Israel reigning over them" (5:10, 5:13). In the Qumran manuscripts, specifically in the War Rule, victory is guaranteed thanks to the strength of the Lord, which is holy, and because "the King of Glory is with us together with the holy ones" (12:8). Beliar's dominion is to be annihilated, as are his allies, the *Kittim*, a cryptic term to describe foreigners and the Romans in particular (15:2-3). The sword of the God of Israel shall be unbeatable (16:1). A text from the first century A.D., the Assumption of Moses, says, "His Kingdom [the Kingdom of God] shall appear throughout all his creation, and then Satan shall be no more, and sorrow shall depart with him" (10:1).

In all these texts, the establishment of God's mighty Kingdom brings a definitive end to the kingdom of Satan and his evil spirits, allies of the enemies of the people of Israel. Jesus also saw his activities as the victorious fight against Satan and his subjects, the demons: "I saw Satan fall like lightning from heaven" (Luke 10:18). However, as G. Theissen points out, he never considered the pagans to be his enemies or the allies of the prince of evil, he who enslaved and destroyed.

This perspective according to which the religious hopes and political utopia of the Jews go hand in hand was the basis for Jesus' proclamation: God wants to make himself manifest with all his royal force of liberation, forgiveness, integration, and mercy. When Jesus talked about the Kingdom to the people, he inspired them with hope. The final triumph of good and justice was brought forward to the present, and this was an invitation to feel fortunate and to live part of history as it is renewed from within. Resignation and fatalism (the bad present would give way to a very good future) were superseded by a good present under God's reign, which would culminate in an even better future. The words Jesus addressed to his disciples were fully justified: "Blessed are the eyes which see what you see! For I tell you that many prophets and kings desired to see what you see, and did not see it, and to hear what you hear, and did not hear it" (Luke 10:23-24 || Matt 13:16-17).

Such a blessing undermines the somewhat stereotypical questions: if the Kingdom of God has already begun, is the end of the world nigh, and when will it come to pass? This could be compared to a lightning strike, an instantaneous and unforeseeable atmospheric phenomenon but still perfectly visible from one end to the other from heaven and earth (Matt 24:27 || Luke 17:24: "For as the lightning comes from the east and shines as far as the west, so will be the coming of the Son of man," the celestial figure who shall come to judge mankind). Similarly surprising images are offered of the master of the house who arrives in the middle of the night (Mark 13:34-36 || Luke 12:36-38) and the thief who turns up without warning (Matt 24:43 || Luke 12:39). It is not possible to make any kind of forecast or offer any clues. It is best to acknowledge our own ignorance about a decision that God has reserved for himself and that no one can influence (Mark 13:32 || Matt 24:36): "But of that day or that hour no one knows, not even the angels in heaven, nor the Son, but only the Father." Jesus did not want to get involved in speculating on the future or the signs that might announce the end of contemporary or current history. In other words, the end of the world can wait.

Jesus did say three things that may imply that the Kingdom is to arrive immediately. However, these sentences do not contradict the statement above, namely, that the end of the world can wait. On the one hand, Jesus wanted to pass on conviction and sureness: "Truly, I say to you, this generation will not pass away before all these things take place. Heaven and earth will pass away, but my words will not pass away" (Mark 13:30-31 || Matt 24:34-35 || Luke 21:32-33). The expression "all these things" does not necessarily mean the end of the world, but the signs that are to precede it: "[W]hen you see things taking place, you know that he is near, at the very gates" (Mark 13:29 || Matt 24:33 || Luke 21:29).

The second of these statements seems to set the date for arrival of the Son of Man, at the end of time: "[F]or truly, I say to you, you will not have gone through all the towns of Israel, before the Son of man comes" (Matt 10:23). However, Jesus may also have been referring somewhat ironically to the great task ahead for the disciples, sent out to take the mission to the people of Israel everywhere; indeed, they would not have finished by the time the Son of Man arrived.

Finally, the date of the arrival of the Kingdom seems to have been definitively set in Mark 9:1 (|| Matt 16:28 || Luke 9:27): "Truly, I say to you, there are some standing here who will not taste death before they see that the kingdom of God has come with power." We should note that this phrase refers only to "some" (it is assumed that the disciples will take longer to die) and that Jesus does not include himself. It is unlikely that he thought the end of the world was imminent; some time had to pass, but the final arrival of the Kingdom was not very far off. The report in Mark 9:1 is the only reference to Jesus talking about the end of the world while some of his disciples are still alive. But it may well have been a modification of the early Christian community.

There is simply not enough evidence to view Jesus as an apocalyptic prophet who, according to A. Schweitzer, considered the Kingdom a reality only in the future, and who believed that the end of the world was imminent.

5.1.1.2. Entering the Kingdom, Now and Later

It is useless to search for signs that allow us to set dates for the arrival of the Kingdom of God. Our attention must be turned to the present time: "the Kingdom of God is in the midst of you" (Luke 17:21). This somewhat ambiguous phrase can be interpreted as meaning that the Kingdom is "within" each of us; its ambit is internal and spiritual, as suggested, in part and similarly, by the Gospel of Thomas 3: "the kingdom is within you and it is outside you." However, logion 113 of Thomas says that the Kingdom "is spread out upon the earth." The Kingdom is not purely internal, but external and visible, since there are signs of its presence in the world. For Jesus, the Kingdom is within reach of those who listen to him here and now; they simply have to keep their eyes and ears wide open in order to welcome it and enter it.

Jesus' words point to another important aspect when he says, "nor will they say, 'Lo, here it is!' or 'There'" (Luke 17:21). The Kingdom is not located at any precise point in history. It cannot be identified like other social, political, or cultural phenomena that have arisen or are to arise. The Kingdom does not encapsulate any ideology or line of thought. Talking about the Kingdom means talking about a new heart, different personal relationships, human ways of working that agree with the way God created and dreamed of this world. The decisive question is, how does one enter the Kingdom, taking part in one's own salvation, happiness, and thanks? God, by making himself manifest, offers everyone these things through Jesus. Fundamentally, there must be a decision, a desire, and unconditional willingness.

Jesus, to the disbelief of his disciples, presents children as role models. One has to welcome the Kingdom of God as a child would, as someone who is needy and weak, someone who cannot do anything on his or her own (Mark 10:15 || Luke 18:17). An even more disconcerting role model is that of the public and notorious sinner, the tax collectors and the prostitutes, who shall "go into the Kingdom of God before you [the law-abiding]" (Matt 21:31). Such individuals would obviously not place any conditions on receiving a life-changing message. The models not to follow are those who see themselves as just and holy and who may refuse Jesus' invitation or even campaign against the message he proclaimed (Matt 13:13 || Luke 12:52). Those who were attached to their riches would not have it easy either, as they were unlikely to take a decision that would lead them to question their own status and to refocus their lives. Jesus invited a rich man to follow him, but the rich man turned down the opportunity and was left sad and depressed. His possessions represented a barrier to the Kingdom of God that he could not overcome (Mark 10:23 || Matt 19:23 || Luke 18:24).

Only those who actively seek admission to the Kingdom above all else will enter (Matt 6:33 || Luke 12:31). Things are not always easy, however, and access to the Kingdom brings with it violence and upheaval; it imposes external and internal conflict, denying oneself and the world. Jesus uses a vibrant metaphor and states that entering the Kingdom requires effort and struggle: "[T]he kingdom of heaven has suffered violence, and men of violence take it by force" (Matt 11:12 || Luke 16:16). Those who love a treasure will fight to get it. Those who want to achieve their wishes have to be tenacious and persevere.

Two parables typify this tenacious and insistent behavior. The first parable describes the importunate neighbor, who arrives at midnight and incessantly calls and knocks at the door to get in. His stubbornness is effective, and he gets what he wants even though he has to kick up a fuss while everyone else is asleep (Luke 11:5-8). At times, what a patient friend cannot achieve an insistent one can. The second parable is that of the widow faced with an unscrupulous and obdurate judge. He did not respect God or man and was isolated from the world by his arrogance and impunity. A figure such as this can be worn down only by constant pressure. The judge finally gives way thanks to the woman's tireless and stubborn complaining, as this is her only choice. The woman's minimal strength multiplied by her tenacity enables her to get what she wants; the judge loses patience and finally capitulates, acceding to her demands and giving her justice (Luke 18:1-8). The Kingdom also requires a ceaseless search, continuous work, like that of the merchant who constantly looks for the finest pearls until he finds the most beautiful of them all, the pearl that is to change his life (Matt 13:45-46); or the fisherman who throws the small fish back and "easily chose the large fish," the only one worth catching (Thomas 8).

Entering the Kingdom of God means, ultimately, accepting, as does Jesus, that God is manifest in the world and that things are not as they were before. Everything has been changed, as hope has been brought closer to people's lives. Entering the Kingdom is, in effect, one's taking part here and now in the good news of this Kingdom and anticipating the peace of a future and eternal Kingdom. Those who welcome the Kingdom that Jesus proclaimed will find their final home in a Kingdom, which will become complete in the end. Jesus himself sees his own future at the banquet in this Kingdom, as proclaimed by the prophets of Israel: "Truly, I say to you, I shall not drink again of the fruit of the vine until that day when I drink it new in the kingdom of God" (Mark 14:25 || Matt 26:29 || Luke 22:18) (see 6.1.3).

The perspectives are not always so appealing. The rich man wanted to "inherit eternal life," and Jesus remarked that he would find it difficult "to enter the kingdom of God" (Mark 10:17, 10:23). Those who provoked scandal would also find it difficult. Those who made others sin and those who misguided the weak would be better off losing one eye now rather than losing the Kingdom forever with both eyes (Mark 9:47 || Matt 18:9). A similar fate awaited those who called God only with their lips but who did not in fact live as he asked them to (Matt 7:21); or those who, despite belonging to the people of Israel, had not welcomed God in his visit through the words and signs of Jesus, unlike the foreigners who came from the east and west and who shared the table in the Kingdom with the patriarchs, Abraham, Isaac, and Jacob (Matt 8:12 || Luke 13:28).

5.1.1.3. Jesus' Urgent Invitation

Jesus makes people see themselves and their lives. If God is manifest in history, and definitive salvation and forgiveness are at hand, each individual's response cannot be put off or watered down. There is to be a future and Final Judgment by God, which will assess the hearts of each person. However, what Jesus forcefully proclaims is that God's intervention has been brought forward against all the odds. As a result, the present (that of two thousand years ago now) has become a time for the renewal of one's heart, a time for the grace of God, and a time for repentance for each and every person.

As soon as Jesus starts preaching, he enthusiastically offers an invitation: "Repent" (Mark 1:15). John the Baptist had also made repentance the basis of his message (see 4.5.2.1). For Jesus, repentance did not represent preparation for judgment but the response to a fundamental message: God is manifest and the Kingdom is at hand. There is a notable change in perspective in the imagery. While John talked about beating and winnowing the grain, once and for all separating the wheat (to be kept) from the chaff (to be burned), Jesus placed emphasis on the sowing and the harvest, in the spreading of the seed and the fruits of the harvest, abundant and ripe ears of corn. For John, now was the time for the farmer to cut the tree without fruit and burn it; Jesus explained that the fig tree that has not produced figs for three years should not be cut down. Before being cut down, it should be dug over and manure used to see "if it bears fruit next year" (Luke 13:9). The call to enter the Kingdom is a mix of urgency and patience.

No one escapes being judged by God and by themselves. Jesus warns against the temptation of thinking that nothing needs to be changed in their lives, or at most only certain insignificant aspects, because they are just, good, and irreproachable people. The other temptation is to think that only the sinners have to repent. Faced with this arrogant error in justice, Jesus insists that setbacks and misfortune crop up, regardless of people's behavior; no one should think that the call to change their lives is addressed only to others and not to them. Jesus reminds people of the Galileans who died when the Roman troops massacred them within the walls of the temple. He also reminds them of the eighteen people who were killed when the Tower of Siloam fell down. None of those who died were guiltier than any of those who survived. The lesson is clear; "[U]nless you repent you will all likewise perish"; anyone can die, and we all have to repent alike (Luke 13:1-5).

Jesus' proclamation confronts the people listening to him with a unique and unrepeatable opportunity. This is not the time to fail. The laborer who digs the field does not fail; having found a treasure, he hides it again, sells all he has, and buys the land. His joy is that of a fortunate man who with a stroke of luck has seen his life change. Likewise, the merchant of fine pearls does not fail when one day he finds a valuable pearl and, like the laborer, decides to sell all his belongings to buy what he has always looked for. With these two parables (Matt 13:44-46), Jesus teaches us that people cannot hesitate if they want to enter the Kingdom now that the chance of a lifetime has come their way. It would be a great mistake to be overcome by doubt or fear. Even though it may mean having to give everything up, people cannot let this opportunity to turn their lives around get away. One's possessions are only relative when compared with what is fullness and enduring, with what offers unrivalled joy and happiness.

If they do not react conscientiously and do not act decisively, they will fail dreadfully, as in the parable of the new wine in the old wine-skins, when the skins burst and the wine spills on the floor; or the piece of new cloth sewn onto the old clothes, which leads to an even greater tear (Mark 2:21-22 || Matt 9:16-17 || Luke 5:36-39). Now is the decisive moment, a privileged and special time, much like a wedding celebration, when everything happens very quickly. Practices, such as fasting, can wait. Would anyone fast during the wedding celebrations (Mark 2:18-20 || Matt 9:14-15 || Luke 5:33-35)? Who would build their house badly on sand or without foundations and have the people laugh at them with the obvious risk that the wind and rain destroy it (Matt 7:24-27 || Luke 6:47-49)?

Likewise, the disciples cannot go back now that they have been called by Jesus to follow him. Faced with the opportunity of a lifetime that the Master offers them, it would be wrong to look for excuses and not realize the importance of this invitation. Failure in life does not involve money or social standing. Failure means not realizing what is at stake in terms of the great window that Jesus has opened: to the loving presence of God.

There are a number of parables that present failure realistically and forcefully. The man who wanted to build a house in a vineyard but had to stop midway through for lack of money was the butt of his neighbors' insults. The king who has taken on a much stronger force and does not send an envoy to broker peace despite his weak position before hostilities break out suffers an embarrassing defeat (Luke 14:28-32). In another parable, ten girls are chosen to be bridesmaids, but half of them find that they cannot undertake their task. At the decisive moment, the torches they are meant to use to welcome the groom go out because they have not thought to bring any extra oil. Half of them have failed in their task, while the other half, who are prepared, can enjoy the wedding celebrations (Matt 25:1-13). In another parable, the men who wait for their master to return, into the early hours of the morning if required, receive all kinds of honors from him (Luke 12:35-38). And in yet another parable, the loyal administrator who treats the servants entrusted to his care well while his master is away is rewarded, while the corrupt administrator who mistreats them and gets drunk fails miserably, loses his job, and is punished (Matt 24:45-51 || Luke 12:42-46). Another example is that of the servant who simply buried the money that his master gave him; he is punished, while the two who took risks and doubled the amount they were given are rewarded (Matt 25:14-30 || Luke 19:11-27).

In short, those who are prepared shall not fail but shall be acknowledged and rewarded greatly. Jesus' invitation to enter the Kingdom of Heaven has to be responded to decisively and generously. Happiness will accompany those who welcome it.

5.1.1.4. The Messenger and the Message

The message and messenger are inseparable. The Kingdom is inseparable from he who proclaims it. Jesus lets it be known that God has started to make himself manifest in his words and acts, which are shafts of light in the cold and hostile darkness: "[W]hoever is far from me is far from the kingdom" (Thomas 82). Right from the start, the exorcisms are probably the most spectacular way of showing this presence. Removing demons who torment the spirit of people is a sign of the force of evil being defeated. There is someone who is stronger than he who is strong by definition, someone capable of tying him up and controlling him, capable of making him powerless. He who enslaves is now enslaved. Jesus is stronger than Satan (Mark 3:27 || Matt 12:29 || Luke 11:21-22).

Right from the start, the parables are metaphors for the Kingdom and communicate it, show it, and make it manifest. Jesus' activities are linked to a personal conviction, which he communicates strongly to his listeners; what God has begun, God himself shall carry out. There is a series of parables that establish a contrast between the small, almost insignificant, beginnings and a spectacular end. After the farmer has sown the seed, it grows. As the days pass, the farmer continues his day-to-day life, the seed grows ceaselessly and the field is filled with the first stalks, then the ears, and finally the wheat. Before you know it, the grain is ready and harvest time has arrived (Mark 4:26-29). There is an obvious contrast between the newly sown field and the one ready to be harvested; the difference between the miniscule mustard seed and the fully grown plant is also enormous; the plant is so lush that even the birds can nest in the shade of its branches (Mark 4:30-32 || Matt 13:31-32 || Luke 13:18-19). The mustard seed planted by the man grows extraordinarily, and the handful of leaven that the woman adds to the three measures of flour makes all the dough rise (Matt 13:33 || Luke 13:20-21). Work in the fields and work in the home are two common sources of inspiration for Jesus' parables: the Kingdom involves God and everyday life. It has begun in an insignificant way, but it is to culminate in a magnificent end.

The parable of the sower has a special place in the Gospel tradition and expresses Jesus' firm belief that the Kingdom was to go ahead and lead to a splendid end. This parable offers a response to the doubts of his followers who have dreamed of immediate and brilliant success and who now see that it has been put off. Jesus replies confident in the knowledge that God is to fully establish his Kingdom, certain that each moment in life is decisive and ideal for receiving the force of the compassion he offers. Jesus is not looking to the future, but to the present; and the present is a blend of success and failure, of small and great events. The results may seem few, but there are blessings and healings that are "successes" for those who are dignified and humanized by the very force of God. The sinner forgiven or the sick person healed find in the Kingdom the anchor for salvation in their lives.

In the parable of the sower, three situations in which the seed is lost are described. In these three situations, the seed either does not grow or grows only a little. The seeds that fall by the roadside do not even enter the earth, and the birds come and eat them. The seeds that fall on rocky soil with little earth soon sprout up, but as they have no roots, the first hot sun burns the little ears and they shrivel up. Other seeds fall in the thorny part of the field. The thorns are stronger than the fragile ears of grain and choke them, so they cannot grow or bear fruit. On the other hand, the seeds that take root in the good ground produce fruit. Here the results are good (thirtyfold), excellent (sixtyfold), and even extraordinary (one hundredfold). Where there is nothing to affect it, the harvest is successful, and this helps us forget earlier failures (Mark 4:3-9 || Matt 13:3-9 || Luke 8:5-8).

With this parable, Jesus not only seeks to justify the modest beginnings of the Kingdom of God but also wants to emphasize the results of his activities (a mixture of success and failure). The parable reflects the way God gets things done. The Kingdom will not suddenly appear triumphantly, rather it will slowly spread, with moments of exaltation and other quieter times. The Kingdom experiences times of great progress and times of sterility and denial. Trust always wins out, however: God himself will ensure that these initial events culminate in a great harvest.

This culmination is highlighted in the prayer of the disciples, the Lord's Prayer, the Christian prayer par excellence (Matt 6:9-13 || Luke 11:2-4). Jesus expresses himself as being close to God and places the name of "Father" in the mouths of those who use it. He talks about closeness to God in the first two requests in the prayer, which are parallel. In the first ("Hallowed be thy name"), the Father is asked to act and show his power and his glory, so that everyone can recognize him as God, Lord of the universe, and friend of the poor and oppressed. In the second ("Thy kingdom come"), God is asked to begin his Kingdom soon, fully and completely, and to let his salvation shine from one side of the earth to the other. The Kingdom of which he is the Holy One shall represent the triumph of justice and peace, of good and truth, beyond the strict boundaries of Israel, meaning that a hope shared by all mankind will come true.

Hope for a future of plenty and fullness is rooted in the sure signs of the Kingdom, which Jesus' activities have testified to. This discreet beginning is essential, as it shows God's commitment to mankind and its needs, and it strengthens people's hopes. There is no contradiction in asking for a complete Kingdom and stating that there are signs of its arrival. This is not a form of logical disjunctive ("the Kingdom is either here or it is not") but a paradox ("the Kingdom is not here and it is starting to be here"). The disciple asks for the Kingdom to come, and Jesus asks him to enter it. Future and present, as G. Stanton points out, are juxtaposed, living together, harmoniously, in Jesus' preaching (and in the lives of every human being!).

In terms of this combination of present and future, the Lord's Prayer continues with three further requests: one refers to bodily well-being (daily bread and also the bread for the celestial banquet), one refers to the relations between God and us and between us and others (the forgiveness received from God corresponds to the forgiveness offered to those who have offended us), and a third refers to spiritual well-being (the decisive aid in the moment of temptation). The tradition in the Gospel according to Matthew underlines the day-to-day dimension of the Lord's Prayer and introduces two pertinent requests: one asks what is meant by God's establishing his Kingdom (what God wants has to be done both in heaven and on earth; "Thy will be done, on earth as it is in heaven"); the other request ("deliver us from evil") adds to the first by asking for help when faced with temptation from the cause (evil, Satan) and its consequences (falling into evil).

If the Lord's Prayer is the prayer par excellence, then the Beatitudes are the focal point of Jesus' message. Where the Lord's Prayer talks of his closeness to God, the Beatitudes come from his closeness to the poor, famished, disconsolate, and downtrodden. The message is based, once again, on the actual experience of mercy and compassion that inspires Jesus, the bearer of the Kingdom, who comes from God himself, he who has sent him (Matt 5:3-4, 5:6, 5:11-12 || Luke 6:20-23). In the Beatitudes, God is placed side by side with people who are struggling and downtrodden, people who have no one to defend them. The less fortunate, those most affected by bad luck or injustice, become happy, blessed people. The Kingdom of God turns situations on their heads, as it is indeed the poor who are God's favorites, his friends. Despite the struggles they may have, they have a life that is full of meaning, as God offers them the gift of his friendship and company. The Kingdom "is" (not merely "will be") for the poor, and the rewards for the calumnies they suffer are said to be "great in heaven." Hopes are set on the present, as God is to accompany those experiencing trials and tribulations on their journey.

Thus, the Kingdom belongs to them, as they have been awarded a celestial reward. The first and fourth Beatitudes strongly stress the reasons for happiness that transform the lives of the poor (Luke 6:20, 6:22-23). Those who are now suffering from hunger and desolation ("those who mourn") are guaranteed that God will give them what they need and ensure they live without pain. The future is also presented for these people as a time and place of plenitude, where God, unique and good, has the keys to life and death and will welcome them into the Kingdom where there is no misery or suffering. As it says in the book of Revelation, "He [God] will wipe away every tear from their eyes, and death shall be no more, neither shall there be mourning nor crying nor pain any more, for the former things have passed away" (21:4). What is new in the Beatitudes is that the present has been transformed as God personally looks after the poor on earth, opening the doors wide to his Kingdom and having them inherit it. Jesus proclaims that the poor are blessed because they are God's friends, here and now, and they shall have a place of honor when his Kingdom is established completely.

As in the case of the Lord's Prayer, Christian tradition has added to the Beatitudes, adapting them to the evolving situations of the early community. The blessing of the downtrodden and persecuted (the fourth Beatitude mentioned) is a sign of the trials and tribulations they underwent (see the description in Matt 10:17-25). By stressing that the Kingdom of God will not be established without judgment to assess each individual's lifestyle, Luke has introduced four obstacles in his Gospel. These obstacles are wake-up calls addressed to those who live self-confidently and who are indifferent to the needs of others (Luke 6:24-26): the rich, who are never hungry, those who never worry about anything, those who show off about their success and high standing. All these have already enjoyed "their" happiness and will find it difficult to join the happiness offered by God.

That the Beatitudes represent a program for life can be seen in the Gospel according to Matthew when it refers to "the poor in spirit," those who are spiritually close to God through humility; those who give themselves up to him and who try carry out his will, even though this may lead to persecution; those who are compassionate, with a sincere and pure heart; those who work for peace. The five Beatitudes that appear only in Matthew outline the profile for Jesus' followers as people who trust in God and who will not give up on the cause of man: their joy, in the Kingdom, is and will be complete (Matt 5:5, 5:7-10).

5.1.1.5. The Final Decisions

The offer of salvation is always present in Jesus' message. With patience and magnanimity, the God that Jesus proclaims brings people nearer to himself and offers them forgiveness and mercy. In the parable of the weeds in the wheat (Matt 13:24-30), the owner of the field does not want to separate the good plants from the bad too soon and tells his workers to let them grow together "until the harvest." The time will come for their separation. Salvation will come for all the people of Israel, for the poor, sick, and children, and it will also go beyond the boundaries of this people; the foreign centurion in Capernaum and the Syrophoenician from Tyre are two good examples.

As we have mentioned (5.1.1.1), one of the differences between the rabbi Jesus' doctrine and the other contemporary Jewish doctrines is that it does not include the defeat and submission of the pagans by the people of Israel. These events were considered to be signs of the restoration of the people of the covenant. In many Jewish texts, including the Song of Solomon (17), the end of the world is characterized by a complete turnaround: Israel's oppressors suffer ignominious defeat at the hands of those they had oppressed. In other texts, foreigners admitted as pilgrims to Zion and Jerusalem acknowledge the God of Israel. However, Jesus' preaching states the opposite: members of the people of Israel, for whom the Kingdom was designed, are expelled, and foreigners coming from the ends of the earth are to sit at the celestial banquet table with the patriarchs of Israel (Matt 8:11-12 || Luke 13:28-29).

This refusal to make salvation dependent on ethnic or religious origin is confirmed in the grand scene of the Final Judgment (Matt 25:31-46), where the criterion to enter the Kingdom is simply compassion for the weakest people: the hungry, the thirsty, the strangers, the naked, the sick, and the imprisoned. Again, this text has the hallmark of Christian tradition, though the core is in complete agreement with what Jesus himself says, namely, that those congregated before the Son of Man, who acts as a universal judge, are "all the nations," without exception or preference. Significantly, the judge, Jesus himself, identifies with the poor and downtrodden on earth wherever they are from, whom he calls his "brethren." This scene represents a new conception in terms of verifying a personal project, in which compassionate and specific behavior takes the place of legal or ritual regulations. The Kingdom is not limited then to the expectations of Israel and the people of the covenant.

However, Jesus kept almost exclusively within the confines of Israel, and the people of Israel represented the framework and audience for his activities. Tangible proof of this comes from the references to salvation, and to judgment (reserved for those who have wanted to turn down the salvation offered to them). Jesus' God, as M. Reiser has pointed out, is a vigorous God, a fire that burns with compassion but that can also devour those who deny it or its messenger. This relationship between heaven and earth, between Jesus and God, contains a clear warning by the Son of Man, the figure who will carry out the Final Judgment. Jesus says, "[E]veryone who acknowledges me before men, the Son of man will also acknowledge before the angels of God; but he who denies me before men will be denied before the angels of God" (Luke 12:8-9 || Matt 10:32-33). Salvation and rebuke are closely related, as both are derived from the royalty that God exercises over the world, people, and history. This royalty, energetic and beseeching, enters into action through Jesus' words and deeds and calls for heartfelt repentance, before the final divine judgment.

Jesus does not use threats to inspire his listeners, but he does refer to the realities that lie between the present and the future. Many examples of this are taken from the Scriptures, contemporary events, or parables coming from popular wisdom. Before the downpour, in the time of Noah, or before the destruction of Sodom and Gomorrah, in the time of Lot, everyone lived peacefully, with their daily routines that ended up a blind alley and in a disaster that took them all by surprise (Matt 24:37-39 || Luke 17:26-30). They also lived in fear of nothing; indeed, they had plenty of projects. A rich man wanted to build new barns to store his possessions and the great harvests he had had. He himself summed his life up saying, "[T]ake your ease, eat, drink and be merry." Death was to come as a surprise to this naive man; he did not even have time to write his will (Luke 12:16-20). Thus, Jesus' warning: "Be passersby" (Thomas 42). Another rich man, who dressed as a king and lived sumptuously, was unconcerned about the poor man who lay at the door of his house. When they die, their situations are reversed completely: Lazarus, the poor injured man ignored by the rich man, was happy to eat the crumbs that fell from his table and found comfort in the bosom of Abraham; whereas the rich man, in torment, asked only for a drop of water from the tip of Lazarus' finger to cool his tongue. It was an impossible request and came at the wrong time, as the injustice could have been redressed only during his life, by taking heed of the Scriptures and repenting (Luke 16:19-31). Those who repent are "good money-changers," people who have known how to make the right decision (*Pseudo-Clementine Homilies* 2:51:1).

The thought of death as a motive for repentance also occurs in two other historical episodes in the life of Jesus. As we have mentioned, these are the case of the Galileans massacred by Pilate and the case of the eighteen victims caused by the fall of the Tower of Siloam (Luke 13:1-5). The future is at stake in the present, and it is not wise to forget, unconsciously or deliberately, the fragile nature of one's existence. The present is not eternal, and the riches may be only a mirage. For this reason, because life is short and because it has a beginning and an end, now is the time to make decisions, to "invest" one's energies in the best way possible. Those who do not make the effort and who take refuge in a fruitless search for security may end up like the third servant in the parable of the talents, who hid the money that he had been entrusted with and ended up with nothing. This shows that those who do not take risks and those who take risks but do not win anything may not be able to enter the Kingdom (Matt 25:14-30 || Luke 19:11-27). People should not be scared by the fact that the path may not be easy or that the door is narrow. They merely have to know in which direction they have to go (Matt 7:13-14 || Luke 13:24). An astute and skillful administrator knew as much when, before being fired from his job, he started reducing the debts of his master's creditors, with the aim of making friends and thus preparing for his future (Luke 16:1-7). The present, for Jesus, is a decisive time and full of decisions.

The question as to who may "have strength . . . to stand before the Son of man" (Luke 21:36) is also present in Jesus' message, which shares the point of view of John the Baptist and his preaching in this respect. The Last Judgment overcomes thoughts of death: death and future judgment are not far off. There is a natural step from one's current situation to the time when one will have to give an account of oneself. Rather than concentrating on the threat of condemnation, Jesus stresses each person's responsibility. The example of the person who goes to the tribunal alongside the person who denounced them reflects the need to resolve arguments before it is too late. Once you have arrived before the judge, he may find against you, and you could end up in prison (Matt 5:25-26). It is necessary to welcome the message of the Kingdom and to change one's life, before the Final Judgment. The judgment clarifies matters and divides them. The end will not be the same for everyone: "[T]hat night there will be two in one bed; one will be taken and the other left. There will be two women grinding together; one will be taken and the other left" (Luke 17:34-35 || Matt 24:40-41). In the parable of the net, the fishermen "sorted the good [fish] into vessels but threw away the bad" (Matt 13:47-49). The selection, however, is made on the shore, not beforehand. Jesus' God is patient, he lets all people have time and space so that they can choose righteousness and tip the balance in their favor.

During his preaching, Jesus experienced people rejecting his message, those who were immune to the gospel. There were those who excluded themselves from salvation, who ignored or disrespected what they saw or heard. Jesus was so convinced of the greatness and importance of his proclamation that he was surprised by the lack of faith of those who should have welcomed it enthusiastically (see Mark 6:6, about the people of Nazareth). Some quotations from the prophets of Israel offer answers to this often incomprehensible reaction. For example, Isaiah 6:9-10 ("Hear and hear, but do not understand; see and see, but do not perceive. Make the heart of this people fat, and their ears heavy, and shut their eyes") serves as a reference in the chapter of parables (Mark 4:12 || Matt 13:14-15 || Luke 8:10). Jesus finds both enthusiastic and cold reactions, acceptance and rejection. On a number of occasions, those furthest from religious practices and the regulations of the Jewish faith responded with uncontained enthusiasm, while the law-abiding distanced themselves and could not bring themselves to trust what the Galilean rabbi proclaimed with the vigor of the prophets.

Jesus used a language reminiscent of the ancient prophets of Israel to describe those who rejected his message of the Kingdom. The most mighty words were reserved for the Galilean towns where Jesus carried out a good part of his miracles: Chorazin, Bethsaida, and Capernaum, the center of his activities. They were towns that had been lucky enough to witness extraordinary scenes of healings and exorcisms firsthand, but, despite this, they had not repented. There is no doubt that the Galilean towns could also be described in the way Jesus described Jerusalem in Luke 19:44: "you did not know the time of your visitation [from God]" (see 4.5.3.1).

The second group that deserved a reproach similar to the one reserved for the Galilean towns was the leaders of Israel, the scribes and Pharisees in particular (Matt 23:13-33 || Luke 11:37-48). Jesus mentioned the rejection that he had experienced from them and criticized their hypocritical and arrogant behavior, careful to keep to the insignificant commandments of the Law but ignorant of the really important things (see 4.5.4).

Criticism was also leveled at a third group or social class, "an evil and adulterous generation" or simply "this generation," which had failed to welcome the wisdom and calls for repentance that Jesus had addressed to them. With this potent rhetoric, he told them that on the day of "judgment" those who accused the children of Israel, who had rejected the message of the Kingdom, should be foreigners such as the Queen of Sheba, who had traveled just to hear the wisdom of Solomon, or the inhabitants of Nineveh, the city that God wanted to destroy for its sins but whose citizens had paid heed to Jonah's preaching, the prophet who had urged them to repent (Matt 12:41-42 || Luke 11:31-32) (see 4.5.3.1).

In summary, Jesus experienced rejection of his preaching and of his own person. This painful and burdensome reaction led to his using strong images that were often borrowed from the popular biblical imagination. He used prophetic language to stress the scope and consequences of this rejection. On no occasion, however, not even in relation to Capernaum, "his hometown," did Jesus condemn anyone eternally and irreversibly, despite the energetic or even threatening nature of his words. The final decisions belonged only to the Father, not the Son or the angels (Mark 13:32), even though the Father is he who has delivered "all things" to the Son (Matt 11:27 || Luke 10:22). We need, then, to ask ourselves about this God that Jesus proclaimed, this Father that Jesus told us about.

5.1.2. God, the Father of All, Through the Parables

Jesus did not "invent" his God. There is not Jesus' God on one side and Abraham's God on the other. The God for whom Jesus is Son is God the creator and provident, the God of the patriarchs, the God of the Exodus and Sinai, the God of David and Solomon, of the prophets and wise men, in short, the God of Israel, to whom each day pious Jews, like Jesus as well, address the *Shema* prayer: "Hear, O Israel: the Lord our God is one Lord" (Deut 6:4). This is how the Master of Nazareth began his reply to an anonymous scribe who was interested in the first and most important commandment of the Jewish Law (Mark 12:28-29). The God that Jesus proclaimed is "merciful and gracious, slow to anger, and abounding in steadfast love and faithfulness," words with which he revealed himself to Moses on Sinai (Exod 34:6) and which have resonated throughout the books of the prophets and the Psalms (e.g., Joel 2:13 and Ps 145:8). Thus, there is no reason to have the God of Sinai, that of the Jewish religion, in opposition to the God of Jesus, that of the Christian religion, as if they were, respectively, evil and good, cruel and merciful. Opposition of this kind goes against the beliefs and message of Jesus of Nazareth.

There are, however, certain aspects in the way Jesus talks about God that give his words a unique character. First, for example, when Jesus refers to God he prefers one way of calling him (Father), above the other possibilities (lord, king, judge, shepherd, saint, highness, etc.). This represents a conscious decision from among the many possibilities offered by the Jewish tradition, from both the Scriptures and other sources. Second, Jesus talks about God and his actions in the world using parables, aphorisms, maxims, and images that are rooted in everyday life and popular wisdom, images the people can understand and recognize, not images reserved for the theologians, Israel's scribes. His world is not one of syllogism, but of metaphor. Thus, he is able to bring a precision to the common religious vocabulary: "God" (or "heaven" in its metonym) and "Father." Third, Jesus did not sweeten the image of God, reducing any hypothetical ills, nor did he lessen his glory, power, or royalty. On the contrary, the expression "Kingdom of God" maintains and reinforces the active and committed presence of God in the history of mankind as a whole and for each individual in particular. His salvation strongly forges a path, overcoming the power of evil and its prince, Satan, allowing righteousness to spread through the world.

5.1.2.1. A Surprising God

The God that Jesus proclaims breaks down the barriers between personal qualities and capabilities, bridging the divisions between people due to their moral virtues or choices in life. Jesus talks about the "Father who is in heaven; . . . he makes the sun rise on the evil and the good, and sends rain on the just and on the unjust" (Matt 5:45). God acts without restrictions or conditions, without prejudgments or half measures. Even the bad and unjust, friends of evil and not of good, have the right to be welcomed close to him. They know that he will treat them all equally. As J. Dupont stresses, Jesus states that the bad also have the right to be loved. This elemental image of the sun and the rain serves to show a fundamental truth: God does not make distinctions between people. Indeed, nor does Jesus, as the Pharisees acknowledge when they ask him about the tribute (Matt 22:16). Jesus' Gospel avoids the initial distinction when evaluating people ("they are a good/bad person") with a somewhat prosaic argument: "the sun shines on us all," both good and bad. In other words, God makes the sun shine on everyone equally each day. This represents irrefutable proof for Jesus of a simple, but almost unexpected, fact: God is the Father of all people, even those who are distanced from him, the sinners.

The parables involve, as we have seen, a suitable, lively, and visual language, which is not subject to or weighed down by the conceptual. This God wants to be the Father to us all, even those who have distanced themselves from him. A good example of this distancing is the lost sheep, which goes its own way, away from the other ninety-nine and the shepherd. Should the shepherd bother to take risks for just one sheep? Perhaps he should not, it may be not advisable or even worthwhile. However, since the shepherd is not willing to give up on any of his sheep, he sets off to find it, and his efforts are rewarded. He can return home with a smile on his face and the lost sheep. God will not resign himself to losing even one of his children, and, for this reason, he is willing to go out and look for them when they get lost so that they can find themselves and the path back to the fold again. It may sound strange, but it is true; the happiness of the shepherd for this sheep is even greater than his happiness for the other ninety-nine. Jesus places no limits on God's joy (Matt 18:12-14 || Luke 15:3-7), nor does he place limits on his friendship with those who have gotten lost.

There is complete harmony between what Jesus says about God and his own actions, which were often criticized by the strictest Jews. The parables act as a neutral territory in which the points of view of the narrator (Jesus) and the audience (in this case, the Pharisees) cross and offer a chance for dialogue. Jesus can thus attract people to his point of view who were initially unwilling to accept it. An exceptional example of this is the parable of the prodigal son, where Jesus' point of view is represented as that of the father and the opinion of those who criticize him is represented as that of the elder brother (Luke 15:11-32). The narrative begins with someone stepping out of line and being dismissed. The younger son rebels against his father and demands part of his inheritance; he renounces his position as a son. Nevertheless, this voluntary loss is followed by a loss brought on by his lack of sense. The son in question ends up without possessions or dignity as a pig farmer, seen by the Jews as the lowest form of employment. He has only one way out: to return to his father's house, but, he believes, as a laborer and not as a son. The surprise comes when his father welcomes him as a son, with a great celebration, proclaiming, "[M]y son was dead, and is alive again; he was lost, and is found." A father's love is unconditional, and this father is not willing to lose his younger son, in the same way that he does not want to lose his elder son. Furthermore, he wants to get him back. The elder son has not left home, but he feels like a laborer, a stranger, someone who wants a few insignificant rights (a party now and then with his friends), and he is indignant that his father still treats his rebellious brother as a son. The elder son has never understood that he has a father; rather, he confuses him with the master of the estate. In the middle of the celebrations, the father goes out to find him, so that he can enter the house as his son ("Son, you are always with me, and all that is mine is yours"), and he also celebrates finding what he had lost. God wants to forgive and does forgive. The son, who returns ashamed of himself, as a laborer, acknowledges this and is welcomed as a son by the Father, but he who did not leave home also has to understand who God is: a Father who, obviously, is happy only when he can see all his children together in happiness and peace.

If there is a parable that contains surprises, then it is the parable of the workers in the vineyard (Matt 20:1-15). The first surprise is that the owner of the vineyard goes to the town square five times to hire workers, at the eleventh hour (!), as the sun is about to go down. This landowner may be worried about the unemployment figures and wants to avoid seeing men standing around without work to do. Maybe he has a very large estate and needs a good number of people to take care of the work that needs doing. The narrator does not initially make clear why. We have to wait. This parable, as with many others, shows the motivations only of those involved indirectly. Evening comes and the time to pay the wages. This is when the second surprise comes: those who have worked only an hour are paid a whole day's pay, one denarius. It is however only a relative surprise as this landowner is a peculiar character, who hires people an hour before the day ends! The real surprise comes when those who have worked from sunup to sundown are paid the same wage: one denarius. They are unanimous in their protests, which seem fully justified. It is not fair that those who work twelve hours get paid the same as those who only work for one. As in the parable of the prodigal son, the elder son complains about the relative injustice he has suffered in comparison to the son who has embezzled his father's money but who is welcomed home again as if nothing had happened. Where are equality and justice? Similarly, in the second parable why are the workers not properly rewarded for the work they have done? These are the protests and complaints from all of those who, in the strictest sense of "justice," even today hear this disconcerting account for the first time.

The response from the owner of the vineyard to those who worked from the earliest hour in the morning represents Jesus' point of view and, fundamentally, God's behavior when he makes himself manifest in the world through his Kingdom. The landowner wants to make it clear, first, that there has been no injustice. He had agreed to pay the first men he hired one denarius, a day's wages, and he had given them what he had promised, a fair wage for the time. What they have earned, they have been given. So why are they complaining? Second, the landowner stresses that he can do whatever he wants with his money. Who can deny him the freedom to pay each of them the same wage? Finally, he offers an explanation for the dismay that those who worked from first light feel: "Is your eye evil because I am good?" (another translation is, "[D]o you begrudge my generosity?"). If his eye were good, his whole body would be filled by the light and there would be no room for envy (Matt 6:22-23 || Luke 11:34-36). This parable highlights the two types of justice that are in play: the distributive and the magnanimous, what is based on strictly rewarding all individuals for what they have done and what is based on freely giving to those who want to be rewarded. There is a reduced justice, which may seem "fairer," and a generous and overflowing justice, that offered by Jesus' God.

The owner of the vineyard offers proof of his tenacious generosity. This is his way of dealing with people, what defines and identifies him. The God that Jesus proclaims is portrayed magnificently in the behavior of this landowner. His righteousness knows no barriers, not even those dictated by what is commonly understood as justice. He wants to be generous to all his children, especially to those whom no one has taken any notice of or, indeed, those whom no one has counted on and who are left waiting in the square. These eleventh-hour workers, alone in the square, without any kind of chance but who still want to go to the vineyard are the sinners, those marginalized by religion, those who were not counted on when Israel needed a new impulse. The law-abiding did not take any notice of them, those who are called first thing in the morning but are unable to understand that Jesus has come "not to call the righteous, but sinners" (Mark 2:17 || Matt 9:13 || Luke 5:32). Unfortunately, they do not understand that their protests are aimed at the God of grace and forgiveness, in whom they say they believe. This God, as proclaimed by Jesus, is generous and bountiful to those who are far from him, to those whom he himself has wanted to go out and find so that they can enter the Kingdom. This surprising search breaks with the traditional Law, whose sole and unique criterion is based on good works and merit. Jesus' friendly manner and welcoming nature with everyone, including the sinners, is based on a God whose righteousness is boundless. This is the way God gets things done.

The banquet is the most common image in Judaism to describe God's final reign. Unsurprisingly, Jesus adopts it in one of his most characteristic parables (Matt 22:1-10 || Luke 14:16-24). The main figure is a man who decides to organize a large celebration for a great number of people. A great banquet is measured in terms of the number of guests attending; and it is for this reason that the banquet is almost a complete disaster. Those who have accepted the invitation decline at the last minute ("I have made ready my dinner"), giving a number of more or less convincing excuses, that show, between the lines, a lack of interest in the event. The host is taken by surprise at this turn of events. He has his home prepared, the food is ready, but he has no guests.

So this man, unable to tolerate a situation that falls somewhere between idleness and ingratitude, reacts quickly, having been offended. He immediately sends his servants to find some guests in the city and the surrounding area, who will not let him down: the poor and the disabled, the blind and the limp, tramps and the homeless, the sick and the downtrodden, those who will make the most of a celebration such as this. The house is soon filled with guests. Those who were never taken into account provide a rapid and enthusiastic response. They just needed someone to invite them and welcome them into their home. The host finally has his banquet, with some unusual, but highly motivated and very grateful, guests.

The Kingdom cannot fail because of people's lack of interest or their arrogance, because of the vain self-sufficiency of those who have been invited to enter but, when it comes to it, back out. These people have not understood what is required, in Jesus' words, "seek first his kingdom" (Matt 6:33 || Luke 12:31); instead they offer a series of excuses, their "urgent" concerns (buying fields or oxen, getting married). Israel's leaders, those who keep strictly to the Law, are not interested in Jesus' message. They do not see it as the only way to encounter God and renew their hearts, which are overly concerned with life's problems. They know that they have received an invitation, but when it comes to entering the banquet hall and deciding whether they are going to accept the message of the Kingdom, all they can do is offer excuses. They resemble the elder son and those who work from first thing in the morning, those who complain about a father's compassion and the generosity of the vineyard's owner. The guests in the parable simply offer a wide range of excuses; for them, obviously, the Kingdom is not a unique pearl or treasure!

On the other hand, those who are not initially taken into consideration are now sitting at the banquet table: the poor and the sick make the gospel of the Kingdom their own and do not hesitate when it comes to entering. God welcomes everyone to the Kingdom, regardless of the condition they are in; but only the simplest people welcome this revelation of God's righteousness and so become the first to enter, whereas the wise and knowledgeable take no notice of what is offered to them. Things are turned on their head when it comes to people's reactions to the news of the Kingdom. This parable shows as much. Those who are furthest away respond, while those who are closest ignore it. Ignoring it and making excuses are, however, subtle ways of showing one's true self to a God who opens the doors of his house to everyone without distinction. He is the Father of all of us, as well as and above all of the poor, those who shall sit at the banquet in his Kingdom.

In the four parables we have looked at above, the figures involved move within the setting of the parable. God is represented as a shepherd, the father of two sons, the owner of a vineyard, and a man organizing a banquet. Nonetheless, in the parable of the Pharisee and the tax collector (Luke 18:10-14), the figures are named; they represent themselves. Here Jesus' objectivity is perfect since the parable is a tool for dialogue and an aid for comprehension that can easily fail if the narrator tries to predispose the audience against one or other participant. For this reason, the descriptions of the Pharisee and the tax collector are absolutely transparent.

The scene takes place in the temple in Jerusalem, where the two men have gone to pray. One is a paradigm of the Jewish religion, law-abiding, diligent, irreproachable, and respected for his virtue. The other is the clearest example of a Jew who ignores the Law, involved in fraud and extortion because of his involvement in the Roman and Herodian tax systems. He is disrespected, and his job is looked down upon. Indeed, the Pharisee, in his prayers, describes himself particularly well, as a man who keeps strictly to the Law, and no one, not even God, can reproach him for any reason. The Pharisee is proud of the fact that he is not a thief, or unjust or adulterous, that he fasts twice a week and that he pays the tithes for everything he buys in the market, even the wild herbs, one of the cheapest goods available. He is self-contented with his virtuous lifestyle and gives thanks to God, as he has granted him a life "not like other men" and, obviously, not "like this tax collector." His prayer is true; God, who knows his heart, knows that he is telling the truth about his life. The Pharisee has a life that is full of good works.

On the other hand, the tax collector cannot present his life as honorable and just to God. He does not keep to the Law. He can show God only his sins. He is at the back of the inner court in the temple and staring at the ground, beating his chest as a sign of repentance. He is a sinner, and he does not hide the fact. He wears his heart on his sleeve and prays to God to be compassionate and to forgive him: "God, be merciful to me a sinner!" His prayer is also true. It is not self-praise, but an authentic prayer. The tax collector prays because he is searching for infinite righteousness. The Pharisee needs God only to rubber-stamp the fact that he is a just man. What does God hear? Whom does he listen to?

This is the question that Jesus answers at the end of the parable with a surprising statement, in both its sense and its form: "I tell you, this man [the tax collector] went down to his house justified [or forgiven] rather than the other." Jesus is clearly talking here from God's perspective, with unquestionable certainty and authority. God has welcomed the tax collector's prayer, but not that of the Pharisee. The words of the Pharisee are redundant and pompous, and they do not enter God's heart, whom he asks to justify what was already justified. For the Pharisee, God, as the guardian of the Law, should limit his actions to corroborating what he has achieved with his irreproachable religiosity. There is no room for free gifts and mercy from he who is, above all else, a Father who feels compassion for his children. The only relationship possible for the Pharisee with his God is that of distributive justice, not that of unbridled generosity.

This generous forgiveness is what the tax collector receives in the temple. He has gone up with a great weight of regret and has come back down again liberated. But the Pharisee returns from the temple with his heart unchanged; indeed, he is probably even more self-satisfied than before. The tax collector is renewed because he has received the forgiveness he was desperately seeking. The Pharisee does not need this forgiveness. Nonetheless, Jesus' God prefers a sinner who asks for forgiveness to a just man who shows off about his good behavior. The Pharisee, lost in his own idea of justice, is not touched by God's warmth and never comes to see him as a righteous Father. It is the same mistake made by the elder brother who accuses his father of not taking into account the years that he has served him: "I never disobeyed your command" (Luke 15:29). The tax collector, who acknowledges his own sins, receives God's friendship and now lives in his company.

5.1.2.2. A Concerned God

The sun and the rain are two gifts from heaven that fall equally on all mankind. The idea of God caring for all the creatures in the universe, including the plants and the animals, is echoed throughout a good number of psalms. God sends the rain to guarantee the fertility of the land, which feeds both men and animals (e.g., Ps 104:13-15). However, what sets Matthew 5:45 apart is that it stresses something otherwise self-evident, that both the good and the bad benefit from the basic elements for existence that come from above, water and sun: "for he [God] is kind to the ungrateful and the selfish" (Luke 6:35). In other words, God is also concerned about those who are not law-abiding, and he never gives up caring for them. He is not quick to offer either salvation or condemnation. Instead, he is willing to hand out the gift of life unconditionally.

The world is built on the equality of all mankind before God and on the righteousness that spreads throughout mankind and creation. God's limitless love includes the unjust; indeed, it is based on loving one's enemies (Matt 5:44-45). His generous and surprising righteousness, which is open to the poor and the sinners, as seen in the parables we have just looked at, is a sign of the care and attention that he pays when dealing with the things he has created. The world takes on another face in the light of the message of the Kingdom; it is recovered as a place of goodness and harmony, just as it was when it was first made by the hands of the Creator.

Thus, from the perspective of a Kingdom that has just begun to grow on earth, we can understand the extraordinarily positive point of view that Jesus has when it comes to the world created as the setting for the manifestation of God's righteousness. As J. Schlosser points out, Jesus sees creation as a mirror of this righteousness. This world that has been created allows us to see the marks left by God's attention to minute detail in his care for each and every one of its inhabitants, his care for the world and for mankind. This acts as the root of the great trust that needs to be placed in God, who will not turn his back on his creation; quite the contrary, he has it in his heart and takes care of it.

The rural setting in which Jesus preaches gives him the inspiration for parables to strengthen trust in God's providence. Jesus' starting point is not some romantic and idyllic representation of nature but his belief in God's care for the things he has created. Jesus sees nature through God's eyes, who, having created the world, "saw that it [what he had created] was good" (Gen 1:10), as it was the result of his righteousness. Jesus echoes the initial righteousness of those things created, which has been maintained by God himself, who is bountiful and magnanimous with what his hands have produced.

The image in the parable of a father giving his son the food and good things he asks for (a fish or an egg) and not what could upset or harm him (a snake or a scorpion) shows God's unwavering goodness toward all those who call to him. Jesus' argument is simple: "If you [fathers of the world] who are evil, know how to give good gifts to your children, how much more will your Father who is in heaven give good things to those who ask him!" (Matt 7:9-11 || Luke 11:11-13). God's care and righteousness are to be found at the center of Jesus' message and beliefs.

God spreads righteousness and offers the "good things" in life, taking care of the basic necessities of life. This is what Jesus focuses on, not on the more spectacular elements in the created world but on the most insignificant and the most abundant: the birds in the sky (ravens, according to Luke) and the lilies of the field (Matt 6:25-33 || Luke 12:22-31). Both the birds and the wild flowers are living things that do not work or produce; they do not harvest or spin; they do not have a "storehouse nor barn"; and, despite all this, they are sustained and fed by the generosity of the Father in heaven, who does not turn his back on anything he has created, no matter how small and insignificant it may seem. Indeed, this Father is not limited to bringing life to the lilies of the field but dresses them in charming clothes that are more beautiful even than Solomon's raiment itself.

Would this God, who is sensitive to beauty, as can be seen in the care he takes with the birds and the flowers, then not pay the same attention to people? If God does not ignore even one single bird sold in the market for four cents, why would he forget about a single human being, whomever they were and wherever they came from? Indeed, "you," any of you, Jesus reminds us insistently "are of more value than many sparrows" (Matt 10:31 || Luke 12:7; Matt 6:26 || Luke 12:24). The conclusion is obvious: "Fear not." Before God, before the Father of all of us, trust wins out. This trust drives out fear and frees us from doubt, concerns, and anxiety. God is bountiful and does not forget the men and women of this world.

The model for creation brings life back to where it belongs, as something that does not belong to us but to the righteous Father. Concerns about food and clothing, the basic needs, are left up to God, who sustains the world he has created in such a way as to allow life (fed and clothed) for all his children. When these concerns are overcome through trust, God's righteousness for mankind can shine from the shadows, as it shines from those things he has created, those things he cares for. Thus, thanks to trust in a God who will not abandon his children, there are no needs that can distract us from the indispensable: preoccupation with the Kingdom, the only concern that it is really worth having. The rest can be left safely up to him. There is a delicate irony in the passage we have just commented on, which is seen in Jesus' reminder that not even the hairs on our head can fall out without God knowing about it (!) (Matt 10:30; Luke 21:18). No matter how hard we try we cannot make our lives any longer or shorter. The righteous care of the Father in heaven is a good reason for "men of little faith" to trust in him.

Nonetheless, we may ask ourselves whether God's goodness has a limit, whether it has any boundaries. In the scene with the rich man called to follow Jesus, he calls him "Good Teacher" and Jesus replies, "[N]o one is good but God alone" (Mark 10:18 || Matt 19:17 || Luke 18:19). If only God is good, we have to assume that his goodness is infinite and that this goodness is unconditional and limitless. Love for one another can have no boundaries, as Jesus shows in inviting us to love our enemies and pray for our persecutors "so that you may be sons of your Father who is in heaven; for he makes his sun rise on the evil and on the good, and sends rain on the just and on the unjust" (Matt 5:44 || Luke 6:35). God's love and righteousness reach out as far as love for one another is needed, to everyone.

The story that most forcibly expresses God and Jesus' closeness to all mankind, without distinction, is the parable of the Good Samaritan (Luke 10:30-37). It is no coincidence that the interpretations of this parable, beginning with the Church Fathers, have identified Jesus as the Samaritan who stops to help an injured man by the wayside, acting as a "neighbor" to the man who had been the victim of an attack by bandits. The scene, as is often the case in Jesus' parables, is described very precisely and without any superfluous information to distract those listening. The action is fast paced, almost on edge. The verbs come one after the other in the three scenes that make up the narrative.

In the first scene, those involved are a man, who remains unidentified and anonymous, traveling on foot from Jerusalem to Jericho, and the ruthless bandits who take his clothes, beat him up, and leave him for dead. We are not told even whether they stole anything of value: the assault is an attack of gratuitous cruelty that leaves the man fighting for his life. In the second scene, the wounded man is lying by the roadside, naked and helpless. Those who could help him see him but pass by on the other side of the road. They are a priest and a Levite from Jerusalem. But neither one nor the other helps him; they avoid this poor man. Why do they not stop? For fear, because of their religious scruples (priests cannot touch dead bodies, and the man must have appeared half dead), because they feel reticence toward someone they are not obliged to aid? They did not consider the wounded man to be any kind of "neighbor" of theirs, and they avoid him. Thus, they still have the benefit of the doubt: Is he a Jew whom they, members of Israel's priesthood, must be the first to help? Or is he just a foreigner?

The third man who passes was not to know either. He is a Samaritan, one excluded from the religion of Israel, traveling through a Jewish land, a land in which he is a stranger and unwelcome. The Samaritan goes up to the injured man and "he saw him, he had compassion." The compassion that he feels in his heart for this defenseless and needy stranger inspires the Samaritan to act. His care becomes the focal point of the scene; he would do no more for one of his own brothers! Even his own journey is relegated to the background. His only concern is to ensure that this stranger has everything he needs. Unlike the priest and the Levite, the Samaritan goes up to the injured man and treats him like a "neighbor," without expecting anything in return. He is motivated purely by his feeling of mercy. This mercy leads to his treating the man's injuries and taking him to a hostel (the hospitals of the time), personally looking after him until the following day and then paying the hostel keeper to look after the man until the Samaritan passes that way again and can pay him for anything else he provides the man.

Jesus' last question as to who behaves like a "neighbor" to the injured man has an easy answer: "The one who shows mercy on him." The Samaritan's care for the man by the roadside is inspired by a feeling of compassion that is translated into extraordinary generosity. There are parallels to the behavior of the father of the prodigal son who is so moved on seeing that the son he has lost has come home again that he organizes a splendid celebration with music and dancing in his honor, for which he has the finest animal in his stables killed. It resembles the surprising attitude of the owner of the vineyard who shows abundant generosity and decides to pay all the workers, even the meekest who has had to spend almost the whole day in the town square waiting to be hired, one denarius, a full day's wage. Wherever the Kingdom is to be found, wherever God is manifest with compassion and generosity, with the care and mercy of a Father, everything is plentiful. Goods are multiplied. God is, indeed, Father to all of us. His righteousness reaches out to everyone. It does not take into account any form of identification, just as the compassion of this Samaritan overflows for this man without a name or identity, recognizing him as a "neighbor" and treating him as one.

The parable that takes exaggeration of language and argument furthest is the one that tells the story of a servant without compassion (Matt 18:23-34). It aims to show how much compassion God has for mankind, to stress his capacity for limitless forgiveness. God's generosity can be seen in all its greatness when he forgives. Jesus even makes forgiveness the fourth request in the Lord's Prayer, the prayer he leads with the disciples: "forgive us our debts." Emphasis is placed by Jesus on God's forgiveness as a gift given and welcomed, a present offered, received, and accepted. This parable is an excellent example of this, with a direct and powerful story line, which at times seems difficult to believe but which is, ultimately, utterly convincing. Fiction and reality come together to form an inseparable whole.

The narrative involves two debts: one enormous and virtually impossible to pay, ten thousand talents (one talent = 21.7 kilograms of silver), and one small and easy to meet, one hundred denarii (one denarius = one day's pay). The first amount is owed by an underling to an important person (a king?), who has administered his master's ten thousand talents disastrously and has been found out. Faced with this financial catastrophe, the master tells this man, who is cornered and obviously unable to pay, that he has to repay him with everything he has (his person, family, and belongings). Indeed, the man himself is to be sold as a slave. This foolish man can appeal only to his master's goodwill and ask not to be imprisoned and that he be allowed to pay him back bit by bit.

It is a highly unlikely proposition; how could he pay back ten thousand talents? However, surprisingly, the master shows this foolish man compassion. He changes the nature of the problem. First, the master accepts the request of his underling and sets him free. Not only does he let him pay him back bit by bit (an impossible task?), but also, unexpectedly and incomprehensibly, he forgives him the debt of ten thousand talents. This gesture resembles the return of the prodigal son and the effect this has on his father, and the compassion shown by the Samaritan for the injured man. There is an overflowing righteousness that overcomes the affront caused by a son who wants to leave home, or that overcomes the Samaritan's inhibitions on seeing a stranger abandoned, half dead by the roadside. This underling had been returned to life, thanks to the generous and unexpected compassion of his master.

The parable could end here, but Jesus seems to want to extract the negative connotations of the second request in the Lord's Prayer, ". . . as we also have forgiven those who have sinned against us." This is the crux of the second section of the parable. The man who has been fortunate enough to receive undeserved compassion grabs one of his colleagues who owes him one hundred denarii, a ridiculous amount compared to the debt that his master has forgiven him. Everything is turned on its head, then, as the man who has been forgiven is incapable himself of forgiving. Instead of compassion, he feels only aggression. Evil replaces goodness. The mercy that should fill the heart of the man who has been forgiven somehow becomes hardness of heart. He who has been freed by his master now has the man who owes him so much less imprisoned

The righteousness of the master who forgives the great debt is lost, twisted by the indignant underling's inability to forgive. The other colleagues are right to feel concerned about what has happened. Why has this man acted the way he has? What is the narrator trying to show us in this upsetting and harsh reaction? As J. Dupont stresses, the contrast between the unexpected generosity of the master and the odious tightfistedness of his underling is absolute. There is a great imbalance between the forgiveness of the master and the forgiveness that the forgiven servant is unable to grant.

The forgiveness that we can offer is insignificant compared to what God has decided to grant us. Despite everything, the underling who was forgiven is unable to forgive. Jesus probably wishes to show that forgiveness is never automatic or easy. To forgive, even if it is only one hundred denarii (!), requires sharing in God's compassion and generosity. Otherwise, if forgiveness is offered and granted by the Father but not welcomed in our hearts, then God's gift may well be lost. The difference between the master and the underling is that one is moved by compassion and the other comes away saying what luck he has had, without understanding the scope of the gift he had been given. The final line that the master addresses to him is said with compassion, which is the basis and mother of forgiveness, the forgiveness of God and man: "[S]hould not you have had mercy on your fellow servant, as I had mercy on you?" The God that Jesus proclaims places no limits on his forgiveness. His forgiveness like his righteousness is constantly renewed. It can, however, be twisted if our hearts are not renewed by compassion.

Those who know that they have been forgiven have a great many reasons to forgive, even to forgive over and over again, tirelessly. The Gospel according to Luke talks about "seven times in the day" (17:3-4), whereas the Gospel of Matthew places the limit (!) at "seventy times seven" (18:22). Jesus' words are so crystal clear that they are somewhat discomforting: "Judge not, and you will not be judged; condemn not, and you will not be condemned; forgive, and you will be forgiven" (Luke 6:37). These words are accompanied by an amusing and striking image, which is full of irony and imagination, stressing the vanity of those who think highly of themselves: "[H]ow can you say to your brother, 'Let me take the speck out of your eye,' when there is a log in your own eye? You hypocrite, first take the log out of your own eye, and then you will see clearly to take the speck out of your brother's eye" (Matt 7:2-5 || Luke 6:41-42). Those who realize the insignificance of their own merits and the greatness of God's compassion are those who forgive.

5.1.2.3. A God Called Father

Jesus talks of a generous and compassionate God, who is good and provident, firm in his decisions and unceasing in his care. All these characteristics come together in the name Father. Jesus' preferred name for God is no coincidence.

Israel's tradition included this metaphor of parenthood (God the father and mother) in referring to God and employed a number of images: from the father who looked after his children to the mother who carried them in her womb and who loved them always with boundless tenderness, for example, Deuteronomy 32:6, "Do you thus requite the Lord, you foolish and senseless people? Is not he your father, who created you, who made you and established you?" or the words that God used to address Israel, his people: "As one whom his mother comforts, so I will comfort you" (Isa 66:13). Both in the First Testament and in subsequent Jewish writings, there are a great many references to what characterizes some form of parenthood, the link between authority and goodness, which corresponds to filial obedience and trust.

At certain times, God's parenthood of Israel, his children, spreads to all peoples and focuses on the protection he offers each and every person. For example, it says in the Wisdom of Solomon, in reference to sailors, "[I]t is thy providence, O Father, that steers its course . . . thou canst save from every danger, so that even if a man lacks skill, he may put to sea" (14:3-4). In the Apocalypse of Moses, written in the first century A.D., God is invoked in the following way: "O God, I have sinned, O God of All, I have sinned against thee" (32). In Philo of Alexandria, God is called "their Father and the Creator of the world" (*Embassy* 115). God is called Father alongside other names, such as King, Highness, Lord of the universe (*Pantocrator*), as can be seen in Eleazar's prayer (3 Macc 6:2-15). We need merely recall the expression "Our Father, Our King" (*Avinu, Malkenu*), in one of the blessings that the Jews of the first century A.D. recited every day.

Jesus, a man of prayer and well versed in the Scriptures, was used to calling God by all the names in Jewish prayer, among which was *Father*. Nonetheless, this name was not the most common at the time. This is what makes it stand out. Jesus clearly prefers the name *Father* when talking about God and, in particular, when invoking him. It is no coincidence that the prayer that he teaches the disciples begins with the words "Our Father" (see 5.4.2, below). Loyal to Jesus' choice, the Christian tradition (above all, in the Gospels of Matthew and John) notably increases the use of the names *Father* and *Son* when referring to God and Jesus. Matthew names God *Father* 40 times; John 119 times. On the other hand, the word *God* is much more common in Mark and Luke together than in Matthew and John. Mark uses *God* some 50 times; Luke over 130 times. Matthew uses *God* almost 60 times; John slightly over 70. In contrast, judging from the extant documents, Jesus uses the word *Lord*, the usual term for the God of Israel, a lot less. Almost a third of the examples in which the Gospels refer to God in this way are quotations from the First Testament.

Jesus primarily called God *Lord*, the generic term common to both Jews and non-Jews, and second, he used the name *Father*. This name (Aramaic, *abba*) (see 5.4.2, below) appears in nearly all Jesus' prayers in the synoptic Gospels: the thanksgiving prayer (Matt 11:25 || Luke 10:21); the prayer in Gethsemane (Mark 14:36 || Matt 26:39, 26:42 || Luke 22:42) ("*Abba*, Father"); the two short prayers on the cross, mentioned only in Luke 23:34 and 23:46; and the Lord's Prayer, the disciples' prayer. The only prayer in which it does not appear is the one on the cross mentioned in Mark (15:34) and Matthew (27:46) ("My God, my God"). In these prayers, and other texts, the rightful parenthood of God is strongly stressed and linked to his universal sovereignty. One example is Jesus' thanksgiving prayer, which starts by saying, "I thank thee, Father, Lord of heaven and earth" (Matt 11:25 || Luke 10:21). In Gethsemane, Jesus confides in God that his future is in his hands and that he could free him from the Passion and death, though he also submits himself to his will (see 6.2.2.3).

The trust placed in God is the result of his generous righteousness, which spreads beyond time and space and which includes the present and the future. Thus, the perspective is opened as far as possible when Jesus says: "Fear not, little flock, for it is your Father's good pleasure to give you the kingdom" (Luke 12:32). Trust in a God who gives his children only good things and who gives and will give them the greatest treasure of all, his friendship, is one of Jesus' profound convictions. No father leaves his children unprotected, and the more desperate their position, the more care he takes, just as the Father in heaven cares for the birds and the lilies in the field. Likewise, the Kingdom belongs to the poor and the insignificant, the downtrodden and those whom no one takes into account. This surprising God proclaimed by Jesus is close to those who are far away and to those who are ignored. One of the last events in Jesus' life takes place in the temple in Jerusalem, in front of the treasury, where all kinds of people come together to bring their offerings. While the wealthy threw much in, a widow could offer only two copper coins. Jesus, keenly aware of what was happening around him, told the disciples how this woman had given the greatest treasure of all of them. Everyone else gave what they had left over, "but she out of her poverty has put in everything she had, her whole living" (Mark 12:44 || Luke 21:4). There is a close, indestructible relationship between the generosity of the poor and their trust in God.

People enter the Kingdom when they receive the great gift of the Lord's compassion. For this reason, one of the culminating statements from the Sermon on the Mount (Matthew) or the Plain (Luke) is, "Be merciful, even as your Father is merciful" (Luke 6:36; a little different in Matt 5:48). Divine compassion has always been a fundamental experience for Israel. This can be seen in the Targum Pseudo-Jonathan on Leviticus (22:28): "My people, children of Israel, as our Father is merciful in heaven, so shall you be merciful on earth." Jesus, however, does not make a distinction between divine and human compassion; instead, he makes the former the point of reference and touchstone for the latter. Is it only in a utopia that we could imagine that man can imitate God's behavior? However, if we do not imitate the behavior of the Father in heaven, what should act as the point of reference for human behavior? Even granting forgiveness, an exclusive prerogative of God's, becomes a right and duty of man: "[W]henever you stand praying, forgive, if you have anything against any one; so that your Father also who is in heaven may forgive you your trespasses" (Mark 11:25). Jesus' God is right at the heart of man and the heart of the world.

5.1.3. Jesus, The Prophet of the Kingdom

Jesus is the bearer of the Kingdom, or perhaps the best way to describe him is as the prophet of the Kingdom. As we have seen, his activities are strongly linked to a core statement, which is potent and recurrent, especially during his time in Galilee: the Kingdom has begun to arrive; God is making himself apparent through the words and signs of the prophet Jesus. The Kingdom is closely linked to he who proclaims it, to he who communicates the gospel, the good news, to those who are willing to listen. Message and messenger are very closely linked and, on occasions, even overlap. Jesus talks of God and his Kingdom from within with words that are authoritative and that ring true. Indeed, it could be no other way, given the weight and novelty of what he was proclaiming: the presence of a God who saves right now in human history, not just in the future.

The prophets of Israel, with John the Baptist the last in a multi-secular series, prophesied the arrival of God ("the Lord will come"). Jesus instead prophesies his presence ("God is here"). For this reason, he can say, in reference to himself, that "something greater than Jonah is here" (Matt 12:41 || Luke 11:32). Jesus offers something extra, an assertion of something new that makes him unique in terms of Israel's prophets. In the words of the wise, Jesus is the (!) eschatological prophet, the only prophet to have preached the presence of the Kingdom of God. Jesus' authority is different to the authority with which the ancient prophets of Israel spoke. Whereas they began their oracles with the phrase "thus says the Lord" or "hear the word of the Lord," Jesus has his own formulae, such as "I say to you," "For truly, I say to you [Greek, *Amēn legōymin*]," or even "I have come," unlike the typical "I have been sent [by God]" of the ancient prophets.

This means, as C. H. Dodd has pointed out, that we find ourselves at a point beyond the sending of emissaries like Isaiah or Jeremiah. Indeed, Jesus states that he had been sent and that welcoming him means also welcoming God himself: "whoever receives me, receives not me but him who sent me" (Mark 9:37 || Luke 9:48; Matt 10:40); or, conversely: "he who rejects me rejects him who sent me" (Luke 10:16). In the case of Jesus, a step further is taken and the emissary becomes part of the message preached. This can be seen in the blessing that ends Jesus' answer to the Baptist's disciples, who come to ask him if he is, or is not, the Messiah: "blessed is he who takes no offence at me [or who does not reject me]" (Matt 11:6 || Luke 7:23).

Accepting the message of the Kingdom and the messenger becomes confused: in this new and different time in history there is a representative, an agent of God, who is not simply an emissary or herald but a plenipotentiary envoy, someone who has received full power to talk and act. He takes a central position within the message he brings. Even the symbolic actions that Jesus carries out in the style of the great prophets of Israel are not simply reinforcing his message but are signs that form part of his person and his mission. In the case of

Jeremiah, the linen waistcloth that was spoiled by the river Euphrates is a sign that God would "spoil the pride of Judah and the great pride of Jerusalem" (Jer 13:1-11); or Ezekiel, who cannot mourn the death of his wife, the light of his life, because the temple in Jerusalem, the light of the life of the people, has also been destroyed and no one will be able to mourn its passing (Ezek 24:15-27). Instead, Jesus, the man, takes center stage in the choosing of the Twelve, in his triumphant entrance into Jerusalem or the farewell supper.

Jesus was considered a prophet and treated as a prophet, given, as we shall see below (5.2), the extraordinary signs that he produced and the healings in particular. When, during his activities in Galilee, he visited Nazareth, his hometown, he was not warmly welcomed by his former neighbors, and he answered them in a proverbial tone: "A prophet is not without honor, except in his own country, and among his own kin, and in his own house." This proverb, created or picked up by Jesus, is witnessed throughout the Christian tradition (Mark 6:4 || Matt 13:57; Luke 4:24; John 4:44; Thomas 31). When he is warned by the Pharisees of Antipas' evil intentions, Jesus offers another proverbial response, again in the third person. He reinforces his desire to continue on his path, despite the threats coming from the tetrarch of Galilee: "I must go on my way today and tomorrow and the day following; for it cannot be that a prophet should perish away from Jerusalem" (Luke 13:33).

We see, in both his visit to Nazareth and his indirect response to Antipas, that Jesus' prophetic activities are related to miraculous events (exorcisms and healings) and the wise words that come from his mouth. In other words, the message of the Kingdom and the miracles are signs of this Kingdom that mark his activities as a prophet. In both scenes, Jesus is presented as a prophet who is rejected or persecuted, a man who has to fight strongly in order to keep going on his mission. This is the destiny that links the ancient prophets of Israel and John the Baptist, "among those born of women there has risen no one greater," to the prophet Jesus. For this reason, Jesus is included as one of these "prophets" who are killed and persecuted, the first of whom was Abel, man of God, a just man who was killed by an uncontrollable and powerful evil (Matt 23:34-36 || Luke 11:49-51).

Jesus speaks clearly of his mission when he answers the disciples sent by the Baptist to ask him whether he is "he who is to come" (Matt

11:2-6 || Luke 7:18-23). As is his wont, Jesus does not answer in the first person about his identity, instead alluding to certain fragments from the book of the prophet Isaiah (26:19, 29:18, 35:5-6, 61:1). It is clear that his activities fulfill the prophecies relating to the last days, the time when God's salvation is to be established definitively among his people. Those to receive this salvation are the poor, those who are needy, who suffer because they have little or because they are marginalized (these are said to receive the good news) and the sick: the blind, the lame, and the deaf are to be healed, the lepers purified, and the dead brought back to life. These are the first people to be attended to by God's envoy. It is highly likely that Jesus identified with this figure of the last days, the Messiah, and that he understood his mission in terms of Isaiah (61:1-3), as does one of the texts from Qumran (4Q521) and as does Luke 4:18-20 (see 5.4.1, below).

The figure of Jesus as a prophet is also described by what is said about him. Nevertheless, the opinions of the people varied somewhat. In Caesarea Philippi, Jesus significantly asked his disciples about the rumors that were going around about him. Their answer was fairly unanimous: the people considered Jesus a prophet (Mark 8:28). Some even thought that he was John the Baptist, the prophet of the Jordan, who Antipas had had decapitated and who had now come back to life. Antipas was one of those who believed this (Mark 6:14, 6:16).

Some saw Jesus as Elijah, the prophet who would be "ready at the appointed time" to restore the people of Israel (Sir 48:10). Elijah was to be the one sent by God to prepare the people and to encourage them to repent before the Day of Judgment (Mal 3:23 and Luke 1:17). Jesus himself said of Elijah that he was the one who had to "come first to restore all things" (Mark 9:12 || Matt 17:11). This did not mean, however, that Jesus was presented as Elijah or that he considered himself as such: Elijah had to come before the arrival of the Kingdom, while Jesus was considered part of the Kingdom of God. In any case, it was only a certain group of people who linked Jesus and Elijah, the prophet who had to restore Israel before Judgment Day (Mark 6:15).

A third view associated Jesus with "one of the prophets," "a prophet who resembled the ancient prophets," possibly Jeremiah or another element of Jewish hopes, "the Prophet" (John 6:14, 7:40). At Qumran, the Prophet was to come in the last days, alongside the sacerdotal Messiah, or Aaron, and the political Messiah, Israel's Messiah

(Community Rule 9:11). The Baptist himself was asked whether he was this prophet for the last days (John 1:21). The picture is made complete by a reference to Jesus as the failed prophet in the Passion. According to Mark 14:65 (|| Matt 26:68 || Luke 22:64), Jesus was subjected to cruel insults: he was blindfolded and had to guess who had hit him. This ridicule was the result of the belief that this man on the cross was a prophet able to foresee what was to happen and to know things that, initially, seemed hidden or secret (see 6.2.3.4).

The tradition concerning Jesus has maintained certain elements related to his ability to read people's thoughts or feelings. When Jesus forgives the sins of the paralytic man carried by four people, he knows what the scribes present are thinking, that they believe him to be committing blasphemy (Mark 2:5-8). At other times, Jesus announces events that are to take place; for example, his own death. When he is anointed by Mary during the meal in Bethany, he says to those present, "[S]he has anointed my body beforehand for burying" (Mark 14:8 || Matt 26:12).

The people saw Jesus as a prophet, a man of God able to utter words that express their hopes and able to carry out extraordinary acts, miracles, and amazing signs. This popular belief is clearly reflected in the Passion where Jesus is questioned by Antipas, the ruler of Galilee, who, "was hoping to see some sign done by him" (Luke 23:8) (see 6.2.4.3). The people's opinion of Jesus was imprecise, and they could as easily link him to John the Baptist (who did not perform miracles!) as they could to Elijah or any of the other prophets. For many, Jesus represented a second Baptist or a second Elijah, prophets linked to the last days. He was a form of reincarnation of both of these figures.

Jesus is presented as a plenipotentiary member of the Kingdom, someone who talks of the royalty of God in the present and with an authority and security that exceed those of a simple emissary. The Kingdom and the person, Jesus, blend together to the extent that devotion to one and the other overlap. The prophet Jesus can talk in a way that resembles the Baptist, or he can perform miracles as did Elijah, but he also offers something new and revolutionary: God has started to make himself manifest in history; his mercy has entered this world. This definitive message makes Jesus the messenger, par excellence; the eschatological prophet. Everything he says and does has a hallmark that inspires the people's enthusiasm: overflowing compassion and righteousness. Those who are devoted to him are devoted to a fire that is ardent and burning. This is thanks to the fact that God's love passes through him: "Whoever is near me is near the fire, and whoever is far from me is far from the kingdom" (Thomas 82).

Finally, we should note that Jesus, though he does on occasion refer to himself as a prophet (but always indirectly, in the third person), does not encourage this form of identification. It is significant that he distances himself from both the Baptist and Elijah and that he does not support people's considering him the reincarnation of the Baptist or Elijah. Jesus is the bearer of the Kingdom, the only unique prophet for the Kingdom of God. The only time when he talks directly about himself, he presents himself as the one to bring good news to the poor and to heal the sick, as the one who is to spread the signs of resurrection. He responds only indirectly when the Baptist's disciples ask him if he is "he who is to come," the Messiah. Jesus neither promotes nor hides his uniqueness.

5.2. The Signs of the Kingdom

The Kingdom that Jesus proclaims is contained in the message he brings in words and deeds. Those who welcome him hear and see new and extraordinary things. Jesus is not limited to just talking. He is not just someone who has created a doctrine that questions the customs and that invites people to renew their hearts. Jesus acts, he brings the Kingdom into the daily lives of the people. He shows his concern for and his desire to help certain groups: the poor and the simple, the sick in body and spirit, those who live marginalized by the Law and society. This concern is part of the care, described by the Scriptures, that the God of Israel takes for those who are downtrodden.

One of the key commitments of the great celebration of the covenant, which took place when the people of Israel came to the land that God had promised them, referred to those who were marginalized: "'Cursed be he who perverts the justice due to the sojourner, the fatherless and the widow.' And all the people shall say 'Amen'" (Deut 27:19). In a similar vein (Jer 22:3), the prophet Jeremiah went to find the king of Judah and demanded that he, and all his people, obey the Lord's will, saying, on behalf of God, "Do justice and righteousness, and deliver from the hand of the oppressor him who has been robbed. And do no wrong or violence to the alien, the fatherless, the widow, nor shed innocent blood in this place." Jesus fulfills the divine will, inspiring the poor with mighty gestures and convincing words, caring for them with an overflowing affection and generous forgiveness.

God's presence, here and now, is proclaimed and happening. It is real, with grace pouring down from heaven to renew and transform people. God is no longer a stranger in the world he created; he is Father to one and all. His Kingdom has begun with the defeat of the powers that oppressed people and took their dignity. All this emerges forcefully in Jesus' life. It is neither a reclusive life nor limited in time or space. Jesus does not set up boundaries, just like the sower who does not measure the radius reached by his arm when he is in the field, throwing out the seed indiscriminately. Jesus' activities are characterized as sowing signs of the Kingdom, seeds that fall on fertile ground in the sick of body and spirit, the sinners and the marginalized; this seed is health, forgiveness, and the welcome he can offer. The Kingdom is on the move, penetrating into the world, and those who are witness to the happiness and blessings are not few in number.

5.2.1. The Miracles

One of the most surprising aspects of Jesus' activities is the great number of amazing events that take place around him. When Josephus tries to summarize in a few words this "wise man," above all else he highlights that "he was a doer of wonderful works [*paradoxōn ergōn*]" (*A.J.* 18:63). When two of Jesus' disciples on their way to Emmaus try to describe who their Master was, he who had died crucified, they say, "a prophet mighty in deed (*dynatos en ergōi*) and word" (Luke 24:19). In the Gospel according to John, when the Sanhedrin deliberates about Jesus, he is "this man [who] performs many signs [*polla sēmeia*]" (John 11:47). The most significant testimony on Jesus is in the Talmud (Babylonian Talmud, *Sanh.* 43a), where his being condemned to death is justified for two reasons: "he practised sorcery and enticed Israel to apostasy." These two reasons can be reduced to just one: he performed miracles.

This is an irrefutable historical fact, with evidence provided throughout the tradition of the Gospels and other sources. Jesus had powers, and he used them to free those who were suffering from illnesses that affected their body and spirit and resolved the difficulties of groups of people. The Gospels contain twenty-seven narratives involving miracles: healings (H, fourteen), expelling demons or exorcisms (E, five), resurrections (R, three), cosmic wonders (C, two), and extraordinary signs (S, three). Below is a list of the twenty-seven Gospel sources: Mark (and the parallel texts in Matthew and Luke), the Q collection, the tradition belonging to Luke, and the tradition belonging to John. After each title, the letter in parentheses shows the type of miracle, in accordance with the above classification.

In the Gospel according to Mark, there are sixteen miracles (multiplying the loaves twice counts as one narrative). A good number of these sixteen (thirteen to be precise) are echoed in Matthew, who has repeated one (number 16). Luke includes twelve of them. John contains only two of them, and these have both been changed markedly (numbers 10 and 11). They are as follows:

1. The possessed man in Capernaum (Mark 1:21-28) (|| Luke 4:31-37) (E)
2. Simon-Peter's mother-in-law (Mark 1:29-31) (|| Matt 8:14-15 || Luke 4:38-39) (H)
3. The Galilean leper (Mark 1:40-45) (|| Matt 8:1-4 || Luke 5:12-16) (H)
4. The paralytic man in Capernaum (Mark 2:1-12) (|| Matt 9:1-8 || Luke 5:17-26) (H)
5. The man with the withered hand (Mark 3:1-6) (|| Matt 12:9-14 || Luke 6:6-11) (H)
6. The calming of the storm (Mark 4:35-41) (|| Matt 8:23-27 || Luke 8:22-25) (C)
7. The possessed man in the Decapolis (Mark 5:1-20) (|| Matt 8:28-34 || Luke 8:26-39) (E)
8. Jairus' daughter (Mark 5:21-24, 5:35-43) (|| Matt 9:18-19, 9:23-26 || Luke 8:40-42, 8:49-56) (R)
9. The woman with hemorrhages (Mark 5:25-34) (|| Matt 9:20-22 || Luke 8:43-48) (H)

10. Multiplying the loaves, the first narrative (Mark 6:32-44) (|| Matt 14:13-21 || Luke 9:10-17) (|| John 6:1-13) and the second narrative (Mark 8:1-10) (|| Matt 15:32-39) (S)
11. Jesus walking on water (Mark 6:45-52) (|| Matt 14:22-33) (|| John 6:16-21) (C)
12. The Syrophoenician's daughter (Mark 7:24-30) (|| Matt 15:21-28) (E)
13. The deaf and dumb man in the Decapolis (Mark 7:31-37) (H)
14. The blind man in Bethsaida (Mark 8:22-26) (H)
15. The possessed epileptic boy (Mark 9:14-29) (|| Matt 17:14-20 || Luke 9:37-43a) (E)
16. Bartimaeus, the blind man in Jericho (Mark 10:46-52) (|| Matt 20:29-34; 9:27-31 || Luke 18:35-43) (H)

The Q collection of sayings provides two further narratives. One of these (number 18) is repeated in Matthew. John also refers to the narrative of the other miracle (number 17), but, as is his wont, it has been modified. They are as follows:

17. The centurion's servant in Capernaum (Matt 8:5-13 || Luke 7:1-10) (John 4:43-54) (H)
18. The possessed dumb man (Matt 9:32-34; 12:22-24 || Luke 11:14-15) (E)

The tradition unique to Luke includes five further miracles in the Gospel. One of these (number 19) also appears in the Gospel according to John, though both narratives have been changed greatly with respect to the tradition that went before them. These narratives are as follows:

19. The miraculous catch (Luke 5:1-11) (John 21:1-19) (S)
20. The widow's son in Nain (Luke 7:11-17) (R)
21. The hunchback woman (Luke 13:10-17) (H)
22. The man with edema (Luke 14:1-6) (H)
23. The ten lepers (Luke 17:11-19) (H)

Finally, the tradition belonging to John has passed down four miracles of its own, as well as remodeling four others found in Mark (numbers 10 and 11), Q (number 17), and Luke (number 19). These four narratives are as follows:

24. The wedding in Cana (John 2:1-11) (S)
25. The paralytic man from Bethzatha or Bethesda (John 5:1-9) (H)
26. The blind man from birth (John 9:1-41) (H)
27. The resurrection of Lazarus (John 11:1-44) (R)

This number is impressive, especially if we consider that Philostratus, biographer of the most famous Greek miracle worker of the first century A.D., Apollonius of Tyana, provides reports of only nine miracles (see 5.2.1.2). In short, extraordinary events form part of Jesus' ordinary life.

The list does not include two amazing events that did not affect people's health, vital needs, or emergencies: the cursed fig tree that dries up (Mark 11:12-14, 11:20-24 || Matt 21:18-22) and the coin found in the mouth of a fish (Matt 17:27). These two symbolic acts are supernatural events rather than actual miracles as such. We should also note that the cursing of the fig tree is the only miracle involving punishment in the Gospels and that the coin in the mouth of the fish is proclaimed only as something that is to happen, not something that has happened.

We have also excluded from this list some of the allusions to Jesus' miraculous activities. The Gospel according to Luke refers to the case of a number of women healed of diabolical possessions and illnesses: Mary Magdalene, Joanna, and Susanna, among others (Luke 8:2-3). The Gospel according to Luke mentions in passing the healing of the high priest's servant, whose ear had been cut off when the officials had tried to detain the Master in Gethsemane (Luke 22:50-51). The summaries of Jesus' miracles, which are regularly repeated throughout the Gospels, have also been excluded (Mark 1:32-34, 1:39, 3:7-11, 6:53-56; Matt 4:23-25, 9:35, 14:34-36, 15:29-31; Luke 4:40-41, 6:17-19, 7:21; John 20:30-31). Jesus' appearance after his resurrection and his transfiguration, signs of his divine nature, involve miraculous elements (see 5.4.2 and 6.3.3.1), but they also go beyond what we have established here as the common denominator for miracles: the help offered by Jesus, the miracle worker, to someone who is in need and who cannot resolve the situation for himself or herself.

Though we are interested only in Jesus' miracles, we should point out that there were also miracles attributed to his disciples, whom he had sent out to proclaim the arrival of the Kingdom. Jesus gives the Twelve powers so that they can do what he can do: heal the bodily and spiritually sick, purify lepers, and even resurrect the dead (Mark 6:7, 6:12; Matt 10:1, 10:8; Luke 9:1, 9:6). The mission of the seventy-two disciples in Luke also has the same characteristics (Luke 10:9, 10:17). Jesus states, "I have given you authority to tread upon serpents and scorpions, and over all the power of the enemy" (Luke 10:19). The activities carried out by the disciples are successful because "even the demons are subject to us in your name!" (Luke 10:17). Only the doubts of the disciples themselves can make the force that Jesus grants them fail, as happens to Peter, who sinks when he tries to walk on water (Matt 14:28-31).

5.2.1.1. Why Does Jesus Perform Miracles?

Miracles in the Gospels are not uncomfortable, or even odious, exceptions to the laws of nature. If the world were immune to any divine intervention and history were formed independently and excluded God completely, miracles would represent ridiculous conceit. In this case, we would simply have to intensify research until we found the scientific reason to explain what seems inexplicable.

This is not the only way of interpreting the Jewish and Greco-Roman cultures of the first century. The popular but not necessarily most intellectual feeling in these cultures and their religions saw miracles not as something to be dismissed but as a natural part of the world. It was where God constantly intervened. People generally believed that miracles were not a parenthesis but simply an intensification of the divine presence, a special manifestation of his power, as he constantly appeared in creation and through his laws.

In other words, miracles did not cause any problems. They were an unusual but not irrational sign of God's force. Their extraordinary nature gave miracles a privileged position within God's presence and activities in our world. Miracles were not some form of holy redoubt but a unique and singular area that could overcome the seemingly immutable and invincible. They represented a new, radical, and absolute development. They were unpredictable and turned the old reality, dominated by resignation, on its head, completely transforming it. Unsurprisingly, miracles inspired enthusiasm and devotion.

Jesus talked about the Kingdom through his miracles because the language of healing and liberation, the language of saving people from sickness and imprisonment, was direct and universally understandable. It would be hard to find a more striking way of communicating God's mercy. For Jesus, miracles were freely given to people, motivated only by compassion, the compassion of God and of Jesus himself. A person healed was living testimony to God's closeness and his involvement in the life of mankind.

Jesus performed miracles with his own authority, without express permission from God. He prayed before performing a miracle only when he resurrected Lazarus (John 11:41-42), and not even here did he have recourse to peremptory words such as "in the name of God, I command." He simply cried, "Lazarus, come out" (John 11:43). The power with which Jesus healed, purified, and, on occasions, resurrected came from God, as he himself admitted: "But if it is by the finger of God that I cast out demons, then the kingdom of God has come upon you" (Luke 11:20) (Matt 12:28 talks about "the Spirit of God"). God acted in and through Jesus, but miracles depended on the freedom and compassion of the prophet from Nazareth. He had been granted an extraordinary power, which, in the words of G. Theissen, emerged spontaneously, without the need for any training or techniques. Jesus healed not because he was an expert in medicine or because he knew some magic formulae or because he could invoke the spirits. Jesus had a charisma that healed; he was able to redress bodies and spirits damaged due to their fragile nature or a destructive power.

Behind any miracle, there is a struggle, a confrontation with the force of evil, and ultimately death, which has destroyed and imprisoned the person in question. For this reason, miracles represent a liberation; they represent the saving of a person from a seemingly impenetrable prison. These miracles overcome apparently impossible obstacles, break boundaries, and go beyond the established limits.

In the framework of the apocalyptic ideas common at the time when Jesus was active, miracles are an arena for the superhuman powers at work in this world, of whatever they are a sign. In other words, an amazing act could be the work of God or of Satan, the two powers that were fighting for control of the world. An evil power could also produce incredible signs to amaze people and inspire their devotion. Casting out demons could be the work of someone in collusion with the devil. One of the accusations that the Jewish leaders use against Jesus is just this, that he exorcises demons because he is possessed by Beelzebub, Satan, and "the prince of demons" had granted him this power (Mark 3:22 || Matt 12:24 || Luke 11:15).

Jesus replied that it was ridiculous to think that Satan could expel himself: What house would pull itself down? How could Jesus, if he were possessed by Satan, dedicate his efforts to casting Satan out of those people who were shackled by his power of death and destruction? Jesus continued his openly ironic argument, stating that if Satan were fighting against himself, then surely he would have divided himself up, and as a result, "he cannot stand and has come to an end" (Mark 3:26). However one looks at it, the fact that Jesus cast out demons as a sign of Satan's domination was untenable. Satan's kingdom was tottering before the Kingdom of God, whose victory and power can be seen in the miracles that Jesus performed.

Jesus' perception of the definitive defeat of Satan and God's complete victory was so clear that he expressed it in global and cosmic terms: "I saw Satan fall like lightning from heaven" (Luke 10:18). In his subjugation of demons, Jesus saw the mighty and compassionate presence of God, the Father, full of omnipotence. He proclaimed the Kingdom in words and signs, miracles, which were simultaneous and complementary. The proclamations of the arrival of God's Kingdom and Satan losing his power in this world (that is why it says that he fell "from heaven" in 10:18) are complementary and logical: the beginning of the Kingdom of God, Lord of history, brings with it the end of the oppressive forces of death and destruction. The miracles are unmistakable signs that a new world has arrived, which is to be home to happiness and hope.

Jesus talks about God's Kingdom and his desire to appear in the world from a position of great closeness (5.1.1). As regards miracles, Jesus is not simply a vehicle for God's power, based on certain techniques for healing and expelling demons. The miracles are mighty acts that Jesus undertakes as part of his mission as the prophet of the Kingdom and that provide a sense of the definitive, the decisive, and the ultimate. Since Jesus sees these miracles as part of the blessing that the coming of the Kingdom of God represents, he lives carrying out miracles rather than living to carry out miracles. The compassion for those around him includes the sick in body and spirit, public sinners, and the marginalized, all those who are needy and can be considered poor.

As the miracles are but signs of the Kingdom, Jesus is free to heal the sick without feeling obliged to heal all the sick. He refuses to perform miracles when they could be interpreted as "a sign from heaven" that people, and their leaders in particular, are expecting (Luke 11:16). Neither miracles nor any of the other amazing signs could replace the fundamental element in his plan: that all individuals respond personally, that they repent. We can see how Jesus concentrated a good part of his miracles in the second phase of his life's journey, when he was working in Galilee and based in Capernaum, the time when his preaching of the Kingdom was most forceful (see 4.6.2), whereas they were few and far between in successive phases.

Jesus did not see miracles as mechanical acts, as if they were carried out without taking those healed or liberated into account. Often, the miracles took place because of the faith of those who wanted to be healed or the faith of those close to them, who were inspired by their conviction and certainty in Jesus' power. In the case of the woman with hemorrhages, the complete opposite took place: the miracle took place without the miracle worker even being aware of the fact and without the person healed even needing to ask. Only afterward, once the woman had been healed, did Jesus realize that "that power had gone forth from him" (Mark 5:30); then the woman, trembling with fear, admits what has happened and Jesus praises her for her strength of faith.

In the other cases, there is an explicit initiative on the part of either Jesus or the sick person. The Galilean leper says, "If you will, you can make me clean" (Mark 1:40). The blind man in Jericho, Bartimaeus, asks him, "Master, let me receive my sight" (Mark 10:51); or Jairus' moving request: "[M]y little daughter is at the point of death. Come and lay your hands on her, so that she may be made well, and live" (Mark 5:23). However, the people of Nazareth distance themselves from Jesus when he comes to visit the town accompanied by his disciples, to the point of turning him away. The Gospel comments that "he could do no mighty work there, except that he laid his hands upon a few sick people and healed them" (Mark 6:5). Clearly miracles do not have an immediate and indisputable effect. Hardness of heart can overcome any response, and a lack of faith acts as an obstacle to repentance. Jesus himself states as much in relation to three Galilean towns (Chorazin, Bethsaida, and Capernaum) that have been witness to many of his miracles but that, despite this, have not repented (Matt 11:21-24 || Luke 10:13-15). In turn, faith is often decisive in leading to miracles becoming sine qua non for Jesus to carry them out. The characteristic phrase "your faith has made you well" is a clear sign of this. Jesus uses it when speaking to the woman with hemorrhages (Mark 5:34 || Matt 9:22 || Luke 8:48), to the blind man in Jericho (Mark 10:52 || Luke 18:42), and to the leprous Samaritan (Luke 17:19) after healing them. Faith does not heal, but it is because of this faith that people are healed. The miracle depends on the freedom of both the one carrying it out and the one receiving.

Jesus did not use miracles to inspire devotion. Instead, when he realized that people were beginning to acclaim and flatter him, he fled from them, as he did after feeding the five thousand (John 6:17). Jesus used miracles to proclaim the Kingdom of God, the merciful Father, and passed on his salvation to those who came to him to ask to be freed from their ills. As faith in God and trust in his messenger merge into one, so Jesus brings the Kingdom with him and the miracles become inseparable from his person and his activities.

An important example is that of the healings on the Sabbath. Jesus seems to heal on the Sabbath often, to the extent that one leader of a synagogue stands up before the people to say, "There are six days on which work ought to be done; come on those days and be healed, and not the Sabbath day" (Luke 13:14). Jesus does on the Sabbath "what is not lawful" according to the interpretation of many rabbis of the time. In their opinion, people could act on the Sabbath only when life was in danger, but Jesus felt that healing a man's withered hand was equivalent to saving his life and thus justified his acting on the Sabbath (Mark 3:4). This argument puts the well-being of the person above the rules. Being able to return full movement to someone's body means the person can recover his or her dignity. Jesus cures on the Sabbath with an authority that shows that this must also be God's will (see 5.3.2.2).

5.2.1.2. Miracles in the Greek and Jewish Worlds

Miracles were phenomena typically manifested among the common people, which normally caused mistrust and skepticism among the most illustrious and leading social sectors. Those who dreamed of miracles were those who were in need of them, knowing no other way out, especially those who had failed in all other attempts to resolve their problems. The Gospels tell of a woman who had suffered hemorrhages for twelve years and who "had spent all that she had" (Mark 5:26) on doctors without success. Great numbers of people went in search of cures, traveling to the sanctuaries of Asclepius and Isis (where medicine and magic were combined) or reacted enthusiastically to certain healings, acclaiming the miracle workers as if they were gods come down to earth. For example, the inhabitants of Lystra, in Asia Minor, tried to offer a sacrifice to Paul and Barnabas, whom they considered Zeus and Hermes, when they healed a man who had been an invalid since birth (Acts 14:8-13).

One figure renowned as a miracle worker was Apollonius of Tyana, a traveling philosopher who was interested in the mystical traditions of the second half of the first century. His life's work was recorded by Philostratus only at the start of the third century, however. As H. C. Kee has shown, the nine miracles attributed to him do not have a very solid historiographical basis. Philostratus, lacking information and without a trustworthy tradition, seems to have made up much of the material or borrowed from other authors when producing his *Vita Apollonii*.

In Jewish lands, healings also attracted crowds, and many holy places were held by the populace to be where miracles took place. A verse (not included in all the manuscripts of the tradition) states that, at the pool of Bethzatha, one of the Lord's angels came down from time to time to stir up the waters, and the next person to enter would be healed (John 5:4). A group of all sorts of sick people kept constant vigil at the poolside.

Naturally, not all Jews were fans of this type of belief. The manuscripts found at Qumran mention only two miracles from the ancient times: where Abraham is said to have expelled an evil spirit that afflicted the pharaoh and his men by praying for him and laying on his hands (1Qap Gen 20:28-29) and a Jewish exorcist who forgave the sins of the king of Babylon in the name of God and freed him from the evil that God himself had sent (4QPrNab 6). The rabbis were very prudent when it came to these marvelous events that could lead to the people abandoning their practice of the Law, the essential goal of the Jewish religion. Rabbis, in accordance with the tradition of great figures in the history of Israel (Moses and Elijah in particular), recognized that God could manifest himself through extraordinary acts, but they insisted that what pleased God was doing good and his will rather than prophesying, expelling demons, or performing a great many miracles. Rabbi Yehoshua ben Levi, a follower of Hillel, said, "[Making a living] is harder than splitting the Red Sea." This is reminiscent of Matthew (7:21-22): those who enter the Kingdom of heaven are not those who perform a great many wonders, like exorcisms or miracles, but those who do the will of the Father in heaven.

Each Sabbath then, people went to the synagogue to read and comment on the Scriptures and the homilies. The wonders of Israel's escape from Egypt were particularly spellbinding for a people that wanted to witness the great liberating gestures from God once more: the ten plagues that overcame the pharaoh; the parting of the waters of the Red Sea and the swamping of the Egyptian army in these waters; the gift of manna, food from heaven, that fed Israel during the forty years in the desert. These were often the focus of the readings from the Torah or Pentateuch. Reading from the Prophets reminded people of the entrance into the Promised Land, accompanied by the great wonders at the time of Joshua; the miracles performed by Elijah or Elisha; the miracles to mark the last days: cosmic wonders, prophecies and visions, healings of the sick and afflicted, freeing of prisoners, cleansing of lepers, and resurrection of the dead, according to the prophetic oracles and Isaiah in particular.

The deep yearning of the Jewish people for freedom from their oppressors and their trust that God would repeat the miracles from the time of the Exodus explain why there were popular, prophetic movements in the first century and why "prophets with signs" appeared on the scene from time to time, who were able to attract a large following. All these figures, whom we know of thanks to Josephus, promised extraordinary events, "signs of their deliverance" (*J.W.* 6:285), which were to be definitive, as God would intervene with a great voice and finally. As we have pointed out (see 3.3.3.3), Theudas wanted to repeat the wondrous crossing of the Jordan from the times of Joshua, when "all Israel were passing over on dry ground" (Josh 3:17). This was to be the start of a new conquest of the country and the expulsion of the Romans, the foreigners occupying the land. The Egyptian aimed to bring down the walls of Jerusalem, as in the time of Joshua the walls of Jericho had fallen (Josh 6). The Romans were to surrender before this great wonder, and a new political regime would be established whereby they would be freed from all oppression. Theudas and the Egyptian took their followers out into the wilderness of Judaea, the place that evoked the great desert that the Israelites had had to cross following their escape from Egypt, when God had guided them and aided them in their victory with his amazing acts. Similarly, other anonymous prophets called people together in the wilderness and promised to free them from their ills, proclaiming a new Exodus.

All these figures, who called themselves prophets, convinced many people to follow them, but, in fact, none of the miracles that they had promised ever came to pass. The Romans massacred them and their leaders were either killed or fled. Josephus accuses them of leading the people astray (*A.J.* 20:97–98). Jesus' case was different. He was also accused of seducing and leading Israel astray "because he practised sorcery" (Sanh. 43a). While the "prophets with signs" between 40 and 60 A.D. promised great signs of deliverance like those in the Exodus (which never actually came to pass), Jesus performed miracles, actual signs of personal repentance that evoked the final days and that brought them forward to the here and now. There was one great sign in Jesus' life reminiscent of the gift of the manna from heaven in the Exodus, a sign that was interpreted as Messianic by his followers: the multiplying of the bread and the fish, after which many wanted to make him king (see 5.2.1.5, below).

Though the rabbis and scribes were not particularly enthusiastic about those who performed miracles (healings and/or casting out demons), they tolerated them to a certain extent. This tolerance turned into enthusiasm in the fourth and fifth centuries A.D., when the Babylonian Talmud was written. The lists of miracles attributed to the rabbis from the past were extended. A clear case of this is rabbi Hanina ben Dosa, who lived before 70 A.D. and who can, thus, be considered a contemporary of Jesus, though we cannot be sure that he lived in Galilee. The Mishnah does not mention where he came from. It does however describe him as the last of the "men of deed" (*Sotah* 9:15), and this expression seems to mean "powerful men" or even "men who perform miracles" (G. Vermes). Others, including J. P. Meier, believe that it means "men who do good," thus, people who keep strictly to the Law. This is not how the Jewish tradition has interpreted it however, as in both Talmuds Hanina ben Dosa is a prototype miracle worker, a rabbi immune to snake bites who heals people from a distance by praying for them and who has powers over demons.

The most informative text on this figure is the Mishnah (Ber. 5:5), where it says that Hanina prayed for the sick and knew, thanks to the fluency of his prayers, whether the sick person would live or die: "If my prayer comes out fluently, I know that he is accepted, but if not, then I know that he is rejected." In this text Hanina does not appear as a man who performs miracles but as someone who has received the gift of potent prayer for the sick, thanks to which he is able even to foresee their fate. Hanina is a holy man, whose prayers can heal, or at least he can foresee what is to become of the person he is praying for. Unlike Jesus, Hanina is not considered "a prophet nor the son of a prophet" (Babylonian Talmud, *Ber.* 34b), though in the Jewish tradition he does have ascetic traits: the austerity of someone who has given up all their belongings. Hanina, furthermore, did not show any special interest in wisdom but instead in fear of sin and good works. This is reflected in the Mishnah (*Avot* 3:10-11).

The other figure to take into account is Honi (Onias) the Circle Drawer, who lived in Jerusalem before 65 B.C. Josephus (*A.J.* 14:22) describes Honi thus: "a righteous man he was, and beloved of God, who, in a certain drought, had prayed to God to put an end to the intense heat, and whose prayers God had heard, and had sent them rain." The same events are described in the Mishnah at greater length and converted into a miracle, the only miracle attributed to a Jewish scribe from the first centuries (*Ta'an.* 3:8). Here it tells of how the people asked Honi to pray for rain but that initially his prayers were not heard. Then, Honi drew a circle on the ground and stood inside it swearing, "by the great name" of God, that he would not leave this circle until it rained. God then made it rain too little and too much, before finally making it rain just enough, until the people had enough water and they asked Honi to pray to God to make it stop.

The narrative of Honi combines magic (the circle, the oath) and a certain impertinence toward God forced to meet the fickle demands of his children and Honi, in particular. Honi is described as a "son of the house [of God]," and the Talmud says that he called God *Abba*, or father. Though this last detail links Honi and Hanina to Jesus, these two cannot be considered miracle workers in the way that Jesus was; they do not show the same levels of authority, and their miracles have nothing to do with the Kingdom of God. They are two holy men who see how their prayers for people, whether sick or in need of water, are answered.

5.2.1.3. Bodily and Spiritual Ills

Jesus is a healer and an exorcist. He himself says, "I cast out demons and perform cures today and tomorrow" (Luke 13:32). These two activities have one common aim, to look after people's health, to remedy those ills that affect the body and the spirit and mind. Illness affects the functions of the human person; it is a distortion of the somatic, psychological, and/or spiritual balance. The personal stability of the sick affects them in their entirety, even though the symptoms and causes of the illness may belong to only a part of them. People are an amalgam, but a local illness does not have localized effects on their lives. Illness is based on a lack of control, produced by a pernicious alteration in a person's internal workings. An illness, especially if it is chronic, constitutes an attack on the dignity of the human being, as the person is reduced and diminished, powerless to overcome his or her affliction.

The expelling of demons

A fundamental question centers on the source of the discomfort or anxiety, the physical or psychological disorder, everything that leads to death. According to a surprisingly common explanation, problems affecting people's health are examples of God's punishment for sins committed. This is the reaction, for example, of the widow of Zarephath when her son dies. She says to the prophet Elijah, "What have you against me, O man of God? You have come to me to bring my sin to remembrance, and to cause the death of my son!" (1 Kgs 17:18). Regarding the man who had been blind since birth, the disciples ask Jesus, "Rabbi, who sinned, this man or his parents, that he was born blind?" (John 9:2). Illness and sin were linked not only because of an ancestral taboo but also because people are an amalgam, and the healing of the body also requires renewal of the spirit. This aspect is illustrated by Jesus' first words to the paralytic man in Capernaum when he is placed before him: "My son, your sins are forgiven" (Mark 2:5). The health of the soul comes before the health of the body. Those who damage their bodies also damage their souls. As Jesus said to the paralytic man at Bethzatha, after healing him, "Sin no more, that nothing worse befall you" (John 5:14).

In the Greco-Roman and Jewish societies of the first century A.D., it was common for the dark forces of evil and destruction to be personified in the figure of Satan; his followers were seen as the ultimate cause of the ills afflicting people. The Gospel of Luke refers to a poor hunchback woman who could not stand up straight. Jesus heals her when he is in the synagogue, even though it is the Sabbath; but the narrative states that the woman "had had a spirit of infirmity." Jesus hammers home the point after curing her, saying that she was "a daughter of Abraham whom Satan bound for eighteen years" and that she had to be "loosed from this bond" (Luke 13:16). Illness is seen here as the result of an act of destruction by the prince of evil.

Another example is that of the epileptic boy possessed by an evil spirit (Mark 9:14-29 || Matt 17:14-20 || Luke 9:37-43a). The boy's father describes the symptoms of the attacks that afflict his son to Jesus (he falls to the ground or into the fire or water, foams at the mouth, grinds his teeth, and becomes rigid). In Matthew (17:15), the father says these words: "Lord, have mercy on my son, for he is an epileptic [literally, a lunatic] and he suffers terribly." The healing of the boy takes place when Jesus faces up to the evil spirit that has brought this illness upon him. The spirit is rebuked and cast out while the boy convulses in the last epileptic fit he is to suffer.

These two examples do not mean that all the exorcisms were healings, where the cause of the illness was the oppressive power of Satan or evil spirits. In a few cases, possessions in the strictest sense are mentioned, people completely dominated by a foreign body that has "eaten" their humanity, to the extent that the will and words of the evil spirit and the person possessed intermingle, the former speaking through the mouth of the latter. The possessed man in Capernaum talks to Jesus in the plural and recognizes his power: "What have you to do with us, Jesus of Nazareth? Have you come to destroy us? I know who you are, the Holy One of God" (Mark 1:24). The possessed man in the Decapolis talks to him in the singular and even asks for pity for what is stronger than he is: "What have you to do with me, Jesus, Son of the Most High God? I adjure you by God, do not torment me" (Mark 5:7). There is a curious role reversal in both cases: "the evil spirit" (just one!) is cast out of the possessed man in Capernaum, whereas the possessed man in Decapolis is freed of a "legion" of them. We should stress that this is both the name of the demons that oppressed him and the name of the Roman army occupying the land. In the narrative, two thousand evil spirits entered a pig, the impure animal par excellence, and ended up at the bottom of the lake, the place that symbolized death.

This shift between the singular and plural shows that it is impossible to determine who the subject(s) is/are that Jesus confronts with his dialectics and that he forces into silence and submission. The destruction going on inside the persons possessed is clearly serious and deep-rooted; Jesus' actions destroy the evil spirits and restore their definitive human identity and their physical and spiritual stability to the afflicted. The possessed man in the Decapolis, once healed, recovers his senses, wears clothes, and settles down, no longer living among the tombs, the place of the dead, but instead sharing the life of the people around him. The possessed mute, when freed from the evil spirit, begins to talk again. The mother of the Syrophoenician girl, once the evil spirit has been expelled, finds her daughter lying peacefully in her bed, freed from the inner turmoil that had controlled her up until then.

Jesus' fame for casting out demons is based on five of the twenty-seven miracles that we mentioned above, at the start of 5.2.1 (numbers 1, 7, 12, 15, and 18). In only two cases does the casting out of demons take place beyond the borders of Jewish lands: the possessed man in the Decapolis and the daughter of the Syrophoenician, the only occasion on which it takes place at a distance. On the other three occasions, these events take place in Galilee: Capernaum (the possessed man) or some unnamed place (the possessed epileptic boy and the mute). The fame of the Master of Nazareth spread quickly, with the result that some cast out demons in his name, even though they were not members of his group. When told of this by his disciples, Jesus did not oppose these actions and said, "Do not forbid him, for no one who does a mighty work in my name will be able soon after to speak evil of me" (Mark 9:39). Over twenty years later, in Ephesus (Asia Minor), some traveling Jewish exorcists tried to cast out demons using the following formula: "I adjure you by the Jesus whom Paul preaches" (Acts 19:13).

The healings

The miracles in the Gospels show the great sense of physicality and sometimes emotion with which Jesus sought to cure people bodily and psychologically. There are fourteen healings mentioned in the Gospels. As with the casting out of demons, they appear both in Mark (eight) and the Q collection of sayings (one); unlike the exorcisms, there are also healings that appear only in Luke (three) and the Gospel according to John (two).

The healings take place in a wide variety of places and involve a wide variety of people and situations. Some are bedridden with fever, some have chronic illnesses affecting their blood (hemorrhages) or bones (the hunchback woman). Some suffer disabilities (the blind, paralytic, deaf, and dumb or the man with the withered hand), some are chronically ill (edema), and one man is bedridden and in great pain. There are many lepers, who have to be kept apart from the rest of the world and who cannot form relationships with anyone ("he suffered them not to come into the city at all, nor to live with any others, as if they were in effect dead persons," as Josephus states in *A.J.* 3:264). All those healed, except one (a Samaritan cleansed of leprosy) (number 23), appear to have been Jews. The healings usually took place in Jewish lands, with the possible exception of the deaf and dumb man, who may have been a Jew or a pagan and lived or was passing though the Decapolis (number 13 from the list at the start of 5.2.1).

Four healings took place in Capernaum. The mother-in-law of Simon-Peter was healed in the house that he and Andrew had in the town (number 2). This house was also where the four men brought the paralytic man on a stretcher, which they have to take up to the roof terrace and pass through a hole they have made in the ceiling in order to get him into the room where Jesus was teaching (number 4). The synagogue in the town was the setting for the healing of the man with the withered hand (number 5). The centurion who asked Jesus to heal his servant also probably lived in Capernaum and may even have paid for the building of the synagogue there (number 17).

In Bethsaida near Capernaum, home to three disciples, Peter, Andrew, and Philip, Jesus healed a blind man outside the town (number 14). The healing of the woman with hemorrhages took place near the side of Lake Galilee (number 9). Galilee was also where Jesus cleansed a leper, whom he told to go and see the priest so that he could certify the healing (number 3).

To these seven healings in Galilee, we need to add three more that the Gospels situate in Judaea. Leaving Jericho, a city in the Jordan Valley, Jesus came across the blind man Bartimaeus, the only person he healed whose name we know; the latter was begging by the roadside (number 16). The Gospel according to John is the only one that refers to two healings that took place in Jerusalem: that of the paralytic by the Bethzatha pool (number 25) and that of the man blind from birth, who was sent to bathe in the pool of Siloam (number 26).

Finally, three healings took pace at unnamed locations. All three are referred to only in the Gospel according to Luke, though this fact (that there is evidence only from one source) does not necessarily mean that the material is not historically reliable. Indeed, the location of these events is fairly specific, and the narrative seems convincing enough. The woman with the hunchback is healed in a synagogue on the Sabbath, despite the vehement protests of the synagogue's leader (number 21). The man with an edema is healed, again on the Sabbath, during a meal that an important Pharisee has prepared for Jesus (number 22). At the entrance to a town, when Jesus is traveling with his disciples, ten lepers ask him to cure them and Jesus accepts, telling them to present themselves to the priests, who have to declare, in accordance with the Law, that the lepers have been cleansed (number 23).

These fourteen healings (thirteen in Jewish lands and one in the Decapolis, possibly involving a deaf mute Jew) appear in one or more of the Gospels; they identify, with some accuracy and in detail, the figures involved, their actions, and the places and circumstances in which they happened. As G. Theissen has shown, the narratives passed down to us follow certain schemes and literary motifs that are repeated, intermingled, and combined. However, there are too many specific details for these narratives simply to be model or synthesized narratives, "created" to express "what Jesus used to do." As J. D. G. Dunn rightly points out, these narratives (and not any others) were passed down by word of mouth from a time when Jesus was at work and thus were passed down as "what Jesus did." Subsequently, they were shaped and molded to match the characteristics required to narrate a miracle, and they have reached us in this form. We know that Jesus healed Peter's mother-in-law and the blind man in Jericho because eyewitnesses there immediately spread news of what had happened. Jesus was famed as a healer, a fame that contributed to embellishing his miracles, but a fame that could exist only because they had happened.

We should also note that none of these fourteen healing narratives seems to test the limits of belief. There are no fantastic or irrational elements. These narratives have a moving humanity to them, on the part of both the healed and the healer. That we are dealing with an area close to Jesus is evident in the wealth of detail in these healing narratives: from the trust felt by the woman with the hemorrhages, who was marginalized socially and religiously because of her illness ("If I touch even his garments, I shall be made well"), to the tenacious and compassionate efforts of Jesus himself in his laying his hands on the blind man's eyes twice in Bethsaida. The two orders for healing (*ephphatha*) and resurrection (*talitha, cumi*) in the original Aramaic, the language used by Jesus, bring us into close contact with the events and the people who witnessed them, the people who first began to hand them down to us (Mark 7:34 and 5:41).

The resurrections

The resurrections carried out by Jesus, or rather the revivals (i.e., returning people to life), amounted to three. Two took place in Galilee: one in Nain, a town some 10 kilometers to the southeast of Nazareth, and the other in an unnamed town near Lake Galilee. Both involved young people: a widow's only son and the twelve-year-old daughter of Jairus (numbers 20 and 8, respectively). They were taking the young man to be buried, when Jesus, who was entering the town, brought him back to life. The girl had just died, when Jesus entered her home and brought her back to life. The third and most spectacular resurrection involved Lazarus, an adult man and brother of Martha and Mary. All three of them were friends of Jesus and lived in Bethany, a town close to Jerusalem. Lazarus had been dead for four days when Jesus arrived in Bethany and resuscitated him (number 27). The resurrection of the widow's son is mentioned only in Luke, and that of Lazarus is mentioned only in John. The resurrection in Nain is very similar to the resurrection of the widow's son in Zarephath involving the prophet Elijah (1 Kgs 17:17-24).

A resurrection represents the ultimate victory over the forces of destruction that attack people. The limit of evil is overcome when it seems irreversible. Those who are brought back to life are reinstated to the condition they had completely lost. Resurrections represent a hundredfold healing, a rescue *in extremis* of the victims from the jaws of death into which they had fallen, a rescue made possible by the divine powers embodied in Jesus. Resurrections are the victory par excellence over the deadly power. Bringing someone back to life is the equivalent of releasing him or her from the bonds of the prince of darkness and hell. As A. Marchadour stresses, resurrection represents an overwhelming victory over the evil spirit that seeks to claim people and take them to the kingdom that is opposed to the kingdom of life. In a resurrection, the person is pulled out of the grip of he who had him or her imprisoned forever, as with an exorcism, where the possessed is freed from he who held him or her captive.

Jesus, the prophet of signs, fulfills through his activities what had been foreseen for the last days of history. When John the Baptist's disciples go to see Jesus on their master's behalf and ask him whether he is "he who is to come," he replies with a description of his plans, which are there for all to see and hear. With fragments from Isaiah, gleaned from here and there, Jesus' reply is a form of summary of his activities: "the blind receive their sight and the lame walk, lepers are cleansed and the deaf hear, and the dead are raised up, and the poor have good news preached to them" (Matt 11:5 || Luke 7:22). Jesus includes resurrection of the dead among the signs of the new times, the signs that show the new dawn of the Kingdom on the horizon of humanity. It is no wonder that the tradition has passed down to us these three narratives involving resurrection in which Jesus, the miracle worker, produces a great sign, a sign for the end of days: bringing the dead back to life.

Resurrection is provisional since the three people he brings back to life return to present life and an inevitable death: they have been freed only provisionally. This does not affect the importance of the resurrections as a sign. It is a sign of the overwhelming victory of life and is even more impressive than expelling demons or healing the sick. In the Gospel according to John, the death and resurrection of Lazarus are seen as events that are to culminate in a victory for the almighty: "This illness is not unto death; it is for the glory of God" (John 11:4).

In all three resurrections, life wins out and evil and the prince of evil fail in their attempts to dominate mankind. Jesus' words are orders that are full of authority, addressed to his dead friend, "Lazarus, come out" (John 11:43), or to Jairus' daughter, "*Talitha, cumi*. . . . Little girl, I say to you, arise" (Mark 5:41), or again to the widow's son in Nain, "Young man, I say to you, arise" (Luke 7:14). The contrast between these words and those pronounced by the prophet Elijah before the dead son of the widow in Zarephath is clear ("O Lord my God, let this child's soul come into him again"; 1 Kgs 17:21). Jesus' potent words dominate the scene majestically. The common denominator in these three narratives is the sign of Jesus' power over life and death: Jesus, the bearer of the Kingdom, God's plenipotentiary envoy in the world.

5.2.1.4. The Cosmic Wonders

There are two incidents that we need to look at: the calming of the storm (number 6 on the list given at the start of 5.2.1) and Jesus' walking on water (number 11). The first is mentioned in three of the synoptic Gospels and the second in Mark and Matthew, and independently in the Gospel according to John.

These events involve both the wind and water (literally: the sea), two forces of nature with human characteristics that take part in the story alongside Jesus and his disciples. The two events take place at night. Nighttime provides a more dramatic setting and leads to a more intuitive and diffused vision of the events. In the calming of the storm, the lake crossing starts "when evening had come" (Mark 4:35). Jesus was already on the boat when he told them to go over to the other side. The storm found him at the stern "asleep on a cushion." The other scene, in which Jesus walks on water to meet his disciples, who are rowing against the wind, takes place in the early morning, "about the fourth watch of the night" (Mark 6:48). The Gospel of John says less specifically that "it was now dark" (6:17).

The focus of the narrative on both occasions is the confrontation between the cosmic powers of the wind and sea and Jesus, who has complete control over them, while some of the awestruck disciples look on expectantly. Jesus commands the wind and the sea, as if it were an order from a powerful and evil spirit, to obey him: "Peace! Be still!" Immediately, the storm ceases and "there was a great calm" (Mark 4:39). The second incident, when Jesus walks "on the sea," not just on water, shows how he controls the cosmic forces of darkness and death. Jesus also controls the wind; according to Mark (6:51), this becomes calm as soon as he gets into the boat, or according to John (6:21), it stops blowing, since, amazingly, the boat touches land when Jesus draws near.

Curiously, these two extraordinary incidents, seen as fantastic or unbelievable by some, are rendered believable by specific details rooted in reality. In the calming of the storm, the narrative includes incidental but significant details; for example, the disciples, in accordance with Jesus' order, set sail, and "they took him with them in the boat, just as he was" (Mark 4:36); Jesus sleeps "in the stern" and "on the cushion" (Mark 4:38); there are "other boats with him," which are not mentioned again in the narrative (Mark 4:36). In the narrative of Jesus walking on water, there is an eyewitness account: Jesus walks toward the disciples but "meant to pass by them" (Mark 6:48); the disciples are not just scared but terrified without exception when they see this figure that they think is a ghost, a spirit come from another world. They are calmed down only when Jesus talks to them and assures them that it is him. The two literary witnesses agree on the words that Jesus spoke to the disciples: "It is I; have no fear" (Mark 6:50; John 6:20).

The disciples must have kept a record of these two extraordinary events on Lake Galilee, when they were in danger and in need: a vicious storm that led to the crew almost drowning and a crossing made difficult by the strong headwinds and increasingly choppy waters. Both events are triggered by a wish expressly made by Jesus himself; on no other occasion are we told that Jesus sailed on the lake after dark or that his disciples sailed without him. On both occasions the disciples are placed in an extreme situation: their lives are endangered by the storm, and they are subjected to an amazing spectacle when half asleep as Jesus miraculously walks on water. As B. J. Malina points out, their state of mind may have been "disturbed" and their memory of the events may not have been clear and distinct. Whatever the case, these memories have transmitted the fact that aid from a holy and mighty Jesus saved them from serious danger from which they felt they would not escape (the calming of the storm) and that he rescued them from a difficult situation (strong headwinds) in the middle of the night, coming to them in the middle of the lake.

The record of these extraordinary events, probably remembered in the shadows of a "disturbed" state of mind, has been evoked time and again through a new understanding of the Scriptures. The miraculous rescue of the disciples by Jesus has been interpreted as another of the great marvels wrought by God at other times to aid the people of Israel. As these two events have been passed down, they may have been added to by other elements from the First Testament, where God is he who "trampled the waves of the sea" (Job 9:8), since he is lord and master, so that the prophet praises him saying: "Thou didst trample the sea with thy horses" (Hab 3:15). The author of a psalm puts it thus: "Thy way was through the sea, thy path through the great waters; yet thy footprints were unseen" (Ps 77:20). Psalm 107:28-29 says, "Then they cried to the Lord in their trouble, and he delivered them from their distress; he made the storm be still, and the waves of the sea were hushed." These and other texts, such as Exodus 33:21-23, which talk about the glorious passing of God (Mark 6:48), or Exodus (3:14), where God manifests himself in an echo of the "It is I" (Mark 6:50; John 6:20), may have influenced the form of the narratives as we have them today.

The fundamental aspects of the events and certain specific and incidental details in the plot of the narratives lead us to conclude that there is a certain historical validity in both of these miracles, where Jesus has absolute control over the wind and sea.

5.2.1.5. The Great Sign: The Loaves and the Fishes

The only miracle to appear in all four Gospels is the feeding of the five thousand. In two of these (Mark and Matthew), the narrative is even told twice. In total, then, there are six (!) narratives about the same event (see number 10 in the list given at the start of 5.2.1). This miracle is Jesus' most written about miracle. The narratives in Mark (6:32-44 || Matt 14:13-21 || Luke 9:10-17) and John 6:1-13 are two separate versions of the same miracle, the result of two different oral traditions. There is third oral tradition in the second narrative of the multiplication of loaves (Mark 8:1-10 || Matt 15:32-39). A notable singularity is that it forms part of a greater sequence of events, which includes a day and a night in the life of Jesus, in both Mark (6:32-53 || Matt 14:13-34) and John 6:1-21. This sequence includes the multiplying of the loaves and the walking on water.

The sequence begins with Jesus and his disciples in an unnamed location to the north of Lake Galilee, probably to the east of Bethsaida, land belonging to Philip and hence not under the jurisdiction of Antipas. The Passover festivities were at hand (John 6:4). Jesus was in the middle of the countryside, away from the centers of population, and had attracted a large crowd: "five thousand men" (Matt 14:21 adds, "besides women and children"; John 6:10 also alludes to this). The second narrative of the multiplication of the loaves brings the figure down to "about four thousand people" (Mark 8:9) (Matt 15:38 again adds that this number did not include the women and children); on this occasion, the narratives point out that the crowd had been with Jesus for three days and their supplies had run out.

The Gospel of Mark sets events by the lakeside (Mark 6:34), while the Gospel of John indicates that Jesus and his disciples and the crowd were on a mountainside not far from the lake (John 6:3, 6:16). Mark states that Jesus spent the day talking and teaching the people (6:34). As the afternoon went on, the disciples suggested that Jesus let the people leave so that they could go home or to the nearby villages to eat. Jesus replied that the disciples should take care of the crowd and the food. The disciples were unable to carry out Jesus' suggestion, so Jesus himself told them to have the people sit down on the grass. He gave thanks to God, as was usual for Jews before they began eating, and broke five loaves and took two fish (seven loaves and a few fish according to Mark 8) and gave them to the disciples so that they could distribute them among the crowd. They all ate as much bread and fish as they wanted, and twelve baskets of bread were left over (seven baskets according to Mark 8).

Popular enthusiasm erupted. Jesus was acclaimed as the prophet everyone was waiting for, Israel's Messiah (John 6:15). In all likelihood the disciples also took part in this acclamation and Jesus wanted them to leave alone on the boat to Bethsaida (Mark 6:45) or Capernaum (John 6:17). Jesus wanted to keep them away from all this messianic enthusiasm he was receiving, especially when the crowd was so passionate and capable of anything. It was already dark when the disciples were on the lake and having problems rowing against the headwind. Meanwhile, Jesus had tempered the people's enthusiasm and made them leave. Subsequently, he went alone to the mountain "to pray" (this is mentioned only in Mark 6:46). All of a sudden (Mark even gives the time as between three and six o'clock in the morning; 6:48), Jesus came up to the disciples, walking on the water. The terrified disciples thought he was a ghost. Jesus identified himself and may have gotten into the boat with them (Mark 6:51). The boat immediately reached the shore in Capernaum (John 6:21), or they continued their crossing and arrived in Gennesaret (Mark 6:53). The sequence lasted approximately one whole day.

It is significant that, as part of a series of events that can be traced fairly exactly, there are a number of differences resulting from the fact that these three traditions were handed down orally before being recorded in the various different narratives in Mark and John. In other words, the main themes in the stories coincide, whereas there is some disagreement as to the specific details and circumstances, which only highlights the authenticity of the three traditions and the narrative's historical roots. The different narratives include a range of details experienced by eyewitnesses, including the reference to the two hundred denarii needed to be able to feed all these people (Mark 6:37) or that even this would be insufficient (John 6:7). Another authentic detail is the figures five and two, with regard to the loaves and the fishes (the figure seven in Mark 8 seems to be incidental). Furthermore, the people ate fish, the most likely source of food in their position by the lake; but they did not drink wine, which would have been unthinkable for so many people and which would have gone against Jesus' wishes (which were simply to feed the hungry crowd). The "green grass" on which the people sat in groups is a detail that shows it must have been the rainy season, spring, the time of year that the great feast took place (Passover is at hand; John 6:4). We should also stress the fleeting appearance of the small boy who brought the five loaves and two fish (a "superfluous" figure who appears only in John 6).

It all leads us to think that Jesus had arranged this great meal where everyone ate bread and fish by Lake Galilee around the time of Passover 29 A.D., in an area (northeast of the lake) where Antipas did not have jurisdiction and which, thus, was completely safe. Thousands of different people (men, women, and children) in the most part from Galilee came together at a pleasant site, some distance from the nearest town. The time of year (near Passover), the place (an unpopulated and deserted spot), and the participants (a great crowd) show that Jesus wanted to offer an important sign, a sign to clearly indicate what his project was. Jesus did not choose a sign involving political or military liberation as would a "prophet of signs," such as the Egyptian, who attracted some four thousand men (Acts 21:38; *J.W.* 2:261 talks of thirty thousand) and took them out into the wilderness, where they waited for the walls of Jerusalem to fall miraculously so that they could destroy the Roman garrison (see 5.2.1.2).

The sign that Jesus produced did not involve violence against the enemy but instead promoted fraternity among those who followed him. Jesus did not evoke the grand military gestures against the Egyptians (the parting of the Red Sea) from the times of Moses or against the Canaanites (the destruction of Jericho) from the times of Joshua, which inspired the Jews of the time and stirred them up against the Romans. Nor did he plan to repeat them. Jesus was unlike the "prophets of signs" who arose as prophets for the people, leaders seeking to free them from the Roman yoke through armed revolt. Jesus did not call the people to fight but to sit down together to a great feast. The marvel recalled by Jesus and related to the Exodus and Passover was the people of Israel's great meal in the wilderness of Sin, when they were miraculously fed by the manna, bread that fell from the sky, and quail (Exod 16). This ended their famine, and manna became their food during the forty years that it took to cross the desert.

In line with Jesus' wishes, the meal by Lake Galilee acted as a sign of God's compassion for his people and the fraternity among those taking part. As in the case of the manna from heaven and the Israelites' meal of bread and quail, they now ate bread and fish, which were shared and multiplied, as a sign of God's commitment to mankind. First, the hungry are provided with abundant amounts of food, as the Beatitudes proclaim (Luke 6:21). This is a sign that a new world is beginning; bread and fish are multiplied and the poor receive good news. Second, the people are welcomed and split into "groups," with no distinctions or separation between the good and the bad, the just and the sinners, the pure and the impure, adults and children, men and women. The God that Jesus proclaims is the God of all of us, the Father of all of us (Matt 5:45). Third, the meal by Lake Galilee is a clear reference to the Kingdom, where people shall come from around the world to sit down alongside Abraham, Isaac, and Jacob (Matt 8:11-12 || Luke 13:28-29). This meal, which is extraordinary in so many ways, offers a splendid image of the Kingdom that is at the heart of Jesus' message and that places him at the center of the people's expectations.

Unfortunately, the people focused their expectations on redressing the religious, social, and political ills of the nation of Israel. The sign was so astounding that the people, not without reason, thought that the man who had performed this great miracle was the one sent by God to free Israel, the new David, the leader they needed. They wanted to make him "king" (John 6:15), so that someone could lead Israel with strength and power. This perfectly understandable reaction, however, showed once again that the level of the people's devotion to Jesus intensified when their immediate and earthly needs were met. They can eat as much bread as they possibly need and that is enough for them. Jesus, however, has spoken to them with the language of the Kingdom, which is the language of abundance, not just an abundance of bread but above all an abundance of compassion and an all-inclusive fraternity. The feeding of the five thousand has made this language real, but the people do not understand everything that Jesus is trying to tell them (see 4.6.2).

The early Christian community came to see the parallel between this meal and another highly significant one, with which Jesus wanted to bring closure to his life: the Last Supper with his disciples, on the eve of his death on the cross (see 6.1.3). The link between these two meals was self-evident, which is why the narrative of the multiplication of the loaves is full of references to the Eucharist. As J. P. Meier has pointed out, Mark 8 is suffused with the words that Jesus used at the Last Supper (cf., e.g., Mark 8:6-7 and 14:22-23). The two events have been inseparably linked in the Christian tradition, as can be seen in the so-called bread of life discourse in chapter 6 of the Gospel according to John.

The other two extraordinary but much more limited signs are those of the water turned into wine and the miraculous catch.

The wedding at Cana, where Jesus converted water into wine, appears only in the Gospel according to John (2:1-12) (see number 24 in the list of miracles given at the start of 5.2.1). This is the only miracle in the Gospels that involves changing one thing into another. Unlike the multiplication of the loaves where the quantities are increased, here they remain the same; the contents of six jars of water are converted into an equivalent quantity of excellent wine. The loaves provided enough food for everyone; when the water is turned into wine, the steward "tastes" this wine without knowing that this superior wine is the result of a transformation produced by Jesus. In the form in which it has reached us, the narrative has undergone some fundamental modifications, no doubt aimed at emphasizing the symbolism in the Gospel text. Converting the water into wine very probably symbolized the replacing of the old Jewish covenant with a new covenant, that of the superior wine and the groom, Jesus Christ, who acts on his mother's wishes. The scene is set in Cana, the town in Galilee that one of the first disciples comes from (Nathanael Bartholomew), during a wedding attended by Jesus, with his mother and disciples.

The story of the miraculous catch is mentioned in two literary documents: the Gospels of Luke and John (see number 19 of the miracles referred to at the start of 5.2.1). There are thus two versions of this incident, the core of which we can glimpse despite the notable changes made by the early Christian tradition. Jesus ensures that Peter has a spectacular catch ("large fish, a hundred and fifty-three of them," according to John 21:11). He also ensures that the net was not torn despite this great number.

This great catch serves to show who Jesus is. According to the Gospel of Luke, Peter, James, and John, once the boats have returned to land with the fish caught, "left everything and followed him" (Luke 5:11). In the Gospel of John, the catch serves for little, as the fish that the disciples eat on the beach have been cooked by Jesus himself on a charcoal fire and are not those that have just been caught (John 21:9-13). The miracle works as part of a separate event, which is vital for Peter: the appearance of the resurrected Jesus, as is mentioned in the First Epistle to the Corinthians (15:5) and narrated in the Gospel of John (21:15-23). This appearance represents the reversal of the Peter's three denials to the Master on the night that he is arrested; these three denials are turned into three opposing affirmations ("you know that I love you"). At the end of his appearance, Jesus says to Peter once again "Follow me" (John 21:19).

This renewed call allows Luke to convert the story handed down orally into a narrative in which Peter is called to follow Jesus, having witnessed and benefited from this miraculous catch (Luke 5:10). The miracle identifies he who calls him and who calls him again; he is Jesus, the mighty Lord. The miraculous catch is an obvious sign of his authority.

5.2.2. His Friendship with the Sinners and the Poor

Those who needed healing, the sick with physical or psychological problems, were not the only ones who suffered in body or spirit. Jesus also addressed another kind of illness: this affected the very foundations of people's behavior, decisions, and convictions; it could be seen in their indifference toward, tolerance of, or connivance with evil: spiritual illness. Jesus could not ignore those who, for whatever reason, whether voluntarily or involuntarily, had unsatisfactory and, often, unfulfilled lives. He went looking for them rather than rejecting them. He became their friend and offered them forgiveness and peace. Jesus himself quoted a saying used against him (and did not deny it), "friend of tax collectors and sinners" (Matt 11:19 || Luke 7:34), which no doubt reflected his lifestyle. Jesus got close to those who were considered suspicious for not keeping to the Law, and he made them the first to hear his message and to receive his friendship. To continue the metaphor of a doctor, Jesus acted as if he were able to offer them the healing they needed and that they often asked for.

When asked about his friendship with those who were looked down upon from a religious point of view, Jesus replied, "Those who are well have no need of a physician, but those who are sick; I came not to call the righteous but the sinners" (Mark 2:17 || Matt 9:12-13 || Luke 5:31-32). Thus, Jesus' friendship with the sinners formed part of his mission. The phrase "I came" shows that his relationship with the sinners was a vital part of his message and the news he brought. The arrival of the Kingdom of God meant that the marginalized were given an opportunity and a place; this was an ethical and religious stance. No matter how much they were looked down upon or the rejection they suffered, God would not marginalize them; his compassion meant that he would support and welcome them; he was counting on them and offered them a new and different life. Once again Jesus made the Kingdom a reality, as his point of view reflected God's.

5.2.2.1. The Gift of Forgiveness

"Sinners" are those who live without obeying the commandments or regulations of Moses' Law, the opposite of the "just," who abide by the law. The Gospels specify two types of people under the general term "sinner": tax collectors and prostitutes. These two groups are mentioned together in the explanation that follows the parable of the two sons (Matt 21:28-32). The parable refers to the two opposing ways of doing things. One son initially refuses to obey his father and does not want to go to work in the vineyard; but he changes his mind ("he repented") and ends up doing as his father told him. The other son neither goes to work in the vineyard nor obeys his father. This second son initially says that he will go, but in the end does not.

The question that Jesus asks his listeners ("Which of the two did the will of his father?") seems unnecessary. Jesus, however, wants to remind those who think that they are "just" and refuse God that they are wrong to feel that they do not need his forgiveness; they feel this way because they overestimate their own virtue and believe themselves to be irreproachable and untainted. These people, who think that the call to repentance is aimed only at the sinners, do not end up going to work in the vineyard. They act like the Pharisee in the parable who goes up to the temple and gives thanks to God as a good and pious man but does not receive God's love in the end. Ultimately, God is the Father of both the just and the unjust, the law-abiding and the sinner, the good and the bad (see 5.1.2.1).

The friendship that Jesus offers the sinners is welcomed by them with great enthusiasm and thanks, as they recognize the call of God, the heavenly Father. Though initially they are far from him, the Gospel that Jesus now preaches has brought them closer to God, who will forgive and save them. Thus, the sinners respond more enthusiastically than the just, to the extent, as Jesus points out to the law-abiding and the Pharisees in particular, that "the tax collectors and the harlots go into the kingdom of God before you" (Matt 21:31). The Kingdom is for those who want to enter it, not for those who think that they are already there. The tax collector in the parable who asks for forgiveness ("God, be merciful to me a sinner!") goes home forgiven.

However, as J. Schlosser points out, Jesus does not demand repentance as a prior condition to forgiveness. The change in people's lives should come as the result of the invitation they receive and the gift that spreads through their heart. Jesus' friendship with sinners is completely free, but it makes a demand that is both subtle and compelling. Nothing can be the same after meeting him. Everything changes with his friendship. This can be seen in two public and notorious sinners, a man and a woman: Zacchaeus, Jericho's chief tax collector, and a prostitute from Galilee, who can probably be identified as Mary of Magdala or Mary Magdalene. Jesus offers them his friendship, and they get close to him and earn his trust, to the general incomprehension of others and the most religious in particular.

Zacchaeus shows an interest in Jesus and, when the latter enters Jericho, Zacchaeus climbs to the top of a sycamore to get a better view of him. Nonetheless, nothing would have happened had Jesus not offered him his friendship: "Zacchaeus, make haste and come down; for I must stay at your house today" (Luke 19:5). The man's initial response is happiness; he is moved by the friendship that Jesus offers him without asking for anything in return, simply that he put him up in his house. It is Zacchaeus himself who reaps the consequences of his friendship with Jesus: he gives half of his possessions away to the poor and generously repays those he had defrauded in the past (see 4.5.3.2). The friendship that Jesus offers him blends in with God's salvation; indeed, as Jesus himself says, "today salvation has come to this house" (Luke 19:9).

The scene with the prostitute takes place in a town (Luke 7:37), probably Magdala. The woman goes to find Jesus in the house of Simon, a Pharisee, who has invited him for a meal, as he wants to show his thanks to the rabbi from Nazareth. The woman kisses Jesus' feet relentlessly and anoints him with perfume in front of Simon and the other guests, who are uncomfortable with this situation or even scandalized by it, since they know "what sort of woman this is." They cannot understand how Jesus can tolerate this sort of behavior. His gestures, however, allow the welling up of the deep-rooted desire for forgiveness and mercy of this woman, whose tears fall on the Master's feet and who uses her hair to dry them.

Jesus, who is willing to share a table and his friendship with a "just" man, a Pharisee, is also willing to do so with this prostitute, a "sinner," who is equally deserving of his friendship. However, the friendship Jesus offers her is part of the forgiveness that God offers everyone, no matter how great the debt owed by each. Everyone has a debt toward God, accumulated through many falls from grace, and we have nothing to pay him back with. Thus, everyone has to accept his free and generous forgiveness. Jesus offers his friendship equally to the Pharisee and the sinners. Jesus makes this clear twice: the woman is forgiven, "her sins, which are many" are cleansed. Her response, which is also free and generous, is a loving response "for she loved much" (Luke 7:47). Her outpouring of emotion toward Jesus pales into insignificance compared to the immeasurable forgiveness she has received.

Jesus had healed this woman and given her back her peace. Receiving forgiveness was the equivalent of being healed, and her trust in this forgiveness led to an outburst of thanks and love. Indeed, Jesus' friendship with sinners was rooted in the compassion that God showed for them. Jesus looked for the company of sinners because God is a Father who welcomes all his children into his house, regardless of the path they have chosen. The paralytic man in Capernaum who was brought to Jesus by four men is told, "My son, your sins are forgiven" (Mark 2:5), and is then healed. The prostitute receives the same assurance: "Your sins are forgiven" (Luke 7:48). Her trust in a God who forgives and in the friendship that Jesus has offered her are vital and for this reason she can go in peace. Jesus also forgives another sinful woman, who has committed adultery; he does not condemn her but tells her instead, "[G]o, and do not sin again" (John

8:11). Friendship with Jesus relegates sin to the past and forgiveness is the way that God makes himself apparent, transforming the lives of those who welcome him.

5.2.2.2. Eating with the Ostracized

One of the most surprising accusations leveled against Jesus refers to his eating habits: "Behold a glutton and a drunkard, a friend of tax collectors and sinners" (Matt 11:19 || Luke 7:34). These accusations come from a fairly unspecific group ("this generation"). However, according to Luke 15:2, those who criticize Jesus because he "receives sinners and eats with them" are clearly specified. They are the Pharisees and scribes who disagree with Jesus' open relationship with people who are suspected of leading lives that do not fall into line with the regulations of the Law, and his willingness to eat with them in particular. We commented above on the negative reaction of the Pharisee Simon and his guests (presumably Pharisees like him) during the meal that Simon had prepared for Jesus in his house. The people around Jesus in Jericho reacted similarly when he decided to go and stay at the house of Zacchaeus, a figure with a dubious reputation.

The fact that Jesus is accused of being a glutton and a drinker has little to do with his eating habits but is instead inspired by the fact that he is wont to dine with people seen to have little or no interest in abiding by the Jewish Law. When Jesus and his disciples are invited to Levi's house to dine with Levi's friends, tax collectors like him, the interrogation of the disciples by the scribes belonging to the Pharisee group is once again centered on the same point: "Why does he [Jesus] eat with tax collectors and sinners?" (Mark 2:16). As R. Aguirre stresses, Jesus expressly cultivates friendships by sharing meals with those marginalized by the religion of the time, those who are looked down upon because of their job or way of life.

In the ancient world, Greco-Roman or Jewish, meals were seen as a special setting for coming together, friendship, and sharing. A meal contributes to the feeling of solidarity and strengthens relations between people belonging to certain social groups (an association, a group of friends, colleagues, or relatives). Thus, the person who organizes a meal by inviting friends and acquaintances makes them feel honored and leads to their acting reciprocally. Sitting at a table with people helps intensify the personal links with them, almost equating them to the members of one's family. Despite the understandable differences between the guests themselves, who occupy a higher or lower place at the banquet, those who sit down at the same table occupy a similar position from a cultural, economic, religious, or ethnic point of view. Thus, meals work on two levels: the inclusive and the exclusive according to social hierarchies and balance. This can be seen in the "canonical" aspect of meals, in their strict protocols and customs (e.g., Sir 31:12–32:13).

Jesus provides his own surprising point of view on the question. In a fragment from the tradition that appears only in the Gospel according to Luke (14:7-14), Jesus offers a series of "rules" for banquets, which have little to do with protocol or ceremony: "[W]hen you give a feast, invite the poor, the maimed, the lame, the blind, and you will be blessed, because they cannot repay you. You will be repaid at the resurrection of the just." Jesus sees graciousness and friendship toward the poor as a replacement for the typical reciprocal nature of social customs (those who invite expect to be invited in return) and as a way of overcoming the exclusion that those who are marginalized by society have to face up to. This is the case of the man in the parable of the banquet, who ends up filling his house with all kinds of anonymous strangers, the poor and the sick and those people who are just happy to accept his invitation (Matt 22:9 || Luke 14:21, 14:23). This is how Jesus acts when he feeds the five thousand by Lake Galilee, having invited a great crowd, welcoming everyone indiscriminately (five thousand men, besides the women and children) (see 5.2.1.5).

The case of the sinners, those people who notoriously and publicly worked in jobs that were looked down upon by the most religious and the Pharisees in particular, was different. The scribes had deemed that certain professions were linked directly to fraud and, thus, impure; they went against the Law of Moses. As J. Jeremias notes, these included usurers, gamblers, those who traded goods during the sabbatical year, shepherds (suspected of injuring other people's property), and money-changers. Publicans, tax collectors, customs officials, and prostitutes were singled out as the professions that were looked down upon most socially. Being employed in one of these professions was the equivalent of living with sin and injustice permanently. For this reason, publicans were deemed pagans, non-Jews (Matt 5:46-47, 18:17), and Jesus had to remind people that Zacchaeus, a tax collector, "also is a son of Abraham" (Luke 19:9); he also belonged to the Jewish people and had the same rights as any Pharisee.

Regardless of a person's behavior, the Pharisees deemed that, for the mere fact that he or she was employed in a certain profession, he or she had entered a permanent state of impurity and could not have any form of relations; if they did, the other person would also be affected by this state of impurity. One of the situations that needed to be avoided at all costs was eating with one of those people considered to be impure "by nature." Those who wanted to abide by the Law had to be sure never to share a table with a "sinner."

However, Jesus did not share this point of view and, right from the start of his public activities, he ate with publicans and tax collectors or similarly stigmatized people who were deemed to have jobs that were considered "impure" and expressed his friendship for them in this way. Jesus invited them and accepted their invitations. This was a provocative public gesture, which led to indignation and protests from the Pharisees and others who kept to the Law, people who could not understand his conduct and reproached him for it. The reasons given by Jesus to justify his behavior were rooted in the heart of his message: the Kingdom of God. Jesus was happy to get close to sinners because God was manifest in the world through mercy and forgiveness and this represented the end to any kind of exclusion. With a language based on acts, friendship, and the meal table, Jesus talks of a God who saves. For Jesus, being a "friend to tax collectors and sinners" is not an ignoble accusation but a reality to be accepted and broadcast, a reality that went beyond the boundaries of the Pharisees' strict interpretation of the Law. All, without exception, poor and sinner, are called to the table in the Kingdom of God.

5.2.2.3. Welcoming the Poor and Marginalized

Signs of the Kingdom spread through a range of people who come to Jesus to ask him to take pity on their wants and needs. They were normally people without anyone else to turn to, without power or influence, who trusted in Jesus and saw in him the solution to the ills that affected them and from which they could not escape on their own. Indeed, the majority of people in the crowds that happily listened to Jesus or that followed him on his travels around Galilee were not the well-to-do but the simple people, who had to work hard to ensure they could meet their daily needs for food and clothing.

It is no coincidence that the third request in the Lord's Prayer, the prayer that Jesus provides for the disciples, refers to the food needed to live (Matt 6:11 || Luke 11:3) or that the first of the Beatitudes is aimed at those who are without all those things needed for a dignified life. In the Beatitudes, Jesus says that blessed are the poor, the hungry, those who cry, in other words all those who now know that both God and Jesus are at their side (Luke 6:20-21). This is the reason for Jesus' constant concern for the poor and downtrodden in his words and deeds; they are the first to receive the good news about the Kingdom and the first to be called to enter it. Material poverty is not a sign of God's rejection; quite the contrary, God shows himself to be close to those who suffer and welcomes them into his Kingdom.

However, those who are concerned only about their possessions in this world have to be reminded that these possessions are fragile and temporary: worms and moths will destroy them and a thief can take them away. This is not the case with the promise of the Kingdom that God offers the poor. This is a safe and guaranteed treasure, which lasts forever. It is worth setting your heart on it and living in the knowledge that God will not fail us. Jesus expresses this idea in a proverb: "For where your treasure is, there will your heart be also" (Matt 6:21 || Luke 12:34).

The welcome received from the people, and the poor in particular, was also extended to the disciples. When a crowd gathered near Lake Galilee and the disciples suggested to Jesus that he tell the people to leave so that they could look for food in the surrounding area, Jesus replied, "You give them something to eat" (Mark 6:37 || Matt 14:16 || Luke 9:13; and similarly, John 6:5). In other words, the disciples could not hold back when it came to the needs of the people. Neither did Jesus hold back when he advised a rich man to give his money away to the poor and follow him (Mark 10:21). This rich man did not follow his advice, but Zacchaeus did, correctly interpreting the message inherent in Jesus' visit to his house (Luke 19:8). The disciples exhibit their meanness in the words they use to criticize the cost of the perfume used to anoint Jesus' feet, but it is the Master's concern for the poor that suffuses the anointing in Bethany. He makes a forceful statement, "For you always have the poor with you" (Mark 14:7 || Matt 26:11 || John 12:8), and Mark continues, "and whenever you will, you can do good to them." In other words, they can hand out money, as charity was a common act for Jesus and his disciples (John 13:29; Didache 1:5). Jesus recommends charitable giving but warns against the pride that may be behind the "good conscience": the left hand should not know what the right hand is doing (Matt 6:3). Concern and welcome for the poor are at the very heart of the Kingdom.

The poor and simple do not know the commandments of the Law, which leads to their marginalization by the Pharisees, who keep strictly to all the Law's prescriptions. Material poverty, low social standing, and lack of knowledge of the regulations referring to ritual cleanliness and the tithes (some of the most important aspects of the Pharisees' interpretation of the Law) are common among a good part of the population, which is poor and illiterate. Nevertheless, the Pharisee scribes and those in similar circles do try to adapt the general regulations to meet each specific situation so that everyone can follow the stipulations of the Law. The Pharisees, apostles of keeping to the Law, show themselves to be patient when it comes to promoting this among the people, but they cannot support those who do not make an effort to abide by the Law in all its forms (regardless of whether this is because they cannot or will not). A sector of the population is deemed by the Pharisees to be irrecoverable, as, according to them, they are simply a "crowd, who do not know the Law, [and] are accursed," excluded by both God and man (John 7:49). The 613 commandments that the scribes summarize into the practice of the Law represent an impossible task for the simplest people.

But Jesus is happy to be surrounded by all these people, he welcomes the "simple," as keeping strictly to the Law does not in itself represent the aim of his message. It is the Kingdom, not the Law, which guides his words, acts, and signs. Those who keep strictly to the Law will not enter the Kingdom; instead, it will be those who welcome the good news of a generous and compassionate God who is manifest in this world and who wants to manifest himself above all to those whom everyone else ignores.

God's way of doing things is expressed by Jesus in a passionate prayer for thanksgiving and is passed down to us in the Q collection: "I thank thee, Father, Lord of heaven and earth, that thou hast hidden these things from the wise and understanding and revealed them to babes" (Matt 11:25 || Luke 10:21). Jesus shows that the Kingdom reaches the simple and the ignorant people, those without hope or future; these are just the people who should be the first to welcome it but are in fact the most reticent. Jesus' friendship with the poor is a direct consequence of the fact that God finds no resistance in those who expect everything from him. His words are an invitation to trust in him: "Fear not, little flock, for it is your Father's good pleasure to give you the kingdom" (Luke 12:32).

Children have a special place in this "little flock," those who are not obliged to keep to the precepts of the Law and thus are seen to be human beings who have yet to be fully formed. The welcome that Jesus offers children is evident in his affectionate gestures that are reminiscent of those of people who look after the sick. He places one child among the disciples to serve as a reference for his words, he takes them in his arms, and he lays his hands on them as a sign of blessing. In the Gospels of Matthew and John, when Jesus multiplies the loaves and the fishes, children are also present at the gathering.

Jesus' care for children is well enough known for people to bring their children to him, but the disciples tell them off, only for Jesus to reproach them and remind them that children should also be welcomed. There is a twofold reason for this. First, the Kingdom of God belongs to them, "for to such belongs the kingdom of God" (Mark 10:14 || Matt 19:14 || Luke 18:16). Like the poor and simple, children are among those whom God has in his heart. Second, children deserve the same welcome that Jesus and the Father in heaven deserve (Mark 9:37 || Matt 18:5 || Luke 9:48). Their dignity is as great as that of God himself and his emissary, Jesus. Once more the notions we take for granted are turned on their head. Jesus values children on their own terms; he does not consider them, as was usual at the time, as some kind of proto-adult. Furthermore, children, because of their weakness, have to ask for everything and are thus the paradigm of the person in need. Welcoming children equates to welcoming the Kingdom.

Regarding exclusion, foreigners were affected most. Foreigners did not belong to the people of the covenant and, thus, could not share in its benefits. However, as we have seen above (5.2.1.3), Jesus healed a number of foreigners: a Samaritan man, cleansed of leprosy; the man from the Decapolis, from whom Jesus expels a legion of demons; and the Phoenician girl, healed of an evil spirit following the pleas from her mother. The servant of the centurion in Capernaum should also be included, as the latter seems to have been a foreign soldier as well as a practicing Jew. There are doubts as to the nationality of the deaf and dumb man in the Decapolis. In total there are four or five occasions where a welcome to foreigners involves a healing (two or three times) or the expulsion of demons (twice).

This is quite a high number. The Gospels contain fourteen stories of healings and five stories of exorcisms, nineteen altogether, four or five of which (20 percent to 25 percent) involve foreigners. Furthermore, Jesus' activities took place fundamentally within the borders of Israel, as evidenced by the instructions to the Twelve sent to proclaim the Kingdom and heal the sick: "Go nowhere amongst the Gentiles [i.e., foreigners], and enter no towns of the Samaritans" (Matt 10:5). But, on the few occasions that Jesus left Israel he continued to expel demons (from the man in the Decapolis and the Phoenician girl) and heal (the deaf and dumb man in the Decapolis?) and, in Israel once again, he healed the servant of a foreign solider living in Capernaum and a Samaritan infected with leprosy.

Foreigners were not to be excluded from the particular welcome that Jesus offered the poor, the sick, and the marginalized (the simple people and children). They were also, though somewhat more sporadically, to witness the coming of a new world where people were freed from the ills that afflicted them and where they could receive the compassion of a God who saves. Foreigners went up to Jesus, the bearer of the Kingdom, with hope and confidence. This is shown by the wishes of a group of Greeks who went up to Philip, one of the Twelve, saying, "Sir, we wish to see Jesus" (John 12:21). After Jesus' death and resurrection, there was a broad willingness to accept people of other faiths into the bosom of the Christian family, which was extended to the Samaritans and other foreigners.

5.2.3. Jesus, The Prophet of the Signs of the Kingdom

Jesus did not limit his actions to proclaiming the Kingdom, to communicating to his listeners that God had started to make his presence felt in the history of mankind, but instead he lived and acted in line with the good news that he brought for everyone, the poor in particular. The Kingdom is a place without borders or limits, a reality that is opening up for many people and that inspires faith in those who welcome it. The Kingdom is accompanied by effective and extraordinary signs of compassion and forgiveness, of mercy and hope, that turn the people's expectations on their head and make God's compassionate presence visible through Jesus' healing activities.

Jesus offered a similar response to two opposing but very important figures in his life (John the Baptist and the tetrarch Antipas). When John sent some of his disciples from his prison to ask Jesus whether he was the person that God had sent (the prophet for the end of time, the Messiah), Jesus reminded them of the miracles he had performed and the words he had spoken that proclaimed the coming of a new dawn. Jesus described himself as the bearer of the Kingdom: he who healed the sick (the blind, lame, leprous, or deaf), he who resurrected the dead and who brought the good news to the poor (Matt 11:2-5 || Luke 7:18-22). Isaiah's prophecies emphasized that all these mighty acts were those of the one to be sent by God. A fragment from Qumran (4Q521), which alludes to Isaiah 61:1, says, "For he [the one anointed by the Lord, the Messiah] will heal the wounded, and revive the dead and bring good news to the poor." Luke (4:18-19) modifies Isaiah (61:1-2) somewhat, saying, "The Spirit of the Lord is upon me, because he has anointed me to preach good news to the poor. He has sent me to proclaim release to the captives and recovering of sight to the blind, to set at liberty those who are oppressed, to proclaim the acceptable year of the Lord." This prophetic Scripture is coming true here and now in the miracles performed by Jesus, the one anointed by God, the Messiah.

Everyone can witness the miraculous words and deeds that bring many people health and freedom. The Kingdom is coming and Jesus is bringing it; those who do not reject him are happy and welcome this emissary as "he who is to come" (Matt 11:3 || Luke 7:20). This is the answer that John's disciples had to pass on to their master, Antipas' prisoner in Machaerus.

On another occasion, a number of Pharisees came up to Jesus to warn him of the danger he is in. Antipas wanted him killed, as he had already killed John. Jesus was not scared, instead defining himself as the victor over the evil spirits that oppress people's minds and self and a healer who returns people to health ("I cast out demons and perform cures today and tomorrow"; Luke 13:31-32). Exorcisms and healings are the two great signs of the Kingdom, which are offered alongside friendship for sinners and the poor. Jesus acts in complete harmony with the God he proclaims, the God of compassion and forgiveness, who gives generously, who shows himself to be caring, who wants to be the Father to everyone, who is happy to welcome the prodigal son and who sides with the downtrodden and ostracized.

The signs of the Kingdom express the Kingdom, they make it clear and real, they form it. Jesus never uses these signs to accredit his own abilities; rather they are always a reason for praising God and giving him thanks. But without these extraordinary and surprising signs, this cornerstone, the message of the Kingdom would be incomplete. Jesus' miracles make people whole again, freeing them from their suffering (or even death) and, on occasions, demonstrating his power over the cosmic forces. The great sign of the loaves and the fishes, halfway through his life's journey, is above all an image of fraternity, of mankind renewed by the force of compassion and overflowing friendship.

The opposite version of events was upheld by Jesus' competitors and adversaries, who saw his miracles as the result of his connivance with the devil (Mark 3:22). According to them, Jesus cheated people and led them astray, amazing them with his marvels and leading them away from what was fundamental: doing God's will as expressed in his Law. Jesus' miracles were traps and his words an artful deception. Jesus was, according to the Jewish authorities, an "impostor" (Matt 27:63), someone who "practised sorcery" (Babylonian Talmud, *Sanh.* 43a). Was Jesus a sorcerer?

The answer has to be no. As we have pointed out, Jesus' miracles had little in common with the miracles that Philostratus attributes to Apollonius of Tyana (see 5.2.1.2). The Greek magical papyri do not permit a clear comparison, nor do they present analogies consistent with the miracles that Jesus performed. As J. D. G. Dunn points out, Josephus does not call Jesus a magician or sorcerer, as he does other "prophets of signs," such as the Egyptian or Theudas (*J.W.* 2:261 and *A.J.* 20:97).

First, there is no evidence of any kind of magic used in Jesus' healings and exorcisms; that is, the use of materials or techniques to expel demons in the ancient world. For example, in the biblical book of Tobit the devil cannot act because, following the Angel Raphael's advice, Tobias has placed the liver and heart of the fish caught in the Tigris over a perfume lamp in the room to ward off evil spirits. Jesus confronts the power of the evil spirits armed only with his mighty and authoritative words. The sentence "Come out of the man, you unclean spirit!" (Mark 5:8) is, for example, the order used on the possessed man in the Decapolis. Nor is there any evidence of magic or esoteric formulae or spells used in the exorcisms or healings—rituals which, as H. C. Kee points out, only served individual and often obscure interests.

Second, Jesus heals in his own name; though the miracle leads to the people thanking God (and not in recognition of any other power!), Jesus does not, in fact, invoke the name of God when he heals the sick of body or spirit, the possessed. When casting out of an evil spirit that torments an epileptic boy and stops him from speaking, Jesus reprimands the evil spirit forcefully saying, "I command you"; as it says in Mark (9:25), "You dumb and deaf spirit, I command you, come out of him, and never enter him again." On other occasions, the power that Jesus possesses as expressed in his words is enough to achieve the desired effect.

In some cases Jesus "touches" the person before or at the exact moment when he healed or revived him or her, as if this gesture were a way of communicating health and life. Jesus takes the hand of Peter's mother-in-law and makes her get up, and the fever is cured. In the case of Jairus' daughter, he also takes her hand and says, "'Talitha, cumi!'; which means, 'Little girl, I say to you, arise'" (Mark 5:41). However, there is no contact with the dead person in the other two resurrections (the widow's daughter in Nain and Lazarus). Jesus does touch the Galilean leper and says, "I will, be clean" (Mark 1:41 || Matt 8:3 || Luke 5:13). Jesus thus transgresses the commandment of the Law that prohibits touching lepers and in this way draws attention to the healing that he is performing. On no occasion, though, does Jesus touch any of the possessed before casting out the evil spirit.

Another common way that Jesus came into direct and personal contact with the sick was by the laying on of his hands. This can be seen in Jairus' request: "Come and lay your hands on her [his daughter who is dying], so that she may be made well, and live" (Mark 5:23; Matt 9:18 talks of "your hand"; see also Mark 7:32, "they besought him to lay his hands upon him [the deaf and dumb man]"). The few people he healed in Nazareth were cured using the same system (Mark 6:5), as was the hunchback woman (Luke 13:13) and the blind man in Bethsaida, who had Jesus lay his hands on him twice (Mark 8:23-25). Jesus heals with his words and/or the gesture of touching the sick person, which was a very unusual thing to do at the time but something he did fairly often. Jesus sought personal contact with the human nature of the ill person, acting almost in synergy with the healed person's internal feelings of trust and faith.

The faith of the healed shows how Jesus' miracles were not just mechanical but took place with the Kingdom in mind and with the hopes that Jesus himself, the healer, inspired. The miracles produced by magical arts could take place even without the consent of the person being healed. They are automatic and essentially impersonal operations, which in the case of black magic do not offer any benefits and, indeed, can be used against people.

The woman with hemorrhages was healed by simply touching Jesus' cloak, where he noticed only "that power had gone forth from him" (Mark 5:30 || Luke 8:46). There has been imperceptible physical contact and, thanks to her great faith, the woman has been able to "capture" some of the healing force present in Jesus. Even the three miracles in which Jesus uses his saliva cannot be considered magical in the strictest sense. In the ancient world, saliva was a popular remedy; famous physicians, such as Galen, and historians such as Pliny the Elder recommended its use, especially if the saliva came from important people, who were said to have healing powers. This appears to have been so in the case of the deaf-mute from the Decapolis, healed after Jesus wets his finger with his own saliva and touches the man's tongue and says, "'*Ephphatha*,' that is, 'Be opened'" (Mark 7:33); or the two blind men, one in Bethsaida and the other blind from birth, whose eyes Jesus anoints with his own saliva (Mark 8:23 and John

9:6, where the saliva is used to make clay). There is no form of special magic involved in these healings, simply the use from time to time of a basic resource that everyone shares. Jesus' healing force comes from his word.

5.3. The Kingdom, A Standard for Life

In relation to the basic pillars of the Jewish religion in the first third of the first century A.D., Jesus shows himself to be a passionate but atypical Jew. There was a certain ambivalence in his attitudes, words, and gestures when it came to the Law and the temple. Jesus was an unusual rabbi, a pious, law-abiding Jew who, surprisingly, did not make the Law the focus of his life. This focus was taken up instead by the Kingdom of God, which he proclaimed and communicated through his convincing and potent words. The Kingdom became in the words of H. Merklein "the basis for action," the standard for life that he advocated for those who followed him; or as B. Chilton and C. A. Evans stress, in an idea that blends poetry and theology, the rising light of God's eschatological reality is Jesus' guiding principle.

Jesus' strong Jewish ethics are guided by God the Father, who has begun to manifest himself through his righteousness, mercy, and generous forgiveness. The basis of this ethical discourse is not some reflection on the nuances of the Law, as was common with the scribes of the time, rather the gift of the Kingdom supersedes all these points of view and opens up new horizons. From this perspective, Jesus creates his own interpretation of the Law that takes advantage of these new horizons, concentrating them. Jesus takes the Law above and beyond itself; he focuses it in terms of a light that catalyzes it in a new way. Jesus makes these new moves basing them on texts from the Law itself, on texts from fragments of the Scriptures, or through authoritative statements that are given the same standing as these Scriptures.

With regard to the temple, the second great pillar of the Jewish religion (see 3.3.1.2), Jesus follows the stipulations of the Law and goes on pilgrimages to Jerusalem with his disciples for some of the Jewish festivals (Passover, Tabernacles, Dedication). Jesus does not, then, oppose the temple as a place of prayer and offerings (respectively, Luke 18:10 and Matt 5:23-24). He cannot tolerate that the temple is used as a marketplace that people and goods pass through, not even when the goods sold were the pigeons to be used as offerings in the sanctuary (Mark 11:15-16). This radical prophetic-style criticism addressed at the temple's leaders and the confrontation it entailed was no doubt one of the causes of his death.

Jesus prophesied, but only to his disciples, the complete destruction of the temple buildings; no stone of these great buildings would remain standing (Mark 13:2). He assured everyone that he could destroy the temple and rebuild it again in just three days (Mark 14:58; John 2:19), thus replacing the current temple with a new one: a material one, or a spiritual one? The current temple is not, then, brought into question as an institution forming part of Israel, but Jesus sees it as lacking a future, since it is destined to be destroyed (and subsequently "rebuilt"). This is made clear in the prophecy in which Jesus laments for Jerusalem, "Behold, your house [i.e., the temple] is forsaken and desolate" (Matt 23:38 || Luke 13:35). The reason for this is that the city has failed to recognize the moment when God visits (Luke 19:44). The current temple, despite being a symbol of God's presence, does not reflect God's wishes and will have to be destroyed or, at the very least, replaced. The Kingdom, meanwhile, is a growing reality that is moving toward a splendid future, of which signs can already be seen in the words and miracles of Jesus, the bearer of this Kingdom. God is manifest in the daily life of the prophet from Nazareth.

5.3.1. Jesus, An Unusual Rabbi

Jesus is commonly called both *rabbi* (a Hebrew word) and *rabboni* (an Aramaic word). The Twelve disciples call him this, for example, Peter on the mountaintop when Jesus is transfigured (Mark 9:5) and Judas when he betrays him in the garden of Gethsemane (Mark 14:45 || Matt 26:49). Other people close to him also address him in this way, including Mary Magdalene, the disciple who recognizes him after his resurrection (John 20:16); and a follower, Nicodemus, who visited him at nighttime so as not to be seen (John 3:2). The blind man in Jericho uses the word normally used by people when they ask him to heal them: "Rabbi, let me receive my sight" (Mark 10:51).

Jesus is called rabbi because the disciples and people in general, even his competitors and adversaries, recognize his authority for teaching, interpreting the Law of Moses, and answering questions relating to the Jewish faith. Like John the Baptist, Jesus attracted loyal disciples who followed him, and this is a clear sign of his position as a teacher. Undoubtedly, Jesus spent some time under the guidance of the Baptist, and this was vital in his being recognized as a rabbi, first of all by the small group of John's disciples who then became his disciples (see 4.5.2.2).

5.3.1.1. Obedient and Free

A rabbi is a religious leader who is respected and listened to by the people. Interest in Jesus increased because he was a rabbi who taught and healed, who offered "a new teaching, taught with authority," which was full of wisdom but also included extraordinary events, such as healings and exorcisms (Mark 1:27). His words demanded attention and the extraordinary deeds that accompanied them inspired enthusiasm.

Likewise, the rabbi Jesus was not beyond going to find people wherever they might be. Jesus was not a conventional rabbi with a fixed abode (a school or synagogue) where he imparted his teachings to those who came to hear him, normally a group of disciples. Jesus was a traveling teacher who not only addressed people in the house in Capernaum or the synagogues of the towns of Galilee but also attracted great crowds at the lakeside, in the countryside, or on the mountainside. His teachings were usually open to everyone. Those who wanted to criticize him had to join the crowds and wait for an opportunity. This does not mean that Jesus did not address his disciples in private, as can be seen in Mark (4:34): "privately to his own disciples he explained everything." There were, then, teachings reserved for them, especially as time went by and he traveled throughout the Jewish and neighboring lands. Jesus announced to those who followed him the tragic end that was to affect Jerusalem (Mark 10:32 || Matt 20:17 || Luke 18:31), the destruction of the temple and the end of the world (Mark 13:3 || Matt 24:3).

Jesus was a well-known and renowned rabbi, who traveled with his disciples and who was accosted wherever he went. He had fringes or knots on each corner of his cloak, as worn by the pious Jews as a reminder that the commandments of the Law had to be kept to: "You shall make yourself tassels on the four corners of your cloak with which to cover yourself" (Deut 22:12). It was this fringe that the woman with hemorrhages touched in the hope of being cured (Matt 9:20 || Luke 8:44), as did the sick who accosted him (Mark 6:56).

As with the pious Jews, and other rabbis, Jesus performed and encouraged others to perform the "good works" of Jewish tradition: charity, prayer, and fasting (Matt 6:1-18). The group's shared purse was used for charity for the poor (John 13:29), and Jesus himself often went away to pray on his own (Mark 6:41, 14:32). Jesus attributed a great power to prayer: "Therefore I tell you, whatever you ask in prayer, believe that you have received it, and it will be yours" (Mark 11:24). Matthew 18:19 says, "[I]f two of you agree on earth about anything they ask, it will be done for them by my Father in heaven." Jesus' trust in God is rooted in Israel's deepest conviction: "Have faith in God" (Mark 11:22). Even the mountains can be moved to the sea if there is faith in God, as "all things are possible to him who believes" (Mark 9:23).

Jesus had certain reservations about fasting. He did not refuse to fast as a practice commanded by the Law and regarded favorably by God as, for example, the fasting on the Day of Atonement; but he refused to adopt the practice of the Pharisees and John the Baptist's disciples (!) which took the observation of the Law to the extreme, fasting two days a week (Tuesdays and Thursdays). His disciples did not have to perform weekly fasts, and the reason was somewhat surprising: "they have the bridegroom with them" (Mark 2:19 || Matt 9:15 || Luke 5:34). In other words, Jesus saw the time he spent preaching as being unique and special, and he did not want the cause of the Kingdom to be affected by anything. The disciples needed all their energy to be able to communicate the good news, the gospel, here and now. He continued, saying, "The days will come, when the bridegroom is taken away from them, and then they will fast in that day" (Mark 2:20).

Jesus' position with regard to fasting is important in relation to the Jewish Law as a whole. The Master from Nazareth did not fail to meet any of the obligations required by the Law, which he had abided by fully since he was a child and in which he saw the expression of God's will. However, unlike the Pharisees, he was not an apostle of the Law with the sole aim of preaching it and ensuring its observation. Jesus looked at the Law from a unique perspective. He did not aim to develop a great number of precepts or to create a "learned" alternative to the interpretations of the Law offered by the Pharisees and Sadducees. For Jesus, the Law was a way of talking about God from the heart. He was not as concerned about fasting as he was about the first commandment: "[Y]ou shall love the Lord your God with all your heart, and with all your soul, and with all your mind, and with all your strength" (Mark 12:30).

Jesus did not sieve through all the Scriptures in order to reduce them to a few hundred precepts (613!), as the Pharisees did. Jesus was concerned only with what he felt was essential for relations with God and with others, the two main points from the Scriptures he chose to focus on. He made a selection and produced a series of questions, which were consciously premeditated, concerning ethics, relating to individual and collective behavior which he prioritized, relegating all the ritual of worship and cleanliness to a clear second place. He said, "[Y]ou tithe mint and dill and cumin [secondary things], and have neglected the weightier matters of the Law, justice, and mercy and faith [fundamental aspects of the Law]" (Matt 23:23). Not everything in the Law has the same importance. Jesus took from the Law those things that he felt to be fundamental so as to make the Kingdom the standard by which his disciples lived their lives. One way of finding out more about this selection is to look at the texts from the Scriptures from which Jesus quoted, as seen in the tradition that has been passed down to us.

5.3.1.2. Interpreter of the Scriptures

Jesus mentioned surprisingly few biblical texts. Jesus abided by the Law, but he did not see himself primarily as an interpreter of it. He used the Scriptures as a tool and a means, not as an aim or end in itself. This set him apart from the rabbis of the time and, later, from both Pharisees and Sadducees. In contrast to the Pharisees, he did not see the "tradition of the elders" (the series of interpretations of the Law that had been produced by earlier rabbis) as regulatory or significant.

In fact, he warned that following this tradition would lead to people's ignoring "the commandment of God," which was essential, and to their violating and invalidating the Law. Thus Jesus never quoted or supported the positions, opinions, rules, or interpretations offered by contemporary or earlier rabbis. Mark (1:22) expresses it thus: "he taught them as one who had authority, and not as the scribes" (see 4.5.4.2).

The Scriptures were not at the center of Jesus' message. As we have said, the Master did not refer to them very often, and when he did so, he would use them in a sardonic way. In relation to the question of the Messiah being a descendant of David, Jesus discusses the interpretation of Psalm 110:1 made by "the scribes" (he does not mention any in particular, but they were linked to the Pharisee group; Mark 12:35-37 || Matt 22:41-46 || Luke 20:41-44). Another contentious case surrounded the so-called Law of corban ("offering to God"), for which Jesus reproached some Pharisees and scribes who had come from Jerusalem to see him. According to this practice, which was accepted by some rabbis but criticized by many others, a son or daughter could "consecrate" to God possessions that they should have used to help their parents, which they would then keep, as they had no obligation to take them to the temple's treasury (Mark 7:10-13 || Matt 15:4-6). Jesus criticizes this practice, which he sees as being a transgression of the precept to honor one's father and mother, part of the Ten Commandments (Exod 20:12 and 21:17). The idea of corban is, according to Jesus, a dishonorable violation of Moses' Law and goes against God's commandments.

Jesus uses the book of Exodus (3:6) to argue in favor of the resurrection of the dead, which was denied by the scribes of the Sadducee group (Mark 12:18-27 || Matt 22:23-33 || Luke 20:27-38). This text has been looked at in 4.5.4.4. The question of divorce was brought up by "some Pharisees," who probably already knew Jesus' position on the subject, offering Deuteronomy 24:1 as proof, a text that justifies the practice. Jesus responded by quoting Genesis 1:27 and 2:24, stressing that it was in force "from the beginning of creation" (Mark 10:1-12 || Matt 19:1-12). It is the only occasion on which Jesus reinterprets a text from the Scriptures (Deut 24:1-4) comparing it with two other texts from these same Scriptures (Gen 1:27 and 2:24) which are seen to be superior to the former (see 5.3.2.2, below). This procedure constitutes the rabbis' seventh rule of interpretation (*mida*), whereby a text has to be interpreted in terms of another similar text, as stipulated by the *baraita* in the introduction to the Midrash HaGadol. Jesus quotes from the Psalms (once) and the Pentateuch (three times) and always in contentious situations.

In noncontentious situations, the Scriptures were also used to call the hardhearted to repent, as may have been the case with the quoting of Isaiah 6:9-10, a biblical text taken from the Targum, the ancient Aramaic translation used at the time in the synagogues of Galilee to help people understand the biblical texts in Hebrew (Mark 4:12). The parable of the murderous workers in the vineyard becomes a plea from Jesus, at the last moment, to the religious leaders of Israel (the tenants in the parable) to recognize his actions and to realize the dreadful catastrophe that Jesus' death will represent (the death of the vineyard owner's son in the parable). The vineyard is the symbol of the people of Israel in Isaiah (5:1-2) (Mark 12:1 || Matt 21:33), and Jesus may be alluding to this text, though we cannot be entirely sure of this (Luke 20:9). In reply to the Baptist's disciples Jesus affirms his messianic activities, performing miracles and bringing good news to the poor, using a series of texts from the prophet Isaiah (26:19, 29:18, 35:5-6, 61:1). Jesus certainly saw his activities as the fulfillment of God's promise that the end of days would be a time of thanks and salvation (Matt 11:5 || Luke 7:22). The prophet Isaiah (61:1-2) is also quoted in the events in the synagogue in Nazareth, as presented by Luke (4:18-19) with certain modifications that stress the arrival of a time of divine mercy. Isaiah 61:1-2 is not quoted in Mark 6 or Matthew 13.

Alongside these texts (four or possibly two) that quote the prophet Isaiah, we need to add some other references to the Ten Commandments and the laws in the Pentateuch. With respect to the most important commandment of the Law (Mark 12:28-34 || Matt 22:34-40 || Luke 10:25-28), the texts cited are Deuteronomy (6:4-5); the famous *Shema Yisrael*, the holiest verse in Judaism, which enshrines the love of God; and Leviticus 19:18, which requires that we love others as we would love ourselves (see 5.3.2.3, below). The commandments from the Decalogue applying to relations with one's neighbors are mentioned by Jesus in the story of the rich man (Mark 10:19), where he quotes Exodus (20:12-16) and Deuteronomy (5:16-20) and in the so-called antitheses, where certain texts from the Pentateuch are quoted: from the books of Exodus, Leviticus, Numbers, and Deuteronomy (see 5.3.2.1, below).

Thus, the Pentateuch, Isaiah (and Micah and Jeremiah), and the Psalms are the parts of the Scriptures that Jesus quoted most often in this order. On other occasions he alluded to biblical texts and even some biblical figures (Moses, David, Solomon, the Queen of Sheba, Elijah, Elisha, Jonah) or cities (Tyre, Sidon, Sodom) in order to move those who listened to him to devotion and repentance. The Scriptures were a means used by Jesus for a number of reasons, but the Scriptures alone did not represent an authority that Jesus respected unquestioningly. God, the Father, was the only authority and righteousness that Jesus bowed down before: "No one is good but God alone" (Mark 10:18), or "what therefore God has joined together, let no man put asunder" (Mark 10:9). He is responsible for everything that happens, and only he knows what is to come. Jesus does not move away from the focus of Israel's covenant, rather he places it before everything else; indeed he himself forms part of it: "no one knows the Father except the Son and any one to whom the Son chooses to reveal him" (Matt 11:27 || Luke 10:22).

5.3.1.3. Jesus and His People

In 3.3 we tried to explain Jewish religiosity in the times of Jesus by what E. P. Sanders calls the "the common Judaism." The basis of the Jewish religion is worship of one God, monotheism. There are three elements that make it up (chosen people, covenant, and Torah) and two characteristics that drive it (forgiveness and repentance). In terms of behavior, the demands are as follows: worship of God in the temple in Jerusalem; prayer on one's own, in the family, and in the synagogue; observance of the ritual precepts of the Law (circumcision, rest on the Sabbath, rules on ritual cleanliness); and observance of the ethical or moral code.

Thus, if we simplify things somewhat, we can see how Jesus highlights certain elements in this list and relegates others. Two points stand out in Jesus' message: devotion to one God, with forgiveness and repentance as characteristics that shape God's way of doing things and people's response; and prayer, centered on the Lord's Prayer, the disciples' prayer, and the importance of an ethical and moral code. The other three points are relegated to the background: the basic elements of Jewish monotheism (chosen people, covenant, and Torah), worship in the temple in Jerusalem, and abiding by ritual precepts (circumcision, Sabbath, rules on ritual cleanliness). We should note that the points relegated to the background are most directly linked to the religious and national identity of the people of Israel, while the main points are linked to more general and common themes. Jesus stresses the ethical norms and shows little interest in the ritual regulations. Significantly, Jesus remains deliberately silent on everything that was central to the Jewish groups and trends of the first century A.D. The term "covenant," for example, appears only four times in the Gospels, three of which occur during the Last Supper and are linked to the spilling of Jesus' blood.

Does this mean that Jesus was not concerned for his people, or was his message being heard in circles that were more cosmopolitan? What did Jesus do for Israel's hopes, for the widely shared longing for national and religious restoration? What role does Israel play as the chosen people with whom God has entered an eternal alliance? What everyone knows and shares does not need to be repeated constantly, the chosen people of Israel and the covenant with God do not seem to rank among Jesus' primary concerns.

As we have already pointed out (see 4.5.3.3), Jesus spent almost all of his time in Israel with his people, but his main aim was not the restoration of Israel. This was Elijah's aim, as typified by certain texts, above all Malachi 3:24 ("He [Elijah] shall reconcile parents with children and children with parents"), Sirach 48:10 ("You [Elijah] who are ready at the appointed time . . . to restore the tribes of Jacob"), and Mark 9:12 ("Elijah does come first to restore all things"). Jesus' main aim was not to rectify the worship in the temple, though at the end of his life he did protest, prophetically, at the way the institution worked, having become a marketplace and driven by consumerism. Even lower on Jesus' list of aims was his desire to become a political leader to head a movement to expel the Romans, the people's oppressors. When he talked about the end of history, Jesus did not envisage God's judgment as the moment for Israel's restoration, or its victory over the pagan peoples, its enemies. He envisaged it as a banquet where everyone (Jews and non-Jews) could share a table with Abraham, Isaac, and

Jacob, Israel's patriarchs: even the "sons of the kingdom," the members of the people of Israel, are warned that they may be left outside (Matt 8:12 || Luke 13:28-29.)

As B. Chilton and C. A. Evans point out, in the incident in the synagogue in Nazareth related in Luke (4:16-30), his compatriots react violently to Jesus when they realize what his intentions are and what his mission is. Again according to Luke 4, Jesus quotes Isaiah 61:1-2, stating that the words of the prophet are fulfilled "today" with the arrival of "the acceptable year of the Lord." It has arrived for everyone, however: not just for the Jews. This is the case of the Phoenician woman whom Elijah protected, even resurrecting her son, and the case of the Syrian leper healed by Elisha. Foreigners also received the divine blessing, as is made clear by the healings of the Syrophoenician woman's daughter (Mark 7:24-30) and the Samaritan leper (Luke 17:11-19). As a result, the Kingdom brings with it restoration, renovation, and transformation, which includes the people of Israel, the primary recipient ("the children" according to the terminology in Mark 7:27), but which also includes those who do not belong to this people ("the dogs" according to this same source).

Jesus' concern for non-Jews and their reciprocal devotion to him can be seen clearly in the events of the healing of the centurion's servant in Capernaum (Matt 8:5-13 || Luke 7:1-10). The centurion shows his complete confidence in Jesus' healing powers and his ability to control the illness thanks to the strength of his words. Jesus admires the man's attitude and publicly praises him, saying, "I tell you, not even in Israel have I found such faith" (Luke 7:9). Pagans are not excluded from Jesus' project. Indeed, on occasions, they even outdo the children of Israel, the people of the covenant (see 5.2.2.3).

Jesus also emphasizes a specific, personal, and inclusive view of Israel, integrating those who are marginalized; marginalized of their own volition or because they have been forced into this position. For Jesus, Israel means "all Israel," each and every one of Abraham's children, without any kind of exception. Primarily, Jesus sees himself as an emissary for those who most need him: the sinners, the spiritually ill (Mark 2:17), the poor, who live in hunger, sadness, and hopelessness (Luke 6:20-21), the physically and psychologically sick (Matt 11:5 || Luke 7:22; Luke 13:32). Obviously, those who observe the Law, the good Jews are not excluded from the Kingdom: God is "your

Father in heaven, . . . he makes his sun rise on the evil and on the good" (Matt 5:45).

Nonetheless, the truth is that Jesus' message has a special effect and reception among the sinners, such as the tax collectors and prostitutes, more so than among those who do not feel the need to repent (Matt 21:31) (see 5.2.2). This was the case with the Baptist as well, who pitied those who were overconfident because they were the children of Abraham and did not bother to enter fully into the profound changes in their lives that he preached (Matt 3:8-9 || Luke 3:8). Belonging to the people of Israel and/or keeping strictly to the commandments of the Law could not be used as an excuse for not paying heed to the great news of the presence of a righteous, liberating God, the beginning of his reign, and the renewal that this meant for the hearts, bodies, and spirits of many.

Jesus did not distance himself from Israel's hopes, but his aim was not the restoration of his people as understood by many groups and circles at the time. Jesus used an inclusive and diffusive concept of Israel. The poor, the sick, and the sinners, those ignorant of the Law, and the children were not marginalized; they were made the focus and given the places of honor at the banquet of the Kingdom. This banquet, furthermore, was not going to exclude foreigners, as God's salvation went beyond the borders of Israel and reached, even though not immediately, those who were not Jews. Jesus, the Jewish rabbi, held his people in his heart and, faced with the rejection he received, it is not surprising the way he felt. This was the case in Jerusalem, the city that represented Israel as a whole: "How often would I have gathered your children together as a hen gathers her brood under her wings" (Matt 23:37 || Luke 13:34). According to John (11:52), the aim of Jesus' life and death is no other than "to gather into one the children of God who are scattered abroad."

5.3.2. The Fulfillment of the Law

Jesus did not go against the Law that God had given the people of Israel on Mount Sinai. He did not contradict it or criticize it or disrespect it. Jesus went to the bottom of the Law, to the core of what made it what it was: the most important aspect being how to carry out God's will.

Nevertheless, would it not be enough to propose the same commandments and rules that teach each Jew how to be loyal to the covenant? Why does Jesus seek to revise the Law, to look again at the series of precepts that form it, and to establish degrees of importance among them? There is one answer to this: the focus of Jesus' message is the Kingdom of God. Thus, the Law cannot remain the same, it has to be "fulfilled" (Matt 5:17). This fulfillment is expressed in three ways: some points of the Law are reinforced (not superseded!), others are made relative (not annulled!), and the twofold commandment of love becomes the focal point for all the light that has to illuminate the world. For this reason, this commandment becomes the center of Jesus' ethics.

Once again we can see how Jesus moves within the framework of Judaism but how he also transcends it. His message contains the seeds that germinate in the life and customs of the early Christian communities.

5.3.2.1. Reinforcing the Ethical Rules

The bases for Jesus' ethics are the Ten Commandments, the Decalogue from Mount Sinai (Exod 20:2-17 || Deut 5:6-21). This can be seen in the answers that Jesus gives the scribe (Mark 12:29-34 || Matt 22:34-40 || Luke 10:25-28) and the rich man who wants eternal life (Mark 10:17-22 || Matt 19:16-22 || Luke 18:18-23). Putting the Ten Commandments into practice meant fulfilling life. The Decalogue inspires the covenant that God makes with Israel on Mount Sinai ("you shall be my own possession among all peoples") and sets out the commitment made by the people, unanimously, to God ("all that the Lord has spoken we will do") (Exod 19:5, 19:8).

For the people of Israel, the basis of the commandments is God's love for his people. For Jesus, living in accordance with the Kingdom is based on a God who is compassionate and forgiving. This can be seen in Mark (1:15), which announces great and good news ("the kingdom of God is at hand") and which is followed by a call to repent and have faith ("repent and believe in the gospel [good news]"). The question is the same in both cases, in the First Testament and asked by Jesus:

what does God want from mankind, both the people of Israel and the other peoples on earth?

Love God with all your heart

The news that God has started to make himself manifest in the world, personally and directly, distinctly and definitively, is the starting point for Jesus' message. Jesus holds God before all else. The first of the Ten Commandments is explicitly reinforced; proclaiming the Kingdom means putting God first, making him mankind's principal aspiration and longing. The scene where the scribe asks Jesus "which commandment is the first of all?" shows Jesus' inner conviction: the first commandment from the Decalogue is also the most important commandment for Jesus (Mark 12:28-34).

Jesus does not, however, quote the biblical text of the Ten Commandments here (Exod 20 or Deut 5); instead he responds with a liturgical prayer that every Jew, including Jesus, recites daily in the synagogue: *Shema Yisrael.* This fragment, which is considered very holy by all Jews, is taken from Deuteronomy 6:4-5 and starts thus: "Hear, O Israel: the Lord our God is one Lord." These words are followed a moment later by the imperative: "[Y]ou shall love the Lord your God with all your heart, and with all your soul [with all your thoughts], and with all your might." For the Jewish religion, and for Jesus, this is the "first of all" the commandments (Mark 12:29).

The Decalogue contains, by way of "explanation" of the first commandment, a prohibition that echoes in Jesus' teachings: "You shall have no other gods before me" (Exod 20:3 || Deut 5:7). On a number of occasions, the gospel tradition contains phrases that insist on the unique nature of the God of the patriarchs and the Exodus, the God that Jesus refers to as the Father of mankind. Thus, when the Q collection refers to the temptation of Christ, it does so with a version of the aforementioned phrase taken from Deuteronomy 6:13: "You shall worship the Lord your God and him only shall you serve" (Matt 4:10 || Luke 4:8; also Exod 20:5 || Deut 5:9). Regarding the tribute to be paid to Caesar (see 3.3.3.2), Jesus seeks to stress God's rights and places all the weight of his answer on the need to put him before all else and to worship him with all your heart: "Render . . . to God the things that are God's" (Mark 12:17 || Matt 22:21 || Luke 20:25). Even when someone calls Jesus "good teacher," he replies quickly saying, "Why do you call me good? No one is good but God alone" (Mark 10:18 || Luke 18:19; Matt 19:17 differs slightly).

There is nothing and no one that can be placed on the same level as God. The prohibition in the Decalogue of having and serving other gods is set in sharp contrast with the specific name of the idol that personifies money: Mammon. Alternating between the two is out of the question: "you cannot serve God and mammon" (Matt 6:24 || Luke 16:13). People cannot carry in their hearts anyone other than God. The god of money, no matter how mighty he may be, has to submit to the one and only God. Jesus reinforces the love of God by highlighting what may appear in its place in a person's heart.

Love your neighbor as yourself

The great surprise is that loving others becomes the second most important commandment for Jesus' way of thinking. In comparison to the Decalogue, we can see that this point undergoes an important change with respect to the Jewish Law. In Exodus (20) and Deuteronomy (5), the first three commandments are reserved for God: adore, love, and worship the one and only God; do not take his name in vain; and rest on the Sabbath. Then come the commandments that refer to relations with other people: honor your father and your mother, do not kill, do not commit adultery, do not steal, do not bear false witness, and do not covet your neighbor's wife or belongings. We should note that the commandments relating to others are all negative ("do not do this or that") and the only positive rule is honoring your parents. The Decalogue, however, does not say anything positive about "neighborliness," about others in general.

Jesus turns to the book of Leviticus for the commandment that he deems to be the second most important in the Law. It comes from a varied list of precepts, which begin with a call to take part in God's holiness ("You shall be holy; for I the Lord your God am holy"). In terms of its literary structure, the second commandment strictly follows the first: "love your neighbor as yourself" (Lev 19:18). Jesus uses this in his answer to the scribe who asks him about the most important commandment, "the first of all" of them (Mark 12:28-34). The Master answers the question, stating that the most important commandment is the one that requires us to love God with all our heart; but he goes on to say, "The second [commandment] is this, 'You shall love your neighbor as yourself.'" In order to hammer home the point, he adds, "There is no commandment greater than these" (Mark 12:31)/"On these two commandments depend all the Law and the prophets" (Matt 22:40).

This is a very important contribution, and fundamental to Christianity. Two commandments, loving God and one another, are set together and in a precise ranking as the first and second commandments of the Law. We can see that, for Jesus, "loving your neighbor" means loving everyone, including those of other races, groups, or ideologies, and even our persecutors, those who place obstacles in our way, our enemies (Matt 5:44). Loving and affectionate relationships with others, whomever they might be, are brought to the forefront and, thus, highly valued. With the commandment to love your neighbors as you would yourself, Jesus reinforces the Law, as he relates the idea of our neighbors to that of mankind as a whole (see 5.3.2.3, below).

Do not swear

In Matthew (5:34-35) and James (5:12), Jesus is seen to prohibit swearing. In the latter text, it says, "do not swear, either by heaven or by earth or with any other oath." Likewise in Matthew, any kind of oath is also prohibited, "either by heaven, for it is the throne of God, or by the earth, for it is his footstool, or by Jerusalem, for it is the city of the great King." Under no circumstances must the name of God be used to add weight or veracity to one's words, as if these words might be made more "true" than any others by adding an oath. It makes no odds whether one swears by God or any other element related to him (heaven, earth, Jerusalem), which might "lessen" the strength of the oath. People must not swear, says Jesus, because God cannot be used to take sides. Jesus' opposition to oaths is head-on and complete: "Do not swear at all" (Matt 5:34). According to Jesus, those who swear take God's name in vain, and thus break the Law.

What does the Decalogue say on the matter? It does not prohibit oaths in general, only false testimony, perjury: "You shall not take the name of the Lord your God in vain" (Exod 20:7 || Deut 5:11). Perjury is a direct and serious affront to God's majesty, as those who use God's name in vain mix their own lies with what is true and the source of all truth. There is, then, a "risk" in swearing, as the lie may spread and supplant, in part or completely, the truth, and this represents an attack on God's holiness. For this reason, the Book of the Sirach (2nd c. B.C.) warns against getting used to swearing: "[T]he man who always swears and utters the Name will not be cleansed from sin" (23:10). Philo of Alexandria (1st c. A.D.) writes along similar lines, but as almost throughout all the Jewish tradition, he does not prohibit oaths; instead as a lesser evil, he recommends the use of expressions that do not involve the name of God (heaven, earth, etc.; see Spec. Laws 2 3–5). The Essenes used oaths in exceptional circumstances; for example, when someone had to be accepted into the community (Community Rule 5:8); but it would seem that they tried to avoid their use in general. Josephus says on the matter, "Swearing is avoided by them, and they esteem it worse than perjury for they say that he who cannot be believed without [swearing by] God is already condemned" (*J.W.* 2:135).

Jesus himself is even stricter: "Let what you say be simply 'Yes' or 'No'" (Matt 5:37; Jas 5:12). For those who speak the truth, oaths are unnecessary. Furthermore, those who invoke the name of God damage his holiness. Those who speak the truth share in his holiness and do not need to use the name of God to reinforce their own words. As a result, according to Jesus, despite the Law's allowing the use of oaths, we should not swear. By opposing oaths, Jesus is not breaking the Law, he is simply reinforcing it, by reinforcing people's commitment to the truth. Indeed, those who do not swear do so because they live in accordance with the wishes of a true God and a God of truth, in their words and in their deeds. Normally, there is no need or reason to swear in everyday life. Only on very special occasions, when one has to declare before a tribunal or when one enters public office, when an oath becomes a legal requirement, is it no longer a personal decision. Swearing is a concession to one's own hardness of heart. The only time one can legitimately invoke God is in prayer. By prohibiting oaths, Jesus safeguards the truth and preserves God's holiness.

Honor your father and your mother

The first commandment in the Decalogue regarding interpersonal relations is honor your father and your mother. Those who fulfill this commandment are guaranteed a long and happy life "in the land which the Lord your God gives you" (Exod 20:12 || Deut 5:16). The Gospels emphasize that the infant Jesus was an obedient child (Luke

2:51). This observation needs to be put in the context of the incident when Jesus, on a pilgrimage to Jerusalem at the age of twelve, stayed in the city without his parents knowing. Anxious as to his whereabouts, they had to turn back to find him. As a young man and adult, until he was over thirty, Jesus lived at home in Nazareth with his parents and, following Joseph's death, with his mother Mary. Jesus dutifully kept to the commandment to honor his father, whose side he was at until his death, and his mother, whom he cared for and supported until she was about fifty.

Once over the age of thirty Jesus left home and left his mother in the care of his brothers and sisters, Joseph's children. In his life that followed, his contact with his mother was only sporadic. The Gospels mention that his mother and brothers visited him in Capernaum, the center of his activities, and a visit by the Master with his disciples to Nazareth, his hometown. Thereafter, mother and son came together again in Jerusalem, at the end of his life (see 4.5.3.2).

Jesus' activities led to a physical distancing from Nazareth and the start of an itinerant lifestyle, in which he and his disciples had to leave the care of their mothers and fathers in the hands of others. Distancing from his own flesh and blood family came after his discovery of a new family, made up of the disciples. The family links to people (father, mother, children, brothers, and sisters) and possessions (fields) were superseded by new family links; those who have to leave their mother "for my sake [Jesus] and the gospel" shall find a hundred (Mark 10:29-30 || Matt 19:29 || Luke 18:29-30); but those who leave their father do not need to look for another because they already have the Father in heaven, God himself (Matt 23:9; Luke 2:49).

When someone decides to follow Jesus and become a disciple of his, family duties, starting with the love and honor of his or her mother and father, are relegated to the background (though not made completely obsolete!), as can be seen in the Gospels (Luke 14:26 || Matt 10:37). The Q collection explains the case of a man who wanted to first go and bury his father before going off to follow Jesus, but he received a cutting response: "leave the dead to bury their own dead" (Matt 8:22 || Luke 9:60). His father is dead and thus the time to honor him has passed; there are more urgent matters at hand! The only absolute is God and his Kingdom, which have to be proclaimed and communicated. The first commandment of the Law is to love him with all your heart and above all else. Honoring your mother and father is not to be belittled or forgotten, but Jesus relegates this below what is at the heart of life: love of God and the commitment to his Kingdom.

Jesus does not invalidate the commandment to honor your father and mother; rather he values it and even denounces certain attempts to undermine it. The most obvious attempt was the application of the so-called corban (i.e., "offering to God") Law, mentioned above (5.3.1.2), by means of which sons and daughters could get out of their obligations to their parents scot-free (Mark 7:10-13 || Matt 15:4-6). The temple provided a pitiful way out. If the children made a public declaration regarding their father and mother ("What you would have gained from me is Corban [consecrated to God]"), the possessions that could have been used to help them are assigned to it. Nevertheless, what was theoretically consecrated to God was never actually handed over to the temple treasury.

The practice of *corban* represented an abuse that Jesus and some rabbis denounced, as it aided the breaking of one of God's commandments. Jesus, who wanted just the opposite (to reinforce the Law's ethical regulations), reacted energetically against this practice that undermined and nullified one of the commandments. Not helping one's father and mother equates to hurting them, and those who hurt their own parents deserve the most severe of punishments (Exod 21:17, quoted in Mark 7:10). On the other hand, honoring one's father and mother forms part of the Law's second commandment: love your neighbor as yourself. This is how it is interpreted in the Gospel according to Matthew in the incident involving the rich man who has kept to all the commandments and whom Jesus invites to follow him (19:19). For Jesus, the Decalogue is the path that leads to people being able to enjoy an eternal happy life, and one of the guidelines to follow on this path is honoring your father and mother (Mark 10:19 || Matt 19:19 || Luke 18:20).

Do not kill

The prohibition of taking someone else's life is forcefully stipulated in Moses' Law. Murder is strictly forbidden, as it is the most serious crime that can be committed against another. Killing is an irreversible action, the final and complete aggression. Those who kill break the Law (Exod 20:13 || Deut 5:17); and, according to the Law, they deserve to be "put to death" (Exod 21:12 || Lev 24:17; Num 35:16-18). Jesus quotes the commandment from the Decalogue but later avoids having to talk about the death penalty, saying, "whoever kills shall be liable to judgment" (Matt 5:21). He does not talk about the death penalty as a necessary or automatic consequence and guides the questions toward the great many nuances that usually accompany an event as serious as killing or murder. These nuances are included in the Law of Moses under the terms involuntary or unintentional homicide and the institution of the cities of refuge (Exod 21:13; Num 35:10-15). Jesus stresses that all killings have to be judged and condemned, but he does not say what punishment they deserve.

He was concerned not with killings but with what led to them and what made them inevitable. Jesus was not interested in the penalties deriving from breaking the Law but with the causes that lead to them and, as a result, with what can be done to avoid these situations. The main question does not concern knowing what has to be avoided but rather how to avoid it. The rabbi Jesus wanted the Law to be feasible, and for this reason, he focused his attention on the three most serious sins: idolatry, murder, and adultery.

Jesus looked at the roots of the behavior patterns that could culminate in someone breaking the Law in such a serious way as killing someone else. There is a first step, an initial indecision that may seem innocuous, but which in fact has unforeseeable consequences. What is at the root of a killing? Jesus' answer is quite simple: heartfelt violence. A rabbi, Eliezer ben Hyrcanus, who lived at the end of the first century A.D., stated something similar: "Those who hate their neighbours, have to be considered murderers" (*Der. Er. Rab.* 11 [Yotse], 13). When hate enters one's heart, the destruction has begun, as hate does not normally remain inside and secret. Violence against others is expressed externally in a number of ways, sometimes seemingly inoffensively (an impatient word or a raised voice) and sometimes more ferociously (biting criticism or insults). Though "verbal aggression" against others can always be played down, Jesus does not treat violent words as any less important. On the contrary, in deliberately strong tones, he lifts the veil off harsh and disrespectful relationships, which hide a fundamental problem.

The text regarding murder is in Matthew (5:21-22), and it is the first of the so-called antitheses, literary forms that contrast two sentences. Jesus begins by quoting from the Law ("You have heard that it was said to the men of old") and then offers his point of view ("But I say to you"). These antitheses are in Matthew (5:21-47). With regard to murder, Jesus quotes the commandment from the Law: "You shall not kill; and whoever kills shall be liable to judgement." He then continues, "But I say to you that everyone who is angry with his brother shall be liable to judgment." The same punishment is deserved by those who are angry with someone else: they are to be brought before the courts! In other words, it is just as serious to be angry with someone as it is to kill him or her. There is one simple reason for this: the anger that sprouts from someone's mouth is a root cause for killings. The three types of violence (of the heart, mouth, and hands) are triggered one by the other. Those who do not want to reach the third of these (hands that kill) should not fall into the trap of the second (words that kill).

The violence of words can lead to things worse than anger: insults. Those who insult other people (literally: "anyone who says to his brother 'Raca'") shall be liable to the Sanhedrin, that is, the great council in charge of the most important matters. Finally, if someone curses someone else, "whoever says 'You fool!' [literally: rebel against God, they are asking God to have them killed] shall be liable to the fire of hell." Insults and curses are close to killings and deserve a particularly strong warning. Those who curse bring on themselves the eternal death that they had demanded for the other. Jesus calls on God himself in an attempt to show the seriousness of verbal aggression against others. Wrath is a poison that seriously damages interpersonal relations when it gets into our hearts; indeed, it is an underground form of killing. Personal relationships are at the heart of Jesus' ethics, and reinforcing these is a way of avoiding killings in all their forms.

The opposite is true of reconciliation with the other person, after offence has been caused and damage made to the bridges of friendship and understanding. Closing a wound created by irritation, insult, or even cursing (the desire to see them dead) is not easy. There is always the problem of making the first step and who has to make it. It would seem reasonable to assume that the person causing the offence asks for forgiveness and that the wounded party expects to receive the corresponding satisfaction. This may be why there are arguments and discussions that are never resolved! For Jesus, the vindication of the person offended becomes a reason to offer forgiveness and reconciliation. This can be seen clearly in the narrative of the Galilean who goes to the altar in the temple in Jerusalem to make an offering and remembers that he has offended someone, so he travels four hundred kilometers (!) there and back to reconcile himself with this person. We can see the subtle sense of humor that typifies Jesus, the rabbi of Nazareth (Matt 5:23-24), and the fact that he is right. It is more important to reestablish relations with someone else than it is to present God with an offering of a lamb or flour. God is in no hurry and can wait for the man to return to Jerusalem to present his offering, but he cannot live with those who have burnt their bridges of friendship.

Forgiveness offered to other people is vital in Jesus' message as it is seen to be an essential condition for the safeguarding of the second commandment ("you shall love your neighbor as yourself"). The only commitment contained in the Lord's Prayer is that "we ourselves forgive every one who is indebted to us" (Luke 11:4 || Matt 6:12). Jesus proposes limitless and reiterated forgiveness, to counteract the weakness that characterizes relations between people. He uses powerful words to reinforce his point: "[I]f he sins against you seven times in the day, and turns to you seven times, and says, 'I repent,' you must forgive him" (Luke 17:4; in Matt 18:22 the number is multiplied, becoming "seventy times seven"). Jesus' ethics are positive and extreme, where the commandment not to kill becomes a commandment to love one another, where heartfelt violence is replaced by a forgiveness that encourages us to start again.

Do not commit adultery

Relations between a man and a woman are at the center of what Jesus has to say about divorce and adultery. As Jesus sought to safeguard people from heartfelt violence through the fifth commandment ("do not kill"), with respect to the sixth commandment ("do not commit adultery") he wanted to protect the fidelity between men and women who share the same life purpose. Jesus showed himself to be a firm believer in the defense of conjugal relations between men and women, and his position differs from that of other Jewish groups and trends of the time, even from that of the Essenes at Qumran, who were also fairly strict in terms of divorce. Jesus strongly valued couples' relationships and the union between men and women as, for him, they were based on the project designed by God himself. For this reason, he did not accept the idea of divorce.

Divorce is, however, allowed by the Law of Moses. This is pointed out to Jesus by some Pharisees who want to trip him up on a particularly sensitive point: his stand against divorce. The scene is in Mark 10:2-9 (|| Matt 19:3-8). Jesus' response to the comments from the Pharisees is anything but evasive. The Pharisees themselves are the ones who state that Moses gave permission "to write a certificate of divorce, and to put her away" (Mark 10:4). Deuteronomy 24:1 says that a man can act thus with his wife if "he has found some indecency in her." This ambiguous expression allows for a wide range of interpretations. According to the rabbi Akiba and the school of the rabbi Hillel, a man could divorce his wife "for any cause" (Matt 19:3): because he felt attracted to another woman or even because of his wife's cooking! The rabbi Shammai was against this position, believing the husband could divorce his wife only if she committed adultery; this would be the only "indecency" alluded to in Deuteronomy 24:1 (Matt 5:32 and 19:9). The cases mentioned here are taken from the Mishnah (*Git.* 9:10) and refer only to the man, as the Law of Moses did not allow women to divorce.

Jesus distanced himself from the debate among the rabbis of the time and, to the surprise of all of them, denied what the Law tolerated or allowed: divorce. First, he stated that the Law on divorce was established "for your hardness of heart." Thus, it was people's own failures that made it inevitable. His second observation was that divorce did not enter God's original plans. Since the creation of the world, there had been a divine project for men and women, who were called to become "one flesh," one thing, invited to form a faithful relationship, not destined to destroy it. Jesus quoted Genesis (2:24), "Therefore a man leaves his father and his mother and cleaves to his wife, and they become one flesh." The union between man and woman is based on God's own creation. According to Genesis (1:27), another text quoted by Jesus, God created human beings in his image, adding that "male and female he created them"; the relations between men and women are "from the beginning of creation," at the start of everything, and are a reflection of God's first wish. Matrimony, as a life project for men and women, exists since human beings began to walk on the earth, and it is God himself who encourages it. Thus, Jesus' final conclusion is authoritative and well-founded: "What therefore God has joined together, let not man put asunder" (Mark 10:9 || Matt 19:6).

Jesus' point of view reappears in the early Christian tradition. Paul, for example, says, "[T]he wife should not separate from her husband . . . the husband should not divorce his wife" (1 Cor 7:10-11). The reason given by Jesus is that divorce did not form part of God's original plan for men and women and that, if it was introduced by Moses, it was due to people's hardness of heart. Once again we see at the center of Jesus' ethics the importance of the heart and each person's most profound intentions as the key to their decisions and acts. In the commandment not to kill, the heart is seen to be the root cause of violence and where destruction of others begins. In the case of adultery, relations with the wife (or husband) of another are, above all, inspired by desire: "[E]very one who looks at a woman lustfully has already committed adultery with her in his heart" (Matt 5:28).

The Law stigmatized sexual relations with those who were already united to someone else. Jesus, however, looked at the causes of adultery, focusing on what led to the breaking of the Law. The first spark is the lustful look that leads to someone destroying someone else's marriage. Some rabbinical texts that postdate Jesus came back to this perspective. We can read in Leviticus Rabba 23:12 (18:3), "Adultery can be committed with the eyes"; similarly, in Pesiqta Rabbati 24 (18:3), "Even those who commit adultery with their eyes have to be considered adulterers." The Decalogue itself ends with a commandment regarding desire, which, among other things, says, "you shall not covet your neighbor's wife" (Exod 20:17 || Deut 5:21).

Heartfelt fidelity, which can overcome desire, is vital in ensuring faithful eyes and, ultimately, faithful actions. Adultery builds up inside people before being consummated. Jesus states that there is an "adultery in the heart," before it takes place in the body. If one's heart can confront and overcome the hardness (Mark 10:5) and not commit adultery, when moved by the desire to possess someone else's partner (Matt 5:28), if someone can maintain love and fidelity in their eyes and heart, then God's original plan can be fulfilled. The prophet Malachi offers a statement along these lines: "I hate divorce, says the Lord the God of Israel" (2:16).

The eyes are the antennae of desire and can lead us to break the Law or into temptation. Jesus offers two pieces of "advice," in an exaggerated and ironic tone, which show his point of view with regard to the seriousness of the question: pull out your right eye and cut off your right hand. Here is the sentence about the eye: "If your right eye causes you to sin, pluck it out and throw it away; it is better that you lose one of your members than that your whole body be thrown into hell" (Matt 5:29; similarly, Mark 9:47). The eye is one of the most useful and valuable parts of the body, and of our two eyes, the one on the right is considered to hold the place of honor. Losing it would be a great loss, but losing oneself forever is irreparable. Having both eyes is of little use if your whole body is to be lost forever. We must sacrifice whatever is required, no matter how valuable it may seem, before falling victim to uncontrolled desire, in terms of sexuality or anything else. This is the meaning of this striking image.

Would it not then be better (in order to be able to keep both eyes!) to avoid all contact with those people who could inspire desire and lead to sin? More than one rabbi advised that men should not look at other women, so as to avoid the inherent "dangers." Ben Sirach says, "Turn your eyes away from a shapely woman, and do not look intently at beauty belonging to another" (9:8). According to Jewish Law, the menstrual cycle leads to women being in a frequent state of ritual impurity, which can be transmitted if one comes into physical contact with them. In Jesus' case, all these extremes do not seem to have any importance. His dealings with women are characterized by either a complete naturalness or a carefulness in line with the strict social norms. Among those in his closest circles there was a former prostitute, Mary Magdalene, who followed him as a disciple right up to the end. Likewise, women, whether single or married, played an active part in his group. Purity of heart, distanced from any desire to possess, seems to be the best way to understand the beliefs and practices of Jesus and his group when it came to the viability, and the importance, of relationships and friendships between men and women.

In the light of the above, we can see how Jesus links divorce and adultery, as both constitute an "attack" on God's original project. His statements on the question are direct, cutting, and (why hide the fact?) somewhat discomforting: "Whoever divorces his wife and marries another, commits adultery against her" (Mark 10:11 || Matt 19:9; also

Luke 16:18; also Matt 5:32 || Luke 16:18). Obviously, what is at stake is not divorce in itself, but the subsequent remarriage. For this reason, Paul states that if the wife leaves her husband "let her remain single or else be reconciled to her husband" (1 Cor 7:11). The only exceptions to a second marriage found in the Christian communities are when a non-Christian wants to separate from his or her Christian partner (1 Cor 7:15) and, above all, when there are illegitimate extramatrimonial relations (Matt 5:32 and 19:9).

In short, the prohibition of divorce and remarriage is one of the most surprising and courageous proposals to be found in Jesus' ethics. The definitive reason for what may be deemed an unrealistic proposal is the great trust that Jesus places in people's ability to successfully respond to God's project for marriage. Divorce ultimately represents the failure and defeat of his project and his will. Likewise, as U. Luz points out in his commentary on Matthew, the triumph of the faithfulness of the heart over the desire for possession outside of marriage equates to honoring and safeguarding God's holiness. Finally, a legislation such as that of the Jewish religion that allows a man, but not a woman, to divorce, and on occasion for somewhat trivial reasons, places women at the complete mercy of their husbands. In this way, the emphasis that Jesus places on God's original plan, according to which man and woman were created and viewed as two beings destined to come together in one relationship, stresses their equality with respect to each other.

Do not steal

The commandment not to steal occupies a somewhat discreet place in Jesus' ethics. The subject of taking possessions from someone else attracts little attention from the rabbi of Nazareth. The fifth and sixth commandments, which affect people's relationships ("do not kill" and "do not commit adultery") are much more important to Jesus. The seventh commandment does not directly affect people's relationships; instead, it focuses on their possessions and assets. This is maybe why it is relegated to the background. The same can be said of contemporary and later Jewish rabbis. Jesus contrasts riches to the Kingdom to the point that people have to make a decision between being a friend of God or of money. One of the most striking and well-known sentences refers to the difficulties that riches represent: "It is easier for a camel to go through the eye of the needle than for a rich man to enter the kingdom of God" (Mark 10:25 || Matt 19:24 || Luke 18:25).

Jesus said this to his disciples when a rich and pious man, who was both law-abiding and wealthy, decided not to follow him. Indeed, Jesus had reminded the rich man of the commandments in the Decalogue relating to others, which included, "you shall not steal" (Exod 20:15 || Deut 5:19; Mark 10:19 || Matt 19:18-19 || Luke 18:20). This man asked what he needed to do to gain eternal life, and Jesus replied that he, a law-abiding man, only needed to do one thing: get rid of his worldly goods, sell everything he had, and distribute it among the poor, so as to be able to share in Jesus' poor and itinerant lifestyle. Only thus would he be able to gain the greatest treasure of all, "treasure in heaven." For this rich man entering the Kingdom of God meant having to renounce everything he had; but he was unable to, as the lure of his worldly riches was stronger than that of the treasure in heaven, and he went away sad and dejected.

Life's aim is not to accumulate riches and guard over them jealously. According to Jesus' ethics, which focus on the Kingdom, possessions are something of a handicap. Jesus often spoke about simple people, those who lived in the countryside, people who were not rich and thus unlikely to fall into temptation because of avarice or greed. It was normally the people with a great many possessions, which may have been gained unjustly, who were the target for Jesus' words. A prime example was that of Zacchaeus, the chief tax collector in Jericho, who had gotten rich thanks to the fraud he had committed through his position. Jesus' coming to his house led to a retroactive fulfillment of the seventh commandment: Zacchaeus, touched to the core by Jesus' visit, said that he would return all the money he had defrauded multiplied by four (!), when all the Law required was that he return the money gained illegally with a fine of 20 percent. However, unlike the rich man who decided not to follow Jesus, Zacchaeus also understood the generosity inspired by the Kingdom and gave the poor half of what he owned. Jesus had freed him from his riches (Luke 19:8-10).

Zacchaeus put into practice the commandment not to steal and returned the money he had defrauded from people because he had undergone a change of heart and was no longer obsessed with the riches that had oppressed him up to then. He had always defended his possessions, even turning to theft and fraud, but now he understood that he could simply get rid of them. As Jesus says, "For where your treasure is, there will your heart be also" (Matt 6:21 || Luke 12:34). Once again, the heart is seen to be crucial to Jesus' ethics. Those who do not set their heart on worldly goods accept that these should be given to and shared with the poor, as they have their heart set on the riches in heaven (Matt 6:19-20 || Luke 12:33). Someone who is giving and generous will not be led astray by "unrighteous mammon" (Luke 16:9). Riches can be treacherous and at times useless, as in the case of the foolish rich man who planned to build a great barn to keep his excellent harvest in, believing that the time had come to take his ease, eat, drink, and be merry, only for him to die that same night (Luke 12:16-20).

It is a risk to set your heart on the riches of this world. There is a warning in the Decalogue: "you shall not covet your neighbor's house . . . or anything that is your neighbour's" (Exod 20:17 || Deut 5:21). Jesus insists on seeing money as an obstacle to entry to the Kingdom, and he proposes making use of it for the poor and needy, so that people with a free heart can set their sights on the treasures of heaven. In the end, it is a question not of stealing but rather of not becoming obsessed with money, one of the most powerful idols, since as Jesus says, "it is more blessed to give than to receive" (Acts 20:35).

Do not bear false witness

Jesus is a champion of righteousness and truth. His actions are never ambiguous; even his enemies acknowledge this. In Jerusalem, the Pharisees, allied to Herod's supporters, met Jesus in order to set a trap for him with regard to the payment of the tribute to Caesar. They began, however, by praising him: "Teacher, we know that you are true" (Mark 12:14 || Matt 22:16). Luke changes the sentence slightly, saying, "Teacher, we know that you speak and teach rightly" (20:21). Beyond an attempt to flatter Jesus with words that could be used against him, this sentence also reflects a common and shared feeling that Jesus was a man who spoke without lies or deception. His words had the authority of being right and truthful. Even when he criticized his competitors and/or adversaries, he always expressed himself truthfully. His teachings formed part of his life and his behavior.

In Jesus' life there are no situations (or at least no record of any situations) where he is falsely accused. Only before the Sanhedrin does the Gospel of Mark say that "someone stood up and bore false witness" against Jesus (Mark 14:57). However, Jesus had actually announced the destruction of the temple in Jerusalem; so, rather than bearing false testimony, the witnesses probably harbored evil intentions in their statements against him in order to justify his being condemned to death (Mark 14:55-56 || Matt 26:59-60). Ironically, the Sanhedrin, the maximum authority on the Law, is presented as the body encouraging the "false witness" and, thus, encouraging the breaking of the eighth commandment from the Decalogue: "you shall not bear false witness against your neighbor" (Exod 20:16 || Deut 5:20).

Jesus' most important statement regarding truthful words comes at the end of the antithesis that talks about oaths (Matt 5:33-37). We have commented on the commandment not to swear earlier in this section, showing how Jesus closed the door to the possibility of swearing that the Law had left open. Honest and truthful words do not leave any possibility for lies. There is no need then to swear. There is enough in simply saying yes, when it is yes, and no, when it is no, regardless of the situation and circumstances. The truth of one's words is the best guarantee when it comes to fulfilling the Law's eighth commandment. False accusation always comes from the desire to lie, from a heart that is not true, from fear or self-interest, permanently or from time to time. Jesus' answer to this lack of inner rectitude highlights the error in employing half-truths and, in turn, the integrity of sincere truthfulness: "let what you say be simply 'yes' or 'no.'" Words have their own worth, to the extent that they can lead to life or death. Words save and condemn. Jesus stresses that all words are important and that "every careless word they utter" (calumny or insult) will be brought to account (Matt 12:36-37). Good words, which console and construct, are born within people, in their hearts. Evil intentions, which lead to hurting and upsetting people, are also born in the heart (Mark 7:21-22). "Out of the abundance of the heart the mouth speaks" (Matt 12:34 || Luke 6:45). Good and evil find ways into the hearts of each of us and are translated into our words and deeds. The fruit gives us an insight into the tree: a good tree must bear good fruit. In the words of Jesus, grapes are not harvested from thorns, or figs from thistles. We can get an insight into people from the fruits they produce (Matt 7:16-17 || Luke 6:43-44).

5.3.2.2. The Relative Nature of the Ritual Rules

Jesus' prioritizing of the ethical rules contrasts with the importance he ascribes to the ritual rules and those for worship. In Jesus' eyes, the ethical dimension is fundamental. As G. Theissen points out, Jesus follows the line of Israel's great prophets, who denounce worship without justice, offering a great many victims in sacrifice without paying attention to those in need. Similarly, Jesus makes people the focus of attention, and not the often meticulous ritual observance prescribed by the Law and the scribes.

The Sabbath

Among the commandments from the Decalogue that refer to God, one refers to the Sabbath rest (Exod 20:8-11 || Deut 5:12-15). The Sabbath is a day set apart from the rest of the days of the week, as "the seventh day is a Sabbath to the Lord your God." God has given man six days that can be used in any way they want ("six days you shall labor and do all your work"), and man has to respond by dedicating the seventh day to God and resting. The Sabbath is a hallmark of Judaism in the first century, for those living in Israel and those living in the Diaspora, within the borders of the Roman Empire or beyond. Jews were distinguished from other peoples because they observed a day of complete rest every seven days.

According to Jewish tradition, however, it was an active rest, marked by prayer, outer calm, and heartfelt peace. No business or commerce could take place on the Sabbath, nor work in the fields, such as plowing or harvesting. Only short journeys were allowed on the day of rest, and domestic tasks had to be left for another day (such as going for firewood, starting the fire, and kneading dough). In short, nothing that could be considered "work" was allowed. In very strict areas, such as near Qumran, the number of activities that were prohibited increased: maintaining sexual relations, talking about business, lifting weights, loading an animal, sailing, hunting, and making war (*Jubilees* 50:6-13). Indeed, one of the great questions regarding the Sabbath affected the legitimacy of defending oneself with weapons if attacked or, simply, having to accept death, as was the case with one thousand Jews at the time of Antiochus IV Epiphanes (2nd c.

B.C.) who refused to violate the Sabbath (1 Macc 2:29-41). The Sabbath is sacred to the Jewish people.

There were two reasons for these rules regarding the Sabbath. First, sabbatical rest reminded people of the rest taken on the seventh day of creation: "[F]or in six days the Lord made heaven and earth, the sea, and all that is in them, and rested the seventh day" (Exod 20:11). Second, the Sabbath was a day consecrated to God, so that the people of Israel could remember that thanks to him they were freed from slavery in Egypt: "You shall remember that you were a servant in the land of Egypt, and the Lord your God brought you out thence with a mighty hand and an outstretched arm" (Deut 5:15). The rest on the Sabbath is a sign of thanksgiving and acknowledgment to God for his love of mankind, in creating the world, and for Israel, in freeing them from oppression. Each week, there is a visible sign of Israel's love for God; the Sabbath is a holy day offered up to a holy God.

Jesus had been brought up in the observance of the Sabbath and kept to it throughout his life, just like any other Jew of the time (see 3.3.1). There was no invitation to needlessly go against the Sabbath rest in his teachings. He did not take the Sabbath rest to be meaningless. The Sabbath was also observed by Jesus' disciples. Nevertheless, the question that affects the rabbi of Nazareth is what it means, to him, to observe the Sabbath rest. What activities are allowed on the day of the week consecrated for God? The stances adopted by different groups on this point vary greatly: the Essenes and Sadducees stand by strict regulations, while the Pharisees, and above all Jesus, show themselves to be much more tolerant. Jesus did not make the Sabbath rest something absolute. Unlike the Pharisees, who sought to adapt the rules on the Sabbath to life's different circumstances, he went to the root of the question: the importance of people (their life and health) above that of the law on the Sabbath rest. The Sabbath was not ignored, but it was made relative.

Jesus even created controversy with regard to the Pharisee interpretation of the Sabbath rest. We should remember that, of the fourteen miracles narrated in the Gospels (see 5.2.1), five took place on the Sabbath: the man with the withered hand (Mark 3:1-6 || Matt 12:9-14 || Luke 6:6-11) and the hunchback woman (Luke 13:10-17) were healed in a synagogue, while the man with dropsy (Luke 14:1-6), the paralytic man at Bethzatha (John 5:1-16), and the blind man from birth (John 9:1-41) were healed in other places. In other words, a third of the healings narrated in the Gospels (but none of the exorcisms) took place on the weekly day of rest, the day consecrated to God. This is no coincidence. Jesus wanted to heal a number of chronically ill people on the Sabbath, whom he could easily have cured on any other day of the week, and the protests from the head of the synagogue seem perfectly justified: "There are six days on which work ought to be done; come on those days and be healed; and not on the Sabbath day" (Luke 13:14). With regard to the healings, the Pharisees and their associates interpreted the law on Sabbath rest as a prohibition of activity and, for this reason, they came into conflict with Jesus. The Gospel of Mark mentions that some Pharisees went to the synagogue in Capernaum to spy on Jesus "to see whether he would heal him [the man with a withered hand] on the Sabbath" (Mark 3:2). So, it was well known that Jesus healed people on the day of rest.

Why did Jesus insist on healing people on the Sabbath and thus upset and anger the Pharisees? Why could he not have shown himself to be more "flexible" and avoid coming into conflict with them? The healings on the Sabbath were linked to what Jesus had to say about God, to whom the Sabbath was dedicated, and his feeling of compassion for the sick and the needy, the first in line for the Kingdom that he proclaimed. For Jesus, returning someone to health, restoring someone, was a sign of the Kingdom. Healing a sick person was an expression of the arrival of God's salvation in his or her life and, thus, any day of the week was a good day for this person to be freed from the evil that oppressed him or her and to recuperate the dignified humanity shared by all mankind. This is the root of the question that Jesus asks the Pharisees and that they were unable to answer: "Is it lawful on the Sabbath to do good or to do harm, to save life or to kill?" (Mark 3:4 || Luke 6:9).

Indeed, if there was one day of the week on which good and life were reaffirmed, then that day was the day dedicated to God, lord of life and source of all righteousness. If healing is doing good and saving life, then the Sabbath is the ideal day for it, as the compassionate God is manifested as a friend to the sick through Jesus' healing activities. Healing on the Sabbath does not go against the day of rest but makes it nobler. In fact according to the Pharisee scribes, the Sabbath rest could be broken if someone's life was in danger, whether one's own or somebody else's: "Saving a life supersedes the *Shabbat* [Sabbath rest]" (Tosefta, *Šhab.* 15:11-16). Jesus reproached them, saying, "Which of you, having a son or an ox that has fallen into a well, will not immediately pull him out on a Sabbath day?" (Luke 14:5). Lifesaving emergencies are more important than the Sabbath; and healing is precisely this, saving someone's life, pulling him or her out of the dark well that seemingly has no end. Jesus applies this exception accepted by the Pharisees (saving lives that are in immediate danger) to illness, which he also sees as a life that has to be saved here and now, in terms of the urgency inspired by the Kingdom. A person's health is more important than the Law.

That people have to be the object of compassion and care, no matter what day it is, is made clear in the argument that compares people and domesticated animals. While the Essenes prohibited doing anything for an animal that had fallen into a well or pit on the Sabbath (*Damascus Document* 11:13-14), the Pharisee scribes allowed owners to rescue an ox or "a single sheep" (the only one they had!) from wells they had fallen into, as the loss of the animal would seriously hinder their meager finances (Luke 14:5; Matt 12:11). However, Jesus states, "Of how much more value is a man than a sheep! So it is lawful to do good on the Sabbath" (Matt 12:12). His reasoning is unquestionable. The comparison of people and domesticated animals is found again in the healing of the hunchback woman, who is oppressed by Satan and freed of her illness by Jesus on the Sabbath, since, "Does not each of you on the Sabbath untie his ox or his ass from the manger, and lead it away to water it?" (Luke 13:15). If this was not the case, the animal would die of dehydration, and its loss would no doubt have serious repercussions on its owner. Thus, it has to be much more reasonable to be able to heal on the Sabbath; there is a person's health at stake and this has to come before everything else.

Jesus offers his definitive opinion during the incident involving plucking heads of grain on the Sabbath: "The Sabbath was made for man, not man for the Sabbath" (Mark 2:27). A rabbi from the end of the second century A.D., Shimon ben Menasia, said something similar: "The Sabbath is holy for those who keep it. It is for you [the children of Israel] that the Sabbath has been given, and not you for the Sabbath" (Mekhilta of Rabbi Ishmael on Exod 31:13-14). In this case, the context is different. Jesus was not referring to the Law given on Sinai to the children of Israel but to any human being ("man") for whom the Sabbath has been made or created.

In the incident of the heads of grain (Mark 2:24-28 || Matt 12:1-8 || Luke 6:1-5), the exception to the day of rest had nothing to do with sick people but Jesus' famished disciples, who started to pluck heads of grain because they needed to eat. Faced with the expected question from the Pharisees, who saw the plucking of heads of grain as the equivalent of harvesting or "working," which is prohibited on the Sabbath, Jesus responded by saying that they were allowed, exceptionally, to see to their basic needs on the Sabbath, as was the case with David. Faced with the need to eat, he and his men resorted to the bread to be used as offerings and reserved for the priests. Here again, as was the case with the healings, a person's life is deemed more important than the Law. It is a case that affects the survival of human beings, and for this reason their lives, even though only "indirectly," are at stake, and life has to be protected at all costs. In Jesus' opinion, this idea justifies the disciples' plucking heads of corn on the Sabbath.

To sum up, Jesus places a person's life and his or her needs, whether for health or food, above all else. Jesus does not concern himself as to whether they are extreme cases, life-or-death situations, as he feels that "doing good" or "saving a life" is always an extreme case and handling them should never be limited by any kind of Law. The fact that a person needs help on the Sabbath should not act as an obstacle to action. The Sabbath, the day dedicated to God, remains a holy day for mankind, as God gave them this day to benefit them. God's compassion is unlimited, and barriers and prohibitions should not be placed in the way of his being able to show it. The arrival of the Kingdom means that its bearer, Jesus, God's emissary, relegates the Sabbath rest to the background. Jesus does not preach for the arbitrary breaking of this rest, which God wants, but he does make it subject to the needs of people, God's children. Despite the Sabbath laws being broken on exceptional occasions and thus being made relative, the Sabbath is ennobled, dedicated to goodness and life to benefit people.

Ritual purity

In the Jewish religion there are things that are not in harmony with God's holiness and that are thus impure. First, there are species of animals that are impure and cannot be offered in sacrifice to

God or eaten, such as the hare and pig (the list of pure and impure animals is in Lev 11:1-23 and Deut 14:3-21). Therefore, only pure or kosher animals (and food in general) are permitted. Second, there are people, animals, and objects that are a source of ritual impurity. Their impurity is spread by contact. Among these sources of ritual impurity are bodily secretions (semen, menstrual fluids, blood loss), skin diseases and infections (leprosy, burns, ringworm), sexual relations taking place under certain conditions, moldy houses or clothes, and coming into contact with bones or bodies.

If, through contact with a source of impurity, people or objects became ritually impure, then they had to be purified. Objects were washed with water or, if the impurity was irreversible, burned. People were purified by washing (Mark 7:4) or bathing themselves completely in what was known as the *mikvah* or pool designed for ritual bathing. Wherever there was an important Jewish community, there would be ritual baths. If they were not purified, the ritually impure could not enter the temple, nor were they allowed to touch other people. Others could not go near or touch them either. Ritual impurity was a source of religious and social ostracism.

The insistence of the Pharisees, and even more so the Essenes, on the rules regarding ritual impurity led to their keeping to them meticulously and to their convincing people that they had to observe them closely. The Pharisees were veritable apostles of ritual purity, and their tradition had increased the practices involving cleanliness as a sign of holiness that the people of Israel had to maintain. One such practice promoted by the Pharisees (which was not shared by all the trends in contemporary Judaism) was the rule of washing one's hands ritually before eating. Jesus' group certainly did not practice this, and the rabbis close to the Pharisees brought him up on the fact: "Why do your disciples not live according to the tradition of the elders, but eat with hands defiled?" (Mark 7:5). Nor does it seem that Jesus observed the Pharisee rule regarding entering the temple only after a ritual bathing (Oxyrhynchus 840, quoted in 2.1.2.4).

In fact, Jesus does not oppose the regulations on ritual purity in the Law of Moses; indeed, he respects them (the particular traditions of the different religious groups of the time, such as the Pharisees, are something completely different). The two healings of lepers in the Gospels (Mark 1:40-45; Luke 17:11-19) include an order from Jesus for those who have been healed to go to the priest to be examined for cleanliness, as required by the Law of Moses (Lev 14:1-32). The priest has to certify that the leper no longer has the illness, as only then can the leper take full part once again in society. Jesus commands the Galilean leper to present the offering "that Moses commanded" at the temple: animals for sacrifice, flour, and oil. However, in order to heal him, Jesus "touches" him as a sign of the purification taking place, something that was forbidden by the Law.

Though Jesus did not declare the Law's rules on ritual purity invalid, he did feel they were not as important as what a person held inside: the person's heartfelt intentions. According to Jesus' ethics (and the biblical tradition!), the heart is the center of thoughts, wishes, and decisions. This is where people's lives are played out. The heart is what "directs" the senses (above all, sight), word and deed (hands and feet). As a first step, the announcement of the Kingdom of God represents a change of heart, repentance. Jesus places all the weight of his project on everyone's ability to change, in the possibilities for opening up to the forgiveness and mercy that are offered to them. We can see that Jesus does not share the Pharisee emphasis on fulfilling the rules for external ritual purity, instead stressing the ethical side of things, heartfelt devotion to a God who is making himself manifest, to a God who saves. External cleanliness, that involving ritual rules, is not completely unconnected to purity of heart. Indeed, what is on the outside reflects what is on the inside, and people's principal concern should not be the ritual regulations but inner purity.

The fundamental statement is found in Mark 7:15 (|| Matt 15:11): "[T]here is nothing outside a man which by going into him can defile him; but the things which come out of a man are what defile him." Hillel, one of the great rabbis before Jesus, had already defended that the inside of a jar, whether pure or impure, determined the purity or impurity of the jar as a whole: "If [a vessel's] inner part becomes unclean, the whole [both inside and out] is unclean" (Mishnah, *Kelim* 25:6). As B. Chilton points out, Jesus felt that what was inside a person was what really made him or her impure. No matter how many external ritual purifications he or she undergoes, if the heart is full of evil, the person shall remain impure.

This is demonstrated by Jesus in a critical remark made against those who fiercely defended ritual purity: "[Y]ou Pharisees cleanse the outside of the cup and of the dish, but inside you are full of extortion and wickedness" (Luke 11:39 || Matt 23:35). The harmony between inside and out, between the heart and the ritual rules has to be complete. Ethical and ritual purity have to coincide. Impurity in its fullest sense is that of the heart. The other impurity relating to people and things as a source of ritual impurity, which is caused by contact with them, does not affect a person's moral rectitude. What is on the inside determines what is on the outside, and not the reverse. It is what is in people's hearts that makes them impure.

Jesus relegates external purity to the background, bringing internal purity to the foreground, relegating what comes from fulfilling the ritual regulations and stressing what comes from the purity that is born from and inspired by a good, generous, and compassionate heart that does not harbor evil. The rules regarding ritual purity cannot be separated from what is really important: a person's heart. Observing the rules on ritual purification makes sense only when these rules reflect a cleanliness of heart and purity of intention. In any case, the heart is put before all else in Jesus' ethics, and this opens the door to the break in the observance of the commandments on ritual purity in the early Christian community.

The tithes

Jesus' position with regard to the Sabbath and ritual purity is confirmed by his stand on tithes. The tithes were taxes benefiting the temple that equated to a tenth of the harvest or the value of a given product. Leviticus (27:30) sets out the rule referring to the tithes: "All the tithe of the land, whether of the seed of the land or of the fruit of the trees, is the Lord's; it is holy to the Lord." The money raised from the tithes was deposited in the treasury at the temple in Jerusalem and used to pay the salaries of the priests and Levites who worked in the temple (Num 18:21-32). We do not know to what extent the laws relating to the tithes were kept to by the Jews who lived in Israel and, above all, those who lived abroad, in the Diaspora.

In any case, the Pharisees insisted on the meticulous payment to the temple of the tithes for any product. This was one of the most salient points in their program to renew the people's religiosity. In the parable of the Pharisee and the tax collector, the former gives thanks to God, with an immodest self-satisfaction, because he gives "tithes of all (!) that he gets" (Luke 18:12). The Pharisees reached the point where they paid tithes for items as tiny and worthless as wild herbs: "mint and dill and cummin" (Matt 23:23; the parallel text, Luke 11:42, mentions "mint and rue and every herb"). According to the Pharisees, the scrupulous payment of the tithes was a defense of God's holiness, a sign of people's acknowledgment of his gifts.

Faced with this, Jesus once again stressed the value of what was essential in the Law, and he did so in a statement that contrasted the payment of the tithes for tiny objects to the practice of great deeds as inspired by the Law itself. Jesus reminded those who defended the tithes, the Pharisees, that one could not regularly pay one's tithes for wild herbs while ignoring "justice and mercy and faith" (Matt 23:25 || Luke 11:42). It makes sense to meticulously pay all these tithes only when one lives in accordance with these fundamental pillars of the message of the Kingdom that Jesus was communicating. As in the case of ritual purity, this external practice, the payment of tithes, cannot be separated from what is at the crux of the Law and Jesus' teachings. Without a pure heart to support it, it remains merely an external act. As Jesus says, "[T]hese you ought to have done, without neglecting the others" (Matt 23:23 || Luke 11:42). Even the most insignificant commandments in the Law have to be fulfilled (Matt 5:19), but in the knowledge that the essentials are justice, love, and faith.

Jesus did not disagree with the Law, but he did show an attitude that assessed and weighed the nuances involved. Not everything has the same value, not everything is the same in terms of the Law. The ethical precepts are fundamental, while the rules regarding rituals and worship are subordinate to these and must be a faithful expression of them. The Pharisees tended to assign equal importance to all 613 commandments, into which all the laws of the Scriptures and their traditions had been distilled and ran the risk of making the Law imbalanced. In order to overcome the confusion deriving from this leveling out of the commandments, Jesus stressed the importance of what was essential. The Law was not cancelled out or disrespected, but Jesus did interpret it in terms of ethics led by the heart, the focus of which was the commandment to love.

5.3.2.3. The Focus: The Commandment to Love

As G. Theissen points out, the heart and focus of Jesus' ethics is the commandment to love God and each other. In Jesus' own words, these were the Law's "first" and "second" commandments. As we have already seen (5.3.2.1), the commandment to love your neighbor becomes the second most important in the Law and is given the same rank and importance as the first ("love God with all your heart"). The other commandments, regardless of what they relate to, cannot be compared to these two, which are the nucleus and concentration of all the Law; as A. Men states, they free us from our own "I" as the center of the universe.

That said, Jesus' perspective was neither unusual nor far from the reality of the Jewish religion at the time. When Jesus put forward the twofold commandment for love to the teacher of the Law who asked him for the most important commandment, there was an agreement and harmony shared by both rabbis. This teacher may have wanted "to put [Jesus] to the test" (Luke 10:25; also Matt 22:35) by putting forward a captious question, but it may also have simply been an honest, though difficult, inquiry. A famous rabbi from before Jesus' time, Shammai, had refused to answer it for a nonbeliever who had demanded, in order to convert to Judaism, that he teach him all the Law, the Torah, in the time he could remain standing on one leg. It was rabbi Hillel, Shammai's rival, who gave him the answer in the so-called "golden rule": "What is hateful to you, do not to your neighbor: that is the whole Torah, while the rest is the commentary thereof; go and learn it" (Babylonian Talmud, *Šabb.* 31a). In fact, Hillel's response already existed in the biblical book of Tobit ("what you hate, do not do to any one"; 4:15) and in extrabiblical literature (in the Wisdom of Ahikar). Jesus also knew it but preferred to quote it with positive connotations: "So whatever you wish that men would do to you, do so to them" (Matt 7:12 || Luke 6:31).

Rabbi Akiba too, who was martyred in 135 A.D., refers to the commandment "you shall love your neighbor as yourself" (Lev 19:18) as the most important principle of the Torah, thus siding with the answer that Jesus gave the teacher of the Law. A Jewish writing from the time of Jesus, the Testaments of the Twelve Patriarchs, among a series of exhortations, states, "[L]ove the Lord and your neighbor"

(*T. Iss.* 5:2). Among the Jews of the Diaspora, Philo of Alexandria, who died in 65 A.D., explained that there were two basic principles in the Jewish religion to which the other specific principles and rules were subordinate: "regulating . . . one's conduct towards God by the rules of piety and holiness, and of one's conduct towards men by the rules of humanity and justice" (*Spec. Laws* 2.63). At the end of the first century A.D., Josephus used these same two principles to typify the teachings of John the Baptist: "to exercise virtue, both as to righteousness towards one another, and piety towards God" (*A.J.* 18:117). The love of God and of others forms the foundations for personal behavior and is a common theme at the time of Jesus. The question asked by the teacher of the Law about the most important commandment and Jesus' answer regarding the commandment to love are both perfectly in tune with the Jewish world of the time.

Nonetheless, we should point out that the twofold commandment to love as Jesus states it does not have precedents in the above parallels. First, as B. Chilton points out, the Master of Nazareth is the only one to quote Deuteronomy (6:4-5) and Leviticus (19:18) together, two texts that share the construction "you shall love" (God, in the former, and your neighbor, in the latter). Second, only Jesus ranks these two commandments relating to love (not just one!) as the two most important, thus promoting them above all others. Loving God and others constitutes the basis of a person's ethics and religion. In this he differs from Philo, who limits himself to taking up a common idea from antiquity of two main groups of duties or virtues (those relating to God and those relating to fellow man), adapting them to the Jewish religion. Third, only Jesus asks himself what it means to love your "neighbor": are they people from your town, group or ideology, or all human beings, including your enemies and persecutors? As G. Theissen points out with regard to the parable of the Good Samaritan, it is not being physically their neighbor or close to others that is important, but carrying out actions that are touched by love, which bring people closer together. Love for others is built on friendships involving compassion and generosity and specific feelings and, above all, actions. The parable of the Good Samaritan ends with an invitation from Jesus to act with love, as the foreigner had done when he found this man, a stranger, lying and injured by the roadside: "Go and do likewise" (Luke 10:37).

One of the most surprising and characteristic elements of Jesus' ethics is his attitude toward his enemies, which comes to symbolize the extension and definitive application of his love for his neighbors: "Love your enemies, do good to those who hate you, bless those who curse you, pray for those who abuse you" (Luke 6:27-28 || Matt 5:44). The most representative image of this may be that of being slapped, one of the most serious offences in Mediterranean culture that one can receive. Jesus said, "To him who strikes you on the cheek, offer the other also" (Luke 6:29 || Matt 5:39). This statement from Jesus is exactly the opposite of the so-called Law of Talio ("an eye for an eye and a tooth for a tooth") in the Law of Moses (e.g., Exod 21:23-25). What Jesus said about the way people should react to someone's suing them and taking their coat that covered and protected them also differs from the Law (in going further): the person should be given everything, tunic and cloak, the most valuable item of clothing (Matt 5:40 || Luke 6:29). The Law protected the poor, who could not be left without a cloak, which they used as a blanket at night (Exod 22:25-26), but Jesus wanted to use extreme images to show that people had to come to love their enemies.

The enemy whether personal or collective (ideological or religious opposition, economic or political oppressors), whether large or small, has the same antagonistic intention, to hurt and cause suffering. Vengeance, however, is the wrong answer: "Do not resist one who is evil" (Matt 5:39). Evil can be beaten only by good and not by more evil, which simply creates a vicious circle. Jesus proposes undermining this vicious circle by never letting it start and by renouncing a response that also employs evil. Instead of resigning oneself to revenge, whether mitigated or contained, and instead of employing the dangerous strategy of siding with an enemy, Jesus proposes responding to our enemies with love, with the same attitude and feelings with which we would treat a friend. A friend is not hated, but loved; a friend is not cursed, but blessed; a friend is welcomed, and we pray that God blesses him or her. A friend is given everything, even those things we need, often receiving more than the friend asked for. In short, a friend is, by definition, someone we love. According to Jesus we should also love our enemies.

The reason is the same throughout Jesus' message: the constant references to the behavior and attitude of God, who is making himself manifest in the world through his Kingdom. As U. Luz stresses in his commentary on Matthew, with the commandment to love your enemies, Jesus is presenting himself as a defender not of some form of universal harmony but simply of God's will: do what God wants and, we could add, what God does. Imitating the way God, the Father, acts and lives and above all loving one's enemies is the basis of Jesus' words, deeds, and particularly ethics. Loving them is possible because people know that God treats everyone lovingly, the good and the bad, the just and the unjust, and we simply need to copy him. This can be seen in the fact that the sun rises each day on all of us or in the fact that the rain does not make distinctions among people's qualities (Matt 5:45). The fact that God is the Father of all of us and that he treats us all as his children allows us to love our enemies. Jesus' ethics end up reflecting those of God: "Be merciful/perfect, even as your Father is merciful/perfect" (Luke 6:36 || Matt 5:48). If God's limitless compassion, care, generosity, and righteousness show that the Kingdom is at hand and at work among mankind, then loving one's enemies indicates that there are those who receive and welcome this Kingdom.

Ultimately, loving one's enemies (and those we sometimes associate with them—foreigners, evildoers, etc.) is the extreme application of the second commandment: "love your neighbor as yourself." If enemies are included among the circle of people who are to be loved, then no one can be left out, the whole of mankind has to be included. Jesus is convinced of the strength of love and denounces hate and vengeance as fatal to interpersonal relations and contrary to his message. He shows himself to be radical on this question. Vengeance on a low level or violence in one's heart (with no external effects!) reflects a life of confusion and bars entrance to the Kingdom. Those who are devoted to the Kingdom are those who truly renounce being someone's enemy, those who decide to treat the enemy as a friend, "expecting nothing in return" (Luke 6:35), with no stratagems or self-interest (Matt 5:46-47 || Luke 6:32-34). God's forgiveness is gracious, and he offers it because he wants to, not because we deserve it, but because he is "kind to the ungrateful and the selfish" (Luke 6:35). The grateful response comes later, and it is loving one's enemies. This response warrants a "great reward": being God's children (Matt 5:45 || Luke 6:35). Jesus' proposal is clear: live as children who imitate the behavior of the Father, children who have received his compassion and who spread it infinitely.

5.3.3. Jesus, The Authoritative Teacher

Jesus is a unique rabbi, who abided by the Law but who had a personal way of interpreting it and who was not linked to any of the Jewish groups, trends, or schools of the time. In his hands, the Law was not made invalid, but it was opened up to new ways of thinking that led to its limits being superseded. The Law was still valid, however, as it says in Matthew 5:17: "I have not come to abolish them [the laws] but to fulfill them"; there is a before and after with regard to Jesus. Jesus does not limit himself to reading and commenting on the Decalogue. He rereads it and brings a new face to it, he restructures the system of internal relations, making the twofold commandment to love the focus for the rest of the commandments, reinforcing the ethical rules and making the ritual precepts relative, strengthening the Law and opening up cracks. His ethics are ethics for the heart and specific actions with regard to others, where God's righteousness and compassion are the points of reference that have to be imitated. The Kingdom is the constant backdrop to these ethics, and God's reign and not the letter of the Law is the definitive standard to be met.

Jesus places himself before the Law, or indeed at its limit, because he often sees it to be insufficient. His position with regard to divorce and his refusal to condemn an adulterer to death by stoning are striking proof of this. Jesus sought to protect and safeguard God's overriding will and his ability to forgive and care for the people's illnesses and needs. The case of the Sabbath shows that the Law cannot be placed above the person, above God's project for them and above the unstoppable growth of affectionate relationships that know no limits, including even one's enemies.

Jesus places himself before the Law authoritatively, with the same authority that he usually speaks with. In the eyes of the people he was, in the words of Josephus, "a wise man . . . a teacher of such men as receive the truth with pleasure" (*A.J.* 18:63). However, the scribes and religious leaders in Jerusalem, disconcerted by Jesus' activities, asked him for the source of this authority: "By what authority are you doing these things?" (Mark 11:28). Jesus refused to respond. In contrast to other rabbis, Jesus did not look for his arguments in the Scriptures, basing his authority on these or using the tradition of the elders as a resource to confirm his own position (Mark 1:22).

The question remains, however, where did Jesus get the authority he spoke with?

Although Jesus did on occasions interpret the Scriptures, and the Ten Commandments formed the backbone of his ethics, his teachings were much broader. The phrases and aphorisms he used, and above all the parables, provide a much larger corpus of material than do his references to the Scriptures. Like John the Baptist, Jesus was a Master, who was also known as a rabbi by the people, as he bore a message of the imminent arrival of God; unlike the Baptist, Jesus proclaimed that the Kingdom had arrived. God was making himself manifest through Jesus' words, which were good news for the poor, and through his amazing deeds, which healed all kinds of sick people, cleansed lepers, and resurrected the dead. The centurion in Capernaum recognized a potent word in Jesus, a word able to make his servant well again (Matt 8:8 || Luke 7:7; John 4:50). The power of these deeds and the strength of these words came from the same source: God, the Father, for whom Jesus was the plenipotentiary emissary. He had given him authority. A phrase from the Q collection says, "All things have been delivered to me by my Father" (Matt 11:27 || Luke 10:22).

Peculiarities in the language used by Jesus indicate the authority with which he expressed himself. First, many of his statements started with the term Amen, which is identical in Hebrew and Aramaic (and in all other languages) and is translated as "I assure you" or "so be it." These are statements that Jesus wanted to stress particularly to his listeners. Second, a good number of his statements started with a similar formula ("I say to you"), which is sometimes translated as "I assure you" (e.g., Matt 12:31). Jesus' words had a strength all of their own. This is how the disciples, who listened to them intently and passed them on carefully and faithfully, saw them. Nonetheless, they were also words that had to be put into practice in order to be made complete, as can be seen in Matthew 7:24 (|| Luke 6:47). Jesus is a teacher who invited his disciples to follow him, a decision that involved every aspect of their lives.

Finally, Jesus asserted his authority by comparing his message and person to some of the figures from the First Testament. In the debate over divorce, Jesus indirectly compared the words of Moses, who "wrote you this commandment," and his own words, where he denied the possibility of divorce with the conclusive statement that "[w]hat therefore God has joined together, let not man put asunder" (Mark 10:5, 10:9). In the so-called antitheses, what was said by "the elders," and Moses on Mount Sinai in particular, is given a new meaning (Matt 5:21, 5:33). There is something extra in Jesus, which can be seen in two other figures from the First Testament: the prophet Jonah, who preached repentance to the city of Nineveh, and King Solomon, whose wisdom was worthy of a visit from the Queen of the South. The inhabitants of Nineveh and the Queen of Sheba listened and paid heed to Jonah and Solomon, respectively. Jesus concluded, when addressing those who demanded signs but who were unwilling to repent, that "something greater than Jonah is here" (Matt 12:41 || Luke 11:32); likewise, "something greater than Solomon is here" (Matt 12:42 || Luke 11:31). As V. Fusco points out, the Torah (Moses), the Prophets (Jonah), and the Writings (Solomon) illustrate the authority that God himself had given Jesus' words and mission.

5.4. Jesus' Identity

Personal identity is an amalgam of two indivisible and, normally, contradictory points of view: the image that other people have of us and the image that we each have of ourselves, our realities and dreams, our project and life. The case of Jesus of Nazareth, rabbi and prophet, itinerant preacher of the Kingdom of God and miracle worker, is no exception. Though it is worthwhile to look at his person in terms of his activities, it is also helpful to focus on his definitive identity, what we human beings each know as a person's "secret."

For this aspect of our research into the Master of Nazareth, we have sufficient information to offer a provisional answer to this "secret"; I say *provisional* because we have yet to describe Jesus' death and the circumstances surrounding it. Bearing in mind the necessary precautions, we can start to look more closely at a complex and fascinating area, where we have to avoid limiting ourselves to a purely psychological investigation and ensure that we stick strictly to the point we have reached: Jesus was on the threshold of a violent end, with his life about to be cut short at its zenith by a death sentence. Fundamentally, we cannot conclude our reflection on Jesus' message and activities without looking at his identity. So, who was Jesus of Nazareth?

5.4.1. Jesus, The Messiah

The first answer to this question involves seeing Jesus as the Messiah of Israel, his people. This was the opinion of his disciples and a good proportion of the people; even Jesus' adversaries had doubts as to whether he was not in fact the emissary sent by God to free Israel. Jesus showed himself to be the Messiah, but he did so indirectly, with a good number of reservations and precautions. Jesus' awareness of himself as the Messiah does not mean that he referred to himself as such or that he had no problem with people calling him such, unlike Simon, the leader of the Second Jewish Revolt (132–135 A.D.), exalted by the great rabbi Akiba and given the messianic nickname *Bar Kokhba*, the "Son of the Star." There were too many stereotypes attached to the word *Messiah* at that time for Jesus to be able to use the title without being confused with the pretenders to the throne, someone aiming to lead Israel in the conquest of their land and their capital, Jerusalem, occupied by the Romans. Undoubtedly Jesus was a descendant of David, and this circumstance would not have gone unnoticed by anyone, whether friends or enemies, the disciples or the people (see 4.3.2). People took up a wide range of positions in regard to Jesus being the Messiah (John 7:42).

During his public activities, the opinions of the people and the disciples led to Jesus sometimes being seen as the Messiah. The most striking incident was the feeding of the five thousand on the northwest coast of Lake Galilee, in Philip's tetrarchy, where five thousand, not counting the women and children, were miraculously fed by Jesus. This meal, a major sign of God's Kingdom and the all-inclusive fraternity, echoed the great events that had taken place in the desert with the manna and quail sent from heaven in particular (see 5.2.1.5), and led to an explosion of enthusiasm in the people: Jesus was acclaimed as a prophet and king, the Messiah (John 6:14-15).

Further acknowledgment comes from the mouth of Peter, the spokesman for the Twelve, when Jesus and the disciples were traveling incognito through the towns around Caesarea, the capital of Philip's tetrarchy. Jesus, who was far from the Jewish lands, asked his disciples for the first and last time about his identity, both what the people thought of him and what they thought: "Who do men say that I am?" (Mark 8:27). Peter, on behalf of all of them, responded, "You are the Christ [Messiah]" (Mark 8:29). If we are to believe that Peter then rebuked Jesus (!) because the latter had said that he had to suffer and die (Mark 8:31-33), then the disciple must have seen the Master as the glorious and mighty Messiah who was to free Israel. This is how the crowd at the feeding of the five thousand also saw him or the sons of Zebedee, another two of the Twelve, who asked for places of honor beside the throne that was to be occupied by Jesus, the Messiah-King (Mark 10:37).

The disciples and the people concurred in what the Messiah had to be and do: defeat Israel's enemies in battle and establish a kingdom characterized by peace and justice. This popular Messianism can be seen in the calls of the blind man, Bartimaeus, when Jesus passed through Jericho on his way to Jerusalem. Bartimaeus demanded that the Messiah have pity on him and heal him, saying, "Jesus, Son of David, have mercy on me!" (Mark 10:47-48). Both David and Solomon, his son, were figures from Israel's history who were popularly linked with healings. Jesus inspired enthusiastic devotion in his disciples, who accompanied him on his last journey to Jerusalem. The disciples were convinced that the Kingdom of God was to manifest itself there, thanks to the miraculous deeds performed by their master, Israel's Messiah (Luke 19:11 and Acts 1:6).

Jesus' attitude toward the enthusiasm of his followers was one of caution. When they wanted to make him king, following the miraculous sign of the multiplication of the loaves and the fishes, he refused to act as the Messiah, as a political and social leader, and escaped to the mountains. When Peter stated in the name of all of the disciples that Jesus was the Messiah, he did not deny it, but he strictly forbade them from telling anyone. What is Jesus scared of? That his disciples, like the people before them, should want to acclaim him publicly as Israel's victorious king, their liberator? Or, did he think that the time had not yet come to make his identity public, that the time had not yet come to die in Jerusalem? He showed the same reticence to go into more detail in the case of Zebedee's two sons, when he said that the places of honor in the Kingdom were not to be assigned by the Messiah but by the one who sent him, God himself. These places could be granted to James and John only once they had drunk from the cup that Jesus drank from. The allusion to suffering and, ultimately, death seems clear. Peter, after calling Jesus the Messiah, also felt that the Master was announcing a difficult and dramatic end.

On one occasion it was Jesus not who asked the question but who responded. The question came from his guide, John the Baptist, who had sent his disciples from his prison to find out whether Jesus was indeed the Messiah sent by God. John's question ("Are you he who is to come, or shall we look for another?") has clear messianic tones. Jesus started his answer indirectly, describing the deeds he had performed, the healings, the resurrections, the bringing of the good news to the poor, which echoed the prophecies of Isaiah concerning the end of time, when God was to manifest himself definitively (Matt 11:4-5 || Luke 7:20-22). Jesus said, in other words, that his works were the works of the Messiah, the Lord's Anointed One; and he ended with a generic blessing ("blessed is he who takes no offence at me"; Matt 11:6 || Luke 7:23), which was a call for the Baptist and all those who doubted him to accept that he really had been sent by God.

In his reply, Jesus puts faithfulness to himself at the center, a faithfulness upon which his identity is based. The Baptist, a holy man and knowledgeable in the Scriptures, should have had enough evidence to see that Jesus was the Messiah, filled with the Lord's Spirit, as proclaimed by Isaiah 61:1 (also 4Q521). The people of Nazareth should also have had enough evidence, when Jesus said, possibly of this same prophecy, "The Spirit of the Lord is upon me, because he has anointed me [i.e., I am his Messiah]" (Luke 4:18). According to the prophecy in Isaiah 61, this Anointed One, or Messiah, was to bring good news to the poor, heal the sick, free the captives, and proclaim the Lord's year of grace. In short, the works of the Messiah had begun. This was how Jesus saw his own activities.

Only when Jesus triumphantly entered Jerusalem just a few days before his death did he let people clearly see that he really was the Messiah. Following the feeding of the five thousand, Jesus refused to let the people acclaim him as king, but now, in Jerusalem, he himself decided to enter the city as if under a messianic banner: the very image of Jesus on a donkey left little room for doubt. It is worth our while looking at Zechariah 9:9-10a, a prophecy that shows what this entrance meant to Jesus, who saw himself as the king of peace: "Rejoice greatly, O daughter of Zion! Shout aloud, O daughter of

Jerusalem! Lo, your king comes to you; triumphant and victorious is he, humble and riding on an ass, on a colt the foal of an ass. I will cut off the chariot from Ephraim [the Israelites from the north] and the war horse from Jerusalem [the Israelites from the south]; and the battle bow shall be cut off, and he shall command peace to the nations." This prophecy, which is quoted in part in the Gospel according to Matthew (21:5), announces the coming of a Messiah of peace who is the antithesis of the Messiah of war who destroys enemies and who was popularly expected by the people of Israel.

Thus, Jesus' entry into Jerusalem was the entrance of a king, who was accustomed to having cloaks placed at his feet, but it was also a peaceful and festive entrance of a king of peace, a different Messiah (!), acclaimed by the people who carried palms and branches, not swords (!), in their hands. The proof that this entrance attracted great crowds but that it was still pacific can be seen in the fact that it provoked no reaction from the Roman garrison stationed in the Antonia Tower and in charge of keeping an eye on public order. Now, finally, Jesus had accepted and, indeed to a certain extent, sought to be acclaimed as the Messiah, as his triumphant entrance into Jerusalem made it clear what it meant to him to be the Lord's Anointed One.

On this occasion, the disciples and people hailed him as "Son of David" (Matt 21:9) and "King of Israel" (Luke 19:38; John 12:13) or exclaimed, "Blessed is the kingdom of our father David that is coming!" (Mark 11:10). The messianic acclamation "Hosanna," which means "[Lord], save us," shows what the people were feeling at the time (Mark 11:9-10; Matt 21:9; John 12:13). On the other hand, the important people (Luke talks of the Pharisees), the leaders (Matthew refers to the temple chiefs and scribes), attacked Jesus for allowing himself to be acclaimed. Was their attitude the result of political prudence, or did they want to close their eyes to the reality of Jesus as Messiah? Did they see his triumphant and surprising entrance as a threat or provocation that could lead to violent repression of the crowds by the Romans and the consequent loss of life? Or did they find Jesus' decision to allow, or even encourage, his followers to acclaim him as the Messiah strange, since until then he had never proclaimed himself as such and, in their eyes, he had no divine authority for such?

In any case, it seems that Jesus' entrance into Jerusalem led to a quantitative change in terms of his being recognized as the Messiah;

what to date had been hidden (Peter's statement and the request from Zebedee's sons were reserved for the circle of the disciples), what had been strongly denied (Jesus disappeared after the feeding of the five thousand, when the people wanted to make him king) or merely tolerated (Jesus acted indifferently to the calls from the blind man Bartimaeus), was now brought to light. Shortly before his death, Jesus surprised everyone, both his disciples and his adversaries, in making his identity clear, though he did not seem to be making any preparations to occupy a throne or establish a kingdom. The entrance into Jerusalem was an outburst that did not seem to be leading anywhere.

The question of Jesus' identity was something that the Jewish leaders, who kept their eyes open for any messianic sign, were aware of; had Jesus been sent by God? His jubilant entrance into Jerusalem may have left them even more disconcerted than ever, and this eruption of messianic fervor may have led them to ask themselves more and more about Jesus' identity. He only added to their confusion, making matters more difficult for the scribes by his interpretation of Psalm 110: is the Messiah less than David (his son) or greater than him (his Lord) (Mark 12:35-37 || Matt 22:41-46 || Luke 20:41-44)? Other leaders, those responsible for the temple, with the high priest as their head, saw in the entrance into Jerusalem confirmation of their fears and were convinced of Jesus' ability to lead an insurrection against the Romans, that he could act as the new David. Thus, the plans against Jesus had to be sped up, though they had already been decided upon. For them, Jesus represented a threat (John 12:47-48). The people's great appreciation of the rabbi of Nazareth was plain to see ("every one will believe in him"). The question as to whether Jesus was or was not the Messiah became a weight around the necks of the people's leaders.

When Jesus was arrested and taken before Caiaphas, the latter asked him whether he was the Messiah, and Jesus replied with an elliptic statement: "You have said so" (Matt 26:64; also Matt 27:11; Mark 15:2; Luke 23:3; only in Mark 14:62 does it say that Jesus replied with a clear "I am"). Obviously this elliptic reply is not a negative, but simply ambiguous. Jesus did not want to manifest his identity in front of adversaries who simply wanted to condemn him. Nonetheless, Pilate condemned Jesus as "king of the Jews," as a messianic pretender to the throne and, thus, an enemy of the Roman Empire and Caesar. This can be seen in the *titulus* or plaque that the Roman governor had nailed to the top of the cross: "[Jesus of Nazareth] king of the Jews" (Matt 27:37 || Mark 15:26 || Luke 23:38 || John 19:19).

The last days of Jesus' life were marked by one constant factor: Jesus is the Messiah; he was acknowledged or feared, accused and condemned, but he was not understood by either his friends or his enemies. The Messiah was to suffer and die on a cross, something that went beyond all expectations and represented a volte-face in the messianic expectations of the people of Israel.

5.4.2. Jesus and the Father

The second perspective in terms of Jesus' identity comes from a second occasion on which the expectations of the time were not met. There were firm convictions surrounding the figure that God was to send at the decisive moment in history, but Jesus went beyond all that which could have been expected of Israel's Messiah. The authority with which Jesus spoke and acted, the fact that his teachings depended on himself (and not just the Scriptures), and the unique nature of his prayers meant that his identity could not be explained in the usual terms. Jesus was seen to be strangely close to God, to his decisions and his definitive plans for mankind and the world.

Obviously, this did not mean that Jesus identified himself as some kind of superman. Quite the contrary, Jesus spoke of himself using the expression the "Son of Man"—which, above all else, simply meant a "man," a human person seen from an earthly perspective, with the weakness and frailty that this implied. However, this expression was also used in a text in the Old Testament (Dan 7:13-14), which talks about a heavenly figure: "[W]ith the clouds of heaven there came one like a son of man. . . . And to him was given dominion and glory and kingdom" by the "Ancient of Days." Thus, the "Son of Man" (*bar nash*; Aramaic, *bar nasha*) is an ambivalent expression that is used only by Jesus, and no one ever uses it to address him; it may well have been common and unspecific. Despite this, it is the name that Jesus uses repeatedly to define himself in a wide range of circumstances.

First, Jesus uses the expression Son of Man when referring to himself and his usual activities, without eliciting any kind of reaction or curiosity. In this way, the Son of Man, unlike the foxes that have their holes and the birds that have their nests, has no fixed abode, nowhere to lay his head (Matt 8:20 || Luke 9:58 || Thomas 86). Furthermore, the Son of Man, unlike John the Baptist, who led an ascetic lifestyle, eats and drinks (often in the company of people of disreputable character) and is accused of being a glutton and a drunkard (Matt 11:18-19 || Luke 7:33-34). Jesus, as with anyone else, is the object of criticism and disrespect, insult and attack: there are those who speak out against the Son of Man (Matt 12:32 || Luke 12:10).

Two further references to the authority possessed by the Son of Man are seen in somewhat different circumstances. While healing the paralytic man in Capernaum, Jesus talks of himself as someone who can forgive, and he forgives the sins of this paralytic man. He shows his authority and power in healing the man and forgiving him his sins. The teachers of the Law privately accuse him of blasphemy, because only God can forgive, but Jesus replies, "[T]he Son of man has authority on earth to forgive sins" (Mark 2:10 || Matt 9:6 || Luke 5:24) (see 6.2.1.1). Another similar authority can be seen with regard to the Sabbath rest, which God himself had instituted on Sinai when he gave Moses the Ten Commandments. Jesus reinterprets it, insisting that people are always more important than the Sabbath: "so the Son of man is lord even of the Sabbath" (Mark 2:28 || Matt 12:8 || Luke 6:5) (see 5.3.2.2).

Jesus refers to a heavenly figure when he uses the expression Son of Man, a figure who, at the end of time, is to come down from the clouds with power and glory to bring the chosen people together from around the world (Mark 13:26-27 || Matt 24:30-31 || Luke 21:27). This image is reminiscent of chapter 7 from the book of Daniel, though the mysterious figure ("one like a son of man") starts to govern once God's enemies have been defeated. But in the Gospel texts, the Son of Man comes only to save the chosen ones and to act as a universal judge. Jesus states before Caiaphas that "you will see the Son of man seated at the right hand of Power, and coming with the clouds of heaven" (Mark 14:62 || Matt 26:64; Luke 22:69). The Son of Man occupies the place of honor at God's right-hand side and has full authority to judge all of mankind (Mark 8:38 || Matt 16:27 || Luke 9:26).

Apparently, we are working within the framework of apocalyptic Jewish thinking: Jesus mentions a heavenly figure to be found in

Daniel 7 and with some variations in the Parables of Enoch and the Fourth Book of Esdras. The phrase mentioned led to a vehement reaction from Caiaphas, the high priest, who tore at his robes and exclaimed that Jesus had just blasphemed (though the phrase is, in fact, ambiguous). Caiaphas interpreted Jesus' words as blasphemy because he felt that Jesus was saying that they should be applied to him, that he identified himself with this heavenly figure, the Son of Man, which would represent a serious offence to the holiness of the one and only God. How could this rabbi from Nazareth (a simple "Son of Man," or simply a man) dare identify himself as "the [heavenly] Son of Man" as prophesied by Daniel?

This identification, which Caiaphas qualifies as blasphemy, relates to Jesus' deepest identity, as he says. In one of the phrases passed down by the Q collection of sayings (Matt 10:32-33 || Luke 12:8-9) and by Mark (8:38 || Matt 16:27 || Luke 9:26), Jesus states that there is a correlation between being denied (or acknowledged) here on earth by men and being denied (or acknowledged) by the Son of Man at the time of judgment before God. The phrase does not directly identify Jesus as the Son of Man, though this is how it has been interpreted by Matthew 10:32: "So every one who acknowledges me before men, I [Luke 12:8: the Son of Man] also will acknowledge before my Father who is in heaven." However, the correlation established between devotion to or denial of Jesus and the welcome or condemnation from the Son of Man is so closely linked that the most obvious explanation has to be that they are in fact the same person.

Jesus represents the start of God's reign over mankind, which is transformed and renewed. This means that the last days are just over the horizon and that, in consequence, the figure of the last days, the anonymous, almighty Son of Man announced by Daniel, can be identified in the person who views himself as the Messiah and God's emissary here on earth. In other words, Jesus is the bearer of the Kingdom, and his authority goes beyond this world and present time, stretching into the future. For this reason, he dares talk about future realities such as the banquet in the Kingdom. Jesus is not presented as some sort of superman, who blends heaven and earth; rather he provides a name and a face for the Son of Man as described in Daniel 7, a figure for the future made manifest in him. This complete correlation (not confusion!) between heaven and earth is the final result of the indestructible link between the message of the Kingdom and the messenger (see 5.1.1.4). Jesus occupies a central position in the Kingdom, and the present authority and future authority, received from God the Father, come together in one expression: Son of Man, who is no stranger to day-to-day life, and to suffering and death in particular.

On a number of occasions, the expression *Son of Man* is used in relation to Jesus' tragic destiny, as someone who was to suffer and die. During the third phase of Jesus' life's journey, while he and his disciples were traveling through Galilee incognito, the Master used a play on words to announce, "The Son of man is to be delivered into the hands of men" (Mark 9:31 || Matt 17:22 || Luke 9:44). The disciples are speechless in reaction to what Jesus is suggesting: his upcoming death. Both here and in other examples (Mark 8:31 and 10:33, with the corresponding parallels in Matthew and Luke, where the marks left by Christian tradition can be seen), the Son of Man mentioned is not only the heavenly and triumphant figure who comes down from the clouds but also "that man," Jesus, who is to undergo great suffering, death, rejection, and disrespect. This can be seen in Luke 17:25, "first he [the Son of Man] must suffer many things and be rejected by this generation," and in Mark 9:12 (|| Matt 17:12), "the Son of man . . . should suffer many things and be treated with contempt." Once the drama reaches its climax and Jesus is arrested in the garden of Gethsemane, the Christian tradition points out that what Jesus himself had said about the Son of Man has come to pass (Mark 14:41 || Matt 26:45). In the Gospel according to John, the reference to the crucifixion says that the Son of Man is to be "lifted up from the earth" (12:32, 12:34) and "glorified" (John 12:23). This is a variation of the same idea in the synoptic Gospels: the Son of Man is to suffer death, but he will not lose his life.

Jesus wanted to connect the expression *Son of Man* to his life's destiny, his having to suffer a violent death brought about and carried out by "men." His humanity is associated with passion and suffering, which cannot be separated from a future of authority and glory that has already started to take root in the present. Again from chapter 7 of the book of Daniel, the people of the saints were first crushed, and then God restored justice, whereby they received an everlasting kingdom. Jesus sees his life and destiny reflected in the expression *Son of Man* and the wide range of meanings this can take on. Jesus, like anyone else who trusts in God, places his life in the hands of the Almighty. The key to understanding Jesus' identity and mission is his closeness to God.

Jesus said little about himself, and when he did so he tended to use allusions and evocations. He revealed his identity only in the last days and hours of his life. The gestures and words used on his triumphant entrance into Jerusalem show, as we have seen above (5.4.1), that he was Israel's Messiah sent by God to bring peace and not destruction on its enemies. When he was brought before Caiaphas in the hands of his adversaries, his response to the high priest referred to the Son of Man, God's emissary, who was full of authority and glory and who was to come to judge mankind. On the other hand, during his public activities, Jesus proclaimed God's reign, his aim being to communicate that God was making himself manifest in the world and that this fact, which brought with it his grace and forgiveness, was to turn people's lives and expectations on their head. Jesus was not, however, simply a spokesman for this Kingdom but its messenger, the divine emissary, legitimized by a strong, truthful, original, and mighty word. This word was mostly aimed at helping the poor; it also contained miraculous actions that healed and saved, bringing together a happy fraternity. All this is based on a unique and very close relationship between Jesus and God.

An allusion to this closeness can be seen in the parable of the murderous tenants in the vineyard (Mark 12:1-9 || Matt 21:33-41 || Luke 20:9-16 || Thomas 65). The parable reaches its climax when the father, who has seen how his servants have been turned away or even beaten by the tenants, decides to send his only son, sure that they will respect him. The tenants, however, decide to kill him and keep his inheritance. It is difficult not to see this parable as a kind of autobiography of Jesus, announcing his forthcoming death (see 6.1.2.2, below). Jesus appears in the parable as the son sent to the vineyard (Israel), while the father figure offers clear allusions to the loving and generous behavior of God to the leaders of Israel, his people. In this parable and the indirect language of a parable (which Jesus is so fond of!), he compares his relationship with God to that of the (only) Son and his Father.

A direct indication of Jesus' closeness to God is the three prayers attributed to him in the synoptic Gospels: the two that he leads personally and the one he teaches to his disciples (see 5.1.1.4 and 5.1.2.3). All three start with the word "Father," though in the last of them, the prayer for the disciples, the invocation is "Our Father." This is an eloquent difference: one thing is a prayer for the disciples and another a prayer for Jesus. God is the Father of all mankind, "Our Father," but for Jesus, he is "the Father," "My Father." In the prayer in Gethsemane, even the term *Abba* appears, which was originally used by Jesus. The prayer starts thus: "*Abba*, Father" (Mark 14:36). Jesus is the only Jew of his era to invoke God using this name unaccompanied by any other. He does not always do so in exactly the same way; in the thanksgiving prayer, he uses a well-documented custom from the time, addressing God saying, "Lord of heaven and earth" (i.e., "Lord of the universe"), but preceded by the characteristic "Father" (Matt 11:25 || Luke 10:21). For the most part, Jesus invokes God in his prayers by calling him *Abba*, "Father." This is seen specifically in two texts from the epistles of the Apostle Paul, which state that the Spirit moves people's hearts to invoke God with this cry: "*Abba*! Father!" (Rom 8:15; Gal 4:6; also Luke 23:34 and 23:46).

If Jesus used the name Father to address God it was because he lived and felt very close to him and wanted to involve those who surrounded him. As J. Schlosser stresses, *Abba* is the opposite of distant, faraway, and separated. Behind this name shine trust and obedience, the fact that he gave himself up to the divine will, recognizing that God is the Lord of life and death. Jesus insists on addressing God in a common and familiar way, as if he were someone he could turn to directly, without the need for intermediaries or any kind of wait. The prayer in Gethsemane and the thanksgiving prayer are in no way conventional, neither in form nor in content. Jesus talks from the heart, expressing two feelings fundamental to human beings: thanks for the love shown to the most insignificant and the trust to overcome fear and make us strong in adversity.

In the thanksgiving prayer, Jesus expresses his message of the Kingdom that he proclaims, the good news that he brings: God's goodness has arrived for the poor and the simple; he has opened up a new world of righteousness, forgiveness, and fraternity for them. God has made himself manifest as a Father to all mankind, especially the marginalized and the needy. The arrival of the Kingdom brings with it God's compassionate and active presence. The prayer ends saying, "Yea, Father, for such was your will" (Matt 11:26 || Luke 10:21). God's free decision is contrasted in the prayer in Gethsemane, in which Jesus addresses the Father with two requests that highlight the difficult nature of the test he has to go through ("remove this cup from me") and his trust in he who has led him to where he is and who will not leave him helpless ("not what I will, but what thou wilt [be done]") (Mark 14:36; see 6.2.2.3). The praise and joy, on the one hand, and the trust, on the other, characterize these two prayers of Jesus and show his great intimacy with the Father, during his life as the messenger of the Kingdom and now at the threshold of his humble and obedient death.

The prayer in John 12:27-28 represents one of John's typical enhancements, this time affecting the prayer in Gethsemane: "Now is my soul troubled. And what shall I say? 'Father, save me from this hour?' No, for this purpose I have come to this hour. Father, glorify thy name." The relationship between Jesus and his God, between the Father and Son, is based on trust ("All things have been delivered to me by my Father") and reciprocal understanding that, through the Son, also spreads to his disciples (Matt 11:27 || Luke 10:22).

Jesus revealed his identity as the Son to some of these disciples: Peter, James, and John, the inner circle of the Twelve. The events took place on a high mountain (Mount Tabor, according to the Christian tradition), where Jesus was transfigured and talked to Elijah and Moses, who appeared with him and accompanied him (Mark 9:2-13 || Matt 17:1-13 || Luke 9:28-36). The three disciples underwent an intense religious experience, which combined a state of indescribable happiness and great shock. The focal point for the events was the voice that spoke from within a cloud and that revealed and proclaimed Jesus' identity: "This is my beloved Son." It was God's voice that disclosed who Jesus was.

All the elements of the story are linked to the central message, the essential core of the scene. The fact that Jesus took on a radically different aspect as he appeared with bright glistening clothes indicates that he was more than a man, that his definitive identity was divine. Moses and Elijah took part in the scene as two great figures from Israel's history (Moses, the man of Law, and Elijah, the prophet to come before the Messiah) and also represented the celestial world, having gone up to heaven miraculously and suddenly. The three disciples act as trusted witnesses of what they saw and heard, and which could have been discredited as a simple hallucination. Instead, it should be seen to be an altered state of consciousness, which leaves a blurred memory of what took place (see 5.2.1.4).

The cloud and voice are traditional instruments for divine revelation, for the mysterious and glorious presence of God. When Moses received the tablets with the Law on Mount Sinai, a cloud covered the mountains and he went inside it (Exod 24:12, 24:15-18). As with Moses, the disciples were covered by the cloud and received a new revelation directly from God: he revealed Jesus' definitive identity, which could be revealed only in this way. Jesus was his beloved Son. He had to be listened to in the same way that the divine word was listened to on Mount Sinai. There was an invitation from the voice, addressed to everyone, both in heaven and on earth: "listen to him."

However, the great revelation that the three disciples experienced had to remain a secret, as Jesus' identity in relation to the Father was to be made clear to everyone only once God had freed him from the bonds of death. Following Jesus' resurrection, the revelation of his definitive identity and his closeness to the Father start to make sense. This is how the early community saw matters, thus linking the transfiguration to the appearances of the resurrected Jesus (see 6.3.3).

6

From Death to Life

As with any other human existence, Jesus' life ended in his death. It was a cruel death that took place when the Galilean Master was at the height of his powers. Jesus of Nazareth ended his days sentenced to death by crucifixion, as dictated by the governor Pontius Pilate, the Romans' highest authority in the province of Judaea, and instigated by the people's religious leaders, and those responsible for the temple in Jerusalem in particular, with Caiaphas as their head. These events, when Jesus was treated as an evildoer and an enemy of Rome and accused of blasphemy by Israel's leaders, developed very quickly, though there had been a number of indications of what was to come during Jesus' life, and especially in his last days. Following a farewell supper with his close circle of Twelve and his shameful abandonment by these men when he was arrested, Jesus was interrogated by the Jewish authorities and sentenced to death by the Roman governor. The sentence was executed immediately by Jerusalem's walls on Friday, April 7, 30 A.D., the eve of the Passover, the great Jewish festival.

On this same day, before sunset, Jesus was buried in a tomb near to where he had been executed. Following the day of rest (on which the annual Passover festivities and the weekly Sabbath coincided that year), some Galilean women, disciples of Jesus, went to the tomb and found that his body was not there. Also on this same day, some disciples, among them the Eleven, stated that Jesus had gone to find them and that they had seen him. They said that Jesus had been resurrected and that he was alive. The last page of his existence was not his death but his life. This is where the memory of and faith in Jesus Christ, dead and resurrected, begin. This is where Christianity begins.

6.1. Jesus Facing Death

Wondering about the attitudes and feelings of people as they face up to their end is neither impossible nor inappropriate. Human beings often find themselves facing up to the consequences of the decisions they take, and the possibility of death can be clearly seen on the horizon of life on occasions. For example, in the Psalms, there are a number of calls to God to save the supplicant from the "flood" that threatens to sweep over him "or the pit [which threatens to] close its mouth over me" (Ps 69:15). In the Psalms, there are calls to "[s]ave my soul from the sword, my life from the power of the dog!" (Ps 22:20). Imminent death becomes part of life for many human beings as a result, for example, of illness or threats. Many people can say that they have continued living but that they were prepared for the worst. Obviously, this does not mean they were completely sure or knew exactly how or when they were to die. Jesus is no different and said as much, especially indirectly, about his impending fate. Nevertheless, he also made clear the link among his person, his mission, and his death; he gave his death meaning.

6.1.1. A Foreseeable Death

6.1.1.1. The Hostility of Competitors and Adversaries

One of the constant themes in Jesus' life is the danger that Antipas, the tetrarch of Galilee and Peraea, represented. If we look back at his life's journey (see 4.6), we can see that, as soon as he left Nazareth to travel to the Jordan to be baptized by John the Baptist and to form part of his group of followers, the long shadow of Antipas started to determine some of his decisions. John, the prophet who was not afraid to denounce the tetrarch's behavior with Herodias, his second wife, had to take refuge in Aenon, not far from Scythopolis, beyond the borders of Peraea governed by Antipas. Jesus and the first disciples followed a similar course and, after Passover 28 A.D., did not return to Peraea, remaining in Judaea instead. When John was imprisoned at Machaerus (in mid-28 A.D.), Jesus continued his public activities in Galilee from his base at Capernaum.

Jesus did not seek to confront Antipas directly, who, if we take into account Luke 9:7-9, seems to be more intrigued than anything else by the miraculous deeds that Jesus carried out. Nonetheless, Antipas was a "fox" according to Jesus (Luke 13:32), a coward and untrustworthy, as, suddenly, his threat once again presented a real danger for Jesus: "Get away from here as Herod [Antipas] wants to kill you" was the warning that Jesus received from some Pharisee friends (Luke 13:31). It is likely that Antipas, having had John decapitated, now turned his attention to the rabbi of Nazareth, whom the tetrarch believed to be John the Baptist "raised" (Mark 6:16) from the dead. Jesus was well aware of the danger that the Baptist's executioner represented for him and his disciples, and he warned them to be alert and careful with respect to the "leaven of Herod [Antipas]" (Mark 8:15).

Driven by the pressure that Antipas placed on him, Jesus was forced to go beyond the boundaries of Galilee, which until then had been the only place he had carried out his activities, traveling to the neighboring lands (Philip's tetrarchy, Phoenicia, the Decapolis) or in Galilee itself, but never staying very long in any one place. Antipas had succeeded in getting what he wanted, having become aware of Jesus' popularity, as seen at the feeding of the five thousand, when thousands of people, for the most part Galileans, came together near the border to his territory. Antipas, whose subjects Jesus and his disciples were, was alarmed by these events and resorted to all means of ensuring that Jesus stopped his activities in Galilee. The tetrarch wanted to deactivate what he considered a potential danger, a rising against him and against Rome.

Jesus never again spent a long time (eight or nine months) in any one place, as he had in Capernaum. From now on, his constant traveling went on until the end of his life, with brief and intermittent stays in a number of towns in Judaea and Peraea, including Jerusalem. His life became clandestine and secretive because of Antipas' hostility. He had had a continued public presence during his time in Capernaum, which became more intermittent now that he began his forced flight from Galilee.

Antipas' hostility was a thorn in Jesus' side that made it more difficult to freely proclaim the message of the Kingdom and led to his and his followers having to live without a home, with no nest or hole, and having to keep an eye on Antipas' movements and those of his acolytes, the so-called Herodians (see 3.4.2). The statement in Mark 3:6, according to which Herod Antipas' supporters played an active role in the plans against Jesus "to destroy him," is evidence of his hostile and threatening attitude, though it was not always at the same level of intensity and vehemence. Nonetheless, Jesus would not suffer the same fate as his guide, John the Baptist, beheaded at the hands of Antipas, but as victim of the enmity of the temple authorities. The historical "adversary," the tetrarch of Galilee, reappeared only briefly during Jesus' trial, since Jesus had for some time lived far from Galilee and no longer represented a need for concern for him (Luke 23:6-12; and 6.2.4.3).

It is difficult to know exactly what sort of relations there were between Jesus and the temple leaders before his triumphal entrance into Jerusalem, only a few days before his death. It seems that a statement by Jesus referring to the destruction and reconstruction of the temple played an important role in affecting the decisions made by the Jewish authorities: "[I will] destroy this temple, and in three days I will raise it up." According to John 2:19, Jesus said this during a discussion on his first trip to Jerusalem, whereas Mark 14:58 dates it to the end of his life. What value and repercussions did this statement have on the opinion of the authorities in Jerusalem? Did they see it as a direct attack on the temple or as simply naive and not worthy of being taken into consideration (wanting to raise up a building that thousands of men had been working on for the past forty-six years!)?

The authorities in Jerusalem were well aware of all of the movements taking place in Jewish territories. In the same way that the Baptist received a visit from "priests and Levites" sent from Jerusalem to interrogate him (John 1:19), so too did Jesus from "scribes" coming from Jerusalem to investigate the miracles he was carrying out. Their verdict was overwhelming: Jesus was possessed by the devil, with whom he was working in harmony, and that is how he was able to expel demons from the possessed (Mark 3:22). This accusation was worthy of the death penalty, as can be seen in the Mishnah (*Sanh.* 7:4): "The following are stoned: . . . a necromancer or a wizard." This was the official accusation made against Jesus according to the Babylonian Talmud (*Sanh.* 43a): "Yeshu, the Nazarene, . . . is going forth to be stoned because he has practised sorcery and enticed Israel to apostasy" (*Sanh.* 107b) (see 2.2.1.2).

Nonetheless, the accusation of practicing sorcery, expelling demons, did not appear in Jesus' trial, though he was accused of blasphemy and being a false prophet, and there were a good number of concerns that he might upset the fragile political balance with the Romans. Jesus, to the leaders, was someone who tricked and led the people astray with his doctrines. Matthew 27:63 agrees with the point of view of the Talmud, calling Jesus an "impostor [someone leading the people to apostasy]" and with John 7:12 and 7:47, which say that he was someone who "is leading the people astray."

If we follow the information from the Gospel according to John, Jesus traveled to Jerusalem at least twice during the last part of his life: for the Feast of Tabernacles, in September–October 29 A.D. (John 7:1) and for the Feast of Dedication, in November–December of the same year (John 10:22). In both cases, his stay in the city was marked by exchanges with the teachers of the Law and was the setting for healings (the man who had been blind from birth and the paralytic man at Bethzatha). It is likely that Jesus spoke in public in the temple and debated, to varying degrees of intensity, with the Pharisee and Sadducee teachers, though much more with the former than the latter.

The Gospel tradition refers to only one explicit argument between Jesus and the Sadducees, with respect to the resurrection of the dead (Mark 12:18-27 and synoptic parallels), which ended with an overwhelming "you are quite wrong," when Jesus sided with the point of view of the Pharisees, who defended the final resurrection. However, other dialectic exchanges, such as the question put to Jesus about the authority with which he acted (Mark 11:27-33 and synoptic parallels) and the parable of the murderous tenants (Mark 12:1-9 and synoptic parallels), were almost certainly addressed to the temple authorities. Jesus used the story of the murderous tenants to allude to the growing hostility against him from the temple leaders and other important figures in Jerusalem (scribes and nobles). The tenants are described as people who show an unequalled hardness of heart toward the owner of the vineyard. Their evil is translated into the cold-blooded murder of the owner's only son and heir, with the explicit intention of taking over the land. It is more than likely that this parable was used toward the end of Jesus' life, when his death was imminent and irreversible in his eyes (see 6.1.2.2).

In respect of the possible hostility from the Pharisees, we have to take into account a great number of nuances. On one occasion, Pharisee scribes were sent from Jerusalem to find Jesus, whom they argued with about issues relating to ritual purity, and specifically the need to wash one's hands before eating (Mark 7:5). Obviously, this is a very different kind issue, and not one that can be considered worthy of the death penalty (see 5.3.2.2). The Pharisees seem to have been divided when it came to Jesus. While some of them were willing to warn him about Antipas' evil intentions, or may even have secretly been followers of his, others sided with the Herodians and joined in with the tetrarch's plans. This was the case in the healing of the man with the withered hand (Mark 3:6), to the extent that Jesus warned his disciples about the dangers of the leaven of the two groups (Mark 8:15).

Nonetheless, neither the Pharisees nor the Herodians played any role in the machinations that led to Jesus' arrest, trial, and sentence. Only the tribute to Caesar was a trap set by both of these groups for Jesus, in order to see whether he would pronounce himself for or against Roman power. It was, in fact, an issue that could have led to a serious political accusation against him (see 3.3.3.2).

Those who were openly hostile to Jesus and who directly led to his death were his main adversaries, the temple leaders, people linked or belonging to the Sadducee group. The temple staff, led by Caiaphas, acted quickly and effectively, but only once Jesus had entered the city triumphantly as the Messiah and after carrying out the prophetic act against the commercial activities taking place in the temple's atria. These events were the straw that broke the camel's back and accelerated the execution of a decision that had already been taken by the Sanhedrin with respect to Jesus (6.2.3.1).

The decision came because the distrust and concerns vis-à-vis the Galilean rabbi had turned into outright and deeply felt hostility, which they attempted to keep in check but which came to the fore in the decision to have him killed. The hawks are to win the battle, the high priests, the temple's leading figures, and the doves are to lose, that is, a small group of influential Pharisees (among whom was Nicodemus, who may not have been a member of the Sanhedrin, and, possibly, the rabbi Gamaliel), led by Joseph of Arimathea (a secret follower of Jesus, a nobleman from Jerusalem and member of the Sanhedrin). The Roman authorities were not involved until the last moment, when they intervened (not without certain apprehensions) and sanctioned the accusation brought against Jesus: that this Galilean was a threat to Rome, a pretender to the throne who wanted to take Caesar's place, "the king of the Jews."

6.1.1.2. The Destiny of the Prophets

In the words of Jesus, John the Baptist was "more than a prophet," the greatest of those born to a woman, the greatest of the prophets (Matt 11:9-11 || Luke 7:26-28). His destiny was as foreseen for all of those sent by God to his people: rejection and violent death. John preached by the Jordan, but the leaders in Jerusalem, the temple authorities and the scribes, did not take any notice of him, they did not come to define him or acknowledge him as a prophet acting and speaking with inspiration from the divine Spirit. John was not believed by Israel's religious elites, as can be seen when Jesus was asked about the authority with which he acted. Nonetheless, the people definitely saw John as being sent by God, as being a prophet (Mark 11:27-33 || Matt 21:23-27 || Luke 20:1-8). Jesus emphasized the positive feelings of the people toward John and referred bitterly to the opposition he faced despite this from the religious authorities and Antipas in particular, the man who had him killed and who "did to him whatever they pleased" (Mark 9:13 || Matt 17:12). John and his message of repentance were not accepted, and he was killed, beheaded, at Machaerus following a lengthy spell of imprisonment.

In the eyes of Jesus, the Baptist was a prophet and a martyr, the last of a long line of prophets who had all shared the same end. The example of the Baptist could not leave him indifferent, as the rabbi of Nazareth had welcomed John's baptism and had even become one of his followers. His closeness to the Baptist represented a point of reference for Jesus, placing both himself and John among those in the long line of prophets who were martyred for Israel (see 4.5.2.3).

In Jesus' case, his destiny as a martyr was explicitly linked to Jerusalem. This can be seen in a highly significant statement that he made: "[I]t cannot be that a prophet should perish away from Jerusalem" (Luke 13:33). In other words, this is where a prophet has to die. Jesus believed this: he, the prophet of the Kingdom, had to die in the great King's city. The last year of Jesus' public activities, from Passover 29 A.D. to Passover 30 A.D., represented a period of waiting, a long journey through Galilee, Peraea, and Judaea that led him to Jerusalem. During this time, Jesus stayed briefly on a number of occasions in the city, which was to be the final destination of his travels through Jewish and non-Jewish lands.

Jesus reacted to the threat from Antipas by explaining, "today and tomorrow," that for some time yet he could continue to carry out healings and exorcisms, and that on "the third day," an uncertain point in the future, "I will finish my course"; in other words, the time would come for his death and all that this is to imply. There was a great serenity in this somewhat enigmatic look into the future that Jesus offered of his own life (Luke 13:32). Nevertheless, Jesus did not try to speed up or slow down his life's rhythm. There were a series of steps or stages, a path that he followed decisively and with a sense of the responsibility. It is clear that his "course" had a precise nature, but in the meantime, "today and tomorrow, and the third day," that is, while life went on, Jesus would not deviate from or dawdle on this path. His mission as messenger for the Kingdom would continue until the end.

What was awaiting Jesus in Jerusalem? What idea did he have of his own future? Why did Jesus see Jerusalem as the setting for his death, and what was this death to entail? The most direct answer to these questions is to be found in a lamentation about the city that Jesus utters, probably at the end of his life. It is a fragment handed down by the Q collection, which exudes strong feelings and which echoes in style the oracles of the great prophets of Israel. With his feelings hurt, Jesus talks of the city, saying, "O Jerusalem, Jerusalem, killing the prophets and stoning those who are sent to you!" (Matt 23:37 || Luke 13:34).

Rejection and suffering form part of the destiny of the martyred prophets, victims of a city that has become hardened and unable to recognize those sent by God himself. The city and its people, however, have become deaf and want to silence the voices of those sent by

God through an ignominious death that Moses' Law stipulates ironically for those who are enemies of the Almighty: stoning (see 6.1.1.1). This was the destiny of Zechariah, who accused the people of having abandoned their God and who was stoned to death in Jerusalem at the orders of King Joash (2 Chr 24:21), and of Stephen, the early Church's first martyr, who was also stoned in Jerusalem (Acts 7:58-59). Jesus was to be executed in accordance with the Roman laws and was to die on the cross. Jesus foresaw a violent death, but not the way in which it was to happen.

Nevertheless, Jesus' feelings for Jerusalem, the city and people who are to lead to his climactic death, which represents the end of a long line of prophets, are full of warm tenderness. His lamentation for Jerusalem continues with an image of care and protection: "How often would I have gathered your children together as a hen gathers her brood under her wings, and you would not!" (Matt 23:37 || Luke 13:34). The city did not want Jesus to get close to it, offering the warmth of his salvation. The metaphor that Jesus uses involves a domestic family setting full of maternal color: the image of the farmyard where the chicks run anxiously behind their mother and search for protection under her wings. There is, however, a one 180-degree turn that indicates their unnatural behavior: the chicks run away from their mother; they do not search for her, despite her wanting to cover them with her wings.

Jesus' preaching in Jerusalem had not, on the whole, been welcomed, and his invitation to enter the Kingdom to the inhabitants of the city had been turned down. As in the Galilean towns, which were witness to his miracles, the people of Jerusalem had been offered many gestures of welcome and compassion by Jesus, but these gestures had been fruitless. Jesus' relationship with Jerusalem reminds us of the way God treated Israel, his people, when he freed them from Egypt and established the covenant with them: "I bore you on eagles' wings" (Exod 19:4; Deut 32:11). Jesus had sought to bring the people of Jerusalem together under the message of the Kingdom, but he had encountered only indifference and rejection. He concludes, "Behold your house is forsaken and desolate" (Matt 23:38 || Luke 13:35).

The indifference shown to his message and the direct opposition to Jesus himself were to have serious consequences for those who had spilt the blood of the prophets: God was to abandon them, and they were to be called to account (Matt 23:34-36 || Luke 11:49-51). Jesus' words, pronounced with sadness and unrequited love, are not unlike those that the prophet Jeremiah used, in the name of God, to address the people in the temple's atrium: "I am bringing upon this city [Jerusalem] . . . all the evil that I have pronounced upon it [the destruction of the city], because they have stiffened their neck, refusing to hear my words" (Jer 19:15).

Jesus foresees that he is to share the violent destiny of the prophets of Israel, his people, especially that of John the Baptist, and that Jerusalem is to be the setting for his martyrdom. This death is to act as the climax to the city's indifferent rejection. They have not welcomed his preaching, and they have not believed in it. His certainty that he is to share a similar destiny to the other prophets is taking shape and can clearly be seen in the last days of his life.

6.1.1.3. The Forewarnings to the Disciples

Nonetheless, the references, whether indirect or alluded to, to his own death are not exclusive to the last days of Jesus' life. Beforehand, there were also suggestions and signs of this, which he himself had communicated to his disciples. On a number of occasions, Jesus pointed out the difficulties that the disciples were going to come across and that were to lead to their losing their lives. Each disciple had to take "his cross" and carry it if he really wanted to follow the Master (Matt 10:38 || Luke 14:27; also Mark 8:34 || Matt 16:24 || Luke 9:23). Carrying the cross meant incorporating the gospel into his life and making it the focal point (see 4.5.3.2). It is significant that Jesus explained what it meant to deny oneself by using the image of the sentenced on their way to the scaffold, themselves carrying the instrument of torture: this image represents, maybe more than any other, the denial of one's own ego. Death on the cross is an ignominious torture that crushes a person's dignity. This is the torture to be applied to Jesus.

In another similar statement, Jesus put forward the idea of having to lose one's life in order to save it: "[W]hoever would save his life will lose it; and whoever loses his life for my sake and the gospel's will save it" (Mark 8:35). This statement is also found in the Q source (Matt 10:39 || Luke 17:33) and in the Gospel according to John (12:25). It is a paradoxical phrase that puts the importance of conserving one's life for whatever price into perspective by stressing the value of losing it in order to be saved for eternity. The most important thing is that we experience a death that saves us in life, that is, not losing one's life forever. According to Jesus, we should not be afraid of those who "kill the body but cannot kill the soul" (Matt 10:28 || Luke 12:4-5).

In addition to these general references to death and carrying the cross, Jesus frequently alluded directly to his own death. The oldest core of the so-called "three Passion predictions" is most probably the phrase from Mark 9:31: "The Son of man will be delivered into the hands of men." Here, as J. D. G. Dunn points out, there is a highly expressive play on words in the original Aramaic, between *man* and *men*. This sentence is fairly vague, both the *man* who is to die and the *men* who are to kill him. The three Passion predictions all state, in the three synoptic Gospels (and somewhat differently in the Gospel of John), that Jesus is to follow the path to his death, from Caesarea Philippi (in the far north of the country) to Jerusalem (Mark 8:31, 9:31, 10:33-34 and the parallels in Matthew and Luke). The Gospel tradition is solid in its agreement on when Jesus announced his death to his disciples in the final stages of his life, before traveling to Jerusalem for the last time.

It is, however, an announcement that his followers cannot come to accept, if we bear in mind the request made by James and John, two of the Twelve, to Jesus and the response they received. Zebedee's two sons asked for places of honor in the glorious kingdom of the Messiah Jesus, and he reminded them that they must first experience suffering and death. Jesus used images of baptism (Mark 10:38-39 || Luke 12:50) and the cup (Mark 10:38-39 || Matt 20:22-23). Jesus assured James and John that they would be baptized with the same baptism as him and that they would drink from the same cup. It is a prophecy with broad implications, since Jesus would in fact have to suffer the Passion and die on the cross alone, and accompanied not by these two loyal disciples but by two bandits. Jesus stressed that the same destiny was to unite them in the future and that this destiny involved suffering and death.

The hints, whether direct or indirect, that Jesus made to his disciples with regard to his imminent death became more frequent following his jubilant entrance into Jerusalem. His subsequent actions against the trading in the temple and the Last Supper, which Jesus shared with the Twelve, were the result of consciously made decisions. Jesus prepared his great entrance into the city meticulously, sending two disciples ahead to search for the donkey he was to ride on during the procession. Jesus gave them precise instructions: the disciples had to go to the neighboring town and take the donkey that no one had ridden, which they would find tied up in the street by a door. Jesus' entrance alerted the Jewish authorities (not the Romans!), and the tension increased when Jesus entered the temple and carried out a prophetic act, attacking the money-changers and pigeon sellers, overturning their tables and stopping anyone from carrying anything through the atrium of this holy place.

The disciples, clearly active participants in the Master's entrance into the city and direct witnesses to his actions in the temple, must have detected a greater intensity in the attitude of the temple leaders toward Jesus. It is not at all clear, however, how they interpreted it: as a sign of the imminent establishment of the Kingdom, under the guidance of Jesus the Messiah, or as part of the growing tensions that could lead to the Master's violent death and the failure of his project. The reactions of the Twelve during the Last Supper and in Gethsemane and the words of the disciples on their way to Emmaus ("we had hoped that he was the one to redeem Israel"; Luke 24:21) would seem to show that they were more inclined toward the former. We can be sure, however, that doubts must have been sown by the warnings they were receiving from Jesus.

During the last days of Jesus' life, he gave the disciples two fairly explicit hints as to his imminent death. The Master and the Twelve had been invited to Simon the Leper's house in Bethany, a town in Judaea just three kilometers from Jerusalem. Bethany was the town where Jesus and his disciples spent the night, at least following his triumphal entrance into Jerusalem. In Simon's house, a woman, Mary, sister of Lazarus and Martha, started anointing Jesus' head, scandalizing the disciples, according to whom the money that the perfume cost, three hundred denarii, should have been given to the poor. But Jesus praised what Mary had done, saying, "She has anointed my body beforehand for burying"/"Let her alone, let her keep it for the day of my burial" (Mark 14:8; John 12:7). Jesus' statement did not implicitly mean that his death was imminent, but this was the most obvious meaning. Jesus saw the anointing as a sign that he was soon to die and be buried, and he made this known to his disciples who, scandalized and miserable, probably did not fully understand the scope of their Master's words. Jesus' response was stern: "They that are with me have not understood me" (Acts of Peter 10).

The last indication that Jesus gave the disciples came in his speech during the Last Supper, on the Thursday night, the day before his death. This meal, like Jesus' entrance into Jerusalem, had been carefully planned and organized by Jesus himself as his farewell meal. The supper was characterized by a series of extraordinary gestures and words regarding the bread and wine. After the supper, while they were still sitting at the table, Jesus, among other things, said to the Twelve, "Truly, I say to you, I shall not drink again of the fruit of the vine until that day when I drink it new in the Kingdom of God/until the Kingdom of God comes" (Mark 14:25 || Luke 22:18). It is clear that Jesus wants to show that this is the last time he is going to eat with his disciples. His words show that he can sense that his death is imminent and that there will not be time to celebrate the Passover, on Friday night, less than twenty-four hours away. For this reason, he had decided to organize this unique farewell supper in Jerusalem, the city that kills the prophets that God sends them. Jesus openly explained here the meaning that he gave his death and the meaning he gave his life (see 6.1.3).

6.1.2. A Meaningful Death

Jesus of Nazareth intuitively knew about his forthcoming death, but he had not looked for it, as those do who seek to sacrifice themselves. This death was the result of many factors that had gradually become interwoven into a form of spider's web that enveloped him and which, in the end, he could not overcome. Jesus found himself facing a death that he did not seek, but, similarly, which he did not try to avoid or run away from. He simply placed himself in front it, faced up to it and accepted it. Despite his doubts at the last minute in the garden of Gethsemane, he did not reject his imminent death, rather he saw it as the result of God's will for him. Jesus saw meaning in death, a meaning that came not from him but from his intimate relationship with God, the Father. God brought meaning to Jesus' death, as his suffering became a means by which liberation and salvation could be spread. As B. F. Meyer states, Jesus did not aim to be rejected and killed; his aim was instead to take on this rejection and death and bring them meaning. Or as N. T. Wright has pointed out, in the final analysis, Jesus died because that was his vocation.

6.1.2.1. A Life and Death for Others

Throughout his life, Jesus constantly offered his care in the service of others and received demands for it. The God, of which Jesus talked, who is manifest in his healings, is generous and inspires generosity. Jesus invites those who listen to him to make mercy their guiding principle, imitating God's behavior: "Be merciful, even as your Father is merciful" (Luke 6:36). Jesus himself uses the image of serving a table as the best example of loving others. Loving means being at the service of others, as when waiting on them, making sure they have everything they need. The Last Supper is, no doubt, the setting for a statement addressed by Jesus to his disciples: "[W]hich is the greater, one who sits at table, or one who serves? Is it not the one who sits at table? But I am among you as one who serves" (Luke 22:27). Furthermore, during this farewell supper, Jesus, the Master, made a gesture of serving reserved for servants and slaves: he washed the feet of those present, in this case his own disciples. He also shared the bread and wine with them as a sign of giving and love taken to the extreme (see 6.1.3.2, below).

Words regarding freely chosen and voluntary service are frequent in Jesus' message, for example, the parable of the man who returns from a wedding and praises his servants for having stayed up throughout the night, waiting for their master to return. His reaction is somewhat surprising: he makes them sit at the table and serves them (Luke 12:36-38). Serving acts as a common denominator in the reciprocal situation between servants and master. Jesus overcomes the distinction between those who have to serve and those who are privileged enough to be served. For his people, "if any one would be first, he must be last of all and servant of all" (Mark 9:35). The first have to take the place destined for the last, those who are overlooked, becoming their servant, and not think of themselves, but take care of the poor, the hungry, and the sad.

The humble service to which the disciples are called is in contrast to the arrogance of those who control and oppress, those who are enslaved by their self-interest. Jesus reminded the Twelve that, unlike those who have power and influence who use these to annihilate the weak, "it shall not be so among you; but whoever would be great among you must be your servant" (Mark 10:43 || Matt 20:26). Being the first means being a slave to everyone: this is a fundamental rule for Jesus' disciples.

The image of freely accepting service was chosen by Jesus in order to summarize his mission and so as to act as a focal point for his life: "For the Son of man also came not to be served but to serve" (Mark 10:45 || Matt 20:28). Jesus' life is a great gesture of committed and active service in favor of the sinners and the poor. God offers those marginalized for religious reasons forgiveness through Jesus, and the poor are, beyond doubt, the chosen people for the Kingdom, the audience for the good news, the gospel, which is to transform their lives. Jesus takes on, as part of his activities, God's desire to ensure that he does not lose any of his children, whether good or bad, just or unjust. From this perspective, everyone is welcomed, even his enemies, those who hate him, who persecute and try to eliminate him. Jesus preached and practiced love for one's enemies, convinced that violence had to be removed from our hearts. In the Lord's Prayer, the prayer for the disciples, loving one's enemies is as an explicit commitment: "forgive us our debts, as also we have forgiven our debtors/every one who is indebted to us" (Matt 6:12 || Luke 11:4).

If Jesus' life was a great gesture of serving and giving, of giving himself up for others, his death could not be any different. If Jesus, loyal to God, his Father, lived bringing salvation to everyone, then he could not see his death any differently. If his life was a continuous offering to others, his death had to represent his giving his life for others, as God himself wished and accepted. His death was not complete on its own, instead it was projected out to those he had served, each and every one of us. Jesus' death is the (harmonious and dramatic) continuation of his life.

If while alive Jesus had accepted his role as the chosen instrument for God's salvation to reach everyone, now his freely accepted death was, paradoxically, to become the means by which this salvation was to be spread. This can be seen in Mark 10:45 (|| Matt 20:28): "[T]he Son of man [has come] . . . to give his life as a ransom for many." Reading between the lines, we can see the Servant figure as prophesied by Isaiah, a figure who offers his life in sacrifice in order to expiate the sins of everyone else, a figure who "bore the sin of many" (Isa 53:10-12). As J. B. Green states, Jesus' death becomes a microcosm of his life.

6.1.2.2. A Meaning from God, the Father

Many Jewish writings from the second and first centuries B.C. refer to the suffering experienced by the people of Israel or some of the members of this people, persecuted by enemies of God and the Law. The virulent aggression of Antiochus IV Epiphanes against the Jewish religion led to the execution or murder of large numbers of people, people who preferred death to having to submit themselves to the king's wishes or to abandon the Law and go against the covenant. For example, the elder Eleazar and the seven brothers, who they wanted to force to eat pork, paid with their lives, martyred for their loyalty to the Law of the ancestors (2 Macc 6, 7). Indeed, "very great wrath came upon Israel" (1 Macc 1:64). The book of Daniel comes from the same era and also mentions the persecution suffered by "the people of the saints of the Most High" who "shall be given into his hand," the hand of King Antiochus, leader of the enemy, the fourth kingdom (Dan 7:23-25). In particular, the "wise" among them, the people's leaders, who are honest and law-abiding, fell, so as "to refine and cleanse them" (Dan 11:35).

The suffering of the just also appears in the Book of Wisdom. Here, the just are vividly presented as people who avoid contact with those who do not abide by the Law and see themselves as children of God. The impious seek to test them with insults and torture, they seek to sentence them to an ignominious death, to see whether "[God] will help him, and will deliver him from the hand of his adversaries" (Wisdom 2:18). This image strongly echoes that of the Passion of Christ and is similar to the images in some of the Psalms, especially 22, 31, and 69. In Psalm 22:9, the just are subjected to the people's taunts, in a way that closely mirrors the Book of Wisdom, and which is taken up again in Matthew 27:43: "He trusts in God; let God deliver him now, if he desires him."

The fourth song of God's Suffering Servant (Isa 52:13–53:12) is not interpreted by the Jewish writings as referring to the Messiah. And neither is this Old Testament figure introduced in the Gospel narratives on the Passion. The only exception is Luke 22:37, which quotes Isaiah 53:12 ("he was reckoned with transgressors"). This is a surprising omission given the analogies existing between the situation of Isaiah's Suffering Servant and the Passion of Christ. It is probably down to the fact that Jesus did not seem to have identified himself with the figure of God's Servant during the Passion, as set out in the book of the prophet Isaiah, whereas, as we shall see later (6.1.3.3), on the cross he does identify himself with the persecuted and suffering figure in Psalm 22: the man who has fallen into the hands of his adversaries and who, overcome by a feeling of profound loneliness, asks God to free him and to save him.

Nonetheless, all this does not mean that Jesus did not give a sense of salvation to his death. The sense that Jesus gave to his death, as with the sense that he had given to his life, is linked to his experience of God. In other words, Jesus accepted the Passion and death on the cross because he saw this as being his Father's will, so that his salvation could take root in the very heart of mankind. This can be seen in Jesus' solemn statement, referred to in Luke 13:33: "I must go on my way today and tomorrow and the day following; for it cannot be that a prophet should perish away from Jerusalem."

The prophets' deaths are not peaceful affairs but deaths preceded by rejection and accompanied by suffering (Matt 27:37-39 || Luke 13:34-35, a text we have already commented on in 6.1.1.2). The case of the prophet Jeremiah is a paradigm of how God's emissaries were victims of insult and attack, hostility and betrayal, and who, despite this, still trusted in him who sent them to be a prophet among his people (e.g., the so-called fifth confession of Jeremiah at 20:7-13). The prophet states how he was always at the mercy of the sword that devours "like a ravening lion" (Jer 2:30). The divine envoy acts as a stumbling block for many because he calls for repentance and is seen as an annoyance and has to be killed (Neh 9:26).

Nonetheless, the difficult path followed by the prophets, which involves suffering and death, is the path laid out by God. Jesus says that the reason he goes to Jerusalem is because "he has to," as this is God's will. His death makes sense in that it is in accordance with a will that is difficult to understand from the point of view of the safety of the one who has to experience it: the prophet is martyred because of his loyalty to God and the message that he has entrusted him with. The path that the prophets have to follow is the path of a martyr: a path that has been both chosen for them and entrusted to them. Their death is given the meaning that God wants to give it. It is not the result of arrogance or temerity but the result of loyalty to a destiny and a meaning. Jesus, who was always close to the Father in everything, sees his death in this way, making the salvation and liberation that the Father instills in the Passion his own.

Probably Jesus' most expressive look at the why and wherefore of his own future comes in the parable of the murderous tenants (Mark 12:1-9 || Matt 21:33-41 || Luke 20:9-16 || Thomas 65). The image created fits perfectly with the situation at the end of Jesus' life. There are three figures in the narrative: the vineyard's owner, his son, and his tenants. The parable tells the story of a vineyard owner who has taken good care of his property, who leases it out for a year to some tenants and who has traveled to some distant part. When the time comes for the harvest, he sends servants three times to collect the part of the fruit that belongs to him, but on all three occasions the tenants abuse, attack, and insult them and they have to return empty-handed. Then, the owner decides to send his only son, sure that the tenants will at least respect him; but the tenants not only do not respect him, they decide to kill him so as to be able to take his inheritance, which is not rightfully theirs and which the father has been keeping for his son. The tenants show a brutal determination: they take the son, kill him, and throw his body out of the vineyard, leaving him unburied.

The analogies between this parable and the situation that Jesus found himself in are striking and show how Jesus foresaw his own death at the hands of his own people's authorities (the tenants), who abused their responsibility for Israel (the vineyard) to the extent that they rejected the prophets (the servants) and appropriated an inheritance that belonged to God (the owner) alone. The climax of the narrative comes with the appearance of the son. He represents a key part of the father's project for the vineyard, a project that is full of patience and forgiveness for these unworthy tenants who have attacked the people sent to them and who, for this alone, deserve punishment and rejection. The father, however, responds to this evil with goodness and decides to send them what is most valuable to him, his own son. He still trusts the tenants and believes that they will know how to respond to this great gesture of affection. This is where the son enters, as his father's emissary. However, instead of accepting and respecting him, as his father has expected, they end up killing him (a premeditated and conspiratorial killing, without warning) and go on to carry out an even more despicable act (leaving the son's body unburied). The narrative is intense and dramatic, as the subject matter demands.

We should stress that the parable, which is dense in both form and content, is not intended to be a portrayal of what is to happen to Jesus, but instead it seeks to show what is happening to him in the present. Two details point to the parable's not acting as some kind of trailer to the upcoming film. First, unlike the son in the parable, Jesus is not actually killed by Israel's religious authorities but sentenced to death and executed by the Romans. Second, unlike what happens to the son's body, Jesus' body does not remain unburied, as one of the people's leaders, a member of the Sanhedrin and follower of Jesus, Joseph of Arimathea, takes charge of burying him in a tomb that he himself owns (see 6.2.6).

The main point of the parable for us is that Jesus identified with the figure of the son sent by the vineyard's owner. Jesus is the last of the emissaries sent by God, the Father, who is to suffer and die as a result of his benevolence toward Israel, his people and their leaders. In the parable, the reason for the son's death and what gives it meaning is the father's wish to send him to the vineyard and to the tenants. Their response is an insult to the father's infinite goodwill, and that of the son.

Nevertheless, beyond the boundaries of the parable, the death of the son does not affect the Father's intention which Jesus, the Son, has accepted: to go to the vineyard as a sign of love and benevolence. The death of the Son is the result of a decision made by the Father, who wants to save the tenants from the evil they have committed by offering them the presence and company of his own Son. The exaggerated and incomprehensible hardness of heart shown by the authorities/

tenants leads to Jesus'/the son's cruel death, but this death has meaning in the equally exaggerated and incomprehensible love of God/the owner for his people. Jesus' death is not only an unjust condemnation of a defenseless and innocent man but also the martyrdom of the Son sent by the Father. God's wishes and his plans for love and forgiveness are the foundation for the cross on which Jesus is crucified.

6.1.3. The Last Supper

Jesus talked about the meaning of his death most when he was with the Twelve, his closest circle of disciples, for the last time. On Thursday, April 6, 30 A.D., the day before the Passion and his death, Jesus, who was staying in Bethany, decided to have supper with the Twelve in a house within the walls of Jerusalem, and he sent two of his disciples to prepare the meal (Mark 14:12-16 || Matt 26:17-19 || Luke 22:7-13). The disciples entered Jerusalem with their errand and discretely, almost secretively, organized the meal in a large room in a house in the city, which had already been prepared with curtains and cushions. The two disciples did not know the exact address of the house and, in accordance with the instructions they had received from Jesus, they were to be guided by a man carrying a jar of water who they were to find once they had entered the city. As the sun set, Jesus turned up at this house with the Twelve.

For him, though no doubt not for them, this was a farewell meal. As well as washing the feet of his disciples, Jesus also pronounced some words when breaking the bread (at the start of the meal) and over the cup of wine (when it ends). The reason for these words, and the gestures that were designed to explain them, reflected the sense that Jesus explicitly gave his imminent death. Here, on the threshold of the Passion, Jesus "saw" deep into events, placing his death in the context of the past, present, and future. Jesus focused and summed up his whole life in the Last Supper. This valedictory meal shows, more than any other event in Jesus' life, the meaning that he wanted to give to his death.

Jesus' Last Supper with the Twelve is recounted in the three main New Testament traditions: the synoptic Gospels, the Gospel according to John, and the record of the Apostle Paul. This supper became

Jesus' spiritual testament, and this is how it was interpreted by the Gospels of Luke (22:14-38) and, in particular, John, which presents it as his farewell. John dedicates no fewer than five chapters of his Gospel to it (13–17)! The oldest historical source that we have on it, however, is the First Epistle to the Corinthians, written by the Apostle Paul between the years 55 and 56 A.D. (11:23-26). In this letter, Paul refers to Jesus' words and gestures regarding the bread and wine "on the night when he was betrayed," stressing that it was a tradition "received from the Lord"; it comes from the very life of Jesus. Paul states that he received the tradition personally and that he has passed it on to the Corinthians, as the core to the celebration of the Eucharist. Separately from Paul, the Gospel according to Mark (14:22-25), which the Gospel according to Matthew is dependent upon (26:26-29), also reports what Jesus did and said when breaking the bread and sharing the wine among those present, the Twelve. The Gospel according to Luke (22:15-20) relies heavily on what is related in the First Epistle to the Corinthians.

All four of these narratives show signs of the influence of the liturgical celebrations of the Eucharist as practiced by the early Christian communities, in both the stylized and hierarchical language and some of the expressions and additions. More proof of this influence can be seen in the passage of the Gospel according to John (6:51-58) that talks about eating the flesh and drinking the blood of the Son of Man.

6.1.3.1. A Farewell Meal in the Context of the Passover

The first question we need to ask ourselves relates to the nature of this Last Supper. We can be absolutely sure that Jesus' last meal began on a Thursday "evening" (Mark 14:17) and continued into the night. It was a Friday as, in accordance with Jewish custom, the days began at sunset (on the day before). Paul dates it as "the night when he [Jesus] was betrayed" (1 Cor 11:23), and the Gospel of John states that, when Judas left, "it was night" (John 13:30).

The meal took place in a house in Jerusalem belonging to an acquaintance of Jesus, which had a "large," spacious room on the top floor, traditionally known as the "cenacle" or upper room. There were probably thirteen men present, Jesus and his closest circle of disciples, the Twelve, though one of them, Judas, left before it was over. We should not dismiss out of hand, though, that, as an exception, there may have been women present, including Mary, Jesus' mother. It is most likely that they were served while seated at the table by a servant provided by the house's owner for the occasion, in accordance with Jewish custom. There may be an indication of this in Luke 22:27: "[W]hich is the greater, one who sits at table, or one who serves?" The room had been prepared with "curtains and cushions," and they ate almost "lying down" (Mark 14:14, 14:18) or reclining on divans placed around the table in a U shape (John 13:12). They were not seated on chairs but reclined, and they did not have individual plates, instead taking food or dipping in sauces from the shared dishes on the table. Each person had his own cup for wine, though.

The scene that we have just described based on the information from the texts constitutes a festive meal, which, in this case, was presided over not by the head of the family or household but by Jesus, the Master. However, that Thursday evening in 30 A.D. was not a feast day; the great meal, the most important of the year, the Passover supper, was to take place the following day, the Friday, the fourteenth day of Nisan, after sunset when the Passover had begun. The Last Supper that Jesus had with the Twelve was festive and extraordinary because this was how he wanted it to be.

The meal followed the usual customs of Jewish festive meals: a blessing/thanksgiving prayer over the bread at the start of the meal; the meal itself, which was abundant, and shared between them all; and a blessing/thanksgiving prayer over the wine following the meal. This is detailed by Paul, who refers to "the cup of blessing," the cup drunk "after supper" (1 Cor 10:16 and 11:25). Obviously, a festive and abundant meal did not come to an abrupt end, but continued; and this farewell meal merited some last words from Jesus to his disciples. The Gospels of Luke (22:14-38) and John (chaps. 13–17) state that this was the setting for a long speech from Jesus, accompanied by some questions and remarks from the disciples.

The most surprising thing about this meal was that Jesus converted the blessings (Hebrew, *berakha*; Greek, *eulogia*) or thanksgiving prayers (Hebrew, *toda*; Greek, *eucharistia*), which are given at the start and end of the meal, into something very different. During Jewish festive meals, the person presiding takes a small round bun at the start and blesses it, to which those present respond with an "Amen." The person presiding breaks a bit of bread for each of those present and gives it to them. Jesus did the same, but he accompanied his action of breaking the bread with these words: "This is my body which is [given] for you." At the end of the meal, the person presiding took his or her cup full of wine, raised it, and gave a blessing, which was responded to by the others with an "Amen." Starting with the person who had made the blessing, everyone drank wine from their own cup. Jesus, however, did not keep to the established custom; instead, he gave the blessing over his own cup and passed this on to his disciples, so that they could each drink from it. This action was accompanied by the following words: "This cup [full of wine] is the new covenant [sealed] in my blood." Jesus wanted those present at the meal, the Twelve, to eat from one bread, broken and shared, and to drink from one cup of wine, shared among them all.

As was common during festive meals, those present remained at the table after drinking from the blessing cup, which Jesus had converted into the cup of the covenant and a powerful union between himself and the Twelve. There was still time to listen to the Master. His words now referred to another meal, the banquet at the end of time, which was to take place in the Kingdom of God. In the book of the prophet Isaiah, it is described in these words: "[T]he Lord of hosts will make for all his peoples a feast of fat things, a feast of wine on the lees" (Isa 25:6). Good wine is a characteristic of this great meal, and Jesus alludes to the banquet in the Kingdom by poetically making reference to the "fruit of the vine": "Truly, I say to you, I shall not drink again of the fruit of the vine until that day when I drink it new in the kingdom of God" (Mark 14:25 || Matt 26:29). In Luke 22:18, the phrase ends similarly: "until the kingdom of God comes." Jesus emphatically states that this is the farewell supper, as the next meal that he is to share with his disciples, the next time he will "drink wine" with them, will be at the final banquet of the Kingdom. Jesus' Last Supper is not the end but simply the turning of a page; it is a meal that is to continue and culminate in the Kingdom of God. This is how the early Christian communities rightly understood it, as can be seen in their liturgies that continued to celebrate Jesus' Last Supper, the Eucharist, as can be seen in the sentence "Do this in remembrance of me," which is found in Paul (1 Cor 11:24, 25) and in the Gospel of Luke (22:19) and which comes to make complete sense only following his resurrection after crucifixion. The early Christian Church picked up on and continued this meaning of the farewell supper, celebrating it.

The impact of these gestures and words of Jesus during the Last Supper was so great that the oldest Christian tradition had already brought them all together, as if everything had taken place simultaneously. Nevertheless, the model for Jewish festive meals has shown us that the three elements mentioned (the gesture and words regarding the bread, the gesture and words regarding the cup, and the words about the banquet in the Kingdom) would not have taken place one after the other: the first came at the start of the meal, the second when the meal had ended, and the third during the subsequent conversation. However, the Gospels according to Mark and Matthew have passed it down as one whole, whereby all three originally separate elements took place at the same time (Mark 14:22, 14:23-24, 14:25). Because of the demands of the narrative, Mark has to report Judas' betrayal of Jesus separately (Mark 14:18-21 || Matt 26:21-25). This announcement (and we need to stress that Jesus did not mention the name of Judas, the disciple who betrayed him) most likely took place during the meal ("at table eating"; Mark 14:18), and not before it, as an inattentive reading of the Gospel of Mark would have us believe. It is clear that the tradition of Mark and Matthew has stylized and fused the events of the Last Supper between Jesus and his disciples.

With respect to the Gospel of Luke, which depends greatly on what is related by the Apostle Paul, there is an even greater remodeling of events (Luke 22:14-23). The main development in Luke is that Jesus' Last Supper is presented as the Jewish Passover feast from the start, where Jesus said, "I have earnestly desired to eat this Passover with you before I suffer" (Luke 22:15). It goes on to talk about a first cup of wine that the disciples shared as a sign that their next meal with Jesus was going to be the banquet of the Kingdom; and only then are the gestures and words about the bread and cup of wine introduced (Luke 22:17-20). However, this order (first the cup or Kiddush cup, the breaking of the bread, and another cup or the blessing cup) is echoed in the Jewish ritual for the Passover meal, as referred to in the Mishnah (*Pesah.* 10). It does not match, however, the order of the Jewish festive meal (blessing and breaking of the bread, meal, blessing of the cup of wine), which was followed by Jesus in his farewell meal. Luke, as do Mark and Matthew, tells of Judas' betrayal separately, but, unlike the others, he places it right at the end (Luke 22:21-23).

Although Luke is the only Gospel that describes Jesus' farewell supper as if it were a Passover meal, the three synoptic Gospels (Matthew, Mark, and Luke) agree that the setting for this Last Supper was the Passover celebrations. Indeed, all three of them unanimously state that the supper took place "on the first day of the Unleavened Bread, when they sacrificed the passover lamb" (Mark 14:12 || Matt 26:17 || Luke 22:7), and all three mention Jesus' desire "to eat the passover with my disciples" (Mark 14:14 || Matt 26:18 || Luke 22:8, 22:11). Mark 14:26 and Matthew 26:30 explain that the meal ended with the singing of "psalms," in reference to the so-called *Hallel* (a hymn made of Ps 115–118) which is sung at the end of the Passover meal. The synoptic Gospels see this Thursday as the eve of Passover, the fourteenth day of Nisan, and have Jesus die on the day of Passover.

Nevertheless, the synoptic Gospels also contain a series of historically incongruous details and features in terms of this dating and seem to cast doubt on Jesus' Last Supper as a Passover meal (see 4.5.1.2). Therefore, despite referring to Jesus' Last Supper as a Passover meal, the synoptic Gospels do not contain any mention of the Passover lamb (which has to be sacrificed at the temple) or the unleavened bread or bitter herbs, which are all basic elements in the celebration of the Jewish Passover. However, the Gospel of John presents Jesus' farewell meal as a celebratory meal that begins on "the day of Preparation of the Passover" (John 19:14 and 31), Friday, the fourteenth day of Nisan, 30 A.D. The supper did not coincide with the celebration of the Jewish Passover meal that year. As a result, for both chronological and historical reasons, the circumstances surrounding the meal and its very structure, it seems obvious that the farewell meal between Jesus and the Twelve was an extraordinary and festive event, but not a Passover meal. This can be seen from the information provided by the Apostle Paul and the Gospel of John.

Despite all this, Passover symbolism surrounds Jesus' Last Supper both in Paul and in the Gospel according to John. In the latter, Jesus' death is directly linked to the regulations regarding the Passover lamb. The Gospel stresses that Jesus, after his death, does not have his legs broken (unlike the other two men crucified with him), and he is compared to the Passover lamb which, according to Exodus (12:46), had to be cooked and eaten without breaking a single bone (John 19:36). Right at the start of the Gospel, Jesus is presented as "the Lamb of God, who takes away the sin of the world!" (John 1:29, 1:36). While he died on the cross, the lambs that everyone in Jerusalem were to eat that night, the night of Passover, were being sacrificed in the temple. Thus, in the fourth Gospel, Jesus' death is a redeeming death and fully integrated into the Passover, where Jesus takes the place of the sacrificed lamb.

In the First Epistle to the Corinthians, written by the Apostle Paul, Jesus is called "our paschal lamb," which "has been sacrificed" like those lambs that are slaughtered for the Jewish Passover (5:7). The memory of being saved and freed from Egypt is now converted into salvation brought by Jesus' death and resurrection. Paul contrasts the old leaven of evil and those who have been liberated thanks to Jesus Christ: the unleavened bread, the Passover bread, has become a symbol of new life.

Jesus himself decided to organize a farewell meal with his disciples, the Twelve (and some women from his group?), in Jerusalem, the city that had failed to recognize him, a few hours before the start of the Jewish Passover festivities in the year 30 A.D. He wanted it to take place as close to this feast day as possible, because the acts he was to perform during the meal were aimed at salvation and he interpreted them as the covenant. However, the Passover as a liberating action of God and the covenant he had made with his people on Sinai are closely linked in the Jewish mind and literature. Jesus spoke of a "new" covenant, and this idea of "newness," which was also present in the "new" wine that would be drunk at the banquet of the Kingdom, gave a sense of the Passover to everything Jesus did and said. Later, on the Friday, there was to be a sacrifice, that of Jesus on the cross, with a letting of blood that evoked that of the lamb, which was a sign of the presence of God, who freed Israel (Exod 12:13).

Thus, there was a closeness to the Passover, a paschal context to Jesus' Last Supper, which can be seen in his intentions and which goes to explain the rapid development of the early Christian tradition. The step from a farewell supper taking place in a paschal setting and with paschal overtones to a meal presented as paschal in itself is relatively small, which would explain the tradition upon which the synoptic Gospels are based. We cannot be more precise when it comes to the circumstances in which this tradition was shaped, but the paschal interpretation of Jesus' death may well have played a decisive role. Nonetheless, the synoptic Gospels themselves have maintained enough clues as to the nature of Jesus' farewell supper.

6.1.3.2. Gestures and Words of Giving and Serving

The bread and cup of wine

The gestures and words at the Last Supper regarding the bread and cup of wine form an inseparable whole. The words explain the gestures, which represent an effective symbolic act to link the life and death of Jesus, his person, with the future for his disciples. As H. Schürmann points out, Jesus lived his life serving others, he gave his life for them, he gave everything for them, bringing them God's salvation, his Kingdom; his imminent death was simply a continuation of his life. Jesus saw his death as another form of giving, in the same way that he saw his life. His death, as his life, was the result of a freedom that accepts and forms part of another freedom, that given by God (see 6.1.1 and 6.1.2).

His death took on a strength of salvation embodied in the ultimate weakness of someone rejected and sentenced: Jesus, when hanging from the cross, was seen by those who had sentenced him as someone whom God himself had rejected. The bread and the wine came to symbolize effectively the direct relationship between Jesus' death (less than twenty-four hours later!) and the Kingdom, which is both present and future, and a new covenant. Jesus incorporated himself into the Kingdom and the covenant when he said that this bread was his body (Latin, *corpus*) and that this wine was the new covenant in his blood. Christian theology talks of this powerful symbol, of the sacrament of the Eucharistic bread and wine, as the "sacrament of the Kingdom."

Jesus' words at the Last Supper were passed down to those who wrote the first documents via two parallel traditions: the Gospels of Mark (14:22-25) and Matthew (26:26-29) on the one hand and, on the other, the texts provided by the Apostle Paul in the First Epistle to the Corinthians (11:23-26) and the Gospel according to Luke (22:15-20). These two traditions come, however, from one single event and, despite the differences, have to be looked at together. Similarly, we have seen that Jesus' words regarding the bread and the wine have to be seen in two prior acts: blessing the bread/giving thanks and breaking it so that all can share in it; and offering those present the same cup so that they can all drink from it. These are two gestures of offering that can be seen as gestures of the giving of himself. Jesus offered the bread and wine as a gift of affection and love for his disciples, who shared in the food and drink and received (though, no doubt, without fully being aware of the fact) a gift that saved them.

Despite the lack of information on the reaction of those who were sitting at the table with Jesus, we can reasonably assume that they were surprised, shocked, and even taken aback by this unprecedented proposal. While Jesus broke the bread and gave it to them to eat, he said to them, "This [the bread] is my body which is [given] for you." Later, when he gave them his cup to drink from, he similarly said, "This cup [full of wine] is the new covenant [sealed] in my blood." These brief words provide an insight into the gestures of offering that Jesus carried out with the bread and the wine and help us to fully understand the scope of these gestures.

With respect to the bread, Jesus stated that it was his body offered "for you" (1 Cor 11:24; Luke 22:19). With this expression, Jesus referred mainly to the fact that he was to be betrayed and killed. Nevertheless, this death had a meaning; Jesus was not going to die meaninglessly, unwittingly, but instead he was going to offer himself up for others, to benefit them, in favor of them, "for" them. His death was to bring salvation. As a result, Jesus' gesture that symbolized this death was a gesture of salvation, and all those who shared in this bread were to take part in this salvation.

This salvation, hidden in the bread that saves, in the Eucharistic bread, was destined for everyone. Although Jesus refers to "you," the Twelve (and the women present?), this is a symbolic figure that has to be linked to the twelve tribes of Israel, all the people (good and bad, just and unjust, healthy and sick, poor and children, comfortable and marginalized, Jews and non-Jews), in accordance with what has always between fundamental to Jesus' activities: a people without distinctions and without exceptions. The word you is not meant as a separation or alternative, but as everyone without exception, whom the Twelve represent. It would not make sense to see Jesus' words as being in any way restrictive, when, during his life, his activities were never restricted, de facto, to Israel or any group within Israel. We merely have to remember the words with which Jesus talked of the banquet for the Kingdom: "many will come from east and west and sit at the table with Abraham, Isaac and Jacob [the patriarchs and prophets of Israel] in the kingdom of heaven" (Matt 8:11 || Luke 13:28-29), accompanied by the Twelve, of whom Jesus himself said, "you may eat and drink at my table in the kingdom" (Luke 22:30).

The inclusive, global sense of Jesus' words about the bread can be seen clearly in the expression in Mark 14:24 (|| Matt 26:28), where, with respect to the cup, he said that it was "my blood . . . which is poured out for many." The expression "for many" is the literal translation of the Greek *hyper pollōn*, which seems to imply exclusivity, and it may be better to translate it as "for everyone." The Semitic languages, including Aramaic, the mother tongue of Jesus and the Twelve, use many words to refer to everything and, both here and in Mark 10:45 (|| Matt 20:28), it is best to translate the Greek according to the original Semitic meaning. The contrary is not supported by the way in which Jesus lived and acted. The words regarding the bread and wine are addressed to all mankind: the salvation that they inspire is boundless. Everyone has a right to take part.

Opening up the possibility to everyone to share in the promised goodness, peace, joy, and forgiveness is clearly shown by Jesus' words regarding the cup of wine: "This cup [full of wine] is the new covenant [sealed] in my blood" (1 Cor 11:25; Luke 22:20, which adds "poured out for you"). The fundamental and surprising expression in this sentence is "the new covenant." Israel called itself the people of the covenant because of the covenant that God entered into with them on Mount Sinai, which was one of the pillars of their identity: God pledges to take care of and protect, to nurture and comfort Israel throughout history, and the people pledge to live in accordance with his Law and his will. The covenant is sealed thus: "I will be their God, and they shall be my people" (Jer 31:33).

The covenant on Sinai renewed the covenant with Abraham and, to a degree, was the precursor of the covenant with David. Nevertheless, it would be the prophets who encouraged a renewal of Israel's loyal commitment to God, as the people had often broken it. Jeremiah, in particular, proclaimed "a new covenant," which consisted of welcoming the Lord into one's heart and forever: "Behold, the days are coming, says the Lord, when I will make a new covenant with the house of Israel and the house of Judah" (Jer 31:31). It is to be "an everlasting covenant" (Jer 32:40). It is to be a new covenant, not because the covenant from Sinai is to be annulled, but so as to renew the pledge, to make it perfect and unbroken, "with one heart and one way" (Jer 32:39). This new covenant is to be broad in scope, global, including "from the least to the greatest": everyone shall get to know the God who forgives and forgets our sins (Jer 31:34).

The echoes seen in Jeremiah's prophecy are indicated by the expression "the new covenant" which Jesus makes his own, for the first and last time, on this special and unique occasion of the Last Supper. Jesus' new covenant is twofold. First, it is established through Jesus' death, his giving of his life. Second, people take part in this covenant, drinking from the cup that he himself offered. Those who drink from the cup offered by Jesus take part in the salvation that his death, this symbolic gift, inspires.

We should also note that the covenant from Sinai was sealed with the offering of burnt offerings and sacrifices of well-being, as can be seen in chapter 24 of the book of Exodus. The sacrifice that sealed the new covenant announced by Jesus at the Last Supper was his own death, the culmination of a life of giving to and for others. In celebration of the covenant established between God and Israel on Sinai, Moses showered the people with the blood of slaughtered oxen and said, "Behold the blood of the covenant which the Lord has made with you" (Exod 24:8). Jesus' violent death, when he is to shed blood, is the sacrifice for the new covenant. This is how he himself seems to interpret his upcoming violent death. As J. D. G. Dunn states, the words used by Jesus over the cup with regard to the pouring of blood point to his death being a sacrifice that seals the establishment of a new covenant. In both Mark 14:24 and Matthew 26:28 we find the expression "blood of the covenant," echoing Exodus 24, an expression that Matthew feels has to be complemented by another expression: "[blood] which is poured out for many for the forgiveness of sins."

The washing of the feet

In addition to the gestures of the bread and the wine, another gesture involved Jesus as a servant and characterized the Last Supper:

the washing of the feet of the Twelve by the Master. This second act by Jesus is only mentioned in one documentary source, the Gospel according to John (13:1-20), which for many experts represents an insurmountable obstacle when it comes to asserting its historical accuracy. Nonetheless, there are a good number of historical materials on Jesus that are to be found in just one source. For example, many people accept that Jesus' farewell meal did not coincide with the Jewish Passover feast, despite this position being attested to only in the Gospel of John; the synoptic Gospels state just the opposite (see 6.1.3.1, above). It is hard to imagine that someone wanted to attribute such a precise series of actions to Jesus as those described in John 13:4-5 about a specific event (the washing of feet), without this having any relation to an actual incident in his life. Finally, the gesture of washing the feet (an unusual act, as we shall see below) is plausible and likely because of the very nature of this extraordinary and unique meal. It seems that there is no reason strong enough to force us to remove the washing of the feet from our files on the historical Jesus.

In Jewish society in the first century A.D., the hierarchies and the roles of individuals and groups were strictly determined and, as in any other Mediterranean society, could not be broken. One of the most consolidated restrictions affected one's behavior toward one's superior and vice versa. For example, in the case of a festive meal, a guest should never serve at the table, and much less so the person presiding over the meal. This task was reserved for the servants or, even, slaves. If it was incomprehensible for a guest to serve at the table, it would have been scandalous for one of the guests to have washed the feet of the others, and simply unthinkable for this task to have been carried out by the person at the head of the table. The most important person present, the person presiding over the meal, could not undertake a task reserved for a slave, for those who occupied the lowest rung on the social ladder.

Well, this is exactly what Jesus did. The head of the table suddenly started acting like a slave and washed the feet of those present, his Twelve Disciples. According to John 13:2, he did so at the wrong time, when they were already seated at the table and once the meal had started, breaking one of the clearest rules regarding festive meals. In fact, with regard to the washing of the feet, the only situation when it would have been thinkable would have been if everyone had washed their own feet before taking their places at the table. The head of the table had "broken" two regulations: first, abandoning his place at the head of the table and, second, washing the feet of those present (which is the contrary of what is becoming of someone of his status), once the meal had already begun!

As with the bread and the wine, Jesus' gesture is surprising and unexpected, and the disciples' shock must have been even greater. The blessing of the bread and wine by the head of the table formed part of the ritual for a festive meal, though Jesus had brought a new and different meaning to them, whereas the fact that the person who occupied the position of greatest honor at the meal should wash the feet of those present was completely unexpected. We can see in Peter's response a mixture of shock and irony ("Lord, do you wash my feet?"; John 13:6).

Jesus removed his cloak, leaving him in just his tunic. He wrapped a towel around himself to dry their feet, once washed, and poured water into a basin. He walked behind each of the disciples, who were lying back, grouped in a semicircle, and washed their feet (John 13:4-5). We have to assume that the room they had been eating in had the necessary preparations for the ritual ablutions required before meals (recipients with water, basins, towels). We do not know, however, whether they had been used and whether they had washed their hands in accordance with the rituals: Mark 7:2 says that "some of his disciples ate with hands defiled." Obviously, they started eating without having washed their feet. This last point fits with the reports that come from Papyrus Oxyrhynchus 840, according to which some Pharisees accused Jesus' disciples of not having ritually washed their feet before entering the temple. Unlike the Pharisees, Jesus does not have a strict position when it came to ritual purity (see 5.3.2.2). It makes sense that Jesus made this gesture of washing the feet of the Twelve once the meal had begun, and not before, since its significance had nothing to do with keeping to the ritual regulations.

Jesus stated that "he who has bathed does not need to wash, except for his feet" (John 13:10). This is a reference to the Jewish practice of preparation for the Passover. Many Jews and proselytes went to Jerusalem a week before the Passover festivities in accordance with the regulations on ritual bathing, which guaranteed the ritual purification required to be able to eat the Passover meal (John 11:55). It seems that, since Jesus and his disciples arrived in Jerusalem (the triumphant entrance into the city had taken place four or five days earlier), they had undergone the ritual bathing required before the Passover festival in the bathing area not far from the temple. Jesus says to his disciples that they have already bathed.

However, the disciples did not wash their own feet ritually, but it was someone else, Jesus, the Master (!), who washed them once the meal had started, something which, obviously, was not part of any of the ritual regulations. There are many unique aspects in Jesus' gesture, and each one stresses the specific meaning he gave to this act. This meaning can be summed up in one word: service. The washing of the feet was a meaningful act, an example of the humble service that characterized the whole of Jesus' life and which now pointed toward his violent, cruel death; a death worthy of a slave, of someone with no kind of rights, someone at the complete mercy of his enemies.

Above (see 6.1.2.1) we stressed that Jesus' life constituted a great parable of generous and humble service, with the poor, the sinners, and the sick being his priorities. Jesus summed up his life and mission when he said that he had come "not to be served but to serve" (Mark 10:45 || Matt 20:28) or "I am among you as one who serves" (Luke 22:27). Service is a vital element, a paradigm, of his existence. When faced with some disciples who were arguing as to who was the most important among them, Jesus said that he who most wanted to be first "must be last of all and servant of all" (Mark 9:35) or "slave of all" (Mark 10:44 || Matt 20:27). In the parable of the servants who wait up, Jesus had already presented a master serving his subordinates at the table, happy to see that they had stayed up all night for him (Luke 12:36-38). During the Last Supper, Jesus, when washing the disciples' feet, actually acted like a slave and, in this way, showed them how they should see life and, in consequence, how they should see his death. It is necessary to have witnessed this death in order to be able to understand the meaning behind his life as a whole. This can be seen in Jesus' response to Peter, the disciple who disagreed with Jesus' bending down to wash his feet. Jesus said to him, "What I am doing you do not know now, but afterward you will understand" (John 13:7).

Jesus' gesture expressed a turning of the tables in the social relations established between a master (he whom the disciples have to serve) and his disciples (those who have to serve their master), and accordingly it required a radical change in the disciples themselves. Jesus' gesture was an invitation for the disciples to live as a fraternity based on humble service. The washing of the feet formed part of his spiritual testament, as it pointed toward a new model for people's relations (John 13:12-17). Imitating this model constituted one of the key points in following Jesus.

Jesus' gesture formed part of the promise of salvation, which is present and future, and which culminates in the banquet in the Kingdom. It was a gesture of service, made now, during the Last Supper with the disciples, but which related to the final and definitive meal to take place in the Kingdom of God. Jesus says to Peter, "If I do not wash you, you have no part in me" (John 13:8). In other words, those who take part in Jesus' gesture of service will join him at the table in the Kingdom. This phrase expresses in a similar, though not identical, fashion what Jesus said toward the end of his farewell meal: "I shall not drink again of the fruit of the vine until that day when I drink it new in the kingdom of God" (Mark 14:25 || Matt 26:29; and slightly differently in Luke 22:18). Giving and serving are the reasons for Jesus' life and death and are projected into the future with the banquet, with guests coming from all corners of the earth, with the disciples and Jesus himself at its head. The table in the Kingdom is "my table" (Luke 22:30). The Last Supper was the result of an invitation from Jesus, and the same will be true of the banquet in the Kingdom.

6.1.3.3. The Kingdom and the Covenant

Jesus' announcement had involved proclaiming to all and sundry the arrival of God's Kingdom, his enlightening and amazing presence among men. His message was new and innovative, as Israel's hopes came true and salvation entered many people's lives abundantly. Nonetheless, as the time of his death approached and Jesus' perception of it became clearer, he became increasingly convinced that the Kingdom had only just begun and that Israel's repentance was still far off; a sign of this was the coldness or even rejection that his message received in the city of Jerusalem, as it had earlier in the towns of Galilee. Did his imminent death represent the failure of the Kingdom? If, to date, the message of the Kingdom had been closely linked to the messenger, to what or to whom would God's salvation now be linked? Or should we believe that the Kingdom was soon to establish itself?

One possibility would be that the Kingdom was to arrive immediately, but nothing leads us to think that Jesus considered this a possibility. The only thing that he considered imminent was his own death. Jesus talked of the future Kingdom, but not of an immediate one. In the four versions of his words regarding the bread and the wine, there is one reference to this future banquet, the final banquet. Jesus stated that there, in the Kingdom of God, he would "drink [wine] new" (Mark 14:25 || Matt 26:29, where it says that he would drink accompanied by the disciples). In Luke, Jesus admits to a similar hope. The fruit of the vine that Jesus shares with the disciples at the farewell supper will not pass his lips again "until the kingdom of God comes" (Luke 22:18; 1 Cor 11:26 expresses this in the language of the early Christian community). The wine at the supper is to be followed by the wine at the final banquet, when God is to manifest himself fully and when his reign is to be established forever, with people coming from all around the world. Nonetheless, the date for the final establishment of the Kingdom, the time of the banquet, to use Jesus' image, remains undefined. It is impossible to say when it will come. As J. Schlosser stresses, Jesus announced only his forthcoming death and displayed certainty about taking part in the banquet in the Kingdom beyond death. The future remains completely open.

Jesus saw his life as a time of salvation that was open to everyone, without exception. He knew that he was the bearer of the Kingdom, the one who brought the good news to the poor, the one who healed the sick and forgave the sinners. He wanted to indicate by a sign the salvation that he had proclaimed and brought to so many people. He wanted to link this sign to his imminent death, which he was facing with fear and trust, and which he saw, paradoxically, as the means for salvation wished for by God. During the Last Supper, he talked of this death as a "new covenant," the consolidation of his Kingdom, his continuation. The sign chosen, the bread and the wine, had to contain the fullness of the Kingdom, the fullness of God. The "new covenant" meant that a different relationship between God and mankind was to begin with his death, and his life (!), a relationship that passed through him. This death was not to be a hiatus, but a continuation. Jesus' death did not represent the defeat of the Kingdom, the end of the dream, a dreadful failure. Quite the contrary, the words and gestures over the bread and the wine expressed and contained present and future salvation, which was inseparable from the giving of Jesus' own life. The words "do this in remembrance of me" were a guide for the future.

Jesus saw himself in terms of his unique relationship with God, the Father, and his Kingdom. He knew he was the Son. The final, new, and effective sign, the bread and wine, passed through him: in the narratives of the Last Supper, the expressions "my body" and "my blood" are repeated a total of eight times! Jesus, the man, was the focal point. The bread represented his personal "I," his specific and tangible being, given and offered, undergoing suffering and death. The wine represented the personal giving of his life, where the pouring of his blood was a sign of the new covenant and, together with the body, the means for salvation. Jesus, the messenger of the Kingdom, who announced that a God who saved was becoming manifest in the life of many, became the intermediary for the Kingdom, as God's salvation was made available and present through him, and through his death and the signs of the bread and wine. The presence of God's reign continued in the presence of Jesus beyond his death, but not without it, and will do so until the consummation of the Kingdom.

There is a stumbling block, however, in Jesus fully accepting his death and giving it this sense of salvation: the words of Psalm 22, which Jesus spoke (at least the first line of the Psalm) when crucified and suffering on the cross: "My God, my God, why hast thou forsaken me?" (Mark 15:34 || Matt 27:46). It seems that Jesus bitterly reproached God for having left him to his fate and that this abandonment was the cause of all his ills and, in the end, his death he was about to endure.

The facts that Jesus used the words from the Psalm and spoke them in Aramaic, his mother tongue (*Eloi, Eloi, lama sabachthani?*), indicate that he recognizes himself in the figure from this Psalm. This figure presents himself as someone mocked, "a worm," who urgently needs God's help, as he is at the mercy of numerous persecutors, characterized as "bulls," "oxen," "lions," and "dogs." He has fallen into the hands of these "evildoers" and now finds himself alone in a position of great physical and mental vulnerability. His enemies have tied him up and stripped him, even sharing out his clothing. Satisfied that they have him in their grasp, they are about to fulfill their intentions. This can be seen in the line "for trouble is near"; he will soon lie "in the dust of death." It seems that there is no way out for him now.

This man, despite his extreme situation, does not give up hope in God and trusts that he is to be freed, as were his ancestors, the people of Israel. The reason for this resides in what he has known throughout his life: since he was born, God was his God. "Thou hast been my God," he claims and insists: "Be not far from me," "save me." His trust is so great that the prayer ends with him giving thanks for the favors received. God has listened to this prayer and, unlike the fate meted out to his enemies, he has not rejected or disrespected him. His life is not lost forever. A new people will rise and all the countries shall recognize his strength and wonders.

The inevitable conclusion is that Jesus, on the cross, recognizes himself as the figure who suffers in Psalm 22, who, while enduring the pain and attacks from his enemies, undergoes the greatest uncertainty that one who trusts in God can experience: he feels abandoned. Nevertheless, Jesus also uses the words from this Psalm in order to stress his absolute trust in receiving help from God, in being freed from death. The divine response will not be long in coming: God cannot leave the one who has experienced this death as a gesture of salvation, offering his own life, in the pit of death.

6.2. The Passion

This classical word, which is used even in the world of the arts, designates the last period of Jesus' life, the part of his life from his arrest in the garden of Gethsemane (to the northeast of Jerusalem) to his burial in another garden, near Golgotha (to the northwest of the city). Jesus' journey takes him to Annas' house, Caiaphas' house, Pilate's praetorium, and Antipas' palace and, finally, from the praetorium to Golgotha, or the place of the skull, the hill where executions were carried out, by which was his tomb. This itinerary, which began and ended in a garden beyond the city walls, took place for the most part within the city, and in the Upper City. It did not take very long: it began well into the night of April 6/7 30 A.D. and ended with sunset on the next day, Friday, coinciding that year with the eve of the Passover.

In this section, we follow Jesus' footsteps in these last hours of his life, up to his death and burial. We should review the reasons that led to his arrest, trial, being sentenced to death, and execution.

6.2.1. Why Was Jesus Sentenced to Death on the Cross?

Two sets of authorities were involved in sentencing Jesus of Nazareth: the Roman authorities and the Jewish authorities. The links between the actions of each of these groups were rightly pointed out by the historian Josephus, who wrote at the end of the first century A.D., "Pilate, at the suggestion of the principal men among us, had him sentenced to the cross" (*A.J.* 18:64). This sentence shows us, first, that the man directly responsible for Jesus' death was he who decreed that he die crucified: Pontius Pilate, the governor of the Roman province of Judaea. Second, Josephus' words indicate who pulled the strings and worked behind the scenes in the cause against Jesus: the "principal men" or leaders—Josephus talks of *tōn prōtōn andrōn* of the Jewish people who lived in Jerusalem. There was a synergy, a joint action, between one group and the other that led to Jesus' death.

If we do not maintain a balance between the involvement of both the Roman and Jewish authorities and if we give one of these sides preference over the other, we run the risk of not doing justice to the historical facts. It would also be inaccurate, as R. A. Horsley stresses, to think that the Jewish leaders were only religious leaders, as they also had political influence. It is clear that the Jewish religious groups from the first century A.D., both Pharisees and Sadducees, held specific political positions within the Roman occupation, which had lasted over one hundred years (see 3.3.2). Therefore, the arguments used by the Jewish authorities, in the case of Jesus and others, were both religious and political, and not simply religious; though, as we shall see, this was the main accusation brought against Jesus. As for Pilate, he kept himself distanced from internal issues relating to the Jewish religion and believed that Jesus' sentencing could be based only on Roman law. His position did not differ greatly from that of Gallio, proconsul of Achaia, who refused to judge Paul because he did not consider that he was being accused of "a wrongdoing or vicious crime" but rather that the question related to Jewish Law (Acts 18:12-15).

6.2.1.1. The Jewish Authorities' Reasons

One of the darkest pages in the history of Christianity and the West, in general, has been anti-Semitism. The ideological basis for anti-Semitism has been a generic accusation against the Jewish people for having "decided," for having brought about the death of Jesus, the Son of God. In the course of history, a biased interpretation of the Gospels has served as justification for all kinds of excesses and pogroms against Jesus' people, as if the prophet of Nazareth needed to be protected from his own people! The last and most terrible attack was the Shoah or extermination carried out as part of the Nazism of the twentieth century. The Gospels have been used even as an arsenal of reasons for anti-Semitic standpoints, and this, voluntary or involuntary, error has led to dreadful consequences. As the Second Vatican Council proclaimed and as modern biblical exegesis has forcefully shown, the Gospels are not documents that attack the Jewish people and cannot be used to justify any anti-Semitic attitudes. One simply has to read them and interpret them with intellectual integrity, without any kind of manipulation that might disfigure them.

With regard to Jesus' Passion, the four Gospels have to be seen as one great historical document on the events that took place at the end of the life of the rabbi of Nazareth. Without these texts we would not know even the tiniest part of what we do about his last hours. However, as with any historical source, the Gospels are not exempt from their own subjective interpretations. In general terms, the four narratives of the Passion of Christ tend to stress Jewish responsibility for his death and lessen that of Pilate, the Roman authority. However, this tendency is not uniform. Where, for example, Matthew (the most "Jewish" of the Gospels!) makes the Jewish people, not just their leaders, explicitly and openly responsible for Jesus' death (Matt 27:25), the Gospel of John sees the "people" play a less important role in events. It should be pointed out that this tendency does not represent a falsification of history, since, in truth, those who led the accusations against Jesus were in fact the Jewish authorities, though not all of them, and the people did take some part as well. We need to specify what is meant by the terms "authorities" and "people" and the reasons that led to their respective encouragement and intervention in Jesus' trial. Only in this way can we be reasonably sure of establishing the historical reasons that led to Pilate sentencing him to death.

The reasons that may have had the most weight in the Jewish authorities' wish to have Jesus killed were fourfold (though they are not mutually exclusive): (a) they saw Jesus as opposition to the great Jewish institutions, someone who declared the temple, worship, the ritual system, and the Law to be out of date; (b) they saw his messianic pretensions as a threat to political stability (the status quo maintained with the Romans); (c) they saw him as a false prophet, an impostor, who led the people astray with his doctrines and/or his "sorcery" (his miracles); and (d) they saw him as a blasphemer, someone who acted as if given divine powers, thus usurping the position reserved for God.

Which authorities?

The four reasons just mentioned contribute, to varying degrees, to the Jewish authorities' conviction that Jesus had to be eliminated, since, in their opinion, he represented a threat to the people and the religion. This conviction, however, was not shared by all of the Jewish leaders. J. Klausner's opinion is still true, namely, that those ultimately responsible for Jesus' death were the high priests, who belonged to one of the small number of influential and aristocratic families in the city who controlled the temple and had a notable presence in the Sanhedrin. They were linked to the Sadducee group (see 3.3.3.3).

The high priests, the highest Jewish authority, came from one of these families, and their members were given the generic name of "high priests" (Acts 4:6 mentions some of the members of the "high-priestly family") (see 3.3.1). According to a lament from the first century A.D., which criticized these families, there were almost exclusively only three (!) who monopolized the position of highest authority in Judaism up until 70 A.D.: those of Boethus, Phiabi, and Annas. In the year of Jesus' death (30 A.D.), the position of high priest was in the hands of Joseph, known as Caiaphas, who had been named by the governor Valerius Gratus in 18 A.D. and who remained in the post throughout the time that Pontius Pilate was governor, until 36 A.D., an exceptionally long time. Caiaphas was married to a daughter of Annas, the highest Jewish authority from 6 to 15 A.D., having been named by Coponius, the first Roman governor to take charge of Judaea. Furthermore, a son of Annas called Eleazar had also been high priest in the years 16–17 A.D. Undoubtedly, when Jesus was sentenced, the same family had held the highest authority in the temple and the Sanhedrin for nearly a quarter of a century. It seems likely that this family was well trusted by the Roman authorities, whom they depended on to be named as high priest. According to the unanimous testimony of the Gospels, the figure of the high priest (a title shared by Caiaphas and Annas) was key in Jesus' trial.

Thus, the group that pulled all the strings in having Jesus sentenced to death was made up of the high priests, headed by Caiaphas, with the full backing (and participation) of Annas, his father-in-law. Within this group, there were other members of the highest temple authorities, including chief priests, in particular the military leader, or commander of the guard, who was second only to the high priest and in charge of ensuring public order in the temple itself (Luke 22:4 and 22:52, where it talks generically and in the plural of "officers," the temple's commanders). According to the synoptic Gospels, there were also "nobles" in this group, members of Jerusalem's well-to-do families, the nonsacerdotal aristocracy but related to these, and "scribes," rabbis, teachers expert in the Law of Moses.

These three groups (high priests, nobles, and scribes), who formed the Sanhedrin, were responsible for Jesus' arrest (Mark 14:43). They acted together in Caiaphas' house, once he had been arrested (Mark 14:53) and together took him to Pilate's praetorium (Mark 15:1). In this last episode, Luke talks about "the chief priests and the rulers of the people" (Luke 23:13; cf. Luke 23:35). The role of the Sanhedrin in Jesus' death is confirmed by all four Gospels. Mark twice emphatically stresses the role of the great Jewish Council ("the whole council") (Mark 14:55, 15:1), while Matthew (26:59) and Luke (22:66) are somewhat more discreet. The Gospel of John also shows the Sanhedrin as making the decision to have Jesus killed (11:47-53). All this evidence raises questions about the reasons for and nature of the participation of the Sanhedrin, controlled by the Sadducee and Pharisee groups, in Jesus' trial.

The three sections of the Sanhedrin represented the institutional power (religious and political), specifically the temple (the high priests), the economic power (the nobles), and the ideological power (the scribes). While the high priests and the majority of the nobles were aligned with the Sadducee group, those belonging or linked to the Pharisees dominated among the scribes, though there were also Sadducees. The power and influence of each group were balanced within the Sanhedrin, but the Sadducees, who were in favor of having Jesus killed, seem to have come out on top in the accusations brought against him.

In the narratives of the Passion, there is an important bias toward the Sadducee group. The high priests, all of whom were Sadducees, are mentioned sixty-two times (sixty-four if we include the two mentions that Luke makes of the temple "officers"), whereas the Pharisees are mentioned on only two occasions (John 18:3 and Matt 27:62), when they acted alongside the Sadducees. The nobles (mentioned thirteen times) have to be aligned with the Sadducees, which only increases the difference. The scribes (mentioned twice) are more difficult to place and were either Sadducees or Pharisees. In summary, the balance is clearly tipped in favor of the Sadducee group, with the high priests in charge and most interested in having Jesus killed. The leaders belonging to the Pharisee group always remain relegated to the background (see 6.2.3, below).

This initial conclusion is reinforced by a consideration of the reasons put forward by the temple leaders—with possible support from other members of the Sanhedrin—when it came to their advocating Jesus' execution.

Jesus' attitude toward the Law

First, it is obvious that the points of disagreement between Jesus and the Pharisees were not great enough to warrant his death. As we have seen above (6.1.1.1), the hostility toward Jesus, as expressed in Mark 3:6 (the Pharisees and Herodians are making plans "to destroy him"), cannot strictly be given any weight. The Pharisees are Jesus' competitors and debate with him on questions relating to the Law of Moses and the tradition of the elders that interprets it: ritual purity, increased fasting, resting on the Sabbath, divorce, and so on. But he also has Pharisee friends who invite him to eat with them, who warn him about Antipas' evil intentions, or even sympathizers. Jesus does not distance himself from Israel's cultural system, though he does make certain specific rules relating to ritual purity relative, but he never annuls them or provocatively goes against them, which would have led to antagonism with all the people, not just the Pharisees. We simply have to remember that Jesus and his disciples, in the days before Passover (and his death!), went up to the temple each day and fulfilled the ritual purification as required for the week preceding this great Jewish feast. Jesus' position on the Law, worship, and ritual purity could not be considered sufficient reason for his being sentenced to death: Jesus acted (on occasions!) as an outsider, but he never placed himself beyond or against Jewish Law (see 5.3.2, above).

On the other hand, in the eyes of the Pharisees Jesus was an atypical rabbi who ignored the tradition of the elders, who did not base his arguments on what had been said by any of the great rabbis who had gone before him (e.g., Hillel or Shammai), and he did not seem overly concerned with the rules on ritual purity, which was one of the key aspects in the Pharisees' observance of the Law. Thus, there was a division of opinions between Jesus' interpretation of the Law and that of the Pharisees; as a result, a sector of this group may not have felt any sympathy for him. Jesus had insisted on carrying out healings on the Sabbath, justifying them for the good of the sick person, but these were often interpreted as his refusal to acknowledge the sacred nature of the Sabbath as a day of rest. John 5:18 states that Jesus deserved to die because, according to the Mishnah (Sanh. 7:4), those who did not respect the Sabbath had to be stoned. A majority of the Pharisees may well have abstained from the Sadducees' proposal and tolerated their determination to have Jesus killed. The Pharisees, as a group, did not directly promote his death. They hardly appear at all in the Gospel narratives of the Passion (they are not mentioned once in Mark or Luke), which would seem to be an important indication as to their role in events.

Jesus' attitude toward the temple

What reasons could have been given by the high priests, the leading powers in the temple and those with most institutional weight on the Sanhedrin? The most obvious answer (and the one that has won the most support over the past twenty years) is linked to his position toward the temple. The temple was the center of religion in Israel and, furthermore, an institution that accumulated religious, political, and economic power, controlled by a small number of people, the high priests.

A sign of Jesus' attitude is seen in his symbolic "purification" of the temple, which he carried out in the style of the prophets of Israel: throwing over the tables of the money-changers and knocking over the stalls belonging to the pigeon sellers, in protest against the commercialism that was tolerated and promoted by the high priests themselves, who were the main beneficiaries of the system in place. Obviously the temple leaders were not happy with Jesus' actions, given the public scandal they would have inspired. Jesus was not attacking or complaining about the sacrificial worship at the temple; had this been the case, he would immediately have had the people turn against him and the Pharisees in particular, as they were zealous defenders of the sanctity of the temple and the worship taking place there.

This prophetic gesture by Jesus echoed one of the strong points in his message: God's cause has an absolute priority, which is incompatible with any other. You cannot serve two lords: God and money. God has to be given what he deserves, without letting one's own interests become involved. Authentic purity comes from the heart, and this heart has to belong to God and not any other idol, such as money. With this prophetic, energetic, and vigorous action, Jesus may have tried, for one last time, to touch the hearts of those leaders and individuals who had become hardhearted and sure of their own roles and power, hoping to provoke a reaction from them. By presenting this as the image of a hen and her chicks, the prophet Jesus wanted to bring these people together under the wings of the messenger of the Kingdom, calling them to repent as a necessary step in receiving the message. His actions in the temple could have been his last attempt to persuade these recalcitrant and hardened leaders, who had failed to listen to John the Baptist when he had preached by the Jordan for the repentance of sins.

However, in the accusations made against Jesus, there is no mention of his attack on the trading within the temple, which took place only days before his death, which is another sign that it was not and could not have been interpreted as an attack on Israel's most important institution. In the charges brought against him, great weight was given to an earlier prophetic announcement of his, which he had made at the start of his public activities about the temple: "I will destroy this temple, and in three days I will build another" (Mark 14:58; John 2:19). These words about the destruction and reconstruction of the temple are used as evidence against him when he stands before Caiaphas (Mark 14:58) and are echoed again later, as an insult by the passers-by at Golgotha while Jesus hung from the cross: "Aha! You who would destroy the temple and build it in three days" (Mark 15:29 || Matt 27:40). The insult is aimed at Jesus because his prophecy about the temple had not come true and, as a result, he was a false prophet, another cruel insult he was subjected to following his interrogation by Annas (Mark 14:65 || Matt 26:67-68) (see 6.2.3.4).

Nevertheless, we should stress that the prophetic announcement of the destruction and reconstruction of the temple alone does not merit the death penalty. First, Jesus stated that he wanted to destroy the temple in order to rebuild it, though he did not say how or what the results would be (a material temple? a spiritual temple?). The words quoted do not indicate on their own that Jesus sought to destroy the holiest place in Israel. Second, we should stress, as does G. Theissen, that two other prophets also announced the destruction of the temple in Jerusalem and suffered fierce opposition from their leaders but were not executed for it: Jeremiah, around 607 B.C. (some twenty years before the destruction of the first temple), and Jesus, son of Ananias, in 62 A.D. (eight years before the destruction of the second). The ultimate criterion is not dependent on what a prophet announced, but whether the prophet spoke in the name of God or not. Nowhere in the Gospels does it say that Jesus deserved to be sentenced to death for his attitude toward the temple. As we shall see, the religious charges brought against Jesus are those of false prophecy (in relation to the temple!) and blasphemy. These are the weightiest charges that tip the balance of the Sanhedrin in favor of having Jesus killed.

Jesus' messianic pretensions

From a Jewish point of view, Jesus' messianic pretensions do not merit capital punishment. These pretensions, as we have explained (see 5.4.1), were never encouraged by Jesus himself; indeed, he tried to stop people from proclaiming him as the Messiah because he did not wish to be a political leader, a pretender to the throne, and a direct rival to the Roman emperor. Only a few days before his death he organized a festive entrance to Jerusalem with crowds lining the streets, an entrance that had a fully messianic form and character (the donkey, the cloaks spread along the way, the cries of hosanna, his acclamation as the son of David, and the proclamation of the arrival of the Kingdom). These events, however, had little in common with the arrival of the Messiah who had defeated his enemies, which was what the people had dreamed of.

Jesus' entrance into Jerusalem represented the arrival of a peaceful Messiah, which inspired his followers, which disconcerted his competitors and adversaries (the Pharisees and temple leaders, respectively), and which left the Roman garrison watching over the eastern gates to the city from the Antonia Tower unconcerned. Following this initial confusion, the Jewish authorities sought to have Jesus tone down the enthusiasm of his followers, who surrounded him acclaiming him, chanting, and brandishing palms. This entrance, they told Jesus, could destabilize the fragile public order in the city, especially with Passover coming up. Jesus, in the true style of a prophet, replied, "[I]f these were silent the very stones would cry out" (Luke 19:40). What were the reasons behind this call for prudence from the Jewish leaders (Pharisees, according to Luke; high priests and scribes, according to Matthew)? Fear of a violent reaction from the Romans or a feeling of "envy" (Mark 15:10 || Matt 27:18)? Or maybe concerns and doubts about someone who had so clearly shown, for the first time and not in his own words, that he was the Messiah, sent by God?

Regardless of the interpretation that the Jewish authorities (the temple leaders and nobles) and the other important people in Jerusalem (the Pharisees) put on Jesus' triumphant arrival in the city, never in the history of the Jewish people had a messianic pretender, for the simple fact of being such, been accused of being an enemy of God's and sentenced to death. Such messianic pretenders either were considered to be naive visionaries taking advantage of the situation or were acclaimed as the promised Messiah. We know of the leader of the Second Jewish Revolt (132–135 A.D.), Simon ben Kosiba or bar Kochba, greeted by the great rabbi Akiba as the Messiah and relating his name to the word "star" (Hebrew, *kokhav*) in the prophecy in Numbers 24:17. Obviously, none of the Jewish leaders accused Bar Kochba, the "son of the star," of being an enemy of the people or an impostor, despite his being defeated and killed by the Romans and having failed completely (Jerusalem Talmud, *Ta'an.* IV:68d). Jesus could not have merited the reproaches of the Jewish authorities for his messianic pretensions: the interrogation in Mark 14:61-64 reaches its climax when Jesus identifies himself (or at least this is how his accusers see it) as the celestial Son of Man. When facing Pilate, Jesus was accused by the Jewish leaders of wanting to be "king" (the Roman "translation" of Messiah), and Pilate ended up sentencing him as an enemy of Caesar, the only king of the Jews.

Does this mean that the Jewish authorities, in accusing Jesus of being a pretender to the throne, made up charges against him so that Pilate could sentence him? John 11:47-53 states that the Jewish leaders saw Jesus as a charismatic leader, who acted independently, without taking into account the established authorities (the temple leaders and the Sanhedrin) and with some popular success. Jesus became a great concern for these authorities, who, with the "prudence" of those in charge, feared the worst, for example, that Jesus could lead a revolt against Rome.

Clearly, the fact that Jesus was considered a potential political leader, a Messiah, who could lead the Jewish people in arms meant that they had not understood either the message or the man. Nonetheless, political reasons motivated the Jewish leaders: the Romans could have thought that Jesus would lead a bloody revolt; they themselves thought that Jesus could question their leadership, and all this must have had some sort of effect. Jesus the man inspired contrasting feelings in Israel's leaders.

This is the crucial point. Jesus provoked confusion and surprise, inspired questions without providing all the answers that the leaders would have wanted, and spoke in a different language, while behaving irreproachably. He allowed himself to be acclaimed as the Messiah, but he did not try to bring together an army willing to fight against the Romans. He energetically attacked the trading in the temple yet prepared for the Passover by carrying out the ritual ablutions required each day near the temple. What were his aims? What did he want to achieve? Furthermore, where was he from and who was he?

Jesus, a false prophet

The question of Jesus' identity and legitimacy had concerned the authorities in Jerusalem since the start of his public activities. This was the main concern facing Israel's leaders. As I see it, the issues cannot be simplified by saying that the high priests and those who supported them were overtaken by hate and envy for Jesus, which took shape in their desire to have him killed at all costs. However, nor can we oversimplify in the other direction and say that the most conspicuous Jewish leaders (the high priests and some of his councillors) wanted to save Jesus from the Romans (actually responsible for his arrest) for fear of the popularity of the prophet from Nazareth among the people, thus avoiding a riot.

It is vital to understand Jesus' case from the perspective of the Jewish leaders, the high priests in particular, and the questions that Jesus inspired in them and the contrasting points of view among themselves. Otherwise, his death would simply have been a miserable and arbitrary decision made by the established powers, acting with impunity against the son of the people.

The case of the prophet Jeremiah is revealing. Some twenty years before the destruction of the temple in Jerusalem at the hands of the Babylonians, around 607 B.C., Jeremiah, in accordance with what God had told him, went to the temple court and warned the people that if they did not keep to the Law and listen to the prophets that God had sent them, the temple and city would be destroyed. The temple leaders immediately turned against Jeremiah, accusing him of having prophesied "in the name of the Lord" against the temple and Jerusalem and exclaimed that he deserved to be sentenced to death. The Judaean magistrates had to decide the case, and Jeremiah explained that God had sent him to make the prophecy; if they converted to God, he would take back this punishment, otherwise destruction would come. The magistrates took heed of what Jeremiah said and pronounced their sentence: "This man does not deserve the sentence of death, for he has spoken to us in the name of the Lord, our God" (Jer 26:16). Jeremiah was acknowledged as an authentic prophet, as an emissary from God, and this fact saved his life. Sentencing him would have meant spilling innocent blood, which is a terrible crime.

It seems that this narrative is the exact opposite of the Passion of Christ. Faced with Jeremiah's prophecy of terrible consequences, the authorities in Jerusalem were divided. The religious leaders, the priests, the temple leaders, saw him as a "false prophet," someone who was not really speaking in the name of God and who they wanted to kill: what authentic prophet could proclaim the destruction of the temple, the holy place that symbolized his presence and where his glory resided? The judicial authorities recognized him as a true prophet, as someone who "has spoken to us in the name of the Lord," and they saved his life.

This was not the case for Jesus. The leaders of his people had him killed. However, beforehand, as in the case of Jeremiah, there was also an assessment of the man, which again was not unanimous (see 6.2.3.1). The fundamental question lies in what took place in the case of the ancient prophet. In whose name was Jesus acting and speaking? In God's name or not? Was he a (or possibly the) legitimate emissary from God, or was he an impostor, a fraud, someone pretending to be a prophet and thus a blasphemer? Who, in reality, was Jesus, the rabbi of Nazareth? This was the overriding concern when Jesus was brought before the high priest or when Pilate asked him during his trial, "Where are you from?" (John 19:9). This question resembles another in the synoptic Gospels: "By what authority are you doing these things, or who gave you this authority to do them?" (Mark 11:28 || Matt 21:23 || Luke 20:2; similarly, Egerton 2).

The incident regarding Jesus' authority took place in the temple grounds and involved the three sections making up the Sanhedrin (high priests, scribes, and nobles), who appeared together only during the Passion and sentencing of Jesus (Mark 11:27 || Luke 20:1; Matt 21:23 does not mention the scribes). According to all three synoptic Gospels, this took place on the day after Jesus' attack on the trading in the temple. The question he was asked ("By what authority are you doing these things?") would seem to refer to this prophet-like action (and this is the interpretation in the Gospel of Mark), but both Matthew and Luke say that Jesus "was teaching" (Matt 21:23) and "teaching the people" (Luke 20:1). The question has a wider meaning (possibly in Mark as well) and refers to the whole series of Jesus' activities, what he had said and done, his words and miracles. Annas also interrogated Jesus in general "about his disciples and his teaching" (John 18:19).

The question as to Jesus' authority may have taken place at some indeterminate time, on one of the occasions when he made a pilgrimage to Jerusalem for one of the Jewish festivals. The question is not threatening or insidious. It is a religious question, focusing on Jesus' relationship with God. The Jewish leaders' concern centered on finding out the truth about Jesus, not on finding reasons for sentencing him. Reading between the lines, though, we can see a serious doubt concerning Jesus' real identity: are Jesus' activities legitimized because he has been given a mission by God and the authority that goes with it, or is he acting without a divine mandate according to his own criteria that do not go beyond the merely human? In short, is he an emissary from God or not? Is God the source of his authority?

Jesus' response is indirect but absolutely clear. Jesus, a master in the art of parables and oblique discourses, takes the question to another level, where the Jewish leaders are seen to be implicated personally: the authority with which John the Baptist baptized, the origin of his baptisms. He said to them, "Was the baptism of John from heaven or from men?" (Mark 11:30 || Matt 21:25 || Luke 20:4). The best answer is a good question. It is not a matter of Jesus proving himself to be right, but instead that his opponents, the people's leaders, show their hand and state who they think he is. If they think he is an emissary of God, they have to believe him. Otherwise, they are perfectly justified in not paying him any attention and in disrespecting him as a false prophet, as someone who is misleading the people.

This was not the case with the Baptist because "all held that John was a real prophet" (Mark 11:32 || Matt 21:26 || Luke 20:6), nor was it the case for Jesus, a former follower of the Baptist, whom the people welcomed and listened to gladly. There is an obvious conclusion to be drawn; Jesus, as was John, had been sent by God and had the authority that came from him. The leaders, who did not take any notice of the Baptist, now, for fear of the prestige that he had among the people, did not dare respond and were equally distanced from Jesus and his message. The response "we do not know" (Mark 11:33 || Matt 21:27 || Luke 20:7) could be considered to mean "we do not want to know"; and this is the stumbling block: Jesus was to die as a false prophet, someone who led his people astray. This is how the Sanhedrin, dominated by the temple authorities, had determined his fate.

The high priests and those who offered them support came to the conclusion that Jesus was a false prophet, an impostor. The accusation of masquerading hung over his figure: Jesus was not what he claimed to be. In the story narrated in Matthew 27:62-66 relating to the conditions demanded of Pilate to ensure the tomb was watched over, the Jewish authorities justified themselves on the grounds that Jesus' actions were a masquerade; he had announced that he would rise again. Jesus was an "impostor," a false prophet who had made a prophecy that was not to come true (!) and which was false. This echoes the insults hurled by the passers-by at Jesus when nailed to the cross. Jesus had prophesied the destruction and reconstruction of the temple in an unbelievable time frame (three days!) (John 2:19; Mark 14:58), but now, dying on the cross, it did not seem that this was to come to pass. The people mocked him and saw this as confirmation of the fact that he was a false prophet, as what he proclaimed had not come true (Mark 15:29 || Matt 27:40). The cruel and bloody insult that Jesus was subjected to after being interrogated by Annas also seems to be related to the failure of this prophecy. The temple guards covered his face and challenged him to tell them who had hit him. Their mocking calls ("Prophesy!") echoed this accusation of being a false prophet and impostor. Jesus was disrespected and could do nothing about it (Mark 14:65 || Matt 26:68).

While the majority of the leaders accused Jesus of acting falsely, of "cheating" and leading the people astray, others, however, saw him as "a good man" and said, "No man ever spoke like this man!" (John 7:12, 7:46). Nevertheless, the former opinion won out: Jesus had misled the people. In the narrative in the Gospel according to Luke, the leaders repeated this accusation three times (!) before Pilate: "we found this man perverting our nation" (Luke 23:2), "He stirs up the people" (23:5), "one who was perverting the people" (23:14). The Babylonian Talmud, a subsequent Jewish source (5th c. A.D.), expresses itself in similar terms to the Gospels of Luke and John, Christian documents of the first century A.D., and agrees significantly with these Gospels and with Matthew (27:63-64). All this agreement in the documentation shows the "common" Jewish opinion of Jesus in the first centuries. The text can be found in the Talmud (*Sanh.* 43a): "He has practised sorcery and enticed Israel to apostasy." Even in the Middle Ages, the Jews saw Jesus as "the enticer" (in the words of the Catalan Misteri de la Selva sobre l'Assumpció de Madona Santa Maria, from the end of the fourteenth century, verses 433-34: "façam que no haja honor/la mare de l'enganyador [enticer]"). Throughout the Jewish tradition, Jesus is seen as an impostor who has deceived people with his miracles (the work of the devil and not of God) and led them astray with his words and false prophecies. He thus deserved death.

The punishment reserved for false prophets and impostors is stoning. This can be seen in the Mishnah (*Sanh.* 7:4) and, applied specifically to Jesus, in the Babylonian Talmud (*Sanh.* 43a and 107b). A specific, and terrible, case of stoning for deception and masquerading can be seen in the authentic prophets who were not recognized as such and sentenced to death as false prophets. Above, we mentioned the case of the prophet Jeremiah, who was very nearly stoned to death since the temple's priests and "official" prophets stated that he was not speaking in the name of the Lord (Jer 26:1-19). Others sent by God, though, were stoned as false prophets in Jerusalem itself; Jesus says of the city, "Jerusalem, killing the prophets and stoning those who are sent to you!" (Matt 23:37 || Luke 13:34). There is another reference to stoning of prophets in Matthew 21:35. Jesus is to share in the destiny of the prophets, and though he is not to be stoned, he is accused of charges that warrant the death penalty: the charge of being a false prophet.

Jesus, a "blasphemer"

In the interrogation to which Caiaphas, the high priest, subjected Jesus, there is one charge that appears in both the Gospels of Mark and Matthew: the accusation of blasphemy. According to Mark 14:63-64, Jesus stated that he was the Messiah and Son of God and talked of himself as the Son of Man. Caiaphas saw this as Jesus' identification of himself as this celestial figure and cried out, tearing at his robes, "You have now heard his blasphemy." Matthew stresses the fact, adding, "He has uttered blasphemy" (26:65). In the Gospel of John, the accusation of blasphemy is linked to Jesus' desire to attribute to himself divine status: "Do you say . . . 'You are blaspheming,' because I said 'I am the Son of God'?" (John 10:36). This sentence does not come from John's narrative of the Passion, but it does indicate why, according to the Jewish leaders, Jesus deserved to be sentenced to death: "We have a Law [the Law of Moses], and by that Law he ought to die, because he has made himself the Son of God" (John 19:7). When Jesus appeared before the Sanhedrin, as described in the Gospel of Luke, there was no express allusion to his blasphemy, but the reason for his being sentenced was, as it is in Mark and Matthew, because he had identified himself with the celestial Son of Man. The members of the Sanhedrin replied that, faced with this self-incrimination, no more witnesses were required (Luke 22:69-71; Mark 14:63 || Matt 26:65). According to the Gospel narratives of the Passion (Luke, implicitly), Jesus had been sentenced to death for blasphemy.

This accusation of blasphemy should not be seen as breaking the Law on pronouncing the Lord's name, which is prohibited by Judaism, or cursing God, but, as R. E. Brown states, in the sense of claiming for oneself what belongs to God. Jesus was seen to have blasphemed because, arrogantly and presumptuously, he saw himself as "equal with God"; as it says in John 5:18, "[Jesus] called God his Father, making himself equal with God."

Significantly, the accusation of blasphemy appears twice during Jesus' public activities, when linked to his forgiveness and to his expulsion of demons. On both occasions, it is a teacher of the Law who accuses him. In the incident of the paralytic man in Capernaum, Jesus says to the sick man, "My son, your sins are forgiven." The reaction of the scribes is not long in coming: "It is blasphemy! Who can forgive sins but God alone?" (Mark 2:5, 2:7 || Matt 9:2-3 || Luke 5:20-21). It is not said where these scribes come from; however, we do know that other scribes "came down from Jerusalem," presumably sent by the authorities to investigate the healing and exorcisms carried out by Jesus. The experts' final conclusion leaves no room for doubt: "[Jesus] is possessed by Beelzebub" (Mark 3:22 || Matt 12:24 || Luke 11:15). That is why he can expel demons so easily! His power is a false power, because if he can expel demons, it is thanks to a previous alliance with the devil. It was not God who had given him such an extraordinary power. Jesus was a false exorcist, someone who, arrogantly and misleadingly, said he had powers that only God could possess. Only God has greater power than Satan. He was behaving blasphemously.

On a third occasion, connected to his prophecy for the temple, we can interpret Jesus' words as a claim for divine prerogative. Jesus said, "[I will] destroy the temple, and in three days I will raise it up" (John 2:19; Mark 14:58). There are two surprising elements in his words. First, as is often the case with him, he talks with an authority that is all his own, not needing to fall back on the usual prophetic formula to legitimize his words ("Thus says the Lord"). Second, he does not state that the temple is to be destroyed, by God, but that he himself is to destroy it and raise it up again. Nevertheless, only God can decree the destruction of a temple that he himself ordered to be built and that he has protected against destruction for centuries. Prophecies, such as Jeremiah's, always stress that they are simply passing on God's wishes, for example the destruction of the temple, with a foreign army responsible for carrying it out. It is God who, definitively, allows his home here on earth to be destroyed. But with the prophecy of the destruction of the temple, Jesus puts himself in a position of authority that belongs to God, giving himself a role, in deciding on this destruction, that can be taken only by God himself.

We should note that God had spoken to the prophet Jeremiah, saying, "I have set you this day over nations and over kingdoms . . . to destroy and to overthrow, to build and to plant" (Jer 1:10). Jesus states that he has this power, but he does not say that it has been given to him by God. He himself has his own authority. Unlike Jeremiah, Jesus states that he will destroy the temple, and in three days (!) rebuild it again. Obviously, he is taking the place of God when he says that three days are enough to raise it up again! Maybe the authority with which Jesus talks of destroying and reconstructing the temple is a prophet-like response to the fundamental questions regarding his person: Has God sent him? On whose authority does he act? This response may have been key in the accusations of blasphemy.

Blasphemers, such as false prophets, are stoned to death. Naboth the Jezreelite was falsely accused of blasphemy against "God and the king" and stoned to death (1 Kgs 21:13). Stephen suffers the same fate, accused of speaking "blasphemous words against Moses and God," "against this holy place [the temple] and the Law" (Acts 6:11-13). Jesus is accused of blasphemy not because he spoke against God or for having pronounced his name but for having made himself equal to him. Those who accuse him do so in the Gospel of John: "It is not for a good work that we stone you but for blasphemy, because you, being a man, make yourself God" (John 10:33).

Jesus is a "blasphemer" because he claims prerogatives that are divine, and he is a false prophet because he tries to make people believe that he speaks and acts in the name of God. The common denominator in both accusations is, however, the same: Jesus has not received any authority from God, although he attributes his mission and his own person to a divine origin. He is an impostor, as is demonstrated by the failure of his prophecy that he himself (!) is to destroy and rebuild the temple in three (!) days. This is the conclusion reached by the majority of the leaders (the high priests, many nobles, and a number of scribes, meeting as the Sanhedrin), and this becomes the reason for having Jesus killed. This reasoning can be seen in Caiaphas' interrogation (Jesus is a blasphemer) and in some of the insults that he is victim to during the Passion (Jesus is a false prophet). Jesus is seen to be a threat to the status quo, as he leads the people astray and could lead them to rise up against the Romans. The leaders believe that, all things considered, it is convenient and necessary to have him killed.

6.2.1.2. The People's Reasons

The different stages involving the people in the Passion of Christ are analyzed later (see 6.2.4 and 6.2.5). Here we focus on the reasons that led them to demand that Pontius Pilate decree death for Jesus. The request came in the form of a popular acclamation and consisted of their demand that Barabbas, a bandit and criminal imprisoned by the Romans, be freed and that Jesus be crucified. The crowds before Pilate insisted over and again that Jesus be condemned. As the Gospel according to Luke concludes, "their voices prevailed" (Luke 23:23; Matt 27:24 and Mark 15:15).

The people's hostility on the Friday morning, during Jesus' trial before Pilate, is surprising given their attitude in the past to the prophet from Nazareth. Up to this point, there is no historical evidence of the people's rejecting him. Indeed, all the indications are to the contrary. The people of Jerusalem knew Jesus well, as he had traveled to the city on a number of occasions, accompanied by his disciples, for the main Jewish festivals and had taught openly in the temple to those who had wanted to listen to him (John 18:20). On the days leading up to his arrest, Jesus, despite staying in Bethany, had gone to Jerusalem every day to carry out the ritual bathing in preparation for the Passover, probably in the main facilities near the temple, and if we pay heed to the information in the synoptic Gospels, he entered the temple and spoke to the crowd gathered at the gates.

Days before, Jesus had entered the city surrounded by throngs of people, an entrance that had revived the messianic hopes among the people and left a pleasant taste in their mouths, if we are to judge from the enthusiasm with which they took part and the festive and good-hearted nature that characterized proceedings. His actions against the trading in the temple may have disconcerted some, but he had not provoked any general reaction among the people of Jerusalem; though Jesus' gesture did directly upset those affected (the money-changers and pigeon sellers) and, above all, the temple authorities, who saw it as a reproach to the way they ran things and an attack on God's preeminence. It is true that not everyone appreciated Jesus, the prophet from Nazareth, in the same way, although he had even carried out some of his miracles in Jerusalem (the healings of the man blind from birth and the paralytic man from Bethzatha). The rabbi of Nazareth may have had some critics, but it would not seem that there was any special animosity toward him among the people.

With some slight exaggeration, we read in John 11:48 words reportedly spoken by the Jewish authorities meeting as the Sanhedrin in reference to Jesus: "If we let him go on, every one will believe in him." Jesus finds acceptance in the people, to the extent that, when the temple leaders meet to plan his arrest and death, they agree that it should not take place during the seven days of the Passover festivities "lest there be a tumult of the people" (Mark 14:2 || Matt 26:5), since, as Luke 22:2 says, "they feared the people."

According to Mark 14:1, the high priests and scribes had come to this conclusion "two days before the Passover," on the Wednesday, according to the chronology of the synoptic Gospels. What led, in such a short space of time (two days!), to things changing so significantly? The clues offered by the Gospel narratives point toward the leaders successfully applying pressure on the people. They would not have acted this way of their own free will, but instead because they had been persuaded by the authorities to coerce Pilate into sentencing Jesus to crucifixion. We read in Matthew 27:20 that "the chief priests and the elders persuaded the people to ask for Barabbas and destroy Jesus." Similarly, according to Mark 15:11, "the chief priests stirred up the crowd to have him release for them Barabbas instead."

In the other two Gospels, Luke and John, little is said on the subject, and the responsibility of the people is reduced to a minimum. In the narrative of the Passion according to Luke, the people appear only alongside the high priests and other leaders, with a seemingly hostile attitude toward Jesus, when he is brought before Pilate (Luke 23:4) and at the start of the scene with Barabbas (Luke 23:13). But after this, as this scene develops, those calling for Jesus' crucifixion are "they," which does not shed any light on the picture. Furthermore, after Jesus' death, the Gospel of Luke emphasizes that the people at Golgotha returned to Jerusalem "beating their breasts" as a sign of penitence (Luke 23:48). Similarly, the Gospel according to John makes only one direct allusion to the intervention of the "nation" in Jesus' sentence. Pilate addresses Jesus and says, "Your own nation and the chief priests have handed you over to me" (John 18:35). In the Gospels of Luke and John, we have to almost search between the lines to find the role of the people alongside the temple leaders, the high priests, in the condemnation of Jesus.

There is no evidence to contradict that the people adopted the ideas put forward by the authorities and became convinced that it was best that Jesus die. However, we have to ask ourselves whether this sudden change of heart regarding Jesus is credible. It is obvious that a change such as this is not unheard of, especially if we are to judge what happened to Jeremiah when he was accused by the leaders at the temple in Jerusalem (by the priests and "official" prophets) of being a false prophet. Initially, the people side with them saying that Jeremiah deserves to die, having dared to prophesy against the temple. Subsequently, however, when the prophet is allowed to express himself and states that he has spoken in the name of God, that he has been commissioned by him, the people change their mind and side with the magistrates and against the temple leaders: Jeremiah does not, in the end, die (Jer 26:1-19). The case of Jesus is just the opposite. The people remain on the side of the temple leaders and give them their full support to press Pilate into condemning Jesus to death, despite having often listened to and felt sympathy for the Galilean rabbi who had spoken in the temple atria or entered Jerusalem so jubilantly.

This abrupt change in the people's feelings for Jesus has led even some experts, such as G. Theissen, to conclude that those who accompanied him when he entered the city or who gladly listened to him in the temple and those who called for his crucifixion were not the same people. The former were probably Galileans who, like Jesus, had come to celebrate the Passover in Jerusalem, while the latter were those swayed over by the high priests, inhabitants of the city who were not in favor of Jesus. Jerusalem could expand to some one hundred thousand inhabitants for Passover, and it would be easy to imagine two very distinct crowds: one on Palm Sunday and the other on Good Friday, one crying out in favor of Jesus and the other against him. This proposal is not beyond the realm of possibility, but it does lack support from the texts. We are better off explaining this sudden change in feelings toward Jesus, who was censured before Pilate and killed without anyone coming to his defense, in terms of fearful silence, cold indifference, and even aggressive disrespect from the people who were present in Jerusalem, whether locals or pilgrims.

The people's attitude changed radically because the leaders were skillful enough not to accuse Jesus of a theoretical or doctrinal crime but a specific and very sensitive one, one that touched a nerve. Jesus was not presented as a man of dangerous doctrines, who refused to say whether he came from God or not, and who, at times, attributed divine prerogatives to himself. The accusation of blasphemy was theological in nature and would have little effect among the people. What could really impress them (and it did impress them!) was Jesus' prophecy about the temple. Jesus had dared to say that he was capable of destroying the temple and reconstructing it (when? how?) in three days: an amazing, majestic temple, which was admired around the world and the glory of the Jewish nation; a temple that had been built over five centuries before to replace Solomon's temple and which for the past forty-six years had been subject to a radical and magnificent restoration.

This prophecy was an intolerable attack on the holiness of God's residence among his people. Who could proclaim the destruction of this temple? Only a false prophet, someone who did not speak in the name of God, but who wanted to make people believe that his words represented the divine will. What did it mean that this Galilean said that he himself (!) could destroy and reconstruct the temple? Why did he want to leave the Jewish people without their temple, even if it was only temporarily? Or, indeed, did he want to destroy it and not rebuild it, despite having said the contrary?

Furthermore, this prophecy from the rabbi of Nazareth had not come true. The temple was still in the same place, firm and solid, apparently indestructible; and a prophecy that does not come true is a false prophecy. The book of Deuteronomy refers to the criteria used to distinguish between authentic and false prophets: "when a prophet speaks in the name of the Lord, if the word does not come to pass or come true, that is a word which the Lord has not spoken; the prophet has spoken it presumptuously, you need not be afraid of him" (Deut 18:22). Nonetheless, Jesus, tied up and in custody, did not inspire any fear. Undoubtedly, he was a man defeated, at the mercy of those who had captured him. He was defenseless and vulnerable, a failed prophet without any force, and almost without words. There were even those who cruelly insulted him, blindfolding him and telling him to prophesy, to guess who had hit him.

The people had radically changed their opinion of Jesus because of the reports spread by the leaders, which constituted a full-frontal attack on his reputation. Bringing Jesus' prophecy about the destruction of the temple to light is the equivalent of bringing him into conflict with Jerusalem itself, a city about to celebrate the Passover in the temple, the temple that this Galilean wanted to destroy! However, Jesus, unlike Jeremiah, could not, or did not want to, explain himself. His focused and cryptic prophecy left many things up in the air, but it may have been his intention to express the great authority that he had received from God, even over the temple, Israel's holiest institution (see 6.2.1.1).

Neither the people nor their leaders understood the meaning of Jesus' prophecy, seeing it as a threat to the temple, which resulted in failure. The people accepted the reasons given by the authorities. They were concerned and angry at this prophecy of the destruction of the temple, which affected one of the focal points for their beliefs. It was fair and necessary that Jesus die. Ultimately, did his arrest (orchestrated by the high priest himself) and sentencing to ignominious crucifixion not constitute reliable proof of his being a false prophet, who had no support from God?

6.2.1.3. The Roman Authorities' Reasons

Josephus explains that in the year 62 A.D., during the Feast of Tabernacles, with the city of Jerusalem packed full of pilgrims, a peasant called Jesus, son of Ananus, suddenly started crying out in the temple atrium that the temple and the city were to be destroyed. For some time, during day and night, he went through the streets of Jerusalem repeating his prophecy of destruction, until "the most eminent among the populace," upset by his preaching, caught him and gave him a good beating. However, he did nothing to try and protect himself and continued to cry out his warning. Finally, the Jewish "rulers" arrested him and took him before Lucceius Albinus, the Roman governor. Presumably it was he who decided to teach him a lesson and who had him whipped "till his bones were laid bare." However, he did not ask for mercy nor cry a single tear, and with each whiplash he received he continued to say in a plaintive voice, "Woe, woe to Jerusalem!" When Albinus asked him who he was, where he was from, and why he cried out so, Jesus, son of Ananus, did not reply, not to these or any other question addressed to him by the governor. The only thing that passed his lips was the laments for Jerusalem. In the end, "Albinus took him to be a madman and dismissed him" (*J.W.* 6:300–306).

Readers will have noticed some interesting parallels between this incident and a similar one involving another Jesus, Jesus of Nazareth, who was also from a rural background and who also proclaimed the destruction of the temple (and its reconstruction in three days), which, among other factors, led to his arrest by the authorities and, finally, his being brought before the Roman procurator, Pontius Pilate, accused of proclaiming himself as king of the Jews (not for wanting to destroy the temple!). As with the other Jesus, the prophet of Nazareth was also interrogated by the Roman governor and whipped; neither did he respond to the accusations he was charged with, but, unlike the son of Ananus, he was sentenced and executed by the Roman authorities.

The only reason the Roman governor sentenced Jesus was because he had been found guilty of threatening the empire with his pretensions of becoming "king of the Jews." The punishment corresponding to this sentence was clearly stipulated in Roman law: death by crucifixion.

Despite the Gospel according to John (18:3, 18:12), everything leads us to think that Jesus was not arrested by Roman soldiers but by some temple guards, sent expressly by the Jewish authorities (see 6.2.2, below). It was not the Roman governor who ordered his arrest but the high priests, the temple leaders. This means that the Roman trial was not preceded by the usual procedures: accusation, arrest warrant, and arrest. Pilate had to judge a man whom he had not ordered to be arrested, a man accused of a serious crime that merited the death penalty.

Nonetheless, if the governor had not ordered the arrest of the Galilean, it was because he had not been accused of anything, nor, up to that point, was there any reason for him to be arrested: he had not upset the public order or made any attempt to. This Jew from Galilee did not mean anything to Pilate. If this had been the case, the Roman authorities, who were always alert in a city such as Jerusalem, the focal point for Jewish aspirations, and at a particularly sensitive time of the year (the city's population increased fourfold with pilgrims arriving for Passover, the main Jewish festival), would not have thought twice about intervening. Pilate himself, who usually lived in Caesarea, the Roman port in the province of Judaea, went each year to Jerusalem around the time of Passover in order to keep a close eye on events and to be able to act as quickly as possible. Jesus' arrest was a purely Jewish affair and Pilate, at most, watched from a distance.

It seems clear that the governor met Jesus for the first time on the Friday morning when he was brought to him by the Jewish authorities. Nothing leads us to think that he already knew him. Nor are there any signs that he would have heard of him either. Indeed, there is no record of any direct contact between Jesus and the Roman administration in Judaea. The political point of reference in the life and activities of the rabbi from Nazareth had always been the tetrarch Herod Antipas, sovereign of Galilee and Peraea, of whom Jesus was a subject. Jesus' stays in Judaea had always been short and intermittent, and had increased only in the last months of his life. Furthermore, during these months, Jesus was based in the area between Jerusalem and the river Jordan, to the east of the city, in the opposite direction to Caesarea, the Roman capital of Judaea and where Pilate usually resided. As a result, though we cannot say for sure that Pilate had not received some information about Jesus in the past, there does not seem to have been an open police file on him. Jesus had not been "booked" by the Romans.

Pilate had to depend on the information provided by the Jewish authorities, and this obviously explains his reticence when it came to accepting some of the charges presented against Jesus. Pilate did not simply add his signature, rather he ensured that the trial had all the necessary legal guarantees, which led to his deciding that the accusation made against Jesus was true and thus he sentenced him (see 6.2.4).

The accusation that the temple leaders and other members of the Sanhedrin (all of whom were important people from Jerusalem) presented to Pilate can be deduced from the question that he asked Jesus as soon as the interrogation began: "Are you the King of the Jews?" (Mark 15:2 || Matt 27:11 || Luke 23:3 || John 18:33). There is unanimity in all four Gospels as to this question that makes reference to the identity of the accused. This is how all Roman trials would normally begin, and this is how Pilate probably began his interrogation. We should stress that the governor did not ask for the personal identity of the accused ("Are you Jesus of Nazareth?"), which would be a more obvious question; he asked about the identity that he had been provided with by Jesus' accusers: "king of the Jews." It seems as if Pilate did not know the name of the person standing in front of him! When he asked the people to decide on Jesus' fate, he asked them, "[W]hat shall I do with the man you call [as if it were something common!] the King of the Jews?" (Mark 15:12). The wording in John 18:39 changes slightly ("[W]ill you have me release for you the King of the Jews?"), but it maintains the name used by Pilate to address Jesus throughout the trial.

During the break in Pilate's interrogation, Jesus, as we shall see, was the victim of insults from the Roman soldiers belonging to the praetorium garrison. The soldiers covered him in a purple cloak, the color of royalty, and placed a crown of thorns on his head as another sign of royalty, they passed before him and saluted him, saying, "Hail, King of the Jews!" (Mark 15:18 || Matt 27:29 || John 19:3). The soldiers' insults clearly showed the reason for Jesus being sentenced. This is seen in the plaque or *titulus* hung on the cross, where Pilate had someone write in three languages "the charge against him" (Mark 15:26 || Matt 27:37). This sign showed publicly and shamefully and possibly in summarized form the charge for which Jesus had been crucified: for making himself "the King of the Jews," a rival to the Roman emperor. This plaque is reliable evidence of Pilate's sentencing: "[This is/Jesus of Nazareth,] the King of the Jews" (Mark 15:26 || Matt 27:37 || Luke 23:38 || John 19:19, 19:21). Once again, the four Gospels, despite some small variations in the text of the *titulus* on the cross, are unanimous in saying that the expression "the king of the Jews" above the cross was the official reason for Jesus' condemnation (see 6.2.5.3).

The accusation of pretender to the throne was the only one that could sway the Roman governor when judging Jesus' case and when sentencing him to capital punishment. We should stress that the Greek language uses the same word (*basileus*) to describe a "king" and the Roman "emperor." The two figures are clearly placed in opposition to each other, even more so if we consider that the royal sovereign and highest authority in the Jewish country at the time was Tiberius Caesar. The inhabitants of the Roman province of Judaea and of the tetrarchies of Antipas and Philip were subjects of the Emperor. So it made no difference that Jesus, as a Galilean, fell under the jurisdiction of Antipas. There was only one "king" (*basileus*) in all the empire, and anyone who sought to replace him was committing high treason against Caesar.

From Pilate's point of view, the accusation against Jesus was clear. The problem, for the Jewish authorities, was the evidence. How could they prove to the governor that Jesus was an enemy of Rome? First, as we have said, they could not accuse Jesus or his followers of violent action against the Roman powers, nor could they accuse him of planning or plotting to end Roman domination of the Jewish country through possible military action. The figure of Jesus is unlike the other pretenders to the throne that Josephus refers to, who arose around the time of the death of Herod the Great, the last "king of the Jews" to hold this title, in 4 B.C. Jesus had not sacked any royal palaces, as had Simon, nor had he, as had Athronges, dedicated his life to eliminating the Herodians and Romans whom he accused of arrogance and injustice, nor had he been involved in banditry and extortion like the Galilean Judas, son of Hezekiah. Jesus' disciples did not receive any instructions or recommendations from their Master to take up an armed fight, not even if it were to restore social justice (see 3.3.3.1).

There is no evidence of any systematic armed resistance against Rome, in the style of the Zealots who came later, though there were isolated groups of "bandits" or "thieves," people acting in the grey area among delinquency, social revolt, and anti-Roman theocratic ideals, from time to time in the cities. There was no contact between Jesus' group and these armed bands (see 3.3.3.4). Since the uprising in 6 A.D., led by Judas the Galilean and inspired by the first Roman census, ordered by Quirinius, a theocratic ideological movement had gained force. This had been galvanized by the nonpayment of the tribute to the Roman emperor, based on the idea that God was the only king of the country. Jesus also responded to this question (one of the most controversial of the time) in an extraordinarily skillful and new way: "Render therefore to Caesar the things that are Caesar's, and to God the things that are God's." A clearly negative position (do not pay the tribute) cannot be deduced from this statement, nor can a positive one (see 3.3.3.2). An accusation based on the first position, as that attributed to the Jewish authorities in Luke 23:2, is not well founded: Jesus did not manifest a well-defined and explicit political opposition to Rome.

Second, it is obvious that the reasons given by the Sanhedrin, which they assumed to be serious enough to warrant Jesus' death, had little or no effect on Pilate. We cannot see any evidence that Pilate was sensitive to the subject of the temple or the charges of false prophecy or blasphemy, which were decisive from the Jewish perspective regarding the legal framework of the Law of Moses (see 6.2.1.1). Pilate judged Jesus according to Roman law, as the Jewish leaders well knew. For this reason, in the trial before Pilate, there is no mention of any accusation other than that of being the "king of the Jews," which was the backbone of the trial and the sentencing (the soldiers' insults and the plaque or *titulus* on the cross).

Nevertheless, Jesus' messianic pretensions constituted one of the charges that the Jewish leaders leveled at him. Jesus had let it be understood that he was the Messiah for Israel, his people. He had let it be known almost *sotto voce* with gestures rather than words, suggesting it rather than proclaiming it and entering Jerusalem as a different kind of Messiah for peace and not for war, but a Messiah, nonetheless! Furthermore, he was a Messiah with a certain power to attract people, people who listened to him intently, and he had a group of loyal followers who had been with him for many months (just over two years!), followers who remained with him day and night, who lived with him. The temple leaders, with Caiaphas as their head, were unsure and alarmed when they saw how Jesus attracted people (John 11:47-53). All told, he represented a threat: the consolidation of a Messiah like Jesus could lead to the worst. To date, he had shown his friendly and peaceful side, but who knows what his actual intentions might be! Jesus' Messianism frightened the Jewish leaders, who were afraid that Jesus might lead the people into the disaster represented by military confrontation with the Romans. We simply have to "translate" the accusation: instead of accusing Jesus of presenting himself as the "Messiah," a charge that was not envisioned in Roman law, they had to call him "the king [*basileus*] of the Jews." This was a language that the Roman authorities and judicial system could understand.

The line of reasoning employed by the Jewish leaders with Pilate was probably the one we have just outlined. Rather than focusing on what Jesus had done against Rome (as he had done nothing against Caesar, and Pilate acknowledged this!), they insisted instead on what he had yet to do. Jesus represented a potential threat not just to Rome but to the Jewish people themselves who, they said, should live happily for many years to come under the protection of the emperor. Maintaining the status quo meant eliminating Jesus of Nazareth, who would, more than likely, become a stumbling block, a stone in the shoe of the Jewish people. Faced with the lack of real evidence against him, the leaders may have turned to presenting him as a future threat: can Rome afford to let this man free, who states that he is "the king of the Jews" (Luke 23:2)? According to John 19:12, the Jewish leaders' reasoning was clear: "[E]very one who makes himself a king sets himself against Caesar." Apparently, calling oneself king and thereby putting oneself on an equal footing with the Roman emperor was enough to merit the death penalty. The evidence, which Pilate ended up accepting, did not comprise actual transgressions of the Roman law but the potential and very real threat of subversion against Caesar. There was enough in the fact that Jesus did not deny that he was the "king of the Jews." Indeed, when asked about this, he responded to Pilate saying, "You have said so" (Mark 15:2 || Matt 27:11 || Luke 23:3 || John 18:37). Subsequently, Pilate simply had to give in to the pressure from the people and the authorities for Jesus' punishment to become, for Pilate, the lesser of two evils. It was better for one man to die than for all the people to rise up.

In summary, although Pilate felt strongly that he should be the one sitting in judgment and should sentence Jesus, without being influenced by the Jewish leaders, the Roman governor did end up endorsing the accusation and reasoning that they had put forward. Pilate ended up accepting what had been adduced by the Jewish authorities, who portrayed Jesus as a great threat (albeit only potential, very real!). This Galilean who considered himself "the king of the Jews" was not mad or deluded but a dangerous rival to Caesar and guilty of *lese-majesty* against him.

6.2.2. His Arrest

The historical sources are the four Gospels (Mark 14:26-52 || Matt 26:30-56 || Luke 23:39-53 || and John 18:1-12). As is often the case in the narrative of the Passion, Matthew closely follows Mark. Luke, who also follows Mark, introduces some traditions of his own. On the other hand, John, together with Mark, is another torchbearer for the material relating to the Passion, but his narrative agrees with the other three synoptic Gospels only as far as the plot is concerned.

6.2.2.1. The Scene

The first of the five scenes of the Passion takes place in a garden or plot of land known as Gethsemane, a Hebrew or Aramaic word meaning "oil mill" or "press." The garden was on the other side of the brook of Cedron, which ran down parallel to the eastern flank of the walls of Jerusalem to the foot of the Mount of Olives. It was toward this hill to the east of the city that Jesus went with the Twelve, once they had left the table and the house where they had celebrated his farewell supper. This house, known traditionally as the cenacle, was probably in the Upper City in west Jerusalem. If this traditional location for the upper room is correct, Jesus had to cross the whole city; more than a kilometer separates these two points as the crow flies. The journey is quite long, and the most obvious route would have been to go down toward the Tyropoeon, the stream that separates the Upper City from the Lower City, and go beyond the walls and follow the brook of Cedron, with the ancient city of David and the temple on the left, and on to Gethsemane.

This was not the first time that Jesus had gone to Gethsemane. According to Luke 22:39, it was something he did often. The Gospel according to John goes on to say that he often met his disciples there (John 18:2). The land was a garden, or a plot bordered by a stone wall, with some olive tress and a press, whose owner was anonymous, as was the case of the house where Jesus had just had supper with the Twelve. It seems clear that both in Bethany and in Jerusalem, and possibly in Bethphage (a town near Bethany), there was an inconspicuous network of Jesus' followers, some of whom we know about (the siblings, Lazarus, Martha, and Mary, and Simon, the Leper, in Bethany; Joseph of Arimathea and Nicodemus in Jerusalem) and others who remain anonymous (the owner of the donkey used to enter the city, the owner of the upper room, the owner of the garden of Gethsemane).

What led Jesus to go to Gethsemane? If we look at the three synoptic Gospels, the answer is that Jesus, having eaten, wanted to go off to pray at this place that he knew well, not far from the road that passes the Mount of Olives on its way to Bethany, the town where he had stayed with his disciples since arriving in Jerusalem to celebrate the Passover. Jesus liked praying at night and in isolated places, "in the morning, a great while before day" when it was still dark (Mark 1:35) or in the evening on a mountainside (Mark 6:47). This idea was something normal for him; his group of disciples were not surprised, since stopping off in Gethsemane to pray would not have affected their expected route. The distance between Gethsemane and Bethany is less than three kilometers. We need to bear in mind, however, how Jesus looked upon and lived that night internally.

The festive supper that the disciples had just shared with Jesus had been a surprising and intense event, with extraordinary words and gestures from the Master. Jesus had invited them to eat the bread he had broken, saying that it was his body, and to drink from the same cup of wine, saying that it was the new covenant in his blood. All of a sudden, when they were already seated at the table, he wanted to wash their feet one by one. The meal had ended with an announcement: this was the last time that Jesus would share a festive table with them until the arrival of the Kingdom of God. Was this Kingdom close at hand, and was this meal some kind of anticipation? What was going to happen? Or, on the contrary, was great disappointment at hand, of which the disciples were unaware? Their behavior in Gethsemane (sleeping instead of keeping watch) shows that they were disconcerted more than anything else and that they lacked any perception of the way events were going. Despite some signs that must have left them somewhat concerned, the disciples were sure that they were to pass that night in Bethany, where they normally stayed, and that the following day they would have the Passover meal with Jesus. The disciples' perception of events is well reflected in the comment to be found in the Gospel according to John, when Judas leaves the upper room once the meal has started: "Some [of the disciples] thought that, because Judas had the money-box, Jesus was telling him, 'Buy what we need for the [Passover] feast'" (John 13:29).

6.2.2.2. The Predictions

The Gospel tradition refers to three prophecies of what was to come, made by Jesus during or after the supper. These prophecies affected the Twelve as a whole and two of them in particular: Peter and Judas. At the Last Supper, Jesus referred indirectly to his imminent death. The subject of giving his life had been the inspiration for his words and gestures with the bread and the wine. Jesus considered that this meal had a decisive farewell aspect, and he had wanted to celebrate this with his disciples as a form of testament. The Master had shown inner clarity and lucidity in expressing himself about his future. He knew that events were speeding up and that the end (what end?) could come at any moment.

Jesus, furthermore, knew his disciples and knew their limits. His path had never involved violence or aggression. The disciples had not been led or instructed to react to force with more force. The recent arrival in Jerusalem had been the triumph of a Messiah of peace. Despite the initial idea that the arrival of the Kingdom would see the proliferation of power and those who were to occupy the positions of government, Jesus had instead talked in different terms. His message had always been against violent or arrogant solutions, based on the acquisition of power and control. Shortly before, following the meal, Jesus had spoken to them about buying a sword ("let him who has no sword sell his mantle and buy one"; Luke 22:36), and they had taken him at his word. Nevertheless, Jesus was talking about being willing to give everything and to lose, if necessary, life itself, while the disciples took pains to remind him that there were two swords there. "It is enough" was Jesus' half ironic, half annoyed reply (Luke 22:38). Jesus predicted that the disciples would let him down because not letting him down would mean dying with him, without defending themselves, or running away. This was a test that these men were not yet able to overcome. He said to them, "You will all fall away" (Mark 14:27 || Matt 26:31; John 16:32).

Linked to the prediction of the disciples letting him down, Jesus also told Peter another prophecy. The leader of the Twelve was to fail him personally and famously, more obviously than the others. The specific detail was the precise time when Peter was to fail him: before the rooster crowed for the second time, before the rooster's crow signaled the dawning of a new day (Mark 14:30 || Matt 26:34; John 13:38). According to Mark, upon whom Matthew and John depend, Jesus made a prediction referring to that same night according to which Peter in particular, the spokesman and leader of the Twelve, was to fail him. Jesus singled Peter out as the only one to deny him in public, and that he would deny him three times, to hammer home the point. As we shall see, denying Jesus did not mean that Peter rejected the Master, but rather, when he was put to the test, he was afraid and denied being a disciple of his.

Despite the emphasis on Peter's unfortunate actions, at heart, his behavior is not very different from the rest of the disciples: the whole of the group of Twelve (except Judas, obviously!) denied being disciples of Jesus, ran away, and left him alone in the hands of his enemies. Faced with the announcement that they were all to fail him, and Peter in particular, both he and the others assured him that they were willing to "die" for him (Mark 14:31 || Matt 26:35), to "lay down my life for you" (John 13:37, here just Peter). This statement sounds excessive and rhetorical and has the overblown, exaggeratedly indignant tone of those who have doubts. The disciples wanted to counter Jesus' announcement ("You will all fall away") with a statement of great élan ("if necessary, we are willing to die for you"), which sounded too courageous to be true. The Twelve did not know that what they had just said fit perfectly with the events that were about to take place, as they would soon find out. As soon as they got to Gethsemane, the first thing that the three most conspicuous members of the group did was not give their life for Jesus but fall asleep, unable to protect him or pray with him.

However, is it credible that Jesus predicted Peter's denials so exactly? Is this exactitude not a sign of an element that was added later? We should note that the prediction of Peter's denials contained a precise reference to the time when they were to take place (that same night, before the rooster announced the new day!), but the prediction did not specify the context or circumstances, or before whom Peter was to deny Jesus. Jesus showed the inner clarity characteristic of the prophets, but his words were not a precise augury of what was to happen to him and the others. The predictions of the disciples' failures and Peter's in particular show Jesus' firm convictions concerning that night: the time was drawing near for him to be handed over to those who wanted to do him harm.

The third prediction refers to the very accomplice in his death, to the man who made it possible for Jesus' adversaries to get their hands on him. It took place during the Last Supper. Jesus had already started to eat with the Twelve when he predicted that one of them ("one of you") was to betray him (Mark 14:18 || Matt 26:26 || John 13:21; similarly, Luke 22:21). There was a great uproar. Some two years before, in Galilee, Jesus had chosen, from among his disciples and followers, twelve men to share his life with him. From then on, they had all been loyal to him. There had been no defections from the circle of the Twelve. None of them had abandoned him or flagged during the difficult times. Jesus himself recognized this: "You are those who have continued with me in my trials" (Luke 22:28). Why then did Jesus now say that one of them was to hand him over to his enemies?

At no time did Jesus mention Judas' name in the company of the other disciples. The Master simply talked about the one who was to "hand him over," from the Greek word *paradidōmi*, which is usually translated as "betray" (Mark 14:18). Although the word "traitor" (Greek, *prodotēs*) is applied to Judas only in Luke 6:16 and although the other Gospel texts limit themselves to describing him as the one "who handed Jesus over" (reading between the lines, to death), Judas' actions are explained in all four Gospels as a betrayal of the trust that the Master had deposited in him. Judas goes to see the high priests behind Jesus' back. It is not unreasonable to talk of betrayal, though the exact sense of the word has to be specified in Judas' case (see 6.2.2.5, below).

Did Jesus know the name and intentions of the disciple who was to betray him? If, as is more than likely, he knew, he did not tell the other disciples, who found out only when Judas carried out the act of betrayal in Gethsemane. During the meal with Jesus and Judas

(!), they make no mention of it, though Jesus' allusion to the betrayal and Judas' enigmatic behavior established a certain level of complicity between the two: neither of them openly showed what they knew or what they planned to do. In John 13:27, this situation can be seen in a short phrase: "What you are going to do, do quickly." The Gospel continues, saying, "no one at the table knew why he said this to him." Judas probably left the upper room during the meal, when Jesus was pronouncing his words over the bread and washing the disciples' feet (see 6.2.2.5). The subject of Judas' betrayal acted as a dramatic counterpoint to Jesus' words and gestures during this farewell meal: the Master was giving his life for all men, and one of his disciples would give him over to death by placing him in the hands of those few men who sought to have him killed.

6.2.2.3. The Prayer

As soon as Jesus entered the garden of Gethsemane with his disciples (all of them, except Judas), the Master clearly wanted to be alone to pray. He asked the disciples to sit down and wait. The Gospels of Mark and Matthew agree in presenting Jesus' prayer not as one whole but as broken down into three parts that were not exactly short (Mark 14:37 talks about the first period of Jesus' prayer lasting "one hour"). In fact, Jesus took three disciples with him to the place where he wanted to pray, those who had accompanied him during the particularly intense moments in his life (Peter, James, and John), and he asked them to keep an eye out and to stay with him and, no doubt, to pray with him. According to the narrative in Mark, which is echoed in Matthew, Jesus prayed for a while and then went to get the three disciples (Luke 22:41 states that Jesus "withdrew them [from the rest of the disciples?] about a stone's throw").

Each of the three times that he stopped praying he went to Peter, James, and John to find them in the same position: the disciples were not keeping an eye out, but fast asleep. After the festive supper, with abundant food and wine, and now well into the night, it is understandable that the three men fell asleep. They were unaware of the seriousness of the situation and what was soon to befall both them and their Master. They were not in tune with what was going on; they were almost absent. Jesus' allusions and indications about what was about to happen had not had any effect. They could not stay awake and fell asleep. There is a hiatus between what Jesus was undergoing and what they were undergoing. According to the Gospels of Mark and Matthew, Jesus made a proverbial statement to interpret this behavior and to typify the inner conflict faced by the three disciples: "[T]he spirit indeed is willing, but the flesh is weak" (Mark 14:38 || Matt 26:41).

The focus of the scene is not the somewhat disappointing attitude of the disciples, who were unable to keep guard or pray, but Jesus' prayer. R. E. Brown sums it up, saying that Jesus was struggling inside and praying to God concerning his imminent death with a feeling of anguish. The synoptic Gospel tradition places this prayer in the garden of Gethsemane and on the night of his arrest. The Gospel according to John, however, introduces the content of the Gethsemane prayers into Jesus' last public act, where he stressed that his time had come. From all four Gospels and the tradition continued into the Epistle to the Hebrews (5:7-10), we can see that Jesus called on God as his Father, asking him to free him from his imminent death but, despite everything, stated that he would do his will. These three elements are shared by the synoptic Gospels and John and thus belong to a very ancient tradition regarding Gethsemane. For example, Mark 14:36 states, "Abba, Father, all things are possible to thee; remove this cup from me; yet not what I will, but what thou wilt" (also Matt 26:29 and Luke 22:42). The underlying similarities with John 12:27-28a are remarkable: "And what shall I say 'Father, save me from this hour'? No, for this purpose I have come to this hour. Father, glorify thy name."

Second, these prayers were said in anxiety and expressed his feeling of abandonment by God. In the second century A.D., the philosopher Celsus, who was opposed to Christianity, observed that if Jesus was a divine being, he should not have been afraid of death (Origen, *Against Celsus* 2:24). These were, however, Jesus' feelings, according to the oldest Christian documents: "In the days of his flesh, Jesus offered up prayers and supplications, with loud cries and tears, to him who was able to save him from death" (Heb 5:7). The same text continues, "and he was heard for his godly fear," because he showed himself willing to continue along the chosen path until the end.

At the Last Supper, Jesus had given his death a meaning; his death sealed the new covenant, which was to continue until the Kingdom of God manifested itself completely. However, in Gethsemane the Passion momentarily seemed to be the victory of evil, of the Devil, and represented the failure of the proclamation of the Kingdom: the Kingdom had only just started to manifest itself and its bearer, God's emissary, was about to die. This is, probably, the real reason for Jesus' apprehension and for his cries during the prayer: the fear that God's cause could fail, and not the fact that he had to die. A tension was created at the Last Supper: on the one hand, it looked forward to the future Kingdom and the covenant; and on the other, Gethsemane was the start of a testing period, in which Jesus was to experience the harsh reality of death and the uncertainty of not knowing God's response, which he was able to overcome only thanks to the boundless trust of a Son.

The scene of the angel confronting Jesus shows this in dramatic fashion. The Gospel of Luke is the only one that recounts these events (Luke 22:43-44, verses that are missing from some older manuscripts but that should be considered original). When faced with this period of trial and temptation, Jesus received a heavenly sign of divine help that assured him that he would not have to undergo the Passion alone. His reaction consisted of praying with more energy and intensity, to the point where his sweat looked like "drops of blood falling to the ground" (Luke 22:44). This is the preferable way to interpret a phrase that some have wanted to see as Jesus actually sweating blood. Jesus' abundant sweat was a physical sign of his suffering and the intensity with which he was praying.

The prayers in Gethsemane, said with concern and apprehension, were interrupted three times by Jesus' attempts to involve Peter, James, and John. They were full of contrasts and supported by the Father, who was present during these trials, and brought to an end by the sudden appearance of a band of armed men who had come to detain Jesus.

6.2.2.4. The Arrest

The band of men that entered the garden of Gethsemane comprised a group of men commissioned by the Jewish authorities to arrest Jesus. This militia, formed for the occasion and acting at this untimely hour of the night, consisted of people who were employed by the high priests and nobles of Jerusalem, or in their household as servants, or members of the temple guard. In fact, among them, there was "the slave of the high priest," their leader (Mark 14:47 || Matt 26:52 || Luke 22:50 || John 18:19). The Gospel according to John gives him a name: Malchus. It is not clear whether this figure is Caiaphas' servant (as the Gospel according to Matthew assumes, as do, possibly, Mark and Luke) or Annas' (as the Gospel according to John states). Caiaphas was the current high priest, but Annas, his father-in-law, had been the high priest and maintained the title and the power. The band had come prepared in case Jesus' disciples offered resistance and carried swords and clubs. Thanks to the information presumably provided by Judas to the high priests, they almost certainly expected a response from the disciples, who would have had some weapons. Nothing, however, leads us to believe that the disciples had foreseen any kind of attack or that they had organized any kind of resistance in the case of an attack. According to Luke 22:38, all the weapons they had were "two swords" (!). The arrival of this band of men took them by surprise and half asleep.

Judas led the way, as he knew the place and in the relative darkness (there was a full moon) identified Jesus. The Gospel according to John describes the band as fully equipped with "lanterns and torches" (18:3); the Gospel describes the scene thus: "some officers from the chief priests" had come to Gethsemane, guided by Judas, together with the Roman cohort usually stationed in Jerusalem with the captain at its head, in total, a few hundred (!) professional soldiers (John 18:3, 18:12-13). This is an unlikely figure from a historical point of view, since, without a direct order from Pilate, an imposing military force such as this could not have left Jerusalem at night; and, should this order have existed, the prisoner would have been taken to the Roman cells at the praetorium and not the house of the Jewish leader, Annas. By referring to the presence of the Roman cohort in Gethsemane, the Gospel of John seeks to indicate the control over the events and powers that Jesus had, as he had had the initiative throughout. In this light, we should stress two events: first, Jesus identified himself and called himself by the powerful divine name "I am he," causing the large military contingent to retreat en masse and fall to the ground; and second, he allowed himself to be taken without a struggle and had them let the disciples go to ensure that not even one of them be lost.

The band, guided by Judas, entered Gethsemane, and from then on everything happened very quickly. First, Judas greeted Jesus, calling him by his usual name ("Rabbi!"), and kissed him. The kiss was the sign, agreed to beforehand, to identify him: Jesus was the only one who had to be arrested; they were not interested in his disciples. Then the members of the band got hold of Jesus. At that point, faced with Jesus' attitude (he did not defend himself or call for help) and faced with the fear of being arrested themselves, all his followers fled Gethsemane. One of Jesus' followers made an armed attack (though it was not exactly resistance), and a member of the band was injured.

This armed attack warrants a lengthy report in the four Gospel sources. We know the name of this man injured in Gethsemane (Malchus), his position (he was a servant of the high priest, a trusted henchman, probably the leader of the band), and how and where he was injured: "one of those who stood by" (a disciple according to Matthew and Luke; John singles Peter out as the assailant) "cut off his ear" (Mark 14:47). Luke and John specify that it was "his right ear," which is more honorable than the left ear (Luke 22:50; John 18:10). According to Mark, the identity of the person who injured the high priest's servant remains unclear ("one of those who stood by"). Could it be another member of the same band who had made a mistake in the darkness? Or was it, as the other three Gospels suppose, one of the group of Twelve, or even another of Jesus' followers, who wanted to come to his defense? An anonymous young man, covered only by a linen cloth, also appeared at the scene who was about to be detained, but at the last moment managed to escape. Does this mean that, as well as the Twelve, other followers of Jesus were present at that time, including the assailant and this young man? In my opinion, rather than an unfortunate accident involving two comrades, it was an attack on the band's leader carried out by one of the Twelve. If it was an accident, it could have been the result of self-defense by the men of the band, faced with the hostile reaction of Jesus' disciples; this is the only explanation why they had to unsheathe their swords.

However, according to Mark, the attack on the high priest's servant took place after Jesus had been arrested. This means that the disciples had not stood up directly to the band guided by Judas when they had entered the garden and that Jesus had been taken without problems. Only then did one of the disciples take advantage of the night and confusion to attack the high priest's servant, who was probably the leader of this militia, without being seen (from behind?). In any case, it did not lead to anything else, as Jesus' arrest and the disciples' flight were both done and dusted. Immediately after, the assailant managed to slip away, like the others, into the night in an area they knew well, and avoided getting caught. Jesus was left alone, in the hands of his enemies. The men of the band did manage to catch the young man covered in the linen cloth (apparently a disciple?), but he preferred the dishonor of escaping naked to sharing in his Master's fate (Mark 14:51-52).

After Gethsemane, the presence of the male disciples in the Passion is all but nonexistent. Judas disappeared from Jesus' life, as if the earth had swallowed him up. Only the Gospel according to Matthew speaks momentarily of his violent death a few hours later (27:3-10) (see 6.2.2.5). Of the others, only Peter made it to the courtyard of the high priest's house, following the band that had detained Jesus from a distance, and there, with his denials, he saw his willingness to follow him to the end diminished. "You will all fall away" was what Jesus had predicted, and they all failed him, without exception. Only the Gospel according to John says that "another disciple . . . known to the high priest" entered his house (John 18:15-16); he subsequently appears as "the disciple whom he loved" at the foot of Jesus' cross (John 19:26-27). It is likely that this was John, one of the Twelve. Nevertheless, the Twelve, as a group, had ceased to exist in Gethsemane and reappeared again only with the discovery of the empty tomb after the Master's death.

Jesus, abandoned completely by the disciples, was left alone with those who had come to arrest him. At this dramatic point, his words, however, remain ironic (Mark 14:48-49 || Matt 26:55-56 || Luke 22:52-53; John 18:20-21). He observed that they had come to detain him with a force and means in keeping with those needed for a bandit, rather than for a good person like himself. Indirectly he was saying that his arrest was unjustified. Furthermore, he stressed that if they wanted to detain him, they need not have waited until that hour of the night and this out-of-the-way spot; they were all connected to the temple and could simply have taken him in the light of day while he was teaching publicly there. He also alluded here to the fact that those who used the darkness and surprise to carry out their work could not have a clear conscience; in this case, the fear of a negative reaction from the people had led them to plan to arrest him secretly.

Jesus' arrest is, like the rest of his life and his death, God's will. He was arrested not because the authorities had decided so but because this was the "right" course of affairs. In the Gospel according to Matthew, this point is expressed with the image of the twelve legions of angels (each legion representing six thousand soldiers!) who could have come to Jesus' defense against this ridiculous band, made up, at most, of two or three dozen people (Matt 26:53). The ultimate explanation for his arrest and subsequent death goes much further than the will of the few men who instigated it and a few others who carried it out. Behind everything is the will of God, the Father (see 6.1.2.2).

6.2.2.5. And Judas?

The questions regarding the disciple who handed Jesus over to his adversaries are many and not easy to answer. In the Christian tradition this figure has been seen as evil incarnate, the representative par excellence of betrayal, a form of scapegoat who has taken on the responsibility for the violence meted out to Jesus during the Passion. Nonetheless, we need to distinguish between the tradition's view of Judas and the figure of Judas, a man chosen by Jesus to form part of the Twelve and who ended up betraying him and handing him over to the Jewish authorities who wanted to have him killed, a man who was to meet a sudden and violent end. Son of Simon Iscariot, and known as Judas Iscariot (see 4.5.3.3), he acted as the treasurer for Jesus' group. This function, however, did not make him stand out from the rest of the disciples during Jesus' public activities. It is only in the days leading up to his death that the synoptic Gospels tell us about Judas' contacts with the high priests with the aim of handing over the rabbi of Nazareth.

Nevertheless, the crisis took shape only really during the Last Supper, and without the other disciples realizing. Judas arrived at the upper room with Jesus and the rest of the Twelve to celebrate the festive meal that Jesus wanted to share with them. The treacherous disciple started the meal with all the others and, according to John 13, left only when Jesus dropped a hint that he knew that Judas was to betray him. Beforehand, however, Judas had seen how Jesus had washed his feet as he had the other disciples'. Luke is the only Gospel that has Judas' betrayal announced during the Last Supper, right at its end, and it is also the only Gospel where the words referring to the banquet in the Kingdom come at the beginning. It is secondary information, as we have suggested (see 6.1.3.1). In Mark and Matthew, this announcement comes at the start of the meal, but from the very words used the meal had clearly already started: "as they were at table eating" (Mark 14:18 || Matt 26:21). The Gospel according to John also testifies that Jesus announced the betrayal of a disciple while they were sitting eating, following the washing of the feet. According to this Gospel, Judas left the meal at the exact moment when Jesus offered him a piece of bread he had dipped and said, "What you are going to do, do quickly" (John 13:27). However, the synoptic Gospels do not specify the exact moment during the meal when Judas left the upper room. In the end, we have to conclude that Jesus' announcement of his betrayal by Judas and the latter's immediate flight from the room must have taken place when the meal had already begun and once everyone had sat down to eat (see 6.2.2.2).

In order to understand the extent of Judas' participation in Jesus' arrest, we need to know the exact role he played. There are two possible answers to this question: (a) Judas played an important role, as someone closely involved in Jesus' death and the main protagonist in his arrest; (b) Judas was simply an informant to the Jewish authorities, and after Gethsemane he disappeared without leaving a trace.

Generally speaking, the Gospels tend to take the former view, that is, they emphasize Judas' role. In Luke and John, it says that the Devil possessed Judas. Luke, specifically, states that the Devil entered him (Luke 22:3) and that, as a result, the disciple ran to speak to the temple leaders and prepare the plot to hand Jesus over to them, with complete discretion. In the Gospel according John, Judas' decision to betray Jesus came as the result of the Devil having entered his heart (John 13:2, 13:27). Judas' betrayal is so incomprehensible that the sources look to the prince of evil in order to try and explain it. As R. E. Brown points out, Judas was at the service of the Devil and he was the first in a series of agents who led Jesus to his death: the disciple handed Jesus over to the high priests, who handed him over to Pilate; Pilate placed him in the hands of the soldiers, and they crucified him. However, many authors have tried to portray Judas as a loyal disciple who fulfilled God's will and acted in accordance with Jesus' instructions: his betrayal made salvation possible (!). Jesus, however, did not "schedule" the Passion. He, not Judas, was the instrument of God's will.

The second position, which is preferable, sees Judas as the person who passed on the necessary information to the Jewish authorities so that they could act discreetly, quickly, and efficiently, without being seen by the people who would not have stood for Jesus being detained in public and broad daylight. Judas formed part of the high priests' strategy, according to which they had to act without the people knowing in order to avoid any kind of uprising when someone who taught openly in the temple and who had done no wrong was arrested. The authorities wanted to put into practice their decision to have Jesus killed. Nonetheless, they were not sure how to get hold of him, since Jesus was staying outside Jerusalem and, furthermore, only went to the temple, which was full of people now that Passover was at hand. John 11:57 leads us to think that the authorities were making moves to get hold of Jesus and that there were rumors to this effect.

These rumors help explain Judas' initiative in presenting himself voluntarily to the authorities, making life easier for them. Judas, one of the Twelve, knew Jesus' movements and could indicate "an opportunity" for the high priests to arrest him (Mark 14:11). They wanted to sort the issue out as quickly as possible and "not during the feast"; they wanted to have it out of the way before the Passover. They needed only the band to be ready and for Judas to tell them when to act. We do not know when or how Judas let them know the information that Jesus was at Gethsemane, but the armed men who entered the garden were guided by the disciple. These men probably had their weapons hidden so as not to arouse the suspicions of the disciples who were at Gethsemane and not cause them alarm at seeing Judas, one of their own, leading the group. Nor were they surprised that this disciple greeted the Master and kissed him affectionately on the cheek as a sign of friendship. The kiss was, however, to identify Jesus, a prearranged sign. While the disciples stood perplexed, they took hold of Jesus. Judas' work was done.

The pertinent question is, what were the motives that led Judas to act this once on his own initiative and so decisively, as a collaborator with the Jewish authorities? What reasons could have led him to present himself before the enemies of his Master, betraying his trust and friendship? Any answer has to attempt to understand this disciple's actions from within. The Gospels of Luke and John, as we have indicated above, see Judas' betrayal as such a perverse act that can have been dictated only by the lord of evil, he who constantly betrays and tricks people with his arts. Judas acted as an instrument of the Devil's will. Furthermore, in the Gospel of John, a voracious and mean greed is attributed to Judas, and he is called a "thief," who steals from the offerings made to their shared money-box, for which he was responsible (John 12:6). This extreme greed led him, according to Matthew 26:14-16, to collaborate with the authorities in return for a certain quantity of money: thirty denarii or silver coins, the equivalent of thirty days' work. This is the amount that the life of a slave killed by a bull is valued at (Exod 21:32). Obviously, the fact that Judas was possessed by the Devil or a blind love of money means that Judas' betrayal cannot be explained in terms of a person's complete freedom of action; at heart, it is Satan or money that is the force of death and destruction that cancels out or disfigures the personal "I."

Possibly, along these same lines, we need to look at what could have disfigured Judas and distanced him internally from Jesus to the point where he took this decision that was so unworthy of a disciple. Judas was a member of the Twelve who, like the others, had lived enthusiastically for a Kingdom that was to bring, and indeed had begun to bring, good news to the poor, health to the sick, food to the hungry, consolation to the sad, and salvation to the sinners. Judas had shared with the other disciples the great hopes, and nothing leads us to believe that he did not believe in them; but this is where the drama began: had he believed so much that he now felt "betrayed" by Jesus? Judas had wanted, as had all the disciples, the Kingdom to manifest itself in splendor and for Israel to be liberated. He did not care about the means: weapons or miracles, or both! He had blind faith in Jesus and was sure that he was the man sent by God, Israel's Messiah. Jesus, however, spoke a different language, and his Kingdom, which had only just begun, required heartfelt repentance and spread through forgiveness and compassion, righteousness and giving one's life, not through a war of liberation or a spectacular miracle that decimated Israel's enemies.

It is likely that Jesus' triumphal entrance into Jerusalem had been the straw that broke the camel's back: Judas had seen what Jesus was not going to do. This distanced him from the Master with a great bitterness in his heart, the result of his own frustration. Betraying Jesus became a legitimate action because he had betrayed the hopes that many, and Judas himself in particular, had placed in him. There is then a strange agreement between Judas and the Jewish authorities concerning Jesus: they both saw the rabbi of Nazareth as a false prophet, someone who had led the people astray and someone who represented a threat to the people. The motives may differ but at heart they share the same feeling. For the authorities, Jesus was a false prophet. For Judas, he was a false Messiah. Resentment can be diabolical. A false Messiah cannot act as an obstacle to the cause for the liberation of Israel. It was legitimate to want him out of the way.

Judas did not survive much longer than Jesus. The Acts of the Apostles states that "this man bought a field with the reward of his wickedness" and there he died a terrible death ("falling headlong he burst open in the middle and all his bowels gushed out") (Acts 1:18), a death that is analogous to those of other figures from the Scriptures who were considered blasphemers. Thus, Antiochus IV Epiphanes, the impious king who profaned the temple in Jerusalem, is said to have died undergoing atrocious suffering (2 Macc 9:5-28). Similarly, Agrippa I, who "did not give God the glory," also suffered a horrible end: "eaten by worms" (Acts 12:23).

The Gospel according to Matthew brings Judas' death forward to the very night when he betrayed Jesus. According to this Gospel, Judas "hanged himself" (Matt 27:5). Judas' suicide was preceded by his repentance, as he acknowledged his crime before the authorities. His death resembled that of another biblical figure who, like Judas, also saw his intentions frustrated: Ahithophel, David's counselor. "When Ahithophel saw that his counsel was not followed . . . [he] hanged himself" (2 Sam 17:23). The Acts of the Apostles and the Gospel according to Matthew agree in associating Judas' betrayal to a field near Jerusalem called Akeldama or the Field of Blood, in remembrance of the price paid to buy it.

6.2.3. The Jewish Interrogation

The historical sources are once again the four canonical Gospels (Mark 14:53–15:1 || Matt 26:57–27:10 || Luke 22:54–23:1 || John 18:12-28). Mark, echoed by Matthew, refers successively to Jesus' appearance before the Sanhedrin, which culminated in his death sentence, the incident where he was insulted, Peter's three denials, and the Sanhedrin's agreement to take Jesus to Pilate. Matthew adds Judas' death to this sequence of events. In Luke, the order is different: Peter's three denials, the incident of the insults, and one single session of the Sanhedrin. The Gospel of John does not include the Sanhedrin's session and alternates Peter's denials with Jesus' interrogation by Annas and his being taken to Caiaphas' house.

6.2.3.1. The Sanhedrin's Preliminary Session

In relation to Jesus' death, the four Gospels agree in mentioning a session of the Sanhedrin or Great Jewish Council, which was made up of seventy-one members and presided over by the high priest. The synoptic Gospels report its taking place on the same night as the arrest of the rabbi of Nazareth. In Mark and Matthew, the Sanhedrin even met twice, whereas in the Gospel according to John it took place on an indeterminate date, after Jesus had brought Lazarus back to life and before he retreated, in the knowledge of the Sanhedrin's decision and as a precaution, "to the country near the wilderness [the Judaean Desert], to a town called Ephraim, and there he stayed with the disciples" (John 11:54). Obviously, according to this version of events, there were still some weeks before Jesus was to return to Jerusalem, when he was to be welcomed by enthusiastic crowds.

The report in John seems the more likely historically. According to the Mishnah Tractate Sanhedrin (4:1, 11:2), a verdict of guilt that warranted the death penalty had to meet the following conditions: (a) the trial and verdict could take place only during the day and not at night; (b) the verdict could not be issued on the same day as the trial, rather they had to wait until the next day—for this reason, a trial could not take place the day before the Sabbath or the day before a feast, and obviously, no trials could take place on the Sabbath or a feast day; (c) the normal setting for sessions of the Sanhedrin was the Chamber of Hewn Stone in the temple. Thus, what is described by the synoptic Gospels does not meet these conditions. According to the synoptic Gospels, Jesus would have been judged in one or two sessions, once the day of Passover had begun and, furthermore, at night, which goes against points a and b. The Sanhedrin would have met in the high priest's house, which goes against point c.

Mark 14:1 (|| Matt 26:3-4 || Luke 22:1) states that "two days before the Passover," Wednesday (according to the calculations in the synoptic Gospels), the authorities had already decided to have Jesus killed and were looking only for the opportunity to arrest him and put their plan into action. If events indeed had gone thus, then the nighttime session of the Sanhedrin in Jerusalem presided over, as to be expected, by the high priest, was a sham (for what purpose?), a simple ratification of a decision already made. We should conclude that the session of the Sanhedrin that looked at and decided Jesus' fate did not take place on the night he was arrested but rather must have taken place earlier, probably in the institution's official setting and without Jesus present. On the night of his arrest, Jesus underwent successive "private" interrogations at Annas' house and before Caiaphas. Annas and Caiaphas were the two figures who had probably worked hardest to have him arrested.

What, then, was the nature of the Sanhedrin or Great Jewish Council in Jerusalem, and what decisions were made with regard to Jesus? In this respect, we need to mention an important report from a subsequent Jewish source, Tractate Sanhedrin 43a from the Babylonian Talmud (5th c. A.D.), which seems to be based on a fairly old tradition. In the Talmud, it specifies that for forty days before Jesus' execution (by stoning!) on the day before Passover, a crier proclaimed the reason for his being sentenced and invited proof in his defense to be presented in order to help revoke the sentence: "[A]ny one who can say anything in his favor, let him come forward and plead on his behalf." This was common practice (Mishnah, *Sanh.* 3:8). The text from the Talmud concludes that no proof was brought forward and Jesus, "who enticed Israel to apostasy," was executed.

This information seems to back up the existence of a firm sentence against Jesus, issued by an official court, and the term "apostasy" indicates the reason behind his being sentenced. We have looked closely at the reasons that led the Jewish authorities to sentence Jesus (see 6.2.1.1). We can see that Jesus was sentenced for blasphemy and false prophecy, as an impostor who had led the people astray, making them believe that he had been sent by God. According to his adversaries, Jesus had not received any authority from God, since his prophecy of the temple's destruction and rebuilding in three days had not come to pass, a prophecy that, according to them, was an attack on Israel's holiest institution. The corresponding punishment, according to the Law, was death by stoning. This is stated in the Torah (Deut 18:20) for false prophecy and in the Mishnah (*Sanh.* 7:4) for blasphemy. Both Jeremiah's case, who was to be killed for having made a prophecy (considered false) against the temple in Jerusalem (Jer 26:8-9), and that of Naboth, stoned for having been falsely accused of blasphemy against God (1 Kgs 21:13), exemplify the capital punishment reserved for false prophecy and blasphemy. Only in one document from Qumran, the Temple Scroll (64), does the death penalty reserved for rebels against God seem to be crucifixion, but this seems to reflect the Roman influence on Jewish customs.

The most enlightening analogy to Jesus' sentencing and death can be seen in the fate of his own brother, James, the leader of Jerusalem's Christian community (see 4.3.4.1). Josephus explains that in 62 A.D., the High Priest Ananus (or Annas the Younger) took advantage of the power vacuum between the death of the Roman governor Festus and the arrival of Albinus, the new governor, to have James, "the brother of Jesus, who was called Christ," killed. This Ananus, who was the son of Annas (the Elder) and brother-in-law of Caiaphas, the two high priests who played the most important roles in Jesus' trial, "assembled the Sanhedrin of judges and brought before them" the aforementioned James, brother of Jesus, "and some others" (evidently, other Christians from the community in Jerusalem). Ananus "formed an accusation against them as breakers of the Law [and] he delivered them to be stoned." Josephus stresses that Ananus belonged to the Sadducee group, "who are very rigid in judging offenders, above all the rest of the Jews." Citizens of Jerusalem denounced Ananus' behavior to the new governor and to king Agrippa II, who was in charge of the temple at the time and who had Ananus removed from the post. It is highly likely that these anonymous law-abiding citizens were Jerusalem's Pharisees (*A.J.* 20:199–203).

This narrative of James' death closely resembles Jesus' death, thirty-two years before: at the initiative of the high priest; intervention by the Sanhedrin; disagreement between the Sadducees (in favor of the execution of James and other Christians) and the Pharisees (against); the death sentence under the accusation of having broken the Law; and execution. The most obvious differences are that, unlike Jesus, James appeared before the Sanhedrin and was judged, sentenced, and executed alongside other people (probably leaders of the community in Jerusalem like him); furthermore, James was stoned, while Jesus was crucified. Ananus' actions were a flagrant abuse of power, since between the years 6 and 66 A.D., Jerusalem's Sanhedrin did not have the so-called *ius gladii* or right to mete out the death penalty: this power was reserved for the Roman governors (and King Agrippa I between the years 41 and 44 A.D.), the only representatives of Caesar. Death by stoning, which was typically Jewish and not included in Roman penal law, was probably applied to James based on the transgressions of the Law detailed in the Mishnah (*Sanh.* 7:4). We do not know what transgression Ananus accused him of during the trial before the Sanhedrin, but it is significant that the most law-abiding among them felt that James had not gone against the Law of Moses.

As in the case of Jesus, there was also probably a division between the Sadducee group, who were in favor of his being killed for blasphemy and false prophecy, and the other leaders, including Pharisees, who defended the religious integrity of the rabbi from Nazareth. There are two possible scenarios: either the confrontation between the two groups took place within the Sanhedrin, or on the other hand, the Sanhedrin was against Jesus, with those who defended him being important people acting from outside. The parallels with James lead us to believe that his sentencing may not have come as a unanimous decision from the Jewish authorities, contrary to the impression gained from a superficial reading of the Gospels. Reading between the lines, we can see that Jesus had those who stood up for him among the Jewish authorities, though it has to be stressed that they were few in number: notably, Joseph of Arimathea, "a respected member of the council" (Mark 15:43), of whom it is said that he "had not consented to their purpose and deed" (Luke 23:51). Joseph was a rich man, belonging to the group of "nobles," or the nonsacerdotal aristocracy, who was a sympathizer of Jesus to the extent that he asked Pilate for his body and buried him in a tomb that belonged to him. Another important sympathizer, despite not belonging to the Sanhedrin, was Nicodemus, a "Pharisee" (John 3:1), who also took part in Jesus' burial.

If we center our attention on the reports in Mark and Luke, Joseph of Arimathea was probably at the head of the minority within the Sanhedrin which was not in favor of Jesus being sentenced, a minority that received support from some of the Pharisees. One of the arguments used may be the interpretation that the Gospel according to John attributes to Nicodemus: "Does our Law judge a man without first giving him a hearing and learning what he does?" (John 7:51). The minority, however, could not defeat the ample majority led by the High Priest Caiaphas himself, who was in favor of Jesus being killed. This majority, linked to the Sadducee group, was made up of the high priests, many nobles, and a good number of scribes. In Jesus' case, the key lay in the weighty personal involvement of Annas and Caiaphas, the temple's and Sanhedrin's highest authorities (Annas, the de facto authority; Caiaphas, the official authority), and the abstention of an important group of Pharisees who were unwilling to side with the minority defending Jesus.

In the session of the Sanhedrin presided over by Caiaphas, which decided on Jesus' death, no heed was paid to the argument of rabbi Gamaliel I, "the Elder" (indeed if it was even given) regarding Peter and John reported in the book of the Acts of the Apostles. With regard to these two disciples of Jesus, this great teacher of the Law made the following observation: "Keep away from these men and let them alone; for if this plan or this undertaking is of men, it will fail; but if it is of God, you will not be able to overthrow them. You might even be found opposing God!" (Acts 5:38-39). With regard to Jesus, in a similar though opposite fashion, it was simply concluded that neither he nor his message came from God. While the intervention from rabbi Gamaliel led to the Sanhedrin deciding not to have the two disciples killed, Jesus was sentenced as an enemy of God by the highest Jewish judicial authority.

There is just one more doubt concerning the type of session held by the Jerusalem Sanhedrin. We know very little about the Jewish judicial procedures of the first century A.D. that could help us clear this matter up. Jesus, the accused, was absent and could not have been asked any kind of question. We can deduce this from a report in John (11:47-53), who points out this irregularity (7:50-51). Mark (14:53-64; 15:1) reports on the appearance of a great many mostly contradictory witnesses, but the only explicit accusation is the destruction and reconstruction of the temple in three days. This leads us to think that there were witnesses at the Sanhedrin session who had heard Jesus prophesy the destruction and rebuilding of the temple and whose declaration contributed to strengthening the accusation against Jesus of false prophecy and blasphemy, making him out to be someone who had wrongly arrogated to himself the prerogatives reserved for God.

In short, the Sanhedrin, led by Caiaphas and basing itself on the interpretation of Jesus' announcement about the temple as the blasphemy of a false prophet, came to the majority decision that this man deserved to die, in accordance with the Law of Moses. Furthermore, it was opportune that he die, given the negative influence he had over the people and the danger of all this leading to an uprising against Rome. A Galilean, a popular preacher, and someone who acted like a prophet was a potential threat to the Sadducees, defenders of the status quo with the Romans. The following key statement is attributed to Caiaphas: "[I]t is expedient for you that one man should die for the people, and that the whole nation should not perish" (John 11:50). Alongside the innate justice in punishing a blasphemer and false prophet, there was also the need to protect the interests of the Jewish people as a whole. On the other hand, the minority did not interpret the announcement about the temple as blasphemy and, in line with what Gamaliel would say about Peter and John following Jesus' death, left the door open: Jesus may have been sent by God, and he did not represent any threat of a violent uprising against Rome.

6.2.3.2. A Prior Agreement

The session of the Sanhedrin ended with a clear agreement: Jesus had to be executed legally and publicly. The Sanhedrin did not decide to have him murdered, to have him eliminated violently and secretly, but rather (as was the case for Jesus, son of Ananias) they opted to act within the Law openly. The inevitable next step was for the Sanhedrin to take their decision to the Roman governor, the only authority able to hand down the death penalty. As it states in Mark 15:1, the Sanhedrin "delivered him [Jesus] to Pilate" once they had decided to have him killed. John says (11:53), "So from that day on they took counsel how to put him to death." This agreement in the Sanhedrin saw the start of a difficult period for Jesus and his disciples: "Jesus therefore no longer went about openly among the Jews, but went from there [Bethany, near Jerusalem] to the country near the wilderness . . . and there he stayed with the disciples" (John 11:54). We cannot dismiss out of hand the possibility that the intentions of the Sanhedrin had been leaked: "[T]he chief priests . . . had given orders that if anyone knew where he was, he should let them know, so that they might arrest him" (John 11:57).

The question is, by whom, when, and how was the decision taken in the highest Jewish council? Those responsible for carrying out the agreement and for delivering Jesus to Pilate and accusing him before the governor were the same people who had encouraged the Sanhedrin to reach this decision: the high priests, led by Annas and Caiaphas, the temple authorities, with the occasional involvement of the members of the other two sections of the Sanhedrin (the nobles and the scribes), all or almost all of whom were members or supporters of the Sadducee group. The Pharisees, as we have stressed, were conspicuous in their absence in the Passion of Christ.

At the time of the agreement, the situation was still not clear. The Jewish authorities had two options: either before or after Passover, the great Jewish feast, which was relatively close at hand. It could not be "during the feast" (Mark 14:2), as the people could have risen up, and it would not have been at all convenient for disturbances or riots to take place in Jerusalem at this time of the year when it was fit to burst, and with Roman reinforcements in place under the direct command of the governor. The massacre of 4 B.C. could be repeated when, at Passover, Archelaus' troops attacked the pilgrims camped out on the plain to the north of the city and killed three thousand (*A.J.* 17:213–18). They could wait until after the week of Passover, when the pilgrims had left and things had gotten back to normal. We know that in the year 43 or 44 A.D. Agrippa I ordered Peter's arrest at the time of Passover, but the king decided to keep him in prison and not judge him until after the festivities (Acts 12:3-4). What led to Jesus' death being brought forward to before the Passover was, very probably, the crowds that welcomed his entrance to Jerusalem and his actions against the trading in the temple. These two incidents, taking place one after the other, greatly concerned the temple authorities and led to events being sped up. When Jesus entered Jerusalem lauded by the people, there were only a few days to go to the great Jewish feast.

The high priests, led by Annas and Caiaphas, started to plot how to have Jesus arrested and judged by Pilate before Saturday that week, the day of the Passover, and how to have him sentenced to death and executed on the orders of the governor. According to Matthew 26:3, the leaders (high priests and nobles) met in Caiaphas' house. Jesus was staying in Bethany and traveled to Jerusalem and the temple every day, where he talked to people and also took the ritual baths, like any other pilgrim, in order to prepare for the Passover (John 11:55). He did all this in broad daylight. At dusk, he returned to Bethany, a friendly town, where he was out of reach of his adversaries. It was in this context that one of the Twelve, Judas Iscariot, went to meet the high priests and agreed to lead them to Jesus so that they could arrest him easily and discreetly. The arrest was to take place in Gethsemane, on the Thursday night/Friday morning, that same week.

6.2.3.3. Annas' Interrogation

Jesus was not judged in person by the Jewish authorities. When he was arrested and taken to Annas, the Sanhedrin's firm agreement was already in place. It is likely that Annas, who was highly influential and possibly the only person in complete control of the situation, wanted to prepare the accusations that were to be brought before Pilate in the morning. Annas' interrogation was in line with the strategy employed by the high priests as to how Jesus was to die. Annas, the former high priest, was a wise and experienced man, who was used to dealing with the Romans and knew Pilate well, so he knew the best way to proceed.

According to the Gospel of John, the only one that gives us information on this interrogation, Annas concentrated on finding out details "about his disciples and his teaching" (18:19). The choice of these two issues is understandable. Though the resistance shown by the disciples in the garden of Gethsemane was virtually nonexistent (and at no time encouraged by Jesus himself), it is clear that he was accompanied by a group of Galileans who were unconditional followers. If the charges that had to be presented to Pilate involved Jesus being a potential threat to Caesar, it would be useful to be able to offer details about the "subversive" activities of this group and demonstrate to the Roman authorities that they were all dangerous activists. This would contribute to Jesus' portrayal as the head of a group of anti-Roman extremists. The questions relating to his doctrine could offer valuable arguments to indicate Jesus' disaffection and disloyalty to the emperor, holding views similar to those of Judas, the Galilean rabbi who had vindicated a theocratic system as an alternative to Rome over twenty years before.

Jesus' response to Annas was clearly evasive; he did not give anything away. Throughout the Passion, Jesus never responded directly to the accusations made or questions asked. Either he remained silent or ambivalent or, as in this case, he replied with a self-evident statement. Generally speaking, Jesus did not want to acknowledge anything about himself, about his activities, doctrine, or disciples, and deflected Annas' questioning. He had spoken in public, and everyone could testify to what he had said: let the people reply! Jesus knew well enough that everything was already done and dusted, that the Sanhedrin had already made its decision, astutely orchestrated by the authorities representing his people. His wise silence represented an accusation against his accusers.

If he did speak, what he said was going to be taken only as an opportunity to attack and disrespect him. His evasive response led to Annas feeling that he "deserved" to be struck by an angry temple guard, a strong symbol of dishonor. Jesus did not fight back, replying, "If I have spoken wrongly, bear witness to the wrong; but if I have spoken rightly, why do you strike me?" (John 18:23). It would seem that the scene was witnessed by someone who belonged to Jesus' group: one of his disciples, "known to the high priest," who had entered the courtyard of Annas' house (John 18:15). Thanks to this disciple we have evidence of this meeting between Annas and Jesus.

6.2.3.4. The Taunts of the Guards and Servants

We do not know at what time of night Annas' interrogation ended, nor can we be sure what time Jesus arrived at the high priest's house, bound and under arrest. Many disconcerting events took place that night: Jesus' supper with the disciples in the Upper City, the half-hour journey to the garden of Gethsemane, his arrest and being taken prisoner to Annas' house in Jerusalem, and the subsequent interrogation. This sequence of events may well not have ended before midnight. Once the interrogation was over, the members of the band who had arrested Jesus brought him down from the first floor where Annas had probably interrogated him and left him in the courtyard. He had to wait a few hours here until day broke and they took him, still bound, to Caiaphas' house.

Jesus was held in the courtyard of Annas' house until daybreak. We have little information as to his exact situation. The band of "servants [of the high priests] and officers" had ensconced themselves and started a fire in the middle of the courtyard to warm themselves, as the night was cold (John 18:18; Mark 14:66; Luke 22:55). Among Annas' servants was a relative of Malchus, the band's leader who had had his ear cut off in Gethsemane (John 18:26). There were also some of the high priest's maids, including the "maid who kept the door" to Annas' house (John 18:16; Mark 14:66, 14:69 || Matt 26:69, 26:71 || Luke 22:56). Among all these people, there was Jesus, a prisoner, and Peter, hidden. We do not know whether there was also the disciple of Jesus who was known to the high priest and who, having spoken to the maid, had Peter let in to the courtyard.

It is likely that Jesus was bound in a corner of the courtyard, far from the fire where the group of men and women were warming themselves together with Peter. This was the scene for a series of cruel taunts by the guards and servants, "the men who were holding Jesus" (Luke 22:63). The taunts were sarcastic and related to the accusation that had led to his detention, and which was deemed worthy of the death penalty: that of being a false prophet. The members of the band, who may have been joined by some of Annas' servants who had not taken part directly in his arrest, attacked Jesus harshly, insulting him as a fraud, a prophet whose dreadful prediction regarding the temple had not come true. Jesus was spat at and hit, signs of great disrespect and dishonor. They blindfolded him, striking and punching him, they challenged him to tell them who had hit him: "Prophesy!" Jesus did not react. These men humiliated their prisoner with physical and psychological attacks throughout the night.

6.2.3.5. Peter' Denials

Once the disciples had fled Gethsemane, upset by the arrest of their Master and scared of also falling into the hands of the band that had taken Jesus, they split up and dispersed. Jesus arrived bound at Annas' house; Peter, the leader of the Twelve, also followed him there, though at some distance. We do not know the exact location of Annas' house, but it may have been in the Upper City, Jerusalem's well-to-do neighborhood, not far from the temple and, possibly, the Hasmonean Palace. Nor do we know what route the band took from Gethsemane to the high priest's residence, but the shortest would have been across the temple esplanade.

When Peter reached Annas' house, he was let in, according to John 18:16, by "another disciple," a follower of Jesus known to the high priest and his servants, who had spoken to the maid on the door at the time. Meanwhile, Jesus had already been taken upstairs to Annas' house to be interrogated. Peter entered the courtyard of the house and joined the group of servants and temple guards who had detained Jesus and who were warming themselves by the fire. There were also servants and maids, Annas' domestic service, in the courtyard.

However, Peter was a stranger and soon had to answer queries and questions, especially from one of the high priest's maids. The disciple would have wanted to pass incognito so as to be able to pick up as much information as possible as to his Master's fate. Nevertheless, his presence did not go unnoticed, and he was identified. The maid in question, who had been on the door according to John 18:16, recognized him as one of the disciples of the man from Nazareth who had been arrested and who was now being interrogated by Annas. Jesus' group had certainly been seen around Jerusalem on a number of occasions, in both the city and the temple, and this perceptive woman, a maid to one of the temple leaders, may well have found Peter's face familiar (Mark 14:67 and John 18:17). She was not absolutely certain, but she did alert the others to this stranger's real identity.

The second sign that gave Peter away was his Galilean origins. The disciple had inevitably started to speak to the people standing around the fire, and they had all noticed his accent. Galilean Aramaic, the mother tongue of Jesus and his disciples, had certain phonetic peculiarities that were easily recognized, especially by the people of

Jerusalem, who were used to dealing with the many Galilean pilgrims in the city for the great feasts. The Galileans coming to Jerusalem for the Passover that year must have been numerous, and it would not have been strange to come across them throughout the city. However, the combination of Jesus' Galilean origins and the Galilean accent of this man must have alerted those present. What was a Galilean doing there and at this late hour? Is this stranger somehow linked to the man from Nazareth who is being interrogated by the high priest right now? According to Mark 14:69, the maid who first raised the alarm was quite sure: "This man [Peter] is one of them." According to John 18:26, someone else was also quite sure, one of the servants of the group that arrested Jesus and who now recognized one of those from Gethsemane in this stranger.

Faced with the questions addressed to him (the Gospels tell of three questions, which the disciple replies to with three denials), Peter felt increasingly hemmed in and insecure. There were successive negative, evasive responses, which culminated in an unsustainable situation for someone who had to ensure that his being a follower of the Nazarene remained secret. From "I neither know nor understand what you mean," a phrase with an undeniable Semitic tone, to the flat denial "I do not know this man," supported by his swearing oaths, Peter increasingly excused himself and protested before those who wanted to have him suffer the same fate as Jesus (Mark 14:68, 14:71). The disciple did not turn against the Master, he did not insult or injure him, he did not renege on him, but he did distance himself, hiding his relationship with Jesus and denying it, as he denied and reneged on his being a disciple. Fear of losing his life overcame the deep love that he professed for his Master. He managed to remain anonymous, but it meant he had to temporarily conceal his true identity.

How long did Peter spend in the courtyard of Annas' house? According to the four Gospels, until the (second) rooster's crow, the call that indicated the arrival of dawn, the coming of a new day. All four Gospels agree in saying that the last time that Peter denied knowing Jesus or having anything to do with him was when the rooster crowed. The synoptic Gospels recall the prediction made by Jesus, according to which that same night, before the rooster crowed and the new day was heralded, his disciple was to deny him (see 6.2.2.2). If we take this information into account, Peter spent the second half of the night of Jesus' arrest in the courtyard of Annas' house, no distance from where his master was being held prisoner.

As we pointed out earlier, this courtyard was almost certainly the place where Jesus had been held until the coming of the new day following his interrogation and where he had been subject to insults for his prophetic pretensions. If this was the correct setting, Jesus and Peter must have been relatively close to each other for a good part of the night. This would have been the context for Luke 22:61: "[Jesus] turned and looked at Peter." Peter's denials, at least to some extent, took place in Jesus' presence, and Peter could have witnessed the insults Jesus received from the temple guards and servants of the high priest.

Finally, faced with the pressure to which he was subjected and the possibility of being recognized, Peter decided to leave Annas' house. If he had stayed in the courtyard until daybreak, his departure would have coincided with Jesus being taken from Annas' house to Caiaphas' house. Peter's departure marked the end of his particular involvement in the events taking place with regard to Jesus: the paths of one and other now led in different directions after the arrest in Gethsemane. Now, after what had happened during the night, we have confirmation of Jesus being abandoned by his disciples and by Peter in particular, who fled not once but twice. Peter lost himself in the city and, as the synoptic Gospels report, burst into tears.

6.2.3.6. The Meeting in Caiaphas' House

Caiaphas' house welcomed members of the Sanhedrin who had conspicuously found against Jesus during the session of the Great Jewish Council and had approved the plan to have him killed. The plan was made up of two parts: first, to arrest Jesus and, second, to have Pilate sentence him to death. Now was the time to put the second part into action. The group that was to take Jesus to the Roman authorities met at Caiaphas' house at dawn for this purpose.

On the one hand, some Jewish leaders (the majority high priests, but there were also some nobles and scribes) were responsible for proving the weight of the accusations against Jesus to Pilate; on the other, a band of men were there to escort the prisoner, in a pitiful state following the attacks and abuse that he had been subjected to during the night. The day had just begun and the prisoner had to be brought before Pilate soon. Nevertheless, before appearing before the Roman governor, it seems that his accusers had to agree on the charges to be brought and the arguments to sustain them. News of this informal meeting and updating for some members of the Sanhedrin (not all of them, obviously) at Caiaphas' house is reported in the Gospels of Mark, Matthew, and Luke (the latter describing it as a meeting of the whole of the Sanhedrin) and indirectly in John.

Jesus' appearance before this (somewhat small) group of members of the Sanhedrin was presided over by Caiaphas in his house. We do not know if Annas was also present, though the conclusions he had reached following the interrogation during the night were communicated to those present, who had to decide on the wording of the accusation to be presented to Pilate. There was little time, and it was highly likely that they had already been appointed a time for the trial before the governor.

According to the Gospels of Mark and Matthew, Caiaphas asked Jesus some questions (Luke attributes them to the leaders present). The aim of these questions was to find out what Jesus would say of himself and who he saw himself as. The leaders had probably already reached an agreement to accuse Jesus as a pretender to the throne and to present him before Pilate as an enemy of Caesar. They would now have wanted to hear in his own words whether he considered himself the Messiah-King of Israel, sent by God to save his people. Jesus responded to Caiaphas with an elliptic statement: "You have said so" (Matt 26:64; Luke 22:70). Immediately, however, he added a reference to the Son of Man, the heavenly figure who has to come at the end of time. Caiaphas saw Jesus as identifying himself with this Son of Man and attributing to himself divine prerogatives. This was sacrilege and confirmed the Sanhedrin's decision to consider Jesus deserving of death for blasphemy and false prophecy (see 6.2.1.1).

The high priest's ritual gesture of tearing his robes shows that he interpreted these words as blasphemy, although Jesus had merely insinuated (without directly stating) that he had taken on the heavenly functions reserved for the Son of Man. Tearing one's robes as a response to blasphemy is seen on other occasions in the Bible (2 Kgs 18:37, 19:1) and the Mishnah (*Sanh.* 7:5). Despite the difficulties in historically recreating the exact words of the dialogue between

Caiaphas and Jesus, the high priest's gesture (which Luke omits) was clearly an outward sign of the inner feeling that moved the Jewish leaders: this man was a blasphemer and a false prophet, and according to Jewish Law deserved to die. Now, they simply had to have him sentenced by Roman law and executed.

6.2.4. The Roman Trial

The historical sources for this section are the four canonical Gospels (Mark 15:1-20; Matt 27:11-31; Luke 23:1-25; John 18:28–19:16) and the Gospel of Peter (1–9). Mark condenses and summarizes the events. Matthew echoes Mark, though he does add some elements of his own, including Pilate's wife's dream and his washing his hands before the crowds, which emphasizes the Jewish responsibility for Jesus' death. Luke also adds his own material, including Jesus' appearance before Herod Antipas and Pilate's acknowledgment of Jesus' innocence three times. John also stresses Jesus' innocence, but unlike the synoptic Gospels, Jesus and Pilate have a wide-ranging dialogue involving theology and texts. The Gospel of Peter, an apocryphal text from the second century, though incomplete, contains certain early elements and excuses Pilate and instead presents Herod Antipas and the Jewish leaders as solely responsible for Jesus' sentence.

6.2.4.1. The Setting and Judicial Procedure

Pontius Pilate, the prefect or governor of the Roman province of Judaea from 26 to 36 A.D., named by the Emperor Tiberius, was the judge who handed down the sentence of death by crucifixion for Jesus of Nazareth on the morning of Friday, April 7, 30 A.D. in the city of Jerusalem. The Roman, Jewish, and Christian sources all report that it was Pilate who sentenced Jesus. The Roman historian Tacitus (2nd c. A.D.) wrote, "Christus . . . suffered the extreme penalty [*supplicio adfectus erat*] during the reign of Tiberius at the hands of one of our procurators, Pontius Pilate" (*Annals* 15:44). The Jewish historian Josephus (1st c. A.D.) described the role of the Jewish authorities in his sentence, "Pilate, at the suggestion of the principal men among us, had him sentenced to [die on] the cross" (*A.J.* 18:64). Similarly, it says in the Babylonian Talmud (5th c. A.D.), "On the eve of the Passover Yeshu [i.e., Jesus], the Nazarene, was hanged. . . . With Yeshu however it was different, for he was connected with [the Roman] government" (*Sanh.* 43a) (see 2.2.1 and 2.2.2). Pilate's responsibility is unanimously confirmed by the four canonical Gospels, the oldest Christian sources (1st c. A.D.), as we shall see in this section. Thus, if Jesus died crucified, it was because a Roman judge, Pontius Pilate, sentenced him.

The court where the trial took place was located in Herod's palace, the usual residence for the Roman governors when they stayed in Jerusalem. The palace, located on a hill in the northeast corner of the city, was a large building, which had been magnificently decorated by King Herod, who had used it as his official residence (from 23 to 4 B.C.). It was built as a fort, with impressive defenses and three high towers that dominated the city's skyline and looked out over its accesses. Together with the so-called Antonia Tower, the fort at the northeast of the temple complex, Herod's palace was the headquarters for the Roman garrison in Jerusalem and at the highest point in the city. The Roman cohort stationed in the city occupied Jerusalem's two fortified buildings, from which they could ensure public order and put down any attempted uprising.

While the Antonia Tower, as its name suggests, was a military fort, Herod's palace acted both as a residence (the building had been built to include every detail necessary) and as a line of defense, being a citadel that was safe from any form of attack. Within the palace, a wing was reserved to accommodate the garrison, called the praetorium (Mark 15:16); the prison cells were located in this wing. Paul, the apostle, was held in one of these cells (cf. Acts 23:35, which calls the place "Herod's praetorium"). There appears to be enough evidence to support the idea that Herod's palace, and not the Antonia Tower, was the most likely setting for Jesus' trial before Pilate (see 3.2.1).

Jesus' trial was carried out in accordance with the Roman judicial procedures, known as *cognitio extra ordinem*, which consisted of four parts: the accusation, the interrogation, the confession of the accused (if there was one), and the sentencing. Unlike an ordinary criminal trial, where the sentence was pronounced by a tribunal chaired by a praetor (who did not take part in the sentencing), extraordinary or *extra ordinem* trials were carried out exclusively by a high-ranking member of the administration. This figure was responsible for the whole process and the sentencing. For criminal cases, *extra ordinem* trials were common in the provinces, where the highest authority (a legate, consul, proconsul, prefect or procurator, or praetor) was the only or highest jurisdiction to turn to for sentences involving the death penalty. This authority, or *ius gladii*, had been conferred, as Josephus explains (*J.W.* 2:117), on Coponius, the first Roman governor of Judaea, and his successors in the position, in 6 A.D.

As a result, the Jewish authorities could decide who deserved death according to the Law of Moses, but they could not put it into practice. In effect, as of 6 A.D. legal executions had to be ordered by the Roman authorities; only in the cases where there was a vacuum of power did the Jewish authorities dare to kill people abusively using the traditional Jewish system, that is, by stoning (see 6.2.3.1). If the Roman courts were the only ones that had the authority to judge criminal cases, then only Roman legislation counted when presenting charges against the accused. The Law of Moses was not accepted by the Romans in judicial terms, whether regarding the accusation or the sentencing. John's report of the Passion clearly shows this. The Jewish authorities said to Pilate, "We have a Law, and by that Law he ought to die, because he has made himself the Son of God" (John 19:7). Nevertheless, this accusation was in no way decisive for Pilate, who, on hearing these words, was shocked, but not moved to sentence Jesus to death. Obviously, the Jewish leaders were unable to sentence him, and acknowledged this: "It is not lawful for us to put any man to death" (John 18:31). The *ius gladii* could be exercised only by Pilate, as he himself emphatically showed when addressing Jesus: "Do you not know that I have the power to release you, and power to crucify you?" (John 19:10).

This last statement indicates the complete and limitless power held by the Roman governors and allied sovereigns in their respective territories: Pilate in Judaea and Antipas in Galilee and Peraea (but not in Jerusalem). Judicially and according to Roman law, Jesus was a *peregrinus*, an inhabitant of the empire who did not hold Roman citizenship. He was completely at the mercy of Pilate's authority, the first and only judge of his charges, and he was not able, as Paul did, to appeal to a higher judicial authority (the Roman emperor).

This does not mean that an *extra ordinem* trial such as Jesus' lacked judicial guarantees, though the *cognitio* did depend on just one person, without a jury or advisory board. The judge, in this case Pilate, had to ascertain the nature of the accusation presented for the accused's death sentence and had to conclude whether the charges had been proven, whether they deserved the death penalty according to Roman law. However, in a trial of this kind the claims of the accused himself were decisive, as the accused acted as his own defense lawyer. As a result, the figure of the interpreter was vital, as the judge and accused often spoke different languages: Pilate spoke Latin and Greek and Jesus spoke Aramaic and, more than likely, some Greek (see 4.4.1.1). Thus, during Jesus' trial, the judge may well have had an interpreter, though the historical sources do not mention this figure or the role the interpreter may have played in the interrogations.

With regard to the official register of the sentence, we cannot be at all sure that a secretary recorded it in writing, to include it in the archives for the Roman province of Judaea, as would be assumed, for example, from the Acts of Pilate, a Christian manuscript from the fifth century A.D., with traditions that may date back to the second century. Jesus was a provincial subject who underwent an *extra ordinem* or summary conviction trial away from Caesarea, the usual setting for the governor's tribunals and where the important and serious cases were tried with all their legal formalities (juries, counselors, secretaries, etc.). In Pilate's eyes, Jesus' case was undoubtedly a minor affair.

6.2.4.2. The Start of the Trial: Accusations and Interrogation

Early in the morning, the entourage moved from Caiaphas' house to Herod's palace, where the governor was waiting for them. Roman courts opened at first light, as Seneca says (*De Ira* 2:7: *prima luce*), and in Jesus' case, this is confirmed by the Gospels of Mark (15:1) and John (18:28). This means that Jesus' trial was the first to take place that Friday. Pilate traveled to Jerusalem only from time to time, for the most important festivals, and one of his tasks there was to act as the judicial administrator. There were at least three other prisoners in the cells in Herod's palace who were also waiting to be tried. Jesus' case was special, for at least two reasons: his arrest had been organized and carried out by the Jewish authorities and not by the Romans and, second, his accusers were preeminent members of the temple's staff and important people from the city. Pilate may have wanted to prioritize this noteworthy case and accepted its being tried first. It was also the day before Passover and the temple would have been especially busy, which would have affected the high priests: thousands of lambs had to be sacrificed so that they could be eaten that same night in Jerusalem as part of the Passover meals to be celebrated by the locals and the pilgrims who had come from all around.

We do not know exactly who formed part of the entourage that escorted Jesus. Obviously, the prisoner was bound and led by members of the band who had arrested him in Gethsemane and watched over him during the night. There were also members of the Sanhedrin who had met at Caiaphas' house, important members of the Sadducee group who had orchestrated the events that were now to culminate in Jesus' appearance before Pilate and their demanding the death penalty for the Nazarene. Annas and Caiaphas almost certainly did not feel it opportune or necessary to be seen alongside Jesus' accusers; at the end of the day he was a Jew who was to be tried for political rebellion against the Roman emperor and presented as a dangerous threat to his own people. Moreover, the High Priest Joseph, known as Caiaphas, had to be ready to officiate in the temple during the Passover, the feast of feasts, which began that same day at dusk. Thus, the strategy to be used by the accusers before Pilate had been prepared carefully, and failure was not likely.

The journey from Caiaphas' house to Herod's palace, the praetorium or governor's headquarters, was short and slightly uphill. The praetorium was known as *Gabatha* (John 19:13), which in Aramaic means "high [place]." Within the complex there was a large courtyard, laid with big stones, the Greek name for which alluded to its appearance: *Lithostrotos*, "the Pavement" (John 19:13). At one end of this courtyard there was a door that led to the praetorium itself. The Jewish band handed Jesus over to the Roman soldiers and Pilate came out of the praetorium to meet those who had just arrived. This gesture from the governor was not out of courtesy but dictated by Jewish rules on ritual purity: if a Jew entered the house of a pagan on the eve of Passover, he or she would be deemed ritually impure and unable to eat the Passover meal either that day, that week, or that month (Num 9:10-11). According to the Gospel of John, Pilate's initial reaction on seeing this prisoner whom he had not ordered to be arrested was unease. It seems that he wanted to get away from the people who accused this man of being an "evildoer" (John 18:30). Nonetheless, the trial began.

The accusation was not very specific, but it became more so as the trial went on: the accused proclaimed himself to be "king" of the Jewish people and represented a direct rival to the legitimate sovereign of the Jewish people, the Roman emperor, Tiberius (6.2.1.3). The first question asked of Jesus by Pilate during the interrogation was, according to all four Gospels, "Are you the King of the Jews?" The Gospel according to Luke (23:2) sets out three accusations, two of which (prohibiting the payment of the tribute to Caesar and considering himself Messiah, a king) clearly reflect this stance. These and other accusations may have been presented by the Jewish leaders (Mark 15:3 says that they "accused him of many things"), but from what we can deduce from subsequent events, they were not taken into separate consideration during the trial. There was only one main accusation: Jesus was a pretender to the throne. Other possible charges (leading the people astray and stirring them up to revolt with his doctrines; Luke 23:2, 23:5) were simply variations on this theme. In any case, we do not know if any of these accusations were included in the fundamental accusation or in the sentence handed down by Pilate.

It is not completely clear where Pilate's interrogation took place. The Gospel according to John alternates between interior scenes (between Pilate and Jesus), in the praetorium, and external scenes (Pilate and Jesus with the Jewish authorities and the people), outside the praetorium, in the Pavement courtyard. According to the synoptic Gospels, everything seems to have taken place in one and the same place, outside the building. The external location is preferable since the accusers could not have presented the charges against Jesus, unable as they were to enter because of the rules on ritual purity regulating their entering a non-Jewish building. Nonetheless, there was nothing to stop a "private" interrogation involving just Jesus and Pilate.

The four Gospels agree on Jesus' response to Pilate ("You have said so"), which is both elliptic and ambivalent. It could be understood to mean "You, not I, say I am king" or "You, quite rightly, say I am king." It is neither confirmation nor denial. In fact, Jesus is not a "king" in the political sense of the word that Pilate and his accusers give it, and he cannot say that he is. However, he cannot say that he is not either since he considers himself God's emissary, his Anointed

One (the Messiah), the humble king who brings peace. His response included a wide range of nuances that reflected the misguided question. In the Gospel according to John, this first dialogue between Jesus and Pilate was marked by a statement along the same lines: "My kingship is not of this world; if my kingship were of this world, my servants would fight, that I might not be handed over to the Jews." This is the truth regarding Jesus, which Pilate is unable to take on because he is unwilling to accept his testimony (John 18:33-38).

Following this short response, Jesus did not defend himself against the other accusations. He responded to the fundamental question and now held his tongue. He refused to reply to those who presented the charges against him. Nonetheless, the accused did not remain in complete silence, and, according to Roman law, Pilate could not assume that this silence was evidence of his guilt, representing a confession. The accusations by the Jewish leaders were met, however, with silence from Jesus. Either these accusations were general (such as "he is a rebel who wants to stir the people into rising against Rome") or, if they were specific, they could not be proven ("he has prepared an army to fight against the Romans"). The lack of consistent or specific proof made these accusations judicially tenuous. Pilate, who had no reason to act partially, came to the conclusion that there was not a sufficient basis to sentence Jesus. The interrogation had not shown there to be any proof of guilt. The leaders' carefully studied strategy was not watertight. Pilate was by no means convinced that Jesus should be sentenced to death.

In the terminology of Roman law, the governor had started the trial with a de plano procedure, without sitting in the judge's chair on the tribunal bench, and thus had no intention of dictating the sentence immediately. The tenuous nature of the accusations and the fact that none of the charges against Jesus could be proven led him to decide, for the moment, not to offer a verdict of guilty or not guilty. Mark 15:10 and Matthew 27:18 point out that "[Pilate] perceived that it was out of envy that the chief priests had delivered him up." Pilate was undecided. He was not sure what he should do with this man accused of wanting to overthrow Caesar. So he ordered the soldiers to take Jesus away and to bring before him the other defendants, including two "bandits" imprisoned in the praetorium also to be sentenced to death on the cross like him.

6.2.4.3. Interval: Taunts from Herod Antipas and the Roman Soldiers

Pilate temporarily stopped proceedings in Jesus' trial; he did not sentence him for the moment. As J. P. Lémonon stresses, the Roman governor did not want to be manipulated by the Jewish leaders, who were stubborn and insistent on charges they had not been able to prove. They may have taken for granted that Rome's representative would sentence the accused. Jesus' trial did not start up again for a while. Pilate now took time out to judge the other prisoners, two of whom were to be sentenced to death on the cross, which was to take place without more ado on that same day, as was usual in Roman procedures.

What happened to Jesus in the meantime? The Gospels of Mark, Matthew, and John tell of a scene involving his being insulted by members of the Roman garrison within the praetorium. John places it in the middle of the trial and not at the end, unlike Mark and Matthew. The Gospel according to Luke describes the scene of the taunts and insults in the Hasmonean palace, the residence of Herod Antipas, tetrarch of Galilee. In this version of events, it was Antipas and his guards who insulted Jesus. According to Mark, Matthew, and John, Jesus did not leave the praetorium, while Luke says that he was taken to Antipas' residence and returned to Pilate's praetorium. Obviously, we could also see them as two successive incidents. Pilate may have wanted to make a gesture of deference to Antipas and thus had the Galilean prisoner taken to him; when the latter was brought back to the praetorium, he had to face the taunts and insults of the soldiers of the cohort, before being called back to the trial again.

Meanwhile, what had happened to Jesus' accusers? Where were they while Pilate took charge of the other trials and while Jesus was probably taken before Antipas and held in the praetorium with the soldiers from the Roman cohort? According to Luke 23:10, "the chief priests and the scribes," the same men who had accused Jesus before Pilate, had gone to the palace where Herod Antipas was residing and there continued "vehemently accusing him." However, Pilate had not sent Jesus to Antipas for him to hand down the sentence but as a sign of respect from the Roman governor. In all likelihood, the majority of Jesus' accusers were busy preparing the strategy that they would use when the trial restarted, in which a character who had not yet appeared on the scene was to play an important part: the people.

Jesus arrived at the Hasmonean palace, located halfway between Herod's palace, where Pilate had his praetorium, and the temple. He was probably escorted by a small band of soldiers (one centurion and four soldiers?) like the one that would later lead him to the place of execution. He was also accompanied by some (few) of his accusers. Relations between Antipas and Jesus had always been tense. Antipas had executed John the Baptist, the prophet who had baptized Jesus and acted as his guide at the start. The rabbi of Nazareth's subsequent activities had been so strongly overshadowed by the threat of Antipas, that he had had to live his life on the road in the territories neighboring Galilee, making only discreet public appearances in Galilee itself (see 6.1.1.1) for around the preceding year. Over the previous few months, Jesus had kept exclusively to Judaea and, on occasions, Peraea, which had led to Antipas' strength of feeling against him being lessened, as Jesus had no longer represented a problem for him.

For this reason, the meeting between Antipas and Jesus took place in a fairly relaxed atmosphere. Finally, the sovereign could see with his own eyes the man who had always managed to escape him, despite his failed attempts to have him killed (Luke 13:31). Antipas knew firsthand the fame that accompanied Jesus when he traveled through Galilee and his reputation as a miracle worker in particular. It should come as no surprise that, now that he had him before him for the first time, he expected some sort of miracle. Jesus, however, did not show any interest in this untrustworthy little king who had tried to have him killed and remained unmoved by his requests and enquiries. Antipas responded with the only weapon he had: disrespect and sarcasm. He knew from the few leaders present the charges that had been brought against Jesus, and the insult was almost self-evident: while his guards taunted and attacked him, Antipas had Jesus clothed in a bright shiny robe, a robe for someone of high standing, worthy of a "king," which was Jesus' pretension, according to his accusers.

Then, the band of Roman soldiers took Jesus back to the praetorium. Luke concludes his narrative of events, "Herod [Antipas] and Pilate became friends with each other that very day, for before this they had been at enmity with each other" (Luke 23:12).

The sarcastic insults that Jesus had suffered at the hands of Antipas and his guards continued in the praetorium. Following Pilate's interrogation and Herod's taunts, the soldiers of the cohort knew well enough about the royal pretensions of this Galilean prisoner. They had before them "the King of the Jews" in person! They were not about to let this chance to pay homage get away. The soldiers stationed in Jerusalem came from a wide range of places (Samaritans, Syrians, Nabateans, etc.) and held deeply anti-Jewish feelings (see 3.4.2.2). Moreover, they were professional soldiers sent to a city that was clearly hostile. They would have held Jesus in little esteem. Jesus had not yet been sentenced, but those accused of a crime worthy of the death penalty, despite being absolved, were never cleared completely: they were always chastised with a whipping (Luke 23:22). Thus, these men felt within their rights to taunt and insult Jesus ferociously for his pretensions of being "king," and king of the Jews, a people they hated.

We cannot state for sure whether the insults against Jesus were based on the so-called "king game" or *basilinda*, where someone was chosen as king and the others had to obey the king's orders; evidence of this game can probably be seen on the Pavement of the Antonia Tower (though the pavement that remains today is from the second c. A.D. and not from the times of Jesus). The Gospels of Mark, Matthew, and John agree in describing a harsh and wild scene, involving all the soldiers stationed in the praetorium, in which Jesus had the clothes he was wearing removed (John omits this detail) and instead had to wear purple clothes according to Mark and John, or scarlet, according to Matthew; a robe according to John, or a (soldier's) cloak, according to Matthew. Or was it the royal cloak that Herod Antipas made him wear?

Despite the differences among the Gospels due to oral tradition, the essential message is obvious: the color of the clothing is that of the royal dynasty. The taunt was inspired by the prisoner's pretension to the throne, the basis of the accusations against him. For a royal crown, the soldiers had a crown of thorns that they placed on Jesus' head. As a scepter, they had a reed, which they placed in the prisoner's right hand (according to Matthew) and with which they hit him over the head. The taunts were completed with a sarcastic salute, accompanied by their kneeling down as a sign of homage: "Hail, King of the

Jews!" According to Mark and Matthew, they also spat at him, and John says that there were also physical attacks, with his being slapped. This all went on until the order came to take the prisoner outside to the Pavement, where Pilate had to complete his trial and sentence him.

6.2.4.4. The Trial Restarts: The Pressure on Pilate

When Jesus, with the crown of thorns and purple robe, ironic royal accoutrements, was brought out to the *Lithostrotos* or Pavement, the courtyard was full of people waiting for him. The leaders of the temple and Sanhedrin who had accused him earlier were there and, significantly, there were now more of them, and they were accompanied by a threatening angry crowd, which had been gathered together by these same leaders. The arrival of a great number of people at the praetorium's courtyard had been orchestrated during the interval when the trial was suspended, while Jesus was with Herod Antipas and Pilate had judged the others on trial. The organizational powers of the temple leaders and the city's leading figures involved in Jesus' trial were impressive, and their associates had been able to summon a crowd with relative ease. Faced with Pilate's wavering, they needed to apply pressure in order to ensure Jesus was sentenced to the penalty reserved for enemies of Rome: crucifixion. We should remember that the temple was Jerusalem's great economic motor and that many families depended on it, whether directly or indirectly. Presenting Jesus as an enemy of the temple was a fine strategy that was bound to reap immediate rewards. As well as Jesus' prophecy regarding the destruction of the temple, his actions against the trading taking place there were also fresh in people's minds.

The hundreds of people who went up to the praetorium to call for the death of the prophet from Nazareth were not victims of some kind of blackmail by the leaders who had power over their work and subsistence and who would have forced them to play their part. Nor had these people been bribed to show themselves against (or in favor of, had it been necessary!) Jesus. The Jewish leaders, Jesus' accusers, were absolutely convinced that the Nazarene was a blasphemer and a false prophet and that he was a threat to the Jewish people. The people who now called for his crucifixion would have been equally convinced that he deserved this end for being a false prophet who wanted to destroy the temple, Israel's holiest place.

Above, we have set out the reasons why the authorities (see 6.2.1.1) and the people (see 6.2.1.2) wanted to have Jesus killed. Nonetheless, the authorities could employ only one strategy when it came to Pilate: they had to present Jesus as a pretender to the throne, someone who wanted to be "king" (*basileus*) and thus a direct rival to the actual "king" (*basileus*), the Roman emperor. The people accepted this strategy and right from the start demanded that Pilate sentence Jesus to the Roman punishment of crucifixion, the cruelest way to die, reserved for those who wanted to usurp Caesar's sovereignty.

Nevertheless, was it really credible for a Roman judge, as impartial and cold as Pilate, who held all the power, to succumb to the pressure of a crowd that wanted to influence his decision through its cries? The first observation is, as we shall see in 6.2.4.5, that the people did not decide Jesus' fate; it was Pilate, and only Pilate, who could hand down the sentence. The people's and their leaders' insistent calls for Jesus' death were not decisive; at most they were intimidating. We should stress that, in the Gospels of Luke and John, Pilate did ask the people if he should sentence Jesus. According to John 18:39, the only question that he asked them was if they wanted him to release their king, "the King of the Jews." However, in the Gospels of Mark and Matthew, the governor asked a question that laid emphasis on the Jews' responsibility for Jesus' death, a question that almost exonerated Pilate ("Thus, what shall I do with the man whom you call the King of the Jews?"; Mark 15:12; also Matt 27:22). In Matthew, the Roman governor even went to the extent of declaring himself innocent of Jesus' death, publicly washing his hands, while "all the people" accepted direct responsibility for the decision and its terrible consequences: "His blood be on us and on our children!" (Matt 27:25). This sentence was written with the catastrophe of the First Jewish Revolt in mind, when, forty years after Jesus' death, the generation that followed on from those who called for his death ("our children") was defeated. Pilate came under pressure from the crowd brought together in the courtyard of the praetorium, but this did not affect his responsibility as governor and judge.

During other events in his career as governor of Judaea, Pilate also came under pressure from the people, though not in the circumstances of a trial. On two occasions, Pilate was willing to change his decision according to the wishes of the people who had come to protest: in the affair of the standards with the Emperor's medal (*A.J.* 18:55-59; *J.W.* 2:169–74) and the affair of the golden shields (*Embassy* 299–305), in which Jewish religious feelings were offended by pagan symbolism in Jerusalem. During the aqueduct riot (*A.J.* 18:60-62; *J.W.* 2:175–77), a great crowd laid siege to the praetorium in protest against Pilate's wish to take money from the temple's treasury. Pilate ordered his soldiers to disperse the protesters, but things got out of hand as they went beyond the orders given and carried out an authentic massacre. Standing up to public pressure was not something new to Pilate, and it never represented a threat to his authority.

Before we turn again to Jesus' trial, let us take note of the information provided by the Gospels of Mark, Matthew, and John regarding the "custom" of freeing a prisoner for the Passover, "one prisoner for whom they asked" as it says in Mark 15:6. This was not an amnesty or collective pardon that meant the quashing of the punishment, which, in the times of Jesus, was something only the emperor could order. As R. E. Brown points out, it was more akin to a pardon, a gracious gesture applied to the accused who had been sentenced or was still to be sentenced (but not for violent crimes).

In fact, the pardon most resembling the case of Barabbas was the freeing of prisoners by the procurator Albinus in 64 A.D.; those sentenced to capital punishment were executed, and only those convicted of lesser crimes were set free (*A.J.* 20:208–9). However, this act of clemency (which was not completely gracious, as Albinus made those freed pay him!) had nothing to do with the Passover festivities and even less to do with the calls of any crowd that had gathered. The Jewish sources (Josephus, Philo, the Mishnah, and the Talmud), and obviously the Roman sources, make no mention of this Passover custom described in the New Testament (the Gospels and Acts 3:14), according to which the Roman authorities freed the prisoner that the Jewish people asked for.

The Roman sources mention occasional, specific cases where the authorities decided, as a gesture of goodwill, to free someone at the request of the people. The Florentine papyrus (61:59 et seq.) refers to the case of a prisoner sentenced to a whipping who, following calls from the people, was freed by the governor of Egypt G. Septimius

Vegetus (85 A.D.). The Emperor Tiberius, under pressure from the calls of the people, freed a slave who had fought well in the amphitheater (as explained by Suetonius in the *Life of Tiberius* 47). The crowd's insistence together with the governor's willingness meant that, what had seemed insurmountable in strictly judicial terms, could be overlooked on occasions. This was neither a desirable situation nor an infrequent one, as can be seen in the Justinian Code (9:47:12), which rules with regard to those in authority: "When the people cry out, they should not be paid heed; nor should their voice be taken into account when they call for someone guilty of a crime to be freed or for an innocent party to be sentenced."

It does not seem that Pilate agreed at all with this advice on good government. The Roman prefect for Judaea was not inflexible when faced with popular pressure to have Jesus sentenced. It is worth pointing out that, in his defense, his wavering was understandable since the guilt of the accused had not been irrefutably proven by the evidence provided, as was to be seen in the events that took place in the second part of the trial.

Jesus' arrival at the Pavement, the purple robe over his body, the crown of thorns on his head, his hands tied, and escorted by soldiers, inspired a unanimous cry of aversion from the people gathered there. In Roman law, trials were public and, as long as order was maintained, anyone could be present. The crowd of a few hundred, headed by important members of the temple staff and Jerusalem's leading families, had gathered in response to the calls from the Jewish authorities. They may have been waiting and calling for the accused for some time because they had gone up to the praetorium not to witness how the trial ended but to call for Jesus' sentencing. They were fairly overwrought because they had before them someone they considered to be a fraud and an impostor; a prophet whose prophecies had not come true; a blasphemer who had wanted to destroy and rebuild the temple (something that only God could have done); a messiah who had fallen into the hands of the Romans, and was thus like a fallen tree for anyone to use for firewood; and now they had the chance to kick him while he was down. In this context, there was nothing and no one on Jesus' side. The only thing in his favor was the indecision of a distant Pilate, who did not see things clearly and who was made uncomfortable by the insistence of the Jewish authorities (now backed by a vociferous crowd) and by the lack of proof of the crime for which this man was accused.

The governor, from the top of the stairs at the door to the praetorium, presented the accused to the people below in the courtyard calling for him for some time. According to John 19:5-6, Pilate presented him with an almost indifferent statement: "Behold the man!" Their response was not long in coming: "Crucify him, crucify him!" This call was repeated over and over again. The people forcefully demanded Jesus' death, and Pilate was taken aback. The trial had begun with an active and motivated group of accusers who had presented Jesus as a pretender to the throne, as "the King of the Jews," and they had unsuccessfully called for his death as an enemy of Caesar, yet they had no proof! Now, however, it was the people who demanded his sentencing, the very people whom the accused wanted to free from the Romans, their enemies. How was it possible, Pilate must have thought, that the people demanded the death of someone who proposed to fight for their freedom? Does it make sense, he must have wondered, that the Jews call for the death of someone who wanted to take Caesar's place and free them from the Roman occupation?

Evidently, the situation made little sense. There was something incongruous in this Galilean, accused of serious charges that could not be proven and inspiring aversion in a crowd of his own people as if he were an enemy of Israel and not of Rome (which was the most important charge that had been brought against him!). Pilate did not know the whole story, he did not know what really motivated the leaders and the people in obstinately demanding the death of this prisoner: his being a blasphemer and a false prophet. The Roman governor could sense, however, that there was something hidden in the background, something that a non-Jew like himself could not understand.

The strategy of the high priests and the other leaders seemed to be on the brink of failure. Pilate was wavering and seemed willing to turn down the accusations brought against Jesus ("to make himself king") as they lacked any foundation. According to Luke 23:16 and 23:22, Pilate wanted to overcome this error by offering the incensed crowd some form of satisfaction: Jesus would be sentenced to a whipping, to be chastised, and then freed. According to Mark 15:9 and John 18:39, Pilate asked the people in the courtyard a key question, which they could respond to only positively (or at least that was what the governor thought): "Do you want me to release for you the King of the Jews?" (Mark 15:9; John 18:39). Who could turn down the release of their own king and deliverance from death? Or, on the contrary, who could call for the death of their king, whether real or only possible, whether called Jesus or some other name? It seemed as though Pilate had found the way to avoid this poor Galilean's execution.

The astute reaction from the leaders was not long in coming, however. Pilate wanted to let someone go, either because he wanted to respect an (unwritten) custom linked to the Jewish Passover or because he felt he should show some clemency in a case that was anything but clear-cut. The governor wanted to pardon him. He wanted to make a gracious gesture for the accused, who had yet to be sentenced. The leaders understood that they could not go against the wishes of the governor and turn down his proposal that Jesus be freed. They could not respond negatively to the Roman authorities! Instead, they had to respect Pilate's proposal but modify its objective: have the prisoner freed not be Jesus, as the governor proposed, but Barabbas, another of the prisoners held in the cells of the praetorium. Pilate's initiative had quickly been hijacked. The people began calling out Barabbas' name and demanding his release. The Jewish leaders had been able to neutralize Pilate's proposal and had left him with only one alternative: to sentence Jesus.

Who was this Barabbas though? Someone known to the people ("notorious," as Matthew says), who had been involved in disturbances that had taken place in Jerusalem and in which someone had been murdered. Mark calls him a "rebel" and John a "robber." Luke goes even further, openly calling him a "murderer." The surname *Barabbas* is a Greek adaptation of the Aramaic patronymic *Bar Abba* (which, etymologically, means "son of the father"); it was not uncommon at the time, nor was *Abba*. It is not beyond the realms of possibility that his full name may have been Jesus/Joshua Barabbas, as some manuscripts of the Gospel according to Matthew state in 27:16-17.

The description of this figure leads us to think that he must have been involved in a band of criminals who had committed a planned murder (someone linked to the Roman authorities?) during *the* disturbances. The group and their crime were probably well known at the time but not important enough to warrant being reported by Josephus or any other historical source. It was in the grey area between common crime and terrorist action aimed at undermining the Roman occupation of the country, carried out by an urban guerrilla group. Though we do not have information on Barabbas' legal situation, he had probably been detained and was waiting to go to trial. Pilate was very unlikely to have agreed to release a man who had been sentenced for murder. Either Barabbas had yet to be judged, according to Mark 15:7-15 or, as was more unlikely, he had been judged that same day with the other "bandits" (those who were to die with Jesus on the cross) but had not been sentenced to death.

The people demanded with their cries that Pilate release Barabbas and crucify Jesus. Pilate found himself stuck between Scylla and Charybdis. He had not initially mentioned Barabbas' name. It was the crowd that called it out, as can be seen in the Gospels of Mark (15:9-11), Luke (23:16, 23:18) and John (18:39-40). The governor had not offered the people a choice, as in Matthew 27:17: "Whom do you want me to release for you, Barabbas, or Jesus who is called Christ [the Messiah]?" It was the people who called for Barabbas to be freed and who caught Pilate off balance. The governor's strategy (which he was not at heart convinced of) fell apart. Jesus' presumed innocence began to fade as the crowd's calls got ever louder and formed a weighty argument.

What did this Galilean represent to Pilate and the Roman authorities? What proof was offered in his defense against these serious allegations against him? An almost total silence. Moreover, why should Pilate turn down the accusations made by the Jewish leaders, respectable people whom he knew well enough and who were absolutely convinced of the truth of their allegations? Were these accusations not in defense of the state's highest interests, denouncing someone who represented a potential threat to Rome, someone who dared to call himself "king"? If he did not sentence this Galilean, would he not create more problems than he would solve? Why make problems for himself with the Jewish authorities on the eve of Passover and in Jerusalem, where one hundred thousand Jews had come together and when anti-Roman feeling was at is height? Finally, why turn the Jewish leaders against him, provoking them to send an ambassador to the Emperor Tiberius (a man who was particularly alert to criminal cases involving high treason against the state) accusing Pilate of being lenient with the enemies of Rome? John 19:12 offers the last and definitive argument used by the Jewish leaders to persuade the governor: "If you release this man, you are not Caesar's friend."

The external pressure on Pilate and his internal doubts tipped the scales against Jesus in the decision made by the Roman administration's highest authority, the man with absolute power over life and death, who gave in and sentenced Jesus according to the wishes of his accusers. Finally, following the uncertainty and faltering, the Jewish leaders' proposal won out: Jesus was found guilty. Pilate had sided with them and would now punish him legally, in accordance with Roman law. Finally, according to John 19:11, Jesus addressed these words to the governor, explaining the way in which the trial had gone: "You would have no power over me unless it had been given you from above; therefore he who delivered me to you has the greater sin." Responsibility for his death had to be shared among those who unjustly accused Jesus and the judge who sentenced him without regard for justice.

6.2.4.5. The Closing of the Trial: The Sentence

Pilate released Barabbas. The former now sat in the judge's seat at the door to the praetorium possibly at the top of the staircase leading from the Pavement courtyard or possibly on a platform built in front of the praetorium (*J.W.* 2:301). The *pro tribunali* judicial process began, which had to end in the sentencing in front of the crowd (John 19:13). According to the Gospel of John, it was around midday on Friday, April 7, 30 A.D., the day before Passover (John 19:14). We do not know the wording of Jesus' sentencing. As we have suggested above (see 6.2.4.1), it was probably not reported in any official document. Jesus was a *peregrinus*, a provincial subject, without the legal rights of a Roman citizen, and his trial was *extra ordinem*. There was no need to have written evidence of the case or the judge's sentence. Nevertheless, it seems that Pilate was unable to ignore the formalities of Roman law and gave his verdict summarizing the reasons leading to the death sentence for Jesus of Nazareth and the type of punishment he was to receive: crucifixion.

Crucifixion was a punishment reserved, infamously, for slaves sentenced to death and subjects of the empire who were not Roman citizens and who had been accused of treason against the emperor. This was Jesus' case more or less. Although there was no proof of his acting directly against Tiberius or the Roman state, his attempt to make and/or call himself "king" had been interpreted, though without any definitive proof, as a threat to Rome and its "king," Caesar. Pilate may have based his decision on the so-called *Lex Iulia de maiestate* when assessing the charges against Jesus. However, he made very little effort to back up his verdict with legal arguments that could not be appealed against. There was enough, in the governor's opinion, to conclude that Jesus represented a threat (though possibly only potential) to the stability of the Roman state and its maximum authority, the emperor. This can be seen indirectly in the sentence attributed by the Gospel of John to Pilate: "Behold your King!" (John 19:14). In other words, the judicial concept of *crimen laesae maiestatis populi romani* was sufficient. Both Tacitus and Suetonius mention that, in the times of Tiberius, the law relating to crimes against his majesty were dealt with severely and often involved capital punishment (*Annals* 2:50, 3:38; *Life of Tiberius* 58).

The final confirmation of the sentence is the text of the plaque or titulus that Pilate had placed over the cross and that stated that the man crucified had been sentenced for being "the king of the Jews." The governor did not accept the rectification proposed by the high priests ("This man said, I am the King of the Jews"; John 19:21) and kept the sign in its legally valid form. Jesus' pretensions to the throne were interpreted as political in nature and accepted as true by Pilate; hence they constituted the official reason for his sentence. Pilate's response shows a level of objectivity in his sentencing of Jesus. The governor had sentenced him not simply because of some of the statements he had made but because he saw him as a real threat: if Jesus saw himself and was seen by others to be the king of the Jews, if he really was a pretender to the throne, then he was a direct threat to the empire. Pilate's sentence was based on an objective charge. The crime was proportionate to the penalty that had to be applied: death on the cross.

6.2.5. His Death on the Cross

The historical sources on the execution of Jesus' death sentence are the canonical Gospels of Mark (15:15, 15:20-41), Matthew (27:26, 27:31-56), Luke (23:26-49), and John (19:1, 19:16-37) and the Gospel of Peter (10–20, 25–27), an apocryphal document. The sequence of events generally agrees in each of the three synoptic Gospels, though Luke does contain some of his own traditions, for example, the laments of the women from Jerusalem and the good thief. He also narrates the events with a great sensibility. Matthew is more akin to Mark, on which he depends (as does Luke), adding a short passage: the reactions and effects brought on by Jesus' death. John has his own structure that has a number of points in common with Mark, though the material from this tradition has been reworked a great deal, for example, the throwing of lots for Jesus' tunic or the spear. In the canonical Gospels are related both the events that took place and the subsequent interpretation they inspired (in the earliest tradition) based on texts from the Old Testament. This can be seen, for example, in the so-called "seven words" of Jesus on the cross, which Christian tradition has taken from a number of Gospel sources (one from Mark-Matthew, three from Luke, and three from John):

1. "Father, forgive them; for they know not what they do." (Luke 23:34)
2. "Woman, behold, your son!" "Behold, your mother!" (John 19:26-27)
3. "Truly, I say to you, today you will be with me in Paradise." (Luke 23:43)
4. "'*Eloi, Eloi, lama sabachthani?*' which means, 'My God, my God, why hast thou forsaken me?'" (Mark 15:34 || Matt 27:46, which reads "*Eli*" instead of "*Eloi*"); "My power, my power, thou hast forsaken me." (Gospel of Peter 19; Ps 22:2)
5. "I thirst." (John 19:28; Ps 22:16; Ps 69:22)
6. "[Everything] is finished." (John 19:30)
7. "Father, into thy hands I commit my spirit!" (Luke 23:46; Ps 31:6)

6.2.5.1. The Whipping

The Romans had three kinds of capital punishment, which got increasingly worse in line with the ignominy of the crime: beheading (*decollatio*), burning (*crematio*), and crucifixion (*crux*). There was also the punishment of being devoured by beasts (*ferae*), which was on a similar level to crucifixion. Cicero describes crucifixion as "the cruellest and most disgusting penalty" (*Against Verres* 2:5:165). Death on the cross arouses compassion among its witnesses by its level of cruelty and monstrosity, since it is, in Josephus' opinion, beyond the limits of human suffering (*A.J.* 13:381). It is a "passion," a suffering that inspires compassion (*J.W.* 5:450) and that is reserved for slaves and those who have committed the worst crimes. The physical and psychological violence that those sentenced to the cross have to support make this punishment more than just an execution, turning it into a torture, with a liberating end in death. This is how Seneca expresses it, asking, "Can any man be found willing to be fastened to the accursed tree, long sickly, already deformed, swelling with ugly tumours on chest and shoulders, and draw the breath of life amid long drawn-out agony?" (*Letters* 101:12). Crucifixion was a form of torture that aimed at killing the condemned while making them suffer and shaming them terribly.

Furthermore, the torture of the capital punishment itself was usually preceded by another form of punishment, flagellation. This whipping accompanied the crucifixion; the punishment consisted of two parts: the flagellation and the crucifixion itself. Josephus describes how the last Roman procurator before the First Jewish Revolt, Gessius Florus, ordered (illegally according to the empire's laws) a number of Jewish leaders with Roman citizenship to be "whipped and nailed to the cross before his tribunal [a platform built in the Pavement courtyard, in front of the praetorium]" (*J.W.* 2:308). Similarly, those who had defended Jerusalem and were captured by the Romans during the First Jewish Revolt "were first whipped, and tormented with all sorts of tortures, before they died, and were then crucified before the wall of the city" (*J.W.* 5:449).

The whipping, a common part of someone's crucifixion, was applied to Jesus at the express request of Pilate almost as an aside, according to the Gospels of Mark (15:15), Matthew (27:26), and John (19:1). We do not know whether the two "robbers" crucified with him where also whipped at the same time or whether they had already been whipped, after having received their sentence. As for Jesus, everything leads us to believe that his execution began as soon as Pilate had pronounced the sentence.

We do not know whether Pilate was present when he was whipped or whether he had returned inside the praetorium (it would have been time for lunch). The soldiers of the cohort assigned to execute Jesus that day (and the other two condemned men) made him come down from where he was, possibly at the top of the stairs to the door, or on the platform that had been built for the trial and where Pilate had handed down his sentence. They led him to the *Lithostrotos* or Pavement courtyard, also known as the *Gabatha*. There they removed the purple robe that had been used to taunt him in his position as "king." Immediately afterward, a number of executioners (or possibly these same soldiers) went on to whip him publicly. The leaders and the people, having witnessed the proceedings in the praetorium courtyard and heard the sentence, moved on. Whippings were carried out on the naked bodies of the condemned, and this was repugnant to Jewish sensibilities.

We do not know how long he was whipped for nor what kind of whip was used (lead balls, leather strips, metal spikes, etc.), but the effects on Jesus' body must have been devastating. When in 62 A.D. the procurator Albinus ordered the whipping of Jesus, son of Ananus, Josephus describes how he was "whipped till his bones were laid bare" (*J.W.* 6:304). The brutality of this punishment was so insupportable that it was not uncommon for some of the condemned to be unable to withstand it, falling dead from the suffering.

Once the whipping was over, they dressed Jesus in his clothes again (a tunic with, possibly, a belt and a cloak) over the flesh torn by the whipping. In order to respect Jewish sensibilities, the Romans made an effort to avoid having the condemned walk naked through the streets of Jerusalem, so Jesus went up to Golgotha clothed.

6.2.5.2. The Road to Golgotha

The escort came together in the praetorium's courtyard after midday. The three condemned men were led by four soldiers with their regular equipment, one of whom was probably a centurion or lesser officer (a decurion?). The Gospel according to John does not mention a centurion, referring specifically instead to a squadron (four men), one of whom acted as their leader. The synoptic Gospels all mention a centurion and an indeterminate group of soldiers (three? four?). A squadron (Greek, *tetradion*; Latin, *quaternion*) was the smallest military unit, and this shows that Pilate was not concerned about any last-minute attempts by Jesus' followers to free him, someone who had been sentenced as a presumed political leader of the people, the "king of the Jews." The security in place seems to have been as usual and not increased in any way. This is another sign of the weakness of the charges brought against Jesus; the Roman authorities did not, when it came down to it, see this man or his followers as a real threat to public order or security. Nonetheless, it is also evidence of the consent of the people of Jerusalem regarding the sentence, whether through their active implication before Pilate, their distant indifference, or their fearful silence.

Jesus left the *Lithostrotos* or *Gabatha* with the *patibulum* or horizontal crossbeam to the crucifix over his shoulders. When he and the other two condemned men reached the rocky hill of Golgotha, the *patibulum* was tied to the vertical pole (*stipes*), which was permanently rooted in the ground and used for all the executions. Plautus writes, in reference to a crucifixion, "[T]hey'll be so pinking you with goads, as you carry your gibbet through the streets" (*Mostellaria* 56–57). Jesus probably had the plaque, ordered by Pilate and explaining the reason for his sentence, around his neck; this was later placed above the cross. Dio Cassius (*Roman History* 54:3:7) offers proof of this procedure with regard to a slave who had been sentenced and who was made to cross the forum. It is less likely that this sign was carried by someone else walking before the condemned man, a Roman practice described by Suetonius (*Life of Caligula* 32).

This other person may have been an executioner who also carried the tools needed for the three executions that day (if it was not the soldiers themselves who carried them): the nails (at least nine: three for each of the condemned), hammers, rope, forks to raise the crossbeam, and other items including a sponge (as mentioned in Mark 15:36 || Matt 27:48 and John 19:29). Following the events of the night and morning that culminated in the harsh punishment of the whipping, Jesus would have been so weak that the soldiers must have been concerned that he would not make it alive to the place where he was to be crucified; thus, they would not have been able to carry out their orders to execute him. As was common among the Roman troops stationed in the provinces, they turned to the practice of press-ganging. They made a man who was simply passing by take up the *patibulum* of the cross that Jesus was no longer able to carry.

This man was called Simon, a Jew from the city of Cyrene in the North African province of Cyrenaica (now Libya), who had immigrated with his family to Jerusalem, where he now lived. We know that there was a colony of Greek-speaking Jews in Jerusalem, which included "Cyrenians" and "Alexandrians" (Acts 6:9). It should come as no surprise that Simon's two sons had non-Jewish names: the name of one was Greek (Alexander) and of the other Latin (Rufus). These two brothers were to become Christians and well-known figures in the early community, being mentioned in the Gospel of Mark (15:21). At that time, after midday, Simon of Cyrene was returning home from work in the fields early, as that Friday was the day before Passover and he had to prepare for the Passover meal at dusk. It says in the Mishnah that in Judaea the custom was to work until midday on the eve of Passover (*Pesah.* 4:5). Simon kept to this custom, but, out of the blue, he was suddenly made to carry Jesus' cross up to the top of Golgotha and thus became an important witness to this part of the Passion.

The streets of northwest Jerusalem were very busy at that time. The locals and great numbers of pilgrims were making last-minute purchases in the markets before the important Passover ceremonies. The temple was a hive of activity, as thousands of paschal lambs were being slaughtered at the time to be eaten that night. The passing of this procession of three condemned men obviously attracted people's attention, and their reactions, especially with regard to Jesus, were contradictory: insults, compassion, disrespect, or shame. According to the Gospel of Luke (23:27-31), a large number of women took interest in him and lamented and cried for the fate of the Galilean prophet. According to this Gospel, Jesus had announced the destruction of Jerusalem with deep regret for the fate of the city. The last sentence was symbolic: "[I]f they do this when the wood is green, what will happen when it is dry?" (Luke 23:31).

The route taken by Jesus from Herod's palace, in the northwest of the city and the site of the praetorium, to Golgotha beyond the city walls where crucifixions took place, is not difficult to trace because it was only some 300 meters as the crow flies. The name Golgotha (John 19:17) is the Greek adaptation of a Semitic word (Aramaic, *gugulta*; Hebrew, *gulgolet*) that means skull (Latin, *calvaria*, which is the origin of the English word "Calvary"). In the Gospels, the place is called "the place of a skull" (Mark 15:22; Matt 27:33; John 19:17) or, simply, "The Skull" (Luke 23:33). Christian tradition, from the third century A.D. onward sought to link this name with the skull and bones of Adam, which were apparently buried there, so as to present Jesus as the sign of a new humanity. This led to a very common iconography in crucifixes and icons. The name Golgotha probably arose because the execution hill was a rocky, barren outcrop, which had nothing else visible except for the vertical poles of the crosses sticking out of the ground. The hill was some meters higher than the surrounding area. It had been part of a quarry, but since the first century B.C. it had been filled in with earth and used for cultivation or burials (taking advantage of the cavities in the rocks). Some 250 meters from Golgotha was one of the gateways to Jerusalem, the so-called Garden (*Gennath*) Gate, beside which, according to Josephus (*J.W.* 5:146), the second or northern city wall began, which ran between Herod's palace and the Antonia Tower. It also seems that there was another gateway in this second wall, called the Gate of Ephraim or Benjamin, which was less than 100 meters from Calvary.

For the Romans, crucifixions were to act as an example and warning; thus, the crosses were at high places by the gates to cities, busy spots. Plautus writes in *Miles Gloriosus* (359–60), "I think that in that self-same position you will have to die outside the gates [*extra portam*], when, with hands outstretched, you will be carrying your cross." Jesus' case was no different. The Gospel according to John 19:20 states that Golgotha "was near the city"; and the Epistle to the Hebrews says, "Jesus also suffered outside the gate" (13:12). It is likely that the gate to Jerusalem through which Jesus passed from the walled city was the gate of Ephraim, which led straight to Golgotha or Calvary. If this hypothesis is correct, the actual distance traveled from Herod's palace (the setting for Pilate's trial) to Golgotha (the setting for Jesus' execution) was some five hundred meters, mostly through Jerusalem itself. Jesus was on his last legs and, for the most part, was not able to carry the crossbeam, which Simon the Cyrene bore. This setting for the *via crucis* agrees only partially with the traditional portrayal, dating from the Middle Ages and going from the Antonia Tower to Golgotha or Calvary.

6.2.5.3. The Crucifixion and Suffering

As soon as the procession reached Golgotha, the soldiers carried out the sentence. Though the Gospel of Mark (15:25) sets the time of the crucifixion as being at nine in the morning, the version in the Gospel of John seems more likely: Pilate pronounced the sentence at "about noon" (John 19:14), and the crucifixion took place before one o'clock in the afternoon. This is approximately the time ("about noon") when the three Gospels and the Gospel of Peter, which depends greatly on them, have an extraordinary phenomenon take place (a "darkness"), which accompanied Jesus' suffering and which went on until three in the afternoon, the time when he died.

Before crucifying him, the soldiers offered Jesus wine spiked with myrrh (Mark 15:23, to be preferred to Matt 27:34, which talks of wine mixed with bile). On occasions, those sentenced to death by crucifixion drank strong drinks to anaesthetise them and make them more able to support the pain and torment. The myrrh did not have any narcotic effects on its own, instead being used for medicinal purposes, as shown by Dioscorides Pedanius (*De Materia Medica* 1:64:3). However, the best wine was spiked with myrrh according to the ancients ("the wines that were most esteemed among the ancient Romans were those perfumed with myrrh"; Pliny the Elder, *Natural History* 14:15) and assisted sleep. The Babylonian Talmud (*Sanh.* 43a) mentions wine containing a grain of frankincense to reduce pain. This offering to Jesus would seem to have been a pious and friendly act.

Nonetheless, it seems unlikely that the soldiers, who up to that moment had shown no consideration for Jesus, now showed compassion for the condemned man by offering him a refined offering designed to lessen the pain of crucifixion, a torture aimed to kill slowly and cruelly. The only possibility is that someone close to Jesus had prepared this drink and, with a bribe, managed to get the soldiers to give it to him. In the fragment from the Talmud mentioned above, a group of women from Jerusalem felt compassion for the condemned man and offered the wine with frankincense. Indeed, a group of women linked to Jesus (his relatives and/or followers) may have reached Golgotha (following the procession of the condemned men?) and wanted to help in his time of great need. These women saw the events on Golgotha firsthand. Jesus, however, was to turn down the drink that the women had been able to get to him via the soldiers.

The crucifixion

Simon of Cyrene left the *patibulum* or crossbeam on the ground by the stipes or vertical pole sticking from the ground and left. The soldiers removed Jesus' clothes (the cloak, tunic, and, possibly, a belt) and made him lie down on the rocky ground of Golgotha, with his arms outstretched over the crucifix's crossbeam. The Roman custom was to have the crucified person hanging naked from the cross, the person's nakedness on public show. This is referred to by Artemidorus Daldianus (*Oneirocritica* 2:53). However, the Jewish revulsion at seeing a nude body in public may have led to a change in the Roman custom, which consequently allowed those crucified to wear a loincloth tied below the stomach (*subligaculum*). For just this reason, Jesus (and the other two condemned men obviously) arrived clothed at Golgotha, which was not the usual Roman custom. We cannot be sure if Jesus was completely naked on the cross. The earliest Christian testimonies, whether literary or artistic, are divided on this issue.

There were two ways of attaching the extremities of the condemned to the cross: tying them and nailing them. The parts of the body attached to the cross could be either the hands or the arms and either the feet or the legs. Moreover, some were crucified upside down and others were impaled. Crucifixions underwent a number of variations, depending on local customs and the macabre creativity of the executioner. Jesus seems to have been nailed by the hands and feet, with his head the right way up. Many think that the nails in his hands were introduced at the wrist, since, if they had been driven through his palms, they would not have been able to support the weight of his body and he would have been torn apart. In any case, Luke 24:39-40 and John 20:25, 20:27 assume that Jesus' "hands" and "feet" were pierced by nails.

With Jesus' hands nailed to the crossbeam (at the wrist), the soldiers raised his body and the beam using two forks and fixed it to the vertical pole. There were two ways of fixing it according to two different types of cross: the cross with three arms in a T-shape (*crux comissa*), where the cross beam fit into a V-shaped notch at the top of the cross; and the cross with four arms, which is the most common in Christian art (*crux immissa*), where the notch was some distance from the top of the vertical pole. The crossbeam was made secure with a rope knot at the point where it was joined. The Gospels assume that it was the latter of these two types of cross, as Matthew (27:37: "over his head"), Luke (23:38: "over him"), and John (19:19: "on the cross") all state that the plaque or *titulus* with the reason for his sentence was placed above Jesus' head.

Jesus' feet were held in place by one or two nails. In 1968, an ossuary was found at Giv'at ha-Mivtar (Jerusalem) with the bones of a man called Johanan, who had been crucified in the mid-first century A.D. at around thirty years of age. This man's feet appear to have been nailed separately to the vertical pole of the cross: the two nails (one for each foot) were first driven through a piece of olive wood (to ensure that the feet could not come away from the nail), the heels, and finally the wood of the pole. The arms of this crucified man were held with ropes, not nails. In Jesus' case, the iconographic representations do not agree on the number of nails in his feet, though the finding of the cross in the fourth century by Saint Helena, mother of the Emperor Constantine, was accompanied by the discovery of three nails (two for the hands and one for the feet).

The image of Christ crucified is completed with other elements that appear in the iconography. The oldest testimonies talked about the so-called *sedile* or seat, a piece of wood placed halfway up the vertical pole, on which the condemned could rest some of their weight, which meant that their suffering could go on a little longer. The other traditional element is the *suppedaneum* or footrest, a piece of wood located at the bottom of the vertical pole, which was not mentioned until the second to third centuries A.D. As with the *sedile*, its function was not to alleviate the suffering of those crucified but to prolong it.

Jesus' cross (we do not know about those of the other two) was crowned with the *titulus* or plaque that Pilate had ordered to show the reason for his sentence, the *causa poenae*: his pretensions to be "the king" of the Jewish people and a direct rival to he who, according to the Roman state, was the only legitimate sovereign, the Emperor Tiberius (see 6.2.1.3 and 6.2.4.5, above). The soldiers had placed this plaque at the top of the cross so that it could be easily seen by all those who passed by Golgotha.

The four Gospels do not agree on the exact wording of this plaque or board, but all four confirm that it included the expression "king of the Jews," which had been key in Jesus' trial and the basis of the accusations and his sentencing. The text in the Gospel of Peter ("This is the King of Israel") is clearly secondary. The wording used here and in the Gospels of Matthew and Luke may date back to the earliest times: "This [is]." Less likely is the mention of the condemned man's name ("Jesus"), which appears only in the Gospels of Matthew and John. The latter reinforces this with his surname "the Nazarene," completing the identification of the figure: "Jesus of Nazareth, the King of the Jews" (Latin, *Iesus Nazarenus Rex Iudaeorum*, hence the acronym INRI). The solemnity and universality that the Gospel of John seeks to give this plaque above the cross can be seen in its trilingual nature: "in Hebrew [or Aramaic], in Latin [literally: Roman] and in Greek" (John 19:20). They are the holy language of the people of Israel, the official language of the empire, and the common language of the Orient, respectively. When the Jewish leaders wanted Pilate to change the text, he responded from his position of authority, saying, "[W]hat I have written, I have written," the concise Latin formula, "*Quod scripsi, scripsi*" (John 19:22).

The crucifixion is completed with the report, found in the four Gospels, that Jesus was crucified with two other men, one on either side of him. This means that the two other condemned men had to suffer the same torture as Jesus and that the conditions and circumstances of their crucifixions must have greatly resembled those of Jesus (the type of cross and system of crucifixion). However, Jesus had been sentenced for an "important" reason, as a pretender to the throne. His position in the middle was probably no coincidence but formed part of the soldiers' taunts started in the praetorium who wanted to "honor" him once again as the "king of the Jews" by placing him in a position of respect.

Up until the last moment of his execution, Jesus' royal pretensions were a source of vicious taunts. The Gospel of Luke (23:32-33) and the Gospel of Peter (10) call those beside him during his suffering "criminals," while Mark 15:27 and Matthew 27:38 call them "robbers." On no occasion are they linked to Barabbas, a "rebel." They had probably been sentenced for common crimes, not political ones, though, as we have suggested, it is difficult to draw a clear line between the violence of petty criminals and what was politically inspired against the Romans and their collaborators.

The Gospel according to Luke is the only source that mentions a "response" from Jesus to his crucifixion. It consists of a short prayer in which he asks for the forgiveness of those who have crucified him: "Father, forgive them; for they know not what they do" (Luke 23:34). Underlying these words, which do not appear in some manuscripts, is a strong echo of the part of the Lord's Prayer that refers to forgiving: "for we ourselves forgive every one who is indebted to us" (Luke 11:4).

The suffering

Jesus' suffering was so short that Pilate was surprised (Mark 15:44). According to the most likely calculations, Jesus was crucified before one o'clock in the afternoon and he died "at three o'clock" (Mark 15:34; Matt 27:46; Luke 23:44), between two and three hours later. It was common for death on the cross to take hours or even days, with the bodies being deformed by infections in the great number of wounds and suffering gradual asphyxia and attack from birds and dogs, which came to tear flesh from those unfortunate enough to still be alive (*Apotelesmatica* 4:198–200, a work attributed to Manetho). The two other men sentenced alongside Jesus were to die after him. The soldiers who were watching over them and who had crucified them put them out of their misery.

Three groups of people were at Calvary: the two men crucified with Jesus, one on either side of him; near them, there were four (or three) soldiers and the centurion (the person in charge), who could not leave the place of execution until the condemned had died; finally, there were some of Jesus' friends and acquaintances (among them, a group of women) who watched him from a distance and who would take charge of his burial.

Other people made an appearance on Golgotha but left before Jesus died. Given the location of the hill where executions took place by one of the gates to Jerusalem (a city full of pilgrims on that particular day), many people would have been passing by Golgotha and may have stopped to look at this spectacle of torment and ignominy. Among these there may have been some of the leaders who had pulled out all the stops to have the Galilean rabbi killed or some of those who had gone to the praetorium to pressure Pilate into sentencing him.

The two men crucified with Jesus, among their cries of desperation, pain, and anger at their own fate, probably insulted and taunted the man who "presided" over this execution, the man with pretensions to be "the king of the Jews." This is certainly the case in the Gospels of Mark and Matthew. Luke, echoed by the Gospel of Peter, is the only one that reports on the events surrounding the figure traditionally known as the "good thief": one of the two criminals sided with Jesus, a just man among the unjust, and he asked him whether he could take part in the future in his Kingdom. Jesus emphatically ("truly, I say to you") accepted and guaranteed that this criminal was to receive heavenly blessing: "today you will be with me in Paradise" (Luke 23:43). The disciples had received a similar promise at the Last Supper: "you may eat and drink at my table in the kingdom" (Luke 22:30). The curious coincidence between the disciples and the good thief is that the promise is the fulfillment of the loyalty in the face of a trial shared with Jesus. For the good thief, there was only the one extreme test; for the disciples, their loyalty showed itself in their continued perseverance. The Gospel indicated (with the word today) that salvation would be soon in coming; the good thief would be able to take part in it immediately.

The soldiers from the cohort, after having nailed the three condemned men to the crosses, simply had to wait and keep watch to ensure that no one tried to take them down from the cross and save them from this inevitable death. This is confirmed by the Roman writer Petronius (*Satyricon* 111). The soldiers did no more than follow orders as was their duty (only Luke shows them as mocking Jesus). That said, all four Gospels tell of how the soldiers raffled the clothes of those crucified. As we know, Jesus went up to Calvary dressed in a cloak and tunic, which may have been bound by a belt. Now, the soldiers took part in a practice that apparently was allowed by Roman law, whereby they could keep the personal belongings of those crucified. The Gospel according to John reports that they shared out Jesus' belongings. First, they divided them up into four parts that could be shared among them: the cloak and, possibly, the belt. The cloak could easily be torn into four parts. Jesus' tunic had no seams down the back or sides, being made of one single piece of fabric from top to bottom (a somewhat unusual design). If it were torn it would be useless, so the soldiers decided to leave it up to fate and the roll of the dice.

The third group that did not move from Golgotha while Jesus suffered consisted of his relatives and sympathizers, in particular a group of women. This group made the unsuccessful attempt to give Jesus some wine mixed with myrrh before his crucifixion. This group remained at some distance from Golgotha, since the soldiers did not allow anyone to come near those on the cross at the very top of the execution hill. They remained apart according to Mark 15:40 (|| Matt 27:55): "There were also women looking on from afar." Luke 23:49 also indicates the distance from which they are looking on. The Gospel of John (19:25) has this group "by the cross" itself, though, like Mark, it indicates that they were not right by Jesus. This group of relatives and followers must have been at some distance, but not all that far away. In all likelihood these sympathizers were at the foot of the hill of Golgotha, at some distance but from where they could observe everything happening to him.

The Gospels of Mark (echoed by Matthew) and John agree on the name of one of the women present: Mary Magdalene. The Gospels of Mark and Matthew also talk of two other women: Mary, wife of Alphaeus and mother of James the Younger and Joseph, and Salome, who can be identified as Zebedee's wife and the mother of James and John according to the Gospel of Matthew. The Gospel of John mentions three further women: "[Jesus'] mother, and his mother's sister, [and] Mary the wife of Clopas" (John 19:25). In total, the sources name six women, all of whom were apparently Galilean and some of whom were close relatives of Jesus' (his mother, his paternal aunt, and his maternal aunt). The Gospel of Luke does not mention the name of any women specifically as witnesses to Jesus' death (do we need to add, however, Joanna, Chuza's wife, from Luke 24:10?). The female group was certainly the more numerous.

With respect to the male group, the Gospel of John refers to the so-called "disciple whom [Jesus] loved" (19:26) and the Gospel of Luke talks of "[Jesus'] acquaintances" (23:49), a somewhat imprecise expression. Should we think that, with Jesus' death being close, Joseph of Arimathea and some other follower (Nicodemus?), who were to intervene directly in his burial, were present at Golgotha? The Twelve were not at Calvary, because they had fled and had ceased to exist at Gethsemane as a group. The Gospel of Peter (26) tries to forgive the attitude of complete capitulation by the disciples and attributes the following words to Peter: "I with my fellows was in grief, and we were wounded in our minds and would have hid ourselves; for we were sought after by them as malefactors, and as thinking to set the temple on fire." It is an excuse that may have some basis in the truth but that clearly shows the Twelve's fear and their flight, as well as indicating that the destruction of the temple was one of the elements involved in Jesus' trial.

We have already pointed out that, according to the synoptic Gospels, the group of Jesus' sympathizers, where the women clearly outnumbered the men, simply watched the scene from a distance. The Gospel of John (the only one that refers to the scene) states that they were near Golgotha ("by the cross"), and some words were addressed by Jesus to his mother and the disciple whom he loved, when he realized that they were there and beside one another: "Woman, behold your son!" (to Mary, his mother) and "Behold, your mother!" (to the disciple, who probably has to be identified as John, one of the Twelve) (John 19:26-27). We should note that no mention is made of any dialogue between Jesus and his mother or the disciple (the soldiers would not have allowed this anyway); only these two short lines that came unexpectedly from the lips of the man on the cross.

Unlike John, the synoptic Gospels refer to but do not name the other people who pass by Golgotha, which was very close to the Gate of Ephraim, one of the access points to Jerusalem. As well as the travelers entering or leaving the city who came across the crucifixes, there were those who went there expressly (people who were hostile to Jesus, the leaders who had brought about his death). Word about Jesus' crucifixion spread throughout the city as the day, the eve of Passover, went on. The speed of events and the surprise factor lessened reactions. Nonetheless, the temple leaders promoted the affair, spreading the news through the city that Jesus had been deemed an enemy of the temple, a false prophet, and a blasphemer and that, during his arrest and crucifixion, he had been unable to carry out any miracles to save himself and that he had not miraculously been saved from the cross.

There were certainly taunts and insults inspired by the fact that this man, who had wished to destroy the sanctuary and rebuild it in three days, could not now save himself. These remarks on Jesus' inability to save himself, repeated only moments before his death, were reminiscent of the remarks about his fame as a miracle worker, which arose during his appearance before Antipas. He who had healed people from illnesses and saved people from death was now unable to free himself from the torture he had to undergo. Jesus offered no response when faced with these hurtful, vexing, humiliating, and disrespectful jibes (we do not know if they were many or few). The same heavy accusing silence that surprised Pilate was used again (against those accused him!).

6.2.5.4. His Death

After a little over two hours of suffering, Jesus came face to face with death. It was around three in the afternoon on April 7, 30 A.D. The Gospel tradition describes the exceptional nature of those final hours of Jesus' life, referring to an extraordinary cosmic phenomenon, "darkness over all the land." According to the Gospel of Peter (15, 18), the phenomenon affected only "all Judaea" (which is even more miraculous), so much so that people had to use lamps in the streets (!). Luke tries to explain this highly symbolic phenomenon in astronomical terms, suggesting that it was an eclipse of the sun, which, in Greco-Roman literature, often accompanied mournful events. It says, "the sun's light failed" (Luke 23:45). However, if there is a full moon (and Passover always takes place on a full moon), an eclipse of the sun is impossible. Nevertheless, Luke may have introduced a solar eclipse that he remembered, such as that on November 24, 29 A.D., or indeed a lunar eclipse, such as the one visible from Jerusalem on April 3, 33 A.D., the day before Passover. Whatever kind of cosmic phenomenon it was, it is clear that the Gospels seek to link Jesus' death to the coming of the day when God, in accordance with what had been predicted by the ancient prophets, was to manifest himself with all his power: "'And on that day,' says the Lord God, 'I will make the sun go down at noon, and darken the earth in broad daylight'" (Amos 8:9).

His last moments

The final moments of Jesus' life were characterized by a prayer that he offered with all the strength left in a man who had been weakened terribly by his suffering: "'*Eloi, eloi, lama sabachthani?*' which means 'My God, my God, why hast thou forsaken me?'" (Mark 15:34 || Matt 27:46). These words, which were almost "cried out" by Jesus in Aramaic, his mother tongue, show his feeling of loneliness and abandonment, a feeling that must have pulsated through him at the time. Death was approaching after the torments he had suffered had left his humanity almost destroyed. The long, sustained suffering (both psychical and psychological) that he had supported with dignity and obedience finally led to Jesus' opening his heart to God with an overwhelming sincerity.

At Gethsemane, his prayer clearly expressed the difficulties he was about to face, the cup he was to drink from, his imminent death. At Golgotha, with his death at hand and the cup almost empty, Jesus cried out again, in the form of prayer, showing the state of his heart. The Passion was a time of God's silence. Jesus appealed to this God, his God!, who seemed to be absent, who seemed not to respond. Jesus chose a well-known prayer, Psalm 22 verse 2, because it is neither desperate nor damning: it is impossible to curse God with a prayer that starts with his name! Jesus did not criticize God, just as the author of the Psalm did not. On the contrary, as if something had exploded within him, he opened his heart and manifested the definitive reason for his suffering: to experience the distance from the Father, his Father and his God ("My God, my God!"). These words of Jesus on the cross show the ultimate scope of this trial, the deepest wound caused by the Passion.

However, this pain had not defeated his trust. The second part of his prayer in Gethsemane remained true: Jesus accepted, trustingly, what God wanted him to do, despite the "loud cries and tears" (Heb 5:7) this might entail. The Gospel of Luke places the stress of this abandonment of his trust and replaces the prayer from Mark–Matthew, taken from Psalm 22:2, with a different one from Psalm 31:6. This is the origin of the words that Jesus pronounced, according to the Gospel of Luke, on his death: "Father, into thy hands I commit my spirit!" (Luke 23:46). These words show, as R. E. Brown points out, that the trial that Jesus had undergone did not separate him from the Father; his trust in him remained, despite his having intensely experienced the distance from God. The prayers from Mark–Matthew and Luke are the two complementary sides to Jesus' behavior at Gethsemane (see 6.1.2.2).

When Jesus cried out "*Eloi, Eloi, lama sabachthani?*" some of those present, Jews who spoke Aramaic (probably not the soldiers), thought that Jesus was crying "Elijah." This confusion can be explained by the resemblance of *Eloi* ("my God" in Aramaic) and *Eli* (an abbreviation of the name of the prophet Elijah [Hebrew, *Eliyyahu*]). Eli is, in fact, the popular name for this great prophet of Israel. We should note that in the Gospel according to Matthew, *Eloi* has been replaced by *Eli* ("my God" in Hebrew) so as to maximize the similarities between the two and stress the possible confusion.

Elijah was seen to be a prophet and miracle worker able to help those in mortal danger; thus, the group of people watching at that time did not find it strange that Jesus, with his strength almost finished and as a last resort, called for help from Elijah. Everyone knew that Jesus was a prophet able, like Elijah, to carry out miracles, and there must have been a common feeling of "disappointment" that the Galilean rabbi, who had been followed by disciples and crowds, who had spoken firmly and powerfully, could accept death without fighting back, without attempting some form of escape. They must have thought that there would be one last surprise, heavenly intervention from Elijah, the prophet of fire, the man of God who did not die. Jesus' life had to go on a little longer, as they could not rule out the possibility that, at the last minute, an extraordinary event might take place.

This idea must have led to one of those present (a soldier?) running to get a sponge, dipped in a vinegary red wine, that was kept in the trunk that the soldiers had brought up to Calvary, so as to quench his thirst. This was the so-called *oxos*, in Greek, or *posca*, in Latin, a strong drink that was very popular among the Roman soldiers and those who worked in the fields for its invigorating effect. They placed the damp sponge on a reed (Mark and Matthew) or hyssop (John); the hyssop was a plant that was about a meter long that grew among the stones (1 Kgs 5:13) and that could be found easily on Golgotha. In this case, it would have been cut and trimmed at the bottom to create a bunch strong enough to take the weight of the sponge dipped in vinegar. Finally, they held the sponge up to Jesus' lips and offered him the vinegary wine so that he could drink and live on a little longer. The intention behind this gesture is clear: "Let's see if Elijah can bring him down from the cross." It would have been a spectacular event to witness Elijah, at the last minute, come and save this man from death!

In the Gospel according to John, the incident of the sponge is not linked to the confusion regarding Eli/Elijah and is instead linked to the fulfilling of the Scriptures, in particular Psalm 22:15 ("my strength is dried up like a potsherd") and Psalm 69:21 ("for my thirst they gave me vinegar to drink"). Jesus (in this Gospel only) says, "I thirst," and the words of the Scriptures are fulfilled, as the Gospel itself states (John 19:28). Then, when he had drunk the vinegar, he solemnly stated that everything had been fulfilled. These are, according to the Gospel of John, his last words, confirming that Jesus has done exactly as God wanted him to. Jesus' mission was completed with his death.

The four canonical Gospels relate Jesus' death concisely and laconically. Mark (15:37) and Matthew (27:50) accompany it with a "loud cry" from Jesus, immediately after the seemingly unsuccessful attempt to give him the vinegar wine. John (19:30) also has his death come after this same incident, though he does explicitly say that Jesus drank the vinegar and said one last sentence before dying: "It is finished." Then, "he bowed his head and gave up his spirit." According to the Gospel of John, Jesus' bowing his head does not mean that he fell unconscious but that, in death, he addressed his followers who were below him, near the cross, giving them the Holy Spirit. As we have mentioned above, according to the Gospel of Luke, Jesus' last words were a prayer of trust in God: "Father, into thy hands I commit my spirit!" (Luke 23:46).

Jesus' death was a real, physical death that came after a long series of outrages, injuries, vexations, and torments, beginning with his arrest in Gethsemane on the Thursday night/Friday morning and culminating in his crucifixion on Golgotha, more than twelve hours later. The physical and psychological attacks came one after another, to the point where his humanity and dignity were left destroyed, as seen in the silence of the one who had always spoken to him, the Father, who was (and is) closely united to the Son. The relative speed of his suffering confirms the loss of the strength and life that he had undergone in the preceding hours. The sentencing of this innocent man fell like a shadow over the events as they took place. Finally, with his body and spirit destroyed by the hostility of man and the silence of God, Jesus died.

From a medical point of view, the exact cause of Jesus' death seems to be impossible to determine. Was the problem that the intercostal muscles could no longer function properly and his lungs filled with carbon dioxide leading to asphyxia? Did his circulation stop working and lead to hypovolemic shock? Was this shock the result of dehydration and the great loss of blood from the numerous wounds all over his body? The only thing we know for sure is that Jesus died as a result of the suffering on the cross to which he had been sentenced.

After his death

According to the Roman custom, the torture on the cross went on for hours, or even days. When the condemned died, the bodies were left to the mercy of the vultures and birds, who would eat the remains. Guards ensured that neither relatives nor friends came to take the bodies down from the crosses because one of the ignominies linked to death on the cross or by wild animals was that the bodies remained unburied. Tacitus wrote, "[T]he condemned, besides forfeiture of their property, were deprived burial" (*Annals* 6:29).

However, Jewish sensibilities did not tolerate the body of one who had been tried not to be buried on the day one died. The rule, and its justification, can be found in Deuteronomy 21:22-23: "[The] body [of someone executed] shall not remain all night upon the tree, but you shall bury him the same day." Josephus notes that "the Jews used to take so much care of the burial of men that they took down those that were sentenced and crucified, and buried them before the going down of the sun" (*J.W.* 4:317). If, moreover, the day after the crucifixion was a day of rest (a feast or the Sabbath), those crucified had to be taken down from the crosses; where necessary, their death had to be brought on so that they could be buried before the sun went down and the day of rest began. In the case of Jesus and the other two condemned men, that Friday was the day before the most important Jewish festival, Passover, and they had to die and be buried before the day came to an end.

This is the reason why, according to John 19:31, Pilate accepted the request from the Jewish authorities; he ordered his people to speed up deaths of the three crucified men and to bury them immediately. The usual system was to break the leg bones of those hanging from the cross, while still alive, so that their legs could no longer hold them, which meant that their body fell forward and they would die quickly of asphyxia. This was the so-called *crurifragium*, mentioned, among others, by Plautus (*Poenulus* 886), which was applied to the two men crucified with Jesus. It was not necessary for Jesus. It came as a surprise, especially to Pilate (Mark 15:44), that Jesus' suffering should end so quickly. When the soldiers went to break the legs of the three men on the crosses and arrived under Jesus' cross, they realized that he had already died. One of them, to make sure, speared him in the side, in an attempt to put him out of his misery. The hole made by the lance was so big that a hand could have passed through it (John 20:25); and out of it came "blood and water" (John 19:34).

By "water," we have to assume they meant some kind of bodily fluid that looked like a watery liquid (pleural or pericardial fluid?). The fact that "blood" came out of the wound made by the spear shows that Jesus had not been dead for very long (his body was still vertical and there were blood vessels where the blood had yet to coagulate). Unlike the other two men, whose bodies had leant forward after their legs had been broken, Jesus remained upright and rigid on the cross.

The incident of the spear is mentioned only in the Gospel according to John. In the synoptic Gospels, the intervention of the soldiers is limited to the words of the centurion, the official responsible for Jesus' execution, who talked like a Christian convinced, confessing his faith: "Truly this man was the Son of God" (Mark 15:39); or like an impartial and overawed observer, reporting on what had taken place: Jesus had the power of the Son of God (Matt 27:54); or like an enthusiastic witness, who gave glory to God and acknowledged the innocence of the condemned man and the injustice perpetrated (Luke 23:47).

Jesus' followers (friends and relatives) witnessed the events in silence from a certain distance; after his death they were desolate and left or remained, or they attempted to ensure that he was given a dignified burial. The day was coming to an end, and that year's Passover supper was about to begin. It is likely that this small group was reduced even further, leaving only a few people. Those who certainly went away from the scene were the curious and expectant, disappointed at not having seen Elijah come to save the Galilean rabbi. The Jewish leaders who had prompted Jesus' death did not want to become ritually impure by coming into contact with dead bodies, which would have prevented them from celebrating the Passover that night, and also would have left. Someone must have ensured that the two men crucified alongside Jesus were buried. It was Joseph of Arimathea who took care of Jesus' body. The squadron of soldiers, following orders, returned to the praetorium.

The Gospels of Mark and Matthew and the Gospel of Peter seek to bring meaning to this death in their narratives and refer to an extraordinary event that took place at the same time: the curtain hanging before the sanctuary in the temple was torn in two (this is also mentioned in Luke, who has the incident take place before Jesus' death). The forthcoming destruction of the temple was thus foreseen. This was a sign showing that it was no longer God's chosen place. The torn curtain meant that God had decided the fate of the temple. Josephus explains that the temple's destruction in 70 A.D. was preceded by similar miraculous events (*J.W.* 6:288–309). Jesus marked the start of a new covenant, in which the temple had been replaced by Jesus himself, the bridge between God and humanity.

The Gospel according to Matthew goes into more detail regarding this vision and mentions a series of miraculous cosmic events that took place when Jesus died (earthquakes, rocks splitting, tombs opening, the resurrection of the bodies that lay in them, and their appearance before people); in all, a great apocalyptic scene that showed that Jesus' death had, in a certain way, brought on the end of the world. Jesus' death is seen as a turning point in history; a new vision of the present and the future has taken center stage.

The Gospel according to John links Jesus' end to the sacrifice of the paschal lambs that takes place on the day before Passover. Jesus is presented as the new paschal lamb, who, in accordance with the Law, shall have no bone broken and shall die in an act of giving, giving life and giving himself completely to bring about a new covenant between God and man. This is how "he who saw it" refers to it; they can state that they have seen it *with their own eyes* and *bear witness to it*, concluding, "he knows that he tells the truth, that you may also believe" (John 19:35-37).

6.2.6. THE SEPULCHRE

The historical sources are the canonical Gospels of Mark (15:42-47), Matthew (27:57-66), Luke (23:50-56), and John (19:38-42) and the Gospel of Peter (21–24, 28–32, 34). The narratives in Mark and John follow a common, early structure, in which Joseph of Arimathea is the main protagonist and responsible for Jesus' burial. The most obvious difference between the two is that in Mark, and the other two synoptic Gospels (Matthew and Luke), some of the women present at the crucifixion, suffering, and death of Jesus are witnesses to his being brought down off the cross and his burial. However, in the Gospel of John, two men are involved in Jesus' burial (the aforementioned Joseph and Nicodemus), while no women are mentioned. The Gospel according to Matthew and the Gospel of Peter add the incident of the guard at the tomb, which the Jewish leaders demanded from Pilate the day after Jesus' death, as they wanted to avoid the possible robbery of Jesus' body by his disciples and the resulting masquerade to make people believe that he had been resurrected. Pilate accepted and ordered a detachment of Roman soldiers to watch over Jesus' tomb.

6.2.6.1. The Descent from the Cross

The body of someone sentenced to death was property of the Roman state, and its representatives could do with it as they pleased. Pilate was the only one able to authorize the burial of Jesus' body. As we have already said, Jewish Law required that the body of the executed be buried on the same day the executed died. It was intolerable for the body to remain on the cross and unburied. The land would have been desecrated: "you shall bury him [the unburied executed man] the same day, for a hanged man is accursed by God" (Deut 21:23). The governor respected Jewish Law regarding hanging and burial and accepted the request from Israel's authorities. Following the acceleration of their deaths, the three men crucified on Golgotha were taken down from their crosses and buried (John 19:31).

Who took charge of removing the nails and burying the two criminals crucified alongside Jesus? Were they non-Jewish executioners paid by the Roman administration or the very soldiers who had executed them? It is highly unlikely that it would have been pious Jews since coming into physical contact with a cadaver would have led to their becoming ritually unclean, which would have meant that they could not celebrate the Passover supper. It was more likely that the Roman administration provided an anonymous grave for the two men crucified with Jesus in one of the numerous caves in the rocks, which were easy to find in the vicinity as it had once been a quarry. Moreover, the area of Golgotha was over twenty-five meters from the walls of Jerusalem and sufficiently far away for burials to take place, in accordance with Jewish Law (Mishnah, *B. Bat.* 2:9).

It was Joseph of Arimathea who took responsibility for Jesus' burial. Without his intervention, Jesus may well have also ended up in a vertical, anonymous hole in the rocky ground around Golgotha, with his remains lost among those of other bodies, far from the family tomb in Nazareth. Instead, Joseph, a "nobleman" who belonged to Jerusalem's lay aristocracy, "a respected member of the council," and no doubt known to the governor, "took courage and went to Pilate, and asked for the body of Jesus" (Mark 15:43). Joseph was a sympathizer of Jesus, a secret sedentary disciple, who held a position of influence and maybe had not openly shown his devotion to the rabbi of Nazareth until this time (see 4.5.3.2). This Joseph seems to have been the head of a minority group in the Sanhedrin (many of whom were Pharisees) who opposed the sentencing of Jesus and lost out to the hostile majority (made up of the Sadducees) who had enjoyed the complicit silence of a good number of Pharisees (see 6.2.3.1).

During Jesus' trial, Joseph of Arimathea had remained at a certain distance from events, but now (once the death sentence handed down by Pilate had been carried out) he took a more active role. He may have been present at Golgotha before Jesus died to support the family members and friends present. It is clear that now with Jesus dead this nobleman from Arimathea, a member of Jerusalem's upper classes and one of the "nobles" on the Sanhedrin, acted as a guardian for the small number of frightened members of Jesus' family who had traveled to Jerusalem and who, together with some of his friends, were living through this terrible series of events.

Joseph of Arimathea's devotion to the man crucified, the man sentenced to death by the Roman authorities, goes beyond the duties of a pious Jew. First, if the information provided in Mark 15:43 is true, according to which he "went to" Pilate, he would have had to accept ritual impurity and thus not have been able to celebrate the Passover that night. John 19:38 simply says that he "asked Pilate that he might take away the body of Jesus [from the cross]." However, it would have been difficult for these delicate negotiations to have taken place outside Pilate's house, as he is unlikely to have met him outside the praetorium. However, we can assume that Joseph was a well-respected man with links to the governor, and Pilate may not have made him go against the Jewish Law.

Second, by asking for Jesus' body, Joseph would have been compromising his position before Pilate, showing himself to have links to the man who had been sentenced as a dangerous element for the empire. Joseph took the place of the members of Jesus' family, who should have been the ones to go to the governor to ask for the body of their relative (but with what chance of success?). Joseph also showed himself, publicly, to be linked to the man who had been accused of being a false prophet to the other members of the Sanhedrin. To an extent, Joseph was standing up to the decision taken by the Great Jewish Council, according to which Jesus was a blasphemer and wicked. He ensured that he got the dignified burial that a blasphemer did not deserve (as it states in the Mishnah, *Sanh.* 6:5-6).

Third, according to Mark 15:46 and John 19:38, Joseph took Jesus down from the cross personally. It seems that he carried out this complicated operation all on his own (!). The inevitable physical contact with Jesus' body would have made him ritually impure and meant that he could not have shared in the paschal supper.

Last, he buried Jesus in a tomb that, according to Matthew 27:60 and the Gospel of Peter 24, was his (!), and where, according to Matthew 27:60, Luke 23:53, and John 19:41, no one else had yet been buried. We have to conclude that this public act of personal dedication by Joseph of Arimathea can be understood only as the act of a convinced supporter or, as John (19:38) puts it, "a disciple of Jesus, but secretly."

Events were straightforward and took place quickly. According to Mark 15:43-44, Joseph of Arimathea went to find Pilate and asked for Jesus' body. A request of this kind would not have been unusual. We know from Philo of Alexandria (*Flacc.* 83) that, with the birth of a member of the imperial family, the families of men who had been crucified were allowed to give their relatives a decent burial. In Jesus' case, Joseph acted as one of Jesus' relatives and took the request to Pilate. The Roman governor was surprised that Jesus was already dead and called for the centurion, the person in charge of the execution, to make sure that this was the case. This means that, as soon as Jesus died, Joseph (who knew that there was not much time to bury him) went straight to the praetorium to get the necessary authorization for his burial.

He had to get moving because the day was coming to an end and, when three stars could be seen in the sky, the new day and Passover, a day of complete rest, would begin; Jesus had to be buried by this time. When Joseph went to get the authorization from Pilate, the latter had accepted the request from the Jewish authorities and had given orders for the death of those on the cross to be sped up before sunset by breaking their legs, so that they could be buried that same day (John 19:31, 19:38). According to Mark 15:44-45, Pilate authorized Joseph's request only once he had found out from the centurion that Jesus was definitely dead.

With this authorization granted, Joseph of Arimathea returned to Golgotha with a new linen shroud that he "had bought" (it does not say when; Mark 15:46). Meanwhile, Jesus, now dead, had been speared in the side, his final wound and no doubt the largest. Taking out the nails and bringing the body down from the cross could not have been easy for one man alone. It is likely that Joseph (a well-to-do nobleman) brought some servants and the tools necessary from his home with him, though he took an active part in the operation. Mark (15:46), echoed by Matthew (27:59), Luke (23:53), and John (19:38), portrays Joseph as the person directly responsible for taking Jesus down from the cross. According to John 19:39, Nicodemus (another influential figure from the Pharisee group and also a sympathizer of the Master's) was also there at Golgotha with one hundred pounds of aromatic spices. Nicodemus seems to have taken part with Joseph of Arimathea in Jesus' descent from the cross.

However, there is no mention of the active participation of the women present, among whom, according to John 19:25, was Jesus' mother, neither in the descent from the cross nor in his burial. According to Mark 15:47, they only "saw," closely watched what was happening. Jesus' dead body was the center of their attention and compassion. We do not know if these were the same women who had formed the group at Golgotha from the time Jesus arrived there to be crucified or whether these women had already returned home. The apparent inactivity of the women has to be the result of two factors. First, everything had to take place so quickly, as time was running out: Jesus had to be taken down from the cross and buried soon, as the day was coming to an end. There was no time for anything else. Second, Jesus had died crucified, and anyone hanging from a cross is, according to Jewish Law, "accursed by God." For this reason, there would have been a mixture of deep sorrow and dreadful shame for what had happened. Their cries and laments would have been drowned out by the scale of his terrible death, leaving room for only tenderness and silence.

6.2.6.2. The Burial

A body could not be buried on the Sabbath or on a feast day, which were days of rest, and could be washed and anointed on one of these days only if no part of the body was moved. This is what it says in the Mishnah (*Šabb.* 23:5). The two operations carried out with Jesus' lifeless body following Pilate's authorizing Joseph of Arimathea to bury him (his being taken down from the cross and buried) had to take place in a short space of time: a little over an hour. They worked hastily and avoided any possible complications. The distance between Golgotha and the tomb was short: some fifty meters as the crow flies, though there was the slope down from the hill where the executions had taken place to the flat plain where people were buried. Even today, despite the destruction and conflict throughout history, one can still see in Jerusalem, in the so-called Anastasia (Resurrection) basilica or Church of the Holy Sepulchre, the original location of Golgotha or Calvary and the tomb where Jesus was buried.

As soon as Joseph of Arimathea and those who helped him (probably servants under his orders, and Nicodemus) had got Jesus down from the cross, his rigid body was placed on the shroud that he had bought, probably held by the few women present, among whom was his mother. This "shroud" is mentioned in the Gospels as a piece of linen used to cover Jesus' body (Mark 15:46; Matt 27:59; Luke 23:53; John 19:40; Gospel of Peter 24). The use of a shroud to wrap a body was common practice in Jewish funerals.

This shroud was probably a piece of linen in the form of a long towel that could be wrapped round the body completely, in front and behind, and which covered it entirely. It was nothing like the strips of cloth, which resembled bandages, that were wrapped round the body and hands and feet (John 11:44) and used for mummification. The Turin Shroud, which many people view to be a venerable relic worthy of consideration (covered in pollen grain from the first century and with a positive print of the unsettling face of a man who had been whipped and crucified) and which others dismiss out of hand (the carbon-14 testing, which few call into doubt, dates the material to the medieval era), is 4.36 meters long and 1.11 meters wide.

Wrapped or shrouded in the linen cloth, Jesus' body could have been taken down the hill of Golgotha to the tomb, located in one of the gardens in the area (the Gospel of Peter 24 calls it the "Garden of Joseph"). The distance that they traveled was so short that a stretcher was not necessary. They would have moved his body between a few people, taking his weight in their arms. Nonetheless, before wrapping the front of his body in the shroud, they had tied "a napkin" round his head to keep his jawbone in place, so that his mouth would remain closed (John 20:7, 11:44).

Everything leads us to believe that Jesus' body reached the entrance to the tomb without having been washed or anointed (the Gospel of Peter 24 notes this "irregularity"). The main reason for this is the lack of time to carry out these two basic preparations of the dead man's body before his burial, especially its being washed. The washing of the body, which included closing all the body's orifices and, on occasion, anointing it with aromatic oils, was a fundamental part of Jewish funerals. It was normally a somewhat laborious operation, but it was carried out for all those who passed away. This can be seen from the text in the Mishnah mentioned above and a text from the Acts of the Apostles (9:37), which talks about the recently deceased Tabitha, who was "washed" as soon as she died.

Jesus' case was different. Washing his body would have been an intricate and time-consuming operation, given the great number of wounds and scratches, splinters and thorns covering his body, as a result of the taunts, whipping, and crucifixion. Lacking time and means, and with a death stigmatized by the Law itself (someone crucified is deemed "accursed by God"), they simply buried him.

Jesus was placed in a tomb "hewn out of the rock," as the Gospels state, while the Gospel of John is even more specific, saying that it was located "in the garden" where he had been crucified. These two reports complement each other and place the tomb in the site of the former quarry to the northwest of Jerusalem, which had been partially filled in with earth and made into an area with gardens, beyond the city walls. As Matthew 27:60 and the Gospel of Peter (24) state, one of these gardens, with a tomb for his family, may have belonged to Joseph of Arimathea. The Gospels specify that it was "a new tomb" (Matthew and John), "where no one had ever been laid" (Luke and John). What must Jesus' tomb have been like?

There were two basic types of tombs for Jews living in first-century Israel: those with a vertical opening, used for one person, with a stone or slab to cover the hole (John 11:38), and those with a horizontal opening, which would have led on to one or more chambers, to the side or behind walls, and which would have been used to bury a number of people (in vaults or *loculi*, niches, or even sarcophagi). This second type of tomb was for families or groups and was closed with a stone that was rolled over to seal the entrance completely. With regard to Jesus' tomb, all the Gospels refer to a "stone" that was "rolled" into place, and there is no doubt as to the type of tomb he was buried in. Mark (16:4) and Matthew (27:60) specify, respectively, that the stone at the entrance "was very large"/"a great stone," to the extent that once rolled across it was possible to sit on it (Matt 28:2).

Nonetheless, the great size of the stone does not necessarily mean that the entrance to the tomb was monumental. Other group tombs in Jerusalem from around the same time as Jesus (such as the so-called "Tombs of the Kings" and the "Sanhedrin Tombs," which were also located in former quarries) lead us to think that the entrance was not more than a meter tall. From outside the tomb, one would have had to bend over to see in (Luke 24:12; John 20:5, 20:11; Gospel of Peter 55). The fact that the stone was big and heavy would have made it difficult to open the tomb; this was aimed at dissuading those who might want to desecrate it.

A second element confirms the above conclusion as to the type of tomb that Jesus was buried in: the fact that it could be entered, as stated by Mark (16:5), Luke (23:3), John (20:4-8), and the Gospel of Peter (54). These Gospels place a number of people and other figures resembling humans in the tomb: three women with aromatic oils and a young man dressed in white waiting for them (Mark); some women with aromatic oils and two men in dazzling robes (Luke); two disciples, Peter and the disciple whom he loved, probably John, and two angels dressed in white robes who talk to Mary Magdalene, who was outside (John); two heavenly figures and, later, a young man in bright clothes (Gospel of Peter).

Obviously, the door gave access to a chamber that was reasonably big, high enough to stand up in and spacious enough for the people who had to bury the deceased to move in. It is likely that the floor of this chamber was lower than outside. Since it was a recently built tomb and hence unused, we should assume that it would have had only the one burial chamber (tombs could be expanded with tunnels and other chambers as required). This chamber was visible from outside the tomb, as long as the stone was not blocking the entrance—though, as we have said, one needed to bend down to see in.

As soon as the group with Jesus' body entered the tomb, the body was placed on a stone bench inside on the right (this detail is provided by Mark 16:5), which probably touched the side wall. John 20:12 also assumes that there was a stone or earth bench in the tomb. This bench probably measured up to two meters long and sixty centimeters wide and was built to support ossuaries, the stone urns used to hold the bones of the deceased once their bodies had decomposed (see the start of 2.1). Possibly, rather than a bench, it was a niche, at the foot of which, around a meter from the ground, there may have been a flat surface or plinth to support the body of the deceased. Nonetheless, the first option would seem to be preferable, given the information provided by John 20:12: "[Mary Magdalene, from outside the tomb] saw two angels in white, sitting where the body of Jesus had lain, one at the head and one at the feet."

Jesus was wrapped in a shroud "with the spices" that Nicodemus had brought (John 19:40). R. E. Brown points out that Nicodemus' blend of myrrh and aloe consisted of powder and solid particles, which made a soft mixture that was placed where the body was to be laid to rest and may have been sprinkled over it, that is, over the shroud in which he was wrapped. Brown also cites the burial of Asa, king of Judaea: "they laid him on a bier which had been filled with various kinds of spices" (2 Chr 16:14).

The myrrh and aloe, two precious aromatic substances, were designed to lessen the effects of the smell of the body and stop its decomposition. However, they could not be applied directly to a body that was covered with wounds as was Jesus', which had not been washed either; the results would have been disastrous. At no time does the Gospel according to John state that the items brought by Nicodemus were used to anoint Jesus' body. He simply states that "they took the body of Jesus, and bound it in linen cloths with spices" (John 19:40). These spices, "accompanied" the body; they were not a part of it. With a certain level of exaggeration, the Gospel according to John offers a round and solemn number, a quantity fit for a king: one hundred pounds, or some thirty kilograms, of spices! We can assume that a reasonable amount of aromatic spices, specifically myrrh and aloe, would have been used to create a kind of bed on which Jesus was placed.

The funeral formalities were dealt with quickly. Time was running out and the Passover festivities were about to begin. Joseph of Arimathea, the owner of the tomb, was the man responsible for rolling the great stone door into place, with the help of the other men present (Nicodemus and the servants). The stone sealed the opening to the tomb, which may have been cut from the rock wall. They all left with just enough time to get home, within Jerusalem's city walls, as the Sabbath was beginning, and they had to respect the rest prescribed by the Law.

Jesus was not buried as a criminal, in a dishonorable manner, though his funeral did involve a blend of tenderness and inconvenience. Everything that had happened had been highly significant, and his death had inspired conflicting feelings, because of both the injustice (his was the death of an innocent man) and disbelief (God had not "done" anything to stop it happening). Everything now seemed over, but people's feeling of friendship for Jesus had not disappeared. Joseph of Arimathea placed his body in the tomb that belonged to his own family, a tomb that was new and unused, rather than an anonymous mass grave. Similarly, Nicodemus sprinkled the Master's body with a great amount of aromatic spices as a sign of dignity and acknowledgment. The women were seen, for the moment, to be less active. Their time, however, would come, following the Sabbath rest. Then, they took the brave personal initiative to return to the tomb to wash and anoint the dead body of the one they loved. It is true that Nicodemus had already taken care to dignify Jesus' body, shrouding it and placing it on a bed of aromatic spices, but these women wanted to ensure the greatest levels of dignity possible for this man who had had to suffer so and die on the cross; they decided to wash his body and anoint it with aromatic oils. However, their desires would not be possible following a dramatic and unexpected turn of events: the disappearance of Jesus' body from the tomb.

6.3. The Resurrection

The biographical profile of a figure normally ends with his or her death, the definitive end to his or her life. There would then come the summing up and epilogues. In the case of Jesus of Nazareth, however, before the epilogue we need to look at a unique event that has inspired all sorts of different reactions, from skepticism to devotion, from curiosity to conviction, from doubt to faith. This event is his resurrection. We see that Jesus passed from life to death by means of crucifixion, but immediately after this he took another step in the opposite direction, an unforeseen and unforeseeable step: the step from death to life, a new and completely different life, which embraced the present and the future, heaven and earth, God and man, the present world and the world to come. For this reason, Christianity sees Jesus as "the living," and not just "the one who lived": he represents the start of the new world. Christian faith focuses on a Jesus who has passed over the threshold of death and places this statement above all others: "God raised [him] from the dead." Right from the start, it was clear that there would be no Christianity without the resurrection of Christ.

Bearing this in mind, it would seem that the resurrection is simply a question of faith and that it should not be included in a book such as this, which does not necessarily assume that its readers have any given religious convictions. Nevertheless, if we opted to leave this subject out or consign it to an epilogue, we could not do justice to the figure to whom this book is dedicated and we would have to ignore a section of the historical sources that relate his life story. These sources state, directly or indirectly, that Jesus' body disappeared from the tomb that he had been buried in and that he was seen, in person and on a number of different occasions, by a significant number of disciples and followers, who spoke to him and even touched him. As a result, we need to present these historical materials and assess what they say and mean. In other words, we need to evaluate the historical impact of an event that cannot be proven but that constitutes a unique and defining moment for the figure we are looking at. What is there from the start of the earliest Christian tradition that states that Jesus was resurrected? What is meant by the fact that some people "saw" him alive following his death? What does "resurrect" mean? Metaphorically speaking, how can we trace the rays of sunshine back to the sun itself?

Up to this point, this book has sought to offer an outline of Jesus' message and life, based on a historical method, attempting to reconstruct the facts, connecting them and interpreting the meaning. The best example of this was the last twenty-four hours of his life: his Passion and death. Here, the historical sources allow us to closely follow the events of the last day in Jesus' life. Now, once the stone is rolled over, sealing the opening to the tomb, these sources seem to turn into a handful of ashes that offer little help in shedding light on an event that is difficult to explain, an event that cannot be pinned down with evidence and demonstrations but which, despite all this, is forcefully and powerfully here.

The information concerning Jesus' resurrection is not harmonious or clear-cut; rather, it appears like flashes of light that make the invisible visible for a moment before burning out, which reflects an air of authenticity from the outset. Indeed, a made-up story would have to avoid gaps and seek to find the greatest levels of coherence to be believable. In our case, the narratives and references to the resurrection agree on certain basic elements but refuse to come together as a consistent whole; instead, they display a surprising and attractive diversity. We have to conclude that the Christian tradition, an organic entity, has brought together references from personal and collective memories, while maintaining (rather than hiding) the rough edges and grey areas.

6.3.1. Jesus and His Future

If, as we saw in 6.1, Jesus took up a stand and position before his death, we need to ask ourselves how he prepared himself for the future after his death. First, it should be pointed out that Jesus (like most of the Jews from the time) was convinced that his death was not the last word on his person and that, at the end of time, there would be a general resurrection affecting everyone, without exception. In his own words, he said, "[T]hey neither marry nor are given in marriage, but are like angels in heaven." For Jesus, it is an unquestionable fact that "the dead are raised." This can be seen in what he said to the Sadducees, who denied that there was to be a general resurrection at the end of time. The reason given by Jesus is clear: "He is not God of the dead, but of the living" (Mark 12:25-27) (see 3.3.2.3).

Jesus' belief (and in this instance also that of the Pharisees) in resurrection was firm. Jesus shared fully in one of the main prongs of Jewish hopes at the time, and it was embodied in his teachings and practice: the end of days included the reuniting of all the chosen ones. This was to be the event prior to the judgment that was to assess the good and the bad that each had done.

Nonetheless, Jesus' resurrection did not mean that everyone was resurrected, nor did it represent the end of the world. His resurrection is presented as a unique and personal experience, in anticipation of humanity's final destiny. In this way, the documents in the New Testament state that there is a link between what happened before and after his death, stressing the identity connecting Christ crucified and Christ resurrected. Jesus had lived through God, the Father; he had been linked to him closely and intimately. Jesus, the messenger for the Kingdom, had spoken directly about the things of God as if they were his own, and he had done so authoritatively and by getting to the root of the commandments of the Law. He had been God's plenipotentiary emissary, endowed with a power to heal and console. He had seen himself as the bearer of a message: to announce the coming of the Kingdom, to make real the compassionate God and the Father of all. He made trust in God his own, as seen in his cries of abandonment moments before his death. Jesus had lived his position as the Son completely, expressing it (and herein lies his secret) indirectly, allusively.

If we look at his project as a whole, it makes sense that he, sent to liberate people and able to liberate them from so many different types of slavery, also be liberated from the strongest bond, from the bond of death. Did Jesus actually experience this hope? Jesus lived in the hope that God would complete the coming of the Kingdom that had begun to emerge in the world. The supreme gift of life had to be a possibility for he who "is good" and he alone! In Jesus' own words, "all things are possible with God" (Mark 10:27), or, in the words of the Baptist, God could make a son of Abraham come from a cold, hard stone (Matt 3:9 || Luke 3:8). Jesus could not stop trusting in God, he who creates and recreates life.

The certainty arising from his absolute trust in God, together with the anxiety as he faced an imminent death while the Father remained silent, accompanied Jesus during the last hours of his life. At the Last Supper, Jesus had said farewell to his disciples (who were overcome by events) and had stated that the next time that they were to sit down together would be at the banquet in the Kingdom. For him, the future remained open. Death was not the end of hope (see 6.1.3.3). And while this Kingdom did not manifest itself wholly, Jesus would not leave his disciples without salvation and company: the sign of breaking the bread and sharing the wine among them was a sign of the "new covenant."

From then on, Jesus became something more than just a messenger: he became the means, as God's salvation came through his very person, given as an offering. For Christian theology, the Eucharist (the sacrament of the bread and the wine) became the sacrament of the Kingdom. Jesus' presence, beyond death, was the guarantee that God would continue at humanity's side. Moreover, this presence was not in death but in life, thanks to the resurrection of Christ crucified. If the symbol of the bread and the wine (giving his own life) was a projection into the future for the disciples, then the underlying reality could not end in death. The gestures and words used at the Last Supper showed a certainty and conviction regarding a future that only God controlled.

Of course, there was a sense of suffering underlying the Passion, suffering he had to undergo as a result of injustice, but which he had freely accepted. Jesus' silence before Pilate was highly significant, a silence that left the governor completely surprised: why does he not want to defend himself from the accusations made? Faced with stubborn adversaries who wanted him to be sentenced and a judge who was willing to allow strategy to defeat truth, Jesus had only one way out: to accept death trusting in the God of life.

Faced with this injustice, it is only to be expected that someone like him, who had lived close to the Father, invoked some prayers from the Psalms: "Many are the afflictions of the righteous; but the Lord delivers him out of them all. He keeps all his bones; not one of them is broken" (Ps 34:19-20); or, "He [God] raises the poor from the dust, and lifts the needy from the ash heap, to make them sit with princes, with the princes of his people" (Ps 113:7-8); or even, "[You, O God,] thou dost not give me up to Sheol [the grave], or let thy godly one see the Pit" (Ps 16:10). Trust in God did not save him, however, from the pain of the silence that was the response to the intense, painful cry that he let out on the cross: "My God, my God, why hast thou forsaken me?" (Ps 22:2). This cry was a call to a God who was present and absent, he who, in the words of the canticle of Anna, an ancient piece from the tradition of Israel, "kills and brings to life, he brings down to *Sheol* and raises up" (1 Sam 2:6).

During the Passion, Jesus looked deeply into his future, beyond the hostility of his adversaries and the abandonment of the disciples, beyond the agony of death and the silence of the Father; he looked on it as a new leaf, on which God would write whatever he wanted to write. This present, made up of suffering and death, made sense thanks to God: Jesus was the instrument for his salvation. The future was not to be a senseless pit; God was to speak, not when Jesus was on the cross but when he had passed over the boundary into death. Then, the Son would be vindicated, and his identity and role at God's side made clear. What Caiaphas understood to be blasphemy (his description of himself as the heavenly Son of Man) would be seen to be the definitive truth about his identity. As B. Holmberg indicates, Jesus' resurrection confirmed his "restored communication" with the Father, who raised him from the dead.

6.3.2. Jesus' Body Missing from the Tomb

The first thing that provoked disbelief and shock in the witnesses was the disappearance of Jesus' body from the tomb. The tomb was discovered empty with Jesus' body missing on the Sunday, the first day of the week in the Jewish (and Christian) calendar, first thing in the morning. It was the third day since Jesus' death (if we include the Friday). The texts that refer to the discovery of the empty tomb are to be found in the canonical Gospels of Mark (16:1-8), Matthew (28:1-8),

Luke (24:1-12), and John (20:1-10) as well as in the Gospel of Peter (50–54, 55–57).

All these texts agree on the following basic pattern. As the new day broke, some women followers of the Master, led by Mary Magdalene, arrived in the garden with the tomb where he had been buried. They realized that the stone at the entrance had been rolled away. The tomb was open. According to the synoptic Gospels and the Gospel of Peter, a heavenly figure told them, "He has risen, he is not here" (Mark 16:6; Matt 28:6; Gospel of Peter 56; Luke 24:6, where there are two heavenly messengers). The women ran to tell the disciples what had happened. Some of these, such as Peter and the disciple whom Jesus loved, returned to the tomb to check that Jesus' body was really not there.

Nonetheless, an empty tomb does not prove anything on its own. Many things could have happened: someone might have stolen the body that had been buried there, someone might have moved it to another tomb, or the deceased may not actually have died, and found his own way out of this place where they had left him. These three possibilities were all defended by various rationalist scholars in the second half of the eighteenth century (especially H. S. Reimarus and H. E. G. Paulus). In fact, those who denied Jesus' resurrection had already put forward similar ideas in the first century A.D.

The hypothesis of the theft of the body by the disciples (who would have wanted to make people believe that he had in fact been resurrected) is attributed to the Jewish leaders in the Gospel of Matthew. The high priests had spread "this story among the Jews to this day" (Matt 28:15). It is, however, a misrepresentation. According to this Gospel (only), Pilate had posted Roman soldiers to guard the tomb, to satisfy the demands of the Jewish leaders and to ensure that the disciples could not steal Jesus' body; but a powerful angel had come down from heaven and rolled the stone away, provoking terror among the soldiers (who "trembled and became like dead men"; Matt 28:4). Once they had recovered from the shock, the soldiers returned to Jerusalem to tell the Jewish leaders what had happened, who then bribed them to spread the rumor that it had been Jesus' disciples who had come at night to steal the body "while we were asleep" (Matt 28:13).

The words that the Gospel of John attributes to Mary Magdalene on Easter morning seem to echo through the hypothesis of the body being taken and moved (which would have led people to believe that he had been resurrected). As soon as she realized that the stone sealing the tomb had been moved, she told Peter and the disciple whom Jesus loved, "They have taken the Lord out of the tomb, and we do not know where they have laid him"(John 20:2). She later repeated similar words, addressed this time to the two angels who appeared in the tomb: "[T]hey have taken away my Lord, and I do not know where they have laid him" (John 20:13). Mary Magdalene insists for a third time, and this time before Jesus himself (!), whom she confused for the gardener: "if you have carried him away, tell me where you have laid him, and I will take him away" (John 20:15).

The third hypothesis, that Jesus did not really die, is too fantastical to merit consideration: all the historical sources on Jesus (whether Christian or non-Christian) assert that Jesus' crucifixion culminated, as to be expected by the sentence handed down by Pilate, in his death on the cross.

A tomb is, as Euripides (*Alcestis* 363–67) said, the house of the dead, and there is no reason for it to be emptied. However, if it appears empty, nothing is proven, but, as they say in French, *ceci donne à penser*, it gives us something to think about, even more so if the circumstances in which the discovery is made are like those seen in Jesus' case. The discovery was made and first witnessed by four women. This is a surprising fact since Jewish customs stated that the testimony of a woman was not valid. It is also surprising that the sources concerning the empty tomb place Mary Magdalene in such an important position, as the leader of a group of women going to the tomb. Mary ran to tell the news to the disciples on behalf of all of those who had witnessed this turn of events: "They have taken the Lord out of the tomb, and we [plural!] do not know where they have laid him" (John 20:2) are Mary's words to Peter and John. Obviously, the other women went to tell the other male disciples what had taken place (Matt 28:8; Luke 24:9-11, 24:22-23). The place of honor, however, is reserved for the female disciple who followed Jesus most fervently.

Alongside Mary Magdalene, we also need to mention another Mary, mother of James, one of the Twelve, and Joseph and wife of Alphaeus, who was with her when the tomb was found empty. The Gospel of Mark also mentions Salome, who was probably the wife of Zebedee and mother of James and John, two further members of the

Twelve. The Gospel of Luke adds Joanna to this group, the wife of Chuza, a steward of Herod Antipas and a man of high standing. This group of (three?) women went to the tomb with jars full of aromatic oils, as their intention was to wash and anoint Jesus' body. The haste of the burial and, above all, the fact that Jesus had died as a man "accursed," on a cross, had meant they could not act earlier. They had not even been able to lament his death and mourn for him as custom dictated.

Joseph of Arimathea brought the shroud and provided a tomb to bury Jesus in; Nicodemus covered Jesus' body with a blend of myrrh and aloe, placed the blend under him, and sprinkled him with it instead of the careful anointing that time had not permitted. The men had dignified a burial carried out in somewhat dramatic circumstances. Nonetheless, these two sympathizers of Jesus, influential people and possibly secret disciples, had completed their tasks. So the anointing of the body with aromatic oils, which some women had decided to carry out when dawn broke that Sunday, lighting up the inside of the tomb, was a personal and courageous initiative on the part of these female disciples, and an idea that did not involve any of their male counterparts. The women ignored the "religious" considerations relating to the death of an "accursed" man and ignored the fear of any possible reprisal if they were found in the burial chamber. They were simply moved by the strong link of friendship that they maintained with Jesus, even after his death. They headed to the tomb with their aromatic oils and one thing on their minds, which was perfectly logical given the spontaneous and solitary nature of their decision: how were they going to move the great stone at the entrance to the tomb? (Mark 16:3). Their concerns would soon disappear, to be replaced by shock, fear, and astonishment.

We have said above that an empty tomb is not proof of a mystical event. In the Gospel of John, two disciples, Peter and the disciple whom Jesus loved, entered the tomb to see whether Jesus' body was there, and all they found was the shroud that had covered him and the napkin that had been tied around his head. Both of them saw the same things, but only the latter correctly interpreted what had happened: Jesus had been raised from the dead. The Gospel of Luke states that Peter "went home marveling at what had happened" (Luke 24:12). Furthermore, in the synoptic Gospels the events are interpreted by a heavenly figure ("a young man . . . dressed in white robe" in Mark; "an angel of the Lord" in Matthew; "two men . . . in dazzling apparel" in Luke). These are two ways of interpreting the same event, in the Gospel of John and the synoptic Gospels, respectively. There was the internal way (faith inspired divinely in the heart of the disciple whom Jesus loved, who sees and believes) and an external way (the message is communicated by a heavenly figure, sent and authorized by God).

Thus, the empty tomb did not prove anything on its own. There had to be an interpretation, the meaning had to be understood. The resurrection of Jesus was not self-evident, but it was a certainty that one had to see for oneself. Finding that Jesus' body was not in the tomb did not answer any questions; instead, it simply raised others: where was this man, who should be buried here, and for whom were the women looking? The interpreting angel pointed the way: Jesus was to show himself to the disciples, and they would see him for themselves.

6.3.3. Jesus Shows Himself to the Disciples

A few years after the discovery of Jesus' empty tomb, the early Christians had produced and handed down a text that could be called "the Gospel of the resurrection." Paul reproduced it in the First Epistle to the Corinthians (15:3-5): "Christ died for our sins in accordance with the scriptures, . . . he was buried, . . . he was raised on the third day in accordance with the scriptures, and . . . he appeared to Cephas [i.e., Peter], then to the Twelve." This brief text contains the two traditions that make up the Christian Easter: the empty tomb ("he was buried") and the manifestations or appearances of the resurrected Jesus before some of his disciples ("he appeared"). We have seen the first tradition. We now look at the second.

6.3.3.1. The Appearances

The documentary sources that tell of the appearances of the resurrected Jesus are the four canonical Gospels: Mark (16:7, 16:9-19), Matthew (28:8-10, 28:16-20), Luke (24:13-35, 24:36-49), and John

(20:11-18, 20:19-29, 21:1-23). We also need to include the Acts of the Apostles (1:3-8) and the First Epistle to the Corinthians (15:5-8), which also refers to an "untimely" appearance, which was witnessed by the Apostle Paul himself. All the other appearances, those in a "timely" fashion, seemingly took place during the first days, weeks, or months after Easter Sunday, the date of the first appearance, and are those that we look at here.

On the next page is a table of Jesus' twelve appearances referred to in the New Testament (apart from Paul's, as we have said).

This detailed table shows the great variety of narratives, in terms of both witnesses and the places where Jesus is said to have made his appearances. It seems that each source has had access to a segment of the tradition and has passed it down as accurately as possible. Obviously, it is very difficult to trace a line that links these details and that allows us to reconstruct the historical sequence of events.

The people to whom Jesus presented himself after the resurrection were, first, women. As we have seen above, they were also responsible for finding the tomb empty. As G. Theissen points out, the lists of women related to Jesus' death and resurrection are almost always headed by Mary Magdalene (though John 19:25 does mention Jesus' mother first). This place of honor may have been due to the fact that Mary Magdalene was the first person to whom the resurrected Jesus appeared by the tomb itself (see row 1 of the table). It is understandable that Peter, the leader of the Twelve (who had denied knowing the Master during the Passion), should be the first of the male disciples to whom Jesus would want to appear (see rows 3 and 8). Subsequently, Peter would have the chance to make up for his triple denial with a triple declaration of unconditional devotion to Jesus (see row 9).

The appearances that took place in Jerusalem on Easter Sunday and that involved a woman and a man, Mary Magdalene and Peter, were accompanied by two further incidents. First, Jesus came across the small group of women (two? three? more than three?) who, still early in the morning, were returning, joyously, from the tomb to tell the disciples that he had been raised from the dead (see row 2). Second, in the afternoon, Jesus encountered two male disciples, who were leaving Jerusalem and heading to the village of Emmaus, sad and disheartened because of the death/failure of their Master (see row 4). We should note that Cleopas was, probably, a relative of Jesus (his uncle)

	Witnesses	*Time*	*Location*	*Sources*
1	Mary Magdalene, the female disciple	Easter Sunday (morning)	Jerusalem (by the tomb)	John 20:11-18 (narrative); Mark 16:9-11 (mention)
2	Two women disciples (Mary Magdalene and Mary, wife of Alphaeus, mother of James and Joseph)	Easter Sunday (morning)	Jerusalem (by the tomb)	Matt 28:8-10 (narrative)
3	Peter, the leader of the Twelve	Easter Sunday	Jerusalem (unnamed place)	Luke 24:34; 1 Cor 15:5 (mention)
4	Two disciples (Cleopas and another)	Easter Sunday (afternoon)	Between Jerusalem and Emmaus	Luke 24:13-35 (narrative); Mark 16:12-13 (mention)
5	The Eleven (and other disciples, except Thomas)	Easter Sunday (evening)	Jerusalem (house)	John 20:19-23; Luke 24:36-49 (narratives); 1 Cor 15:5 (mentions the Twelve)
6	The Eleven (and other disciples, with Thomas)	Sunday after Easter	Jerusalem (house)	John 20:26-29 (narrative)
7	The Eleven	For forty days (?) after Easter	Jerusalem (unnamed place)	Acts 1:3 (mention)
		Fortieth day after Easter	Jerusalem (Mount of Olives)	Acts 1:4-11; Mark 16:14-19 (narratives)
8	The Eleven (especially Peter)		Galilee (mountain)	Mark 16:7 (mention); Matt 28:16-20 (narrative)
9	Seven disciples (of the Eleven?): Peter, Thomas, Nathanael, James, John, and two others		Galilee (Lake Galilee)	John 21:1-23 (narrative)
10	Five hundred disciples (men and women?)		Jerusalem (unnamed place)	1 Cor 15:6 (mention)
11	James, Jesus' brother		Jerusalem (unnamed place)	1 Cor 15:7 (mention)
12	All the apostles		Jerusalem (unnamed place)	1 Cor 15:7 (mention)

and that among the women who had come to Jerusalem from Galilee there was his mother and two aunts (a paternal aunt, Cleopas' wife, and a maternal aunt). The fifth appearance on Easter Sunday also took place in Jerusalem, in the evening, and involved the Eleven (except Thomas) and, according to Luke, other disciples. The disciples were together in a house, traditionally identified as the cenacle or the upper room where Jesus had organized his farewell supper. The disciples' feelings ranged from shock (Luke) to happiness (John). Jesus greeted them ("Peace be with you") and talked to them about their mission (to communicate the gospel) and the gift that was to sustain them (the Holy Spirit) (see row 5).

Thus, five of the twelve appearances took place on the day that the women found his tomb empty: Easter Sunday. The other seven took place at different, often unspecified, times and places. Two appearances took place in Jerusalem itself, at the house where the disciples had come together: the first, eight days after Easter, and the second, forty days after. Both involved the Eleven, and possibly other disciples. On the first occasion, Jesus insisted on showing Thomas, the doubting disciple, the wounds left by the nails in his hands and the spear in his side (see row 6). On the second occasion, Jesus ate with the Eleven and again entrusted them with the mission of communicating the gospel around the world and promising them the gift of the Holy Spirit. This second appearance took place at the end of the period of forty days (marked, according to Acts 1:3, by Jesus coming into repeated contact with his disciples) that culminated in Jesus' ascension to heaven (see row 7).

Two further appearances, on an unspecified date, took place in Galilee, and not Jerusalem as had been the case until then. The first was on a mountaintop and involved the Eleven. The disciples were sent to preach and baptize around the world, and Jesus assured them that he would never abandon them (see row 8). The similarities with the events in row 7 are obvious. The second appearance took place on the shore of Lake Galilee and coincided with an amazing event, the miraculous catch of fish. Jesus showed himself to seven disciples, who belonged to the group of Eleven, if we are to judge from the names given. Jesus ate with these seven on the beach and, then, offered Peter the chance to make up for his triple denial with a triple affirmation of his love for him. Mention is also made of the destiny of the disciple whom Jesus loved (see row 9). It is said of this appearance that "this was now the third time that Jesus was revealed to the disciples after he was raised from the dead" (John 21:14). The first two times are detailed in rows 5 and 6.

There were three further appearances, and we do not know when or where they took place. We know only from the Apostle Paul, who mentions them in the First Epistle to the Corinthians, that the audience was one person (James, Jesus' brother) and two other much more numerous groups (the five hundred and all the apostles). According to Paul, these three personal appearances by the resurrected Jesus took place some time after his appearances to Peter and the Twelve (the Eleven). According to the order provided by Paul, the witnesses were, first, a large group of people, the five hundred (probably, men and women), all of them Christians and most of them still alive in 55 A.D. (the date of Paul's First Epistle to the Corinthians) and able to corroborate what they had seen. Twenty-five years had passed, and only a few of them had died; this means that the average age of these disciples, when Jesus appeared to them, must have been relatively young (see row 10).

The other numerous group that Paul makes reference to comprises "all the apostles," those people who, at the start of Christianity, had been sent out as missionaries (the word "apostle" comes from the verb "to send forth") to spread the gospel (see row 12). The only individual figure is James, Jesus' elder brother, who had acted in Nazareth as the head of the family on the death of Joseph, Jesus' legal father. Subsequently, James became head of the Christian community in Jerusalem and a very influential figure in the early days of Christianity (see 4.3.4.1). The fact that Jesus appeared to him legitimized his position as a unique witness and put him on a level, to a certain extent, with the select group of Twelve (see row 11).

6.3.3.2. Relations between Jesus and the Disciples after Easter

Jesus appeared twelve times to all of the most important people and in the areas where he had been most active and where the early Christian community that had arisen following his death. His appearances were all selective, none of them were indiscriminate, and they affected the inner circles of his closest followers, his disciples, both men and women. The group that benefited most from his appearances was the Twelve, also known as the Eleven, bearing in mind Judas Iscariot's defection. On four occasions, the circle chosen to receive a visit from the Master was that of the disciples, those whom Jesus had called at the start of his public activities.

The most notable appearance was that on the evening of Easter Sunday, in the house in Jerusalem where the Eleven, and probably other disciples, had come together. On another occasion, in Galilee, Jesus appeared to some of them (seven, who may all have belonged to the group of Eleven). We may wonder whether the Eleven were also among the "five hundred" and "all the apostles," the groups that were also visited by the resurrected Jesus. If this is the case, the Eleven were always present when Jesus appeared to an all-male or mixed group of disciples.

Of the other five appearances, three of them involved just one person (Mary Magdalene, Peter, and James) and two were to a small group of men (Cleopas and another anonymous disciple, on their way to Emmaus) or to a group of women (Mary Magdalene, Mary wife of Alphaeus, and others). This group of women had provided support for Jesus and the Twelve when they were in Galilee and were committed followers. The same can be said of Cleopas and his traveling companion, who were disciples belonging to the intermediate circle of followers. The most surprising case was that of James, Jesus' elder brother, who had been somewhat reticent about or even critical of his public activity. He later traveled to Jerusalem with a large part of Jesus' family including his mother, following in his brother's footsteps, and settled there for good. With this unique and individual appearance, even though it was some time after his appearance to Peter and the Eleven/Twelve, Jesus confirmed James' position as one of the pillars of early Christianity and the head of the community in Jerusalem.

The appearances were always the result of a personal initiative on the part of Jesus who took his audience by surprise. They took place in a wide range of settings but were always linked to places that Jesus and his disciples had visited together before his death. In Jerusalem, the sources mention a house in the city where the disciples had come together (the upper room?) and the Mount of Olives, the place where Jesus' group usually met and a stopping-off point between Jerusalem and Bethany. The exception is Emmaus, a town "about seven miles from Jerusalem" (Luke 24:13), and which, in a number of hypotheses, is always deemed to be to the west of the city, an area not mentioned by the Gospels in relation to Jesus' travels. With regard to Galilee, the settings are an unnamed mountain and the lakeside. In Jerusalem again, there is a garden with the tomb and the surrounding area, which was linked to the women and their finding the tomb empty. It was here that Jesus appeared to them before appearing to the male disciples.

These appearances are presented as a real "seeing" and not a "vision" or apparition: Jesus was personally present. The disciples did not have visions or dreams or esoteric experiences or an arcane revelation. They did not experience a state of paranormal perception or some kind of hallucination that allowed them to see dimensions of reality unknown to normal levels of perception. It is not so much that the eyes "saw" but that Jesus let them "see" him, when and where he wanted. The disciples did not choose to see him, nor did they employ techniques to acquire paranormal vision so as to perceive him. Each appearance began and ended when Jesus wanted and when he decided. Moreover, Jesus is not presented surrounded by a piercing light or a halo of superhuman glory; he did not arrive wrapped in clouds or storms, as if he were some heavenly being coming down to visit the earth. Complete normality is the hallmark of the narratives of the appearances. An appearance is not a vision. An appearance involves someone who wants to show himself or herself, whereas a vision involves the exploration of unknown worlds (whether real or imagined).

This does not mean, however, that the disciples "seeing" him was automatic, as when each morning we awake from sleep and open our eyes, immediately starting to perceive objects. The disciples saw Jesus and had access to his presence only once he had identified himself with a word and/or sign, or once they recognized him thanks to something he did. This is why Jesus appeared only to the disciples, people who already knew him and who were able to appreciate who he was.

For example, on the evening of Easter Sunday, Jesus appeared among the disciples and addressed the usual Jewish greeting to them: "Peace be with you" (Luke 24:36; John 20:19). He then showed them the marks on his body left from his being crucified, specifically the holes from the nails in his hands and feet and the spear in his side. Then, and only then, did they realize who he was. According to John

20:22, he said to them, "Receive the Holy Spirit." At times, a personal reference was enough. On the morning of Easter Sunday, Mary Magdalene was in the garden by the tomb, and, according to John 20:14, "[she] saw Jesus standing, but she did not know that it was Jesus." She mistook him for the gardener, until Jesus called her by her name: "Mary." Only then did she exclaim, "*Rabonni*!" ("Teacher" in Aramaic), which was the way the disciples normally addressed Jesus.

With respect to the signs, Jesus' encounter with Cleopas and the other disciple on the road to Emmaus concluded with the sign of the bread, over which he said a blessing, breaking it and sharing it out. Luke 24:31 continues, "[Then, and only then] their eyes were opened and they recognized him." They had in fact been walking and talking with Jesus for some time, "but their eyes were kept from recognizing him" (Luke 24:16). The reason is clear: the hardness of their hearts. They did not believe that he could have been raised from the dead. Similarly, Jesus appeared by Lake Galilee, and "yet the [seven] disciples did not know that it was Jesus" (John 21:4). After failing to catch any fish, they followed Jesus' instructions and ended up filling the boat with fish. Following this miraculous sign, "that disciple whom Jesus loved said to Peter, 'It is the Lord!'" (John 21:7).

Thus, we need to talk of a particular form of "seeing," which is not automatic and which is "activated" only when the right circumstances are in place that allow for the discovery of the identity of the person who is there, before them, before the disciples. Those who know him can recognize him, once they overcome the obstacles set up by doubt and disenchantment. Doubt is a common element in the narratives of the appearances; doubt besieged the disciples who had come together and the Eleven in particular (Matt 28:17; Luke 24:38, 24:41).

Doubt also overwhelmed Thomas, who, during Jesus' first appearance, was not with the others and had not had the chance to see him (John 20:15, 20:27). As we have just pointed out, doubt was present due to a hardness of heart and lack of understanding, as was the case of the two disciples on their way to Emmaus whom Jesus joined as they walked (Luke 24:15). Doubt was the difficulty that had to be overcome so that Jesus' appearance could be "received" and welcomed without suspicion and with an open heart. Often, doubt was not an alternative to faith but a first step, melting away only when it was replaced by the warmth and joy of seeing Jesus. Obviously, the ultimate response can be decided only by the doubters themselves; they have to move step by step toward faith, and this can be tiring. In the case of the appearances, doubt became an inevitable change of spirit, disconcerted by this unparalleled event. Thus, the Eleven, who went up the mountain where Jesus appeared, "worshipped him," despite having "doubted" (Matt 28:17). These two feelings are not contradictory but form part of a necessary step: the step required to believe that Jesus had been raised from the dead and the belief that they were not now seeing a ghost, that they were not hallucinating.

Despite the difficulties involved in "seeing," none of these appearances ended in failure, refusal, or denial. Jesus chose the people, places, and times involved in his appearances to the disciples carefully, as if he were trying to summarize his activities in them. In fact, doubt and the lack of understanding of Jesus' project had characterized the response of his disciples on no small number of occasions in the past. It should come as no surprise now that when Jesus appeared "center stage" doubt continued to besiege his followers. The resurrected Jesus offered few words in response to this doubt, as if he felt that there was enough in his simple appearance before the disciples, as if his only concern should be assuring them of his presence now that a new time was beginning: a time for a mission around the world, a time for building the community and for nurturing the Church.

The relations that Jesus established with the disciples after Easter were very complicated. The central message was, primarily, Jesus himself, who had experienced suffering on the cross and, now, resurrected, went to find his friends. Jesus moved and acted according to certain parameters of closeness; the witnesses to his resurrection, whom he chose, were not strangers or people who had arrived at the last minute; they were people whom he had shared his life with and who were now blessed with seeing him again, with a transformed, glorious body.

6.3.4. Above and Beyond the History

The oldest text on the four fundamental events in Christianity (Jesus' death, burial, resurrection, and appearances) handed down by the Apostle Paul in the First Epistle to the Corinthians (15:3-5) talks about the fulfillment of the Scriptures. The death and resurrection "on the third day" are options that God offered Jesus, his Son, which he accepted. Thus, the Scriptures were fulfilled. Death was the result of Jesus' freedom, whereas the resurrection was a free act by God: Jesus wanted to give his life, and God wanted to free him from death. There is a mutual exchange of gifts, and the beneficiary is humanity, which is now open to hope.

"Resurrect" does not mean return to the previous life, as did Lazarus, nor does it mean the adoption of another form of life, of the many available. Resurrect means entering the presence of God once and forever, accepting it fully and entering heaven. Jesus, once resurrected, inaugurates future life, the definitive world. His body is the manifestation of this state of blessing and peace. The end of history, the great day, is here. The Jewish writings from the time, especially those inspired by the times of persecution, firmly stated that God would reward those who had suffered unjustly with "an everlasting renewal of life" (2 Macc 7:9) and "they who are put to death for the Lord's sake shall awake to life" (*Testament of Judah* 25:4).

So, all this was anticipated in Jesus. His resurrection was to mark the start of the new world. Nonetheless, if this new world was to begin now, it was because the resurrected Jesus did not represent a spirit that was to go up and down to heaven, who would travel without having to be bound to the servitude of a body: his body was not dissolved or corrupted but transformed, it continued alive after death. During his appearances, Jesus chatted, ate, and invited the disciples to touch his flesh and bones or to see for themselves the wounds left on his body by the crucifixion. This body is the guarantee of continuity before and after his death: the man resurrected was the same man who had been crucified, not someone else who died for him.

Nonetheless, Jesus' body was not exactly as it had been, as before he died he was subject, like everyone else, to corruption, while he was now incorruptible and able to defeat the laws of nature. In the narratives of his appearances, Jesus was present among his disciples, even though the doors were locked. What is surprising is not that Jesus could "walk through" walls but that he manifested himself to his disciples when he wanted and where he wanted. The paradox of a body that is and is not the same as it was is expressed by the Apostle Paul when he says that the body of the Jesus resurrected is a "spiritual body," which has to be differentiated from a "physical body," which is apt only for the world in which we live (1 Cor 15:44). Jesus himself stated that after resurrection people were not victim to the same desires as they were in this world, "but are like angels in heaven" (Mark 12:25). The body of the resurrected Jesus was a body transformed, and he was the first to have experienced the journey from death to life.

Nevertheless, this journey remains hidden to human eyes and to any form of measurement or verification. We know only the results, the effects. The canonical Gospels do not explain, nor do they want to explain, how Jesus was raised from the dead, as they are perfectly aware that his resurrection is to be found only at the very frontier of what cannot be verified. The explanations derived from, or supported by, modern physics (that Jesus' dead body was converted into energy) are fragile and questionable attempts at justifying the way his body disappeared from the tomb. In fact, already in the second century A.D., the Gospel of Peter, an apocryphal text, dared go beyond what had been provided in the canonical Gospels. It "described" Jesus' resurrection as follows: two men came down from heaven to look for the man in the tomb, Jesus, and taking him by the hand they took him away to heaven above (35-42) while the astonished guards looked on. Both "explanations," today's and that from the past, agree on one fact that constitutes the starting point: Jesus' body was not strictly of this earth.

The Hellenistic model of the apotheosis of heroes or the heavenly exaltation of figures deemed holy, born again into immortal life, does not help us understand the resurrection either. The resurrection is not merely a person's survival but rather his transformation, the complete recuperation of his humanity in a new world. The body of the resurrected Jesus is immortal, but above all it is a glorious body, a body thanks to which mankind had not been lost in the spirit. On the contrary, the Spirit of God (in capital letters!) had made it different and new, untouched by any weakness or frailty.

It is pointless trying to search for evidence, as if the resurrection could be demonstrated incontrovertibly, almost rationally, or, on the contrary, that it could be denied as absurd. As M. Bockmuehl points out, the way to understand the resurrection is the way taken by the narratives of those who saw Jesus or who found the tomb empty. This way is an open question, which cannot be ignored as an unimportant detail. Both the discovery of the empty tomb and the first appearances of Jesus resurrected (as stated by the witnesses) took place on the same day, Easter Sunday, three days after Jesus' death. Including the Friday, there were three days from Friday evening (when Jesus was buried) to first light on Sunday morning (when the women realized that his body was no longer in the tomb) during which time apparently nothing happened. It was not until the first witnesses found the tomb empty that Jesus showed himself to some disciples.

Nonetheless, the resurrection could have taken place only on the Sunday because Saturday is the day of rest for the Jews. "The third day," Sunday, was the first possible day for the news to break on: the five appearances that are said to have taken place on Easter Sunday show that Jesus had chosen this day, the third after his death, to make his resurrection known. Three days is a short period of time but long enough to certify (in accordance with Jewish customs) that the deceased was really dead. However, the third day, the Sunday, rather than being the day when Jesus' death was corroborated, became the day that marked his resurrection. Thus it is no surprise that for the early Christians, Sunday, or the first day of the week, became the most important day, the day of God's intervention on Jesus' body. Sunday even "attracted" the sign of the bread and the wine (the Eucharist), which had taken place on a Thursday, and the commemoration of Jesus' death, which had taken place on a Friday. The resurrection as an event became the focus of the life of the Christian community right from the start.

Jesus' resurrection was an event that took place on the border between historical, empirical, provable reality and metahistorical reality, which is intuitively taken to be true and, for those who believe, asserted as necessary. Talking about the resurrection leads, as N. T. Wright points out, to the extremes of historical, philosophical, and theological language. However, Jesus' resurrection is not some way of saying that the disciples have experienced God's grace, his light. The resurrection does illuminate (or it would be a scandal!) the life of each individual, but its impact comes from something that predates the personal experience: Jesus, who had been crucified, was no longer in the tomb, and the reason was that he had been raised from the dead.

Jesus' resurrection is an event that exceeds the coordinates set by any historical approach, as it belongs to an area that may or may not be believed. History did not remain silent when faced with Jesus' resurrection, but it cannot manage to grasp its uniqueness and everything that it represents. Here, more than anywhere else in Jesus' life, we find ourselves in the world of notions, though they are reasoned and reasonable notions. However, these pieces of evidence—the empty tomb and the appearances—which are attested to by history, support faith in the resurrection. Considered as a whole, they constitute, in the words of N. T. Wright, the sufficient and necessary condition for Jesus to have physically been resuscitated from death. In fact, resurrection can be spoken of in real terms only if the body of Jesus left the tomb and he appeared frequently before his own people.

The window that lets us look out on to what has happened is the window of faith, since faith, like the resurrection, is historical and metahistorical, rooted in history but able to go beyond it as well. The image of a window is not fortuitous, as the only eyes able to see through the darkness of the tomb are the bright eyes of those who, like the women or the disciple whom Jesus loved, are able to correctly interpret the empty tomb and who do not doubt when faced with the unexpected and surprising appearance of the resurrected Jesus. The eyes of the witnesses have seen clearly and their words should be respected. Nonetheless, they have not "seen" the resurrection. They have, however, seen something more important: the resurrected man himself, who manifested himself to them personally and called them by their name.

Art has helped bring together the two paths that led to this unique event that is Jesus' resurrection. In a Gothic altarpiece from the church of Santa Maria de Guimerà, the work of Ramon de Mur (15th c.) kept in the Episcopal Museum in Vic, there is a representation of the moment when Jesus, glorious and victorious, leaves the tomb—the soldiers petrified with their eyes closed. The only figure who has her eyes open is a woman who looks on from a window in the top-left corner of the altarpiece: Mary, the Mother of God, who represents the heavenly community and faith in the resurrection. The greatest testimony to the resurrected Jesus comprises the people who believe in him. The Gothic altarpiece from Guimerà, inspired by the Western models of iconography, represents history (the empty tomb and the appearances) as seen through faith. In the church of St. Roch in l'Argilaga (Tarragona), an icon produced in the Orthodox monastery of St. Nicholas of Dalmeria (Languedoc) represents the scope and force of Jesus' resurrection through Western iconography. Jesus goes down to hell, to the kingdom of death, where a crowd of people await him, victims of slavery and the chains of imprisonment. Now, with all bonds broken and oppression overthrown, Jesus offers his hand to all humanity, both men and women, as represented by Adam and Eve, and shows himself willing to help them out of the pit of death and to take them to his glorious Kingdom. Humanity is not destined to death but to life. The journey made by he who has gone before has culminated in a new and happy life, the heavenly Kingdom. Now, the mission the disciples are charged with is to ensure that humanity keeps to this path that promises so much.

7
Epilogue

History has taken care of its duty by showing that the memory of Jesus, a Jewish rabbi and prophet from the first century, has not stopped growing over the past two thousand years and that it has spread around the world, in the twentieth century in particular. Indeed, right from the start, those who considered themselves to be his followers and who saw him as the Son of God did not identify themselves with a nation, culture, or language but sought to adapt their message to the many different ways of life. Christianity safeguards the memory of Jesus Christ by continuing his work and putting his person forward as a fundamental point of reference for our existence. Jesus' project, his vision of God and mankind, of the present and the future, of life and death, has supported and continues to support many paths and hopes, as well as involving obstacles and adversities. The questions that could be asked of Jesus and about him are limitless; those who get close to him and his message receive not only answers but also further questions.

Looking back now, from the end of this book, on the whole of Jesus' life, his death on the cross emerges as a stumbling block but as the element that is most difficult to digest. Is death not, ultimately, an unjust and unjustified assault? Did the salvation of humanity require the death of God's emissary? Likewise, why did the almost excessive suffering of torture on the cross have to mark the end of that life, not only from the point of view of God, whose will it was, but also from that of Jesus, who accepted it? Why did the Son of God have to end up hanging from a cross accused of blasphemy, suffering a punishment that, according to the Jewish Law, was reserved for those "accursed by God"? The answer to these questions cannot avoid the pain of the world, of the men and women who live there, nor the suffering of so many innocent people, with whom Jesus identifies and whose fate he shares. Jesus' life replicates that of each and every man and woman who has or is to live on this earth. His humanity is well-known, familiar, and close. His feelings are not above human feelings, but instead he explores their depths. For Jesus, nothing human is strange or foreign, neither suffering or death nor disrespect or injustice.

Jesus identified himself particularly with the poor and insignificant, the ignorant and simple, the sick and children, all those who were marginalized from the centers of power and the important decisions that people take. During his life, he received many pleas and requests from anonymous strangers who saw him as the last or only hope to which they could aspire. Jesus arose as the defender of the weak. He did not shun the company of sinners (the religiously marginalized of the time), and he vociferously criticized self-satisfied and complacent religiosity. Jesus did not fight to bring down the institutions but to reinforce and extend the value of the individual: the Sabbath was for people, not people for the Sabbath. In Jesus' opinion, the cause of other people was sacred and unquestionable. When the poor ask, we should give, without delay and without question. They cannot always remain the victims of a history built on domination and enrichment. For this reason, Christianity, as long as it remains loyal to Jesus' Gospel, defends the weak and acts as a support to those who see their ultimate dignity denied them: being children of the Father in heaven.

The seed sowed by Jesus, of limitless, unconditional solidarity, grew in an unexpected and paradoxical way thanks to his resurrection. The resurrection opened a new path beyond death. Jesus experienced a poor life at every stage, without a "hole" or "nest," a life that his closest disciples, above all the Twelve, agreed to make their own. However, when his project seemed to have been buried by a power that, like all power, sought to affirm itself, there came an unexpected turn of events that relaunched his message of the Kingdom in strength, a message that had been at the heart of his preaching: he who died was now to live forever. Then, from that Easter morning, the emphasis moved from the message to the messenger himself. Jesus' crucified and glorious body, his whole being, both divine and human, became the focal point and nerve center. His resurrection sealed the decision as to God's love for his Son and all humanity. Once his disciples had seen him freed from the bonds of death, the indestructible core of his person and, thus, the Christian faith was made clear: Jesus, the Christ, had died and been resurrected.

The early community, the Church of the first days and of the rest of time, was born from this belief. The Church did not arise from a sociological determinism, or the random coming together of a number of factors or the stubbornness of some followers who wanted to promote a project that, with the tragic death of the man who started it, seemed to be directionless. Jesus wanted to gather a group of disciples around him, calling twelve of them to be with him and entrusting them with the new covenant, the continuity of his words and gestures of healing and mercy. However, Jesus did not turn his disciples whom he sent on the mission into activists, focused unhappily on effectiveness, nor did he seek to lead them toward a speculative wisdom, which would be appropriate only for the initiated. His Gospel was not proselytism or gnosis. Jesus called the Twelve, but he spoke to them alone only relatively infrequently. The instruction of the disciples was based on imitating the essential in Jesus' life since only one thing was truly urgent: to proclaim the preeminence of God and his Kingdom, to spread the word with evocative and effective language, the language of the parable and the miracle, to tell people that he is the Father of all mankind.

For Jesus, reality was never a series of failed or abandoned projects, nor was it where self-defense and mistrust should dominate. For him, the world remained a complicated place, and sometimes even hostile, where violence could be defeated only by compassion. This was the fundamental aspect in his life: love open to everyone, giving of one's own existence as an effective instrument for salvation. In Jesus' gospel, history was dreamed of as a place for construction, not destruction, a place where care replaced rejection and where there was always room for those who wanted to build peace. "Peace be with you" is, indeed, the phrase that the resurrected Jesus addressed to the disciples who had met together and who, for fear, had locked the doors.

Jesus, nonetheless, appeared among them, and their fear was replaced by the happiness of seeing him again. The response to injustice was not confrontation but justice, forgiveness and offering peace. The definitive life of Jesus after his resurrection was not a form of revenge against his adversaries but the seal to a new humanity. Resurrection was not, ultimately, the vindication of the figure of Jesus that God would have engineered in order to destroy those who had brought about his death. If this had been the essential intention, then the resurrected Jesus would have appeared before the high priests and the rest of Israel's leaders and would have reproached their behavior. On the contrary, once resurrected, Jesus appeared only to his disciples, his friends, many of whom had failed him, abandoning him at the moment of truth. These were the ones who had to know that he was alive. Christianity was not to be based on incontrovertible evidence (which can, ultimately, be denied or falsified) but on faithful and trustworthy witnesses.

The message of the Kingdom that Jesus preached sought to bring God closer to people's hearts. Trusting prayer (the model for which is Jesus himself), life's orientation (based on heartfelt repentance), and generosity toward others (like that of the Good Samaritan) are clear expressions of the new path that he had opened. Likewise, in terms of relationships with others, humble and tireless service, interpersonal relations that are maintained despite division or disagreement, and the warmth of a sincere welcome all are signs of the new way of seeing and living. Jesus' impact on human history represented a volte-face, an authentic revolution for people's inner truths and attitudes. Everything begins, however, with a different way of looking at reality, which comes from the heart and which is able to find sweetness in severity, goodness in evil, love in hate. A civilization of love grows alongside the culture of forgiveness, and forgiveness is the cornerstone of Christianity.

What makes Jesus' life unique is the fact that his history, while coinciding with human history, exceeds it. Christianity states that Jesus is to return to judge the living and the dead, that there is to be an assessment of people's intentions and behavior, where love is what will tip the balance. Jesus' resurrection brings with it victory over death and his active presence alongside God, a presence with a cosmic reach. When the time comes for this world to be renewed, he will come gloriously. Jesus, then, not only has personally experienced death but also brings life to any sign of death and pain, of mourning and suffering. Creation is transfigured. There are no limits to hope and no barriers for goodness. It is possible to imagine the end of a world weighed down with evil and mutual destruction, a world disfigured by the Shoah and gulags. Truth will prevail.

Jesus' project is not a dream that has been suspended, awaiting some more or less distant future. Human history cannot be nourished by resignation or revolt. The boundary between time and eternity, between chiaroscuro and bright light, disappears when the lighting strikes of the new world light the earth, when the fire of the Spirit starts. Jesus is a "historical" figure in the way in which he promised he would be "with you always, to the close of the age" (Matt 28:20). Thanks to his saving presence, evil can be defeated and the fear of death is no longer a nightmare. The energies that emanate from Jesus' gospel are strong and strengthening.

Jesus' resurrection is the start of a new creation, which is full of beauty. The future world has started to make itself shown. The appearances of the resurrected Jesus are the first fruit. They can be reproduced in complex situations, even when it seems that there is no place for hope. The resurrection of individuals or whole peoples, whole continents, is reflected in the eruption of life that came out of Jesus' tomb. This tomb was in a garden, a garden in which Jesus revealed himself to a female disciple by her name: "Mary!" Humanity also began in a garden, in the Garden of Eden, where God spoke to the man and the woman, who were his friends. There is a fruitful relationship linking the garden of the first creation, paradise, and the garden of the second creation, of the new humanity, which is personified in the glorious body of Jesus Christ. For this reason, we should and must recover the memory of this paradise by nurturing gardens of fraternity in a world that is called to be made new.

Bibliography

(NOT INCLUDING GOSPEL COMMENTARIES)

Aguirre, R. *La mesa compartida*. Santander: Sal Terrae, 1994.

Aletti, J. N. *Jésus-Christ fait-il l'unité du Nouveau Testament?* Jésus et Jésus Christ 61. Paris: Desclée, 1994.

Allison, D. C. *Jesus of Nazareth: Millenarian Prophet*. Minneapolis: Fortress, 1998.

Barbaglio, G. *Gesù ebreo di Galilea: Indagine Storica*. Bologna: Dehoniane, 2002.

Barnett, P. *After Jesus*. Vol. 3, *Finding the Historical Christ*. Grand Rapids: Eerdmans, 2009.

Bauckham, R. "The Brothers and Sisters of Jesus: An Epiphanian Response to John P. Meier." *Catholic Biblical Quarterly* 56 (1994): 686–700.

———. *Jesus and the Eyewitnesses: The Gospels as Eyewitness Testimony*. Grand Rapids: Eerdmans, 2006.

Becker, J. *Jesus von Nazareth*. Berlin: De Gruyter, 1996.

———. *Maria, Mutter Jesu und erwählte Jungfrau*. Biblische Gestalt 4. Leipzig: Evangelische Verlagsanstalt, 2001.

Benedict XVI, Pope (Joseph Ratzinger). *Jesus of Nazareth: From the Baptism in the Jordan to the Transfiguration*. 7th ed. New York: Doubleday, 2007.

Berger, K. *Jesus*. Munich: Pattloch, 2004.

Bockmuehl, M. (ed.) *The Cambridge Companion to Jesus*. Cambridge: University Press, 2001. Especially the articles by C. A. Evans, P. J. Tomson, M. Meye Thompson, G. Stanton, B. Chilton, J. B. Green, and M. Bockmuehl.

Borg, M. J. *Jesus: A New Vision*. San Francisco: Harper & Row, 1987.

Bornkamm, G. *Jesus von Nazareth*. 7th ed. Stuttgart: Kohlhammer, 1965 (1956) [= *Jesus of Nazareth*. Philadelphia: Fortress, 1995].

Borrell i Viader, A. "L'autoritat de Jesús, és l'autoritat de Déu?" *Revista Catalana de Teologia* 36 (2011) (forthcoming).

Broadhead, E. "Implicit Christology and the Historical Jesus." In *Handbook for the Study of the Historical Jesus*, vol. 2. Edited by T. Holmén and S. E. Porter. Leiden: Brill, 2010.

Brown, R. E. *The Birth of the Messiah: A Commentary on the Infancy Narratives in the Gospels of Matthew and Luke*. Anchor Bible Reference Library. 2nd ed. New York: Doubleday, 1993.

———. *The Death of the Messiah: From Gethsemane to the Grave: A Commentary on the Passion Narratives in the Four Gospels*, 2 vols. Anchor Bible Reference Library. New York: Doubleday, 1994.

Bultmann, R. *Jesus (Die Unsterblichen)*. Berlin: Deutsche Bibliothek, 1926 [= *Jesus and the Word*. New York: Scribner, 1934].

Charlesworth, J. H. "The Historical Jesus in the Fourth Gospel: A Paradigm Shift?" *Journal for the Study of the Historical Jesus* 8 (2010): 3–46.

———. *Jesus and Archaeology*. The Proceedings of the Millennium Celebration in Jerusalem. Grand Rapids: Eerdmans, 2006.

Charlesworth, J. H. and L. L. Johns (eds.) *Hillel and Jesus: Comparative Studies of Two Major Religious Leaders*. Minneapolis: Fortress, 1997.

Charlesworth, J. H. and P. Pokorný (eds.) *Jesus Research: An International Perspective*. Grand Rapids: Eerdmans, 2009.

Chilton, B. *The Temple of Jesus: His Sacrificial Program within a Cultural History of Sacrifice*. College Park: Pennsylvania State University Press, 1992.

———. *Rabbi Jesus: An Intimate Biography*. New York: Doubleday, 2000.

Chilton, B. and C. A. Evans (eds.) *Studying the Historical Jesus. Evaluations of the State of Current Research*. New Testament Tools and Studies 19. Leiden: Brill, 1994. Especially the articles by W. R.

Telford, B. Chilton/C. A. Evans, B. L. Blackburn, R. A. Horsley, and P. Perkins.

———. *Authenticating the Words of Jesus*. New Testament Tools and Studies 28/1. Leiden: Brill, 1999. Especially the articles by T. Holmén, H. C. Kee, and W. Klassen.

———. *Authenticating the Activities of Jesus*. New Testament Tools and Studies 28/2. Leiden: Brill, 1999. Especially the articles by B. F. Meyer, D. C. Allison, D. Zeller, B. J. Malina, W. Klassen, and R. Bauckham.

Chilton, B., C. A. Evans, and J. Neusner (eds.) *The Missing Jesus: Rabbinic Judaism and the New Testament*. Leiden: Brill, 2002.

Crossan, J. D. *The Historical Jesus. The Life of a Mediterranean Jewish Peasant*. Edinburgh: T&T Clark, 1991.

———. *Jesus: A Revolutionary Biography*. San Francisco: Harper, 1994.

DeConick, A. D. *Recovering the Original Gospel of Thomas: A History of the Gospel and Its Growth*. Edinburgh: T&T Clark, 2005.

De Jonge, M. *Jesus: The Servant-Messiah*. New Haven: Yale University, 1991.

Destro, A. and M. Pesce. *L'uomo Gesù: Giorni, luoghi, incontro di una vita*. Milano: Mondadori, 2008.

Dibelius, M. *Jesus*. Berlin: de Gruyter, 1939.

Dodd, C. H. *The Founder of Christianity*. London: Collins, 1971.

Donaldson, T. L. *Judaism and the Gentiles: Jewish Patterns of Universalism (to 135CE)*. Waco, Tex.: Baylor University Press, 2007.

Dunn, J. D. G. *Jesus Remembered*. Christianity in the Making 1. Grand Rapids: Eerdmans, 2003.

———. *A New Perspective on Jesus*. Grand Rapids: Eerdmans, 2006.

———. *Beginning from Jerusalem*. Christianity in the Making 2. Grand Rapids: Eerdmans, 2009.

Dupont, J. "Le Dieu de Jésus." *Nouvelle Revue Théologique* 104 (1987): 321–44.

Dupont, J. (ed.) *Jésus aux origines de la christologie*. Bibliotheca Ephemeridum Theologicarum Lovaniensium 40. 2nd ed. Leuven: University Press–Peeters, 1989.

Ehrman, B. D. *Jesus, Apocalyptic Prophet of the New Millennium*. New York: Oxford University Press, 1999.

Fabris, R. *Gesù di Nazareth: Storia e interpretazione*. Assisi: Citadella, 1983.

Fitzmyer, J. A. "The Languages of Palestine in the First Century A.D." In *A Wandering Aramean: Collected Aramaic Essays*. Missoula: Scholars, 1979, 29–56.

———. *The One Who Is to Come*. Grand Rapids: Eerdmans, 2007.

Flusser, D. *Jesus*. 3rd ed. Jerusalem: Magnes, 2001.

Fredriksen, P. *Jesus of Nazareth, the King of the Jews: A Jewish Life and the Emergence of Christianity*. New York: Alfred A. Knopf, 1999.

Frey, J. "Der historische Jesus und der Christus der Evangelien." In *Der historiche Jesus: Tendenzen und Perspektiven der gegenwärtigen Forschungen*. BZNT 114. Edited by J. Schröter and R. Brucker. Berlin: De Gruyter, 2002, 273–336.

Frey, J. (ed.) *Jesus und die Archäologie Galiläas*. Biblische und Theologische Studien 87. Neukirchen-Vluyn: Neukirchener, 2008.

Freyne, S. *Galilee and Gospel: Selected Essays*. WUNT 125. Tübingen: Mohr Siebeck, 2000.

———. *Jesus, a Jewish Galilean: A New Reading of the Jesus Story*. London: T&T Clark (Continuum), 2004.

Funk, R. W. and R. V. Hoover. *Jesus Seminar, The Five Gospels: What Did Jesus Really Say? The Search for the Authentic Words of Jesus*. San Francisco: Harper, 1993.

Fusco, V. "Gesù e le Scritture di Israele." In E. Norelli (ed.) *La Bibbia nell'antichità cristiana, I: Da Gesù a Origene*. La Bibbia nella storia 15. Bologna: Dehoniane, 1998, 35–63.

Gaventa, B. R. and R. B. Hays (eds.) *Seeking the Identity of Jesus: A Pilgrimage*. Grand Rapids: Eerdmans, 2008.

Gnilka, J. *Jesus von Nazareth: Botschaft und Geschichte*. Herders Theologischer Kommentar Suppl. 3. Freiburg i. Br.: Herder, 1990 [= *Jesus of Nazareth: Message and History*. Peabody, Mass.: Hendrickson, 1997].

Grelot, P. *L'espérance juive à l'heure de Jésus*. Jésus et Jésus Christ 6. Paris: Desclée, 1978.

———. *Jésus de Nazareth, Christ et Seigneur: Une lecture de l'Évangile*. Vol. 1: Lectio Divina 167. Vol. 2: Lectio Divina 170. Paris–Montréal: Cerf–Novalis, 1997, 1998.

Guijarro Oporto, S. *Fidelidades en conflicto: La ruptura con la familia por causa del discipulado y de la misión en la tradición sinóptica*. Plenitudo Temporis 4. Salamanca: Publicaciones Universidad Pontificia, 1998.

Harnack, A. v. *Das Wesen des Christentums*. Leipzig, 1900 [= *What Is Christianity?* London: Williams & Norgate, 1901].

Hengel, M. *Judentum und Hellenismus*. WUNT 10. Tübingen: Mohr Siebeck, [2]1973.

———. *Mors turpissima crucis: die Kreuzigung in der antiken Welt*. Tübingen: Mohr Siebeck, 1976.

Hengel, M. and A. M. Schwemer. *Der messianische Anspruch Jesu und die Anfänge der Christologie. Vier Studien*. WUNT 138. Tübingen: Mohr Siebeck, 2001.

———. *Jesus und das Judentum*. Geschichte des frühen Christentums 1. Tübingen: Mohr Siebeck, 2007.

Holmberg, B. *Människa och mer: Jesus i forskningens ljus*. Lund: Arcus, 2001 ("Man and More: Jesus in the Light of Research").

Holmén, T. "Seven Theses on the So-Called Criteria of Authenticity of Historical Jesus Research." *Revista Catalana de Teologia* 33 (2008): 343–76.

Holmén, T. and S. E. Porter (eds.) *Handbook for the Study of the Historical Jesus*. Leiden: Brill, 2010.

Holtzmann, H. J. *Die synoptischen Evangelien. Ihr Ursprung und geschichtlicher Charakter*. Leipzig: Wilhelm Engelmann, 1863.

Horsley, R. A. *Jesus in Context: Power, People, & Performance*. Minneapolis: Fortress, 2008.

Hurtado, L. W. *Lord Jesus Christ. Devotion to Jesus in Earliest Christianity*. Grand Rapids: Eerdmans, 2003.

Jeremias, J. *Jerusalem zur Zeit Jesus: Eine kulturgeschichtliche Untersuchung zur neutestamentlichen Zeitgeschichte*. 3rd ed. Göttingen: Vandenhoeck & Ruprecht, 1969 [= *Jerusalem in the Time of Jesus: An Investigation into Economic & Social Conditions during the New Testament Period*. Philadelphia: Fortress, 1969].

———. *Unbekannte Jesusworte*. Gütersloh: Monn, [4]1975 [= *Unknown Sayings of Jesus*. London: SPCK, 1964].

———. *Die Gleicnisse Jesu*. 7th ed. Göttingen: Vandenhoeck & Ruprecht, 1965 [= *The Parables of Jesus*. New York: Scribner, 1966].

Johnson, L. T. *The Real Jesus: The Misguided Quest for the Historical Jesus and the Truth of the Traditional Gospels*. San Francisco: Harper, 1997.

Kähler, M. *Der sogennante historische Jesus und der geschichtliche biblische Christus*. 2nd ed. Munich: Chr. Kaiser, 1982 (1956) [= *The*

So-Called Historical Jesus and the Historic, Biblical Christus. Philadelphia: Fortress, 1964].

Käsemann, E. "Das Problem des historischen Jesus." *Zeitschrift für Theologie und Kirche* 51 (1954): 125–53.

Kasper, W. *Jesus der Christus*. Mainz: Matthias Grünewald, 1974 [= *The God of Jesus Christ*. New York: Crossroad, 1984].

Keener, C. S. *The Historical Jesus of the Gospels*. Grand Rapids: Eerdmans, 2009.

Kelber, W. H. and S. Byrskog (eds.) *Jesus in Memory: Traditions in Oral and Scribal Perspectives*. Waco, Tex.: Baylor University Press, 2009.

Klauck, H. J. *Judas*. Freiburg i. Br.: Herder, 1987.

Klausner, J. *Jesus of Nazareth: His Life, Times, and Teaching*. New York: Macmillan, 1925 (Hebrew: 1922).

Koester, H. *Ancien Christian Gospels: Their History and Development*. Philadelphia: Fortress, 1990.

Labahn, M. and A. Schmidt (eds.) *Jesus, Mark and Q: The Teaching of Jesus and Its Earliest Records*. JSNT.S 214. Sheffield: University Press, 2001.

Légasse, S. *Le Procès de Jésus: L'histoire*. Lectio Divina 156. Paris: Cerf 1994.

Levine, A.-J. *The Misunderstood Jew: The Church and the Scandal of the Jewish Jesus*. San Francisco: HarperSanFrancisco, 2006.

Marchadour, A. Lazare. *Histoire d'un récit: Récits d'une histoire*. Lectio Divina 132. Paris: Cerf, 1988.

Marguerat, D. "Jésus le juif selon la Troisième Quête du Jésus de l'histoire." *Revista Catalana de Teologia* 33 (2008): 443–59.

Marguerat, D., E. Norelli, and J. M. Poffet (eds.) *Jésus de Nazareth. Nouvelles approches d'une énigme*. Le Monde de la Bible 38. Genève: Labor et Fides 1998. Especially the articles by V. Fusco, J. P. Jossua, G. Theissen, G. Rochais, E. P. Sanders, J. S. Kloppenborg, D. Marguerat, J. Schlosser, J .P. Lémonon, E. Norelli, and C. Thoma.

Meier, J. P. *A Marginal Jew: Rethinking the Historical Jesus*. Vol. 1, *The Roots of the Problem and the Person*. Anchor Bible Reference Library. New York: Doubleday, 1991.

———. *A Marginal Jew: Rethinking the Historical Jesus*. Vol. 2, *Mentor, Message and Miracles*. Anchor Bible Reference Library. New York: Doubleday, 1994.

———. *A Marginal Jew: Rethinking the Historical Jesus*. Vol. 3, *Companions and Competitors*. Anchor Bible Reference Library. New York: Doubleday, 2001.

———. *A Marginal Jew: Rethinking the Historical Jesus*. Vol. 4, *Law and Love*. New Haven: Yale University Press, 2009.

Men, A. *Jésus, le Maître de Nazareth*. Montrouge: Nouvelle Cité, 1999. (Russian original: Moscow, 1992.)

Merklein, H. *Die Gottesherrschaft als Handlungsprinzip*. Forschung zur Bibel 34. 2nd ed. Würzburg: Echter, 1981.

Meyer, B. F. *The Aims of Jesus*. London: SCM, 1979.

———. "'Phases' in Jesus' Mission." *Gregorianum* 73 (1992): 5-17.

Neufeld, T. R. Y. *Recovering Jesus: The Witness of the New Testament*. Grand Rapids: Brazos, 2007.

Neusner, J. *A Rabbi Talks with Jesus*. 2nd ed. Philadelphia: McGill-Queen's University Press, 2000.

Newman, C. C. (ed.) *Jesus and the Restoration of Israel: A Critical Assessment of N. T. Wright's Jesus and the Victory of God*. Downers Grove, Ill.: InterVarsity, 1999.

Onuki, T. *Jesus: Geschichte und Gegenwart*. BTS 82. Neukirchen-Vluyn: Neukirchener, 2006.

Painter, J. *Just James: The Brother of Jesus in History and Tradition*. Edinburgh: Clark, 1999.

Penna, R. *I ritratti originali di Gesù il Cristo: Inizi e sviluppi della cristologia neotestamentaria*. Vol. 1, *Gli inizi* (SBA). Cinisello Balsamo (Milano): San Paolo, 1996.

Perrin, N. *Rediscovering the Teaching of Jesus*. New York: Harper & Row, 1967.

Perrot, C. *Jésus et l'histoire*. Jésus et Jésus-Christ 11. 2nd ed. Paris: Desclée, 1993.

———. *Jésus*. Que sais-je? 3300. Paris: Presses Universitaires de France, 1998.

Pikaza, X. *La figura de Jesús: profeta, taumaturgo, rabino*. El Mundo de la Biblia. Estella: Verbo Divino, 1992.

Piper, R. *"Love your Enemies": Jesus' Love Command in the Synoptic Gospels and the Early Christian Paraenesis*. SNTS Monograph Series 38. Cambridge: University Press, 1979.

Puig i Tàrrech, A. "Les quêtes récentes du Jésus historique." *Revista Catalana de Teologia* 25 (2000): 95–120.

———. *Jesus: An Uncommon Journey*. WUNT 288. Tübingen: Mohr Siebeck, 2010.

———. "Els relats de la resurrecció de Jesús." *Revista Catalana de Teologia* (2011) (forthcoming).

Reimarus, H. S. "Fragmente eines Ungennanten: Von dem Zwecke der Jesus und seiner Jünger." In G. E. Lessing, *Sämtliche Werke*. Edited by G. Friecke and H.G. Göpfert, vol. 7. Munich: Carl Hauser, 1976 [= *The Goal of Jesus and His Disciples*. Leiden: Brill, 1970].

Reiser, M. *Die Gerichtspredigt Jesu*. Neutestamentliche Abhandlungen NF 23. Münster: Aschendorff, 1990.

Renan, E. *La vie de Jésus*. 69th ed. Paris: Calmann-Lévy, 1925 (1863) [= *The Life of Jesus*, repr. Amherst, N.Y.: Prometheus Books, 1991].

Riesner, R. *Jesus als Lehrer*. WUNT II/7. 2nd ed. Tübingen: Mohr Siebeck, 1984.

Robinson, J. M., P. Hoffmann, and J. S. Kloppenborg. *The Critical Edition of Q*. Minneapolis: Fortress, 2000.

Safrai, S., M. Stern, D. Flusser, and W. C. van Unnik (eds.) *The Jewish People in the First Century*, 2 vols. Compendia Rerum Iudaicarum ad Novum Testamentum. Section I. Assen: van Gorcum, 1974–1976.

Saldarini, A. J. *Pharisees, Scribes and Sadducees*. Wilmington, Del.: Michael Glazier, 1988.

Sanders, E. P. *Paul and Palestinian Judaism*. London: SCM, 1977.

———. *Jesus and Judaism*. London: SCM, 1985.

———. *The Historical Figure of Jesus*. Harmondsworth: Lane, 1993.

Schäfer, P. *Jesus in the Talmud*. Princeton: Princeton University, 2007.

Schlosser, J. *Le Dieu de Jésus: Étude exégétique*. Lectio Divina 129. Paris: Cerf, 1987.

———. *Jésus de Nazareth*. Paris: Noêsis, 1999.

Schmidt, K. L. *Der Rahmen der Geschichte Jesu: Literarkritische Untersuchungen zur ältesten Jesusüberlieferung*. Berlin: Trowitzsch, 1919.

Schnackenburg, R. *Gottes Herrschaft und Reich*. 3rd ed. Freiburg i. Br.: Herder, 1963 [= *God's Rule and Kingdom*. New York: Herder & Herder, 1963].

Schröter, J. *Jesus von Nazareth: Jude aus Galiläa – Retter der Welt*. BG 15. Leipzig: Verlagsanstalt, 2006.

Schröter, J. and R. Brucker (eds.) *Der historiche Jesus: Tendenzen und*

Perspektiven der gegenwärtigen Forschungen. BZNT 114. Berlin: de Gruyter, 2002.

Schürer, E. *Geschichte des jüdischen Volkes im Zeitalter Jesu Christi* I–IIII. Leipzig: Hinrichs, 1901–1909 [= *The History of the Jewish People in the Age of Jesus Christ*, rev. and ed. G. Vermes and F. Millar, 4 vols. Edinburgh: T&T Clark, 1973–1987].

Schürmann, H. *Jesu ureigener Tod*. 2nd ed. Freiburg i Br.: Herder, 1976.

Schweitzer, A. *Vom Reimarus zu Wrede: eine Geschichte der Leben-Jesu-Forschung*. Tübingen: Mohr Siebeck, 1906 [= *The Quest for the Historical Jesus: A Critical Study of Its Progress from Reimarus to Wrede*. London: A. & C. Black, 1910].

———. *Die Geschichte der Leben-Jesu-Forschung*. Tübingen: Mohr Siebeck, 1913 [new ed. of the earlier German work].

Segalla, G. *Evangelo e vangeli. Quattro evangelisti, quattro vangeli, quattro destinatari*. Bologna: EDB, 1993.

———. *Sulle tracce di Gesù: la "Terza Ricerca."* Assisi: Cittadella, 2006.

———. "La 'Terza Ricerca' del Gesù storico e il suo paradigma postmoderno nel quadro della ricerca moderna." *Revista Catalana de Teologia* 33 (2008): 273–99.

Smith, M. D. "Of Jesus and Quirinius." *Catholic Biblical Quarterly* 62 (2000): 278–93.

Stanton, G. *Gospel Truth? New Light on Jesus and the Gospels*. London: HarperCollins, 1995.

Stein, R. H. *Jesus the Messiah: A Survey of the Life of Christ*. London: InterVarsity, 1996.

Strauss, D. F. *Das Leben Jesu kritisch*, I–II. Tübingen: C. F. Osiander 1835–1836; 3rd ed., 1838–1839 [= *The Life of Jesus Critically Examined*. Philadelphia: Fortress, 1972].

Theissen, G. *Urchristliche Wundergeschichten: Ein Beitrag zur formgeschichtlichen Erforschung der synoptischen Evangelien*. Gütersloh: Mohn, 1974 [= *Miracle Stories in the Early Christian Tradition*. Edinburgh: T&T Clark 1983].

———. *Der Schatten des Galiläers: Historische Jesusforschung in erzählender Form*. Munich: Christian Kaiser, 1986 [= *The Shadow of the Galilean: The Quest of the Historical Jesus in Narrative Form*. Minneapolis: Fortress, 1998].

———. *Jesus als historische Gestalt*. FRLANT 202. Göttingen: Vandenhoeck & Ruprecht, 2003.

Theissen, G. and A. Merz. *Der historische Jesus: Ein Lehrbuch*. Göttingen: Vandenhoeck & Ruprecht, 1996 [= *The Historical Jesus: A Comprehensive Guide*. Minneapolis: Fortress, 1998].

Theissen, G. and D. Winter. *Die Kriterienfrage in der Jesusforschung. Vom Differenzkriterium zum Plausibilitätskriterium*. Novum Testamentum et Orbis Antiquus 34. Göttingen: Vandenhoeck & Ruprecht, 1997 [= *The Quest for the Plausible Jesus: The Essential Problem of the Criterion of Dissimilarity*. Louisville, Ky.: Westminster John Knox, 2002].

Tragan, P. R. *La preistoria dei Vangeli. Tradizione cristiana primitiva. Valore storico, forma e contenuto*. Quaderni di ricerca 72. Sotto il Monte: Servitium, 1999.

Tuckett, C. M. *Q and the History of Early Christianity*. Studies on Q. Edinburgh: T&T Clark, 1996.

Vermes, G. *Jesus the Jew: A Historian's Reading of the Gospels*. London: Collins, 1973.

———. *Jesus and the World of Judaism*. London: SCM, 1983.

———. *The Religion of Jesus the Jew*. London: SCM, 1993.

Vidal, S. *Los tres proyectos de Jesús y el cristianismo naciente*. Biblioteca de Estudios Bíblicos 110. Salamanca: Sígueme, 2003.

Weder, H. Die *Gleichnisse Jesu als Metaphern*. Forschungen zur Religion und Literatur des Alten und Neuen Testaments 120. Göttingen: Vandenhoeck & Ruprecht, 1978.

Weiss, J. *Die Predigt Jesu vom Reiche Gottes*. 2nd ed. Göttingen, 1900 (1892) [= *Jesus' Proclamation of the Kingdom of God*. Chico: Scholars Press, 1985].

Witherington, B. *The Jesus Quest: The Third Search for the Jew of Nazareth*. 2nd ed. Downers Grove, Ill.: InterVarsity, 1997.

Wrede, W. *Das Messiasgeheimnis in den Evangelien, zugleich ein Beitrag zum Verständnis des Markusevangeliums*. Göttingen: Vandenhoeck & Ruprecht, 1901.

Wright, N. T. *The New Testament and the People of God*. Christian Origins and the Question of God 1. London: SPCK, 1992.

———. *Jesus and the Victory of God*. Christian Origins and theQuestion of God 2. Minneapolis: Fortress, 1996.

———. "Jesus and the Identity of God." *Ex auditu* 14 (1998): 42–56.

———. *The Resurrection of the Son of God*. Christian Origins and the Question of God 3. Minneapolis: Fortress, 2003.

Index of Ancient Sources

Books of the Prophets

OLD TESTAMENT APOCRYPHA

NEW TESTAMENT APOCRYPHA

APOSTOLIC FATHERS

NAG HAMMADI COPTIC LIBRARY

DEAD SEA SCROLLS (QUMRAN AND OTHERS)

PHILO OF ALEXANDRIA

FLAVIUS JOSEPHUS

MISHNAH, TOSEFTA, AND TALMUDS

Mishnah

CHURCH FATHERS

QURAN

WORKS OF REFERENCE AND OTHERS

Index of Modern Authors